The Libertarian Reader

Classic and contemporary writings
from Lao-tzu to Milton Friedman

Edited by
David Boaz

Simon & Schuster Paperbacks
New York   London   Toronto   Sydney   Singapore

Simon & Schuster Paperbacks
1230 Avenue of the Americas
New York, NY 10020

First Simon & Schuster trade paperback edition February 2015

SIMON & SCHUSTER and colophon are registered trademarks of
Simon & Schuster, Inc.

For information about special discounts for bulk purchases,
please contact Simon & Schuster Special Sales at 1-866-506-1949
or business@simonandschuster.com.

The Simon & Schuster Speakers Bureau can bring authors to
your live event. For more information or to book an event contact
the Simon & Schuster Speakers Bureau at 1-866-248-3049 or
visit our website at www.simonspeakers.com.

Interior design by Claudia Martinez

Manufactured in the United States of America

10 9 8 7 6 5 4 3 2 1

Library of Congress Cataloging-in-Publication Data

The Libertarian reader: classic and contemporary writings from Lao-tzu to
Milton Friedman / [compiled by] David Boaz.
     p.   cm.
  Includes bibliographical references (p.   ).
  1. Libertarianism.   I. Boaz, David, 1953–   .
JC585.L3898   1997
320.51'2—dc21   96–48122
                                                              CIP

ISBN 978-1-4767-5289-1
ISBN 978-1-4767-5292-1 (ebook)

Contents

====

Introduction

The question of the relationship of individuals to one another and to the state has been debated for as long as we have records of human debates, especially in the Western world. The specific perspective on that question known as libertarianism took many centuries to develop, and its intellectual evolution was often intertwined with political struggles. Today, as the brutality, indignity, and inefficacy of coercion become increasingly apparent, more and more people around the world are embracing the philosophy of individual rights, civil society, and free markets.

In 2013, as endless wars, mounting debt, and revelations about the surveillance state dominated political discussion, a *Washington Post* headline declared "Libertarianism is hot." The following year *Financial Times* columnist Edward Luce wrote, "If there is a new spirit in America's rising climate of anti-politics, it is libertarian."

Libertarian ideas have been building over a long period, perhaps since the stumbles of the New Deal–Great Society paradigm in the 1970s. In his 1996 presidential address to the American Sociological Association, Amitai Etzioni noted that libertarianism's "influence has been rising in social science, law, philosophy, and society over the last two decades." A few years later Colin Bird of the University of Virginia wrote, "The prestige of classical liberal and libertarian ideas has been higher than at any time since the end of the nineteenth century. Moreover, it is libertarian, not communitarian, ideas that have had a more direct impact on the politics of the Western countries over the past twenty-five years."

Not everyone likes this way of thinking, of course. *New York Times* columnist David Brooks deplored in 2013 "the distinct strands of libertarianism that are blossoming in this fragmenting age: the deep suspicion of authority, the strong belief that hierarchies and organizations are suspect, the fervent devotion to transparency, the assumption that individual preference should be supreme." Scholars such as Garry Wills, Charles Taylor, Lawrence Lessig, Cass Sunstein, Ellen Willis, Benjamin Barber, and Michael Sandel have written books critical of libertarian ideas.

Libertarian political sentiments are strong, especially among younger Americans. There has been a remarkable efflorescence of libertarian scholarship and policy analysis. The goal of this reader is to offer in one place a necessarily brief introduction to the richness of the libertarian tradition, from the days of John Locke and Adam Smith to F. A. Hayek, Ayn Rand, and Milton Friedman.

THE ROOTS OF LIBERTARIANISM

Although libertarian ideas are evident in the writings of the Chinese philosopher Lao-tzu in the sixth century BCE, the main thread of libertarianism goes back to the Jewish and Greek idea of a higher law, a law by which everyone, even the ruler, could be judged. The simple idea that the will of the ruler was not the ultimate source of authority helped lay the groundwork for a pluralist society, the flowering of individualism, and eventually the scientific and economic miracles of Western civilization.

Libertarianism developed in a civilization that was, by world standards, profoundly decentralized. The many political jurisdictions in a common European culture gave individuals some opportunity to move from repressive to less repressive regimes and thus gave rulers incentives to bargain with their subjects, notably by granting them liberties and immunities. The existence of an independent church played a major role in limiting and dividing power, as did the emergence of chartered towns in the Middle Ages.

A consistent libertarian doctrine began to emerge in the seventeenth century in response to the royal absolutism of the Bourbons in France, the Stuarts in England, and the Habsburgs in the Netherlands. John Milton's *Areopagitica* was an eloquent defense of religious freedom and a free press. The Levellers in the 1640s, led especially by the popular hero John Lilburne, began to put forth a program of religious toleration, low taxes, abolition of monopolies, peace, and freedom of the press, all based on a foundation of self-ownership and natural rights. That is the first recognizably libertarian (or liberal) political platform, though neither term was used at the time.

A generation later, John Locke set forth the philosophical justification for liberty, property, and a government based on consent in his *Second Treatise of Government*, published in 1690. His ideas have been an essential foundation for libertarian thought ever since. They also constitute the fundamental argument underlying modern democratic governments, though modern governments have strayed far from Locke's strict definition of the purpose of government: to protect life, liberty, and estate (all of which constituted property).

Locke's ideas were echoed and developed by John Trenchard and Thomas Gordon's *Cato's Letters* in the 1730s, by the revolutionary pamphleteer Thomas Paine, and by Thomas Jefferson in the Declaration of Independence. With the addition of the economic theory of spontaneous order and free markets—developed by the Spanish School of Salamanca, the French Physiocrats, and the Scottish Enlightenment thinkers, especially Adam Smith—libertarianism was essentially complete. It combined a normative theory of justice, imprescriptible rights, with a positive theory of social analysis, the self-regulating order.

To say the theory was "essentially complete," of course, is not to suggest that liberalism or libertarianism is a closed system. Libertarian ideas have been continually developed and debated: David Hume's analysis of the circumstances that require us to develop a system of property rights; Mary Wollstonecraft's demonstration that the rights of men are also the rights of women; Alexis de Tocqueville's penetrating analysis of liberty and democracy; the abolitionists' view of slavery as "man-stealing"; Wilhelm von Humboldt's and John Stuart Mill's emphasis on the individual's need to develop his own character; Herbert Spencer's consistent application of the "law of equal freedom" to every area of state action; the discovery (or rediscovery) of the marginal theory of value by the economists Carl Menger, W. Stanley Jevons, and Leon Walras; the devastating critique of socialism by Ludwig von Mises; F. A. Hayek's lifelong investigation of spontaneous order; Ayn Rand's radical moral defense of individualism against collectivism; Murray Rothbard's argument that the coercive state is not needed even to supply defense and justice; Robert Nozick's examination of what kind of state can be justified if individuals have rights; the countless studies of the failure of government intervention in the free market by Milton Friedman and his colleagues at the University of Chicago; and much more.

It is easier to define libertarian ideas than to agree on a proper name for those ideas. The advocacy of individual liberty against state power has gone by many names over the centuries, including Whiggism, individualism, voluntaryism, and radical republicanism. In the first years of the nineteenth century the term "liberalism" came into widespread use in France and Spain, and it soon spread. But by the end of that century the meaning of the term "liberalism" had undergone a remarkable change. From a leave-us-alone (*laissez-faire, laissez-passer*) philosophy, it had come to stand for advocacy of substantial government intervention into the marketplace. The economist Joseph Schumpeter noted, "As a supreme, if unintended, compliment, the enemies of private enterprise have thought it wise to appropriate its label." Eventually people began to call the philosophy of individual rights, free markets, and limited government—the philosophy of Locke, Smith, and Jefferson—classical liberalism. Some liberals, such as Hayek and Friedman, continued to call themselves liberals. But to younger generations of Americans, "liberal" had come to mean advocacy of big government—high taxes, the extension of the state into the realm of civil society, and massive intrusion into the personal choices of individuals. Thus in the 1950s Leonard Read, founder of the Foundation for Economic Education, began calling himself a libertarian. That word had long been used for the advocates of free will (as opposed to determinism); and, like the word "liberal," it was derived from the Latin *liber*, free. The name was gradually embraced by a growing band of libertarians in the 1960s and 1970s.

Some old liberals began calling themselves conservatives. After all, what is conservatism in a liberal society? If it means a defense of constitutional liberties and the private enterprise system, then "conservatives" may in fact be conservative liberals. The generally recognized father of modern conservatism, Edmund Burke, was himself a Whig and a liberal. Although most libertarians would agree with Thomas Paine's defense of the French Revolution of 1789 rather than Burke's opposition to it, the liberal essayist William Hazlitt said of Burke's *Reflections on the Revolution in France*: "In arriving at one error, Burke discovered a hundred truths." Still, "conservative" is not a word that seems to imply a firm belief in individual rights, an appreciation of the effects of free markets and spontaneous order, and an optimistic belief in change and progress. In his essay "Why I Am Not a Conservative," Hayek objected to conservatism's "fear of change" and wrote that "order appears to the conservative as the result of the continuous attention of authority," directly opposed to the liberals' appreciation for spontaneous order and progress.

We might define libertarianism as a subset of (classical) liberalism, an advocacy of individual liberty, free markets, and limited government rooted in a commitment to self-ownership, imprescriptible rights, and the moral autonomy of the individual. But today any old-style liberal, who believes in individual choice, private property, and the market process, must by default call himself a libertarian.

THE RESURGENCE OF LIBERTARIANISM

In 1955 the historian Cecelia Kenyon famously described the Anti-Federalist opponents of the U.S. Constitution as "men of little faith"—little faith, that is, in rulers and in the ability of a written constitution to constrain those who would rule a large polity. Today, after six decades characterized by Vietnam, Watergate, domestic spying, police abuse, stagnant educational results, unsustainable entitlement programs, and profligacy at every level of government, we may have more appreciation for the Anti-Federalists' lack of faith in government.

The record of activist government in the past century has generated a rebirth of libertarianism, which had almost disappeared after the triumph of liberalism during the nineteenth century. Today, having witnessed fascism, communism, apartheid, military dictatorship, and the inexorable growth of even democratic states, many people have acquired a renewed appreciation for Lord Acton's warning that power corrupts. Libertarian scholarship is enjoying a resurgence, as is the influence of libertarian ideas on politics and culture.

Around the world states are cutting high tax rates, privatizing state enterprises, and giving up on the attempt to control the flow of ideas in a global economy of satellite television and the Internet. There are many counterexamples, to be sure, but revolutions in transportation and communications are making rulers around the world face the dilemma that European princes encountered in the Middle Ages: high taxes, insecure property rights, and intellectual repression may cause your most productive citizens to flee.

Disillusionment with government failure alone, of course, doesn't mean a resurgence of libertarianism. But the loss of faith in government is inspiring thinkers and activists around the world to rediscover and extend libertarian ideas. In particular, the recognition of the difficulty of limiting the powers of democratic governments has generated a new enthusiasm for rules that would strictly define the role of government rather than leaving majorities (or coalitions of interest groups) with the power to adopt policies that seem attractive at the moment. There is a growing appreciation for the consistency and complexity of libertarian thought.

KEY THEMES OF LIBERTARIANISM

The sections of this reader present several key themes of libertarianism: skepticism about power, the dignity of the individual, individual rights, spontaneous order, free markets, and peace. Other topics and subtopics could of course be included—the role of law in protecting liberty, the idea of civil society, the virtue of production, and limited government, for instance—but constraints of space limit our choices. Because the major themes are discussed in the introductions to each relevant section, they won't be explored here. (They are also discussed at more length in my book *The Libertarian Mind: A Manifesto for Freedom*.) The most important point to note is the interrelatedness of the concepts.

Because libertarians are skeptical about the effects of concentrated power, they support institutions that limit and divide power, such as federalism, separation of powers, private property, and free markets. Capitalism, democracy, and the Western intellectual system are all competitive systems that give no one final authority. Because libertarians respect each individual, they insist that he or she have the right to make choices and pursue projects. Because humans must cooperate to achieve most purposes, we need free markets, a legal system to guarantee the enforcement of contracts, and property rights, to tell us what each of us controls and what we may exchange.

Do libertarians believe in free markets because of a belief in individual rights or an empirical observation that markets produce prosperity and social harmony? The question ultimately makes no sense. As Hume said, the circumstances confronting humans are our self-interestedness, our necessarily limited generosity toward others, and the scarcity of resources available to fulfill our needs. Because of these circumstances, it is necessary for us to cooperate with others and to have rules of justice—especially regarding property and exchange—to define how we can do so. If individuals using their own knowledge for their own purposes didn't generate a spontaneous order of peace and prosperity, then it would make little sense to advocate either natural rights or free markets.

Does civil society produce liberty, or does a firm commitment to natural rights produce civil society? Well, both. Locke, Spencer, Rand, and Rothbard have helped to outline a rigorous and consistent theory of individual rights that, if applied, would protect freedom and allow people to generate all the institutions of civil society. But Hume, Acton, and Hayek would direct our attention to the historical processes by which liberty was actually achieved in the West, and especially in England and America: a long struggle in which the members of civil society demanded specific liberties from their rulers, with those liberties eventually forming a large enough space for freedom of thought and action that we might call it liberty.

As for peace, its relation to the other concepts of libertarianism is obvious. War not only concentrates power and slaughters the innocent, it disrupts social cooperation, the market process, and the rule of law. The earliest libertarians sought to prevent their rulers from wasting the lives and treasure of the people and disrupting their plans in needless wars.

OPPONENTS OF LIBERTARIANISM

Libertarianism arose in opposition to royal absolutism, to kings who sought to govern without constraint. Court intellectuals, of course, had developed elaborate theories to justify monarchy, aristocracy, and imposed order. It would hardly be fair to suggest that "conservatives" were defenders of absolutism, but in time a form of conservatism emerged that defended the existing privileges of the king, the aristocracy, the established church, and the monopolies. In the aftermath of the American and French revolutions, liberalism and conservatism contended for the future of Europe. The poet Robert Southey bemoaned the lost world of happy peasants (with short lifespans and no hope of social mobility) before the Industrial Revolution, and the philosopher Joseph de Maistre urged a return to the age of kings, aristocrats, and hierarchy. When the liberal legal scholar Henry Sumner Maine wrote of the movement from "a society of status" to "a society of contract," he was describing the triumph of liberalism over conservatism.

As liberalism was advancing in Europe—as the Old Order was swept away and replaced by religious freedom, capitalism, and elected constitutional governments—a new opponent arose: socialism. Because of the dominance of economic issues in our time, socialism is usually seen as the antithesis of libertarianism. Rothbard, however, argued that socialism was essentially a "middle-of-the-road movement" between liberalism and conservatism:

> Socialism, like liberalism and against conservatism, accepted the industrial system and the liberal *goals* of freedom, reason, mobility, progress, higher living standards for the masses, and an end to theocracy and war; but it tried to achieve these ends by the use of incompatible, conservative means: statism, central planning, communitarianism, etc.

In practice, of course, full-blown socialism—including the nationalization of property—did prove the antithesis of liberty. The elimination of private property meant the elimination of the principal source of resistance to state power. Socialism promised freedom, prosperity, and community but delivered totalitarianism, poverty, and atomism.

Today the Old Order of monarchy and theocracy is but a memory, and full-fledged socialism is rapidly passing from the scene. The ideological battles of the future seem likely to be fought on liberal ground, with the general principles of private property, market relations, freedom of expression, and democratic government accepted by all sides. Still, libertarians will find much room for disagreement with conservatives and welfare-statists (unfortunately called liberals in the United States) in the battle to protect the rights of the individual and a society of peace, prosperity, and freedom. Politics may become a struggle between conservative paternalists, welfare-state maternalists, and libertarians who believe that adults should make their own decisions. A guide to some of the critics of libertarianism can be found in "The Literature of Liberty" at the end of this book.

WRITINGS ON LIBERTY

The books and articles that have contributed to modern libertarianism would fill a library. This anthology is but a brief introduction to the ideas of liberty. It is designed to introduce the thoughtful reader to the most important thinkers who have helped to develop the libertarian worldview and to identify the key concepts in that worldview.

So much of the vast literature of individualism and libertarianism has been omitted from this necessarily limited collection that it would be hard to single out the most regrettable omissions. However, we might point to a few writers who will surely be missed by some readers: the Spanish Scholastics, such as Francisco de Vitoria and Bartolomé de Las Casas, who built on Thomistic thought to defend the rights of the American Indians and who arguably provided a more solid foundation for modern economics than did Adam Smith; Ralph Waldo Emerson and Henry David Thoreau, whose eloquent defenses of individualism have inspired generations of American students; the Public Choice school of economics, especially James M. Buchanan and Gordon Tullock, who have so cogently examined the reasons that government fails to produce the results that civics books promise; Karl Popper, the philosopher of science, whose political views were not quite libertarian but whose skeptical epistemology should be better known among libertarians. The list could go on indefinitely.

Those who are inspired to do more reading than this anthology offers are directed to the "Literature of Liberty" essay by Tom G. Palmer, itself a valuable introduction to libertarian ideas.

CONCLUSION

Because a pluralist, competitive, individualist society is best suited to intellectual and economic progress, world politics will likely continue to move in the libertarian direction that has been resumed after the twentieth-century catastrophes of national socialism and communism. Globalization has continued to bring more people into the world economy, and billions of people are rising out of poverty. Enlightenment values of tolerance and human rights are spreading to more parts of the world, with particular emphasis on the rights of women, racial and religious minorities, and gay and lesbian people (though to be sure, there are parts of the world where illiberalism is growing). The Internet is giving people more information, more ways to connect, more commercial opportunities, and more choice. Despite what we may be led to think from the flood of information about the world, we are probably living in the most peaceful era in history.

In their article "The Libertarian Moment" in *Reason* magazine, Nick Gillespie and Matt Welch argue that the world is rapidly becoming more libertarian:

This is now a world where it's more possible than ever to live your life on your own terms; it's an early rough draft version of the libertarian philosopher Robert Nozick's glimmering "utopia of utopias." Due to exponential advances in technology, broad-based increases in wealth, the ongoing networking of the world via trade and culture, and the decline of both state and private institutions of repression, never before has it been easier for more individuals to chart their own course and steer their lives by the stars as they see the sky.

They credit the Internet with "entire new economies, modes of scattered and decentralized organization and work, and a hyper-individualization that would have shocked the Founding Fathers." On both left and right there are thinkers and actors who don't like that "hyper-individualization," which might better be characterized as self-reliance, minding your own business, and making your own decisions. But for now it seems to be in the ascendancy.

Still, liberty will not want for challenges. Singaporean strongman Lee Kuan Yew scoffs that Singapore does not "need the kind of free-for-all libertarianism that we see in America." From social democracy to theocratic Islam to "Asian values," there will be no shortage of anti-liberal ideas for the heirs of Locke, Smith, Mises, and Hayek to confront. This reader, and the works from which it draws, will help them explore and extend the ideas of freedom, responsibility, and dignity.

PART ONE

SKEPTICISM ABOUT POWER

The first principle of libertarian social analysis is a concern about the concentration of power. One of the mantras of libertarianism is Lord Acton's dictum, "Power tends to corrupt, and absolute power corrupts absolutely." As the first selection in this section demonstrates, that concern has a long history. God's warning to the people of Israel about "the ways of the king that will reign over you" reminded Jews and Christians for centuries that the state was at best a necessary evil.

The history of the West is characterized by competing centers of power. We may take that for granted, but it was not true everywhere. In most parts of the world, church and state were united, leaving little room for independent power centers to develop. Divided power in the West might be traced to the response of Jesus to the Pharisees: "Render unto Caesar the things that are Caesar's and unto God the things that are God's." In so doing he made it clear that not all of life is under the control of the state. This radical notion took hold in Western Christianity.

The historian Ralph Raico writes, "The essence of the unique European experience is that a civilization developed that felt itself to be a whole—Christendom—and yet was radically decentralized. With the fall of Rome, ... the continent evolved into a mosaic of separate and competing jurisdictions and polities whose internal divisions themselves excluded centralized control." An independent church checked the power of states, just as kings prevented power from becoming centralized in the hands of the church. In the free, chartered towns of the Middle Ages, people developed the institutions of self-government. The towns provided a place for commerce to flourish.

Even law, usually thought of today as a unified product of government, has a pluralist history. As Harold Berman writes in *Law and Revolution,* "Perhaps the most distinctive characteristic of the Western legal tradition is the coexistence and competition within the same community of diverse jurisdictions and diverse legal systems.... Legal pluralism originated in the differentiation of the ecclesiastical polity from secular polities.... Secular law itself was divided into various competing types, including royal law, feudal law, manorial law, urban law, and mercantile law. The same person might be subject to the ecclesiastical courts in one type of case, the king's court in another, his lord's court in a third, the manorial court in a fourth, a town court in a fifth, a merchants' court in a sixth." Even more important, individuals had at least some degree of choice among courts, which encouraged all the legal systems to dispense good law.

In all these ways people in the West developed a deep skepticism about concentrated power. When kings, especially Louis XIV in France and the Stuart kings in Britain, began to claim more power than they had traditionally had, Europeans resisted. The institutions of civil society and self-government proved stronger in England than on the Continent, and the Stuarts' attempt to impose royal absolutism ended ignominiously, with the beheading of Charles I in 1649.

Modern liberal ideas emerged as a response to absolutism, in the attempt to protect liberty from an overweening state. Especially in England, the Levellers, John Locke, and the opposition writers of the eighteenth century developed a defense of religious toleration, private property, freedom of the press, and free markets for labor and commerce.

In the following selections, Thomas Paine takes those opposition ideas a step further: Government itself is at best "a necessary evil." The first king was no doubt just "the principal ruffian of some restless gang," and the English monarchy itself began with a "French bastard, landing with an armed banditti." There was no divinity in the powers that be, and the people were thus justified in rebelling against a government that exceeded its legitimate powers.

Once the American Revolution was successful, James Madison and other Americans set out on another task: creating a government on liberal principles, one that would secure the benefits of civil society and not extend itself beyond that vital but minimal task. His solution was the United States Constitution, which he defended, along with Alexander Hamilton and John Jay, in a series of newspaper essays that came to be known as *The Federalist Papers,* the most important American contribution to political philosophy. In the famous *Federalist* no. 10, he explained how the limited government of a large territory could avoid falling prey to factional influence and majoritarian excesses. If Madison and his colleagues might be viewed as conservative libertarians, many of the Anti-Federalists were more radical libertarians, who feared that the Constitution would not adequately limit the federal government and whose efforts resulted in the addition of a Bill of Rights.

Forty years after the Constitution was ratified, a young Frenchman named Alexis de Tocqueville came to America to observe the world's first liberal country. His reflections became one of the most important works in liberal political theory, *Democracy in America.* He warned that a country based on political equality might develop a new kind of despotism, one that would, like a nurturing parent, "cover the surface of society with a network of small complicated rules, minute and uniform." Americans would have to be eternally vigilant to protect their hard-won liberty.

In one of the most enduring liberal texts, *On Liberty,* John Stuart Mill set forth his principle that "the only purpose for which power can be rightfully exercised over any member of a civilized community, against his will, is to prevent harm to others." (Other libertarian scholars would argue that "harm" is too vague a standard and that the better formulation would be "to protect the well-defined rights of life, liberty, and property.") He also argued that the tasks of government should be limited—even if it might perform some task better than civil society—to avoid "the great evil of adding unnecessarily to its power."

Twentieth-century libertarians have continued to examine the nature of power and to look for ways to limit it. H. L. Mencken excoriated government as a "hostile power" but did not hold out much hope for changing that. Isabel Paterson feared that humanitarian impulses exercised through inappropriate means could lead even good people to wield power in dangerous ways. Murray Rothbard took a radical view among libertarian scholars: that all coercive government is an illegitimate infringement on natural liberty and that all goods and services could be better supplied through voluntary processes than through government. Richard Epstein approached the issue of power differently: Given that we need some coercive government to protect us from each other and allow civil society to flourish, how do we limit it? He offers in his selection a threefold answer: federalism, separation of powers, and strict guarantees for individual rights.

Constraining power is the great challenge for any political system. Libertarians have always put that challenge at the center of their political and social analysis.

I SAMUEL 8

The Bible

The most important book in the development of Western civilization was the Bible, which of course just means "the Book" in Greek. Until recent times it was the touchstone for almost all debate on morality and government. One of its most resonant passages for the study of government was the story of God's warning to the people of Israel when they wanted a king to rule them. Until then, as Judges 21:25 reports, "there was no king in Israel: every man did that which was right in his own eyes," and there were judges to settle disputes. But in I Samuel, the Jews asked for a king, and God told Samuel what it would be like to have a king. This story reminded Europeans for centuries that the state was not divinely inspired. Thomas Paine, Lord Acton, and other liberals cited it frequently.

---

1 And it came to pass, when Samuel was old, that he made his sons judges over Israel.

2 Now the name of his firstborn was Joel; and the name of his second, Abiah: *they were* judges in Beersheba.

3 And his sons walked not in his ways, but turned aside after lucre, and took bribes, and perverted judgment.

4 Then all the elders of Israel gathered themselves together, and came to Samuel unto Ramah,

5 And said unto him, Behold, thou art old, and thy sons walk not in thy ways: now make us a king to judge us like all the nations.

6 But the thing displeased Samuel, when they said, Give us a king to judge us. And Samuel prayed unto the LORD.

7 And the LORD said unto Samuel, Hearken unto the voice of the people in all that they say unto thee: for they have not rejected thee, but they have rejected me, that I should not reign over them.

8 According to all the works which they have done since the day that I brought them up out of Egypt even unto this day, wherewith they have forsaken me, and served other gods, so do they also unto thee.

9 Now therefore hearken unto their voice: howbeit yet protest solemnly unto them, and shew them the manner of the king that shall reign over them.

10 And Samuel told all the words of the LORD unto the people that asked of him a king.

11 And he said, This will be the manner of the king that shall reign over you: He will take your sons, and appoint *them* for himself, for his chariots, and *to be* his horsemen; and *some* shall run before his chariots.

12 And he will appoint him captains over thousands, and captains over fifties; and *will set them* to ear his ground, and to reap his harvest, and to make his instruments of war, and instruments of his chariots.

13 And he will take your daughters *to be* confectionaries, and *to be* cooks, and *to be* bakers.

14 And he will take your fields, and your vineyards, and your oliveyards, *even* the best *of them,* and given *them* to his servants.

15 And he will take the tenth of your seed, and of your vineyards, and give to his officers, and to his servants.

16 And he will take your menservants, and your maidservants, and your goodliest young men, and your asses, and put *them* to his work.

17 He will take the tenth of your sheep: and ye shall be his servants.

18 And ye shall cry out in that day because of your king which ye shall have chosen you; and the LORD will not hear you in that day.

19 Nevertheless the people refused to obey the voice of Samuel; and they said, Nay; but we will have a king over us;

20 That we also may be like all the nations; and that our king may judge us, and go out before us, and fight our battles.

21 And Samuel heard all the words of the people, and he rehearsed them in the ears of the LORD.

22 And the LORD said to Samuel, Hearken unto their voice, and make them a king. And Samuel said unto the men of Israel, Go ye every man unto his city.

OF THE ORIGIN AND DESIGN OF GOVERNMENT

Thomas Paine

Thomas Paine (1737–1809) was an agitator for freedom in England, America, and France and an important theorist as well. His major works were *The Rights of Man,* a response to Edmund Burke's *Reflections on the Revolution in France,* which is often cited as a founding document of modern conservatism, and *The Age of Reason,* a manifesto for what Paine regarded as rational Christianity but others denounced as atheism. This is an excerpt from his fabulously successful 1776 publication *Common Sense.* In this and other writings Paine helped to establish the ideology that became known first as liberalism and then as libertarianism by combining a theory of natural rights and justice with a social theory that emphasized natural harmony and spontaneous order in the absence of coercion.

Some writers have so confounded society with government, as to leave little or no distinction between them; whereas they are not only different, but have different origins. Society is produced by our wants, and government by our wickedness; the former promotes our happiness *positively* by uniting our affections, the latter *negatively* by restraining our vices. The one encourages intercourse, the other creates distinctions. The first is a patron, the last a punisher.

Society in every state is a blessing, but government even in its best state is but a necessary evil; in its worst state an intolerable one; for when we suffer, or are exposed to the same miseries *by a government,* which we might expect in a country *without government,* our calamities are heightened by reflecting that we furnish the means by which we suffer. Government, like dress, is the badge of lost innocence; the palaces of kings are built on the ruins of the bowers of paradise. For were the impulses of conscience clear, uniform, and irresistibly obeyed, man would need no other lawgiver; but that not being the case, he finds it necessary to surrender up a part of his property to furnish means for the protection of the rest; and this he is induced to do by the same prudence which in every other case advises him out of two evils to choose the least. *Wherefore,* security being the true design and end of government, it unanswerably follows that whatever *form* thereof appears most likely to ensure it to us, with the least expense and greatest benefit, is preferable to all others.

In order to gain a clear and just idea of the design and end of government, let us suppose a small number of persons settled in some sequestered part of the earth, unconnected with the rest, they will then represent the first peopling of any country, or of the world. In this state of natural liberty, society will be their first thought. A thousand motives will excite them thereto, the strength of one man is so unequal to his wants, and his mind so unfitted for perpetual solitude, that he is soon obliged to seek assistance and relief of another, who in his turn requires the same. Four or five united would be able to raise a tolerable dwelling in the midst of a wilderness, but *one* man might labour out the common period of life without accomplishing any thing; when he had felled his timber he could not remove it, nor erect it after it was removed; hunger in the mean time would urge him from his work, and every different want call him a different way. Disease, nay even misfortune would be death, for though neither might be mortal, yet either would disable him from living, and reduce him to a state in which he might rather be said to perish than to die.

Thus necessity, like a gravitating power, would soon form our newly arrived emigrants into society, the reciprocal blessings of which, would supersede, and render the obligations of law and government unnecessary while they remained perfectly just to each other; but as nothing but heaven is impregnable to vice, it will unavoidably happen, that in proportion as they surmount the first difficulties of emigration, which bound them together in a common cause, they will begin to relax in their duty and attachment to each other; and this remissness, will point out the necessity, of establishing some form of government to supply the defect of moral virtue.

Some convenient tree will afford them a State-House, under the branches of which, the whole colony may assemble to deliberate on public matters. It is more than probable that their first laws will have the title only of REGULATIONS, and be enforced by no other penalty than public disesteem. In this first parliament every man, by natural right will have a seat.

But as the colony increases, the public concerns will increase likewise, and the distance at which the members may be separated, will render it too inconvenient for all of them to meet on every occasion as at first, when their number was small, their habitations near, and the public concerns few and trifling. This will point out the convenience of their consenting to leave the legislative part to be managed by a select number chosen from the whole body, who are supposed to have the same concerns at stake which those have who appointed them, and who will act in the same manner as the whole body would act were they present. If the colony continue increasing, it will become necessary to augment the number of the representatives, and that the interest of every part of the colony may be attended to, it will be found best to divide the whole into convenient parts, each part sending its proper number; and that the *elected* might never form to themselves an interest separate from the *electors,* prudence will point out the propriety of having elections often; because as the *elected* might by that means return and mix again with the general body of the *electors* in a few months, their fidelity to the public will be secured by the prudent reflection of not making a rod for themselves. And as this frequent interchange will establish a common interest with every part of the community, they will mutually and naturally support each other, and on this (not on the unmeaning name of king) depends the *strength of government, and the happiness of the governed.*

Here then is the origin and rise of government; namely, a mode rendered necessary by the inability of moral virtue to govern the world; here too is the design and end of government, viz. freedom and security. And however our eyes may be dazzled with snow, or our ears deceived by sound; however prejudice may warp our wills, or interest darken our understanding, the simple voice of nature and of reason will say, it is right. . . .

OF MONARCHY AND HEREDITARY SUCCESSION

Mankind being originally equals in the order of creation, the equality could only be destroyed by some subsequent circumstance; the distinctions of rich, and poor, may in a great measure be accounted for, and that without having recourse to the harsh, ill-sounding names of oppression and avarice. Oppression is often the *consequence*, but seldom or never the *means* of riches; and though avarice will preserve a man from being necessitously poor, it generally makes him too timorous to be wealthy.

But there is another and greater distinction for which no truly natural or religious reason can be assigned, and that is, the distinction of men into KINGS and SUBJECTS. Male and female are the distinctions of nature, good and bad the distinctions of heaven; but how a race of men came into the world so exalted above the rest, and distinguished like some new species, is worth inquiring into, and whether they are the means of happiness or of misery to mankind.

In the early ages of the world, according to the scripture chronology, there were no kings; the consequence of which was there were no wars; it is the pride of kings which throw mankind into confusion. Holland without a king hath enjoyed more peace for this last century than any of the monarchial governments in Europe. Antiquity favours the same remark; for the quiet and rural lives of the first patriarchs hath a happy something in them, which vanishes away when we come to the history of Jewish royalty.

Government by kings was first introduced into the world by the Heathens, from whom the children of Israel copied the custom. It was the most prosperous invention the Devil ever set on foot for the promotion of idolatry. The Heathens paid divine honours to their deceased kings, and the Christian world hath improved on the plan by doing the same to their living ones. How impious is the title of *sacred majesty* applied to a worm, who in the midst of his splendour is crumbling into dust.

As the exalting one man so greatly above the rest cannot be justified on the equal rights of nature, so neither can it be defended on the authority of scripture; for the will of the Almighty, as declared by Gideon and the prophet Samuel, expressly disapproves of government by kings. All anti-monarchial parts of scripture have been very smoothly glossed over in monarchial governments, but they undoubtedly merit the attention of countries which have their governments yet to form. *"Render unto Caesar the things which are Caesar's"* is the scriptural doctrine of courts, yet it is no support of monarchial government, for the Jews at that time were without a king, and in a state of vassalage to the Romans.

Near three thousand years passed away from the Mosaic account of the creation, till the Jews under a national delusion requested a king. Till then their form of government (except in extraordinary cases, where the Almighty interposed) was a kind of republic administered by a judge and the elders of the tribes. Kings they had none, and it was held sinful to acknowledge any being under that title but the Lord of Hosts. And when a man seriously reflects on the idolatrous homage which is paid to the persons of kings, he need not wonder, that the Almighty, ever jealous of his honour, should disapprove of a form of government which so impiously invades the prerogative of heaven.

Monarchy is ranked in scripture as one of the sins of the Jews, for which a curse in reserve is denounced against them. The history of that transaction is worth attending to.

The children of Israel being oppressed by the Midianites, Gideon marched against them with a small army, and victory, thro' the divine interposition, decided in his favour. The Jews, elate with success, and attributing it to the generalship of Gideon, proposed making him a king, saying, *Rule thou over us, thou and thy son and thy son's son.* Here was temptation in its fullest extent; not a kingdom only, but an hereditary one, but Gideon in the piety of his soul replied, *I will not rule over you, neither shall my son rule over you,* THE LORD SHALL RULE OVER YOU. Words need not be more explicit; Gideon doth not *decline* the honour but denieth their right to give it; neither doth he compliment them with invented declarations of his thanks, but in the positive style of a prophet charges them with disaffection to their proper sovereign, the King of Heaven.

These portions of scripture are direct and positive. They admit of no equivocal construction. That the Almighty hath here entered his protest against monarchial government is true, or the scripture is false. And a man hath good reason to believe that there is as much of king-craft, as priest-craft in withholding the scripture from the public in Popish countries. For monarchy in every instance is the Popery of government.

To the evil of monarchy we have added that of hereditary succession; and as the first is a degradation and lessening of ourselves, so the second, claimed as a matter of right, is an insult and an imposition on posterity. For all men being originally equals, no *one* by *birth* could have a right to set up his own family in perpetual preference to all others for ever, and though himself might deserve *some* decent degree of honours of his contemporaries, yet his descendants might be far too unworthy to inherit them. One of the strongest *natural* proofs of the folly of hereditary right in kings, is, that nature disapproves it, otherwise she would not so frequently turn it into ridicule by giving mankind an *ass for a lion*.

Secondly, as no man at first could possess any other public honours than were bestowed upon him, so the givers of those honours could have no power to give away the right of posterity, and though they might say "We choose you for *our* head," they could not, without manifest injustice to their children, say "that your children and your children's children shall reign over *ours* for ever." Because such an unwise, unjust, unnatural compact might (perhaps) in the next succession put them under the government of a rogue or a fool. Most wise men, in their private sentiments, have ever treated hereditary right with contempt; yet it is one of those evils, which when once established is not easily removed; many submit from fear, others from superstition, and the more powerful part shares with the king the plunder of the rest.

This is supposing the present race of the kings in the world to have had an honourable origin; whereas it is more than probable, that could we take off the dark covering of antiquity, and trace them to their first rise, that we should find the first of them nothing better than the principal ruffian of some restless gang, whose savage manners or pre-eminence in subtlety obtained him the title of chief among plunderers; and who by increasing in power, and extending his depredations, over-awed the quiet and defenceless to purchase their safety by frequent contributions. Yet his electors could have no idea of giving hereditary right to his descendants, because such a perpetual exclusion of themselves was incompatible with the free and unrestrained principles they professed to live by. Wherefore, hereditary succession in the early ages of monarchy could not take place as a matter of claim, but as something casual or complimental; but as few or no records were extant in those days, and traditionary history stuffed with fables, it was very easy, after the lapse of a few generations, to trump up some superstitious tale, conveniently timed, Mahomet like, to cram hereditary right down the throats of the vulgar. Perhaps the disorders which threatened, or seemed to threaten on the decease of a leader and the choice of a new one (for elections among ruffians could not be very orderly) induced many at first to favour hereditary pretensions; by which means it happened, as it hath happened since, that what at first was submitted to as a convenience, was afterwards claimed as a right.

England, since the conquest, hath known some few good monarchs, but groaned beneath a much larger number of bad ones, yet no man in his senses can say that their claim under William the Conqueror is a very honourable one. A French bastard landing with an armed banditti, and establishing himself king of England against the consent of the natives, is in plain terms a very paltry rascally original.—It certainly hath no divinity in it. However, it is needless to spend much time in exposing the folly of hereditary right, if there are any so weak as to believe it, let them promiscuously worship the ass and lion, and welcome. I shall neither copy their humility, nor disturb their devotion.

Yet I should be glad to ask how they suppose kings came at first? The question admits but of three answers, viz. either by lot, by election, or by usurpation. If the first king was taken by lot, it establishes a precedent for the next, which excludes hereditary succession. Saul was by lot yet the succession was not hereditary, neither does it appear from that transaction there was any intention it ever should. If the first king of any country was by election, that likewise establishes a precedent for the next; for to say, that the *right* of all future generations is taken away, by the act of the first electors, in their choice not only of a king, but of a family of kings for ever, hath no parallel in or out of scripture but the doctrine of original sin, which supposes the free will of all men lost in Adam; and from such comparison, and it will admit of no other, hereditary succession can derive no glory. For as in Adam all sinned, and as in the first electors all men obeyed; as in the one all mankind were subjected to Satan, and in the other to Sovereignty; as our innocence was lost in the first, and our authority in the last; and as both disable us from re-assuming some former state and privilege, it unanswerably follows that original sin and hereditary succession are parallels. Dishonourable rank! Inglorious connection! Yet the most subtle sophist cannot produce a juster simile.

As to usurpation, no man will be so hardy as to defend it; and that William the Conqueror was an usurper is a fact not to be contradicted. The plain truth is, that the antiquity of English monarchy will not bear looking into.

But it is not so much the absurdity as the evil of hereditary succession which concerns mankind. Did it ensure a race of good and wise men it would have the seal of divine authority, but as it opens a door to the *foolish,* the *wicked,* and the *improper,* it hath in it the nature of oppression. Men who look upon themselves born to reign, and others to obey, soon grow insolent; selected from the rest of mankind their minds are early poisoned by importance; and the world they act in differs so materially from the world at large, that they have but little opportunity of knowing its true interests, and when they succeed to the government are frequently the most ignorant and unfit of any throughout the dominions. . . .

In England a king hath little more to do than to make war and give away places; which in plain terms, is to impoverish the nation and set it together by the ears. A pretty business indeed for a man to be allowed eight hundred thousand sterling a year for, and worshipped into the bargain! Of more worth is one honest man to society, and in the sight of God, than all the crowned ruffians that ever lived.

FEDERALIST NO. 10

James Madison

In 1787 James Madison, Alexander Hamilton, and John Jay wrote a series of newspaper articles under the pseudonym "Publius" advocating the ratification of the U.S. Constitution. They are together regarded as the most important work of political philosophy produced by Americans. The authors were dealing with a difficult issue: how to design the world's first republican government to extend over a large geographical area. They believed that they had devised a practical solution to avoid the various pitfalls of monarchy, majoritarian democracy, or anarchy: a federal government of delegated, enumerated, and thus limited powers, with power divided among three branches of government and a bicameral Congress with the two houses selected in different ways. In the bitter debates over ratification, libertarians debated on both sides. All supported individual rights and limited government; their argument was over whether the proposed Constitution would indeed limit government sufficiently. In this, the best known of the Federalist Papers, Madison, who is generally regarded as the chief architect of the Constitution, discusses how a republican government over a large territory would actually have the advantage of being more immune to the effects of faction than governments of smaller communities. In a large territory, he wrote, "you make it less probable that a majority of the whole will have a common motive to invade the rights of other citizens." An Anti-Federalist, the "Federal Farmer," replied that on the contrary "in large territories, the men who govern find it more easy to unite, while people cannot." The Federalists won the political debate; history is still judging the two arguments.

———————

To the People of the State of New York:
Among the numerous advantages promised by a well-constructed Union, none deserves to be more accurately developed than its tendency to break and control the violence of faction. The friend of popular governments never finds himself so much alarmed for their character and fate, as when he contemplates their propensity to this dangerous vice. He will not fail, therefore, to set a due value on any plan which, without violating the principles to which he is attached, provides a proper cure for it. The instability, injustice, and confusion introduced into the public councils, have, in truth, been the mortal diseases under which popular governments have everywhere perished; as they continue to be the favorite and fruitful topics from which the adversaries to liberty derive their most specious declamations. The valuable improvements made by the American constitutions on the popular models, both ancient and modern, cannot certainly be too much admired; but it would be an unwarrantable partiality, to contend that they have as effectually obviated the danger on this side, as was wished and expected. Complaints are everywhere heard from our most considerate and virtuous citizens, equally the friends of public and private faith, and of public and personal liberty, that our governments are too unstable, that the public good is disregarded in the conflicts of rival parties, and that measures are too often decided, not according to the rules of justice and the rights of the minor party, but by the superior force of an interested and overbearing majority. However anxiously we may wish that these complaints had no foundation, the evidence of known facts will not permit us to deny that they are in some degree true. It will be found, indeed, on a candid review of our situation, that some of the distresses under which we labor have been erroneously charged on the operation of our governments; but it will be found, at the same time, that other causes will not alone account for many of our heaviest misfortunes; and, particularly, for that prevailing and increasing

distrust of public engagements, and alarm for private rights, which are echoed from one end of the continent to the other. These must be chiefly, if not wholly, effects of the unsteadiness and injustice with which a factious spirit has tainted our public administrations.

By a faction, I understand a number of citizens, whether amounting to a majority or minority of the whole, who are united and actuated by some common impulse of passion, or of interest, adverse to the rights of other citizens, or to the permanent and aggregate interests of the community.

There are two methods of curing the mischiefs of faction: the one, by removing its causes; the other, by controlling its effects.

There are again two methods of removing the causes of faction: the one, by destroying the liberty which is essential to its existence; the other, by giving to every citizen the same opinions, the same passions, and the same interests.

It could never be more truly said than of the first remedy, that it was worse than the disease. Liberty is to faction what air is to fire, an aliment without which it instantly expires. But it could not be less folly to abolish liberty, which is essential to political life, because it nourishes faction, than it would be to wish the annihilation of air, which is essential to animal life, because it imparts to fire its destructive agency.

The second expedient is as impracticable as the first would be unwise. As long as the reason of man continues fallible, and he is at liberty to exercise it, different opinions will be formed. As long as the connection subsists between his reason and his self-love, his opinions and his passions will have a reciprocal influence on each other; and the former will be objects to which the latter will attach themselves. The diversity in the faculties of men, from which the rights of property originate, is not less an insuperable obstacle to a uniformity of interests. The protection of these faculties is the first object of government. From the protection of different and unequal faculties of acquiring property, the possession of different degrees and kinds of property immediately results; and from the influence of these on the sentiments and views of the respective proprietors, ensues a division of the society into different interests and parties.

The latent causes of faction are thus sown in the nature of man;

and we see them everywhere brought into different degrees of activity, according to the different circumstances of civil society. A zeal for different opinions concerning religion, concerning government, and many other points, as well of speculation as of practice; an attachment to different leaders ambitiously contending for pre-eminence and power; or to persons of other descriptions whose fortunes have been interesting to the human passions, have, in turn, divided mankind into parties, inflamed them with mutual animosity, and rendered them much more disposed to vex and oppress each other than to co-operate for their common good. So strong is this propensity of mankind to fall into mutual animosities, that where no substantial occasion presents itself, the most frivolous and fanciful distinctions have been sufficient to kindle their unfriendly passions and excite their most violent conflicts. But the most common and durable source of factions has been the various and unequal distribution of property. Those who hold and those who are without property have ever formed distinct interests in society. Those who are creditors, and those who are debtors, fall under a like discrimination. A landed interest, a manufacturing interest, a mercantile interest, a moneyed interest, with many lesser interests, grow up of necessity in civilized nations, and divide them into different classes, actuated by different sentiments and views. The regulation of these various and interfering interests forms the principal task of modern legislation, and involves the spirit of party and faction in the necessary and ordinary operations of the government.

No man is allowed to be a judge in his own cause, because his interest would certainly bias his judgment, and, not improbably, corrupt his integrity. With equal, nay with greater reason, a body of men are unfit to be both judges and parties at the same time; yet what are many of the most important acts of legislation, but so many judicial determinations, not indeed concerning the rights of single persons, but concerning the rights of large bodies of citizens? And what are the different classes of legislators but advocates and parties to the causes which they determine? Is a law proposed concerning private debts? It is a question to which the creditors are parties on one side and the debtors on the other. Justice ought to hold the balance between them. Yet the parties are, and must be, themselves the judges;

and the most numerous party, or, in other words, the most powerful faction must be expected to prevail. Shall domestic manufactures be encouraged, and in what degree, by restrictions on foreign manufactures? are questions which would be differently decided by the landed and the manufacturing classes, and probably by neither with a sole regard to justice and the public good. The apportionment of taxes on the various descriptions of property is an act which seems to require the most exact impartiality; yet there is, perhaps, no legislative act in which greater opportunity and temptation are given to a predominant party to trample on the rules of justice. Every shilling with which they overburden the inferior number, is a shilling saved to their own pockets.

It is in vain to say that enlightened statesmen will be able to adjust these clashing interests, and render them all subservient to the public good. Enlightened statesmen will not always be at the helm. Nor, in many cases, can such an adjustment be made at all without taking into view indirect and remote considerations, which will rarely prevail over the immediate interest which one party may find in disregarding the rights of another or the good of the whole.

The inference to which we are brought is, that the *causes* of faction cannot be removed, and that relief is only to be sought in the means of controlling its *effects*.

If a faction consists of less than a majority, relief is supplied by the republican principle, which enables the majority to defeat its sinister views by regular vote. It may clog the administration, it may convulse the society; but it will be unable to execute and mask its violence under the forms of the Constitution. When a majority is included in a faction, the form of popular government, on the other hand, enables it to sacrifice to its ruling passion or interest both the public good and the rights of other citizens. To secure the public good and private rights against the danger of such a faction, and at the same time to preserve the spirit and the form of popular government, is then the great object to which our inquiries are directed. Let me add that it is the great desideratum by which this form of government can be rescued from the opprobrium under which it has so long labored, and be recommended to the esteem and adoption of mankind.

By what means is this object attainable? Evidently by one of two only. Either the existence of the same passion or interest in a majority at the same time must be prevented, or the majority, having such coexistent passion or interest, must be rendered, by their number and local situation, unable to concert and carry into effect schemes of oppression. If the impulse and the opportunity be suffered to coincide, we well know that neither moral nor religious motives can be relied on as an adequate control. They are not found to be such on the injustice and violence of individuals, and lose their efficacy in proportion to the number combined together, that is, in proportion as their efficacy becomes needful.

From this view of the subject it may be concluded that a pure democracy, by which I mean a society consisting of a small number of citizens, who assemble and administer the government in person, can admit of no cure for the mischiefs of faction. A common passion or interest will, in almost every case, be felt by a majority of the whole; a communication and concert result from the form of government itself; and there is nothing to check the inducements to sacrifice the weaker party or an obnoxious individual. Hence it is that such democracies have ever been spectacles of turbulence and contention; have ever been found incompatible with personal security or the rights of property; and have in general been as short in their lives as they have been violent in their deaths. Theoretic politicians, who have patronized this species of government, have erroneously supposed that by reducing mankind to a perfect equality in their political rights, they would, at the same time, be perfectly equalized and assimilated in their possessions, their opinions, and their passions.

A republic, by which I mean a government in which the scheme of representation takes place, opens a different prospect, and promises the cure for which we are seeking. Let us examine the points in which it varies from pure democracy, and we shall comprehend both the nature of the cure and the efficacy which it must derive from the Union.

The two great points of difference between a democracy and a republic are: first, the delegation of the government, in the latter, to a small number of citizens elected by the rest; secondly, the greater number of citizens, and greater sphere of country, over which the latter may be extended.

The effect of the first difference is, on the one hand, to refine and enlarge the public views, by passing them through the medium of a chosen body of citizens, whose wisdom may best discern the true interest of their country, and whose patriotism and love of justice will be least likely to sacrifice it to temporary or partial considerations. Under such a regulation, it may well happen that the public voice, pronounced by the representatives of the people, will be more consonant to the public good than if pronounced by the people themselves, convened for the purpose. On the other hand, the effect may be inverted. Men of factious tempers, of local prejudices, or of sinister designs, may, by intrigue, by corruption, or by other means, first obtain the suffrages, and then betray the interests, of the people. The question resulting is, whether small or extensive republics are more favorable to the election of proper guardians of the public weal; and it is clearly decided in favor of the latter by two obvious considerations:

In the first place, it is to be remarked that, however small the republic may be, the representatives must be raised to a certain number, in order to guard against the cabals of a few; and that, however large it may be, they must be limited to a certain number, in order to guard against the confusion of a multitude. Hence, the number of representatives in the two cases not being in proportion to that of the two constituents, and being proportionally greater in the small republic, it follows that, if the proportion of fit characters be not less in the large than in the small republic, the former will present a greater option, and consequently a greater probability of a fit choice.

In the next place, as each representative will be chosen by a greater number of citizens in the large than in the small republic, it will be more difficult for unworthy candidates to practise with success the vicious arts by which elections are too often carried; and the suffrages of the people being more free, will be more likely to centre on men who possess the most attractive merit and the most diffusive and established characters.

It must be confessed that in this, as in most other cases, there is a mean, on both sides of which inconveniences will be found to lie. By enlarging too much the number of electors, you render the representative too little acquainted with all their local circumstances and lesser interests; as by reducing it too much, you render him unduly attached to these, and too little fit to comprehend and pursue great and national objects. The federal Constitution forms a happy combination in this respect; the great and aggregate interests being referred to the national, the local and particular to the State legislatures.

The other point of difference is, the greater number of citizens and extent of territory which may be brought within the compass of republican than of democratic government; and it is this circumstance principally which renders factious combinations less to be dreaded in the former than in the latter. The smaller the society, the fewer probably will be the distinct parties and interests composing it; the fewer the distinct parties and interests, the more frequently will a majority be found of the same party; and the smaller the number of individuals composing a majority, and the smaller the compass within which they are placed, the more easily will they concert and execute their plans of oppression. Extend the sphere, and you take in a greater variety of parties and interests; you make it less probable that a majority of the whole will have a common motive to invade the rights of other citizens; or if such a common motive exists, it will be more difficult for all who feel it to discover their own strength, and to act in unison with each other. Besides other impediments, it may be remarked that, where there is a consciousness of unjust or dishonorable purposes, communication is always checked by distrust in proportion to the number whose concurrence is necessary.

Hence, it clearly appears, that the same advantage which a republic has over a democracy, in controlling the effects of faction, is enjoyed by a large over a small republic,—is enjoyed by the Union over the States composing it. Does the advantage consist in the substitution of representatives whose enlightened views and virtuous sentiments render them superior to local prejudices and to schemes of injustice? It will not be denied that the representation of the Union will be most likely to possess these requisite endowments. Does it consist in the greater security afforded by a greater variety of parties, against the event of any one party being able to outnumber and oppress the rest? In an equal degree does the increased variety of parties comprised within the Union, increase this security. Does it, in fine, consist in the greater obstacles opposed to the concert and accomplishment of the secret wishes of an unjust and interested majority? Here, again, the extent of the Union gives it the most palpable advantage.

The influence of factious leaders may kindle a flame within their particular States, but will be unable to spread a general conflagration through the other States. A religious sect may degenerate into a political faction in a part of the Confederacy; but the variety of sects dispersed over the entire face of it must secure the national councils against any danger from that source. A rage for paper money, for an abolition of debts, for an equal division of property, or for any other improper or wicked project, will be less apt to pervade the whole body of the Union than a particular member of it; in the same proportion as such a malady is more likely to taint a particular county or district, than an entire State.

In the extent and proper structure of the Union, therefore, we behold a republican remedy for the diseases most incident to republican government. And according to the degree of pleasure and pride we feel in being republicans, ought to be our zeal in cherishing the spirit and supporting the character of Federalists.

WHAT SORT OF DESPOTISM
DEMOCRATIC NATIONS HAVE TO FEAR

Alexis de Tocqueville

As a young man, Alexis de Tocqueville (1805–59) made a trip
to the United States. His observations on that trip, published in
1835 as *Democracy in America,* came to be regarded as one of
the most profound reflections on liberty and democracy ever
written. Tocqueville admired the United States for its attempt to
implement political equality, but he warned of many problems
that democratic nations might confront. He was concerned
about conflicts between liberty and equality and about the
possibility that excessive individualism could turn into majoritarian tyranny. In this selection he warns of the dangers from
a nurturing government "extending its arm over the whole
community."

I had remarked during my stay in the United States, that a democratic
state of society, similar to that of the Americans, might offer singular
facilities for the establishment of despotism; and I perceived, upon
my return to Europe, how much use had already been made by most
of our rulers, of the notions, the sentiments, and the wants engendered by this same social condition, for the purpose of extending the
circle of their power. This led me to think that the nations of Christendom would perhaps eventually undergo some sort of oppression
like that which hung over several of the nations of the ancient world.

A more accurate examination of the subject, and five years of meditations, have not diminished my apprehensions, but they have changed the object of them.

No sovereign ever lived in former ages so absolute or so powerful as to undertake to administer by his own agency, and without the assistance of intermediate powers, all the parts of a great empire: none ever attempted to subject all his subjects indiscriminately to strict uniformity of regulation, and personally to tutor and direct every member of the community. The notion of such an undertaking never occurred to the human mind; and if any man had conceived it, the want of information, the imperfection of the administrative system, and above all, the natural obstacles caused by the inequality of conditions, would speedily have checked the execution of so vast a design.

When the Roman emperors were at the height of their power, the different nations of the empire still preserved manners and customs of great diversity; although they were subject to the same monarch, most of the provinces were separately administered; they abounded in powerful and active municipalities; and although the whole government of the empire was centred in the hands of the emperor alone, and he always remained, upon occasions, the supreme arbiter in all matters, yet the details of social life and private occupations lay for the most part beyond his control. The emperors possessed, it is true, an immense and unchecked power, which allowed them to gratify all their whimsical tastes, and to employ for that purpose the whole strength of the State. They frequently abused that power arbitrarily to deprive their subjects of property or of life; their tyranny was extremely onerous to the few, but it did not reach the greater number; it was fixed to some few main objects, and neglected the rest; it was violent, but its range was limited.

But it would seem that if despotism were to be established amongst the democratic nations of our days, it might assume a different character; it would be more extensive and more mild; it would degrade men without tormenting them. I do not question, that in an age of instruction and equality like our own, sovereigns might more easily succeed in collecting all political power into their own hands, and might interfere more habitually and decidedly within the circle of private interests, than any sovereign of antiquity could ever do. But this same principle of equality which facilitates despotism, tempers its rigour. We have seen how the manners of society become more humane and gentle in proportion as men become more equal and alike. When no member of the community has much power or much wealth, tyranny is, as it were, without opportunities and a field of action. As all fortunes are scanty, the passions of men are naturally circumscribed,—their imagination limited, their pleasures simple. This universal moderation moderates the sovereign himself, and checks within certain limits the inordinate stretch of his desires.

Independently of these reasons drawn from the nature of the state of society itself, I might add many others arising from causes beyond my subject; but I shall keep within the limits I have laid down to myself.

Democratic governments may become violent and even cruel at certain periods of extreme effervescence or of great danger; but these crises will be rare and brief. When I consider the petty passions of our contemporaries, the mildness of their manners, the extent of their education, the purity of their religion, the gentleness of their morality, their regular and industrious habits, and the restraint which they almost all observe in their vices no less than in their virtues, I have no fear that they will meet with tyrants in their rulers, but rather guardians.

I think then that the species of oppression by which democratic nations are menaced is unlike anything which ever before existed in the world: our contemporaries will find no prototype of it in their memories. I am trying myself to choose an expression which will accurately convey the whole of the idea I have formed of it, but in vain; the old words despotism and tyranny are inappropriate: the thing itself is new; and since I cannot name it, I must attempt to define it.

I seek to trace the novel features under which despotism may appear in the world. The first thing that strikes the observation is an innumerable multitude of men all equal and alike, incessantly endeavouring to procure the petty and paltry pleasures with which they glut their lives. Each of them, living apart, is as a stranger to the fate of all the rest,—his children and his private friends constitute to him the whole of mankind; as for the rest of his fellow-citizens, he is close to them, but he sees them not;—he touches them, but he feels them not; he exists but in himself and for himself alone; and if his kindred still remain to him, he may be said at any rate to have lost his country.

Above this race of men stands an immense and tutelary power, which takes upon itself alone to secure their gratifications, and to watch over their fate. That power is absolute, minute, regular, provident, and mild. It would be like the authority of a parent, if, like that authority, its object was to prepare men for manhood; but it seeks on the contrary to keep them in perpetual childhood: it is well content that the people should rejoice, provided they think of nothing but rejoicing. For their happiness such a government willingly labours, but it chooses to be the sole agent and the only arbiter of that happiness: it provides for their security, foresees and supplies their necessities, facilitates their pleasures, manages their principal concerns, directs their industry, regulates the descent of property, and subdivides their inheritances—what remains, but to spare them all the care of thinking and all the trouble of living?

Thus it every day renders the exercise of the free agency of man less useful and less frequent; it circumscribes the will within a narrower range, and gradually robs a man of all the uses of himself. The principle of equality has prepared men for these things: it has predisposed men to endure them, and oftentimes to look on them as benefits.

After having thus successively taken each member of the community in its powerful grasp, and fashioned them at will, the supreme power then extends its arm over the whole community. It covers the surface of society with a network of small complicated rules, minute and uniform, through which the most original minds and the most energetic characters cannot penetrate, to rise above the crowd. The will of man is not shattered, but softened, bent, and guided: men are seldom forced by it to act, but they are constantly restrained from acting: such a power does not destroy, but it prevents existence; it does not tyrannize, but it compresses, enervates, extinguishes, and stupefies a people, till each nation is reduced to be nothing better than a flock of timid and industrious animals, of which the government is the shepherd.

I have always thought that servitude of the regular, quiet, and gentle kind which I have just described, might be combined more easily than is commonly believed with some of the outward forms of freedom; and that it might even establish itself under the wing of the sovereignty of the people.

Our contemporaries are constantly excited by two conflicting passions; they want to be led, and they wish to remain free: as they cannot destroy either one or the other of these contrary propensities, they strive to satisfy them both at once. They devise a sole, tutelary, and all-powerful form of government, but elected by the people. They combine the principle of centralization and that of popular sovereignty; this gives them a respite: they console themselves for being in tutelage by the reflection that they have chosen their own guardians. Every man allows himself to be put in leading-strings, because he sees that it is not a person or a class of persons, but the people at large that holds the end of his chain.

By this system the people shake off their state of dependence just long enough to select their master, and then relapse into it again. A great many persons at the present day are quite contented with this sort of compromise between administrative despotism and the sovereignty of the people; and they think they have done enough for the protection of individual freedom when they have surrendered it to the power of the nation at large. This does not satisfy me: the nature of him I am to obey signifies less to me than the fact of extorted obedience.

I do not however deny that a constitution of this kind appears to me to be infinitely preferable to one, which, after having concentrated all the powers of government, should vest them in the hands of an irresponsible person or body of persons. Of all the forms which democratic despotism could assume, the latter would assuredly be the worst.

When the sovereign is elective, or narrowly watched by a legislature which is really elective and independent, the oppression which he exercises over individuals is sometimes greater, but it is always less degrading; because every man, when he is oppressed and disarmed, may still imagine, that whilst he yields obedience it is to himself he yields it, and that it is to one of his own inclinations that all the rest give way. In like manner I can understand that when the sovereign represents the nation, and is dependent upon the people, the rights and the power of which every citizen is deprived, not only serve the head of the state, but the state itself; and that private persons derive some return from the sacrifice of their independence which they have made to the public. To create a representation of the people in every centralized country is, therefore, to diminish the evil which extreme centralization may produce, but not to get rid of it.

I admit that by this means room is left for the intervention of individuals in the more important affairs; but it is not the less suppressed in the smaller and more private ones. It must not be forgotten that it is especially dangerous to enslave men in the minor details of life. For my own part, I should be inclined to think freedom less necessary in great things than in little ones, if it were possible to be secure of the one without possessing the other.

Subjection in minor affairs breaks out every day, and is felt by the whole community indiscriminately. It does not drive men to resistance, but it crosses them at every turn, till they are led to surrender the exercise of their will. Thus their spirit is gradually broken and their character enervated; whereas that obedience, which is exacted on a few important but rare occasions, only exhibits servitude at certain intervals, and throws the burden of it upon a small number of men. It is in vain to summon a people, which has been rendered so dependent on the central power, to choose from time to time the representatives of that power; this rare and brief exercise of their free choice, however important it may be, will not prevent them from gradually losing the faculties of thinking, feeling, and acting for themselves, and thus gradually falling below the level of humanity.

OBJECTIONS TO GOVERNMENT INTERFERENCE

John Stuart Mill

John Stuart Mill (1806–73) was a key figure in the development of British liberalism. For many people he is the embodiment of nineteenth-century liberalism, and *On Liberty* is a fixture in political philosophy classes. To libertarians he is often seen as the embodiment of the unfortunate change in the nature of liberalism, from a philosophy of individual rights and laissez-faire economics to a mild version of socialism. Hayek blamed Mill for separating the concept of distribution from that of production, allowing intellectuals and planners to take production as a given and then debate how to divide it. In this selection from *On Liberty,* however, he sounds important libertarian themes: that individuals should be free to live as they choose so long as they don't harm others and that the power of government should be strictly limited.

The object of this Essay is to assert one very simple principle, as entitled to govern absolutely the dealings of society with the individual in the way of compulsion and control, whether the means used be physical force in the form of legal penalties, or the moral coercion of public opinion. That principle is, that the sole end for which mankind are warranted, individually or collectively, in interfering with the liberty of action of any of their number, is self-protection. That the only purpose for which power can be rightfully exercised over any member of a civilized community, against his will, is to prevent harm to others. His own good, either physical or moral, is not a sufficient warrant. . . .

The objections to government interference, when it is not such as to involve infringement of liberty, may be of three kinds.

The first is, when the thing to be done is likely to be better done by individuals than by the government. Speaking generally, there is no one so fit to conduct any business, or to determine how or by whom it shall be conducted, as those who are personally interested in it. This principle condemns the interferences, once so common, of the legislature, or the officers of government, with the ordinary processes of industry. . . .

The second objection is more nearly allied to our subject. In many cases, though individuals may not do the particular thing so well, on the average, as the officers of government, it is nevertheless desirable that it should be done by them, rather than by the government, as a means to their own mental education—a mode of strengthening their active faculties, exercising their judgement, and giving them a familiar knowledge of the subjects with which they are thus left to deal. This is a principal, though not the sole, recommendation of jury trial (in cases not political); of free and popular local and municipal institutions; of the conduct of industrial and philanthropic enterprises by voluntary associations. These are not questions of liberty, and are connected with that subject only by remote tendencies; but they are questions of development. It belongs to a different occasion from the present to dwell on these things as parts of national education; as being, in truth, the peculiar training of a citizen, the practical part of the political education of a free people, taking them out of the narrow circle of personal and family selfishness, and accustoming them to the comprehension of joint interests, the management of joint concerns—habituating them to act from public or semi-public motives, and guide their conduct by aims which unite instead of isolating them from one another. Without these habits and powers, a free constitution can neither be worked nor preserved; as is exemplified by the too-often transitory nature of political freedom in countries where it does not rest upon a sufficient basis of local liberties. The management of purely local business by the localities, and of the great enterprises of industry by the union of those who voluntarily supply the pecuniary means, is further recommended by all the advantages which have been set forth in this Essay as belonging to individuality of development, and diversity of modes of action. Government operations tend to be everywhere alike. With individuals and voluntary associations, on the contrary, there are varied experiments, and endless diversity of experience. What the State can usefully do, is to make itself a central depository, and active circulator and diffuser, of the experience resulting from many trials. Its business is to enable each experimentalist to benefit by the experiments of others; instead of tolerating no experiments but its own.

The third, and most cogent reason for restricting the interference of government, is the great evil of adding unnecessarily to its power. Every function superadded to those already exercised by the government, causes its influence over hopes and fears to be more widely diffused, and converts, more and more, the active and ambitious part of the public into hangers-on of the government, or of some party which aims at becoming the government. If the roads, the railways, the banks, the insurance offices, the great joint-stock companies, the universities, and the public charities, were all of them branches of the government; if, in addition, the municipal corporations and local boards, with all that now devolves on them, became departments of the central administration; if the employes of all these different enterprises were appointed and paid by the government, and looked to the government for every rise in life; not all the freedom of the press and popular constitution of the legislature would make this or any other country free otherwise than in name.

MORE OF THE SAME

H. L. Mencken

H. L. Mencken (1880–1956) was one of America's most respected journalists. He was an incredibly prolific writer, turning out columns for the Baltimore *Evening Sun,* essays for *The
Smart Set* and *The American Mercury,* books such as the monu-
mental *The American Language,* memoirs, and a diary that was
published long after his death. Like many libertarians, he found
his position on the political spectrum changing as he held to
the same views throughout his life. Early in his career, during
the Republican era of 1900–1932, he was seen as a liberal critic
of the complacent bourgeoisie; later he was regarded as a re-
actionary opponent of Franklin Roosevelt and the New Deal.
In fact, he was a consistent libertarian throughout, declaring
his preference for "a government that barely escapes being no
government at all." This 1925 essay from *The American Mercury*
was reprinted in *A Mencken Chrestomathy.*

The average man, whatever his errors otherwise, at least sees clearly
that government is something lying outside him and outside the
generality of his fellow men—that it is a separate, independent and
often hostile power, only partly under his control, and capable of
doing him great harm. In his romantic moments, he may think of it
as a benevolent father or even as a sort of *jinn* or god, but he never
thinks of it as part of himself. In time of trouble he looks to it to perform miracles for his benefit; at other times he sees it as an enemy

with which he must do constant battle. Is it a fact of no significance that robbing the government is everywhere regarded as a crime of less magnitude than robbing an individual, or even a corporation? In the United States today it carries a smaller penalty and infinitely less odium than acts that are intrinsically trivial—for example, marrying two wives, both willing.

What lies behind all this, I believe, is a deep sense of the fundamental antagonism between the government and the people it governs. It is apprehended, not as a committee of citizens chosen to carry on the communal business of the whole population, but as a separate and autonomous corporation, mainly devoted to exploiting the population for the benefit of its own members. Robbing it is thus an act almost devoid of infamy—an exploit rather resembling those of Robin Hood and the eminent pirates of tradition. When a private citizen is robbed a worthy man is deprived of the fruits of his industry and thrift; when the government is robbed the worst that happens is that certain rogues and loafers have less money to play with than they had before. The notion that they have earned that money is never entertained; to most sensible men it would seem ludicrous. They are simply rascals who, by accidents of law, have a somewhat dubious right to a share in the earnings of their fellow men. When that share is diminished by private enterprise the business is, on the whole, far more laudable than not.

The intelligent man, when he pays taxes, certainly does not believe that he is making a prudent and productive investment of his money; on the contrary, he feels that he is being mulcted in an excessive amount for services that, in the main, are useless to him, and that, in substantial part, are downright inimical to him. He may be convinced that a police force, say, is necessary for the protection of his life and property, and that an army and navy safeguard him from being reduced to slavery by some vague foreign kaiser, but even so he views these things as extravagantly expensive—he sees in even the most essential of them an agency for making it easier for the exploiters constituting the government to rob him. In those exploiters themselves he has no confidence whatever. He sees them as purely predatory and useless; he believes that he gets no more net benefit from their vast and costly operations than he gets from the money he lends to his wife's brother. They constitute a power that stands over him constantly, ever alert for new chances to squeeze him. If they could do so safely they would strip him to his hide. If they leave him anything at all, it is simply prudentially, as a farmer leaves a hen some of her eggs.

This gang is well-nigh immune to punishment. Its worst extortions, even when they are baldly for private profit, carry no certain penalties under our laws. Since the first days of the Republic less than a dozen of its members have been impeached, and only a few obscure understrappers have ever been put into prison. The number of men sitting at Atlanta and Leavenworth for revolting against the extortions of the government is always ten times as great as the number of government officials condemned for oppressing the taxpayers to their own gain. Government, today, has grown too strong to be safe. There are no longer any citizens in the world; there are only subjects. They work day in and day out for their masters; they are bound to die for their masters at call. Out of this working and dying they tend to get less and less. On some bright tomorrow, a geological epoch or two hence, they will come to the end of their endurance, and then such newspapers as survive will have a first-page story well worth its black headlines.

THE HUMANITARIAN WITH THE GUILLOTINE

Isabel Paterson

In 1943, at one of the lowest points for liberty and humanity in history, three remarkable women published books that could be said to have given birth to the modern libertarian movement. The best known was Ayn Rand's *The Fountainhead,* which eventually sold millions of copies. Rose Wilder Lane, the daughter of Laura Ingalls Wilder, who had written *Little House on the Prairie* and other stories of American rugged individualism, published a passionate historical essay called *The Discovery of Freedom.* Isabel Paterson (1886–1961), a novelist and literary critic, produced *The God of the Machine,* which defended individualism as the source of progress in the world. In this excerpt Paterson argues that the desire to do good for others can lead people to the conclusion that their concept of the good should be enforced by compulsion.

Most of the harm in the world is done by good people, and not by accident, lapse, or omission. It is the result of their deliberate actions, long persevered in, which they hold to be motivated by high ideals toward virtuous ends. This is demonstrably true; nor could it occur otherwise. The percentage of positively malignant, vicious, or depraved persons is necessarily small, for no species could survive if its members were habitually and consciously bent upon injuring one another. Destruction is so easy that even a minority of persistently evil intent could shortly exterminate the unsuspecting majority of well-disposed persons. . . .

The present war, begun with a perjured treaty made by two powerful nations (Russia and Germany), that they might crush their smaller neighbors with impunity, the treaty being broken by a surprise attack on the fellow conspirator, would have been impossible without the internal political power which in both cases was seized on the excuse of doing good to the nation. *The lies, the violence, the wholesale killings, were practiced first on the people of both nations by their own respective governments.* It may be said, and it may be true, that in both cases the wielders of power are vicious hypocrites; that their conscious objective was evil from the beginning; none the less, they could not have come by the power at all except *with the consent and assistance* of good people. The Communist regime in Russia gained control by promising the peasants land, in terms the promisers knew to be a lie as understood. Having gained power, the Communists took from the peasants the land they already owned; and exterminated those who resisted. This was done by plan and intention; and the lie was praised as "social engineering," by socialist admirers in America. . . .

Why did the humanitarian philosophy of eighteenth century Europe usher in the Reign of Terror? It did not happen by chance; it followed from the original premise, objective and means proposed. The objective is to do good to others as a *primary* justification of existence; the means is the power of the collective; and the premise is that "good" is collective.

The root of the matter is ethical, philosophical, and religious, involving the relation of man to the universe, of man's creative faculty to his Creator. The fatal divergence occurs in failing to recognize the norm of human life. Obviously there is a great deal of pain and distress incidental to existence. Poverty, illness, and accident are possibilities which may be reduced to a minimum, but cannot be altogether eliminated from the hazards mankind must encounter. But these are not desirable conditions, to be brought about or perpetuated. Naturally children have parents, while most adults are in fair health most of their lives, and are engaged in useful activity which brings them a livelihood. That is the norm and the natural order. Ills are marginal. They can be alleviated from the marginal surplus of production; otherwise nothing at all could be done. Therefore it cannot be supposed that the producer exists only for the sake of the non-producer, the well for the sake of the ill, the competent for the sake of the incompetent; nor any person merely for the sake of another. (The logical procedure, if it is held that any person exists only for the sake of another, was carried out in semi-barbarous societies, when the widow or followers of a dead man were buried alive in his grave.)

The great religions, which are also great intellectual systems, have always recognized the conditions of the natural order. They enjoin charity, benevolence, as a moral obligation, to be met out of the producer's surplus. That is, they make it *secondary to production*, for the inescapable reason that without production there could be nothing to give. Consequently they prescribe the most severe rule, to be embraced only voluntarily, for those who wish to devote their lives wholly to works of charity, from contributions. Always this is regarded as a special vocation because it could not be a general way of life. Since the almoner must obtain the funds or goods he distributes from the producers, he has no authority to command; he must ask. When he subtracts his own livelihood from such alms, he must take no more than bare subsistence. In proof of his vocation, he must even forgo the happiness of family life, if he were to receive the formal religious sanction. Never was he to derive comfort for himself from the misery of others. . . .

If the primary objective of the philanthropist, his justification for living, is to help others, his ultimate good *requires that others shall be in want*. His happiness is the obverse of their misery. If he wishes to help "humanity," the whole of humanity must be in need. The humanitarian wishes to be a prime mover in the lives of others. He cannot admit either the divine or the natural order, by which men have the power to help themselves. The humanitarian puts himself in the place of God.

But he is confronted by two awkward facts; first, that the competent do not need his assistance; and second, that the majority of people, if unperverted, positively do not want to be "done good" by the humanitarian. When it is said that everyone should live primarily for others, what is the specific course to be pursued? Is each person to do exactly what any other person wants him to do, without limits or reservations? and only what others want him to do? What if various persons make conflicting demands? The scheme is impracticable. Perhaps then he is to do only what is actually "good" for others. But will those others know what is good for them? No, that is ruled out by the same difficulty. Then shall A do what he thinks is good for B, and B do what he thinks is good for A? Or shall A accept only what he thinks is good for B, and vice versa? But that is absurd. Of course what the humanitarian actually proposes is that *he* shall do what he thinks is good for everybody. It is at this point that the humanitarian sets up the guillotine.

What kind of world does the humanitarian contemplate as affording him full scope? It could only be a world filled with breadlines and hospitals, in which nobody retained the natural power of a human being to help himself or to resist having things done to him. And that is precisely the world that the humanitarian arranges when he gets his way. When a humanitarian wishes to see to it that everyone has a quart of milk, it is evident that he hasn't got the milk, and cannot produce it himself, or why should he be merely wishing? Further, if he did have a sufficient quantity of milk to bestow a quart on everyone, as long as his proposed beneficiaries can and do produce milk for themselves, they would say no, thank you. Then how is the humanitarian to contrive that he shall have all the milk to distribute, and that everyone else shall be in want of milk?

There is only one way, and that is by the use of the political power in its fullest extension. Hence the humanitarian feels the utmost gratification when he visits or hears of a country in which everyone is restricted to ration cards. Where subsistence is doled out, the desideratum has been achieved, of general want and a superior power to "relieve" it. The humanitarian in theory is the terrorist in action.

The good people give him the power he demands because they have accepted his false premise. The advance of science lent it a specious plausibility, with the increase in production. Since there is enough for everybody, why cannot the "needy" be provided for first, and the question thus disposed of permanently? . . .

Why do kind-hearted persons call in the political power? They cannot deny that the means for relief must come from production. But they say there is enough and to spare. Then they must assume that the producers are not willing to give what is "right." Further they assume that there is a collective right to impose taxes, for any purpose the collective shall determine. They localize that right in "the government," as if it were self-existent, forgetting the American axiom that government itself is not self-existent, but is instituted by men for limited purposes. The taxpayer himself hopes for protection from the army or navy or police; he uses the roads; hence his right to insist on limiting taxation is self-evident. The government has no "rights" in the matter, but only a delegated authority.

But if taxes are to be imposed for relief, who is the judge of what is possible or beneficial? It must be either the producers, the needy, or some third group. To say it shall be all three together is no answer; the verdict must swing upon majority or plurality drawn from one or other group. Are the needy to vote themselves whatever they want? Are the humanitarians, the third group, to vote themselves control of both the producers and the needy? (That is what they have done.) The government is thus supposed to be empowered to give "security" to the needy. *It cannot.* What it does is to seize the provision made by private persons for their own security, thus depriving everyone of every hope or chance of security. It can do nothing else, if it acts at all. Those who do not understand the nature of the action are like savages who might cut down a tree to get the fruit; they do not think over time and space, as civilized men must think. . . .

As between the private philanthropist and the private capitalist acting as such, take the case of the truly needy man, who is not incapacitated, and suppose that the philanthropist gives him food and clothes and shelter—when he has used them up, he is just where he was before, except that he may have acquired the habit of dependence. But suppose someone with no benevolent motive whatever, simply wanting work done for his own reasons, should hire the needy man for a wage. The employer has not done a good deed. Yet the condition of the employed man has actually been changed. What is the vital difference between the two actions?

It is that the unphilanthropic employer has brought the man he employed *back into the production line,* on the great circuit of energy; whereas the philanthropist can only divert energy in such manner that there can be no return into production, and therefore less likelihood of the object of his benefaction finding employment. . . .

If the full roll of *sincere* philanthropists were called, from the beginning of time, it would be found that all of them together by their strictly philanthropic activities have never conferred upon humanity one-tenth of the benefit derived from the normally self-interested efforts of Thomas Alva Edison, to say nothing of the greater minds who worked out the scientific principles which Edison applied. Innumerable speculative thinkers, inventors, and organizers, have contributed to the comfort, health, and happiness of their fellow men—because that was not their objective. When Robert Owen tried to run a factory for efficient production, the process incidentally improved some very unpromising characters among his employees, who had been on relief, and were therefore sadly degraded; Owen made money for himself; and while so engaged, it occurred to him that if better wages were paid, production could be increased, having made its own market. That was sensible and true. But then Owen became inspired with a humanitarian ambition, to do good to everybody. He collected a lot of humanitarians, in an experimental colony; they were all so intent upon doing good to others that nobody did a lick of work; the colony dissolved acrimoniously; Owen went broke and died mildly crazy. So the important principle he had glimpsed had to wait a century to be rediscovered.

The philanthropist, the politician, and the pimp are inevitably found in alliance because they have the same motives, they seek the same ends, to exist for, through, and by others.

THE STATE

Murray N. Rothbard

Murray N. Rothbard (1926–95) was a prolific scholar who played a key role in the formation of a consciously libertarian intellectual and political movement. He staked out a radical position within libertarian scholarship, arguing that individual rights were absolute and that all goods and services, including law and justice, could be provided without coercive government. He published books in the fields of economics (*Man, Economy, and State* and *Power and Market*), political philosophy (*The Ethics of Liberty*), history (four volumes of *Conceived in Liberty*), and contemporary policy (*For a New Liberty*). In this excerpt from *For a New Liberty* he argues that the state is "the supreme, the eternal, the best organized aggressor against persons and property."

THE STATE AS AGGRESSOR

The central thrust of libertarian thought, then, is to oppose any and all aggression against the property rights of individuals in their own persons and in the material objects they have voluntarily acquired. While individual and gangs of criminals are of course opposed, there is nothing unique here to the libertarian creed, since almost all persons and schools of thought oppose the exercise of random violence against persons and property. . . .

But the critical difference between libertarians and other people is not in the area of private crime; the critical difference is their view of the role of the State—the government. For libertarians regard the State as the supreme, the eternal, the best organized aggressor against the persons and property of the mass of the public. *All* States everywhere, whether democratic, dictatorial, or monarchical, whether red, white, blue, or brown.

The State! Always and ever the government and its rulers and operators have been considered above the general moral law. The "Pentagon Papers" are only one recent instance among innumerable instances in the history of men, most of whom are perfectly honorable in their private lives, who lie in their teeth before the public. Why? For "reasons of State." Service to the State is supposed to excuse all actions that would be considered immoral or criminal if committed by "private" citizens. The distinctive feature of libertarians is that they coolly and uncompromisingly apply the general moral law to people acting in their roles as members of the State apparatus. Libertarians make no exceptions. For centuries, the State (or more strictly, individuals acting in their roles as "members of the government") has cloaked its criminal activity in high-sounding rhetoric. For centuries the State has committed mass murder and called it "war"; then ennobled the mass slaughter that "war" involves. For centuries the State has enslaved people into its armed battalions and called it "conscription" in the "national service." For centuries the State has robbed people at bayonet point and called it "taxation." In fact, if you wish to know how libertarians regard the State and any of its acts, simply think of the State as a criminal band, and all of the libertarian attitudes will logically fall into place.

Let us consider, for example, what it is that sharply distinguishes government from all other organizations in society. Many political scientists and sociologists have blurred this vital distinction, and refer to all organizations and groups as hierarchical, structured, "governmental," etc. Left-wing anarchists, for example, will oppose equally government *and* private organizations such as corporations on the ground that each is equally "elitist" and "coercive." But the "rightist" libertarian is not opposed to inequality, and his concept of "coercion" applies only to the use of violence. The libertarian sees a crucial distinction between government, whether central, state, or local, and all other institutions in society. Or rather, two crucial distinctions. First, every other person or group receives its income by voluntary payment: either by voluntary contribution or gift (such as the local community chest or bridge club), *or* by voluntary purchase of its goods or services on the market (i.e., grocery store owner, baseball player, steel manufacturer, etc.). *Only* the government obtains its income by coercion and violence—i.e., by the direct threat of confiscation or imprisonment if payment is not forthcoming. This coerced levy is "taxation." A second distinction is that, apart from criminal outlaws, *only* the government can use its funds to commit violence against its own or any other subjects; only the government can prohibit pornography, compel a religious observance, or put people in jail for selling goods at a higher price than the government deems fit. Both distinctions, of course, can be summed up as: *only* the government, in society, is empowered to aggress against the property rights of its subjects, whether to extract revenue, to impose its moral code, or to kill those with whom it disagrees. Furthermore, any and all governments, even the least despotic, have always obtained the bulk of their income from the coercive taxing power. And historically, by far the overwhelming portion of all enslavement and murder in the history of the world have come from the hands of government. And since we have seen that the central thrust of the libertarian is to oppose all aggression against the rights of person and property, the libertarian necessarily opposes the institution of the State as the inherent and overwhelmingly the most important enemy of those precious rights.

There is another reason why State aggression has been far more important than private, a reason apart from the greater organization and central mobilizing of resources that the rulers of the State can impose. The reason is the absence of any check upon State depredation, a check that does exist when we have to worry about muggers or the Mafia. To guard against private criminals we have been able to turn to the State and its police; but who can guard us against the State itself? No one. For another critical distinction of the State is that it compels the monopolization of the service of protection; the State arrogates to itself a virtual monopoly of violence and of ultimate decision-making in society. If we don't like the decisions of the

State courts, for example, there are no other agencies of protection to which we may turn.

It is true that, in the United States, at least, we have a constitution that imposes strict limits on some powers of government. But, as we have discovered in the past century, no constitution can interpret or enforce itself; it must be interpreted by *men*. And if the ultimate power to interpret a constitution is given to the government's own Supreme Court, then the inevitable tendency is for the Court to continue to place its imprimatur on ever-broader powers for its own government. Furthermore, the highly touted "checks and balances" and "separation of powers" in the American government are flimsy indeed, since in the final analysis all of these divisions are part of the same government and are governed by the same set of rulers.

One of America's most brilliant political theorists, John C. Calhoun, wrote prophetically of the inherent tendency of a State to break through the limits of its written constitution:

> A written constitution certainly has many and considerable advantages, but it is a great mistake to suppose that the mere insertion of provisions to restrict and limit the powers of the government, without investing those for whose protection they are inserted with the means of enforcing their observance, will be sufficient to prevent the major and dominant party from abusing its powers. Being the party in possession of the government, they will . . . be in favor of the powers granted by the constitution and opposed to the restrictions intended to limit them. As the major and dominant parties, they will have no need of these restrictions for their protection. . . .
>
> The minor or weaker party, on the contrary, would take the opposite direction and regard them as essential to their protection against the dominant party. . . . But where there are no means by which they could compel the major party to observe the restrictions, the only resort left them would be a strict construction of the constitution. . . . To this the major party would oppose a liberal construction—one which would give to the words of the grant the broadest meaning of which they were susceptible. It would then be construction against construction—the one to contract and the

other to enlarge the powers of the government to the utmost. But of what possible avail could the strict construction of the minor party be, against the liberal interpretation of the major, when the one would have all the powers of the government to carry its construction into effect and the other be deprived of all means of enforcing its construction? In a contest so unequal, the result would not be doubtful. The party in favor of the restrictions would be overpowered. . . . The end of the contest would be the subversion of the constitution . . . the restrictions would ultimately be annulled and the government be converted into one of unlimited powers.

Nor would the division of government into separate and, as it regards each other, independent departments prevent this result . . . as each and all the departments—and, of course, the entire government—would be under the control of the numerical majority, it is too clear to require explanation that a mere distribution of its powers among its agents or representatives could do little or nothing to counteract its tendency to oppression and abuse of powers.[1]

But why worry about the weakness of limits on governmental power? Especially in a "democracy," in the phrase so often used by American liberals in their heyday before the mid-1960s when doubts began to creep into the liberal utopia: "Are *we* not the government?" In the phrase "we are the government," the useful collective term "we" has enabled an ideological camouflage to be thrown over the naked exploitative reality of political life. For if *we* truly *are* the government, then *anything* a government does to an individual is not only just and not tyrannical; it is also "voluntary" on the part of the individual concerned. If the government has incurred a huge public debt which must be paid by taxing one group on behalf of another, this reality of burden is conveniently obscured by blithely saying that "we owe it to ourselves" (but *who* are the "we" and *who* the "ourselves"?). If the government drafts a man, or even throws him

[1] John C. Calhoun, *A Disquisition on Government* (New York: Liberal Arts Press, 1953), pp. 25–27.

into jail for dissident opinions, then he is only "doing it to himself" and therefore nothing improper has occurred. Under this reasoning, then, Jews murdered by the Nazi government were *not* murdered; they must have "committed suicide," since they *were* the government (which was democratically chosen), and therefore anything the government did to them was only voluntary on their part. But there is no way out of such grotesqueries for those supporters of government who see the State merely as a benevolent and voluntary agent of the public.

And so we must conclude that "we" are *not* the government; the government is *not* "us." The government does not in any accurate sense "represent" the majority of the people, but even if it did, even if 90% of the people decided to murder or enslave the other 10%, this would *still* be murder and slavery, and would not be voluntary suicide or enslavement on the part of the oppressed minority. Crime is crime, aggression against rights is aggression, no matter how many citizens agree to the oppression. There is nothing sacrosanct about the majority; the lynch mob, too, is the majority in its own domain.

But while, as in the lynch mob, the majority can become actively tyrannical and aggressive, the normal and continuing condition of the State is *oligarchic* rule: rule by a coercive elite which has managed to gain control of the State machinery. There are two basic reasons for this: one is the inequality and division of labor inherent in the nature of man, which gives rise to an "Iron Law of Oligarchy" in all of man's activities; and second is the parasitic nature of the State enterprise itself.

We have said that the individualist is not an egalitarian. Part of the reason for this is the individualist's insight into the vast diversity and individuality within mankind, a diversity that has the chance to flower and expand as civilization and living standards progress. Individuals differ in ability and in interest both within and between occupations; and hence, in all occupations and walks of life, whether it be steel production or the organization of a bridge club, leadership in the activity will inevitably be assumed by a relative handful of the most able and energetic, while the remaining majority will form themselves into rank-and-file followers. This truth applies to all activities, whether they are beneficial or malevolent (as in criminal organizations). Indeed, the discovery of the Iron Law of Oligarchy was made by the Italian sociologist Robert Michels, who found that the Social Democratic Party of Germany, despite its rhetorical commitment to egalitarianism, was rigidly oligarchical and hierarchical in its actual functioning.

A second basic reason for the oligarchic rule of the State is its parasitic nature—the fact that it lives coercively off the production of the citizenry. To be successful to its practitioners, the fruits of parasitic exploitation must be confined to a relative minority, otherwise a meaningless plunder of all by all would result in no gains for anyone. Nowhere has the coercive and parasitic nature of the State been more clearly limned than by the great late nineteenth-century German sociologist Franz Oppenheimer. Oppenheimer pointed out that there are two and only two mutually exclusive means for man to obtain wealth. One, the method of production and voluntary exchange, the method of the free market, Oppenheimer termed the "economic means"; the other, the method of robbery by the use of violence, he called the "political means." The political means is clearly parasitic, for it requires previous production for the exploiters to confiscate, and it subtracts from instead of adding to the total production in society. Oppenheimer then proceeded to define the State as the "organization of the political means"—the systematization of the predatory process over a given territorial area.[2] . . .

If the State is a group of plunderers, *who* then constitutes the State? Clearly, the ruling elite consists at any time of (a) the full-time *apparatus*—the kings, politicians, and bureaucrats who man and operate the State; and (b) the groups who have maneuvered to gain privileges, subsidies, and benefices from the State. The remainder of society constitutes the ruled. It was, again, John C. Calhoun who saw with crystal clarity that, no matter how small the power of government, no matter how low the tax burden or how equal its distribution, the very nature of government creates two unequal and inherently conflicting classes in society: those who, on net, *pay* the taxes (the "tax-payers"), and those who, on net, *live off* taxes (the "tax-consumers"). Suppose that the government imposes a low and

[2] Franz Oppenheimer, *The State* (New York: Vanguard Press, 1926), pp. 24–27 and passim.

seemingly equally distributed tax to pay for building a dam. This very act takes money from most of the public to pay it out to net "tax-consumers": the bureaucrats who run the operation, the contractors and workers who build the dam, etc. . . .

If states have everywhere been run by an oligarchic group of predators, how have they been able to maintain their rule over the mass of the population? The answer, as the philosopher David Hume pointed out over two centuries ago, is that in the long run *every* government, no matter how dictatorial, rests on the support of the majority of its subjects. Now this does not of course render these governments "voluntary," since the very existence of the tax and other coercive powers shows how much compulsion the State must exercise. Nor does the majority support have to be eager and enthusiastic approval; it could well be mere passive acquiescence and resignation. The conjunction in the famous phrase "death and taxes" implies a passive and resigned acceptance to the assumed inevitability of the State and its taxation.

SELF-INTEREST AND THE CONSTITUTION

Richard Epstein

Richard Epstein is a professor of law at New York University and the University of Chicago. In a series of pathbreaking books he has explored the implications of individual rights, common law, and America's founding principles for such issues as property rights *(Takings: Private Property and the Power of Eminent Domain)*, the relationships of individuals with a complex government *(Bargaining with the State)*, and the limited government embodied in the Constitution *(The Classical Liberal Constitution)*. In *Simple Rules for a Complex World*, he challenged the conventional view that a complex society requires complex law and argued that "government works best when it establishes the rules of the road, not when it seeks to determine the composition of the traffic." In this essay he explored how we can effectively limit government, a theme he developed at greater length in his books.

The choice of a constitution rests in large measure upon our conception of human nature. The relation between human nature and human government was well understood by the political writers who influenced the Framers of our own Constitution, but it is often lost sight of today. What I hope to do in this brief essay is to resurrect a lost tradition and to show why we as a nation have gone astray because we have failed to keep a close tab on certain critical fundamentals of political theory.

To the question What is the driving force of human nature with which constitutions must contend?, I give one answer and one answer only: the Hobbesian answer of self-interest. All people are not equally driven, but when it comes to the use of power, those who have excessive amounts of self-interest are apt to be the most influential—and most dangerous. Hence, it is to curb them, not to accommodate benign altruists, that government should be designed. Of course, we must not over-simplify, for it is surely true that, even among the self-interested, all individuals have different natural talents and endowments. Thus, we should not expect that self-interest will manifest itself in the same way in all people. Some people gain more from cooperation; others gain more from competition—hence the organization of firms and the existence of competition (or collusion) between them. But self-interest can express itself in ways other than competition. Sometimes it works through the use of force and violence or the use of deceit. Politics is not immune from these variations that characterize private behavior. If anything, politics brings out the extremes—of both good and evil. Accordingly, we should expect coalitions, competition, confiscation, and violence to be part of the political process, as they are of private affairs. And it is just that array of behaviors and outcomes that we have observed over time.

There is unfortunately no set of institutions which can escape the ravages of misdirected self-interest. The problem, then, is to design a set of institutions which at some real, admitted positive cost curbs the worst of its excesses. In order to design that system of governance, it is not enough simply to condemn self-interest. Such condemnation cuts too broadly, for then there is nothing left to praise. It is necessary, therefore, to distinguish among the different manifestations of self-interest.

One way to clarify the issue is to examine the correspondence between, or the divergence of, the private and the social interest. Competition and violence give very different pictures. Voluntary bargains tend to benefit both parties to trade and, by increasing the store of wealth, tend (with a few minor exceptions—e.g., monopolies) to have positive external effects on the public at large as well. The greater the wealth in the aggregate, the greater the opportunities for third parties to trade with the contracting parties. When one looks at a full array of transactions, therefore, any outsider's particular loss in one case is overridden by the potential for gain from free trade in a myriad of other transactions. I might wish to stop a voluntary trade between A and B because I hope to sell to A. But if I were forced to decide whether I wish to stop all voluntary sales across the board in order to stop this one, my answer would clearly be no. With the strategic options blocked, I will not forfeit the many opportunities for buying and selling that the system of markets affords to me, along with all others. As a general matter, discrete competitive losses are offset by systematic gains from which everyone—the short-term loser included—benefits. What I want is a special exemption from the general rules. I should not get it.

Violence produces very different social effects than does competition, because one individual's gain is necessarily another's loss. Violence yields no mutual benefits. Further, the third-party effect of violence is to spread fear throughout the general population. There is no reason to think that the total level of wealth or happiness in society will remain constant when incursions on liberty and property are routinely tolerated. Vast resources will be spent on attack and defense, so that the total level of wealth (the social pie) will shrink through the process of coerced redistribution. The negative social consequences of violence stand in sharp opposition to the positive consequences of competition.

There is, then, a functional explanation for the durability of the basic distinction between force and persuasion both in constitutional law and political theory. One obvious way to think of a constitution follows. A constitution should vest in "the sovereign" the task of controlling violence and of facilitating voluntary transactions. Our general success in this task should not blind us to its importance.

THREE LIMITATIONS ON SOVEREIGNTY

It is one thing to specify what behavior is legal and what is not. It is quite another to make sure that the rules are observed in practice.

For enforcement we turn to the sovereign. But who is the sovereign? Here any neat theory of governance tends to break down in practice, just as all systems do when one searches for a prime mover. It is hard to identify the sovereign. We cannot rely upon the market, that is, voluntary transactions, to police and protect the market. Someone will break from the post, set up shop as a sovereign, and claim and exert a monopoly on force. The risk is that the sovereign's self-interest will render him faithless to his duty to protect the legal order. He will have the position and face the temptation to extract all he can from the citizens in order to improve his own personal condition. For example, rent-seeking in politics is simply a statement that the sovereign, i.e., those fallible people with sovereign power, will allow the citizen a little something so long as he continues to make the sovereign better off. Thus, the sovereign, the supposed solution to the problem of political union, himself becomes the problem. And the issue of constitutionalism is just this: how to constrain the misconduct of the sovereign while allowing him the necessary power to keep peace and good order.

Our answer to this problem is limited government. If our task is to limit the power of self-interested individuals, it seems clear that a certain *redundancy* is good for the health of the system. Some barriers may bend or break, and the presence of some back-up protection should merely improve the operation of the system as a whole. The key trick is to make sure that no single individual or small faction obtains or maintains the legal monopoly on force for himself or themselves. Of course, it costs a good deal of money and statecraft to abandon the Hobbesian state wherein everybody is at the mercy of the sovereign, but we can try. Here are three possible limitations on sovereignty: federalism, separation of powers, and entrenched individual rights.

FEDERALISM
First, we should try to maintain competition between the separate governments, as a check to the threat of monopoly. The system of federalism, which was familiar to the Founders because of their colonial experience, represents a profound response to the problem

of governance. The individual states are in competition with each other for residents, businesses, and tax dollars. That competition will limit their capacity for the ruinous forms of expropriation that might otherwise take place, at least if the rights of exit and entry across the states are fully preserved in the governing document. This competitive model generally works without direct judicial regulation of the substantive legislation of the various states. But by the same token, it works only if state powers cannot be supplemented by a vast federal power that covers the same domain of economic issues.

The regrettable jurisprudence under the modern commerce clause cases thus becomes critical in this connection because it shows how Justice Hughes (in the Wagner Act cases) and Justice Jackson (in the agricultural production quota cases) had so little understanding of the relationship between government monopoly and private competition that they gave the federal government the trump over local production and employment decisions. By so doing, they weakened the power of private citizens and increased the opportunities for interest-group politics. The power to exit from any given state loses much of its effectiveness when Congress can regulate private market behavior on a national scale. The groups that are bound in state A can no longer escape their restriction by a move to state B, since the federal solution is undercut by a national cartel enforced at the national level. Federalism as a counterweight to the monopoly sovereign is undercut by the massive expansion of federal power under the commerce clause.

SEPARATION OF POWERS

The second restraint on sovereignty is the division of power across separate branches at every level of government, each division acting as a check on the powers of the others. This system of restraints was built into the original Constitution, and in large measure it has held. The most controversial element is the judicial, but the case for judicial review is that while the courts do have the power to trump legislation, they lack (or should lack) other powers: they have no power of appointment, no power to levy taxes and impose regulations, no power to declare war. Thus, no sovereign monopoly is conferred upon the judges, even under the banner of judicial activism.

Administrative agencies, which were not a part of the Constitution's original plan, raise a more controversial issue. My view is that they are flatly unconstitutional—there is no article IIIA—and for good reason. Keeping the cost of running government low is not an unalloyed blessing when there is a persistent risk of government misconduct. Forcing all powers into three distinct branches reduces the total size of the federal government and forces those in power to make hard choices about what should be done. The rigid division of power operates, therefore, as another indirect limit on the size of government and hence upon its total power. The modern regulatory state is quite unthinkable without independent administrative agencies, and that is the way it should be.

ENTRENCHED RIGHTS
The last part of the overall system is the direct protection of individual rights. In part this principle is necessary because the exit rights from the states (or for that matter the nation) are simply not powerful enough to overcome all forms of governmental abuse. Local expropriation in land use contexts continues to be rampant, and the formal school segregation in the Old South (and to a lesser extent elsewhere) indicates that local governments do exercise some substantial element of monopoly power, which can be turned in unprincipled fashion against some determinate group of citizens for the benefit of the rest. If the key peril is the inability of democratic political institutions to preserve the rights of minorities, then the problem of entrenched legal rights against both state and federal government is rightly regarded as critical to our entire scheme of government.

Accordingly, I strongly support limitations upon government power in all areas of life. In addition, I think that the modern distinction between preferred freedoms and ordinary rights is wholly misguided, not because the former receive too much protection but because the latter receive far too little. It is not sufficient to say that the rich can protect themselves by legislation. We are not trying to protect them as such. The concern is social. There is little good to factional struggles that pit industry against industry, rich against rich, or poor against poor. But whatever the configuration of these struggles, the source of concern is social, not private, losses. The defense of private property that I have tried to mount is not a disguised defense of special privilege. I should strike down any legislation that tries to restrict entry to preserve the province of the well-to-do. As Adam Smith demonstrated so long ago, a belief in property and markets is not a belief in mercantilism, high tariffs, and other barriers to trade.

Our basic purpose is to keep the sovereign, that Leviathan, to manageable proportions. That task is not an easy one, because a constitution requires that one make judgments in the abstract, with confidence that they will hold good in the particular cases that arise in the future. That has proved a recurrent difficulty with all substantive guarantees, but not a hopeless one. The ambiguity and error at the margins, be it with property or speech, are well worth tolerating to preserve the core. Over the years we have been able to fashion principles of freedom of speech that control its use as an adjunct to force and fraud, while allowing it the broadest possible sway in other areas. That same generality is applicable in principle to the constitutional protection of contract and property, notwithstanding their shabby treatment at the hands of the Supreme Court.

Recall the observations I made at the beginning of this paper about the effect of ordinary contracts. If they are correct, then we know that voluntary commercial transactions increase the wealth of the contracting parties and generate systematic positive externalities. The use of violence has exactly the opposite social effect. The argument in no way turns on the particulars of the case, such as the type of private contract or the motivation for violence. We have, therefore, the requisite generality to support a constitutional principle. We can protect the contract whether we work with labor or capital markets, whether we deal with restrictions on entry imposed by the minimum-wage laws, with restrictions on entry that prevent banks from selling securities, or with rent-control laws. As a matter of first principle, they are all unconstitutional. The details of each case do not alter the general analysis. They only indicate the way in which fundamentally wrongheaded legislation takes its toll in social loss, whether measured in terms of utility or wealth. Decisions such as *Lochner* v. *New York* were correct because New York's maximum-hour legislation was vintage special-interest legislation: successful attempts by certain unions to impose disproportionate burdens upon rival firms that employed different modes of production and hence had different requirements for their workforce.

The principles of substantive due process, or of takings, *do* deserve constitutional status, precisely because they have a generality, power, and permanence that are immune to future shifts in technology or tastes. While there is surely a need to leave to the legislature the decision whether to declare war on some foreign nations, there is no similar reason to suspend judgment when the question is whether one should regulate wages and prices of ordinary labor and commodities. Since that question can be answered in the negative once and for all, there is no reason to leave it open so that legislature can get it wrong when they succumb to the powerful pressures and blandishments of special-interest groups. There is a powerful normative theory which explains why the protection of liberty and property is good for all ages, and it is that theory which makes it inadvisable to draw the artificial distinction between the protection of speech and the protection of property which is now embedded in the modern law.

IS CONSTITUTIONALISM POSSIBLE?

The above program is an ambitious one. One might ask, therefore, Can all this be done by any constitution? By our Constitution? One's answer in large part depends upon the view one takes of language, of its capacity to guide and inform. If one assumes that all doctrines are mushy, intellectually open, politically adaptable, and morally contestable, then any effort to formulate a constitution is in vain. Sooner or later, and probably sooner, any serious effort at constitutional elaboration will necessarily fall of its own weight. Yet it seems clear that some provisions of our Constitution, most notably those on separation of powers and freedom of speech and religion, have survived the pounding to which generations of cases have exposed them precisely because linguistic skepticism has never dominated judicial approaches to textual interpretation.

I will go further. I think that very few of the wrong steps that have been taken in our constitutional history can be made respectable by celebrating the open-textured nature of constitutional language. In ordinary usage, manufacture does precede commerce; it is not part of it. In ordinary language, there is no watertight distinction between a tax and a taking. In ordinary language, the creation of legislative and executive power does not authorize the use of administrative agencies. I do not want to minimize the interpretive difficulties that arise under the Constitution even when interpreted with an eye to its basic structure and theory. But the difficulties of interpretation cannot explain the current malaise of modern American constitutional law. The remorseless and enormous expansion in government power can only be explained by the systematic repudiation of the basic principles of limited government which informed the original constitutional structure. It is a different political philosophy that lies at the root of the many decisions that have extended the scope of federal (and state) power over individual affairs. The Constitution was drafted by individuals who tried to find a Lockean response to the Hobbesian problem. It has been interpreted by courts and academics who too often forget that big government is often the problem, not the solution.

PART TWO

INDIVIDUALISM
AND CIVIL SOCIETY

Libertarian social analysis begins with the individual. Although man, unlike other animals, can achieve very little without combining with others, still it is individuals who enter into association. Each individual is responsible for his or her own survival and flourishing. Only individuals can assume responsibility for the consequences of their actions.

The heritage of the West is the extension of human dignity to more people. Through the struggles for freedom of conscience, abolition of slavery, the liberation of women and minorities, and freedom of enterprise, libertarian thinkers have sought to achieve for every individual the dignity of freedom and responsibility.

The notion of individual worth took a long time to develop its modern form. Plato presented a "noble lie" of gold, silver, iron, and bronze souls and suggested that people be led to believe that the gold souls should rule the others. Aristotle laid much of the groundwork for modern thought—and stressed the importance of directing one's own life and making one's own decisions for the achievement of happiness—but even he defended the idea that some people "are intended for being ruled." Even in the ancient world, there were those who rejected such notions. In the fifth century B.C., Alcidamas, a member of the relatively libertarian Sophist school, said, "God has given everybody his freedom, nature has made no man a slave."

The concept of individualism developed in the West through the Christian church's emphasis on the dignity of the individual and his personal relationship with God, and was strengthened by the Protestant Reformation theme of individuals reading and understanding the Bible for themselves and by the spread of printing, which made the Bible more widely available. In the thirteenth century Pope Innocent IV warned Crusaders not to injure the person or property of nonbelievers (such as Jews and Muslims), who were rational individuals with rights. The sixteenth-century scholar Francisco de Vitoria was prominent among the Spanish Scholastic thinkers, sometimes known as the school of Salamanca, whose explorations of theology, natural law, and economics anticipated many of the themes later found in the works of Adam Smith and the Austrian School. From his post at the University of Salamanca, Vitoria condemned the Spanish enslavement of the Indians in the New World in terms of individualism and natural rights: "Every Indian is a man and thus capable of achieving salvation or damnation. Every man is a person and is the master of his body and possession. Inasmuch as he is a person, every Indian has free will and, consequently, is the master of his actions. . . . Every man has the right to his own life and to physical and mental integrity."

During the English Revolution of the seventeenth century, individualism emerged as a defense of the rights of Englishmen. The Leveller leader Colonel Thomas Rainborough famously declared in the Putney Debates, "The poorest he that is in England hath a life to live, as the greatest he." Later, in *The Wealth of Nations,* Adam Smith argued that the *real* wealth of a nation is not the gold and silver held by the crown but the consumable goods available to any random individual, and that wealth would be increased by giving free rein to individuals to pursue their own interest, constrained only by laws equally applicable to all. Through Locke and Paine, Kant and Jefferson, von Humboldt and Mill, the modern concept of individualism developed.

The first clear victory for liberalism was the gradual attainment of religious toleration, which was followed by the more radical demand for complete separation of church and state. John Locke's *Letter Concerning Toleration,* excerpted here, is an eloquent argument for placing individual conscience outside the realm of state power. In discussing how individuals come together in civil society, Adam Smith examines the relationship between justice and beneficence. The latter, he says, makes life more pleasant and is essential to a good society. But if necessary, society could exist without beneficence; it could not exist without justice, by which he means the security of each person's life, liberty, and property against injury by others. So long as our life and property are secure, we can combine with others to achieve our purposes; if that were not the case, we would truly find ourselves in a war of all against all.

In the revolutionary eighteenth century, when men in England, America, and France demanded their rights, some people began to insist that women be included in the community of rights- and responsibility-bearing individuals. Indeed, the new individualist order of capitalism and the intellectual ferment for natural rights could hardly fail to generate strong pressures for feminism, as well as for the abolition of slavery. One of the earliest feminist writers was Mary Wollstonecraft, who asked her fellow liberals "whether, when men contend for their freedom . . . it be not inconsistent and unjust to subjugate women?" Feminism and abolitionism inter-twined in England and America in a general context of liberalism and individual rights. The sisters Sarah and Angelina Grimké began to think of their own rights as women while crusading for the rights of African-Americans. They rested their arguments squarely on the notion that every individual is a moral agent who must take responsibility for his or her actions.

Leading abolitionists were consistent libertarians: They shared a commitment to individual rights, private property, free markets, and limited government. The ideas of natural rights and property are woven throughout the selections here from William Lloyd Garrison, Frederick Douglass, and William Ellery Channing. The first property that every person has, of course, is his property in himself, which is why Garrison's appeal on behalf of the American Anti-Slavery Convention refers to the slaveholder as a "man-stealer."

In an important speech in 1833, the French liberal Benjamin Constant set out the nature of individual liberty in the modern world. We are frequently confused between two meanings of freedom: freedom as participation in public affairs and freedom as the individual right to worship, trade, speak, and "come and go as we please." Constant explains that the former definition was that of the ancient world, but it is not suited to the modern world of commerce and the extended society, where people are busy pursuing their own projects and have no time to spend the day in the public square debating politics.

Alexis de Tocqueville thought a great deal about the relationship between individualism and civil society. He argued that association with others is an important way that people pursue their individual goals. In civil associations, he said, "there is no sacrifice of will or reason, rather will and reason are applied to bring success to a common enterprise." The point for modern theorists of civil society is that individualism and community are coextensive, not in conflict.

John Stuart Mill stressed the importance of individual differences and the development of one's own personality as the reason that people need freedom. Even those of us who are content to conform benefit from a society in which others choose new ways of living, some of which may turn out to be worth emulating.

In the twentieth century libertarians even more vigorously pressed the defense of the individual against the growing power of the state and against intellectual collectivism. Ayn Rand's argument that individuals are "the only creators of any tomorrows humanity has ever been granted" was reminiscent of Mill's point that individuals who discover new ideas worthy of emulation "are the salt of the earth; without them, human life would become a stagnant pool." She denounced collectivism as "the subjugation of the individual to a group . . . to a race, class, or state." Libertarians also continued to emphasize that in a pluralist world individualism and equal rights are not only the moral standard for public policy, they are the policy best suited to reduce social conflict. Rand denounced racism as "the lowest, most crudely primitive form of collectivism. It is the notion of ascribing moral, social or political significance to a man's genetic lineage . . . which means, in practice, that a man is to be judged, not by his own character and actions, but by the characters and actions of a collective of ancestors." Murray Rothbard decried the compulsory segregation practiced in the American South and even ventured to inquire why, when everyone was stressing the importance of non-violence in the civil rights movement, it was acceptable for "the white oppressors, whether in the form of Ku Klux Klan–type mobs or as armed police, [to] be armed and violent." As government's intrusions into individual dignity and individual rights took a new form, Clint Bolick wrote, "If American history has taught us anything at all, it is that government's awesome power to discriminate on the basis of immutable characteristics such as race or gender is inherently divisive and incendiary. . . . In a free society, the government should not possess the power either to discriminate among its citizens, nor to deny them basic liberties." Doug Bandow reminded libertarians that those who reject a role for government in enforcing morality have a special responsibility as members of civil society to speak up for justice and individualism. Charles Murray explored how centralization destroys civil society and produces atomized individuals.

Individualism is not just a philosophical commitment and a political demand. For libertarian scholars, it is also a way of understanding the world. The economist Carl Menger pointed out that because we *are* individuals, we can understand something about individuals and how they act, so that the proper method for social analysis is to trace complex phenomena to the plans and intentions of individuals. Parker T. Moon, a scholar of international relations, wrote in his 1926 book *Imperialism and World Politics:*

> Language often obscures truth. More than is ordinarily realized, our eyes are blinded to the facts of international relations by tricks of the tongue. When one uses the simple monosyllable "France" one thinks of France as a unit, an entity. When to avoid awkward repetition we use a personal pronoun in referring to a country— when for example we say "France sent *her* troops to conquer Tunis"—we impute not only unity but personality to the country. The very words conceal the facts and make international relations a glamorous drama in which personalized nations are the actors, and all too easily we forget the flesh-and-blood men and women who are the true actors. How different it would be if we had no such word as "France," and had to say instead—thirty-eight million men, women and children of very diversified interests and beliefs, inhabiting 218,000 square miles of territory! Then we should more accurately describe the Tunis expedition in some such way as this: "A few of these thirty-eight million persons sent thirty thousand others to conquer Tunis." This way of putting the fact

immediately suggests a question, or rather a series of questions. Who were the "few"? Why did they send the thirty thousand to Tunis? And why did these obey?

Empire-building is done not by "nations" but by men. The problem before us is to discover the men, the active, interested minorities in each nation, who are directly interested in imperialism, and then to analyze the reasons why the majorities pay the expenses and fight the wars necessitated by imperialist expansion.

One effect of methodological individualism is to ask the questions that some might prefer to obscure, whether the topic is imperialism or "national economic planning" or "strengthening family values." Both methodologically and philosophically, libertarianism puts the individual at center stage.

UNDERSTANDING CAN NOT BE COMPELLED

John Locke

Libertarianism is often seen primarily as a philosophy of economic freedom, but its historical roots are perhaps more firmly planted in the struggle for religious toleration. From the early Christians who developed theories of toleration in the face of Roman persecution to the observers of the happy Dutch experience with toleration in the seventeenth century, proto-libertarians argued that each person has "a property in his conscience" into which the state should not intrude. John Locke (1632–1704) argued both that "liberty of conscience is every man's natural right" and that truth would emerge from religious pluralism. This selection is drawn from his *Letter Concerning Toleration,* published in 1689.

I esteem it above all things necessary to distinguish exactly the business of civil government from that of religion, and to settle the just bounds that lie between the one and the other. If this be not done, there can be no end put to the controversies that will be always arising between those that have, or at least pretend to have, on the one side, a concernment for the interest of men's souls, and, on the other side, a care of the commonwealth.

The commonwealth seems to me to be a society of men constituted only for the procuring, preserving, and advancing their own civil interests.

Civil interest I call life, liberty, health, and indolency of body; and the possession of outward things, such as money, lands, houses, furniture, and the like. . . .

The care of souls cannot belong to the civil magistrate, because his power consists only in outward force: but true and saving religion consists in the inward persuasion of the mind, without which nothing can be acceptable to God. And such is the nature of the understanding, that it cannot be compelled to the belief of any thing by outward force. . . .

It is one thing to persuade, another to command; one thing to press with arguments, another with penalties. This the civil power alone has a right to do; to the other, good-will is authority enough. Every man has commission to admonish, exhort, convince another of error, and by reasoning to draw him into truth: but to give laws, receive obedience, and compel with the sword, belongs to none but the magistrate. And upon this ground I affirm, that the magistrate's power extends not to the establishing of any articles of faith, or forms of worship, by the force of his laws. For laws are of no force at all without penalties, and penalties in this case are absolutely impertinent; because they are not proper to convince the mind. . . .

Let us now consider what a church is. A church then I take to be a voluntary society of men, joining themselves together of their own accord, in order to the public worshipping of God, in such a manner as they judge acceptable to him, and effectual to the salvation of their souls.

I say, it is a free and voluntary society. Nobody is born a member of any church; otherwise the religion of parents would descend unto children, by the same right of inheritance as their temporal estates, and every one would hold his faith by the same tenure he does his lands; than which nothing can be imagined more absurd. . . .

And first, I hold, that no church is bound by the duty of toleration to retain any such person in her bosom, as after admonition continues obstinately to offend against the laws of society. . . .

Secondly: no private person has any right in any manner to prejudice another person in his civil enjoyments, because he is of another church or religion. . . .

Nobody therefore, in fine, neither single persons, nor churches, nay, nor even commonwealths, have any just title to invade the civil rights and worldly goods of each other, upon pretense of religion. Those that are of another opinion, would do well to consider with themselves how pernicious a seed of discord and war, how powerful a provocation to endless hatreds, rapines, and slaughters, they thereby furnish unto mankind. No peace and security, no, not so much as common friendship, can ever be established or preserved amongst men, so long as this opinion prevails, "that dominion is founded in grace, and that religion is to be propagated by force of arms." . . .

We have already proved, that the care of souls does not belong to the magistrate: not a magisterial care, I mean, if I may so call it, which consists in prescribing by laws, and compelling by punishments. But a charitable care, which consists in teaching, admonishing, and persuading, cannot be denied unto any man. The care therefore of every man's soul belongs unto himself, and is to be left unto himself. But what if he neglect the care of his soul? I answer, what if he neglect the care of his health, or of his estate; which things are nearlier related to the government of the magistrate than the other? Will the magistrate provide by an express law, that such a one shall not become poor or sick? Laws provide, as much as is possible, that the goods and health of subjects be not injured by the fraud or violence of others; they do not guard them from the negligence or ill husbandry of the possessors themselves. No man can be forced to be rich or healthful, whether he will or no. Nay, God himself will not save men against their wills. . . .

In the next place: as the magistrate has no power to impose, by his laws, the use of any rites and ceremonies in any church; so neither has he any power to forbid the use of such rites and ceremonies as are already received, approved, and practiced by any church: because, if he did so, he would destroy the church itself; the end of whose institution is only to worship God with freedom, after its own manner.

You will say, by this rule, if some congregations should have a mind to sacrifice infants, or, as the primitive Christians were falsely accused, lustfully pollute themselves in promiscuous uncleanness, or practice any other such heinous enormities, is the magistrate obliged to tolerate them, because they are committed in a religious assembly? I answer, No. These things are not lawful in the ordinary course of life, nor in any private house; and, therefore, neither are they so in the worship of God, or in any religious meeting. But, indeed, if any people congregated upon account of religion, should be desirous to sacrifice a calf, I deny that that ought to be prohibited by a law. Meliboeus, whose calf it is, may lawfully kill his calf at home, and burn any part of it that he thinks fit: for no injury is thereby done to any one, no prejudice to another man's goods. And for the same reason he may kill his calf also in a religious meeting. Whether the doing so be well-pleasing to God or no, it is their part to consider that do it.— The part of the magistrate is only to take care that the commonwealth receive no prejudice, and that there be no injury done to any man, either in life or estate. . . .

But idolatry, say some, is a sin, and therefore not to be tolerated. If they said it were therefore to be avoided, the inference were good. But it does not follow, that because it is a sin, it ought therefore to be punished by the magistrate. For it does not belong unto the magistrate to make use of his sword in punishing every thing, indifferently, that he takes to be a sin against God. Covetousness, uncharitableness, idleness, and many other things are sins, by the consent of all men, which yet no man ever said were to be punished by the magistrate. The reason is, because they are not prejudicial to other men's rights, nor do they break the public peace of societies. . . .

Speculative opinions, therefore, and articles of faith, as they are called, which are required only to be believed, cannot be imposed on any church by the law of the land; for it is absurd that things should be enjoined by laws which are not in men's power to perform; and to believe this or that to be true does not depend upon our will. . . .

Further, the magistrate ought not to forbid the preaching or professing of any speculative opinions in any church, because they have no manner of relation to the civil rights of the subjects. If a Roman Catholic believe that to be really the body of Christ, which another man calls bread, he does no injury thereby to his neighbor. If a Jew does not believe the New Testament to be the word of God, he does not thereby alter any thing in men's civil rights. If a heathen doubt of both Testaments, he is not therefore to be punished as a pernicious citizen. The power of the magistrate, and the estates of the people, may be equally secure, whether any man believe these things or no. I readily grant that these opinions are false and absurd; but the business of laws is not to provide for the truth of opinions, but for the safety and security of the commonwealth, and of every particular man's goods and person. And so it ought to be; for truth certainly would do well enough, if she were once left to shift for herself. She seldom has received, and I fear never will receive, much assistance from the power of great men, to whom she is but rarely known, and more rarely welcome. She is not taught by laws, not has she any need of force to procure her entrance into the minds of men. . . .

Any one may employ as many exhortations and arguments as he pleases, towards the promoting of another man's salvation. But all force and compulsion are to be forborn. . . .

But to come to particulars. I say, first, no opinions contrary to human society, or to those moral rules which are necessary to the preservation of civil society, are to be tolerated by the magistrate. But of those indeed examples in any church are rare. For no sect can easily arrive to such a degree of madness, as that it should think fit to teach, for doctrines of religion, such things as manifestly undermine the foundations of society, and are therefore condemned by the judgment of all mankind: because their own interest, peace, reputation, every thing would be thereby endangered.

Another more secret evil, but more dangerous to the commonwealth, is when men arrogate to themselves, and to those of their own sect, some peculiar prerogative, covered over with a specious show of deceitful words, but in effect opposite to the civil rights of the community. For example: we cannot find any sect that teaches expressly and openly, that men are not obliged to keep their promise; that princes may be dethroned by those that differ from them in religion; or that the dominion of all things belongs only to themselves. . . . But nevertheless, we find those that say the same things in other words. . . . These therefore, and the like, who attribute unto the faithful, religious, and orthodox, that is, in plain terms, unto themselves, any peculiar privilege or power above other mortals, in civil concernments; or who, upon pretense of religion, do challenge any manner of authority over such as are not associated with them in their ecclesiastical communion; I say these have no right to be tolerated by the magistrate; as neither those that will not own and teach the duty of tolerating all men in matters of mere religion. For what do all these and the like doctrines signify, but that they may, and are ready upon any occasion to seize the government, and possess themselves of the estates and fortunes of their fellow-subjects; and that they only ask leave to be tolerated by the magistrates so long, until they find themselves strong enough to effect it.

Again: that church can have no right to be tolerated by the magistrate, which is constituted upon such a bottom, that all those who enter into it, do thereby, *ipso facto,* deliver themselves up to the protection and service of another prince. . . .

Lastly, those are not at all to be tolerated who deny the being of God. Promises, covenants, and oaths, which are the bonds of human society, can have no hold upon an atheist.

JUSTICE AND BENEFICENCE

Adam Smith

Adam Smith (1723–90) is best known as the father of modern economics, but he was a professor of moral philosophy at the University of Glasgow in Scotland. His first book, *The Theory of Moral Sentiments* (1759), makes clear that the common view of Smith as an advocate of self-interest and obsessive capital accumulation is entirely wrong. In fact, he tried to understand human motivations, including both self-interest and sympathy with others, and offered the metaphor of the Impartial Spectator by which we all weigh the justice and morality of our actions. He urges a balance between the virtues of prudence, justice, and benevolence. In these excerpts from *The Theory of Moral Sentiments,* he explains why benevolence is desirable but justice is essential to civil society and how we measure our behavior in the eyes of others.

It is thus that man, who can subsist only in society, was fitted by nature to that situation for which he was made. All the members of human society stand in need of each other's assistance, and are likewise exposed to mutual injuries. Where the necessary assistance is reciprocally afforded from love, from gratitude, from friendship, and esteem, the society flourishes and is happy. All the different members of it are bound together by the agreeable bands of love and affection, and are, as it were, drawn to one common centre of mutual good offices.

But though the necessary assistance should not be afforded from such generous and disinterested motives, though among the different members of the society there should be no mutual love and affection, the society, though less happy and agreeable, will not necessarily be dissolved. Society may subsist among different men, as among different merchants, from a sense of its utility, without any mutual love or affection; and though no man in it should owe any obligation, or be bound in gratitude to any other, it may still be upheld by a mercenary exchange of good offices according to an agreed valuation.

Society, however, cannot subsist among those who are at all times ready to hurt and injure one another. The moment that injury begins, the moment that mutual resentment and animosity take place, all the bands of it are broken asunder, and the different members of which it consisted, are, as it were, dissipated and scattered abroad by the violence and opposition of their discordant affections. If there is any society among robbers and murderers, they must at least, according to the trite observation, abstain from robbing and murdering one another. Beneficence, therefore, is less essential to the existence of society than justice. Society may subsist, though not in the most comfortable state, without beneficence; but the prevalence of injustice must utterly destroy it.

Though nature, therefore, exhorts mankind to acts of beneficence, by the pleasing consciousness of deserved reward, she has not thought it necessary to guard and enforce the practice of it by the terrors of merited punishment in case it should be neglected. It is the ornament which embellishes, not the foundation which supports the building, and which it was, therefore, sufficient to recommend, but by no means necessary to impose. Justice, on the contrary, is the main pillar that upholds the whole edifice. . . .

The principle by which we naturally either approve or disapprove of our own conduct, seems to be altogether the same with that by which we exercise the like judgments concerning the conduct of other people. We either approve or disapprove of the conduct of another man, according as we feel that, when we bring his case home to ourselves, we either can or cannot entirely sympathize with the sentiments and motives which directed it. And, in the same manner, we either approve or disapprove of our own conduct, according as we feel that, when we place ourselves in the situation of another man, and view it, as it were, with his eyes and from his station, we either can or cannot entirely enter into and sympathize with the sentiments and motives which influenced it. We can never survey our own sentiments and motives, we can never form any judgment concerning them, unless we remove ourselves, as it were, from our own natural station, and endeavour to view them as at a certain distance from us. But we can do this in no other way than by endeavouring to view them with the eyes of other people, or as other people are likely to view them. Whatever judgment we can form concerning them, accordingly, must always bear some secret reference, either to what are, or to what, upon a certain condition, would be, or to what, we imagine, ought to be the judgment of others. We endeavour to examine our own conduct, as we imagine any other fair and impartial spectator would examine it. If, upon placing ourselves in his situation, we thoroughly enter into all the passions and motives which influenced it, we approve of it, by sympathy with the approbation of this supposed equitable judge. If otherwise, we enter into his disapprobation, and condemn it.

Were it possible that a human creature could grow up to manhood in some solitary place, without any communication with his own species, he could no more think of his own character, of the propriety or demerit of his own sentiments and conduct, of the beauty or deformity of his own mind, than of the beauty or deformity of his own face. All these are objects which he cannot easily see, which naturally he does not look at, and with regard to which he is provided with no mirror which can present them to his view. Bring him into society, and he is immediately provided with the mirror which he wanted before. It is placed in the countenance and behaviour of those he lives with, which always mark when they enter into, and when they disapprove of his sentiments; and it is here that he first views the propriety and impropriety of his own passions, the beauty and deformity of his own mind. . . .

When I endeavour to examine my own conduct, when I endeavour to pass sentence upon it, and either to approve or condemn it, it is evident that, in all such cases, I divide myself, as it were, into two persons; and that I, the examiner and judge, represent a different character from that other I, the person whose conduct is examined into and judged of. The first is the spectator, whose sentiments with regard to my own conduct I endeavour to enter into, by placing myself in his situation, and by considering how it would appear to me, when seen from that particular point of view. The second is the agent, the person whom I properly call myself, and of whose conduct, under the character of a spectator, I was endeavouring to form some opinion. The first is the judge; the second the person judged of. But that the judge should, in every respect, be the same with the person judged of, is as impossible as that the cause should, in every respect, be the same with the effect.

To be amiable and to be meritorious; that is, to deserve love and to deserve reward, are the great characters of virtue; and to be odious and punishable, of vice. But all these characters have an immediate reference to the sentiments of others. Virtue is not said to be amiable, or to be meritorious, because it is the object of its own love, or of its own gratitude; but because it excites those sentiments in other men. The consciousness that it is the object of such favourable regards, is the source of that inward tranquillity and self-satisfaction with which it is naturally attended, as the suspicion of the contrary gives occasion to the torments of vice. What so great happiness as to be beloved, and to know that we deserve to be beloved? What so great misery as to be hated, and to know that we deserve to be hated? . . .

Our sensibility to the feelings of others, so far from being inconsistent with the manhood of self-command, is the very principle upon which that manhood is founded. The very same principle or instinct which, in the misfortune of our neighbour, prompts us to compassionate his sorrow, in our own misfortune, prompts us to restrain the abject and miserable lamentations of our own sorrow. The same principle or instinct which, in his prosperity and success, prompts us to congratulate his joy, in our own prosperity and success, prompts us to restrain the levity and intemperance of our own joy. In both cases, the propriety of our own sentiments and feelings seems to be exactly in proportion to the vivacity and force with which we enter into and conceive his sentiments and feelings.

The man of the most perfect virtue, the man whom we naturally love and revere the most, is he who joins, to the most perfect command of his own original and selfish feelings, the most exquisite sensibility both to the original and sympathetic feelings of others. The man who, to all the soft, the amiable, and the gentle virtues, joins all the great, the awful, and the respectable, must surely be the natural and proper object of our highest love and admiration.

The person best fitted by nature for acquiring the former of those two sets of virtues, is likewise necessarily best fitted for acquiring the latter. The man who feels the most for the joys and sorrows of others, is best fitted for acquiring the most complete control of his own joys and sorrows. The man of the most exquisite humanity is naturally the most capable of acquiring the highest degree of self-command.

THE SUBJUGATION OF WOMEN

Mary Wollstonecraft

The fervor for natural rights in the late eighteenth century inevitably led some people to raise the issue of the rights of women. Mary Wollstonecraft (1759–97) responded to Edmund Burke's *Reflections on the Revolution in France* by writing *A Vindication of the Rights of Men,* in which she argued that "the birthright of man . . . is such a degree of liberty, civil and religious, as is compatible with the liberty of every other individual with whom he is united in a social compact." Just two years later she published *A Vindication of the Rights of Woman,* which asked, "Consider . . . whether, when men contend for their freedom . . . it be not inconsistent and unjust to subjugate women?" Her case for women's rights is made entirely in libertarian terms of equal and natural rights. Mary Wollstonecraft and her husband William Godwin, himself a prominent political theorist, were the parents of Mary Wollstonecraft Shelley, the author of *Frankenstein.*

Consider, I address you as a legislator, whether, when men contend for their freedom, and to be allowed to judge for themselves respecting their own happiness, it be not inconsistent and unjust to subjugate women, even though you firmly believe that you are acting in the manner best calculated to promote their happiness? Who made man the exclusive judge, if woman partake with him the gift of reason? . . .

Let there be then no coercion *established* in society, and the common law of gravity prevailing, the sexes will fall into their proper places. And, now that more equitable laws are forming your citizens, marriage may become more sacred: your young men may choose wives from motives of affection, and your maidens allow love to root out vanity. . . .

As to the argument respecting the subjection in which the sex has ever been held, it retorts on man. The many have always been enthralled by the few; and monsters, who scarcely have shewn any discernment of human excellence, have tyrannized over thousands of their fellow-creatures. Why have men of superior endowments submitted to such degradation? For, is it not universally acknowledged that kings, viewed collectively, have ever been inferior, in abilities and virtue, to the same number of men taken from the common mass of mankind—yet, have they not, and are they not still treated with a degree of reverence that is an insult to reason? China is not the only country where a living man has been made a God. *Men* have submitted to superior strength to enjoy with impunity the pleasure of the moment—*women* have only done the same, and therefore till it is proved that the courtier, who servilely resigns the birthright of a man, is not a moral agent, it cannot be demonstrated that woman is essentially inferior to man because she has always been subjugated.

Brutal force has hitherto governed the world, and that the science of politics is in its infancy, is evident from philosophers scrupling to give the knowledge most useful to man that determinate distinction.

I shall not pursue this argument any further than to establish an obvious inference, that as sound politics diffuse liberty, mankind, including woman, will become more wise and virtuous. . . .

Women are, in common with men, rendered weak and luxurious by the relaxing pleasures which wealth procures; but added to this they are made slaves to their persons, and must render them alluring that man may lend them his reason to guide their tottering steps aright. Or should they be ambitious, they must govern their tyrants by sinister tricks, for without rights there cannot be any incumbent duties. The laws respecting woman, which I mean to discuss in a future part, make an absurd unit of a man and his wife; and then, by the easy transition of only considering him as responsible, she is reduced to a mere cypher. . . .

It is a melancholy truth; yet such is the blessed effect of civilization! the most respectable women are the most oppressed; and, unless they have understandings far superiour to the common run of understandings, taking in both sexes, they must, from being treated like contemptible beings, become contemptible. How many women thus waste life away the prey of discontent, who might have practised as physicians, regulated a farm, managed a shop, and stood erect, supported by their own industry, instead of hanging their heads surcharged with the dew of sensibility, that consumes the beauty to which it at first gave lustre; nay, I doubt whether pity and love are so near akin as poets feign, for I have seldom seen much compassion excited by the helplessness of females, unless they were fair; then, perhaps, pity was the soft handmaid of love, or the harbinger of lust.

How much more respectable is the woman who earns her own bread by fulfilling any duty, than the most accomplished beauty!— beauty did I say?—so sensible am I of the beauty of moral loveliness, or the harmonious propriety that attunes the passions of a well-regulated mind, that I blush at making the comparison; yet I sigh to think how few women aim at attaining this respectability by withdrawing from the giddy whirl of pleasure, or the indolent calm that stupifies the good sort of women it sucks in.

Proud of their weakness, however, they must always be protected, guarded from care, and all the rough toils that dignify the mind.—If this be the fiat of fate, if they will make themselves insignificant and contemptible, sweetly to waste "life away," let them not expect to be valued when their beauty fades, for it is the fate of the fairest flowers to be admired and pulled to pieces by the careless hand that plucked them. In how many ways do I wish, from the purest benevolence, to impress this truth on my sex; yet I fear that they will not listen to a truth that dear bought experience has brought home to many an agitated bosom, nor willingly resign the privileges of rank and sex for the privileges of humanity, to which those have no claim who do not discharge its duties.

Those writers are particularly useful, in my opinion, who make man feel for man, independent of the station he fills, or the drapery of factitious sentiments. I then would fain convince reasonable men of the importance of some of my remarks; and prevail on them to weigh dispassionately the whole tenor of my observations.—I appeal to their understandings; and, as a fellow-creature, claim, in the name of my sex, some interest in their hearts. I entreat them to assist to emancipate their companion, to make her a *help meet* for them!

Would men but generously snap our chains, and be content with rational fellowship instead of slavish obedience, they would find us more observant daughters, more affectionate sisters, more faithful wives, more reasonable mothers—in a word, better citizens. We should then love them with true affection, because we should learn to respect ourselves; and the peace of mind of a worthy man would not be interrupted by the idle vanity of his wife, nor the babes sent to nestle in a strange bosom, having never found a home in their mother's.

THE LIBERTY OF THE ANCIENTS
COMPARED WITH THAT OF THE MODERNS

Benjamin Constant

Benjamin Constant (1767–1830) was a prominent French liberal in the postrevolutionary era. He served in the chamber of deputies and helped to shape a parliamentary opposition along the English model. In his political writings he examined the nature of liberty and in particular the differences between the liberty of the ancient city-states and the individual liberty suitable to modern commercial society. He sympathized with the longing for the ancient forms but believed that modernity was both preferable and inevitable. In this essay, delivered as a speech in 1833, he argues that the ancient concept of liberty as political participation was not suited to modern society, in which people were busy with the production of wealth. Modern people want autonomy, the freedom to live their lives as they choose, more than full-time participation in politics. This essay has been enormously influential in the development of Continental liberalism, but it was until recently known in the English-speaking world almost exclusively through the influence it had on the Oxford philosopher Isaiah Berlin.

Gentlemen,
I wish to submit for your attention a few distinctions, still rather new, between two kinds of liberty: these differences have thus far remained unnoticed, or at least insufficiently remarked. The first is

the liberty the exercise of which was so dear to the ancient peoples; the second the one the enjoyment of which is especially precious to the modern nations. If I am right, this investigation will prove interesting from two different angles.

Firstly, the confusion of these two kinds of liberty has been amongst us, in the all too famous days of our revolution, the cause of many an evil. France was exhausted by useless experiments, the authors of which, irritated by their poor success, sought to force her to enjoy the good she did not want, and denied her the good which she did want.

Secondly, called as we are by our happy revolution (I call it happy, despite its excesses, because I concentrate my attention on its results) to enjoy the benefits of representative government, it is curious and interesting to discover why this form of government, the only one in the shelter of which we could find some freedom and peace today, was totally unknown to the free nations of antiquity. . . .

This system is a discovery of the moderns, and you will see, Gentlemen, that the condition of the human race in antiquity did not allow for the introduction or establishment of an institution of this nature. The ancient peoples could neither feel the need for it, nor appreciate its advantages. Their social organization led them to desire an entirely different freedom from the one which this system grants to us.

Tonight's lecture will be devoted to demonstrating this truth to you.

First ask yourselves, Gentlemen, what an Englishman, a Frenchman, and a citizen of the United States of America understand today by the word "liberty."

For each of them it is the right to be subjected only to the laws, and to be neither arrested, detained, put to death or maltreated in any way by the arbitrary will of one or more individuals. It is the right of everyone to express their opinion, choose a profession and practise it, to dispose of property, and even to abuse it; to come and go without permission, and without having to account for their motives or undertakings. It is everyone's right to associate with other individuals, either to discuss their interests, or to profess the religion which they and their associates prefer, or even simply to occupy their days or hours in a way which is most compatible with their inclinations or whims. Finally it is everyone's right to exercise some influence on the administration of the government, either by electing all or particular officials, or through representations, petitions, demands to which the authorities are more or less compelled to pay heed. Now compare this liberty with that of the ancients.

The latter consisted in exercising collectively, but directly, several parts of the complete sovereignty; in deliberating, in the public square, over war and peace; in forming alliances with foreign governments; in voting laws, in pronouncing judgements; in examining the accounts, the acts, the stewardship of the magistrates; in calling them to appear in front of the assembled people, in accusing, condemning or absolving them. But if this was what the ancients called liberty, they admitted as compatible with this collective freedom the complete subjection of the individual to the authority of the community. You find among them almost none of the enjoyments which we have just seen form part of the liberty of the moderns. All private actions were submitted to a severe surveillance. No importance was given to individual independence, neither in relation to opinions, nor to labour, nor, above all, to religion. The right to choose one's own religious affiliation, a right which we regard as one of the most precious, would have seemed to the ancients a crime and a sacrilege. In the domains which seem to us the most useful, the authority of the social body interposed itself and obstructed the will of individuals. Among the Spartans, Therpandrus could not add a string to his lyre without causing offence to the ephors. In the most domestic of relations the public authority again intervened. The young Lacedaemonian could not visit his new bride freely. In Rome, the censors cast a searching eye over family life. The laws regulated customs, and as customs touch on everything, there was hardly anything that the laws did not regulate.

Thus among the ancients the individual, almost always sovereign in public affairs, was a slave in all his private relations. As a citizen, he decided on peace and war; as a private individual, he was constrained, watched and repressed in all his movements; as a member of the collective body, he interrogated, dismissed, condemned, beggared, exiled, or sentenced to death his magistrates and superiors; as a subject of the collective body he could himself be deprived of his status, stripped of his privileges, banished, put to death, by the discretionary will of the whole to which he belonged. Among the moderns, on the contrary, the individual, independent in his private life, is, even in the freest of states, sovereign only in appearance. His sovereignty is restricted and almost always suspended. If, at fixed and rare intervals, in which he is again surrounded by precautions and obstacles, he exercises this sovereignty, it is always only to renounce it.

I must at this point, Gentlemen, pause for a moment to anticipate an objection which may be addressed to me. There was in antiquity a republic where the enslavement of individual existence to the collective body was not as complete as I have described it. This republic was the most famous of all: you will guess that I am speaking of Athens. I shall return to it later, and in subscribing to the truth of this fact, I shall also indicate its cause. We shall see why, of all the ancient states, Athens was the one which most resembles the modern ones. Everywhere else social jurisdiction was unlimited. The ancients, as Condorcet says, had no notion of individual rights. Men were, so to speak, merely machines, whose gears and cog-wheels were regulated by the law. The same subjection characterized the golden centuries of the Roman republic; the individual was in some way lost in the nation, the citizen in the city.

We shall now trace this essential difference between the ancients and ourselves back to its source.

All ancient republics were restricted to a narrow territory. The most populous, the most powerful, the most substantial among them, was not equal in extension to the smallest of modern states. As an inevitable consequence of their narrow territory, the spirit of these republics was bellicose; each people incessantly attacked their neighbours or was attacked by them. Thus driven by necessity against one another, they fought or threatened each other constantly. Those who had no ambition to be conquerors, could still not lay down their weapons, lest they should themselves be conquered. All had to buy their security, their independence, their whole existence at the price of war. This was the constant interest, the almost habitual occupation of the free states of antiquity. Finally, by an equally necessary result of this way of being, all these states had slaves. The mechanical professions and even, among some nations, the industrial ones, were committed to people in chains.

The modern world offers us a completely opposing view. The smallest states of our day are incomparably larger than Sparta or than Rome was over five centuries. Even the division of Europe into several states is, thanks to the progress of enlightenment, more apparent than real. While each people, in the past, formed an isolated family, the born enemy of other families, a mass of human beings now exists, that under different names and under different forms of social organization are essentially homogeneous in their nature. This mass is strong enough to have nothing to fear from barbarian hordes. It is sufficiently civilized to find war a burden. Its uniform tendency is towards peace.

This difference leads to another one. War precedes commerce. War and commerce are only two different means of achieving the same end, that of getting what one wants. Commerce is simply a tribute paid to the strength of the possessor by the aspirant to possession. It is an attempt to conquer, by mutual agreement, what one can no longer hope to obtain through violence. A man who was always the stronger would never conceive the idea of commerce. It is experience, by proving to him that war, that is the use of his strength against the strength of others, exposes him to a variety of obstacles and defeats, that leads him to resort to commerce, that is to a milder and surer means of engaging the interest of others to agree to what suits his own. War is all impulse, commerce, calculation. Hence it follows that an age must come in which commerce replaces war. We have reached this age.

I do not mean that amongst the ancients there were no trading peoples. But these peoples were to some degree an exception to the general rule. The limits of this lecture do not allow me to illustrate all the obstacles which then opposed the progress of commerce; you know them as well as I do; I shall only mention one of them.

Their ignorance of the compass meant that the sailors of antiquity always had to keep close to the coast. To pass through the pillars of Hercules, that is, the straits of Gibraltar, was considered the most daring of enterprises. The Phoenicians and the Carthaginians, the most able of navigators, did not risk it until very late, and their example for long remained without imitators. In Athens, of which we shall talk soon, the interest on maritime enterprises was around 60%, while current interest was only 12%: that was how dangerous the idea of distant navigation seemed.

Moreover, if I could permit myself a digression which would unfortunately prove too long, I would show you, Gentlemen, through the details of the customs, habits, way of trading with others of the trading peoples of antiquity, that their commerce was itself impregnated by the spirit of the age, by the atmosphere of war and hostility which surrounded it. Commerce then was a lucky accident, today it is the normal state of things, the only aim, the universal tendency, the true life of nations. They want repose, and with repose comfort, and as a source of comfort, industry. Every day war becomes a more ineffective means of satisfying their wishes. Its hazards no longer offer to individuals benefits that match the results of peaceful work and regular exchanges. Among the ancients, a successful war increased both private and public wealth in slaves, tributes and lands shared out. For the moderns, even a successful war costs infallibly more than it is worth.

Finally, thanks to commerce, to religion, to the moral and intellectual progress of the human race, there are no longer slaves among the European nations. Free men must exercise all professions, provide for all the needs of society.

It is easy to see, Gentlemen, the inevitable outcome of these differences.

Firstly, the size of a country causes a corresponding decrease of the political importance allotted to each individual. The most obscure republican of Sparta or Rome had power. The same is not true of the simple citizen of Britain or of the United States. His personal influence is an imperceptible part of the social will which impresses on the government its direction.

Secondly, the abolition of slavery has deprived the free population of all the leisure which resulted from the fact that slaves took care of most of the work. Without the slave population of Athens, 20,000 Athenians could never have spent every day at the public square in discussions.

Thirdly, commerce does not, like war, leave in men's lives intervals of inactivity. The constant exercise of political rights, the daily discussion of the affairs of the state, disagreements, confabulations, the whole entourage and movement of factions, necessary agitations, the compulsory filling, if I may use the term, of the life of the peoples of antiquity, who, without this resource would have languished under the weight of painful inaction, would only cause trouble and fatigue to modern nations, where each individual, occupied with his speculations, his enterprises, the pleasures he obtains or hopes for, does not wish to be distracted from them other than momentarily, and as little as possible.

Finally, commerce inspires in men a vivid love of individual independence. Commerce supplies their needs, satisfies their desires, without the intervention of the authorities. This intervention is almost always—and I do not know why I say almost—this intervention is indeed always a trouble and an embarrassment. Every time collective power wishes to meddle with private speculations, it harasses the speculators. Every time governments pretend to do our own business, they do it more incompetently and expensively than we would. . . .

It follows from what I have just indicated that we can no longer enjoy the liberty of the ancients, which consisted in an active and constant participation in collective power. Our freedom must consist of peaceful enjoyment and private independence. The share which in antiquity everyone held in national sovereignty was by no means an abstract presumption as it is in our own day. The will of each individual had real influence: the exercise of this will was a vivid and repeated pleasure. Consequently the ancients were ready to make many a sacrifice to preserve their political rights and their share in the administration of the state. Everybody, feeling with pride all that his suffrage was worth, found in this awareness of his personal importance a great compensation.

This compensation no longer exists for us today. Lost in the multitude, the individual can almost never perceive the influence he exercises. Never does his will impress itself upon the whole; nothing confirms in his eyes his own cooperation.

The exercise of political rights, therefore, offers us but a part of the pleasures that the ancients found in it, while at the same time the progress of civilization, the commercial tendency of the age, the communication amongst peoples, have infinitely multiplied and varied the means of personal happiness.

It follows that we must be far more attached than the ancients to our individual independence. For the ancients when they sacrificed that independence to their political rights, sacrificed less to obtain more; while in making the same sacrifice, we would give more to obtain less.

The aim of the ancients was the sharing of social power among the citizens of the same fatherland: this is what they called liberty. The aim of the moderns is the enjoyment of security in private pleasures; and they call liberty the guarantees accorded by institutions to these pleasures. . . .

The danger of ancient liberty was that men, exclusively concerned with securing their share of social power, might attach too little value to individual rights and enjoyments.

The danger of modern liberty is that, absorbed in the enjoyment of our private independence, and in the pursuit of our particular interests, we should surrender our right to share in political power too easily.

The holders of authority are only too anxious to encourage us to do so. They are so ready to spare us all sort of troubles, except those of obeying and paying! They will say to us: what, in the end, is the aim of your efforts, the motive of your labours, the object of all your hopes? Is it not happiness? Well, leave this happiness to us and we shall give it to you. No, Sirs, we must not leave it to them. No matter how touching such a tender commitment may be, let us ask the authorities to keep within their limits. Let them confine themselves to being just. We shall assume the responsibility of being happy for ourselves.

ASSOCIATIONS IN CIVIL LIFE

Alexis de Tocqueville

Humans are social animals, and individuals choose to cooperate with one another in many ways. Tocqueville was impressed by a particular aspect of civil society, the many associations that Americans founded to undertake all sorts of worthy projects. He contrasted this with his native France, where, during the Revolution that convulsed the country, the church and other intermediary institutions were abolished and power was focused in the centralized state.

The political associations which exist in the United States are only a single feature in the midst of the immense assemblage of associations in that country. Americans of all ages, all conditions, and all dispositions, constantly form associations. They have not only commercial and manufacturing companies, in which all take part, but associations of a thousand other kinds,—religious, moral, serious, futile, extensive or restricted, enormous or diminutive. The Americans make associations to give entertainments, to found establishments for education, to build inns, to construct churches, to diffuse books, to send missionaries to the antipodes; and in this manner they found hospitals, prisons, and schools. If it be proposed to advance some truth, or to foster some feeling by the encouragement of a great example, they form a society. Wherever, at the head of some new undertaking, you see the Government in France, or a man of rank in England, in the United States you will be sure to find an association.

I met with several kinds of associations in America, of which I confess I had no previous notion; and I have often admired the extreme skill with which the inhabitants of the United States succeed in proposing a common object to the exertions of a great many men, and in getting them voluntarily to pursue it.

I have since travelled over England, whence the Americans have taken some of their laws and many of their customs; and it seemed to me that the principle of association was by no means so constantly or so adroitly used in that country. The English often perform great things singly; whereas the Americans form associations for the smallest undertakings. It is evident that the former people consider association as a powerful means of action, but the latter seem to regard it as the only means they have of acting.

Thus the most democratic country on the face of the earth is that in which men have in our time carried to the highest perfection the art of pursuing in common the object of their common desires, and have applied this new science to the greatest number of purposes. Is this the result of accident? or is there in reality any necessary connexion between the principle of association and that of equality?

Aristocratic communities always contain, amongst a multitude of persons who by themselves are powerless, a small number of powerful and wealthy citizens, each of whom can achieve great undertakings single-handed. In aristocratic societies men do not need to combine in order to act, because they are strongly held together. Every wealthy and powerful citizen constitutes the head of a permanent and compulsory association, composed of all those who are dependent upon him, or whom he makes subservient to the execution of his designs.

Amongst democratic nations, on the contrary, all the citizens are independent and feeble; they can do hardly anything by themselves, and none of them can oblige his fellow-men to lend him their assistance. They all, therefore, fall into a state of incapacity, if they do not learn voluntarily to help each other. If men living in democratic countries had no right and no inclination to associate for political purposes, their independence would be in great jeopardy; but they might long preserve their wealth and their cultivation: whereas if they never acquired the habit of forming associations in ordinary life, civilization itself would be endangered. A people amongst which individuals should lose the power of achieving great things single-handed, without acquiring the means of producing them by united exertions, would soon relapse into barbarism. . . .

A Government might perform the part of some of the largest American companies; and several States, members of the Union, have already attempted it; but what political power could ever carry on the vast multitude of lesser undertakings which the American citizens perform every day, with the assistance of the principle of association? It is easy to foresee that the time is drawing near when man will be less and less able to produce, of himself alone, the commonest necessaries of life. The task of the governing power will therefore perpetually increase, and its very efforts will extend it every day. The more it stands in the place of associations, the more will individuals, losing the notion of combining together, require its assistance: these are causes and effects which unceasingly engender each other. Will the administration of the country ultimately assume the management of all the manufactures, which no single citizen is able to carry on? And if a time at length arrives, when, in consequence of the extreme subdivision of landed property, the soil is split into an infinite number of parcels, so that it can only be cultivated by companies of husbandmen, will it be necessary that the head of the government should leave the helm of state to follow the plough? The morals and the intelligence of a democratic people would be as much endangered as its business and manufactures, if the government ever wholly usurped the place of private companies.

Feelings and opinions are recruited, the heart is enlarged, and the human mind is developed by no other means than by the reciprocal influence of men upon each other. I have shown that these influences are almost null in democratic countries; they must therefore be artificially created, and this can only be accomplished by associations.

When the members of an aristocratic community adopt a new opinion, or conceive a new sentiment, they give it a station, as it were, beside themselves, upon the lofty platform where they stand; and opinions or sentiments so conspicuous to the eyes of the multitude are easily introduced into the minds or hearts of all around. In democratic countries the governing power alone is naturally in a condition to act in this manner; but it is easy to see that its action is always inadequate, and often dangerous. A government can no more be competent to keep alive and to renew the circulation of opinions and feelings amongst a great people, than to manage all the speculations of productive industry. No sooner does a government attempt to go beyond its political sphere and to enter upon this new track, than it exercises, even unintentionally, an insupportable tyranny; for a government can only dictate strict rules, the opinions which it favours are rigidly enforced, and it is never easy to discriminate between its advice and its commands. Worse still will be the case if the government really believes itself interested in preventing all circulation of ideas; it will then stand motionless, and oppressed by the heaviness of voluntary torpor. Governments therefore should not be the only active powers: associations ought, in democratic nations, to stand in lieu of those powerful private individuals whom the equality of conditions has swept away.

As soon as several of the inhabitants of the United States have taken up an opinion or a feeling which they wish to promote in the world, they look out for mutual assistance; and as soon as they have found each other out, they combine. From that moment they are no longer isolated men, but a power seen from afar, whose actions serve for an example, and whose language is listened to. The first time I heard in the United States that a hundred thousand men had bound themselves publicly to abstain from spirituous liquors, it appeared to me more like a joke than a serious engagement; and I did not at once perceive why these temperate citizens could not content themselves with drinking water by their own firesides. I at last understood that these hundred thousand Americans, alarmed by the progress of drunkenness around them, had made up their minds to patronize temperance. They acted just in the same way as a man of high rank who should dress very plainly, in order to inspire the humbler orders with a contempt of luxury. It is probable, that if these hundred thousand men had lived in France, each of them would singly have memorialized the government to watch the public-houses all over the kingdom.

Nothing, in my opinion, is more deserving of our attention than the intellectual and moral associations of America. The political and industrial associations of that country strike us forcibly; but the others elude our observation, or if we discover them, we understand them imperfectly, because we have hardly ever seen anything of the kind. It must, however, be acknowledged that they are as necessary to the American people as the former, and perhaps more so.

In democratic countries the science of association is the mother of science; the progress of all the rest depends upon the progress it has made.

Amongst the laws which rule human societies there is one which seems to be more precise and clear than all others. If men are to remain civilized, or to become so, the art of associating together must grow and improve, in the same ratio in which the equality of conditions is increased.

INTEREST RIGHTLY UNDERSTOOD

Alexis de Tocqueville

In this selection Tocqueville discusses the ways that self-interest "rightly understood" disciplines people "in the habits of regularity, temperance, moderation, foresight, [and] self-command."

When the world was managed by a few rich and powerful individuals, these persons loved to entertain a lofty idea of the duties of man. They were fond of professing that it is praiseworthy to forget oneself, and that good should be done without hope of reward, as it is by the Deity himself. Such were the standard opinions of that time in morals.

I doubt whether men were more virtuous in aristocratic ages than in others; but they were incessantly talking of the beauties of virtue, and its utility was only studied in secret. But since the imagination takes less lofty flights and every man's thoughts are centred in himself, moralists are alarmed by this idea of self-sacrifice, and they no longer venture to present it to the human mind. They therefore content themselves with inquiring whether the personal advantage of each member of the community does not consist in working for the good of all; and when they have hit upon some point on which private interest and public interest meet and amalgamate, they are eager to bring it into notice. Observations of this kind are gradually multiplied: what was only a single remark becomes a general principle; and it is held as a truth that man serves himself in serving his fellow-creatures, and that his private interest is to do good.

I have already shown, in several parts of this work, by what means the inhabitants of the United States almost always manage to combine their own advantage with that of their fellow-citizens: my present purpose is to point out the general rule which enables them to do so. In the United States hardly anybody talks of the beauty of virtue; but they maintain that virtue is useful, and prove it every day. The American moralists do not profess that men ought to sacrifice themselves for their fellow-creatures *because* it is noble to make such sacrifices; but they boldly aver that such sacrifices are as necessary to him who imposes them upon himself, as to him for whose sake they are made. . . .

The Americans, on the contrary, are fond of explaining almost all the actions of their lives by the principle of interest rightly understood; they show with complacency how an enlightened regard for themselves constantly prompts them to assist each other. . . .

The principle of interest rightly understood is not a lofty one, but it is clear and sure. It does not aim at mighty objects, but it attains without excessive exertion all those at which it aims. As it lies within the reach of all capacities, every one can without difficulty apprehend and retain it. By its admirable conformity to human weaknesses, it easily obtains great dominion; nor is that dominion precarious, since the principle checks one personal interest by another, and uses, to direct the passions, the very same instrument which excites them.

The principle of interest rightly understood produces no great acts of self-sacrifice, but it suggests daily small acts of self-denial. By itself it cannot suffice to make a man virtuous, but it disciplines a number of citizens in habits of regularity, temperance, moderation, foresight, self-command; and, if it does not lead men straight to virtue by the will, it gradually draws them in that direction by their habits. If the principle of interest rightly understood were to sway the whole moral world, extraordinary virtues would doubtless be more rare; but I think that gross depravity would then also be less common. The principle of interest rightly understood perhaps prevents some men from rising far above the level of mankind; but a great number of other men, who were falling far below it, are caught and restrained by it. Observe some few individuals, they are lowered by it; survey mankind, it is raised.

MAN CANNOT HOLD PROPERTY IN MAN

William Lloyd Garrison

Slavery was about as clear a violation of libertarian principles as could be imagined, so it's no surprise that many leading abolitionists were libertarians. They staked their argument on the natural and imprescriptible rights of life, liberty, and property, noting in particular that each person owns himself—so the slaveholder is, as this *Declaration of Sentiments of the American Anti-Slavery Convention* (1833) argues, a "man-stealer." Abolitionism was not only a crusade for individual rights, it was an important element of the long historical struggle to extend dignity to more individuals. William Lloyd Garrison (1805–79), author of this Declaration, was probably the most prominent leader of the abolitionist movement. He founded and edited *The Liberator* and campaigned vigorously for immediate and complete abolition.

More than fifty-seven years have elapsed, since a band of patriots convened in this place, to devise measures for the deliverance of this country from a foreign yoke. The corner-stone upon which they founded the Temple of Freedom was broadly this—"that all men are created equal; that they are endowed by their Creator with certain inalienable rights; that among these are life, LIBERTY, and the pursuit of happiness." At the sound of their trumpet-call, three millions of people rose up as from the sleep of death, and rushed to the strife of blood; deeming it more glorious to die instantly as freemen, than desirable to live one hour as slaves. They were few in number—poor in resources; but the honest conviction that Truth, Justice and Right were on their side, made them invincible. . . .

Their grievances, great as they were, were trifling in comparison with the wrongs and sufferings of those for whom we plead. Our fathers were never slaves—never bought and sold like cattle—never shut from the light of knowledge and religion—never subjected to the lash of brutal taskmasters.

But those, for whose emancipation we are striving—constituting at the present time at least one-sixth part of our countrymen—are recognized by law, and treated by their fellow-beings, as marketable commodities, as goods and chattels, as brute beasts; are plundered daily of the fruits of their toil without redress; really enjoy no consti-tutional nor legal protection from licentious and murderous outrages upon their persons; and are ruthlessly torn asunder—the tender babe from the arms of its frantic mother—the heart-broken wife from her weeping husband—at the caprice or pleasure of irresponsible tyrants. For the crime of having a dark complexion, they suffer the pangs of hunger, the infliction of stripes, the ignominy of brutal servitude. They are kept in heathenish darkness by laws expressly enacted to make their instruction a criminal offence.

These are the prominent circumstances in the condition of more than two millions of our people, the proof of which may be found in thousands of indisputable facts, and in the laws of the slaveholding States.

Hence we maintain—that, in view of the civil and religious priv-ileges of this nation, the guilt of its oppression is unequalled by any other on the face of the earth; and, therefore, that it is bound to repent instantly, to undo the heavy burdens, and to let the oppressed go free.

We further maintain—that no man has a right to enslave or im-brute his brother—to hold or acknowledge him, for one moment, as a piece of merchandize—to keep back his hire by fraud—or to bru-talize his mind, by denying him the means of intellectual, social and moral improvement.

The right to enjoy liberty is inalienable. To invade it is to usurp the prerogative of Jehovah. Every man has a right to his own body—to the products of his own labor—to the protection of law—and to the common advantages of society. It is piracy to buy or steal a native African, and subject him to servitude. Surely, the sin is as great to enslave an American as an African.

Therefore, we believe and affirm—that there is no difference, in principle, between the African slave trade and American slavery:

That every American citizen, who detains a human being in involuntary bondage as his property, is, according to Scripture (Ex. xxi. 16), a man-stealer:

That the slaves ought instantly to be set free, and brought under the protection of law:

That if they had lived from the time of Pharaoh down to the present period, and had been entailed through successive generations, their right to be free could never have been alienated, but their claims would have constantly risen in solemnity:

That all those laws which are now in force, admitting the right of slavery, are therefore, before God, utterly null and void; being an audacious usurpation of the Divine prerogative, a daring infringement on the law of nature, a base overthrow of the very foundations of the social compact, a complete extinction of all the relations, endearments and obligations of mankind, and a presumptious transgression of all the holy commandments; and that therefore they ought instantly to be abrogated.

We further believe and affirm—that all persons of color, who possess the qualifications which are demanded of others, ought to be admitted forthwith to the enjoyment of the same privileges, and the exercise of the same prerogatives, as others; and that the paths of preferment, of wealth, and of intelligence, should be opened as widely to them as to persons of a white complexion.

We maintain that no compensation should be given to the planters emancipating their slaves:

Because it would be a surrender of the great fundamental principle, that man cannot hold property in man:

Because slavery is a crime, and therefore is not an article to be sold:

Because the holders of slaves are not the just proprietors of what they claim; freeing the slave is not depriving them of property, but restoring it to its rightful owner; it is not wronging the master, but righting the slave—restoring him to himself:

Because immediate and general emancipation would only destroy nominal, not real property; it would not amputate a limb or break a bone of the slaves, but by infusing motives into their breasts, would make them doubly valuable to the masters as free laborers; and

Because, if compensation is to be given at all, it should be given to the outraged and guiltless slaves, and not to those who have plundered and abused them.

We regard as delusive, cruel and dangerous, any scheme of expatriation which pretends to aid, either directly or indirectly, in the emancipation of the slaves, or to be a substitute for the immediate and total abolition of slavery.

We fully and unanimously recognise the sovereignty of each State, to legislate exclusively on the subject of the slavery which is tolerated within its limits; we concede that Congress, under the present national compact, has no right to interfere with any of the slave States, in relation to this momentous subject:

But we maintain that Congress has a right, and is solemnly bound, to suppress the domestic slave trade between the several States, and to abolish slavery in those portions of our territory which the Constitution has placed under its exclusive jurisdiction.

We also maintain that there are, at the present time, the highest obligations resting upon the people of the free States to remove slavery by moral and political action, as prescribed in the Constitution of the United States. They are now living under a pledge of their tremendous physical force, to fasten the galling fetters of tyranny upon the limbs of millions in the Southern States; they are liable to be called at any moment to suppress a general insurrection of the slaves; they authorize the slave owner to vote for three-fifths of his slaves as property, and thus enable him to perpetuate his oppression; they support a standing army at the South for its protection; and they seize the slave, who has escaped into their territories, and send him back to be tortured by an enraged master or a brutal driver. This relation to slavery is criminal, and full of danger: IT MUST BE BROKEN UP.

These are our views and principles—these our designs and measures. With entire confidence in the overruling justice of God, we plant ourselves upon the Declaration of our Independence and the truths of Divine Revelation, as upon the Everlasting Rock.

YOU ARE A MAN, AND SO AM I

Frederick Douglass

Frederick Douglass (c. 1817–95) escaped from slavery in 1838 and became a prominent abolitionist speaker and editor of the *North Star*. In these selections from three essays—"Letter to His Old Master," "The Nature of Slavery," and his 1852 Fourth of July Oration in Rochester, New York—he argues that slavery "destroys the central principle of human responsibility" and that the Constitution nowhere sanctions this odious institution.

LETTER TO HIS OLD MASTER

To My Old Master, Thomas Auld.

Sir—The long and intimate, though by no means friendly, relation which unhappily subsisted between you and myself, leads me to hope that you will easily account for the great liberty which I now take in addressing you in this open and public manner. The same fact may possibly remove any disagreeable surprise which you may experience on again finding your name coupled with mine, in any other way than in an advertisement, accurately describing my person, and offering a large sum for my arrest. In thus dragging you again before the public, I am aware that I shall subject myself to no inconsiderable amount of censure. I shall probably be charged with an unwarrantable, if not a wanton and reckless disregard of the rights and proprieties of private life. There are those north as well as south who entertain a much higher respect for rights which are merely conventional, than they do for rights which are personal and essential. Not a few there are in our country, who, while they have no scruples against robbing the laborer of the hard earned results of his patient industry, will be shocked by the extremely indelicate manner of bringing your name before the public. Believing this to be the case, and wishing to meet every reasonable or plausible objection to my conduct, I will frankly state the ground upon which I justify myself in this instance, as well as on former occasions when I have thought proper to mention your name in public. All will agree that a man guilty of theft, robbery, or murder, has forfeited the right to concealment and private life; that the community have a right to subject such persons to the most complete exposure. However much they may desire retirement, and aim to conceal themselves and their movements from the popular gaze, the public have a right to ferret them out, and bring their conduct before the proper tribunals of the country for investigation. Sir, you will undoubtedly make the proper application of these generally admitted principles, and will easily see the light in which you are regarded by me; I will not therefore manifest ill temper, by calling you hard names. . . .

From that time, I resolved that I would some day run away. The morality of the act I dispose of as follows: I am myself; you are yourself; we are two distinct persons, equal persons. What you are, I am. You are a man, and so am I. God created both, and made us separate beings. I am not by nature bond to you, or you to me. Nature does not make your existence depend upon me, or mine to depend upon yours. I cannot walk upon your legs, or you upon mine. I cannot breathe for you, or you for me; I must breathe for myself, and you for yourself. We are distinct persons, and are each equally provided with faculties necessary to our individual existence. In leaving you, I took nothing but what belonged to me, and in no way lessened your means for obtaining an *honest* living. Your faculties remained yours, and mine became useful to their rightful owner. I therefore see no wrong in any part of the transaction. . . .

After remaining in New Bedford for three years, I met with William Lloyd Garrison, a person of whom you have *possibly* heard, as he is pretty generally known among slaveholders. He put it into my head that I might make myself serviceable to the cause of the slave, by devoting a portion of my time to telling my own sorrows, and those of other slaves, which had come under my observation. This was the commencement of a higher state of existence than any to which I had ever aspired. I was thrown into society the most pure, enlightened, and benevolent, that the country affords. Among these I have never forgotten you, but have invariably made you the topic of conversation—thus giving you all the notoriety I could do. I need not tell you that the opinion formed of you in these circles is far from being favorable. . . .

I will now bring this letter to a close; you shall hear from me again unless you let me hear from you. I intend to make use of you as a weapon with which to assail the system of slavery—as a means of concentrating public attention on the system, and deepening the horror of trafficking in the souls and bodies of men. I shall make use of you as a means of exposing the character of the American church and clergy—and as a means of bringing this guilty nation, with yourself, to repentance. In doing this, I entertain no malice toward you personally. There is no roof under which you would be more safe than mine, and there is nothing in my house which you might need for your comfort, which I would not readily grant. Indeed, I should esteem it a privilege to set you an example as to how mankind ought to treat each other.

I am your fellow-man, but not your slave.

THE NATURE OF SLAVERY

More than twenty years of my life were consumed in a state of slavery. My childhood was environed by the baneful peculiarities of the slave system. I grew up to manhood in the presence of this hydra-headed monster—not as a master—not as an idle spectator—not as the guest of the slaveholder—but as A SLAVE, eating the bread and drinking the cup of slavery with the most degraded of my brother-bondmen, and sharing with them all the painful conditions of their wretched lot. In consideration of these facts, I feel that I have a right to speak, and to speak *strongly*. Yet, my friends, I feel bound to speak truly. . . .

First of all, I will state, as well as I can, the legal and social relation of master and slave. A master is one—to speak in the vocabulary of the southern states—who claims and exercises a right of property in the person of a fellow-man. This he does with the force of the law and the sanction of southern religion. The law gives the master absolute power over the slave. He may work him, flog him, hire him out, sell him, and, in certain contingencies, *kill* him, with perfect impunity. The slave is a human being, divested of all rights—reduced to the level of a brute—a mere "chattel" in the eye of the law—placed beyond the circle of human brotherhood—cut off from his kind—his name, which the "recording angel" may have enrolled in heaven, among the blest, is impiously inserted in a *master's ledger,* with horses, sheep, and swine. In law, the slave has no wife, no children, no country, and no home. He can own nothing, possess nothing, acquire nothing, but what must belong to another. To eat the fruit of his own toil, to clothe his person with the work of his own hands, is considered stealing. He toils that another may reap the fruit; he is industrious that another may live in idleness; he eats unbolted meal that another may eat the bread of fine flour; he labors in chains at home, under a burning sun and biting lash, that another may ride in ease and splendor abroad; he lives in ignorance that another may be educated; he is abused that another may be exalted; he rests his toil-worn limbs on the cold, damp ground that another may repose on the softest pillow; he is clad in coarse and tattered raiment that another may be arrayed in purple and fine linen; he is sheltered only by the wretched hovel that a master may dwell in a magnificent mansion; and to this condition he is bound down as by an arm of iron. . . .

It is, then, the first business of the enslaver of men to blunt, deaden, and destroy the central principle of human responsibility. Conscience is, to the individual soul, and to society, what the law of gravitation is to the universe. It holds society together; it is the basis of all trust and confidence; it is the pillar of all moral rectitude. Without it, suspicion would take the place of trust; vice would be more than a match for virtue; men would prey upon each other, like the wild beasts of the desert; and earth would become a *hell.*

Nor is slavery more adverse to the conscience than it is to the mind. This is shown by the fact, that in every state of the American Union, where slavery exists, except the state of Kentucky, there are laws absolutely prohibitory of education among the slaves. The crime of teaching a slave to read is punishable with severe fines and imprisonment, and, in some instances, with *death itself.*

Nor are the laws respecting this matter a dead letter. Cases may occur in which they are disregarded, and a few instances may be found where slaves may have learned to read; but such are isolated cases, and only prove the rule. The great mass of slaveholders look upon education among the slaves as utterly subversive of the slave system. I well remember when my mistress first announced to my master that she had discovered that I could read. His face colored at once with surprise and chagrin. He said that "I was ruined, and my value as a slave destroyed; that a slave should know nothing but to obey his master; that to give a negro an inch would lead him to take an ell; that having learned how to read, I would soon want to know how to write; and that by-and-by I would be running away." I think my audience will bear witness to the correctness of this philosophy, and to the literal fulfillment of this prophecy. . . .

While this nation is guilty of the enslavement of three millions of innocent men and women, it is as idle to think of having a sound and lasting peace, as it is to think there is no God to take cognizance of the affairs of men. There can be no peace to the wicked while slavery continues in the land. It will be condemned; and while it is condemned there will be agitation. Nature must cease to be nature; men must become monsters; humanity must be transformed; christianity must be exterminated; all ideas of justice and the laws of eternal goodness must be utterly blotted out from the human soul,—ere a system so foul and infernal can escape condemnation, or this guilty republic can have a sound, enduring peace.

FOURTH OF JULY ORATION, 1852

This, for the purpose of this celebration, is the 4th of July. It is the birthday of your National Independence, and of your political freedom. This, to you, is what the Passover was to the emancipated people of God. It carries your minds back to the day, and to the act of your great deliverance; and to the signs, and to the wonders, associated with that act, and that day. This celebration also marks the beginning of another year of your national life; and reminds you that the Republic of America is now 76 years old. . . .

Fellow-citizens, pardon me, allow me to ask, why am I called upon to speak here to-day? What have I, or those I represent, to do with your national independence? Are the great principles of political freedom and of natural justice, embodied in that Declaration of Independence, extended to us? and am I, therefore, called upon to bring our humble offering to the national altar, and to confess the benefits and express devout gratitude for the blessings resulting from your independence to us?

Would to God, both for your sakes and ours, that an affirmative answer could be truthfully returned to these questions! . . .

But, such is not the state of the case. I say it with a sad sense of the disparity between us. I am not included within the pale of this glorious anniversary! Your high independence only reveals the immeasurable distance between us. The blessings in which you, this day, rejoice, are not enjoyed in common. The rich inheritance of justice, liberty, prosperity and independence, bequeathed by your fathers, is shared by you, not by me. The sunlight that brought life and healing to you, has brought stripes and death to me. This Fourth of July is *yours,* not *mine. You* may rejoice, *I* must mourn. To drag a man in fetters into the grand illuminated temple of liberty, and call upon him to join you in joyous anthems, were inhuman mockery and sacrilegious irony. Do you mean, citizens, to mock me, by asking me to speak to-day? . . .

Fellow-citizens; above your national, tumultous joy, I hear the mournful wail of millions! whose chains, heavy and grievous yesterday, are, to-day, rendered more intolerable by the jubilee shouts that reach them. . . . To forget them, to pass lightly over their wrongs, and to chime in with the popular theme, would be treason most scandalous and shocking, and would make me a reproach before God and the world. My subject, then fellow-citizens, is AMERICAN SLAVERY. I shall see, this day, and its popular characteristics, from the slave's point of view. Standing, there, identified with the American bondman, making his wrongs mine, I do not hesitate to declare, with all my soul, that the character and conduct of this nation never looked

blacker to me than on this 4th of July! Whether we turn to the declarations of the past, or to the professions of the present, the conduct
of the nation seems equally hideous and revolting. America is false to
the past, false to the present, and solemnly binds herself to be false to
the future. Standing with God and the crushed and bleeding slave on
this occasion, I will, in the name of humanity which is outraged, in
the name of liberty which is fettered, in the name of the constitution
and the Bible, which are disregarded and trampled upon, dare to call
in question and to denounce, with all the emphasis I can command,
everything that serves to perpetuate slavery—the great sin and shame
of America! . . .

What point in the anti-slavery creed would you have me argue?
On what branch of the subject do the people of this country need
light? Must I undertake to prove that the slave is a man? That point
is conceded already. Nobody doubts it. The slaveholders themselves
acknowledge it in the enactment of laws for their government. They
acknowledge it when they punish disobedience on the part of the
slave. There are seventy-two crimes in the State of Virginia, which, if
committed by a black man, (no matter how ignorant he be), subject
him to the punishment of death; while only two of the same crimes
will subject a white man to the like punishment. What is this but the
acknowledgement that the slave is a moral, intellectual and responsible being? The manhood of the slave is conceded. . . .

Would you have me argue that man is entitled to liberty? that he
is the rightful owner of his own body? You have already declared it.
Must I argue the wrongfulness of slavery? Is that a question for republicans? Is it to be settled by the rules of logic and argumentation,
as a matter beset with great difficulty, involving a doubtful application of the principle of justice, hard to be understood? How should
I look to-day, in the presence of Americans, dividing, and subdividing a discourse, to show that men have a natural right to freedom?
speaking of it relatively, and positively, negatively, and affirmatively.
To do so, would be to make myself ridiculous, and to offer an insult
to your understanding. There is not a man beneath the canopy of
heaven, that does not know that slavery is wrong *for him*. . . .

What, to the American slave, is your 4th of July? I answer: a day
that reveals to him, more than all other days in the year, the gross

injustice and cruelty to which he is the constant victim. To him, your celebration is a sham; your boasted liberty, an unholy license; your national greatness, swelling vanity; your sounds of rejoicing are empty and heartless; your denunciations of tyrants, brass fronted impudence; your shouts of liberty and equality, hollow mockery; your prayers and hymns, your sermons and thanksgivings, with all your religious parade, and solemnity, are, to him, mere bombast, fraud, deception, impiety, and hypocrisy—a thin veil to cover up crimes which would disgrace a nation of savages. There is not a nation on the earth guilty of practices, more shocking and bloody, than are the people of these United States, at this very hour. . . .

Americans! your republican politics, not less than your republican religion, are flagrantly inconsistent. You boast of your love of liberty, your superior civilization, and your pure Christianity, while the whole political power of the nation (as embodied in the two great political parties), is solemnly pledged to support and perpetuate the enslavement of three millions of your countrymen. You hurl your anathemas at the crowned headed tyrants of Russia and Austria, and pride yourselves on your Democratic institutions, while you yourselves consent to be the mere *tools* and *bodyguards* of the tyrants of Virginia and Carolina. You invite to your shores fugitives of oppression from abroad, honor them with banquets, greet them with ovations, cheer them, toast them, salute them, protect them, and pour out your money to them like water; but the fugitives from your own land you advertise, hunt, arrest, shoot and kill. . . .

Fellow-citizens! there is no matter in respect to which, the people of the North have allowed themselves to be so ruinously imposed upon, as that of the pro-slavery character of the Constitution. In *that* instrument I hold there is neither warrant, license, nor sanction of the hateful thing; but, interpreted as it *ought* to be interpreted, the Constitution is a GLORIOUS LIBERTY DOCUMENT. Read its preamble, consider its purposes. Is slavery among them? Is it at the gateway? or is it in the temple? It is neither. While I do not intend to argue this question on the present occasion, let me ask, if it be not somewhat singular that, if the Constitution were intended to be, by its framers and adopters, a slave-holding instrument, why neither *slavery*, *slaveholding*, nor *slave* can anywhere be found in it. What would be thought of an instrument, drawn up, *legally* drawn up, for the purpose of entitling the city of Rochester to a track of land, in which no mention of land was made? . . .

Now, take the constitution according to its plain reading, and I defy the presentation of a single pro-slavery clause in it. On the other hand it will be found to contain principles and purposes, entirely hostile to the existence of slavery.

A HUMAN BEING CANNOT BE JUSTLY OWNED

William Ellery Channing

William Ellery Channing (1780–1842) was a Unitarian minister and a major influence on such New England transcendentalists as Ralph Waldo Emerson. In this extract from *Slavery* (1841), he argues that in the nature of property rights, human beings cannot be the property of others.

The slave-holder claims the slave as his Property. The very idea of a slave is, that he belongs to another, that he is bound to live and labor for another, to be another's instrument, and to make another's will his habitual law, however adverse to his own. Another owns him, and, of course, has a right to his time and strength, a right to the fruits of his labor, a right to task him without his consent, and to determine the kind and duration of his toil, a right to confine him to any bounds, a right to extort the required work by stripes, a right, in a word, to use him as a tool, without contract, against his will, and in denial of his right to dispose of himself, or to use his power for his own good. "A slave," says the Louisiana code, "is in the power of the master to whom he belongs. The master may sell him, dispose of his person, his industry, his labor; he can do nothing, possess nothing, nor acquire any thing, but which must belong to his master." "Slaves shall be deemed, taken, reputed, and adjudged," says the South Carolina laws, "to be chattels personal in the hands of their masters, and possessions to all intents and purposes whatsoever." Such is slavery, a claim to man as property.

Now this claim of property in a human being is altogether false, groundless. No such right of man in man can exist. A human being cannot be justly owned. To hold and treat him as property is to inflict a great wrong, to incur the guilt of oppression. . . .

I will endeavor, however, to illustrate the truth which I have stated.

1. It is plain, that, if one man may be held as property, then every other man may be so held. If there be nothing in human nature, in our common nature, which excludes and forbids the conversion of him who possesses it into an article of property; if the right of the free to liberty is founded, not on their essential attributes as rational and moral beings, but on certain adventitious, accidental circumstances, into which they have been thrown; then every human being, by a change of circumstances, may justly be held and treated by another as property. If one man may be rightfully reduced to slavery, then there is not a human being on whom the same chain may not be imposed. . . . This deep assurance, that we cannot be rightfully made another's property, does not rest on the hue of our skins, or the place of our birth, or our strength, or wealth. These things do not enter our thoughts. The consciousness of indestructible rights is a part of our moral being. The consciousness of our humanity involves the persuasion, that we cannot be owned as a tree or a brute. As men, we cannot justly be made slaves. Then no man can be rightfully enslaved. . . .

2. A man cannot be seized and held as property, because he has *Rights*. What these rights are, whether few or many, or whether all men have the same, are questions for future discussion. All that is assumed now is, that every human being has some rights. This truth cannot be denied, but by denying to a portion of the race that moral nature which is the sure and only foundation of rights. This truth has never, I believe, been disputed. It is even recognized in the very codes of slave legislation, which, while they strip a man of liberty, affirm his right to life, and threaten his murderer with punishment. Now, I say, a being having rights cannot justly be made property; for this claim over him virtually annuls all his rights. It strips him of all power to assert them. It makes it a crime to assert them. The very essence of slavery is, to put a man defenceless into the hands of another. The

right claimed by the master, to task, to force, to imprison, to whip, and to punish the slave, at discretion, and especially to prevent the least resistance to his will, is a virtual denial and subversion of all the rights of the victim of his power. The two cannot stand together. Can we doubt which of them ought to fall? . . .

4. That a human being cannot be justly held and used as property, is apparent from the very nature of property. Property is an exclusive right. It shuts out all claim but that of the possessor. What one man owns, cannot belong to another. What then, is the consequence of holding a human being as property? Plainly this. He can have no right to himself. His limbs are, in truth, not morally his own. He has not a right to his own strength. It belongs to another. His will, intellect, and muscles, all the powers of body and mind which are exercised in labor, he is bound to regard as another's. Now, if there be property in any thing, it is that of a man in his own person, mind, and strength. All other rights are weak, unmeaning, compared with this, and, in denying this, all right is denied. It is true, that an individual may forfeit by crime his right to the use of his limbs, perhaps to his limbs, and even to life. But the very idea of forfeiture implies, that the right was originally possessed. It is true, that a man may by contract give to another a limited right to his strength. But he gives only because he possesses it, and gives it for considerations which he deems beneficial to himself; and the right conferred ceases at once on violation of the conditions on which it was bestowed. To deny the right of a human being to himself, to his own limbs and faculties, to his energy of body and mind, is an absurdity too gross to be confuted by any thing but a simple statement. Yet this absurdity is involved in the idea of his belonging to another. . . .

6. Another argument against the right of property in man, may be drawn from a very obvious principle of moral science. It is a plain truth, universally received, that every right supposes or involves a corresponding obligation. If, then, a man has a right to another's person or powers, the latter is under obligation to give himself up as a chattel to the former. This is his duty. He is bound to be a slave, and

bound not merely by the Christian law, which enjoins submission to injury, not merely by prudential considerations, or by the claims of public order and peace; but bound because another has a right of ownership, has a moral claim to him, so that he would be guilty of dishonesty, of robbery, in withdrawing himself from this other's service. It is his duty to work for his master, though all compulsion were withdrawn; and in deserting him he would commit the crime of taking away another man's property, as truly as if he were to carry off his owner's purse. Now do we not instantly feel, can we help feeling, that this is false? Is the slave thus morally bound? When the African was first brought to these shores, would he have violated a solemn obligation by slipping his chain, and flying back to his native home? Would he not have been bound to seize the precious opportunity of escape? Is the slave under a moral obligation to confine himself, his wife, and children, to a spot where their union in a moment may be forcibly dissolved? Ought he not, if he can, to place himself and his family under the guardianship of equal laws? Should we blame him for leaving his yoke? Do we not feel, that, in the same condition, a sense of duty would quicken our flying steps? Where, then, is the obligation which would necessarily be imposed, if the right existed which the master claims? The absence of obligation proves the want of the right. The claim is groundless. It is a cruel wrong.

7. I come now to what is to my own mind the great argument against seizing and using a man as property. He cannot be property in the sight of God and justice, because he is a Rational, Moral, Immortal Being; because created in God's image, and therefore in the highest sense his child; because created to unfold godlike faculties, and to govern himself by a Divine Law written on his heart, and republished in God's Word. His whole nature forbids that he should be seized as property. From his very nature it follows, that so to seize him is to offer an insult to his Maker, and to inflict aggravated social wrong. Into every human being God has breathed an immortal spirit, more precious than the whole outward creation. No earthly or celestial language can exaggerate the worth of a human being. No matter how obscure his condition. Thought, Reason, Conscience, the capacity

of Virtue, the capacity of Christian Love, an immortal Destiny, an intimate moral connection with God—here are attributes of our common humanity which reduce to insignificance all outward distinctions, and make every human being unspeakably dear to his Maker. No matter how ignorant he may be. The capacity of Improvement allies him to the more instructed of his race, and places within his reach the knowledge and happiness of higher worlds. Every human being has in him the germ of the greatest idea in the universe, the idea of God; and to unfold this is the end of his existence. Every human being has in his breast the elements of that Divine, Everlasting Law, which the highest orders of the creation obey. . . . Every human being has affections, which may be purified and expanded into a Sublime Love. He has, too, the idea of Happiness, and a thirst for it which cannot be appeased. Such is our nature. Wherever we see a man, we see the possessor of these great capacities. Did God make such a being to be owned as a tree or a brute? How plainly was he made to exercise, unfold, improve his highest powers, made for a moral, spiritual good! and how is he wronged, and his Creator opposed, when he is forced and broken into a tool to another's physical enjoyment!

Such a being was plainly made for an End in Himself. He is a Person, not a Thing. He is an End, not a mere Instrument or Means. . . .

Having considered the great fundamental right of human nature, particular rights may easily be deduced. Every man has a right to exercise and invigorate his intellect or the power of knowledge, for knowledge is the essential condition of successful effort for every good; and whoever obstructs or quenches the intellectual life in another, inflicts a grievous and irreparable wrong. Every man has a right to inquire into his duty, and to conform himself to what he learns of it. Every man has a right to use the means, given by God and sanctioned by virtue, for bettering his condition. He has a right to be respected according to his moral worth; a right to be regarded as a member of the community to which he belongs, and to be protected by impartial laws; and a right to be exempted from coercion, stripes, and punishment, as long as he respects the rights of others.

He has a right to an equivalent for his labor. He has a right to sustain domestic relations, to discharge their duties, and to enjoy the happiness which flows from fidelity in these and other domestic relations. Such are a few of human rights; and if so, what a grievous wrong is slavery!

RIGHTS AND RESPONSIBILITIES OF WOMEN

Angelina Grimké

The emphasis on the individual mind in the Enlightenment, the individualist nature of the emerging market order, and the demand for individual rights that inspired the American Revolution naturally led people to think more carefully about the nature of the individual and soon to insist that the dignity of individual rights be extended to all rational individuals. Feminism and abolitionism both developed in that climate, and each drew strength from the other. Angelina Grimké (1805–79) was the daughter of a prominent slaveholder in Charleston, South Carolina. She became a Quaker, moved to the North, and began a career of agitation for the rights of slaves. In this excerpt, drawn from her famous letter to Catherine Beecher, another abolitionist, Grimké argues that the abolitionist cause should not be kept separate from the issue of women's rights. Her claim for women's moral status rests squarely on the traditional libertarian argument that individuals are moral agents possessing both rights and responsibilities.

––––––––––

The investigation of the rights of the slave has led me to a better understanding of my own. I have found the Anti-Slavery cause to be the high school of morals in our land—the school in which *human rights* are more fully investigated, and better understood and taught, than in any other. Here a great fundamental principle is uplifted and illuminated, and from this central light, rays innumerable stream all around. Human beings have *rights,* because they are *moral* beings: the rights of *all* men grow out of their moral nature; and as all men have the same moral nature, they have essentially the same rights. These rights may be wrested from the slave, but they cannot be alienated: his title to himself is as perfect *now,* as is that of Lyman Beecher: it is stamped on his moral being, and is, like it, imperishable. Now if rights are founded in the nature of our moral being, then the *mere circumstance of sex* does not give to man higher rights and responsibilities, than to woman. To suppose that it does, would be to deny the self-evident truth, that the "physical constitution is the mere instrument of the moral nature." To suppose that it does, would be to break up utterly the relations, of the two natures, and to reverse their functions, exalting the animal nature into a monarch, and humbling the moral into a slave; making the former a proprietor, and the latter its property. When human beings are regarded as *moral* beings, *sex,* instead of being enthroned upon the summit, administering upon rights and responsibilities, sinks into insignificance and nothingness. My doctrine then is, that whatever it is morally right for man to do, it is morally right for woman to do. Our duties originate, not from difference of sex, but from the diversity of our relations in life, the various gifts and talents committed to our care, and the different eras in which we live. . . .

I have often been amused at the vain efforts made to define the rights and responsibilities of immortal beings as *men* and *women.* No one has yet found out just where the line of separation between them should be drawn, and for this simple reason, that no one knows just how far below man woman is, whether she be a head shorter in her moral responsibilities, or head and shoulders, or the full length of his noble stature, below him, i.e. under his feet. Confusion, uncertainty, and great inconsistencies, must exist on this point, so long as woman is regarded in the least degree inferior to man; but place her where her Maker placed her, on the same high level of human rights with man, side by side with him, and difficulties vanish, the mountains of perplexity flow down at the presence of this grand equalizing principle. Measure her rights and duties by the unerring standard of *moral being,* not by the false weights and measures of a mere circumstance of her human existence, and then the truth will be self-evident, that whatever it is *morally* right for a man to do, it is *morally* right for a woman to do. I recognize no rights but *human* rights—I know nothing of men's rights and women's rights; for in Christ Jesus, there is neither male nor female.

WOMAN AS A MORAL BEING

Sarah Grimké

Sarah Grimké (1792–1873), the older sister of Angelina Grimké, was also a prominent abolitionist lecturer. In this excerpt from an essay written as a letter to the Boston Female Anti-Slavery Society, she criticizes the legal status of women under English and American law, as described in the famous *Commentaries on the Laws of England* by Sir William Blackstone. Grimké argues that both women and slaves are denied their responsibilities as moral beings by being treated as mere appendages of their husbands or masters.

———————

Blackstone, in the chapter entitled "Of husband and wife," says:—

"By marriage, the husband and wife are one person in law; that is, *the very being, or legal existence of the woman* is suspended during the marriage, or at least is incorporated and consolidated into that of the husband under whose wing, protection and cover she performs everything." "For this reason, a man cannot grant anything to his wife, or enter into covenant with her; for the grant would be to suppose her separate existence, and to covenant with her would be to covenant with himself; and therefore it is also generally true, that all compacts made between husband and wife, when single, are voided by the intermarriage. A woman indeed may be attorney for her husband, but that implies no separation from, but is rather a representation of, her love."

Here now, the very being of a woman, like that of a slave, is absorbed in her master. All contracts made with her, like those made with slaves by their owners, are a mere nullity. Our kind defenders have legislated away almost all our legal rights, and in the true spirit of such injustice and oppression, have kept us in ignorance of those very laws by which we are governed. They have persuaded us, that we have no right to investigate the laws, and that, if we did, we could not comprehend them; they alone are capable of understanding the mysteries of Blackstone, &c. But they are not backward to make us feel the practical operation of their power over our actions. . . .

This law that "a wife can bring no action," &c., is similar to the law respecting slaves. "A slave cannot bring a suit against his master, or any other person, for an injury—his master, must bring it." So if any damages are recovered for an injury committed on a wife, the husband pockets it; in the case of the slave, the master does the same.

> "In criminal prosecutions, the wife may be indicted and punished separately, unless there be evidence of coercion from the fact that the offence was committed in the presence, or by the command of her husband. A wife is excused from punishment for theft committed in the presence, or by the command of her husband."

It would be difficult to frame a law better calculated to destroy the responsibility of woman as a moral being, or a free agent. Her husband is supposed to possess unlimited control over her; and if she can offer the flimsy excuse that he bade her steal, she may break the eighth commandment with impunity, as far as human laws are concerned.

OF INDIVIDUALITY

John Stuart Mill

Mill's concept of individuality in *On Liberty* was greatly influenced by the German author Wilhelm von Humboldt (1767–1835), in his book *The Sphere and Duties of Government*, written in 1792 but published in 1851. (Humboldt's book has also been published in English as *The Limits of State Action*.) As Mill notes here, Humboldt emphasized the individual's need to develop his own character and personality. In order to flourish, individuals need two things: freedom and a wide variety of circumstances or living arrangements so that people can find the circumstances that are best for them.

If all mankind minus one, were of one opinion, and only one person were of the contrary opinion, mankind would be no more justified in silencing that one person, than he, if he had the power, would be justified in silencing mankind. Were an opinion a personal possession of no value except to the owner; if to be obstructed in the enjoyment of it were simply a private injury, it would make some difference whether the injury was inflicted only on a few persons or on many. But the peculiar evil of silencing the expression of an opinion is, that it is robbing the human race; posterity as well as the existing generation, those who dissent from the opinion, still more than those who hold it. If the opinion is right, they are deprived of the opportunity of exchanging error for truth: if wrong, they lose, what is almost as great a benefit, the clearer perception and livelier impression of truth, produced by its collision with error. . . .

It is desirable, in short, that in things which do not primarily concern others, individuality should assert itself. Where, not the person's own character, but the traditions or customs of other people are the rule of conduct, there is wanting one of the principal ingredients of human happiness, and quite the chief ingredient of individual and social progress.

In maintaining this principle, the greatest difficulty to be encountered does not lie in the appreciation of means towards an acknowledged end, but in the indifference of persons in general to the end itself. If it were felt that the free development of individuality is one of the leading essentials of well-being; that it is not only a co-ordinate element with all that is designated by the terms civilization, instruction, education, culture, but is itself a necessary part and condition of all those things; there would be no danger that liberty should be undervalued, and the adjustment of the boundaries between it and social control would present no extraordinary difficulty. But the evil is, that individual spontaneity is hardly recognized by the common modes of thinking, as having any intrinsic worth, or deserving any regard on its own account. The majority, being satisfied with the ways of mankind as they now are (for it is they who make them what they are), cannot comprehend why those ways should not be good enough for everybody; and what is more, spontaneity forms no part of the ideal of the majority of moral and social reformers, but is rather looked on with jealousy, as a troublesome and perhaps rebellious obstruction to the general acceptance of what these reformers, in their own judgement, think would be best for mankind. Few persons, out of Germany, even comprehend the meaning of the doctrine which Wilhelm von Humboldt, so eminent both as a savant and as a politician, made the text of a treatise—that "the end of man, or that which is prescribed by the eternal or immutable dictates of reason, and not suggested by vague and transient desires, is the highest and most harmonious development of his powers to a complete and consistent whole"; that, therefore, the object "towards which every human being must ceaselessly direct his efforts, and on which especially those who design to influence their fellow men must ever keep their eyes, is the individuality of power and development"; that for this there are two requisites, "freedom, and variety of situations"; and that from the union of these arise "individual vigour and manifold diversity," which combine themselves in "originality."[3]

Little, however, as people are accustomed to a doctrine like that of von Humboldt, and surprising as it may be to them to find so high a value attached to individuality, the question, one must nevertheless think, can only be one of degree. No one's idea of excellence in conduct is that people should do absolutely nothing but copy one another. No one would assert that people ought not to put into their mode of life, and into the conduct of their concerns, any impress whatever of their own judgement, or of their own individual character. On the other hand, it would be absurd to pretend that people ought to live as if nothing whatever had been known in the world before they came into it; as if experience had as yet done nothing towards showing that one mode of existence, or of conduct, is preferable to another. Nobody denies that people should be so taught and trained in youth, as to know and benefit by the ascertained results of human experience. But it is the privilege and proper condition of a human being, arrived at the maturity of his faculties, to use and interpret experience in his own way. It is for him to find out what part of recorded experience is properly applicable to his own circumstances and character. The traditions and customs of other people are, to a certain extent, evidence of what their experience has taught *them;* presumptive evidence, and as such, have a claim to his deference: but, in the first place, their experience may be too narrow; or they may not have interpreted it rightly. Secondly, their interpretation of experience may be correct, but unsuitable to him. Customs are made for customary circumstances, and customary characters; and his circumstances or his character may be uncustomary. Thirdly, though the customs be both good as customs, and suitable to him, yet to conform to custom, merely *as* custom, does not educate or develop in him any of the qualities which are the distinctive endowment of a human being. The human faculties of perception, judgement, dis-

---

[3] *The Sphere and Duties of Government,* from the German of Baron Wilhelm von Humboldt, pp. 11–13.

criminative feeling, mental activity, and even moral preference, are exercised only in making a choice. He who does anything because it is the custom, makes no choice. He gains no practice either in discerning or in desiring what is best. The mental and moral, like the muscular powers, are improved only by being used. The faculties are called into no exercise by doing a thing merely because others do it, no more than by believing a thing only because others believe it. If the grounds of an opinion are not conclusive to the person's own reason, his reason cannot be strengthened, but is likely to be weakened, by his adopting it: and if the inducements to an act are not such as are consentaneous to his own feelings and character (where affection, or the rights of others, are not concerned) it is so much done towards rendering his feelings and character inert and torpid, instead of active and energetic.

He who lets the world, or his own portion of it, choose his plan of life for him, has no need of any other faculty than the ape-like one of imitation. He who chooses his plan for himself, employs all his faculties. He must use observation to see, reasoning and judgement to foresee, activity to gather materials for decision, discrimination to decide, and when he has decided, firmness and self-control to hold to his deliberate decision. And these qualities he requires and exercises exactly in proportion as the part of his conduct which he determines according to his own judgement and feelings is a large one. It is possible that he might be guided in some good path, and kept out of harm's way, without any of these things. But what will be his comparative worth as a human being? It really is of importance, not only what men do, but also what manner of men they are that do it. Among the works of man, which human life is rightly employed in perfecting and beautifying, the first in importance surely is man himself. Supposing it were possible to get houses built, corn grown, battles fought, causes tried, and even churches erected and prayers said, by machinery—by automatons in human form—it would be a considerable loss to exchange for these automatons even the men and women who at present inhabit the more civilized parts of the world, and who assuredly are but starved specimens of what nature can and will produce. Human nature is not a machine to be built after a model, and set to do exactly the work prescribed for it, but a tree, which requires to grow and develop itself on all sides, according to the tendency of the inward forces which make it a living thing. . . .

A person whose desires and impulses are his own—are the expression of his own nature, as it has been developed and modified by his own culture—is said to have a character. One whose desires and impulses are not his own, has no character, no more than a steam-engine has a character. If, in addition to being his own, his impulses are strong, and are under the government of a strong will, he has an energetic character. Whoever thinks that individuality of desires and impulses should not be encouraged to unfold itself, must maintain that society has no need of strong natures—is not the better for containing many persons who have much character—and that a high general average of energy is not desirable. . . .

It is not by wearing down into uniformity all that is individual in themselves, but by cultivating it and calling it forth, within the limits imposed by the rights and interests of others, that human beings become a noble and beautiful object of contemplation; and as the works partake the character of those who do them, by the same process human life also becomes rich, diversified, and animating, furnishing more abundant aliment to high thoughts and elevating feelings, and strengthening the tie which binds every individual to the race, by making the race infinitely better worth belonging to. In proportion to the development of his individuality, each person becomes more valuable to himself, and is therefore capable of being more valuable to others. There is a great fullness of life about his own existence, and when there is more life in the units there is more in the mass which is composed of them. As much compression as is necessary to prevent the stronger specimens of human nature from encroaching on the rights of others, cannot be dispensed with; but for this there is ample compensation even in the point of view of human development. The means of development which the individual loses by being prevented from gratifying his inclinations to the injury of others, are chiefly obtained at the expense of the development of other people. And even to himself there is a full equivalent in the better development of the social part of his nature, rendered possible by the restraint put upon the selfish part. To be held to rigid rules of justice for the sake of others, develops the feelings and capacities which have the good of others for their object. But to be restrained in things not affecting their good, by their mere displeasure, develops nothing valuable, except such force of character as may unfold itself in resisting the restraint. If acquiesced in, it dulls and blunts the whole nature. To give any fair play to the nature of each, it is essential that different persons should be allowed to lead different lives. In proportion as this latitude has been exercised in any age, has that age been noteworthy to posterity. Even despotism does not produce its worst effects, so long as individuality exists under it; and whatever crushes individuality is despotism, by whatever name it may be called, and whether it professes to be enforcing the will of God or the injunctions of men.

Having said that Individuality is the same thing with development, and that it is only the cultivation of individuality which produces, or can produce, well-developed human beings, I might here close the argument: for what more or better can be said of any condition of human affairs, than that it brings human beings themselves nearer to the best thing they can be? or what worse can be said of any obstruction to good, than that it prevents this? Doubtless, however, these considerations will not suffice to convince those who most need convincing; and it is necessary further to show, that these developed human beings are of some use to the undeveloped—to point out to those who do not desire liberty, and would not avail themselves of it, that they may be in some intelligible manner rewarded for allowing other people to make use of it without hindrance.

In the first place, then, I would suggest that they might possibly learn something from them. It will not be denied by anybody, that originality is a valuable element in human affairs. There is always need of persons not only to discover new truths, and point out when what were once truths are true no longer, but also to commence new practices, and set the example of more enlightened conduct, and better taste and sense in human life. This cannot well be gainsaid by anybody who does not believe that the world has already attained perfection in all its ways and practices. It is true that this benefit is not capable of being rendered by everybody alike: there are but few persons, in comparison with the whole of mankind, whose experiments, if adopted by others, would be likely to be any improvement on established practice. But these few are the salt of the earth; without them, human life would become a stagnant pool. Not only is it they who introduce good things which did not before exist; it is they who keep the life in those which already existed. If there were nothing new to be done, would human intellect cease to be necessary? Would it be a reason why those who do the old things should forget why they are done, and do them like cattle, not like human beings? There is only too great a tendency in the best beliefs and practices to degenerate into the mechanical; and unless there were a succession of persons whose ever-recurring originality prevents the grounds of those beliefs and practices from becoming merely traditional, such dead matter would not resist the smallest shock from anything really alive, and there would be no reason why civilization should not die out, as in the Byzantine Empire. Persons of genius, it is true, are, and are always likely to be, a small minority; but in order to have them, it is necessary to preserve the soil in which they grow. Genius can only breathe freely in an *atmosphere* of freedom. Persons of genius are, *ex vi termini, more* individual than any other people—less capable, consequently, of fitting themselves, without hurtful compression, into any of the small number of moulds which society provides in order to save its members the trouble of forming their own character. If from timidity they consent to be forced into one of these moulds, and to let all that part of themselves which cannot expand under the pressure remain unexpanded, society will be little the better for their genius. If they are of a strong character, and break their fetters, they become a mark for the society which has not succeeded in reducing them to commonplace, to point at with solemn warning as "wild," "erratic," and the like; much as if one should complain of the Niagara river for not flowing smoothly between its banks like a Dutch canal.

I insist thus emphatically on the importance of genius, and the necessity of allowing it to unfold itself freely both in thought and in practice, being well aware that no one will deny the position in theory, but knowing also that almost every one, in reality, is totally indifferent to it. People think genius a fine thing if it enables a man to write an exciting poem, or paint a picture. But in its true sense, that of originality in thought and action, though no one says that it is not a thing to be admired, nearly all, at heart, think that they can do very well without it. Unhappily this is too natural to be wondered at. Originality is the one thing which unoriginal minds cannot feel the use of. They cannot see what it is to do for them: how should they? If they could see what it would do for them, it would not be originality. The first service which originality has to render then, is that of opening their eyes: which being once fully done, they would have a chance of being themselves original. Meanwhile, recollecting that nothing was ever yet done which some one was not the first to do, and that all good things which exist are the fruits of originality, let them be modest enough to believe that there is something still left for it to accomplish, and assure themselves that they are more in need of originality, the less they are conscious of the want.

In sober truth, whatever homage may be professed, or even paid, to real or supposed mental superiority, the general tendency of things throughout the world is to render mediocrity the ascendant power among mankind. In ancient history, in the middle ages, and in a diminishing degree through the long transition from feudality to the present time, the individual was a power in himself; and if he had either great talents or a high social position, he was a considerable power. At present individuals are lost in the crowd. In politics it is almost a triviality to say that public opinion now rules the world. The only power deserving the name is that of masses, and of governments while they make themselves the organ of the tendencies and instincts of masses. This is as true in the moral and social relations of private life as in public transactions. Those whose opinions go by the name of public opinion, are not always the same sort of public: in America they are the whole white population; in England, chiefly the middle class. But they are always a mass, that is to say, collective mediocrity. And what is a still greater novelty, the mass do not now take their opinions from dignitaries in Church or State, from ostensible leaders, or from books. Their thinking is done for them by men much like themselves, addressing them or speaking in their name, on the spur of the moment, through the newspapers. I am not complaining of all this. I do not assert that anything better is compatible, as a general rule, with the present low state of the human mind. But that does not hinder the government of mediocrity from being mediocre government. No government by a democracy or a numerous aristocracy, either in its political acts or in the opinions, qualities, and tone of mind which it fosters, ever did or could rise above mediocrity, except in so far as the sovereign. Many have let themselves be guided (which in their best times they always have done) by the counsels and influence of a more highly gifted and instructed One or Few. The initiation of all wise or noble things, comes and must come from individuals; generally at first from some one individual. The honour and glory of the average man is that he is capable of following that initiative; that he can respond internally to wise and noble things, and be led to them with his eyes open. I am not countenancing the sort of "hero-worship" which applauds the strong man of genius for forcibly seizing on the government of the world and making it do his bidding in spite of itself. All he can claim is, freedom to point out the way. The power of compelling others into it, is not only inconsistent with the freedom and development of all the rest, but corrupting to the strong man himself. It does seem, however, that when the opinions of masses of merely average men are everywhere become or becoming the dominant power, the counterpoise and corrective to that tendency would be, the more and more pronounced individuality of those who stand on the higher eminences of thought. It is in these circumstances most especially, that exceptional individuals, instead of being deterred, should be encouraged in acting differently from the mass. In other times there was no advantage in their doing so, unless they acted not only differently, but better. In this age, the mere example of nonconformity, the mere refusal to bend the knee to custom, is itself a service. Precisely because the tyranny of opinion is such as to make eccentricity a reproach, it is desirable, in order to break through that tyranny, that people should be eccentric. Eccentricity has always abounded when and where strength of character has abounded; and the amount of eccentricity in a society has generally been proportional to the amount of genius, mental vigour, and moral courage which it contained. That so few now dare to be eccentric, marks the chief danger of the time. . . .

If it were only that people have diversities of taste, that is reason enough for not attempting to shape them all after one model. But different persons also require different conditions for their spiritual development; and can no more exist healthily in the same moral, than all the variety of plants can in the same physical, atmosphere and climate. The same things which are helps to one person towards the cultivation of higher nature, are hindrances to another. . . .

The despotism of custom is everywhere the standing hindrance to human advancement, being in unceasing antagonism to that disposition to aim at something better than customary, which is called, according to circumstances, the spirit of liberty, or that of progress or improvement. The spirit of improvement is not always a spirit of liberty, for it may aim at forcing improvements on an unwilling people; and the spirit of liberty, in so far as it resists such attempts, may ally itself locally and temporarily with the opponents of improvement; but the only unfailing and permanent source of improvement is liberty, since by it there are as many possible independent centres of improvement as there are individuals. The progressive principle, however, in either shape, whether as the love of liberty or of improvement, is antagonistic to the sway of Custom, involving at least emancipation from that yoke; and the contest between the two constitutes the chief interest of the history of mankind. The greater part of the world has, properly speaking, no history, because the despotism of Custom is complete. . . . A people, it appears, may be progressive for a certain length of time, and then stop: when does it stop? When it ceases to possess individuality. . . .

What is it that has hitherto preserved Europe from this lot? What has made the European family of nations an improving, instead of a stationary portion of mankind? Not any superior excellence in them, which, when it exists, exists as the effect, not as the cause; but their remarkable diversity of character and culture. Individuals, classes, nations, have been extremely unlike one another: they have struck out a great variety of paths, each leading to something valuable; and although at every period those who travelled in different paths have been intolerant of one another, and each would have thought it an excellent thing if all the rest could have been compelled to travel his road, their attempts to thwart each other's development have rarely had any permanent success, and each has in time endured to receive the good which the others have offered. Europe is, in my judgement, wholly indebted to this plurality of paths for its progressive and many-sided development. . . .

What, then, is the rightful limit to the sovereignty of the individual over himself? Where does the authority of society begin? How much of human life should be assigned to individuality, and how much to society?

Each will receive its proper share, if each has that which more particularly concerns it. To individuality should belong the part of life in which it is chiefly the individual that is interested; to society, the part which chiefly interests society.

Though society is not founded on a contract, and though no good purpose is answered by inventing a contract in order to deduce social obligations from it, every one who receives the protection of society owes a return for the benefit, and the fact of living in society renders it indispensable that each should be bound to observe a certain line of conduct towards the rest. This conduct consists, first, in not injuring the interests of one another; or rather certain interests, which, either by express legal provision or by tacit understanding, ought to be considered as rights; and secondly, in each person's bearing his share (to be fixed on some equitable principle) of the labours and sacrifices incurred for defending the society or its members from injury and molestation. . . .

That the whole or any large part of the education of the people should be in State hands, I go as far as any one in deprecating. All that has been said of the importance of individuality of character, and diversity in opinions and modes of conduct, involves, as of the same unspeakable importance, diversity of education. A general State education is a mere contrivance for moulding people to be exactly like one another: and as the mould in which it casts them is that which pleases the predominant power in the government, whether this be a monarch, a priesthood, an aristocracy, or the majority of the existing generation in proportion as it is efficient and successful, it establishes a despotism over the mind, leading by natural tendency to one over the body. An education established and controlled by the State should only exist, if it exist at all, as one among many competing experiments, carried on for the purpose of example and stimulus, to keep the others up to a certain standard of excellence.

ON EQUALITY AND INEQUALITY

Ludwig von Mises

From at least the time of the Levellers, libertarians have firmly defended the equal rights of all individuals. But the very term "Levellers" was a libel by their aristocratic opponents. The so-called Levellers did not want to level society, to abolish private property in order to bring about absolute equality; they wanted only to take away legal privileges and make men equal before the law. The chimera of equality has been a mainstay of socialist visionaries. Libertarians have understood that people have different talents and interests. That makes the division of labor both necessary and productive; and in turn the division of labor means that some people will prove better at satisfying the wants of others and will thus profit more in the marketplace. We cannot have a complex economy, in which people can develop their unique talents, without finding that people will achieve unequal results. But, as Ludwig von Mises points out in this selection, in precapitalist societies stronger or more ambitious men got ahead by subjugating and exploiting others; capitalism encourages the talented to prosper by "vying with one another in serving the masses" in order to make money. Mises (1881–1973) was a towering figure in the history of libertarianism and of twentieth-century economics. Born in Austria, in 1934 he sensed trouble ahead, especially for Austrian Jews such as himself, and moved to Switzerland, going on to the United States in 1940. In *Socialism* (1922) he persuaded many young intellectuals of the impracticability of abolishing money and markets—as Marx and his Soviet followers intended—though others unfortunately took much longer to understand and needed overwhelming empirical evidence. His other major books included *The Theory of Money and Credit* (1912), *Omnipotent Government* (1944), *Bureaucracy* (1944), and *Theory and History* (1957). His greatest work was *Human Action* (1949), usually described as an economics treatise but in fact a wide-ranging examination of society, cooperation, spontaneous order, and the market process. In this excerpt from a 1961 essay in the magazine *Modern Age,* he distinguishes between equal rights and the alluring but fanciful notion of equal abilities and equal outcomes.

The doctrine of natural law that inspired the eighteenth century declarations of the rights of man did not imply the obviously fallacious proposition that all men are biologically equal. It proclaimed that all men are born equal in rights and that this equality cannot be abrogated by any man-made law, that it is inalienable or, more precisely, imprescriptible. Only the deadly foes of individual liberty and self-determination, the champions of totalitarianism, interpreted the principle of equality before the law as derived from an alleged physical and physiological equality of all men. The French declaration of the rights of the man and the citizen of November 3, 1789, had pronounced that all men are born and remain equal in rights. But, on the eve of the inauguration of the regime of terror, the new declaration that preceded the Constitution of June 24, 1793, proclaimed that all men are equal *"par la nature."* From then on this thesis, although manifestly contradicting biological experience, remained one of the dogmas of "leftism." Thus we read in the *Encyclopaedia of the Social Sciences* that "at birth human infants, regardless of their heredity, are as equal as Fords."

However, the fact that men are born unequal in regard to physical and mental capacities cannot be argued away. Some surpass their fellow men in health and vigor, in brain and aptitudes, in energy and resolution and are therefore better fitted for the pursuit of earthly affairs than the rest of mankind—a fact that has also been admitted by Marx. He spoke of "the inequality of individual endowment and therefore productive capacity *(Leistungsfähigkeit)*" as "natural privileges" and of "the unequal individuals (and they would not be different individuals if they were not unequal)." In terms of popular psychological teaching we can say that some have the ability to adjust themselves better than others to the conditions of the struggle for survival. We may therefore—without indulging in any judgment of value—distinguish from this point of view between superior men and inferior men.

History shows that from time immemorial superior men took advantage of their superiority by seizing power and subjugating the masses of inferior men. In the status society there is a hierarchy of castes. On the one hand are the lords who have appropriated to themselves all the land and on the other hand their servants, the liegemen, serfs, and slaves, landless and penniless underlings. The inferiors' duty is to drudge for their masters. The institutions of the society aim at the sole benefit of the ruling minority, the princes, and their retinue, the aristocrats.

Such was by and large the state of affairs in all parts of the world before, as both Marxians and conservatives tell us, "the acquisitiveness of the bourgeoisie," in a process that went on for centuries and is still going on in many parts of the world, undermined the political, social, and economic system of the "good old days." The market economy—capitalism—radically transformed the economic and political organization of mankind.

Permit me to recapitulate some well-known facts. While under precapitalistic conditions superior men were the masters on whom the masses of the inferior had to attend, under capitalism the more gifted and more able have no means to profit from their superiority other than to serve to the best of their abilities the wishes of the majority of the less gifted. In the market economic power is vested in the consumers. They ultimately determine, by their buying or abstention from buying, what should be produced, by whom and how, of what quality and in what quantity. The entrepreneurs, capitalists, and landowners who fail to satisfy in the best possible and cheapest way the most urgent of the not yet satisfied wishes of the consumers are forced to go out of business and forfeit their preferred position.

In business offices and in laboratories the keenest minds are busy fructifying the most complex achievements of scientific research for the production of ever better implements and gadgets for people who have no inkling of the theories that make the fabrication of such things possible. The bigger an enterprise is, the more is it forced to adjust its production to the changing whims and fancies of the masses, its masters. The fundamental principle of capitalism is mass production to supply the masses. It is the patronage of the masses that make enterprises grow big. The common man is supreme in the market economy. He is the customer who "is always right."

In the political sphere, representative government is the corollary of the supremacy of the consumers in the market. Office-holders depend on the voters as entrepreneurs and investors depend on the consumers. The same historical process that substituted the capitalistic mode of production for precapitalistic methods substituted popular government—democracy—for royal absolutism and other forms of government by the few. And wherever the market economy is superseded by socialism, autocracy makes a comeback. It does not matter whether the socialist or communist despotism is camouflaged by the use of aliases like "dictatorship of the proletariat" or "people's democracy" or "*Führer* principle." It always amounts to a subjection of the many to the few.

It is hardly possible to misconstrue more thoroughly the state of affairs prevailing in capitalistic society than by calling the capitalists and entrepreneurs a "ruling" class intent upon "exploiting" the masses of decent men. We will not raise the question of how the men who under capitalism are in business would have tried to take advantage of their superior talents in any other thinkable organization of production. Under capitalism they are vying with one another in serving the masses of less gifted men. All their thoughts aim at perfecting the methods of supplying the consumers. Every year, every month, every week something unheard of before appears on the market and is soon made accessible to the many.

What has multiplied the "productivity of labor" is not some degree of effort on the part of manual workers, but the accumulation of capital by the savers and its reasonable employment by the entrepreneurs. Technological inventions would have remained useless trivia if the capital required for their utilization had not been previously accumulated by thrift. Man could not survive as a human being without manual labor. However, what elevates him above the beasts is not manual labor and the performance of routine jobs, but speculation, foresight that provides for the needs of the—always uncertain—future. The characteristic mark of production is that it is behavior directed by the mind. This fact cannot be conjured away by a semantics for which the word "labor" signifies only manual labor.

THE TENDRILS OF COMMUNITY

Charles Murray

As the welfare state transfers power from the individual to the state, so it also saps the power of civil society. Each new task taken on by government means less responsibility, less purpose, for the neighborhood, the community, and the church. In his book *In Pursuit: Of Happiness and Good Government* (1988) Charles Murray explored the nature of happiness and how government can encourage or impede its pursuit. He argued that the growth of the welfare state takes responsibility away from individuals and communities, removing an important source of satisfaction from our lives. Murray is best known as the author of *Losing Ground: American Social Policy, 1950–1980* (1984), which argued that welfare actually harmed the people it was intended to help by creating dependency, illegitimacy, and long-term poverty. In his next book, *In Pursuit,* from which this selection is taken, he broadened his argument to examine the effects of the welfare state on the whole society.

———

Now, to repeat the question: Why, in a nation with the wealth of the United States, would there not be enough people to attend naturally and fully to the functions of community that I have been describing?

The answer I am proposing is indicated by the image in the title, "tendrils" of community. To occur in the first place, then to develop, certain kinds of affiliations must have something to attach themselves to. Communities exist because they have a reason to exist, some core of functions around which the affiliations that constitute a vital community can form and grow. When the government takes away a core function, it depletes not only the source of vitality pertaining to that particular function, but also the vitality of a much larger family of responses. By hiring professional social workers to care for those most in need, it cuts off nourishment to secondary and tertiary behaviors that have nothing to do with formal social work. An illustration: In the logic of the social engineer, there is no causal connection between such apparently disparate events as (1) the establishment of a welfare bureaucracy and (2) the reduced likelihood (after a passage of some years) that, when someone dies, a neighbor will prepare a casserole for the bereaved family's dinner. In the logic I am using, there *is* a causal connection, and one of great importance.

I am arguing ultimately from two premises. One is again straight from Aristotle, that the practice of a virtue has the characteristics of a habit and of a skill. People may be born with the capacity of being generous, but become generous only by practicing generosity. People have the capacity for honesty, but become honest only by practicing honesty. The second, for which I do not have a specific source, is the human response to which I have referred several times: People tend not to do a chore when someone else will do it for them. At the micro-level, the dialogue between the government and the citizen goes roughly like this:

"Do you want to go out and feed the hungry or are you going to sit here
    and watch television?"
"I'm tired. What'll happen if I don't go?"
"Well, if you don't go I guess I'll just have to do it myself."
"In that case, you go."

It shows up in the aggregate as well. In the normal course of events, the personal income that people and corporations contribute to philanthropies "ought" to increase not only in raw dollar amounts, but as a proportion of income, as wealth itself increases: If I can afford to give away 5 percent of my income when I make $10,000, then (ceteris paribus, as always) when I make $11,000 I can afford to give away a higher percentage and still have more money for my personal use than I had before. From the beginning of the 1940s through 1964, this expectation held true: the richer the United States got, the greater the proportion of its wealth that was given to philanthropy. Then, suddenly, sometime during 1964–65, in the middle of an economic boom, this consistent trend was reversed. The proportion of wealth being given away began to fall even though wealth continued to increase. This new and disturbing trend continued through the rest of the 1960s, throughout the 1970s, and then suddenly reversed itself again in 1981 (during a period of hard times), when a new administration came to office that once more seemed to be saying "If you don't do it, nobody will." Figure 1 shows this intriguing history from 1950 through 1985.

I use the graph to illustrate, not as proof. But the causal relationship—government spending crowds out private philanthropy—has been demonstrated in a number of technical analyses. The causal explanation needn't be much more complicated than the private dialogue ("What'll happen if I don't do it?") played out on a national scale.

FIGURE 1

A COINCIDENCE OF POLICY RHETORIC AND PRIVATE PHILANTHROPY.

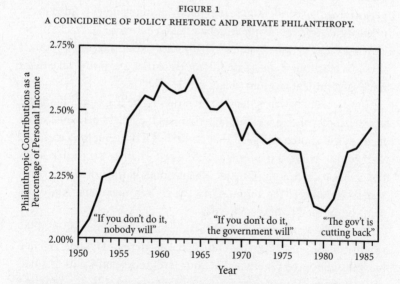

SOURCES: Bureau of the Census, *Historical Statistics of the United States* (Washington, D.C.: Government Printing Office, 1975), Series F297–348 (for personal income), Series 398–411 (for philanthropic contributions), and Bureau of the Census, *Statistical Abstract of the United States 1987* (Washington, D.C.: Government Printing Office, 1987), table 713 and comparables in other volumes (for personal income), table 630 and comparables (for philanthropic contributions).

It seems to be inevitable. If the message is that if people don't do these things themselves then the state will hire people to do these things for them, that knowledge affects behavior. You may once again use yourself as a source of evidence. Suppose, for example, that tomorrow you were told that every bit of government assistance to poor people—federal, state, and municipal—in your neighborhood had ended. If you are a physician, would this have any effect on your availability for pro bono services? If you are a member of a church board, would it have any effect on the agenda items for next week's meeting? If you are an unconnected member of the community, would you give any thought to what you might do to pick up needs that the government had so callously dropped? If you already do volunteer work, would you increase your efforts?

If you would be likely to function more actively as a member of your community under such circumstances, the puzzle to ponder is this: It is very probable that such activities will provide you with satisfactions. You can be fairly confident of this—so why is it that you are not behaving *now* as you would behave if the government stopped performing these functions? After all, the evening news is filled every night with stories of people who have fallen between the cracks of the existing social service system. Why not go out and take for yourself these satisfactions in the same full measure that you would take them if the government were no longer involved?

The correct answer is that "It just wouldn't be the same." If a child in the neighborhood will not be fed unless the neighborhood church feeds it, the church will feed that child. But if the church is merely a distribution point, if it is simply a choice of whether the church feeds the child or a Generous Outside Agency does it, the urgency is gone, and so is some of the response by the church members. And so is some of the vitality of that church.

Recall the formulation: Satisfactions are a product of responsibility, effort, and function. When the Generous Outside Agency has the action, the reality is that your level of responsibility is small and nebulous. Thus voluntary agencies are faced with the problem of either finding something to do that does not have a government program competing with it, or of convincing prospective volunteers that they are doing something that is falling between the cracks. As government responsibilities expand, each of these cases becomes harder to make persuasively. Why donate $500 of your money (which represents a lot, to you) to a local agency when there is a bureaucracy in your city spending $20 million on the same function? Why give up an evening a week, when you're working a full day at your job, to do something for which the city has a full-time paid staff of several hundred people? If the job's not getting done, make them do what they're being paid to do.

None of this is meant to ignore the voluntary and philanthropic programs that exist; rather, I am suggesting that what we observe is the tip of what would exist otherwise, the behavior of a comparative few who are highly motivated. Nor am I at this particular moment making a case for the best way to feed hungry children. The welfare of the fed child is not the issue here; the issue is the vitality of the church as a community institution. The church will be a satisfying institution of community life (not just religious life) to the extent that the members have something important to do; that institutional role will atrophy to the extent that it does not. Similarly for schools, clubs, chambers of commerce, and any other local institution. They have to have something to do, and their responsibility has to be real.

So I am proposing that there is nothing mysterious about why people become atomized in modern urban settings. Individuals are drawn to community affiliations and attach themselves to them in direct proportion to the functional value of those organizations. As people attach themselves to individual community institutions the aggregate intangible called "community" itself takes on a life and values that are greater than the sum of the parts. Take away the functions, and you take away the community. The cause of the problem is not a virus associated with modernity, it is a centralization of functions that shouldn't be centralized, and this is very much a matter of political choice, not ineluctable forces.

PRIVATE PREJUDICE, PRIVATE REMEDY

Doug Bandow

Libertarians believe that government should be limited to protecting the life, liberty, and property of each individual. It should not be empowered to influence our opinions, improve our moral character, or impose legal penalties on people who engage in immoral behavior that does not violate the rights of others. Drawing on an ancient Western tradition, libertarians typically argue that actions are virtuous only when they are freely chosen and that the improvement of character should be left to the voluntary sector of society. In this essay Doug Bandow applies those principles to the problem of racism in modern America. Bandow is a senior fellow at the Cato Institute and the author of several books, including *Beyond Good Intentions: A Biblical View of Politics* (1988) and *The Politics of Plunder* (1990).

———————

There may be no more politically contentious issue than race. The federal government has created a vast racial spoils system that often helps those who least need assistance. To be well-educated and well-connected—that is, successful—is to gain the most from a system supposedly intended to help the victims of discrimination.

But the perversion of such programs is not the most important reason to dismantle racial norming, quotas, preferences, and other forms of discrimination against the "majority." Justice should be based on individual, not group, treatment. To favor someone simply because he or she is black (or Hispanic, or whatever) is morally wrong. Doing so is also, in the long run, socially destructive, causing everyone to look at almost everything through a racial lens. The most elemental decisions about education and employment become political; even private relationships increasingly polarize as everyone squabbles over their supposed "entitlement" by color. . . .

Race also underlies most of the other critical issues facing our society: crime, economic opportunity, education, poverty, welfare. Too many political debates quickly descend into vicious squabbles over race, even though the solutions are usually simple to discern. African-Americans are almost invariably the victims of perverse government policies, which, though racially neutral on their face, have a highly disparate impact. The minimum wage disproportionately bars urban youth from the job market; welfare disproportionately disrupts inner-city families and communities. And so on. Here, too, less state control and more individual freedom and community responsibility are the answer.

Yet to criticize government intervention on race, especially the tendency of people to turn every private dispute, no matter how small, into a public crisis—via a formal lawsuit, government prosecution, or federal program—carries with it a responsibility to criticize acts of private discrimination and intolerance. That is, if we really believe that public law should not reach every obnoxious private act, then people who are moral as well as free should practice the alternative: applying social sanctions.

The need for private action is probably greater than realized by most middle-class whites. Imagine stopping by the mall and buying a shirt that you liked. Imagine returning to the shop the next day wearing the shirt. Imagine being accosted by two security guards, demanding to see the receipt for your shirt—which, not surprisingly, you didn't think to bring with you. Imagine being ordered to strip off the shirt and, even though a cashier remembered selling you one, told to bring in the receipt to retrieve your shirt.

Seem improbable? If you're a middle-aged white, it's inconceivable. Any employee going up to such a customer and saying, "Excuse me, sir—that shirt looks like the type we stock. Where's your receipt?" would earn a quick trip to the unemployment line.

But an Eddie Bauer clothing store in a Washington, D.C., suburb forced Alonzo Jackson, a 16-year-old black male, to literally give the shirt off of his back to store security personnel. He went home in his t-shirt. He did find the receipt, though not without some effort. The store's management wasn't entirely satisfied: explained spokeswoman Cheryl Engstrom, "The amount on the receipt matched the purchase, although the stub didn't specifically indicate whether or not it was the same shirt." However, Engstrom added, the store "gave him the benefit of the doubt and let him keep it anyway." Mr. Jackson was lucky the store guards weren't checking underwear as well as shirts.

The treatment of Alonzo Jackson dramatically demonstrates why race remains such a painful and divisive issue. Store personnel implicitly accused Jackson of being a criminal and took his property—because he was black. It took a torrent of angry letters and phone calls from whites and blacks alike before the company formally apologized.

That young black males are treated badly because they are young black males is not new. Cab drivers are less likely to pick up and jewelers less likely to buzz into locked shops African-American males. Stores are, as Jackson certainly knows, more likely to suspect young black males of shoplifting.

The fear of African-American men is shared by many African-Americans—black cab drivers also pass by black pedestrians. It was Jesse Jackson, of all people, who once observed that "There is nothing more painful to me at this stage in my life than to walk down the street and hear footsteps and start thinking about robbery—then look around and see someone white and feel relieved."

Yet this understandable fear of a small number of predators who commit a disproportionate share of crimes penalizes the vast majority of African-Americans who are not only decent, law-abiding people, but also the primary victims of crime. Explains the Justice Department, "Black households, Hispanic households, and urban households were the most likely to experience crime." In fact, blacks are 50 percent more likely than others to be victimized by a violent crime. People like Alonzo Jackson are paying twice—they are more likely to suffer from crime and be suspected of being criminals.

And that has a larger social impact. Such treatment can only fan anger, frustration, and resentment. Victimology has become big business, with most everyone wanting to be called, and recompensed for allegedly being a victim. But there are real victims, like Jackson.

What can we do? Some of the answers, as noted earlier, are better policy. Crime must be detected, punished, and deterred, especially in poor neighborhoods, where residents are so vulnerable. The government's educational monopoly must be broken, giving disadvantaged students a chance to receive a real education. The economy needs to be deregulated and opened to help everyone, rather than controlled to enrich special interests, such as labor unions, which back laws like the Davis-Bacon Act, which restrict the hiring of minorities.

Racism is harder to address, especially through government. Some race-based decisions, like those of cab drivers who pass by blacks, reflect reasons other than prejudice. Are we really prepared to penalize people who, even if wrongly, believe their lives might be in danger—especially when today's antidiscrimination laws have misfired, creating a quota mentality and encouraging disappointed jobseekers to routinely scream racism?

We especially need to steer clear of the quota temptation that has so entranced politicians in Washington and across the nation. When the high school in Piscataway Township, New Jersey, facing the need to lay off one of ten business education teachers, fired Sharon Taxman because she was white, it compounded rather than alleviated injustice. Cases like this also ensure that anger, frustration, and resentment will rise among whites as well as blacks.

At the same time, the kind of racist behavior exhibited by Eddie Bauer should be criticized and treated as socially unacceptable. As it was when consumers of all races demanded that Eddie Bauer apologize to Alonzo Jackson, else they would take their business elsewhere.

And this is how it should be. As individuals, we need to insist that racism is wrong. That means speaking out and taking action when necessary. The burden for doing so falls especially heavily on those of us who don't believe that every instance of offensive behavior should be a crime. If political society is to do less, as it should, then civil society must do more. It becomes the duty of every one of us to help shape society's moral code.

PART THREE

INDIVIDUAL RIGHTS

The idea of individual rights runs throughout the history of liberal and libertarian thought. Some philosophers have thought that rights came from God; thus the Declaration of Independence says that men are "endowed by their Creator" with inalienable rights. Others have found the source of rights in the nature of human beings—thus "natural" rights—or in the need for social cooperation. But all have agreed that rights are *imprescriptible,* that is, not granted by government.

Much libertarian thought, especially the study of spontaneous order and the market process, is a positive analysis of the consequences of actions. The theory of individual rights provides a normative component to libertarianism, a theory of justice: It is unjust to deprive others of their life, liberty, or property. A distinguishing characteristic of libertarianism within the broader liberal tradition is its emphasis on self-ownership or self-propriety as the origin of rights, a theme that underlies the selections in this reader from Overton, the abolitionists, Spencer, Spooner, Rand, and Rothbard.

The concept of imprescriptible rights was influenced by the Greek and Hebrew concept of a higher law by which everyone, even kings, can be judged and by the Christian emphasis on the dignity of the individual soul. The Spanish Scholastics, whose work influenced Northern European liberals through the Dutch scholar Hugo Grotius and the German Samuel Pufendorf, emphasized the natural rights of every person in their criticisms of the Spanish enslavement of Indians in the New World. In the turmoil of the English Civil War, the Levellers began to enunciate a recognizably liberal program of religious toleration, low taxes, abolition of monopolies, peace, and freedom of the press, all based on a foundation of individual rights.

John Locke produced the great modern defense of individual rights. He claimed that people have rights before the existence of government—thus we call them natural rights, because they exist in nature. People form a government to protect their rights. They could do that without government, but a well-ordered government is an efficient system for protecting rights. And if government exceeds that role, people are justified in revolting. Representative government is the best way to ensure that government sticks to its proper purpose. Echoing a long philosophical tradition, he wrote, "A Government is not free to do as it pleases. . . . The law of nature stands as an eternal rule to all men, legislators as well as others." Although they have been much debated by liberals and others, Locke's ideas are the foundation on which modern Western society rests: individualism, rights to liberty and property, and representative government to protect those rights.

The question is sometimes raised among libertarians: Would you support a firm respect for the rights of life, liberty, and property if they led to devastating or even disappointing results, if they meant a society materially poorer than a planned economy? Many people believe that such a choice must be made. Many American intellectuals in the 1950s and beyond believed that the Soviet Union's planned economy would soon overtake the unplanned United States economy; they debated whether more rapid economic growth would be worth the loss of freedom inherent in central planning. Ira Levin, in his anti-utopian novel *This Perfect Day,* suggested that a destruction of the totalitarian world government would lead to an unfortunate reduction in economic output and an increase in such disorders as electrical outages and plane crashes.

But the question is wrong. We don't have to choose between respecting rights and achieving economic progress. And it is not just coincidental that a society based on the rights of life, liberty, and property also produces social peace and material well-being. As Locke, Hume, and other rights theorists demonstrate, we need a system of rights in order to produce social cooperation, without which people can achieve very little. In the absence of well-defined property rights, we would face constant conflict over who got to use each piece of property. It is our agreement on property rights that allows us to undertake the complex social tasks of cooperation and coordination by which we achieve our purposes.

It would be nice if love or benevolence could accomplish that task, without all the emphasis on self-interest and individual rights, and many opponents of liberalism have offered an appealing vision of society based on universal benevolence. But as Adam Smith pointed out, "In civilized society [man] stands at all times in need of the co-operation and assistance of great multitudes," yet in his whole life he could never befriend a small fraction of the number of people whose cooperation he needs. If we depended entirely on benevolence to produce cooperation, we simply couldn't undertake complex tasks. Reliance on other people's self-interest, in a system of well-defined property rights and free exchange, is the *only* way to organize a society more complicated than a small village.

Because we are unique individuals who take responsibility for the consequences of our actions, we have a moral claim to liberty and to the acquisition of property needed to carry out our projects. Because we need the cooperation of many others in order to achieve our purposes, we need a system of rights. There is no conflict between the moral and the practical analyses of rights, though the nuances provide much opportunity for debate among libertarian scholars.

Locke's theory of rights was never more concisely and eloquently summed up than by Thomas Jefferson in the Declaration of Independence, which continues to inspire fighters for freedom around the world.

Since Locke and Hume began the scientific analysis of the origin and purpose of rights, many other theorists have taken up the subject. Immanuel Kant laid out a theory of inalienable rights, arguing that each person is entitled to the fullest liberty possible consistent with the equal liberty of others. He did not, however, apply that standard to the sovereign, whom he conceived to be above the law of equal freedom. That approach, derived from Hobbes, puts Kant outside the mainstream of liberal theory. Herbert Spencer adopted the law of equal freedom but emphatically did hold the ruler to be subject to the law. Lysander Spooner, an American abolitionist and constitutional lawyer, pressed the theory of individual rights and consent to its ultimate conclusion: that no one was bound by any obligations he had not personally agreed to. Therefore, he said, people were bound by the contracts they signed and by the natural law of justice but not by the United States Constitution or any other positive law.

In the twentieth century, the novelist and philosopher Ayn Rand set forth an uncompromising theory of individual rights derived from the moral philosophy of Aristotle, Aquinas, Locke, and Spencer. Although many sympathetic philosophers have found her theory incomplete, her passionate writing and clear moral vision attracted many young people to the old American belief in individual rights. In 1974 the Harvard philosopher Robert Nozick helped to revive rights theory within the academic world with his book *Anarchy, State, and Utopia*. A central part of his argument was his distinction between "historical principles" of justice and "end-result" principles. He defended the idea of justice as a just process against the notion that justice would mean a particular pattern of distribution of economic goods. He pointed out that any attempt to produce a particular pattern of distribution would require forbidding "capitalist acts between consenting adults."

In our final selection of this section Roger Pilon of the Cato Institute examines a subject that has often inspired opposition to a system of individual rights: the right to do wrong. We have rights because we are moral agents *and* because we need rights to bring about social cooperation. But should we have the right to do things that are—according to someone's moral theory—wrong? David Hume recognized that justice often requires us to make decisions that seem unfortunate in a given context: "However single acts of justice may be contrary, either to public or private interest, 'tis certain, that the whole plan or scheme is highly conducive, or indeed absolutely requisite, both to the support of society, and the well-being of every individual." Thus, he says, we may sometimes have to "restore a great fortune to a miser or a seditious bigot," but "every individual person must find himself a gainer" from the peace, order, and prosperity that a system of property rights establishes in society. Pilon examines two kinds of actions that most Americans regard as immoral: burning the American flag and discriminating against someone on the basis of race. Pilon contends that "if we are born free and equal, with equal moral rights to plan and live out own lives," then that freedom must include the right to pursue our own values even "when doing so offends others." In a free society, those offended by the peaceful actions of others should resort to "moral suasion and public obloquy," not legal force, to press their moral views on others.

The long experience with government excesses has persuaded libertarians that strict limits on government are needed to protect individual freedom. Some libertarians believe that individuals have natural rights, whose legal protection is the best check on power. Others believe that although rights are ultimately a social construction, not a natural reality, the constitution of a free society should limit government in a manner *consistent with* individual rights. Others take a more historical approach, arguing that our constitutional rights reflect a long process of individuals and groups contending with governments to achieve particular liberties, which eventually produce a free society, one in which civil society is left largely free of coercive intervention by the state. All would agree that individuals should be free to live their lives as they choose, so long as they respect the rights of others to do likewise.

AN ARROW AGAINST ALL TYRANTS

Richard Overton

During the English Civil War (1642–49), vigorous debates about the role of government took place. One group on the parliamentary side of the conflict were dubbed the Levellers, because their opponents claimed they wanted to "level" society. The Levellers—including John Lilburne, William Walwyn, and Colonel Thomas Rainborough—responded that they wanted only to eliminate legal privileges, not all differences between people. In fact, the Levellers began to enunciate the ideas that would come to be known as liberalism. They placed the defense of religious liberty and the ancient rights of Englishmen in a context of self-ownership and natural rights. In a famous essay, "An Arrow Against All Tyrants" (1646), written while he was imprisoned by the House of Lords, the Leveller leader Richard Overton (?1600–?60s) argued that every individual has a "self-propriety"; that is, everyone owns himself and thus has rights to life, liberty, and property. (Spelling has been modernized in this excerpt.)

To every individual in nature is given an individual property by nature, not to be invaded or usurped by any: for every one, as he is himself, so he hath a self-propriety, else could he not be himself, and on this no second may presume to deprive any of, without manifest violation and affront to the very principles of nature, and of the rules of equity and justice between man and man; mine and thine cannot be, except this be: No man hath power over my rights and liberties, and I over no man's; I may be but an individual, enjoy myself and my self-propriety, and may right myself no more than myself, or presume any further; if I do, I am an encroacher and an invader upon another man's right, to which I have no right. For by natural birth, all men are equally and alike born to like propriety, liberty, and freedom, and as we are delivered of God by the hand of nature into this world, every-one with a natural, innate freedom and propriety (as it were writ in the table of every man's heart, never to be obliterated) even so are we to live, everyone equally and alike to enjoy his birthright and privi-lege; even all whereof God by nature hath made him free.

And this by nature everyone desires, aims at, and requires, for no man naturally would be befooled of his liberty by his neighbor's craft, or enslaved by his neighbor's might, for it is nature's instinct to preserve itself from all things hurtful and obnoxious, and this in na-ture is granted of all to be most reasonable, equal, and just, not to be rooted out of the kind, even of equal duration with the creature: And from this fountain or root, all just human powers take their original; not immediately from God (as kings usually plead their prerogative) but mediately by the hand of nature, as from the represented to the representors; for originally, God hath implanted them in the crea-ture, and from the creature those powers immediately proceed; and no further: and no more may be communicated than stands for the better being, weal, or safety thereof: and this is man's prerogative and no further, so much and no more may be given or received thereof: even so much as is conducent to a better being, more safety and freedom, and no more; he that gives more, sins against his own flesh; and he that takes more, is a thief and robber to his kind: Every man by nature being a king, priest, and prophet in his own natural circuit and compass, whereof no second may partake, but by deputation, commission, and free consent from him, whose natural right and freedom it is. . . .

For by nature we are the sons of Adam, and from him have legiti-mately derived a natural propriety, right, and freedom, which only we require, and how in equity you can deny us, we cannot see; It is but the just rights and prerogative of mankind (whereunto the people of England are heirs apparent as well as other nations) which we desire:

and sure you will not deny it us, that we may be men, and live like men; if you do, it will be as little safe for your selves and posterity, as for us and our posterity, for Sir, look what bondage, thralldom, or tyranny soever you settle upon us, you certainly, or your posterity will taste of the dregs: if by your present policy and (abused) might, you chance to award it from yourselves in particular, yet your posterity do what you can, will be liable to the hazard thereof.

OF PROPERTY AND GOVERNMENT

John Locke

The length of this section is appropriate, since John Locke (1632–1704) may be regarded as the principal architect both of libertarianism and of the modern world. Immediately after the Glorious Revolution of 1688 and the Bill of Rights the following year, Locke published three important works: *A Letter Concerning Toleration, An Essay Concerning Human Understanding,* and *Two Treatises of Government.* In the *Second Treatise,* Locke made several points that form the basis of liberal political theory: that people have rights before the existence of governments; that the purpose of government is to protect their rights, including their property rights; and that people are justified in dissolving a government that exceeds its just powers. Representative government is the best way to ensure that government sticks to its proper purpose.

———————

27. Though the earth, and all inferior creatures be common to all men, yet every man has a property in his own person. This nobody has any right to but himself. The labour of his body, and the work of his hands, we may say, are properly his. Whatsoever then he removes out of the state that nature hath provided, and left it in, he hath mixed his labour with, and joined to it something that is his own, and thereby makes it his property. It being by him removed from the common state nature placed it in, it hath by this labour something annexed to it, that excludes the common right of other men. For this

labour being the unquestionable property of the labourer, no man but he can have a right to what that is once joined to, at least where there is enough, and as good left in common for others.

28. He that is nourished by the acorns he picked up under an oak, or the apples he gathered from the trees in the wood, has certainly appropriated them to himself. Nobody can deny but the nourishment is his. I ask then, when did they begin to be his? When he digested? Or when he eat? Or when he boiled? Or when he brought them home? Or when he picked them up? And 'tis plain, if the first gathering made them not his, nothing else could. That labour put a distinction between them and common. That added something to them more than nature, the common mother of all, had done; and so they became his private right. And will anyone say he had no right to those acorns or apples he thus appropriated, because he had not the consent of all mankind to make them his? Was it a robbery thus to assume to himself what belonged to all in common? If such a consent as that was necessary, man had starved, notwithstanding the plenty God had given him. We see in commons, which remain so by compact, that 'tis the taking any part of what is common, and removing it out of the state nature leaves it in, which begins the property; without which the common is of no use. And the taking of this or that part, does not depend on the express consent of all the commoners. Thus the grass my horse has bit; the turfs my servant has cut; and the ore I have digged in any place where I have a right to them in common with others, become my property, without the assignation or consent of anybody. The labour that was mine, removing them out of that common state they were in, hath fixed my property in them. . . .

32. But the chief matter of property being now not the fruits of the earth, and the beasts that subsist on it, but the earth itself; as that which takes in and carries with it all the rest: I think it is plain, that property in that too is acquired as the former. As much land as a man tills, plants, improves, cultivates, and can use the product of, so much is his property. He by his labour does, as it were, enclose it from the common. Nor will it invalidate his right to say, everybody else has an equal title to it; and therefore he cannot appropriate, he cannot

enclose, without the consent of all his fellow-commoners, all mankind. God, when he gave the world in common to all mankind, commanded man also to labour, and the penury of his condition required it of him. God and his reason commanded him to subdue the earth, i.e. improve it for the benefit of life, and therein lay out something upon it that was his own, his labour. He that in obedience to this command of God, subdued, tilled and sowed any part of it, thereby annexed to it something that was his property, which another had no title to, nor could without injury take from him. . . .

OF THE BEGINNING OF POLITICAL SOCIETIES

95. Men being, as has been said, by nature, all free, equal and independent, no one can be put out of this estate, and subjected to the political power of another, without his own consent. The only way whereby anyone divests himself of his natural liberty, and puts on the bonds of civil society is by agreeing with other men to join and unite into a community, for their comfortable, safe, and peaceable living one amongst another, in a secure enjoyment of their properties, and a greater security against any that are not of it. This any number of men may do, because it injures not the freedom of the rest; they are left as they were in the liberty of the state of nature. When any number of men have so consented to make one community or government, they are thereby presently incorporated, and make one body politic, wherein the majority have a right to act and conclude the rest.

96. For when any number of men have, by the consent of every individual, made a community, they have thereby made that community one body, with a power to act as one body, which is only by the will and determination of the majority. For that which acts any community, being only the consent of the individuals of it, and it being necessary to that which is one body to move one way; it is necessary the body should move that way whither the greater force carries it, which is the consent of the majority: or else it is impossible it should act or continue one body, one community, which the consent of every individual that united into it, agreed that it should; and so every-

one is bound by that consent to be concluded by the majority. And therefore we see that in assemblies empowered to act by positive laws where no number is set by that positive law which empowers them, the act of the majority passes for the act of the whole, and of course determines, as having by the law of nature and reason, the power of the whole. . . .

OF THE ENDS OF POLITICAL SOCIETY AND GOVERNMENT

123. If man in the state of nature be so free, as has been said; if he be absolute lord of his own person and possessions, equal to the greatest, and subject to nobody, why will he part with his freedom? Why will he give up this empire, and subject himself to the dominion and control of any other power? To which 'tis obvious to answer, that though in the state of nature he hath such a right, yet the enjoyment of it is very uncertain, and constantly exposed to the invasion of others. For all being kings as much as he, every man his equal, and the greater part no strict observers of equity and justice, the enjoyment of the property he has in this state is very unsafe, very insecure. This makes him willing to quit this condition, which however free, is full of fears and continual dangers: and 'tis not without reason, that he seeks out, and is willing to join in society with others who are already united, or have a mind to unite for the mutual preservation of their lives, liberties and estates, which I call by the general name, property.

124. The great and chief end therefore, of men's uniting into commonwealths, and putting themselves under government, is the preservation of their property. To which in the state of nature there are many things wanting.

First, there wants an established, settled, known law, received and allowed by common consent to be the standard of right and wrong, and the common measure to decide all controversies between them. For though the law of nature be plain and intelligible to all rational creatures; yet men being biased by their interest, as well as ignorant for want of study of it, are not apt to allow of it as a law binding to them in the application of it to their particular cases.

125. Secondly, in the state of nature there wants a known and indifferent judge, with authority to determine all differences according to the established law. For everyone in that state being both judge and executioner of the law of nature, men being partial to themselves, passion and revenge is very apt to carry them too far, and with too much heat, in their own cases; as well as negligence, and unconcernedness, to make them too remiss, in other men's.

126. Thirdly, in the state of nature there often wants power to back and support the sentence when right, and to give it due execution. They who by any injustice offended, will seldom fail, where they are able, by force to make good their injustice: such resistance many times makes the punishment dangerous, and frequently destructive, to those who attempt it.

127. Thus mankind, notwithstanding all the privileges of the state of nature, being but in an ill condition, while they remain in it, are quickly driven into society. Hence it comes to pass, that we seldom find any number of men live any time together in this state. The inconveniences, that they are therein exposed to, by the irregular and uncertain exercise of the power every man has of punishing the transgressions of others, make them take sanctuary under the established laws of government, and therein seek the preservation of their property. 'Tis this make them so willingly give up everyone his single power of punishing to be exercised by such alone as shall be appointed to it amongst them; and by such rules as the community, or those authorized by them to that purpose, shall agree on. And in this we have the original right and rise of both the legislative and executive power, as well as of the governments and societies themselves.

131. But though men when they enter into society, give up the equality, liberty, and executive power they had in the state of nature, into the hands of the society, to be so far disposed of by the legislative, as the good of the society shall require; yet it being only with an intention in everyone the better to preserve himself his liberty and property; (for no rational creature can be supposed to change his

condition with an intention to be worse) the power of the society, or legislative constituted by them, can never be supposed to extend further than the common good; but is obliged to secure everyone's property by providing against those three defects above mentioned, that made the state of nature so unsafe and uneasy. And so whoever has the legislative or supreme power of any commonwealth, is bound to govern by established standing laws, promulgated and known to the people, and not by extemporary decrees; by indifferent and upright judges, who are to decide controversies by those laws; and to employ the force of the community at home, only in the execution of such laws, or abroad to prevent or redress foreign injuries, and secure the community from inroads and invasion. And all this to be directed to no other end, but the peace, safety, and public good of the people. . . .

OF THE EXTENT OF THE LEGISLATIVE POWER

134. The great end of men's entering into society, being the enjoyment of their properties in peace and safety, and the great instrument and means of that being the laws established in that society; the first and fundamental positive law of all commonwealths, is the establishing of the legislative power; as the first and fundamental natural law, which is to govern even the legislative itself, is the preservation of the society, and (as far as will consist with the public good) of every person in it. This legislative is not only the supreme power of the commonwealth, but sacred and unalterable in the hands where the community have once placed it; nor can any edict of anybody else, in which form soever conceived, or by what power soever backed, have the force and obligation of a law, which has not its sanction from that legislative, which the public has chosen and appointed. For without this the law could not have that, which is absolutely necessary to its being a law, the consent of the society, over whom nobody can have a power to make laws, but by their own consent, and by authority received from them; and therefore all the obedience, which by the most solemn ties anyone can be obliged to pay, ultimately terminates in this supreme power, and is directed by those laws which it enacts: nor

can any oaths to any foreign power whatsoever, or any domestic subordinate power, discharge any member of the society from his obedience to the legislative, acting pursuant to their trust, nor oblige him
to any obedience contrary to the laws so enacted, or further than they
do allow; it being ridiculous to imagine one can be tied ultimately to
obey any power in the society, which is not the supreme.

135. Though the legislative, whether placed in one or more, whether
it be always in being, or only by intervals, though it be the supreme
power in every commonwealth; yet,

First, it is not, nor can possibly be absolutely arbitrary over the
lives and fortunes of the people. For it being but the joint power of
every member of the society given up to that person, or assembly,
which is legislator, it can be no more than those persons had in a
state of nature before they entered into society, and gave up to the
community. For nobody can transfer to another more power than
he has in himself; and nobody has an absolute arbitrary power over
himself, or over any other, to destroy his own life, or take away the
life or property of another. A man, as has been proved, cannot subject
himself to the arbitrary power of another; and having in the state
of nature no arbitrary power over the life, liberty, or possession of
another, but only so much as the law of nature gave him for the preservation of himself, and the rest of mankind; this is all he doth, or
can give up to the commonwealth, and by it to the legislative power,
so that the legislative can have no more than this. Their power in the
utmost bounds of it, is limited to the public good of the society. It is
a power, that hath no other end but preservation, and therefore can
never have a right to destroy, enslave, or designedly to impoverish the
subjects. The obligations of the law of nature, cease not in society, but
only in many cases are drawn closer, and have by human laws known
penalties annexed to them, to enforce their observation. Thus the
law of nature stands as an eternal rule to all men, legislators as well
as others. The rules that they make for other men's actions, must, as
well as their own and other men's actions, be conformable to the law
of nature, i.e. to the will of God, of which that is a declaration, and
the fundamental law of nature being the preservation of mankind, no
human sanction can be good, or valid against it.

136. Secondly, the legislative, or supreme authority, cannot assume to itself a power to rule by extemporary arbitrary decrees, but is bound to dispense justice, and decide the rights of the subject by promulgated standing laws, and known authorized judges. For the law of nature being unwritten, and so nowhere to be found but in the minds of men, they who through passion or interest shall miscite, or misapply it, cannot so easily be convinced of their mistake where there is no established judge: and so it serves not, as it ought, to determine the rights, and fence the properties of those that live under it, especially where everyone is judge, interpreter, and executioner of it too, and that in his own case: and he that has right on his side, having ordinarily but his own single strength, hath not force enough to defend himself from injuries, or to punish delinquents. To avoid these inconveniences which disorder men's properties in the state of nature, men unite into societies, that they may have the united strength of the whole society to secure and defend their properties, and may have standing rules to bound it, by which everyone may know what is his. To this end it is that men give up all their natural power to the society which they enter into, and the community put the legislative power into such hands as they think fit, with this trust, that they shall be governed by declared laws, or else their peace, quiet, and property will still be at the same uncertainty, as it was in the state of nature.

137. Absolute arbitrary power, or governing without settled standing laws, can neither of them consist with the ends of society and government, which men would not quit the freedom of the state of nature for, and tie themselves up under, were it not to preserve their lives, liberties and fortunes; and by stated rules of right and property to secure their peace and quiet. It cannot be supposed that they should intend, had they a power so to do, to give to any one, or more, an absolute arbitrary power over their persons and estates, and put a force into the magistrate's hand to execute his unlimited will arbitrarily upon them: this were to put themselves into a worse condition than the state of nature, wherein they had a liberty to defend their right against the injuries of others, and were upon equal terms of force to maintain it, whether invaded by a single man, or many in combination. Whereas by supposing they have given up themselves to the

absolute arbitrary power and will of a legislator, they have disarmed themselves, and armed him, to make a prey of them when he pleases. He being in a much worse condition who is exposed to the arbitrary power of one man, who has the command of 100,000 than he that is exposed to the arbitrary power of 100,000 single men: nobody being secure, that his will, who has such a command, is better, than that of other men, though his force be 100,000 times stronger. And therefore whatever form the commonwealth is under, the ruling power ought to govern by declared and received laws, and not by extemporary dictates and undetermined resolutions. For then mankind will be in a far worse condition, than in the state of nature, if they shall have armed one or a few men with the joint power of a multitude, to force them to obey at pleasure the exorbitant and unlimited decrees of their sudden thoughts, or unrestrained, and till that moment unknown wills without having any measures set down which may guide and justify their actions. For all the power the government has, being only for the good of the society, as it ought not to be arbitrary and at pleasure, so it ought to be exercised by established and promulgated laws: that both the people may know their duty, and be safe and secure within the limits of the law, and the rulers too kept within their due bounds, and not to be tempted, by the power they have in their hands, to employ it to such purposes, and by such measures, as they would not have known, and own not willingly.

138. Thirdly, the supreme power cannot take from any man any part of his property without his own consent. For the preservation of property being the end of government, and that for which men enter into society, it necessarily supposes and requires, that the people should have property, without which they must be supposed to lose that by entering into society, which was the end for which they entered into it, too gross an absurdity for any man to own. Men therefore in society having property, they have such a right to the goods, which by the law of the community are theirs, that nobody hath a right to take their substance, or any part of it from them, without their own consent; without this, they have no property at all. For I have truly no property in that, which another can by right take from me, when he pleases, against my consent. Hence it is a mistake to

think, that the supreme or legislative power of any commonwealth, can do what it will, and dispose of the estates of the subject arbitrarily, or take any part of them at pleasure. This is not much to be feared in governments where the legislative consists, wholly or in part, in assemblies which are variable, whose members upon the dissolution of the assembly, are subjects under the common laws of their country, equally with the rest. But in governments, where the legislative is in one lasting assembly always in being, or in one man, as in absolute monarchies, there is danger still, that they will think themselves to have a distinct interest, from the rest of the community; and so will be apt to increase their own riches and power, by taking, what they think fit, from the people. For a man's property is not at all secure, though there be good and equitable laws to set the bounds of it, between him and his fellow subjects, if he who commands those subjects, have power to take from any private man, what part he pleases of his property, and use and dispose of it as he thinks good. . . .

141. Fourthly, the legislative cannot transfer the power of making laws to any other hands. For it being but a delegated power from the people, they, who have it, cannot pass it over to others. The people alone can appoint the form of the commonwealth, which is by constituting the legislative, and appointing in whose hands that shall be. And when the people have said, "we will submit to rules, and be governed by laws made by such men, and in such forms," nobody else can say other men shall make laws for them; nor can the people be bound by any laws but such as are enacted by those, whom they have chosen, and authorized to make laws for them. The power of the legislative being derived from the people by a positive voluntary grant and institution, can be no other, than what that positive grant conveyed, which being only to make laws, and not to make legislators, the legislative can have no power to transfer their authority of making laws, and place it in other hands.

142. These are the bounds which the trust that is put in them by the society, and the law of God and nature, have set to the legislative power of every commonwealth, in all forms of government.

First, they are to govern by promulgated established laws, not to be varied in particular cases, but to have one rule for rich and poor, for the favourite at court, and the countryman at plough.

Secondly, these laws also ought to be designed for no other end ultimately than the good of the people.

Thirdly, they must not raise taxes on the property of the people, without the consent of the people, given by themselves, or their deputies. And this properly concerns only such governments where the legislative is always in being, or at least where the people have not reserved any part of the legislative to deputies, to be from time to time chosen by themselves.

Fourthly, the legislative neither must nor can transfer the power of making laws to anybody else, or place it anywhere but where the people have. . . .

OF TYRANNY

199. As usurpation is the exercise of power, which another hath a right to; so tyranny is the exercise of power beyond right, which nobody can have a right to. And this is making use of the power anyone has in his hands; not for the good of those, who are under it, but for his own private separate advantage. When the governor, however entitled, makes not the law, but his will, the rule; and his commands and actions are not directed to the preservation of the properties of his people, but the satisfaction of his own ambition, revenge, covetousness, or any other irregular passion. . . .

OF THE DISSOLUTION OF GOVERNMENT

211. He that will with any clearness speak of the dissolution of government, ought, in the first place to distinguish between the dissolution of the society, and the dissolution of the government. That which makes the community, and brings men out of the loose state of nature, into one politic society, is the agreement which everyone has with the rest to incorporate, and act as one body, and so be one distinct commonwealth. The usual, and almost only way whereby

this union is dissolved, is the inroad of foreign force making a conquest upon them. For in that case, (not being able to maintain and support themselves, as one entire and independent body) the union belonging to that body which consisted therein, must necessarily cease, and so everyone return to the state he was in before, with a liberty to shift for himself, and provide for his own safety as he thinks fit in some other society. Whenever the society is dissolved, 'tis certain the government of that society cannot remain. Thus conquerors' swords often cut up governments by the roots, and mangle societies to pieces, separating the subdued or scattered multitude from the protection of, and dependence on that society which ought to have preserved them from violence. The world is too well instructed in, and too forward to allow of this way of dissolving of governments to need any more to be said of it: and there wants not much argument to prove, that where the society is dissolved, the government cannot remain; that being as impossible, as for the frame of a house to subsist when the materials of it are scattered, and dissipated by a whirlwind, or jumbled into a confused heap by an earthquake.

212. Besides this overturning from without, governments are dissolved from within,

First, when the legislative is altered. Civil society being a state of peace, amongst those who are of it, from whom the state of war is excluded by the umpirage, which they have provided in their legislative, for the ending all differences, that may arise amongst any of them, 'tis in their legislative, that the members of a commonwealth are united, and combined together into one coherent living body. This is the soul that gives form, life, and unity to the commonwealth: from hence the several members have their mutual influence, sympathy, and connection: and therefore when the legislative is broken, or dissolved, dissolution and death follows. For the essence and union of the society consisting in having one will, the legislative, when once established by the majority, has the declaring, and as it were keeping of that will. The constitution of the legislative is the first and fundamental act of society, whereby provision is made for the continuation of their union, under the direction of persons, and bonds of laws made by persons authorized thereunto, by the consent and appointment of the people, without which no one man, or number of men, amongst them, can have authority of making laws, that shall be binding to the rest. When any one, or more, shall take upon them to make laws, whom the people have not appointed so to do, they make laws without authority, which the people are not therefore bound to obey; by which means they come again to be out of subjection, and may constitute to themselves a new legislative, as they think best, being in full liberty to resist the force of those, who without authority would impose anything upon them. Everyone is at the disposure of his own will, when those who had by the delegation of the society, the declaring of the public will, are excluded from it, and others usurp the place who have no such authority or delegation. . . .

220. In these and the like cases, when the government is dissolved, the people are at liberty to provide for themselves, by erecting a new legislative, differing from the other, by the change of persons, or form, or both as they shall find it most for their safety and good. For the society can never, by the fault of another, lose the native and original right it has to preserve itself, which can only be done by a settled legislative, and a fair and impartial execution of the laws made by it. But the state of mankind is not so miserable that they are not capable of using this remedy, till it be too late to look for any. To tell people they may provide for themselves, by erecting a new legislative, when by oppression, artifice, or being delivered over to a foreign power, their old one is gone, is only to tell them they may expect relief, when it is too late, and the evil is past cure. This is in effect no more than to bid them first be slaves, and then to take care of their liberty; and when their chains are on, tell them, they may act like free men. This, if barely so, is rather mockery than relief; and men can never be secure from tyranny, if there be no means to escape it, till they are perfectly under it: and therefore it is, that they have not only a right to get out of it but to prevent it.

221. There is therefore, secondly, another way whereby governments are dissolved, and that is; when the legislative, or the prince, either of them act contrary to their trust.

First, the legislative acts against the trust reposed in them, when they endeavour to invade the property of the subject, and to make themselves, or any part of the community, masters, or arbitrary disposers of the lives, liberties, or fortunes of the people.

222. The reason why men enter into society, is the preservation of their property; and the end why they choose and authorize a legislative, is, that there may be laws made, and rules set as guards and fences to the properties of all the members of the society, to limit the power, and moderate the dominion of every part and member of the society. For since it can never be supposed to be the will of the society, that the legislative should have a power to destroy that, which everyone designs to secure, by entering into society, and for which the people submitted themselves to the legislators of their own making; whenever the legislators endeavour to take away, and destroy the property of the people, or to reduce them to slavery under arbitrary power, they put themselves into a state of war with the people, who are thereupon absolved from any further obedience, and are left to the common refuge, which God hath provided for all men, against force and violence. Whensoever therefore the legislative shall transgress this fundamental rule of society; and either by ambition, fear, folly or corruption, endeavour to grasp themselves, or put into the hands of any other an absolute power over the lives, liberties, and estates of the people; by this breach of trust they forfeit the power, the people had put into their hands, for quite contrary ends, and it devolves to the people, who have a right to resume their original liberty, and, by the establishment of a new legislative (such as they shall think fit) provide for their own safety and security, which is the end for which they are in society. . . .

223. To this perhaps it will be said, that the people being ignorant, and always discontented, to lay the foundation of government in the unsteady opinion, and uncertain humour of the people, is to expose it to certain ruin; and no government will be able long to subsist, if the people may set up a new legislative, whenever they take offence at the old one. To this, I answer: quite the contrary. People are not so easily got out of their old forms, as some are apt to suggest. They are hardly to be prevailed with to amend the acknowledged faults, in

the frame they have been accustomed to. And if there be any original defects, or adventitious ones introduced by time, or corruption; 'tis not an easy thing to get them changed, even when all the world sees there is an opportunity for it. This slowness and aversion in the people to quit their old constitutions, has, in the many revolutions which have been seen in this kingdom, in this and former ages, still kept us to, or, after some interval of fruitless attempts, still brought us back again to our old legislative of king, lords and commons: and whatever provocations have made the crown be taken from some of our princes' heads, they never carried the people so far, as to place it in another line. . . .

229. The end of government is the good of mankind, and which is best for mankind, that the people should be always exposed to the boundless will of tyranny, or that the rulers should be sometimes liable to be opposed, when they grow exorbitant in the use of their power, and employ it for the destruction, and not the preservation of the properties of their people? . . .

232. Whosoever uses force without right, as everyone does in society, who does it without law, puts himself into a state of war with those, against whom he so uses it, and in that state all former ties are cancelled, all other rights cease, and everyone has a right to defend himself, and to resist the aggressor. . . .

240. Here, 'tis like, the common question will be made, who shall be judge whether the prince or legislative act contrary to their trust? This, perhaps, ill affected and factious men may spread amongst the people, when the prince only makes use of his due prerogative. To this I reply, the people shall be judge; for who shall be judge whether his trustee or deputy acts well, and according to the trust reposed in him, but he who deputes him, and must, by having deputed him have still a power to discard him, when he fails in his trust? If this be reasonable in particular cases of private men, why should it be otherwise in that of the greatest moment; where the welfare of millions is concerned, and also where the evil, if not prevented, is greater, and the redress very difficult, dear, and dangerous?

241. But further, this question, (who shall be judge?) cannot mean, that there is no judge at all. For where there is no judicature on earth, to decide controversies amongst men, God in heaven is judge: he alone, 'tis true, is judge of the right. But every man is judge for himself, as in all other cases, so in this, whether another hath put himself into a state of war with him, and whether he should appeal to the supreme judge, as Jephtha did.

242. If a controversy arise betwixt a prince and some of the people, in a matter where the law is silent, or doubtful, and the thing be of great consequence, I should think the proper umpire, in such a case, should be the body of the people. For in cases where the prince hath a trust reposed in him, and is dispensed from the common ordinary rules of the law; there, if any men find themselves aggrieved, and think the prince acts contrary to, or beyond that trust, who so proper to judge as the body of the people, (who, at first, lodged that trust in him) how far they meant it should extend? But if the prince, or whoever they be in the administration, decline that way of determination, the appeal then lies nowhere but to heaven. Force between either persons, who have no known superior on earth, or which permits no appeal to a judge on earth, being properly a state of war, wherein the appeal lies only to heaven, and in that state the injured party must judge for himself, when he will think fit to make use of that appeal, and put himself upon it.

243. To conclude, the power that every individual gave the society, when he entered into it, can never revert to the individuals again, as long as the society lasts, but will always remain in the community; because without this, there can be no community, no commonwealth, which is contrary to the original agreement: so also when the society hath placed the legislative in any assembly of men, to continue in them and their successors, with direction and authority for providing such successors, the legislative can never revert to the people whilst that government lasts: because having provided a legislative with power to continue forever, they have given up their political power to the legislative, and cannot resume it. But if they have set limits to the duration of their legislative, and made this supreme power in any

person, or assembly, only temporary: or else when by the miscarriages of those in authority, it is forfeited; upon the forfeiture of their rulers, or at the determination of the time set, it reverts to the society, and the people have a right to act as supreme, and continue the legislative in themselves, or erect a new form, or under the old form place it in new hands, as they think good.

JUSTICE AND PROPERTY

David Hume

David Hume (1711–76) was one of the key figures in the Scottish Enlightenment, which contributed significantly to the development of the concept of spontaneous order. In Book III of his *Treatise of Human Nature,* Hume considers the origins and nature of justice. He argues that the rules of justice are the result not of rational calculation but of many individual actions, motivated largely by self-interest and leading to the emergence of general rules. He suggests three conditions of the world that lead to the need for rules of justice and property rights: people seek to improve their lives; they are benevolent toward others but not unlimitedly so; and nature has made "scanty provision" for the fulfillment of human wants. Thus we need a system of rules, especially for the acquisition, use, and transfer of property, to allow us to pursue our own interests and cooperate with others. Hume pointed out that money and language also developed spontaneously, without any conscious design.

———————

Of all the animals, with which this globe is peopled, there is none towards whom nature seems, at first sight, to have exercis'd more cruelty than towards man, in the numberless wants and necessities, with which she has loaded him, and in the slender means, which she affords to the relieving these necessities. In other creatures these two particulars generally compensate each other. If we consider the lion as a voracious and carnivorous animal, we shall easily discover him to be very necessitous; but if we turn our eye to his make and temper, his agility, his courage, his arms, and his force, we shall find, that his advantages hold proportion with his wants. The sheep and ox are depriv'd of all these advantages; but their appetites are moderate, and their food is of easy purchase. In man alone, this unnatural conjunction of infirmity, and of necessity, may be observ'd in its greatest perfection. Not only the food, which is requir'd for his sustenance, flies his search and approach, or at least requires his labour to be produc'd, but he must be possess'd of cloaths and lodging, to defend him against the injuries of the weather; tho' to consider him only in himself, he is provided neither with arms, nor force, nor other natural abilities, which are in any degree answerable to so many necessities.

'Tis by society alone he is able to supply his defects, and raise himself up to an equality with his fellow-creatures, and even acquire a superiority above them. By society all his infirmities are compensated; and tho' in that situation his wants multiply every moment upon him, yet his abilities are still more augmented, and leave him in every respect more satisfied and happy, than 'tis possible for him, in his savage and solitary condition, ever to become. When every individual person labours a-part, and only for himself, his force is too small to execute any considerable work; his labour being employ'd in supplying all his different necessities, he never attains a perfection in any particular art; and as his force and success are not at all times equal, the least failure in either of these particulars must be attended with inevitable ruin and misery. Society provides a remedy for these *three* inconveniences. By the conjunction of forces, our power is augmented: By the partition of employments, our ability encreases: And by mutual succour we are less expos'd to fortune and accidents. 'Tis by this additional *force, ability,* and *security,* that society becomes advantageous. . . .

For it must be confest, that however the circumstances of human nature may render an union necessary, and however those passions of lust and natural affection may seem to render it unavoidable; yet there are other particulars in our *natural temper,* and in our *outward circumstances,* which are very incommodious, and are even contrary to the requisite conjunction. Among the former, we may justly esteem our *selfishness* to be the most considerable. I am sensible, that, generally speaking, the representations of this quality have been carried much too far; and that the descriptions, which certain philosophers delight so much to form of mankind in this particular, are as wide of nature as any accounts of monsters, which we meet with in fables and romances. So far from thinking, that men have no affection for any thing beyond themselves, I am of opinion, that tho' it be rare to meet with one, who loves any single person better than himself; yet 'tis as rare to meet with one, in whom all the kind affections, taken together, do not over-balance all the selfish. Consult common experience: Do you not see, that tho' the whole expence of the family be generally under the direction of the master of it, yet there are few that do not bestow the largest part of their fortunes on the pleasures of their wives, and the education of their children, reserving the smallest portion for their own proper use and entertainment. This is what we may observe concerning such as have those endearing ties; and may presume, that the case would be the same with others, were they plac'd in a like situation.

But tho' this generosity must be acknowledg'd to the honour of human nature, we may at the same time remark, that so noble an affection, instead of fitting men for large societies, is almost as contrary to them, as the most narrow selfishness. For while each person loves himself better than any other single person, and in his love to others bears the greatest affection to his relations and acquaintance, this must necessarily produce an opposition of passions, and a consequent opposition of actions; which cannot but be dangerous to the new-establish'd union.

'Tis however worth while to remark, that this contrariety of passions wou'd be attended with but small danger, did it not concur with a peculiarity in our *outward circumstances,* which affords it an opportunity of exerting itself. There are three different species of goods, which we are possess'd of; the internal satisfaction of our mind, the external advantages of our body, and the enjoyment of such possessions as we have acquir'd by our industry and good fortune. We are perfectly secure in the enjoyment of the first. The second may be ravish'd from us, but can be of no advantage to him who deprives us of them. The last only are both expos'd to the violence of others, and may be transferr'd without suffering any loss or alteration; while at the same time, there is not a sufficient quantity of them to supply every one's desires and necessities. As the improvement, therefore, of these goods is the chief advantage of society, so the *instability* of their possession, along with their *scarcity*, is the chief impediment. . . .

I have already observ'd, that justice takes its rise from human conventions; and that these are intended as a remedy to some inconveniences, which proceed from the concurrence of certain *qualities* of the human mind with the *situation* of external objects. The qualities of the mind are *selfishness* and *limited generosity:* And the situation of external objects is their *easy change,* join'd to their *scarcity* in comparison of the wants and desires of men. . . .

Here then is a proposition, which, I think, may be regarded as certain, *that 'tis only from the selfishness and confin'd generosity of men, along with the scanty provision nature has made for his wants, that justice derives its origin.* If we look backward we shall find, that this proposition bestows an additional force on some of those observations, which we have already made on this subject.

First, we may conclude from it, that a regard to public interest, or a strong extensive benevolence, is not our first and original motive for the observation of the rules of justice; since 'tis allow'd, that if men were endow'd with such a benevolence, these rules would never have been dreamt of.

Secondly, we may conclude from the same principle, that the sense of justice is not founded on reason, or on the discovery of certain connexions and relations of ideas, which are eternal, immutable, and universally obligatory. For since it is confest, that such an alteration as that above-mention'd, in the temper and circumstances of mankind, wou'd entirely alter our duties and obligations, 'tis necessary upon the common system, *that the sense of virtue is deriv'd from reason,* to shew the change which this must produce in the relations and ideas. But 'tis evident, that the only cause, why the extensive generosity of man, and the perfect abundance of every thing, wou'd destroy the very idea of justice, is because they render it useless; and that, on the other hand, his confin'd benevolence, and his necessitous condition, give rise to that virtue, only by making it requisite to the publick interest, and to that of every individual. 'Twas therefore a concern for our own, and the publick interest, which made us establish the laws of justice; and nothing can be more certain, than that it is not any relation of ideas, which gives us this concern, but our impressions and sentiments, without which every thing in nature is perfectly indifferent to us, and can never in the least affect us. The sense of justice, therefore, is not founded on our ideas, but on our impressions.

Thirdly, we may farther confirm the foregoing proposition, *that those impressions, which give rise to this sense of justice, are not natural to the mind of man, but arise from artifice and human conventions.* For since any considerable alteration of temper and circumstances destroys equally justice and injustice; and since such an alteration has an effect only by changing our own and the publick interest; it follows, that the first establishment of the rules of justice depends on these different interests. But if men pursu'd the publick interest naturally, and with a hearty affection, they wou'd never have dream'd of restraining each other by these rules; and if they pursu'd their own interest, without any precaution, they wou'd run headlong into every kind of injustice and violence. These rules, therefore, are artificial, and seek their end in an oblique and indirect manner; nor is the interest, which gives rise to them, of a kind that cou'd be pursu'd by the natural and inartificial passions of men.

To make this more evident, consider, that tho' the rules of justice are establish'd merely by interest, their connexion with interest is somewhat singular, and is different from what may be observ'd on other occasions. A single act of justice is frequently contrary to *public interest;* and were it to stand alone, without being follow'd by other acts, may, in itself, be very prejudicial to society. When a man of merit, of a beneficent disposition, restores a great fortune to a miser, or a seditious bigot, he has acted justly and laudably, but the public is a real sufferer. Nor is every single act of justice, consider'd apart, more conducive to private interest, than to public; and 'tis easily conceiv'd how a man may impoverish himself by a signal instance of integrity, and have reason to wish, that with regard to that single act, the laws of justice were for a moment suspended in the universe. But however single acts of justice may be contrary, either to public or private interest, 'tis certain, that the whole plan or scheme is highly conducive, or indeed absolutely requisite, both to the support of society, and the well-being of every individual. 'Tis impossible to separate the good from the ill. Property must be stable, and must be fix'd by general rules. Tho' in one instance the public be a sufferer, this momentary ill is amply compensated by the steady prosecution of the rule, and by the peace and order, which it establishes in society. And even every individual person must find himself a gainer, on ballancing the account; since, without justice, society must immediately dissolve, and every one must fall into that savage and solitary condition, which is infinitely worse than the worst situation that can possibly be suppos'd in society. When therefore men have had experience enough to observe, that whatever may be the consequence of any single act of justice, perform'd by a single person, yet the whole system of actions, concurr'd in by the whole society, is infinitely advantageous to the whole, and to every part; it is not long before justice and property take place. Every member of society is sensible of this interest: Every one expresses this sense to his fellows, along with the resolution he has taken of squaring his actions by it, on condition that others will do the same. No more is requisite to induce any one of them to perform an act of justice, who has the first opportunity. This becomes an example to others. And thus justice establishes itself by a kind of convention or agreement; that is, by a sense of interest, suppos'd to be common to all, and where every single act is perform'd in expectation that others are to perform the like. Without such a convention, no one wou'd ever have dream'd, that there was such a virtue as justice, or have been induc'd to conform his actions to it. Taking any single act, my justice may be pernicious in every respect; and 'tis only upon the supposition, that others are to imitate my example, that I can be induc'd to embrace that virtue; since nothing but this combination can render justice advantageous, or afford me any motives to conform my self to its rules. . . .

However useful, or even necessary, the stability of possession may be to human society, 'tis attended with very considerable inconveniences. The relation of fitness or suitableness ought never to enter into consideration, in distributing the properties of mankind; but we must govern ourselves by rules, which are more general in their application, and more free from doubt and uncertainty. Of this kind is *present* possession upon the first establishment of society; and afterwards *occupation, prescription, accession,* and *succession.* As these depend very much on chance, they must frequently prove contradictory both to men's wants and desires; and persons and possessions must often be very ill adjusted. This is a grand inconvenience, which calls for a remedy. To apply one directly, and allow every man to seize by violence what he judges to be fit for him, wou'd destroy society; and therefore the rules of justice seek some medium betwixt a rigid sta- bility, and this changeable and uncertain adjustment. But there is no medium better than that obvious one, that possession and property shou'd always be stable, except when the proprietor agrees to bestow them on some other person. This rule can have no ill consequence, in occasioning wars and dissentions; since the proprietor's consent, who alone is concern'd, is taken along in the alienation: And it may serve to many good purposes in adjusting property to persons. Different parts of the earth produce different commodities; and not only so, but different men both are by nature fitted for different employments, and attain to greater perfection in any one, when they confine them- selves to it alone. All this requires a mutual exchange and commerce; for which reason the translation of property by consent is founded on a law of nature, as well as its stability without such a consent. . . .

We have now run over the three fundamental laws of nature, *that of the stability of possession, of its transference by consent,* and *of the performance of promises.* 'Tis on the strict observance of those three laws, that the peace and security of human society entirely depend; nor is there any possibility of establishing a good correspondence among men, where these are neglected. Society is absolutely nec- essary for the well-being of men; and these are as necessary to the support of society.

THE DECLARATION OF INDEPENDENCE

Thomas Jefferson

Perhaps the most eloquent and the most influential piece of libertarian writing in history is the Declaration of Independence, written by Thomas Jefferson (1743–1826), adopted by the Continental Congress on July 2, 1776, and publicly presented on July 4. The key philosophical section is the second paragraph, which concisely sums up John Locke's theories of individual rights and government: that people have natural rights, that the purpose of government is to protect those rights, and that if government exceeds its proper purpose, people have the right "to alter or abolish it." A key feature of Jefferson's argument is his insistence on *in*alienable rights. These are rights that cannot be transferred. We cannot "agree" to transfer all of our rights to the sovereign; here Jefferson struck at the very root of absolutist and tyrannical government. Echoes of Locke's phrasing can be seen in the Declaration, though Jefferson said that he "turned to neither book nor pamphlet in writing it." The most significant change made by the Congress in Jefferson's draft was to eliminate his passionate condemnation of George III for the slave trade. The specific indictments of George III's policies have been omitted from this selection.

———————

When in the Course of human events, it becomes necessary for one people to dissolve the political bonds which have connected them with another, and to assume among the Powers of the earth, the separate and equal station to which the Laws of Nature and of Nature's God entitle them, a decent respect to the opinions of mankind requires that they should declare the causes which impel them to the separation.

We hold these truths to be self-evident, that all men are created equal, that they are endowed by their Creator with certain unalienable Rights, that among these are Life, Liberty, and the pursuit of Happiness. That to secure these rights, Governments are instituted among Men, deriving their just powers from the consent of the governed,—That whenever any Form of Government becomes destructive of these ends, it is the Right of the People to alter or abolish it, and to institute new Government, laying its foundation on such principles and organizing its powers in such form, as to them shall seem most likely to effect their Safety and Happiness. Prudence, indeed, will dictate that Governments long established should not be changed for light and transient causes; and accordingly all experience hath shown, that mankind are more disposed to suffer, while evils are sufferable, than to right themselves by abolishing the forms to which they are accustomed. But when a long train of abuses and usurpations, pursuing invariably the same Object evinces a design to reduce them under absolute Despotism, it is their right, it is their duty, to throw off such Government, and to provide new Guards for their future security.—Such has been the patient sufferance of these Colonies; and such is now the necessity which constrains them to alter their former Systems of Government. The history of the present King of Britain is a history of repeated injuries and usurpations, all having in direct object the establishment of an absolute Tyranny over these States. To prove this, let Facts be submitted to a candid world. . . .

In every stage of these Oppressions We have Petitioned for Redress in the most humble terms: Our repeated Petitions have been answered only by repeated injury. A Prince, whose character is thus marked by every act which may define a Tyrant, is unfit to be the ruler of a free people.

Nor have We been wanting in attention to our British brethren. We have warned them from time to time of attempts by their legislature to extend an unwarrantable jurisdiction over us. We have reminded them of the circumstances of our emigration and settlement here. We have appealed to their native justice and magnanimity, and we have conjured them by the ties of our common kindred to disavow these usurpations, which, would inevitably interrupt our connections and correspondence. They too have been deaf to the voice of justice and of consanguinity. We must, therefore, acquiesce in the necessity, which denounces our separation, and hold them, as we hold the rest of mankind, Enemies in War, in Peace Friends.

We therefore, the Representatives of the United States of America in General Congress, Assembled, appealing to the Supreme Judge of the world for the rectitude of our intentions, do, in the Name, and by the authority of the good People of these Colonies, solemnly publish and declare, That these United Colonies are, and of Right ought to be Free and Independent States; that they are Absolved from all Allegiance to the British Crown, and that all political connection between them and the State of Great Britain, is and ought to be totally dissolved; and that as Free and Independent States; they have full Power to levy War, conclude Peace, contract Alliances, establish Commerce, and to do all other Acts and Things which Independent States may of right do. And for the support of this Declaration, with a firm reliance on the Protection of Divine Providence, we mutually pledge to each other our Lives, our Fortunes, and our sacred Honor.

EQUALITY OF RIGHTS

Immanuel Kant

Immanuel Kant (1724–1804) was one of the greatest philosophers in history, although in the English-speaking world he is not usually regarded as a major *political* philosopher, and his contribution to liberalism has largely gone unrecognized. He did, however, in his political writings lay out a theory of inalienable rights and the formation of government that falls squarely in the Enlightenment liberal tradition. In this excerpt from his essay *Theory and Practice* (1791, reprinted in *Kant: Political Writings,* edited by Hans Reiss [Cambridge University Press, 1991]), Kant discusses the freedom, equality, and independence of each person in a civil commonwealth and argues that laws must be based on the protection of rights, not the attempt to create happiness for the citizens. Two major aspects of Kant's argument put him outside the liberal mainstream: He puts the head of state above the laws and demands complete obedience of the citizens, and—as seen in the last paragraph of this excerpt, taken from *The Metaphysics of Morals* (1797, also reprinted in *Kant: Political Writings*)—he lacks a theory of how social order can emerge in the absence of coercion.

ON THE RELATIONSHIP OF THEORY
TO PRACTICE IN POLITICAL RIGHT

Among all the contracts by which a large group of men unites to form a society (*pactum sociale*), the contract establishing a *civil constitution (pactum unionis civilis)* is of an exceptional nature. For while, so far as its execution is concerned, it has much in common with all others that are likewise directed towards a chosen end to be pursued by joint effort, it is essentially different from all others in the principle of its constitution *(constitutionis civilis)*. In all social contracts, we find a union of many individuals for some common end which they all *share*. But a union as an end in itself which they all *ought to share* and which is thus an absolute and primary duty in all external relationships whatsoever among human beings (who cannot avoid mutually influencing one another), is only found in a society in so far as it constitutes a civil state, i.e. a commonwealth. And the end which is a duty in itself in such external relationships, and which is indeed the highest formal condition *(conditio sine qua non)* of all other external duties, is the *right* of men *under coercive public laws* by which each can be given what is due to him and secured against attack from any others. But the whole concept of an external right is derived entirely from the concept of *freedom* in the mutual external relationships of human beings, and has nothing to do with the end which all men have by nature (i.e. the aim of achieving happiness) or with the recognised means of attaining this end. And thus the latter end must on no account interfere as a determinant with the laws governing external right. *Right* is the restriction of each individual's freedom so that it harmonises with the freedom of everyone else (in so far as this is possible within the terms of a general law). And *public right* is the distinctive quality of the *external laws* which make this constant harmony possible. Since every restriction of freedom through the arbitrary will of another party is termed *coercion,* it follows that a civil constitution is a relationship among *free* men who are subject to coercive laws, while they retain their freedom within the general union with their fellows. Such is the requirement of pure reason, which legislates *a priori,* regardless of all empirical ends (which can all be summed up under the general heading of happiness). Men have different views on the empirical end of happiness and what it consists of, so that as far as happiness is concerned, their will cannot be brought under any common principle nor thus under any external law harmonising with the freedom of everyone.

The civil state, regarded purely as a lawful state, is based on the following *a priori* principles:

1. The *freedom* of every member of society as a *human being.*
2. The *equality* of each with all the others as a *subject.*
3. The *independence* of each member of a commonwealth as a *citizen.*

These principles are not so much laws given by an already established state, as laws by which a state can alone be established in accordance with pure rational principles of external human right. Thus:

1. Man's *freedom* as a human being, as a principle for the constitution of a commonwealth, can be expressed in the following formula. No-one can compel me to be happy in accordance with his conception of the welfare of others, for each may seek his happiness in whatever way he sees fit, so long as he does not infringe upon the freedom of others to pursue a similar end which can be reconciled with the freedom of everyone else within a workable general law—i.e. he must accord to others the same right as he enjoys himself. A government might be established on the principle of benevolence towards the people, like that of a father towards his children. Under such a *paternal government (imperium paternale),* the subjects, as immature children who cannot distinguish what is truly useful or harmful to themselves, would be obliged to behave purely passively and to rely upon the judgement of the head of state as to how they *ought* to be happy, and upon his kindness in willing their happiness at all. Such a government is the greatest conceivable *despotism,* i.e. a constitution which suspends the entire freedom of its subjects, who thenceforth have no rights whatsoever. The only conceivable government for men who are capable of possessing rights, even if the ruler is benevolent, is not a *paternal* but a *patriotic* government *(imperium non paternale, sed patrioticum).* A *patriotic* attitude is one where everyone in the state, not excepting its head, regards the commonwealth as a maternal womb, or the land as the paternal ground from which he himself

sprang and which he must leave to his descendants as a treasured pledge. Each regards himself as authorised to protect the rights of the commonwealth by laws of the general will, but not to submit it to his personal use at his own absolute pleasure. This right of freedom belongs to each member of the commonwealth as a human being, in so far as each is a being capable of possessing rights.

2. Man's *equality* as a subject might be formulated as follows. Each member of the commonwealth has rights of coercion in relation to all the others, except in relation to the head of state. For he alone is not a member of the commonwealth, but its creator or preserver, and he alone is authorised to coerce others without being subject to any coercive law himself. But all who are subject to laws are the subjects of a state, and are thus subject to the right of coercion along with all other members of the commonwealth; the only exception is a single person (in either the physical or the moral sense of the word), the head of state, through whom alone the rightful coercion of all others can be exercised. For if he too could be coerced, he would not be the head of state, and the hierarchy of subordination would ascend infinitely. But if there were two persons exempt from coercion, neither would be subject to coercive laws, and neither could do to the other anything contrary to right, which is impossible.

This uniform equality of human beings as subjects of a state is, however, perfectly consistent with the utmost inequality of the mass in the degree of its possessions, whether these take the form of physical or mental superiority over others, or of fortuitous external property and of particular rights (of which there may be many) with respect to others. Thus the welfare of the one depends very much on the will of the other (the poor depending on the rich), the one must obey the other (as the child its parents or the wife her husband), the one serves (the labourer) while the other pays, etc. Nevertheless, they are all equal as subjects *before the law,* which, as the pronouncement of the general will, can only be single in form, and which concerns the form of right and not the material or object in relation to which I possess rights. For no-one can coerce anyone else other than through the public law and its executor, the head of state, while everyone else can resist the others in the same way and to the same degree. No-one, however, can lose this authority to coerce others and to have rights towards them except through committing a crime. And no-one can voluntarily renounce his rights by a contract or legal transaction to the effect that he has no rights but only duties, for such a contract would deprive him of the right to make a contract, and would thus invalidate the one he had already made.

From this idea of the equality of men as subjects in a commonwealth, there emerges this further formula: every member of the commonwealth must be entitled to reach any degree of rank which a subject can earn through his talent, his industry and his good fortune. And his fellow-subjects may not stand in his way by *hereditary* prerogatives or privileges of rank and thereby hold him and his descendants back indefinitely.

All right consists solely in the restriction of the freedom of others, with the qualification that their freedom can co-exist with my freedom within the terms of a general law; and public right in a commonwealth is simply a state of affairs regulated by a real legislation which conforms to this principle and is backed up by power, and under which a whole people live as subjects in a lawful state *(status iuridicus)*. This is what we call a civil state, and it is characterised by equality in the effects and counter-effects of freely willed actions which limit one another in accordance with the general law of freedom. Thus the *birthright* of each individual in such a state (i.e. before he has performed any acts which can be judged in relation to right) is absolutely *equal* as regards his authority to coerce others to use their freedom in a way which harmonises with his freedom. Since birth is not an act on the part of the one who is born, it cannot create any inequality in his legal position and cannot make him submit to any coercive laws except in so far as he is a subject, along with all the others, of the one supreme legislative power. Thus no member of the commonwealth can have a hereditary privilege as against his fellow-subjects; and no-one can hand down to his descendants the privileges attached to the rank he occupies in the commonwealth, nor act as if he were qualified as a ruler by birth and forcibly prevent others from reaching the higher levels of the hierarchy (which are *superior* and *inferior,* but never *imperans* and *subiectus*) through their own merit. He may hand down everything else, so long as it is material and not pertaining to his person, for it may be acquired and disposed of as property and may over a series of generations create considerable inequalities in wealth among the members of the commonwealth (the employee and the employer, the landowner and the agricultural servants, etc.). But he may not prevent his subordinates from raising themselves to his own level if they are able and entitled to do so by their talent, industry and good fortune. If this were not so, he would be allowed to practise coercion without himself being subject to coercive counter-measures from others, and would thus be more than their fellow-subject. No-one who lives within the lawful state of a commonwealth can forfeit this equality other than through some crime of his own, but never by contract or through military force *(occupatio bellica)*. For no legal transaction on his part or on that of anyone else can make him cease to be his own master. He cannot become like a domestic animal to be employed in any chosen capacity and retained therein without consent for any desired period, even with the reservation (which is at times sanctioned by religion, as among the Indians) that he may not be maimed or killed. He can be considered happy in any condition so long as he is aware that, if he does not reach the same level as others, the fault lies either with himself (i.e. lack of ability or serious endeavour) or with circumstances for which he cannot blame others, and not with the irresistible will of any outside party. For as far as right is concerned, his fellow-subjects have no advantage over him.

3. The *independence (sibisufficientia)* of a member of the commonwealth as a *citizen*, i.e. as a co-legislator, may be defined as follows. In the question of actual legislation, all who are free and equal under existing public laws may be considered equal, but not as regards the right to make these laws. Those who are not entitled to this right are nonetheless obliged, as members of the commonwealth, to comply with these laws, and they thus likewise enjoy their protection (not as *citizens* but as co-beneficiaries of this protection). . . .

As for landowners, we leave aside the question of how anyone can have rightfully acquired more land than he can cultivate with his own hands (for acquisition by military seizure is not primary acquisition), and how it came about that numerous people who might otherwise have acquired permanent property were thereby reduced to serving someone else in order to live at all. It would certainly conflict with the above principle of equality if a law were to grant them a privileged status so that their descendants would always remain feudal landowners, without their land being sold or divided by inheritance and thus made useful to more people; it would also be unjust if only those belonging to an arbitrarily selected class were allowed to acquire land, should the estates in fact be divided. . . .

CONCLUSION

This, then, is an *original contract* by means of which a civil and thus completely lawful constitution and commonwealth can alone be established. But we need by no means assume that this contract (*contractus originarius* or *pactum sociale*), based on a coalition of the wills of all private individuals in a nation to form a common, public will for the purposes of rightful legislation, actually exists as a *fact*, for it cannot possibly be so. Such an assumption would mean that we would first have to prove from history that some nation, whose rights and obligations have been passed down to us, did in fact perform such an act, and handed down some authentic record or legal instrument, orally or in writing, before we could regard ourselves as bound by a pre-existing civil constitution. It is in fact merely an *idea* of reason, which nonetheless has undoubted practical reality; for it can oblige every legislator to frame his laws in such a way that they could have been produced by the united will of a whole nation, and to regard each subject, in so far as he can claim citizenship, as if he had consented within the general will. . . .

No generally valid principle of legislation can be based on happiness. For both the current circumstances and the highly conflicting and variable illusions as to what happiness is (and no-one can prescribe to others how they should attain it) make all fixed principles impossible, so that happiness alone can never be a suitable principle of legislation. The doctrine that *salus publica suprema civitatis lex est* retains its value and authority undiminished; but the public welfare which demands *first* consideration lies precisely in that legal constitution which guarantees everyone his freedom within the law, so that each remains free to seek his happiness in whatever way he thinks best, so long as he does not violate the lawful freedom and rights of his fellow subjects at large. If the supreme power makes laws which are primarily directed towards happiness (the affluence of the citizens, increased population etc.), this cannot be regarded as the end for which a civil constitution was established. . . .

Thus *freedom of the pen* is the only safeguard of the rights of the people, although it must not transcend the bounds of respect and devotion towards the existing constitution, which should itself create a liberal attitude of mind among the subjects. To try to deny the citizen this freedom does not only mean, as Hobbes maintains, that the subject can claim no rights against the supreme ruler. It also means withholding from the ruler all knowledge of those matters which, if he knew about them, he would himself rectify, so that he is thereby put into a self-stultifying position. For his will issues commands to his subjects (as citizens) only in so far as he represents the general will of the people. But to encourage the head of state to fear that independent and public thought might cause political unrest is tantamount to making him distrust his own power and feel hatred towards his people.

The general principle, however, according to which a people may judge negatively whatever it believes was *not decreed* in good will by the supreme legislation, can be summed up as follows: *Whatever a people cannot impose upon itself cannot be imposed upon it by the legislator either. . . .*

FROM "THE METAPHYSICS OF MORALS"

Experience teaches us the maxim that human beings act in a violent and malevolent manner, and that they tend to fight among themselves until an external coercive legislation supervenes. But it is not experience or any kind of factual knowledge which makes public legal coercion necessary. On the contrary, even if we imagine men to be as benevolent and law-abiding as we please, the *a priori* rational idea of a non-lawful state will still tell us that before a public and legal state is established, individual men, peoples and states can never be secure against acts of violence from one another, since each will have his own right to do *what seems right and good to him,* independently of the opinion of others. Thus the first decision the individual is obliged to make, if he does not wish to renounce all concepts of right, will be to adopt the principle that one must abandon the state of nature in which everyone follows his own desires, and unite with everyone else (with whom he cannot avoid having intercourse) in order to submit to external, public and lawful coercion. He must accordingly enter into a state wherein that which is to be recognised as belonging to each person is allotted to him *by law* and guaranteed to him by an adequate power (which is not his own, but external to him). In other words, he should at all costs enter into a state of civil society.

THE RIGHT TO IGNORE THE STATE

Herbert Spencer

Herbert Spencer (1820–1903) was one of the great scholars of the nineteenth century, in an era when one individual could still master current thinking in many disciplines. Along with Charles Darwin and Thomas H. Huxley, he developed the theory of evolution, which allowed critics to charge him unfairly with a belief in some heartless theory of "social Darwinism." He planned a vast work, *Synthetic Philosophy,* that would apply the principle of evolutionary progress to all branches of knowledge; he published volumes on biology, psychology, sociology, and ethics. He was also a political philosopher who vigorously defended liberalism in such works as *Social Statics* (1851) and *The Man versus the State* (1884). In the course of his long life he saw liberalism triumph and then begin to be eroded as Britons forgot the liberal principles that had brought them unprecedented liberty and prosperity. In this excerpt from *Social Statics,* he makes a radical claim: that an individual may sever all connections with the state. Spencer himself may have decided that the time had not yet arrived for so radical a proposal; he omitted this chapter from subsequent editions of the book. Note that Spencer's law of equal freedom echoes Kant's principle of freedom.

---

1. As a corollary to the proposition that all institutions must be subordinated to the law of equal freedom, we cannot choose but admit

the right of the citizen to adopt a condition of voluntary outlawry. If every man has freedom to do all that he wills, provided he infringes not the equal freedom of any other man, then he is free to drop connection with the state—to relinquish its protection and to refuse paying toward its support. It is self-evident that in so behaving he in no way trenches upon the liberty of others, for his position is a passive one, and while passive he cannot become an aggressor. It is equally self-evident that he cannot be compelled to continue one of a political corporation without a breach of the moral law, seeing that citizenship involves payment of taxes; and the taking away of a man's property against his will is an infringement of his rights. Government being simply an agent employed in common by a number of individuals to secure to them certain advantages, the very nature of the connection implies that it is for each to say whether he will employ such an agent or not. If any one of them determines to ignore this mutual-safety confederation, nothing can be said except that he loses all claim to its good offices and exposes himself to the danger of maltreatment—a thing he is quite at liberty to do if he likes. He cannot be coerced into political combination without a breach of the law of equal freedom; he can withdraw from it without committing any such breach, and he has therefore a right so to withdraw.

2. "No human laws are of any validity if contrary to the law of nature; and such of them as are valid derive all their force and all their authority mediately or immediately from this original." Thus writes Blackstone, to whom let all honor be given for having so far outseen the ideas of his time and, indeed, we may say of our time. A good antidote, this, for those political superstitions which so widely prevail. A good check upon that sentiment of power worship which still misleads us by magnifying the prerogatives of constitutional governments as it once did those of monarchs. Let men learn that a legislature is *not* "our God upon earth," though, by the authority they ascribe to it and the things they expect from it, they would seem to think it is. Let them learn rather that it is an institution serving a purely temporary purpose, whose power, when not stolen, is at the best borrowed.

Nay, indeed, have we not seen that government is essentially immoral? Is it not the offspring of evil, bearing about it all the marks of its parentage? Does it not exist because crime exists? Is it not strong—or, as we say, despotic—when crime is great? Is there not more liberty—that is, less government—as crime diminishes? And must not government cease when crime ceases, for very lack of objects on which to perform its function? Not only does magisterial power exist *because* of evil, but it exists *by* evil. Violence is employed to maintain it, and all violence involves criminality. Soldiers, policemen, and jailers; swords, batons, and fetters are instruments for inflicting pain; and all infliction of pain is in the abstract wrong. The state employs evil weapons to subjugate evil and is alike contaminated by the objects with which it deals and the means by which it works. Morality cannot recognize it, for morality, being simply a statement of the perfect law, can give no countenance to anything growing out of, and living by, breaches of that law (Chapter I). Wherefore, legislative authority can never be ethical—must always be conventional merely.

Hence, there is a certain inconsistency in the attempt to determine the right position, structure, and conduct of a government by appeal to the first principles of rectitude. For, as just pointed out, the acts of an institution which is in both nature and origin imperfect cannot be made to square with the perfect law. All that we can do is to ascertain, firstly, in what attitude a legislature must stand to the community to avoid being by its mere existence an embodied wrong; secondly, in what manner it must be constituted so as to exhibit the least incongruity with the moral law; and thirdly, to what sphere its actions must be limited to prevent it from multiplying those breaches of equity it is set up to prevent.

The first condition to be conformed to before a legislature can be established without violating the law of equal freedom is the acknowledgment of the right now under discussion—the right to ignore the state.[4]

3. Upholders of pure despotism may fitly believe state control to be unlimited and unconditional. They who assert that men are made

[4]Hence may be drawn an argument for direct taxation, seeing that only when taxation is direct does repudiation of state burdens become possible.

for governments and not governments for men may consistently hold that no one can remove himself beyond the pale of political organization. But they who maintain that the people are the only legitimate source of power—that legislative authority is not original, but deputed—cannot deny the right to ignore the state without entangling themselves in an absurdity.

For, if legislative authority is deputed, it follows that those from whom it proceeds are the masters of those on whom it is conferred; it follows further that as masters they confer the said authority voluntarily; and this implies that they may give or withhold it as they please. To call that deputed which is wrenched from men, whether they will or not, is nonsense. But what is here true of all collectively is equally true of each separately. As a government can rightly act for the people only when empowered by them, so also can it rightly act for the individual only when empowered by him. If A, B, and C debate whether they shall employ an agent to perform for them a certain service, and if while A and B agree to do so C dissents, C cannot equitably be made a party to the agreement in spite of himself. And this must be equally true of thirty as of three; and if of thirty, why not of three hundred, or three thousand, or three million?

4. Of the political superstitions lately alluded to, none is so universally diffused as the notion that majorities are omnipotent. Under the impression that the preservation of order will ever require power to be wielded by some party, the moral sense of our time feels that such power cannot rightly be conferred on any but the largest moiety of society. It interprets literally the saying that "the voice of the people is the voice of God," and, transferring to the one the sacredness attached to the other, it concludes that from the will of the people— that is, of the majority—there can be no appeal. Yet is this belief entirely erroneous.

Suppose, for the sake of argument, that, struck by some Malthusian panic, a legislature duly representing public opinion were to enact that all children born during the next ten years should be drowned. Does anyone think such an enactment would be warrantable? If not, there is evidently a limit to the power of a majority. Suppose, again, that of two races living together—Celts and Saxons, for example—the most numerous determined to make the others their slaves. Would the authority of the greatest number be in such case valid? If not, there is something to which its authority must be subordinate. Suppose, once more, that all men having incomes under £50 a year were to resolve upon reducing every income above that amount to their own standard, and appropriating the excess for public purposes. Could their resolution be justified? If not, it must be a third time confessed that there is a law to which the popular voice must defer. What, then, is that law, if not the law of pure equity—the law of equal freedom? These restraints, which all would put to the will of the majority, are exactly the restraints set up by that law. We deny the right of a majority to murder, to enslave, or to rob, simply because murder, enslaving, and robbery are violations of that law—violations too gross to be overlooked. But if great violations of it are wrong, so also are smaller ones. If the will of the many cannot supersede the first principle of morality in these cases, neither can it in any. So that, however insignificant the minority, and however trifling the proposed trespass against their rights, no such trespass is permissible.

When we have made our constitution purely democratic, thinks to himself the earnest reformer, we shall have brought government into harmony with absolute justice. Such a faith, though perhaps needful for the age, is a very erroneous one. By no process can coercion be made equitable. The freest form of government is only the least objectional form. The rule of the many by the few we call tyranny; the rule of the few by the many is tyranny also, only of a less intense kind. "You shall do as we will, and not as you will," is in either case the declaration; and if the hundred make it to the ninety-nine, instead of the ninety-nine to the hundred, it is only a fraction less immoral. Of two such parties, whichever fulfills this declaration necessarily breaks the law of equal freedom: the only difference being that by the one it is broken in the persons of ninety-nine, while by the other it is broken in the persons of a hundred. And the merit of the democratic form of government consists solely in this, that it trespasses against the smallest number.

The very existence of majorities and minorities is indicative of an immoral state. The man whose character harmonizes with the moral law, we found to be one who can obtain complete happiness without

diminishing the happiness of his fellows (Chapter III). But the enactment of public arrangements by vote implies a society consisting of
men otherwise constituted—implies that the desires of some cannot
be satisfied without sacrificing the desires of others—implies that in
the pursuit of their happiness the majority inflict a certain amount of
unhappiness on the minority—implies, therefore, organic immoral-
ity. Thus, from another point of view, we again perceive that even in
its most equitable form it is impossible for government to dissociate
itself from evil; and further, that unless the right to ignore the state is
recognized, its acts must be essentially criminal.

5. That a man is free to abandon the benefits and throw off the burdens of citizenship may indeed be inferred from the admissions
of existing authorities and of current opinion. Unprepared as they
probably are for so extreme a doctrine as the one here maintained,
the radicals of our day yet unwittingly profess their belief in a maxim
which obviously embodies this doctrine. Do we not continually hear
them quote Blackstone's assertion that "no subject of England can be
constrained to pay any aids or taxes even for the defence of the realm
or the support of government, but such as are imposed by his own
consent, or that of his representative in parliament"? And what does
this mean? It means, say they, that every man should have a vote.
True, but it means much more. If there is any sense in words it is a
distinct enunciation of the very right now contended for. In affirming
that a man may not be taxed unless he has directly or indirectly given
his consent, it affirms that he may refuse to be so taxed; and to refuse
to be taxed is to cut all connection with the state. Perhaps it will be
said that this consent is not a specific, but a general one, and that the
citizen is understood to have assented to everything his representative may do when he voted for him. But suppose he did not vote for
him, and on the contrary did all in his power to get elected someone
holding opposite views—what then? The reply will probably be that,
by taking part in such an election, he tacitly agreed to abide by the
decision of the majority. And how if he did not vote at all? Why, then
he cannot justly complain of any tax, seeing that he made no protest
against its imposition. So, curiously enough, it seems that he gave his
consent in whatever way he acted—whether he said yes, whether he

said no, or whether he remained neuter! A rather awkward doctrine, this. Here stands an unfortunate citizen who is asked if he will pay money for a certain proffered advantage; and whether he employs the only means of expressing his refusal or does not employ it, we are told that he practically agrees, if only the number of others who agree is greater than the number of those who dissent. And thus we are introduced to the novel principle that A's consent to a thing is not determined by what A says, but by what B may happen to say!

It is for those who quote Blackstone to choose between this absurdity and the doctrine above set forth. Either his maxim implies the right to ignore the state, or it is sheer nonsense.

THE CONSTITUTION OF NO AUTHORITY

Lysander Spooner

Lysander Spooner (1808–87) was a constitutional lawyer and writer active in the abolitionist and other libertarian movements through much of the nineteenth century. In his essay "The Constitution of No Authority" (1870), no. 6 of a series of pamphlets titled *No Treason,* he argues that the Constitution of the United States has no authority over anyone who didn't sign it. Spooner pursued liberal theories of consent and natural rights to what he saw as their natural conclusion: that no one was bound by any agreement he had not personally agreed to. Despite his claim that the Constitution itself was of no authority, he made use of its protections for freedom before the Civil War in his essay *The Unconstitutionality of Slavery.* He also founded a mail-delivery company to compete with the United States Post Office; when he was forced by act of Congress to stop, he wrote *The Unconstitutionality of the Laws of Congress Prohibiting the Private Delivery of Mail.*

The Constitution has no inherent authority or obligation. It has no authority or obligation at all, unless as a contract between man and man. And it does not so much as even purport to be a contract between persons now existing. It purports, at most, to be only a contract between persons living eighty years ago. And it can be supposed to have been a contract then only between persons who had already come to years of discretion, so as to be competent to make reasonable and obligatory contracts. Furthermore, we know, historically, that only a small portion even of the people then existing were consulted on the subject, or asked, or permitted to express either their consent or dissent in any formal manner. Those persons, if any, who did give their consent formally, are all dead now. Most of them have been dead forty, fifty, sixty, or seventy years. *And the Constitution, so far as it was their contract, died with them.* They had no natural power or right to make it obligatory upon their children. It is not only plainly impossible, in the nature of things, that they *could* bind their posterity, but they did not even attempt to bind them. That is to say, the instrument does not purport to be an agreement between any body but "the people" *then* existing; nor does it, either expressly or impliedly, assert any right, power, or disposition, on their part, to bind anybody but themselves. Let us see. Its language is:

> We, the people of the United States (that is, the people *then existing* in the United States), in order to form a more perfect union, insure domestic tranquility, provide for the common defense, promote the general welfare, and secure the blessings of liberty to ourselves *and our posterity,* do ordain and establish this Constitution for the United States of America.

It is plain, in the first place, that this language, *as an agreement,* purports to be only what it at most really was, viz., a contract between the people then existing; and, of necessity, binding, as a contract, only upon those then existing. In the second place, the language neither expresses nor implies that they had any intention or desire, nor that they imagined they had any right or power, to bind their "posterity" to live under it. It does not say that their "posterity" will, shall, or must live under it. It only says, in effect, that their hopes and motives in adopting it were that it might prove useful to their posterity, as well as to themselves, by promoting their union, safety, tranquility, liberty, etc.

Suppose an agreement were entered into, in this form:

We, the people of Boston, agree to maintain a fort on Governor's Island, to protect ourselves and our posterity against invasion.

This agreement, as an agreement, would clearly bind nobody but the people then existing. Secondly, it would assert no right, power, or disposition, on their part, to compel their "posterity" to maintain such a fort. It would only indicate that the supposed welfare of their posterity was one of the motives that induced the original parties to enter into the agreement.

When a man says he is building a house for himself and his posterity, he does not mean to be understood as saying that he has any thought of binding them, nor is it to be inferred that he is so foolish as to imagine that he has any right or power to bind them, to live in it. So far as they are concerned, he only means to be understood as saying that his hopes and motives, in building it, are that they, or at least some of them, may find it for their happiness to live in it.

So when a man says he is planting a tree for himself and his posterity, he does not mean to be understood as saying that he has any thought of compelling them, nor is it to be inferred that he is such a simpleton as to imagine that he has any right or power to compel them, to eat the fruit. So far as they are concerned, he only means to say that his hopes and motives, in planting the tree, are that its fruit may be agreeable to them.

So it was with those who originally adopted the Constitution. Whatever may have been their personal intentions, the legal meaning of their language, so far as their "posterity" was concerned, simply was, that their hopes and motives, in entering into the agreement, were that it might prove useful and acceptable to their posterity; that it might promote their union, safety, tranquility, and welfare; and that it might tend "to secure to them the blessings of liberty." The language does not assert nor at all imply, any right, power, or disposition, on the part of the original parties to the agreement, to compel their "posterity" to live under it. If they had intended to bind their posterity to live under it, they should have said that their object was, not "to secure to them the blessings of liberty," but to make slaves of them; for if their "posterity" are bound to live under it, they are nothing less than the slaves of their foolish, tyrannical, and dead grandfathers.

It cannot be said that the Constitution formed "the people of the

United States," for all time, into a corporation. It does not speak of "the people" as a corporation, but as individuals. A corporation does not describe itself as "we," nor as "people," nor as "ourselves." Nor does a corporation, in legal language, have any "posterity." It supposes itself to have, and speaks of itself as having, perpetual existence, as a single individuality.

Moreover, no body of men, existing at any one time, have the power to create a perpetual corporation. A corporation can become practically perpetual only by the voluntary accession of new members, as the old ones die off. But for this voluntary accession of new members, the corporation necessarily dies with the death of those who originally composed it.

Legally speaking, therefore, there is, in the Constitution, nothing that professes or attempts to bind the "posterity" of those who established it.

If, then, those who established the Constitution, had no power to bind, and did not attempt to bind, their posterity, the question arises, whether their posterity have bound themselves. If they have done so, they can have done so in only one or both of these two ways, viz., by voting, and paying taxes.

Let us consider these two matters, voting and tax paying, separately. And first of voting.

All the voting that has ever taken place under the Constitution, has been of such a kind that it not only did not pledge the whole people to support the Constitution, but it did not even pledge any one of them to do so, as the following considerations show.

1. In the very nature of things, the act of voting could bind nobody but the actual voters. But owing to the property qualifications required, it is probable that, during the first twenty or thirty years under the Constitution, not more than one-tenth, fifteenth, or perhaps twentieth of the whole population (black and white, men, women, and minors) were permitted to vote. Consequently, so far as voting was concerned, not more than one-tenth, fifteenth, or twentieth of those then existing, could have incurred any obligation to support the Constitution.

At the present time, it is probable that not more than one-sixth of the whole population are permitted to vote. Consequently, so far as voting is concerned, the other five-sixths can have given no pledge that they will support the Constitution.

2. Of the one-sixth that are permitted to vote, probably not more than two-thirds (about one-ninth of the whole population) have usually voted. Many never vote at all. Many vote only once in two, three, five, or ten years, in periods of great excitement.

No one, by voting, can be said to pledge himself for any longer period than that for which he votes. If, for example, I vote for an officer who is to hold his office for only a year, I cannot be said to have thereby pledged myself to support the government beyond that term. Therefore, on the ground of actual voting, it probably cannot be said that more than one-ninth or one-eighth, of the whole population are usually under any pledge to support the Constitution.

3. It cannot be said that, by voting, a man pledges himself to support the Constitution, unless the act of voting be a perfectly voluntary one on his part. Yet the act of voting cannot properly be called a voluntary one on the part of any very large number of those who do vote. It is rather a measure of necessity imposed upon them by others, than one of their own choice. . . .

[To quote myself:] "In truth, in the case of individuals, their actual voting is not to be taken as proof of consent, *even for the time being.* On the contrary, it is to be considered that, without his consent having even been asked a man finds himself environed by a government that he cannot resist; a government that forces him to pay money, render service, and forego the exercise of many of his natural rights, under peril of weighty punishments. He sees, too, that other men practice this tyranny over him by the use of the ballot. He sees further, that, if he will but use the ballot himself, he has some chance of relieving himself from this tyranny of others, by subjecting them to his own. In short, he finds himself, without his consent, so situated that, if he use the ballot, he may become a master; if he does not use it, he must become a slave. And he has no other alternative than these two. In self-defence, he attempts the former. His case is analogous to that of a man who has been forced into battle, where he must either kill others, or be killed himself. Because, to save his own life in battle, a man attempts to take the lives of his opponents, it is not to be inferred that the battle is one of his own choosing. Neither in contests with the ballot—which is a mere substitute for a bullet—because, as his only chance of self-preservation, a man uses a ballot, is it to be inferred that the contest is one into which he voluntarily entered; that he voluntarily set up all his own natural rights, as a stake against those of others, to be lost or won by the mere power of numbers. On the contrary, it is to be considered that, in an exigency into which he had been forced by others, and in which no other means of self-defence offered, he, as a matter of necessity, used the only one that was left to him.

"Doubtless the most miserable of men, under the most oppressive government in the world, if allowed the ballot, would use it, if they could see any chance of thereby meliorating their condition. But it would not, therefore, be a legitimate inference that the government itself, that crushes them, was one which they had voluntarily set up, or even consented to.

"Therefore, a man's voting under the Constitution of the United States, is not to be taken as evidence that he ever freely assented to the Constitution, *even for the time being*. Consequently we have no proof that any very large portion, even of the actual voters of the United States, ever really and voluntarily consented to the Constitution, *even for the time being*. Nor can we ever have such proof, until every man is left perfectly free to consent, or not, without thereby subjecting himself or his property to be disturbed or injured by others."

As we can have no legal knowledge as to who votes from choice, and who from the necessity thus forced upon him, we can have no legal knowledge, as to any particular individual, that he voted from choice; or, consequently, that by voting, he consented, or pledged himself, to support the government. Legally speaking, therefore, the act of voting utterly fails to pledge *any one* to support the government. It utterly fails to prove that the government rests upon the voluntary support of anybody. On general principles of law and reason, it cannot be said that the government has any voluntary supporters

at all, until it can be distinctly shown who its voluntary supporters are. . . .

The payment of taxes, being compulsory, of course furnishes no
evidence that any one voluntarily supports the Constitution.

1. It is true that the *theory* of our Constitution is, that all taxes are
paid voluntarily; that our government is a mutual insurance company, voluntarily entered into by the people with each other; that
each man makes a free and purely voluntary contract with all others
who are parties to the Constitution, to pay so much money for so
much protection, the same as he does with any other insurance company; and that he is just as free not to be protected, and not to pay
tax, as he is to pay a tax, and be protected.

But this theory of our government is wholly different from the
practical fact. The fact is that the government, like a highwayman,
says to a man: "Your money, or your life." And many, if not most,
taxes are paid under the compulsion of that threat.

The government does not, indeed, waylay a man in a lonely place,
spring upon him from the roadside, and, holding a pistol to his head,
proceed to rifle his pockets. But the robbery is none the less a robbery on that account; and it is far more dastardly and shameful.

The highwayman takes solely upon himself the responsibility,
danger, and crime of his own act. He does not pretend that he has
any rightful claim to your money, or that he intends to use it for your
own benefit. He does not pretend to be anything but a robber. He has
not acquired impudence enough to profess to be merely a "protector,"
and that he takes men's money against their will, merely to enable
him to "protect" those infatuated travellers, who feel perfectly able to
protect themselves, or do not appreciate his peculiar system of protection. He is too sensible a man to make such professions as these.
Furthermore, having taken your money, he leaves you, as you wish
him to do. He does not persist in following you on the road, against
your will; assuming to be your rightful "sovereign," on account of
the "protection" he affords you. He does not keep "protecting" you,
by commanding you to bow down and serve him; by requiring you
to do this, and forbidding you to do that; by robbing you of more
money as often as he finds it for his interest or pleasure to do so; and

by branding you as a rebel, a traitor, and an enemy to your country, and shooting you down without mercy, if you dispute his authority, or resist his demands. He is too much of a gentleman to be guilty of such impostures, and insults, and villainies as these. In short, he does not, in addition to robbing you, attempt to make you either his dupe or his slave. . . .

For this reason, whoever desires liberty, should understand these vital facts, viz.: 1. That every man who puts money into the hands of a "government" (so called), puts into its hands a sword which will be used against himself, to extort more money from him, and also to keep him in subjection to its arbitrary will. 2. That those who will take his money, without his consent, in the first place, will use it for his further robbery and enslavement, if he presumes to resist their demands in the future. 3. That it is a perfect absurdity to suppose that any body of men would ever take a man's money without his consent, for any such object as they profess to take it for, viz., that of protecting him; for why should they wish to protect him, if he does not wish them to do so? To suppose that they would do so, is just as absurd as it would be to suppose that they would take his money without his consent, for the purpose of buying food or clothing for him, when he did not want it. 4. If a man wants "protection," he is competent to make his own bargains for it; and nobody has any occasion to rob him, in order to "protect" him against his will. 5. That the only security men can have for their political liberty, consists in their keeping their money in their own pockets, until they have assurances, perfectly satisfactory to themselves, that it will be used as they wish it to be used, for their benefit, and not for their injury. 6. That no government, so called, can reasonably be trusted for a moment, or reasonably be supposed to have honest purposes in view, any longer than it depends wholly upon voluntary support.

These facts are all so vital and so self-evident, that it cannot reasonably be supposed that any one will voluntarily pay money to a "government," for the purpose of securing its protection, unless he first makes an explicit and purely voluntary contract with it for that purpose.

It is perfectly evident, therefore, that neither such voting, nor such payment of taxes, as actually takes place, proves anybody's consent, or obligation, to support the Constitution. Consequently we have no evidence at all that the Constitution is binding upon anybody, or that anybody is under any contract or obligation whatever to support it. And nobody is under any obligation to support it.

The Constitution not only binds nobody now, but it never did bind anybody. It never bound anybody, because it was never agreed to by anybody in such a manner as to make it, on general principles of law and reason, binding upon him.

It is a general principle of law and reason, that a *written* instrument binds no one until he has signed it. This principle is so inflexible a one, that even though a man is unable to write his name, he must still "make his mark," before he is bound by a written contract. This custom was established ages ago, when few men could write their names; when a clerk—that is, a man who could write—was so rare and valuable a person, that even if he were guilty of high crimes, he was entitled to pardon, on the ground that the public could not afford to lose his services. Even at that time, a written contract must be signed; and men who could not write, either "made their mark," or signed their contracts by stamping their seals upon wax affixed to the parchment on which their contracts were written. Hence the custom of affixing seals, that has continued to this time.

The law holds, and reason declares, that if a written instrument is not signed, the presumption must be that the party to be bound by it, did not choose to sign it, or to bind himself by it. . . .

Inasmuch as the Constitution was never signed, nor agreed to, by anybody, as a contract, and therefore never bound anybody, and is now binding upon nobody; and is, moreover, such an one as no people can ever hereafter be expected to consent to, except as they may be forced to do so at the point of the bayonet, it is perhaps of no importance what its true legal meaning, as a contract, is. Nevertheless, the writer thinks it proper to say that, in his opinion, the Constitution is no such instrument as it has generally been assumed to be; but that by false interpretations, and naked usurpations, the government has been made in practice a very widely, and almost wholly, different thing from what the Constitution itself purports to authorize. He has heretofore written much, and could write much more, to prove that such is the truth. But whether the Constitution really be one thing, or another, this much is certain—that it has either authorized such a government as we have had, or has been powerless to prevent it. In either case, it is unfit to exist.

THE *PLAYBOY* INTERVIEW WITH AYN RAND

Alvin Toffler

Ayn Rand (1905–82) is one of the most influential and controversial figures in the modern history of libertarianism. Born
Alyssa Rosenbaum in St. Petersburg, she fled Russia after the
Bolshevik Revolution and came to the United States. In her
powerful novels *The Fountainhead* (1943) and *Atlas Shrugged*
(1957) and in a steady series of nonfiction essays, she developed
a philosophy based on reason, egoism, and individual rights,
which she called Objectivism. Her novels sold in the millions
and inspired in thousands of young people a passionate commitment to those ideas. The political philosophy found in her
writings virtually defined libertarianism for a generation of
readers—individual rights, the morality of free markets, and a
government limited to the protection of rights through police,
courts, and national defense. Yet she disclaimed any connection
with libertarianism, insisting that a political philosophy could
not stand on its own, without the metaphysical, epistemological, and ethical foundation that she outlined. Although she attracted many people to libertarian ideas, many libertarians
were uncomfortable with her atheism, her uncompromising
egoism, and what they saw as her peremptory manner and cult
following. Rand's differences with libertarianism are shared by
her heirs, so we are unable to include her major essays in this
reader. But her ideas are clearly presented in this interview
from the March 1964 issue of *Playboy*. The interviewer was

Alvin Toffler, who went on to write *Future Shock* and other books.*

_____

PLAYBOY: Miss Rand, your novels and essays, especially your controversial best seller, *Atlas Shrugged,* present a carefully engineered, internally consistent world view. They are, in effect, the expression of an all-encompassing philosophical system. What do you seek to accomplish with this new philosophy?

RAND: I seek to provide men—or those who care to think—with an integrated, consistent and rational view of life.

PLAYBOY: What are the basic premises of Objectivism? Where does it begin?

RAND: It begins with the axiom that existence exists, which means that an objective reality exists independent of any perceiver or of the perceiver's emotions, feelings, wishes, hopes or fears. Objectivism holds that reason is man's only means of perceiving reality and his only guide to action. By reason, I mean the faculty which identifies and integrates the material provided by man's senses.

PLAYBOY: In *Atlas Shrugged* your hero, John Galt, declares, "I swear—by my life and my love of it—that I will never live for the sake of another man, nor ask another man to live for mine." How is this related to your basic principles?

RAND: Galt's statement is a dramatized summation of the Objectivist ethics. Any system of ethics is based on and derived, implicitly or explicitly, from a metaphysics. The ethic derived from the metaphysical base of Objectivism holds that, since reason is man's basic tool of survival, rationality is his highest virtue. To use his mind, to perceive reality and to act accordingly, is man's moral imperative. The standard of value of the Objectivist ethics is: man's life—man's survival qua man—or that which the nature of a rational being requires for his proper survival. The Objectivist ethics, in essence, hold that man exists for his own sake, that the pursuit of his own happiness is his highest moral purpose, that he must not sacrifice himself to others, not sacrifice others to himself. It is this last that Galt's statement summarizes. . . .

_____

*Interview reprinted by permission of *Playboy* and Alvin Toffler.

PLAYBOY: Would you be willing to die for your cause, and should your followers be willing to die for it? And for the truly nonsacrificial Objectivist, is *any* cause worth dying for?

RAND: The answer to this is made plain in my book. In *Atlas Shrugged* I explain that a man has to live for, and when necessary, fight for, his values—because the whole process of living consists of the achievement of values. Man does not survive automatically. He must live like a rational being and accept nothing less. He cannot survive as a brute. Even the simplest value, such as food, has to be created by man, has to be planted, has to be produced. The same is true of his more interesting, more important achievements. All values have to be gained and kept by man, and, if they are threatened, he has to be willing to fight and die, if necessary, for his right to live like a rational being. You ask me, would I be willing to die for Objectivism? I would. But what is more important, I am willing *to live* for it—which is much more difficult. . . .

PLAYBOY: In your early novel, *Anthem,* your protagonist declares, "It is my will which chooses, and the choice of my will is the only edict I respect." Isn't this anarchism? Is one's own desire or will the *only* law one must respect?

RAND: Not one's own will. This is, more or less, a poetic expression made clear by the total context of the story in *Anthem.* One's own rational judgment. You see, I use the term free will in a totally different sense from the one usually attached to it. Free will consists of man's ability to think or not to think. The act of thinking is man's primary act of choice. A rational man will never be guided by desires or whims, only by values based on his rational judgment. That is the only authority he can recognize. This does not mean anarchy, because, if a man wants to live in a free, civilized society, he would, in reason, have to choose to observe the laws, when those laws are objective, rational and valid. I have written an article on this subject for *The Objectivist Newsletter*—on the need and proper function of a government.

PLAYBOY: What, in your view, *is* the proper function of a government?

RAND: Basically, there is really only one proper function: the protection of individual rights. Since rights can be violated only by physical force, and by certain derivatives of physical force, the proper function of government is to protect men from those who initiate the use of physical force: from those who are criminals. Force, in a free society, may be used only in retaliation and only against those who initiate its use. This is the proper task of government: to serve as a policeman who protects men from the use of force.

PLAYBOY: If force may be used only in retaliation against force, does the government have the right to use force to collect taxes, for example, or to draft soldiers?

RAND: In principle, I believe that taxation should be voluntary, like everything else. But how one would implement this is a very complex question. I can only suggest certain methods, but I would not attempt to insist on them as a definitive answer. A government lottery, for instance, used in many countries in Europe, is one good method of voluntary taxation. There are others. Taxes should be voluntary contributions for the proper governmental services which people do need and therefore would be and should be willing to pay for—as they pay for insurance. But, of course, this is a problem for a distant future, for the time when men will establish a fully free social system. It would be the last, *not* the first, reform to advocate. As to the draft, it is improper and unconstitutional. It is a violation of fundamental rights, of a man's right to his own life. No man has the right to send another man to fight and die for his, the sender's, cause. A country has no right to force men into involuntary servitude. Armies should be strictly voluntary; and, as military authorities will tell you, volunteer armies are the best armies.

PLAYBOY: What about other public needs? Do you consider the post office, for example, a legitimate function of government?

RAND: Now let's get this straight. My position is fully consistent. Not only the post office, but streets, roads, and above all, schools, should all be privately owned and privately run. I advocate the separation of state and economics. The government should be concerned only with those issues which involve the use of force. This means: the police, the armed services, and the law courts to settle disputes among men. Nothing else. Everything else should be privately run and would be much better run.

PLAYBOY: Would you create any new government departments or agencies?

RAND: No, and I truly cannot discuss things that way. I am not a government planner nor do I spend my time inventing Utopias. I'm talking about principles whose practical applications are clear. If I have said that I am opposed to the initiation of force, what else has to be discussed?

PLAYBOY: What about force in foreign policy? You have said that any free nation had the right to invade Nazi Germany during World War II . . .

RAND: Certainly.

PLAYBOY: . . . And that any free nation today has the moral right—though not the duty—to invade Soviet Russia, Cuba, or any other "slave pen." Correct?

RAND: Correct. A dictatorship—a country that violates the rights of its own citizens—is an outlaw and can claim no rights.

PLAYBOY: Would you actively advocate that the United States invade Cuba or the Soviet Union?

RAND: Not at present. I don't think it's necessary. I would advocate that which the Soviet Union fears above all else: economic boycott. I would advocate a blockade of Cuba and an economic boycott of Soviet Russia; and you would see both those regimes collapse without the loss of a single American life.

PLAYBOY: Would you favor U.S. withdrawal from the United Nations?

RAND: Yes. I do not sanction the grotesque pretense of an organization allegedly devoted to world peace and human rights, which includes Soviet Russia, the worst aggressor and bloodiest butcher in history, as one of its members. The notion of protecting rights, with Soviet Russia among the protectors, is an insult to the concept of rights and to the intelligence of any man who is asked to endorse or sanction such an organization. I do not believe that an individual should cooperate with criminals, and, for all the same reasons, I do not believe that free countries should cooperate with dictatorships.

PLAYBOY: Would you advocate severing diplomatic relations with Russia?

RAND: Yes.

PLAYBOY: How do you feel about the test-ban treaty which was recently signed?

RAND: I agree with Barry Goldwater's speech on this subject on the Senate floor. The best military authorities, and above all, the best scientific authority, Dr. Teller, the author of the hydrogen bomb, have stated that this treaty is not merely meaningless but positively dangerous to America's defense.

PLAYBOY: If Senator Goldwater is nominated as the Republican presidential candidate this July, would you vote for him?

RAND: At present, yes. When I say "at present," I mean the date when this interview is being recorded. I disagree with him on a great many things, but I do agree, predominantly, with his foreign policy. Of any candidates available today, I regard Barry Goldwater as the best. I would vote for him, if he offers us a plausible, or at least semiconsistent, platform.

PLAYBOY: How about Richard Nixon?

RAND: I'm opposed to him. I'm opposed to any compromiser or me-tooer, and Mr. Nixon is probably the champion in this regard.

PLAYBOY: What about President Johnson?

RAND: I have no particular opinion about him.

PLAYBOY: You are a declared anti-communist, antisocialist and anti-liberal. Yet you reject the notion that you are a conservative. In fact, you have reserved some of your angriest criticism for conservatives. Where *do* you stand politically?

RAND: Correction. I never describe my position in terms of negatives. I am an advocate of *laissez-faire* capitalism, of individual rights—there are no others—of individual freedom. It is on this ground that I oppose any doctrine which proposes the sacrifice of the individual to the collective, such as communism, socialism, the welfare state, fascism, Nazism and modern liberalism. I oppose the conservatives on the same ground. The conservatives are advocates of a mixed economy and of a welfare state. Their difference from the liberals is only one of degree, not of principle.

PLAYBOY: You have charged that America suffers from intellectual bankruptcy. Do you include in this condemnation such right-wing publications as the *National Review?* Isn't that magazine a powerful voice against all the things you regard as "statism"?

RAND: I consider *National Review* the worst and most dangerous magazine in America. The kind of defense that it offers to capitalism results in nothing except the discrediting and destruction of capitalism. Do you want me to tell you why?

PLAYBOY: Yes, please.

RAND: Because it ties capitalism to religion. The ideological position of *National Review* amounts, in effect, to the following: In order to accept freedom and capitalism, one has to believe in God or in some form of religion, some form of supernatural mysticism. Which means that there are no rational grounds on which one can defend capitalism. Which amounts to an admission that reason is on the side of capitalism's enemies, that a slave society or a dictatorship is a rational system, and that only on the ground of mystic faith can one believe in freedom. Nothing more derogatory to capitalism could ever be alleged, and the exact opposite is true. Capitalism is the only system that can be defended and validated by reason.

PLAYBOY: You have attacked Governor Nelson Rockefeller for "lumping all opponents of the welfare state with actual crackpots." It was clear from his remarks that among others, he was aiming his criticism at the John Birch Society. Do you resent being lumped with the John Birchers? Do you consider them "crackpots" or a force for good?

RAND: I resent being lumped with anyone. I resent the modern method of never defining ideas, and lumping totally different people into a collective by means of smears and derogatory terms. I resent Governor Rockefeller's smear tactics: his refusal to identify specifically whom and what he meant. As far as I'm concerned, I repeat, I don't want to be lumped with anyone, and certainly not with the John Birch Society. Do I consider them crackpots? No, not necessarily. What is wrong with them is that they don't seem to have any specific, clearly defined political philosophy. Therefore, some of them may be crackpots, others may be very well-meaning citizens. I consider the Birch Society futile, because they are not *for* capitalism, but merely *against* communism. I gather they believe that the disastrous state of today's world is caused by a communist conspiracy. This is childishly naive and superficial. No country can be destroyed by a mere conspiracy, it can be destroyed only by *ideas*. The Birchers seem to be either nonintellectual or anti-intellectual. They do not attach importance to ideas. They do not realize that the great battle in the world today is a philosophical, ideological conflict.

PLAYBOY: Are there any political groups in the United States today of which you approve?

RAND: Political groups, as such—no. Is there any political group today which is fully consistent? Such groups today are guided by or advocate blatant contradictions.

PLAYBOY: Do you have any personal political aspirations yourself? Have you ever considered running for office?

RAND: Certainly not. And I trust that you don't hate me enough to wish such a thing on me.

PLAYBOY: But you are interested in politics, or at least in political theory, aren't you?

RAND: Let me answer you this way: When I came here from Soviet Russia, I was interested in politics for only one reason—to reach the day when I would not have to be interested in politics. I wanted to secure a society in which I would be free to pursue my own concerns and goals, knowing that the government would not interfere to wreck them, knowing that my life, my work, my future were not at the mercy of the state or of a dictator's whim. This is still my attitude today. Only today I know that such a society is an ideal not yet achieved, that I cannot expect others to achieve it for me, and that I, like every other responsible citizen, must do everything possible to achieve it. In other words, I am interested in politics only in order to secure and protect freedom.

PLAYBOY: Throughout your work you argue that the way in which the contemporary world is organized, even in the capitalist countries, submerges the individual and stifles initiative. In *Atlas Shrugged,* John Galt leads a strike of the men of the mind—which results in the collapse of the collectivist society around them. Do you think the time has come for the artists, intellectuals and creative businessmen of today to withdraw their talents from society in this way?

RAND: No, not yet. But before I explain, I must correct one part of your question. What we have today is not a capitalist society, but a mixed economy—that is, a mixture of freedom and controls, which, by the presently dominant trend, is moving toward dictatorship. The action in *Atlas Shrugged* takes place at a time when society has reached the stage of dictatorship. When and if this happens, that will be the time to go on strike, but not until then.

PLAYBOY: What do you mean by dictatorship? How would you define it?

RAND: A dictatorship is a country that does not recognize individual rights, whose government holds total, unlimited power over men.

PLAYBOY: What is the dividing line, by your definition, between a mixed economy and a dictatorship?

RAND: A dictatorship has four characteristics: one-party rule, executions without trial for political offenses, expropriation or nationalization of private property, and censorship. Above all, this last. So long as men can speak and write freely, so long as there is no censorship, they still have a chance to reform their society or to put it on a better road. When censorship is imposed, *that* is the sign that men should go on strike intellectually, by which I mean, should not cooperate with the social system in any way whatever.

PLAYBOY: Short of such a strike, what do you believe ought to be done to bring about the societal changes you deem desirable?

RAND: It is *ideas* that determine social trends, that create or destroy social systems. Therefore, the right ideas, the right philosophy, should be advocated and spread. The disasters of the modern world, including the destruction of capitalism, were caused by the altruist-collectivist philosophy. It is altruism that men should reject.

PLAYBOY: And how would you define altruism?

RAND: It is a moral system which holds that man has no right to exist for his own sake, that service to others is the sole justification of his existence, and that self-sacrifice is his highest moral duty, value and virtue. This is the moral base of collectivism, of all dictatorships. In order to seek freedom and capitalism, men need a nonmystical, non-altruistic, *rational* code of ethics—a morality which holds that man is not a sacrificial animal, that he has the right to exist for his own sake, neither sacrificing himself to others, nor others to himself. In other words, what is desperately needed today is the ethics of Objectivism.

PLAYBOY: Then what you are saying is that to achieve these changes one must use essentially educational or propagandistic methods?

RAND: Yes, of course.

PLAYBOY: What do you think of your antagonists' contention that the moral and political principles of Objectivism place you outside the mainstream of American thought?

RAND: I don't acknowledge or recognize such a concept as a "mainstream of *thought*." That might be appropriate to a dictatorship, to a collectivist society in which thought is controlled and in which there exists a collective mainstream—of slogans, not of thought. There is no such thing in America. There never was. However, I have heard that expression used for the purpose of barring from public communication any innovator, any nonconformist, anyone who has anything original to offer. I am an innovator. This is a term of distinction, a term of honor, rather than something to hide or apologize for. Anyone who has new or valuable ideas to offer stands outside the intellectual status quo. But the status quo is not a stream, let alone a "mainstream." It is a stagnant swamp. It is the innovators who carry mankind forward.

PLAYBOY: Do you believe that Objectivism as a philosophy will eventually sweep the world?

RAND: Nobody can answer a question of that kind. Men have free will. There is no guarantee that they will choose to be rational, at any one time or in any one generation. Nor is it necessary for a philosophy to "sweep the world." If you ask the question in a somewhat different form, if you say, do I think that Objectivism will be the philosophy of the future, I would say yes, but with this qualification: If men turn to reason, if they are not destroyed by dictatorship and precipitated into another Dark Ages, if men remain free long enough to have time to think, then Objectivism is the philosophy they will accept.

PLAYBOY: Why?

RAND: In any historical period when men were free, it has always been the most rational philosophy that won. It is from this perspective that I would say, yes, Objectivism will win. But there is no guarantee, no predetermined necessity about it.

PLAYBOY: You are sharply critical of the world as you see it today, and your books offer radical proposals for changing not merely the shape of society, but the very way in which most men work, think and love. Are you optimistic about man's future?

RAND: Yes, I am optimistic. Collectivism, as an intellectual power and a moral ideal, is dead. But freedom and individualism, and their political expression, capitalism, have not yet been discovered. I think men *will* have time to discover them. It is significant that the dying collectivist philosophy of today has produced nothing but a cult of depravity, impotence and despair. Look at modern art and literature with their image of man as a helpless, mindless creature doomed to failure, frustration and destruction. This may be the collectivists' psychological confession, but it is not an image of man. If it were, we would never have risen from the cave. But we did. Look around you and look at history. You will see the achievements of man's mind. You will see man's unlimited potentiality for greatness, and the faculty that makes it possible. You will see that man is not a helpless monster by nature, but he becomes one when he discards that faculty: his mind. And if you ask me, what is greatness?—I will answer, it is the capacity to live by the three fundamental values of John Galt: reason, purpose, self-esteem.

AYN RAND ON RIGHTS AND CAPITALISM

Douglas J. Den Uyl and Douglas B. Rasmussen

This essay from *The Philosophic Thought of Ayn Rand* (1984), edited by Den Uyl and Rasmussen, lays out Rand's theory of rights and her moral justification for capitalism and limited government. Footnotes have been omitted. The major sources are the essays "Man's Rights," "What Is Capitalism?" and "The Nature of Government," all of which are reprinted in Ayn Rand, *Capitalism: The Unknown Ideal* (New York: New American Library, 1967), and "The Objectivist Ethics," in Ayn Rand, *The Virtue of Selfishness* (New York: New American Library, 1964). Den Uyl and Rasmussen are contemporary philosophers and the authors of *Liberty and Nature: An Aristotelian Defense of Liberal Order* (La Salle, Ill.: Open Court, 1991).

With the possible exception of her ethical views, Ayn Rand's political philosophy is the most notorious feature of her philosophic system. Her unabashed defense of laissez-faire capitalism coupled with a firm denunciation of all forms of collectivism has made her political positions the object of widespread critical attack. Nevertheless, most of the criticisms leveled at Rand's political theories lack an appreciation of the philosophic foundations that support the theory. Whether Rand is wrong or right in her conclusions, any objective reader of her political writings must admit: (1) that her political views flow from a comprehensive philosophy of man and nature, and (2) that her defense of capitalism is insightful and original. The latter point should become evident as we outline Rand's political theory below. A brief discussion of the first point is the natural place to begin that outline.

Rand's political theory centers around her doctrine of human rights. Yet human rights must themselves be understood in light of a prior moral theory. Consider the following passage from Rand.

> "Rights" are a moral concept—the concept that provides a logical transition from the principles guiding an individual's actions to the principles guiding his relationship with others—the concept that preserves and protects individual morality in a social context—the link between the moral code of a man and the legal code of a society, between ethics and politics. *Individual rights are a means of subordinating society to moral law.*

Notice that to understand Rand's theory of rights one must first grasp her ethical doctrine and that to grasp her ethical theory one must appreciate her philosophy of man.

In the preceding introductory essays, Rand's theory of human nature was discussed in some detail. In those sections we learned that the mode of activity appropriate to and necessary for human existence is the use of our rational (i.e., conceptual) capacity. This capacity was seen as the foundation for all *human* acts and institutions. Rand's essentially Aristotelian conception of man is modified by her heavy emphasis on the *creative* power of the human mind. Since human beings are not omniscient or infallible, their success in life depends upon their ability to increase their knowledge. The degree to which one's knowledge increases is a function of one's ability to effectively solve the problems confronted. There is no static set of rules that, if followed, will lead automatically to new insights into a given problem. To be sure, there are epistemological constraints, but the creative mind is one that looks beyond the common understanding. Men of genius in both the sciences and the arts are those who do not allow themselves to be held down by received wisdom. In both Rand's fictional and nonfictional writings the creative mind is presented as the motive force of all human progress. Stagnation is synonymous with death, and thus human creativity and innovation must be protected at all cost.

One may justifiably conclude that Rand's doctrine of rights is designed to secure those conditions necessary for the operation of the most significant asset of human nature—the mind. There is ample evidence that Rand links her theory of rights with her conception of human nature. In an article entitled "Man's Rights," for example, she says that "the source of rights is man's nature" and that "rights are a necessary condition of his [man's] particular mode of survival." Elsewhere Rand argues that "it is the basic, metaphysical fact of man's nature—the connection between his survival and his use of reason— that capitalism recognizes and protects." Capitalism is itself "a social system based on the recognition of individual rights."

Reason for Rand is the ability to conceptualize the material provided by the senses. Our survival as human beings depends upon our ability to conceptually attend to the world, to properly interpret and judge the data we confront at each waking moment. The fundamental choice human beings make is whether to direct our full attention to the situations we experience.

If we now add together the foregoing remarks about the choice to think and the creative element of thought necessary for progress, we shall gain a clearer understanding of Rand's doctrine of rights. When Rand claims that rights specify norms necessary for man's survival qua man, she does not mean that any violation of rights results in instant death. Rather, she means that the principle implied by a rights violation is contrary to the principles required for human life. Since men are (and must be) creatures that act and think in terms of principles, a doctrine of rights is meant to insure that the choice to live by those principles required for human life is not impeded by other human beings. Both the choice to think and the creative element of thought are characterized by a process that is volitional and judgmental. What must, therefore, be insured by a system of rights is that those actions not be permitted which limit or destroy the free operation of choice and judgment in action; for any other principle of action would necessarily imply that something besides choice and judgment be the fundamental norm for human action. All this is to say that the moral propriety of attending to the world through the use of our conceptual faculty requires the freedom to act on our judgment. The right of free choice means the right to act on our choices.

Rand argues, as we have seen, that the fundamental alternative facing living things is existence or nonexistence. In the case of human beings, those courses of action necessary for the furtherance of our existence are not automatically determined. Because we are given no automatic means for the furtherance of our lives, we are bound to make choices about which course of action to take. Ethics may give us certain objective standards for the guidance of those choices, but ethics cannot directly dictate how to apply those standards in particular concrete cases. Ethical rules do not tell us *when* we are in a situation that calls for one or another of the rules. We must, therefore, use our judgment in those particular cases and choose accordingly. It is appropriate to conclude, then, that the volitional nature of man's consciousness implies a principle of freedom. To act as if there is some substitute for this volitional feature of human nature is to ignore a fundamental metaphysical fact about our nature.

Now there are numerous ways in which an individual can act that imply principles contrary to the volitional principle just discussed. One such way is to act on the basis of faith. But in the interpersonal realm it is coercion that represents the most significant violation of the volitional principle. Coercion is the attempt to substitute force for judgment and choice—"force and mind are opposites; morality ends where a gun begins." Coercion implies that an independent assessment of the facts is unnecessary and that we can accomplish the business of living a human life by circumventing the necessity of judgment and choice. Since coercive acts violate the volitional principle, rights are meant to be those principles that protect freedom of judgment. Rand puts it this way:

> Thus for every individual, a right is the moral sanction of a *positive*—of his freedom to act on his own judgment, for his own goals, by his own *voluntary*, uncoerced choice. As to his neighbors, his rights impose no obligations on them except of a *negative* kind: to abstain from violating his rights.

In essence then, the indispensability of judgment and choice for human existence is given its social expression in Rand's doctrine of individual rights.

It should also be noted at this stage of our discussion that one implication of Rand's view of choice is that choice becomes the foundation for virtue in society. In order to attribute moral worth to an individual's actions it is necessary that the individual be a moral agent, i.e., that his actions be chosen. Liberty is inherently connected with the process of moral perfection. Tibor Machan has made this point in the following way:

> The choice to learn, to judge, to evaluate, to appraise, to decide what he ought to do in order to live his life must be each person's own, otherwise he simply has no opportunity to excel or fail at the task. His moral aspirations cannot be fulfilled (or left unfulfilled) if he is not the source of his own actions, if they are imposed or forced upon him by others.

The implication of the preceding remarks for social theory is that even though freedom permits evil actions as well as good ones, the *only* way a society can properly be seen as moral is if its members *choose* the good.

Life, by its very nature, is not guaranteed. In recognition of this metaphysical fact, Rand holds that rights are freedoms of action and not guarantees of anything. Even property rights are not conceived by her to be rights to things, but only the freedom to pursue courses of action with respect to material goods. A system or theory of rights that gives the pretense of guaranteeing certain goods is neither a consistent practice nor a coherent theory. If certain goods are to be guaranteed to individuals—as modern "welfare" rights would have it—some people must be coerced to provide for others. Apart from the fact that what is guaranteed is conditional upon the productivity of some (and hence no guarantee at all), there is in principle no limit to what one could claim must be guaranteed. If the Democratic Party Platform of 1960 can demand that everyone have a right to a "decent home," then there is virtually nothing human beings desire that cannot also be "guaranteed." But this view of rights makes a mockery of the notion of a guarantee; for if there is no object to which one may not claim a right, then we could conceivably ask the state to guarantee all things equally to everyone.

Even if we were to ignore the foregoing remarks, there are further problems with a welfare conception of rights. In the first place, few arguments are ever advanced for why the coercive apparatus of the state should be the vehicle for guaranteeing certain goods to individuals. It is not enough to assume that the state should provide the goods demanded. One must *show* why initiatory acts of force by the state are not subject to the same moral condemnation we apply to individuals who take such actions. Furthermore, it is imperative to recognize that the welfare conception of rights is inherently discriminatory. That conception of rights demands that the state treat some individuals differently from others, depending on their particular status in society at a particular time (e.g., whether they are rich or poor). Since one's status in society may change over time, the only guarantee we have is that we cannot expect consistent treatment in the course of our lifetime. Robert Nozick makes this very point in *Anarchy, State, and Utopia*. Finally, despite any rhetoric to the contrary, welfare rights do not suppose that people possess rights, but rather that rights are gifts of the state. And like all gifts, the one who has the power to make the gift also has the power to take it away.

Rand's theory of rights avoids the preceding theoretical problems, since all individuals possess the same right to freely pursue their own goals—though there is no guarantee that they will be successful in that pursuit. Since no guarantees are given in nature that men will lead successful lives, it is a kind of metaphysical fraud to act as if this fact were not true in social life. The best we can do is try to establish those *conditions* that will allow for the pursuit of a proper human life, if people so choose to seek that end. Establishing these conditions can be done without reference to anyone's particular circumstances—that is, equally.

It may appear as though Rand is just asking the state to guarantee a different set of goods from those demanded by welfare-rights advocates. One must keep in mind, however, that there is an important difference between a reactive course of action and an assertive one. In Rand's scheme, the state reacts to rights violations—it does not assert itself in the creation of rights. It might be said that the state protects those rights we possess by nature, rather than acting as the instrument of their creation. In other words, the state acts on the recognition of a moral truth, rather than merely stipulating a mode of behavior. Herein lies one reason for considering Rand a natural-rights theorist.

Although we have sketched the basic elements of Rand's theory of rights, we have yet to speak of the importance she attaches to property rights. It has already been noted that her conception of property rights means the right to certain courses of action rather than to particular things. In this sense property rights reduce to the right to life—that is, the right of an individual to pursue courses of action he deems best, provided he does not coercively interact with others. Yet the special importance Rand accords to property rights is expressed in the following passage:

> The right to life is the source of all rights—and the right to property is their only implementation. Without property rights, no other rights are possible. Since man has to sustain his life by his own effort, the man who has no right to the product of his effort has no means to sustain his life. The man who produces while others dispose of his product is a slave.

Since human beings are material entities that require material goods to sustain their existence, the use, creation, and disposal of material things must be permitted. Moreover, Rand holds that only individuals act; collectivities are in no sense individuals and cannot act as such. Collectivities, therefore, possess no rights. Since rights specify freedom of action and collectivities do not act, property rights are rights possessed by individuals. Individuals can, of course, form groups and consent to be treated *as if* they were one individual (e.g., a corporation), but this does not detract from the essential truth that rights belong to individual human beings.

But what does it mean to say that an individual has a right to property? In the first place, it means that the individual must not be kept from seeking material goods. Second and more important, the individual must be free to utilize those goods he has noncoercively acquired as he sees fit; for otherwise we have violated the already established principle that it is impermissible to restrict another's freedom of action by the initiation of force. Thus, when Rand says that "without property rights, no other rights are possible," she means simply that freedom of action with respect to material goods is the only way to make manifest the basic right to life. To coercively restrict someone's freedom of action is to say, in effect, that one is free to judge but not to act on one's judgment. This is to advance the principle that there is no necessary connection for human existence between judgments about a course of action and the overt actions implied by those judgments. It would be wrong to suppose that one's judgment about a course of action will necessarily be life-enhancing when the action is performed. What is implied by Rand's comment is that, in principle, the life-enhancing implications of a judgment can never be known unless the judgment is made manifest in overt action. In sum, freedom of choice or judgment implies the freedom to act on one's judgment, and such actions will occur in the material world. All of the foregoing is itself justified in terms of what is necessary for the achievement of a good human life.

Needless to say, freedom of action does not mean the freedom to plunge a knife into someone's stomach, for that would be a violation of the basic right to life. In this connection, Rand holds that a violation of one's property rights is an expression of force against the individual himself. In a very real sense, to steal, to defraud, or to expropriate another's property is to initiate an act of violence against that person. It only follows that if our lives find their expression in the realm of objects—whether those objects be scholarly books or business enterprises—the nonconsensual use of that property constitutes a direct attack on the person himself. Unfortunately, we often tend to see a person's life as extending only to that person's outer epidermic layer. When a new law is passed that forcibly extracts a portion of one's income, we speak of that event as a tax on one's property and not on one's life or personhood. Indeed, we even tend to think of criminal actions, such as theft, as deplorable only because they violate a social rule and not because they represent an assault on someone's life. Rand's argument is that one cannot divorce what one has produced from one's personhood without thereby destroying the proper picture of human existence.

The foregoing argument can be expressed by saying that human beings are ends in themselves and not means to the ends of others.

Since life is an end in itself and since life does not exist in the abstract but only in individuals, each individual's life is an end in itself. Rand's doctrine of individual rights is merely the *social* expression of the previous point. In a social context, we show our respect for the concept of each person's being an end in himself by not demanding that he deal with us on any terms but consent. Voluntary agreement is the operative principle of Rand's theory of rights. She calls it the "principle of trade"—exchanging value for value. Granted, there are many complications in determining when one has initiated force, rightfully owns a piece of property, has violated or not lived up to an agreement, and so forth. Rand, however, is more concerned with providing an overall view of the proper social order than with working out its details. The principle of trade and the theory of rights behind that principle constitute the basic structure of that vision. While some may hold that merely arguing for basic principles is not enough to test a doctrine's validity, we believe that the kind of challenge Rand poses for conventional thinking on these issues demands that the overall outline be established before the details can be worked on. Any other procedure would have lost sight of the end to be achieved.

Rand's theory of rights is what informs her defense of capitalism. She defines *capitalism* as follows: "capitalism is a social system based on the recognition of individual rights, including property rights, in which all property is privately owned." Notice that the foundation of Rand's definition is in terms of individual rights and not in terms of the class in control of the means of production or the degree to which government interferes with business enterprise. Capitalism is not simply an economic system. Indeed, for Rand, the essence of capitalism is represented by a moral rather than an economic doctrine. If individual rights are respected in a society, then that society is capitalistic. Rand's conception of capitalism is, in principle, a novel one; for it allows for a society that values primarily art and literature to be just as capitalistic as one that values automobiles and boats—so long as both respect individual rights.

One of the unique features of Rand's defense of capitalism is that she neither considers capitalism a necessary evil (as do many conservatives) nor tries to defend it simply in terms of the benefits it produces (as do many economists). It is not that we must put up with the system to reap its benefits, as we put up with manure to grow a flower garden. Rather, Rand defends the thesis that the very mode of human interaction called for by capitalism is the only morally justifiable way for people to socialize. Consider this passage:

> The *moral* justification of capitalism does not lie in the altruist claim that it represents the best way to achieve "the common good." . . . The moral justification of capitalism lies in the fact that it is the only system consonant with man's rational nature, that it protects man's survival *qua* man, and that its ruling principle is: *justice.*

This is not Adam Smith, F. A. Hayek, or Milton Friedman's defense of capitalism, for these thinkers defend capitalism in terms of its overall social product. Rand, on the other hand, goes to the heart of the issue, because only she has been willing to say that capitalism is an inherently moral social structure.

To make her case for capitalism more plausible, however, Rand does have to overcome some rather widely held misconceptions about the social effects of capitalism. For example, in one chapter of *Capitalism: The Unknown Ideal* the issues of monopoly, depression, labor unions, public education, inherited wealth, and the practicability of a laissez-faire system are discussed. We cannot undertake an examination of these issues here, and we refer the reader to the aforementioned chapter and the bibliography at the end of that volume. Nevertheless, we can at least indicate Rand's attitude on a few general and more philosophic matters.

It has often been asserted that capitalism is a system that extols the pursuit of self-interest. This statement is usually meant to be a strike against capitalism; but for Rand it is not only descriptively accurate but morally acceptable as well. Some of the issues surrounding the role of self-interest in society have already been discussed in this volume and are further detailed in the following essay by Antony Flew. One does not, however, capture Rand's full view if one's analysis merely shows that capitalism is a social system based on principles that accord with rational self-interest. Rand also seems to hold that capitalism is a system which provides incentives for *advancing* one's self-interest. In the first place, capitalism promotes one of Rand's cardinal virtues—productivity. Whatever one's line of work, a competitive and free market tends to push one toward the achievement of the best one is able to produce within a given context. Because there are no guarantees that past achievements will not be bettered, there are strong incentives to continue to produce at the maximum level. Moreover, those who are innovative and hard-working are not held to the level of the mediocre and the slothful, since there is the full expectation of reaping the rewards of one's efforts. In short, capitalism is a system directed toward achievement.

The push for achievement is given its motive force by the competitive nature of a capitalistic economy. Rand argues that competition is neither the law of the jungle nor a "dog-eat-dog" mode of existence. As Rand put it, "The motto 'dog eat dog' . . . is *not* applicable to capitalism nor to dogs." Competition is not a zero-sum game where someone wins and another loses, such that there is no overall gain between parties. Competition is rather a method of coordinating activities in which those who are most efficient at utilizing a given resource are in a position to do so. A kind of human ecological balance is promoted by the market. An economy of resources develops with the result that the appropriate quantity of goods of optimal quality are directed into those areas where they are most needed or desired. The arguments on the efficiency of the market are not new with Rand, but the emphasis she places upon the market's beneficial effects on one's own sense of worth or efficacy is a novel perspective.

In any case, since the market tends to put resources into the hands of those most adept at using them, all stand to benefit—even those who may have been overcome by a more efficient competitor. As the economists tell us, the benefit of an efficient allocation of resources— through competitive markets—is a higher standard of living for all. Another's success in the market is not achieved at the expense of someone else; for if that were the case, there would be no advance in the standard of living—everyone would simply be changing positions. If we see competition as a directive device, however, we realize that the success of some and the failure of others is a signal about where resources ought to be directed. And since the market order allows the mobility to follow those signals quickly and fully, the efficiency thereby obtained permits sufficient surplus to raise everyone's standard of living.

In this connection it is important to realize that profits (contrary to popular belief) are also not achieved at someone else's expense. In opposition to the Marxist contention that progress in a capitalist order is the result of exploiting the surplus labor of the workers, Rand argues that capitalism is the only system that entirely removes sacrifice from human interaction. Collectivism, in whatever variety, is a system wherein some are sacrificed for the sake of others. The sacrificial character of collectivist social systems stems from their willingness to consider the "needs of society" as overriding the individual's own interests. Rand dramatically states the issue in the following passage:

> The social theory of ethics substitutes "society" for God—and though it claims that its chief concern is life on earth, it is *not* the life of man, not the life of an individual, but the life of a disembodied entity, *the collective*. . . . As far as the individual is concerned, *his* ethical duty is to be the selfless, voiceless, rightless slave of any need, claim or demand asserted by others.

The Marxists are, indeed, correct to speak of surplus (i.e., profit) as the motive force for progress in a capitalist society; but that surplus is an individual phenomenon and *not* a class phenomenon. In a capitalist society, production is a process of individual efforts coordinated by a network of contractual agreements. No one is forced to associate with those one finds detrimental to one's interests. This is not to say that capitalism is a fantasy land where one never confronts difficult choices or finds oneself in disagreeable situations. Capitalism, however, does hold out the promise that the products of one's efforts will not be expropriated without one's consent and that one will not have to exert oneself for the sake of an end one has not chosen. It is true that what one has to offer others may not be wanted by them, but the freedom to refuse a product is just the flip side of the freedom to offer it. Thus human relationships are nonsacrificial in the sense that they are consummated only when all parties agree to a specific course of action.

If voluntary interaction among men is morally superior to coerced interaction, then there are no grounds for the forcible rectification of the results of voluntary interaction. Individuals who engage in just exchanges—that is, who voluntarily contract for mutually agreed upon purposes—cannot then be forced to engage in involuntary exchange. [Robert] Nozick has termed the theory of justice that looks only to past actions to see if current holdings were voluntarily gained an historical entitlement theory. The entitlement theory is opposed to a theory that relies on "end-state" principles—that is, principles which demand that society conform to some specific pattern. The upshot of Nozick's argument is that if past actions were voluntarily undertaken by all parties concerned, there are no grounds for a later attempt to rectify the results of those interactions.

The fundamental place accorded to freedom of choice by both Rand and Nozick would imply that choices to engage in trade detrimental to one's objective interest (e.g., the choice to consume cigarettes) is morally superior to coercive attempts to prohibit the detrimental behavior. Thus, all forced redistributive schemes and all attempts to keep people from harming themselves are inherently pernicious. A society that mixes free and coerced exchanges is one which has chosen to mix two incompatible theories of the appropriate form of human interaction. And just as mixed economies are inherently unstable because the pockets of free trade tend to upset the plans imposed by the state, so also does the mixture of voluntary and coerced exchanges tend to unsettle a society's moral values.

Today we find mass confusion about what are appropriate and inappropriate ways for human beings to interact. The result must be either further restriction on liberty or further removal of already existing restrictions. That is the choice we face. And even though we seem to be choosing the former course, the very fact that we do have a choice means we are not doomed to that alternative.

In all of Rand's discussions of the virtues of capitalism one must remember that no system of laissez-faire capitalism has ever existed. Many of the alleged abuses of capitalism—such as depression, poverty, and war—cannot be attributed to capitalism itself, but to the actions of the state. Thus many of the examples used against capitalism are simply beside the point. To justify this last claim is beyond the scope of this essay. We mention it only to alert the reader to the fact that one must distinguish the results that can be directly attributable to the market from those attributable to the state (or a mixture of state and market). Rand holds that when one has carefully examined the evidence, one will find that governmental action is usually responsible for the abuses normally attributed to the market order.

To claim that the state is often guilty of promoting problems that would have been otherwise nonexistent or less severe in a market order requires at least a general outline of Rand's view of the role and nature of the state. We must know, in other words, what Rand takes to be the permissible limits of state power before we can determine whether a given state has gone beyond those limits. Rand restricts the state's function to the retaliatory use of physical force. The basic principle behind the permissibility of the retaliatory use of physical force is the right of self-defense. Individuals have the right of self-defense, because without that right their other rights could not be protected. The state acts in behalf of this right of self-defense, and the reason the state does so rather than individuals themselves seems to be because of the potential for excessive responses to minor rights violations. Moreover, without a set of rules for evidence and for punishment, there would be no way to adjudicate claims concerning rights violations. And without some method of adjudication, people would be able to deal with one another in *whatever* way their desires happened to push them. Under such a system no rights would be protected at all. Rand does not, however, seem to have either an explicit theory of punishment or a detailed theory about the structure of proper rules of evidence.

The essential role of government is to protect people's rights, not only by preventing physical violence, but also by the enforcement of contractual agreements. Rand considers a breach of contract (together with fraud and extortion) to be an indirect initiation of force. In such cases, values are obtained without consent and then, by mere possession, are retained by force and not by right. Yet it is not only because rights must be protected that governments are justified. A further justification for government lies in the fact that without such protection civilization would be impossible, and civilization is necessary for people to achieve their proper end as human beings. This defense of the existence of government follows, given the fact that rights themselves are seen in terms of what is necessary for a proper human life.

Rand adopts the essentially Weberian view that governments possess a monopoly on the legal use of physical force. The monopoly status of government means that the government possesses great potential to violate rights. The strictures on governmental action are, therefore, the same as the strictures placed upon individuals—actions that initiate force must not be taken. Moreover, since the government possesses a monopoly on the legal use of force, the potential consequences of its violation of rights is more serious than the criminal's violation of rights (even if we collectively aggregate the potential consequences of all criminals at any given time). These potential consequences of governmental abuse require that specific limitations be placed upon government. The regimes of Stalin, Hitler, and Mao are constant reminders that the violation of rights is more often and to a greater degree perpetrated by governments than by criminals.

Now that we have sketched the basic areas of Rand's political theory, we face the question of just where Rand's contribution in this area lies. Apart from the many interesting specifics one might mention, perhaps the most general statement of her contribution is the following. Rand attempts to combine an essentially classical or pre-modern view of man with a modern political doctrine; that is to say, an Aristotelian view of man's nature is integrated with a liberal political doctrine. The argument, as we have seen, is that freedom of action in society is a function of what is proper to living a good human life—indeed, what is necessary for the fulfillment of our human potential. There have been other intellectuals who have held a basically classical view of man and who were also political liberals. But no one else has shown the connection between those two outlooks as explicitly and successfully as Ayn Rand. Many details still need to be given thought, and there are certainly controversies that must be settled. Nevertheless, Rand offers us the outline of a theory that can motivate much scholarly research and debate. The present volume is the first step in that effort to discuss the merits of the Randian teaching.

Like the ancients, Rand has always strongly adhered to the view that ideas not only have consequences, but also have an important impact on culture. Moreover, Rand never wavers from the belief in the primacy of philosophy. Her emphasis on the role of the intellect culminates in the importance she attaches to the most intellectual of all subject matters—philosophy. Her advice to philosophers, and to other intellectuals as well, is summed up in the following passage:

> The best among the present intellectuals should consider the tremendous power which they are holding, but have never fully exercised or understood. If any man among them feels that he is the helpless, ineffectual stepson of a "materialistic" culture that grants him neither wealth nor recognition . . . let him realize that ideas are not an escape from reality, not a hobby for "disinterested" neurotics in ivory towers, but the most crucial and productive power in human existence.

THE ENTITLEMENT THEORY OF JUSTICE

Robert Nozick

Harvard University philosopher Robert Nozick's 1974 book
Anarchy, State, and Utopia brought the idea of individual rights
back to center stage among academic philosophers. Nozick
(1938–2002) argued that "a minimal state, limited to the narrow functions of protection against force, theft, [and] fraud,
enforcement of contracts, and so on, is justified; [and] that any
more extensive state will violate persons' rights not to be forced
to do certain things." Since the publication of *Anarchy, State,
and Utopia,* philosophers who seek to justify a more extensive
state have been compelled to address Nozick's arguments,
though they still often avoid responding to the different arguments of Mises, Rand, and Rothbard. In this excerpt Nozick
lays out his entitlement theory of justice and argues that any
end-state theory of justice requires constant interference with
the choices of adults.

The minimal state is the most extensive state that can be justified.
Any state more extensive violates people's rights. Yet many persons
have put forth reasons purporting to justify a more extensive state.
It is impossible within the compass of this book to examine all the
reasons that have been put forth. Therefore, I shall focus upon those
generally acknowledged to be most weighty and influential, to see
precisely wherein they fail. In this chapter we consider the claim that
a more extensive state is justified, because necessary (or the best in-

strument) to achieve distributive justice; in the next chapter we shall take up diverse other claims.

The term "distributive justice" is not a neutral one. Hearing the term "distribution," most people presume that some thing or mechanism uses some principle or criterion to give out a supply of things. Into this process of distributing shares some error may have crept. So it is an open question, at least, whether *re*distribution should take place; whether we should do again what has already been done once, though poorly. However, we are not in the position of children who have been given portions of pie by someone who now makes last-minute adjustments to rectify careless cutting. There is no *central* distribution, no person or group entitled to control all the resources, jointly deciding how they are to be doled out. What each person gets, he gets from others who give to him in exchange for something, or as a gift. In a free society, diverse persons control different resources, and new holdings arise out of the voluntary exchanges and actions of persons. There is no more a distributing or distribution of shares than there is a distributing of mates in a society in which persons choose whom they shall marry. The total result is the product of many individual decisions which the different individuals involved are entitled to make. Some uses of the term "distribution," it is true, do not imply a previous distributing appropriately judged by some criterion (for example, "probability distribution"); nevertheless, despite the title of this chapter [Distributive Justice], it would be best to use a terminology that clearly is neutral. We shall speak of people's holdings; a principle of justice in holdings describes (part of) what justice tells us (requires) about holdings. I shall state first what I take to be the correct view about justice in holdings, and then turn to the discussion of alternate views.

The subject of justice in holdings consists of three major topics. The first is the *original acquisition of holdings,* the appropriation of unheld things. This includes the issues of how unheld things may come to be held, the process, or processes, by which unheld things may come to be held, the things that may come to be held by these processes, the extent of what comes to be held by a particular process, and so on. We shall refer to the complicated truth about this topic, which we shall not formulate here, as the principle of justice in acquisition. The second topic concerns the *transfer of holdings* from one person to another. By what processes may a person transfer holdings to another? How may a person acquire a holding from another who holds it? Under this topic come general descriptions of voluntary exchange, and gift and (on the other hand) fraud, as well as reference to particular conventional details fixed upon in a given society. The complicated truth about this subject (with placeholders for conventional details) we shall call the principle of justice in transfer. (And we shall suppose it also includes principles governing how a person may divest himself of a holding, passing it into an unheld state.)

If the world were wholly just, the following inductive definition would exhaustively cover the subject of justice in holdings.

1. A person who acquires a holding in accordance with the principle of justice in acquisition is entitled to that holding.
2. A person who acquires a holding in accordance with the principle of justice in transfer, from someone else entitled to the holding, is entitled to the holding.
3. No one is entitled to a holding except by (repeated) applications of 1 and 2.

The complete principle of distributive justice would say simply that a distribution is just if everyone is entitled to the holdings they possess under the distribution.

A distribution is just if it arises from another just distribution by legitimate means. The legitimate means of moving from one distribution to another are specified by the principle of justice in transfer. The legitimate first "moves" are specified by the principle of justice in acquisition. Whatever arises from a just situation by just steps is itself just. The means of change specified by the principle of justice in transfer preserve justice. As correct rules of inference are truth-preserving, and any conclusion deduced via repeated application of such rules from only true premises is itself true, so the means of transition from one situation to another specified by the principle of justice in transfer are justice-preserving, and any situation actually arising from repeated transitions in accordance with the principle from a just situation is itself just. The parallel between justice-preserving transformations and truth-preserving transformations illuminates where it fails as well as where it holds. That a conclusion could have been deduced by truth-preserving means from premises that are true suffices to show its truth. That from a just situation a situation *could* have arisen via justice-preserving means does *not* suffice to show its justice. The fact that a thief's victims voluntarily *could* have presented him with gifts does not entitle the thief to his ill-gotten gains. Justice in holdings is historical; it depends upon what actually has happened. We shall return to this point later.

Not all actual situations are generated in accordance with the two principles of justice in holdings: the principle of justice in acquisition and the principle of justice in transfer. Some people steal from others, or defraud them, or enslave them, seizing their product and preventing them from living as they choose, or forcibly exclude others from competing in exchanges. None of these are permissible modes of transition from one situation to another. And some persons acquire holdings by means not sanctioned by the principle of justice in acquisition. The existence of past injustice (previous violations of the first two principles of justice in holdings) raises the third major topic under justice in holdings: the rectification of injustice in holdings. If past injustice has shaped present holdings in various ways, some identifiable and some not, what now, if anything, ought to be done to rectify these injustices? What obligations do the performers of injustice have toward those whose position is worse than it would have been had the injustice not been done? Or, than it would have been had compensation been paid promptly? How, if at all, do things change if the beneficiaries and those made worse off are not the direct parties in the act of injustice, but, for example, their descendants? Is an injustice done to someone whose holding was itself based upon an unrectified injustice? How far back must one go in wiping clean the historical slate of injustices? What may victims of injustice permissibly do in order to rectify the injustices being done to them, including the many injustices done by persons acting through their government? I do not know of a thorough or theoretically sophisticated treatment of such issues. Idealizing greatly, let us suppose theoretical investigation will produce a principle of rectification. This principle uses historical information about previous situations and injustices done in them (as defined by the first two principles of justice and rights against interference), and information about the actual course of events that flowed from these injustices, until the present, and it yields a description (or descriptions) of holdings in the society. The principle of rectification presumably will make use of its best estimate of subjunctive information about what would have occurred (or a probability distribution over what might have occurred, using the expected value) if the injustice had not taken place. If the actual description of holdings turns out not to be one of the descriptions yielded by the principle, then one of the descriptions yielded must be realized.

The general outlines of the theory of justice in holdings are that the holdings of a person are just if he is entitled to them by the principles of justice in acquisition and transfer, or by the principle of rectification of injustice (as specified by the first two principles). If each person's holdings are just, then the total set (distribution) of holdings is just. To turn these general outlines into a specific theory we would have to specify the details of each of the three principles of justice in holdings: the principle of acquisition of holdings, the principle of transfer of holdings, and the principle of rectification of violations of the first two principles. I shall not attempt that task here. . . .

HISTORICAL PRINCIPLES AND END-RESULT PRINCIPLES

The general outlines of the entitlement theory illuminate the nature and defects of other conceptions of distributive justice. The entitlement theory of justice in distribution is *historical;* whether a distribution is just depends upon how it came about. In contrast, *current time-slice principles* of justice hold that the justice of a distribution is determined by how things are distributed (who has what) as judged by some *structural* principle(s) of just distribution. A utilitarian who judges between any two distributions by seeing which has the greater sum of utility and, if the sums tie, applies some fixed equality criterion to choose the more equal distribution, would hold a current time-slice principle of justice. As would someone who had a fixed schedule of trade-offs between the sum of happiness and equality. According to a current time-slice principle, all that needs to be looked at, in judging the justice of a distribution, is who ends up with what; in comparing any two distributions one need look only at the matrix presenting the distributions. No further information need be fed into a principle of justice. It is a consequence of such principles of justice that any two structurally identical distributions are equally just. (Two distributions are structurally identical if they present the same profile, but perhaps have different persons occupying the particular slots. My having ten and your having five, and my having five and your having ten are structurally identical distributions.) Welfare economics is the theory of current time-slice principles of justice. The subject is conceived as operating on matrices representing only current information about distribution. This, as well as some of the usual conditions (for example, the choice of distribution is invariant under relabeling of columns), guarantees that welfare economics will be a current time-slice theory, with all of its inadequacies.

Most persons do not accept current time-slice principles as constituting the whole story about distributive shares. They think it relevant in assessing the justice of a situation to consider not only the distribution it embodies, but also how that distribution came about. If some persons are in prison for murder or war crimes, we do not say that to assess the justice of the distribution in the society we must look only at what this person has, and that person has, and that person has, . . . at the current time. We think it relevant to ask whether someone did something so that he *deserved* to be punished, deserved to have a lower share. Most will agree to the relevance of further information with regard to punishments and penalties. Consider also desired things. One traditional socialist view is that workers are entitled to the product and full fruits of their labor; they have earned it; a distribution is unjust if it does not give the workers what they are entitled to. Such entitlements are based upon some past history. No socialist holding this view would find it comforting to be told that because the actual distribution A happens to coincide structurally with the one he desires D, A therefore is no less just than D; it differs only in that the "parasitic" owners of capital receive under A what the workers are entitled to under D, and the workers receive under A what the owners are entitled to under D, namely very little. This socialist rightly, in my view, holds onto the notions of earning, producing, entitlement, desert, and so forth, and he rejects current time-slice principles that look only to the structure of the resulting set of holdings. (The set of holdings resulting from what? Isn't it implausible that how holdings are produced and come to exist has no effect at all on who should hold what?) His mistake lies in his view of what entitlements arise out of what sorts of productive processes.

We construe the position we discuss too narrowly by speaking of *current* time-slice principles. Nothing is changed if structural principles operate upon a time sequence of current time-slice profiles and, for example, give someone more now to counterbalance the less he has had earlier. A utilitarian or an egalitarian or any mixture of the two over time will inherit the difficulties of his more myopic comrades. He is not helped by the fact that *some* of the information others consider relevant in assessing a distribution is reflected, unrecoverably, in past matrices. Henceforth, we shall refer to such unhistorical principles of distributive justice, including the current time-slice principles, as *end-result principles* or *end-state principles*.

In contrast to end-result principles of justice, *historical principles* of justice hold that past circumstances or actions of people can create differential entitlements or differential deserts to things. An injustice can be worked by moving from one distribution to another structurally identical one, for the second, in profile the same, may violate people's entitlements or deserts; it may not fit the actual history.

PATTERNING

The entitlement principles of justice in holdings that we have sketched are historical principles of justice. To better understand their precise character, we shall distinguish them from another subclass of the historical principles. Consider, as an example, the principle of distribution according to moral merit. This principle requires that total distributive shares vary directly with moral merit; no person should have a greater share than anyone whose moral merit is greater. (If moral merit could be not merely ordered but measured on an interval or ratio scale, stronger principles could be formulated.) Or consider the principle that results by substituting "usefulness to society" for "moral merit" in the previous principle. Or instead of "distribute according to moral merit," or "distribute according to usefulness to society," we might consider "distribute according to the weighted sum of moral merit, usefulness to society, and need," with the weights of the different dimensions equal. Let us call a principle of distribution *patterned* if it specifies that a distribution is to vary along with some natural dimension, weighted sum of natural dimensions, or lexicographic ordering of natural dimensions. And let us say a distribution is patterned if it accords with some patterned principle. (I speak of natural dimensions, admittedly without a general criterion for them, because for any set of holdings some artificial dimensions can be gimmicked up to vary along with the distribution of the set.) The principle of distribution in accordance with moral merit is a patterned historical principle, which specifies a patterned distribution. "Distribute according to I.Q." is a patterned principle that looks to information not contained in distributional matrices. It is not historical, however, in that it does not look to any past actions creating differential entitlements to evaluate a distribution; it requires only distributional matrices whose columns are labeled by I.Q. scores. The distribution in a society, however, may be composed of such simple patterned distributions, without itself being simply patterned. Different sectors may operate different patterns, or some combination of patterns may operate in different proportions across a society. A distribution composed in this manner, from a small number of patterned distributions, we also shall term "patterned." And we extend the use of "pattern" to include the overall designs put forth by combinations of end-state principles.

Almost every suggested principle of distributive justice is patterned: to each according to his moral merit, or needs, or marginal product, or how hard he tries, or the weighted sum of the foregoing, and so on. The principle of entitlement we have sketched is *not* patterned. There is no one natural dimension or weighted sum or combination of a small number of natural dimensions that yields the distributions generated in accordance with the principle of entitlement. The set of holdings that results when some persons receive their marginal products, others win at gambling, others receive a share of their mate's income, others receive gifts from foundations, others receive interest on loans, others receive gifts from admirers, others receive returns on investment, others make for themselves much of what they have, others find things, and so on, will not be patterned. Heavy strands of patterns will run through it; significant portions of the variance in holdings will be accounted for by pattern-variables. If most people most of the time choose to transfer some of their entitlements to others only in exchange for something from them, then a large part of what many people hold will vary with what they held that others wanted. More details are provided by the theory of marginal productivity. But gifts to relatives, charitable donations, bequests to children, and the like, are not best conceived, in the first instance, in this manner. Ignoring the strands of pattern, let us suppose for the moment that a distribution actually arrived at by the operation of the principle of entitlement is random with respect to any pattern. Though the resulting set of holdings will be unpatterned, it will not be incomprehensible, for it can be seen as arising from the operation of a small number of principles. These principles specify how an initial distribution may arise (the principle of acquisition of holdings) and how distributions may be transformed into others (the principle of transfer of holdings). The process whereby the set of holdings is generated will be intelligible, though the set of holdings itself that results from this process will be unpatterned.

The writings of F. A. Hayek focus less than is usually done upon what patterning distributive justice requires. Hayek argues that we cannot know enough about each person's situation to distribute to each according to his moral merit (but would justice demand we do so if we did have this knowledge?); and he goes on to say, "our objection is against all attempts to impress upon society a deliberately chosen pattern of distribution, whether it be an order of equality or of inequality." However, Hayek concludes that in a free society there will be distribution in accordance with value rather than moral merit; that is, in accordance with the perceived value of a person's actions and services to others. Despite his rejection of a patterned conception of distributive justice, Hayek himself suggests a pattern he thinks justifiable: distribution in accordance with the perceived benefits given to others, leaving room for the complaint that a free society does not realize exactly this pattern. Stating this patterned strand of a free capitalist society more precisely, we get "To each according to how much he benefits others who have the resources for benefiting those who benefit them." This will seem arbitrary unless some acceptable initial set of holdings is specified, or unless it is held that the operation of the system over time washes out any significant effects from the initial set of holdings. As an example of the latter, if almost anyone would have bought a car from Henry Ford, the supposition that it was an arbitrary matter who held the money then (and so bought) would not place Henry Ford's earnings under a cloud. In any event, *his* coming to hold it is not arbitrary. Distribution according to benefits to others *is* a major patterned strand in a free capitalist society, as Hayek correctly points out, but it is only a strand and does not constitute the whole pattern of a system of entitlements (namely, inheritance, gifts for arbitrary reasons, charity, and so on) or a standard that one should insist a society fit. Will people tolerate for long a system yielding distributions that they believe are unpatterned? No doubt people will not long accept a distribution they believe is *unjust.* People want their society to be and to look just. But must the look of justice reside in a resulting pattern rather than in the underlying generating principles? We are in no position to conclude that the inhabitants of a society embodying an entitlement conception of justice in holdings will find it unacceptable. Still, it must be granted that were people's reasons for transferring some of their holdings to others always irrational or arbitrary, we would find this disturbing. (Suppose people always determined what holdings they would transfer, and to whom, by using a random device.) We feel more comfortable upholding the justice of an entitlement system if most of the transfers under it are done for reasons. This does not mean necessarily that all deserve what holdings they receive. It means only that there is a purpose or point to someone's transferring a holding to one person rather than to another; that usually we can see what the transferrer thinks he's gaining, what cause he thinks he's serving, what goals he thinks he's helping to achieve, and so forth. Since in a capitalist society people often transfer holdings to others in accordance with how much they perceive these others benefiting them, the fabric constituted by the individual transactions and transfers is largely reasonable and intelligible. (Gifts to loved ones, bequests to children, charity to the needy also are nonarbitrary components of the fabric.) In stressing the large strand of distribution in accordance with benefit to others, Hayek shows the point of many transfers, and so shows that the system of transfer of entitlements is not just spinning its gears aimlessly. The system of entitlements is defensible when constituted by the individual aims of individual transactions. No overarching aim is needed, no distributional pattern is required.

To think that the task of a theory of distributive justice is to fill in the blank in "to each according to his _____" is to be predisposed to search for a pattern; and the separate treatment of "from each according to his _____" treats production and distribution as two separate and independent issues. On an entitlement view these are *not* two separate questions. Whoever makes something, having bought or contracted for all other held resources used in the process (transferring some of his holdings for these cooperating factors), is entitled to it. The situation is *not* one of something's getting made, and there being an open question of who is to get it. Things come into the world already attached to people having entitlements over them. From the point of view of the historical entitlement conception of justice in holdings, those who start afresh to complete "to each according to his _____" treat objects as if they appeared from nowhere, out of nothing. A complete theory of justice might cover this limit case as well; perhaps here is a use for the usual conceptions of distributive justice.

So entrenched are maxims of the usual form that perhaps we should present the entitlement conception as a competitor. Ignoring acquisition and rectification, we might say:

> From each according to what he chooses to do, to each according to what he makes for himself (perhaps with the contracted aid of others) and what others choose to do for him and choose to give him of what they've been given previously (under this maxim) and haven't yet expended or transferred.

This, the discerning reader will have noticed, has its defects as a slogan. So as a summary and great simplification (and not as a maxim with any independent meaning) we have:

> *From each as they choose, to each as they are chosen.*

HOW LIBERTY UPSETS PATTERNS

It is not clear how those holding alternative conceptions of distributive justice can reject the entitlement conception of justice in holdings. For suppose a distribution favored by one of these non-entitlement conceptions is realized. Let us suppose it is your favorite one and let us call this distribution D_1; perhaps everyone has an equal share, perhaps shares vary in accordance with some dimension you treasure. Now suppose that Wilt Chamberlain is greatly in demand by basketball teams, being a great gate attraction. (Also suppose contracts run only for a year, with players being free agents.) He signs the following sort of contract with a team: In each home game, twenty-five cents from the price of each ticket of admission goes to him. (We ignore the question of whether he is "gouging" the owners, letting them look out for themselves.) The season starts, and people cheerfully attend his team's games; they buy their tickets, each time dropping a separate twenty-five cents of their admission price into a special box with Chamberlain's name on it. They are excited about seeing him play; it is worth the total admission price to them. Let us suppose that in one season one million persons attend his home games, and Wilt Chamberlain winds up with $250,000, a much larger sum than the average income and larger even than anyone else has. Is he entitled to this income? Is this new distribution D_2, unjust? If so, why? There is *no* question about whether each of the people was entitled to the control over the resources they held in D_1; because that was the distribution (your favorite) that (for the purposes of argument) we assumed was acceptable. Each of these persons *chose* to give twenty-five cents of their money to Chamberlain. They could have spent it on going to the movies, or on candy bars, or on copies of *Dissent* magazine, or of *Monthly Review*. But they all, at least one million of them, converged on giving it to Wilt Chamberlain in exchange for watching him play basketball. If D_1 was a just distribution, and people voluntarily moved from it to D_2, transferring parts of their shares they were given under D_1 (what was it for if not to do something with?), isn't D_2 also just? If the people were entitled to dispose of the resources to which they were entitled (under D_1), didn't this include their being entitled to give it to, or exchange it with,

Wilt Chamberlain? Can anyone else complain on grounds of justice?
Each other person already has his legitimate share under D_1. Under
D_1, there is nothing that anyone has that anyone else has a claim of
justice against. After someone transfers something to Wilt Chamberlain, third parties *still* have their legitimate shares; *their* shares are not
changed. By what process could such a transfer among two persons
give rise to a legitimate claim of distributive justice on a portion of
what was transferred, by a third party who had no claim of justice
on any holding of the others *before* the transfer? To cut off objections
irrelevant here, we might imagine the exchanges occurring in a socialist society, after hours. After playing whatever basketball he does
in his daily work, or doing whatever other daily work he does, Wilt
Chamberlain decides to put in *overtime* to earn additional money.
(First his work quota is set; he works time over that.) Or imagine it
is a skilled juggler people like to see, who puts on shows after hours.

Why might someone work overtime in a society in which it is
assumed their needs are satisfied? Perhaps because they care about
things other than needs. I like to write in books that I read, and to
have easy access to books for browsing at odd hours. It would be very
pleasant and convenient to have the resources of Widener Library in
my back yard. No society, I assume, will provide such resources close
to each person who would like them as part of his regular allotment
(under D_1). Thus, persons either must do without some extra things
that they want, or be allowed to do something extra to get some of
these things. On what basis could the inequalities that would eventuate be forbidden? Notice also that small factories would spring up
in a socialist society, unless forbidden. I melt down some of my personal possessions (under D_1) and build a machine out of the material.
I offer you, and others, a philosophy lecture once a week in exchange
for your cranking the handle on my machine, whose products I exchange for yet other things, and so on. (The raw materials used by the
machine are given to me by others who possess them under D_1, in
exchange for hearing lectures.) Each person might participate to gain
things over and above their allotment under D_1. Some persons even
might want to leave their job in socialist industry and work full time
in this private sector. I shall say something more about these issues
in the next chapter. Here I wish merely to note how private property

even in means of production would occur in a socialist society that did not forbid people to use as they wished some of the resources they are given under the socialist distribution D_1. The socialist society would have to forbid capitalist acts between consenting adults.

The general point illustrated by the Wilt Chamberlain example and the example of the entrepreneur in a socialist society is that no end-state principle or distributional patterned principle of justice can be continuously realized without continuous interference with people's lives. Any favored pattern would be transformed into one unfavored by the principle, by people choosing to act in various ways; for example, by people exchanging goods and services with other people, or giving things to other people, things the transferrers are entitled to under the favored distributional pattern. To maintain a pattern one must either continually interfere to stop people from transferring resources as they wish to, or continually (or periodically) interfere to take from some persons resources that others for some reason chose to transfer to them. (But if some time limit is to be set on how long people may keep resources others voluntarily transfer to them, why let them keep these resources for *any* period of time? Why not have immediate confiscation?) It might be objected that all persons voluntarily will choose to refrain from actions which would upset the pattern. This presupposes unrealistically (1) that all will most want to maintain the pattern (are those who don't, to be "reeducated" or forced to undergo "self-criticism"?), (2) that each can gather enough information about his own actions and the ongoing activities of others to discover which of his actions will upset the pattern, and (3) that diverse and far-flung persons can coordinate their actions to dove-tail into the pattern. Compare the manner in which the market is neutral among persons' desires, as it reflects and transmits widely scattered information via prices, and coordinates persons' activities.

It puts things perhaps a bit too strongly to say that every patterned (or end-state) principle is liable to be thwarted by the voluntary actions of the individual parties transferring some of their shares they receive under the principle. For perhaps some *very* weak patterns are not so thwarted. Any distributional pattern with any egalitarian component is overturnable by the voluntary actions of individual persons over time; as is every patterned condition with sufficient content so as actually to have been proposed as presenting the central core of distributive justice. Still, given the possibility that some weak conditions or patterns may not be unstable in this way, it would be better to formulate an explicit description of the kind of interesting and contentful patterns under discussion, and to prove a theorem about their instability. Since the weaker the patterning, the more likely it is that the entitlement system itself satisfies it, a plausible conjecture is that any patterning either is unstable or is satisfied by the entitlement system. . . .

REDISTRIBUTION AND PROPERTY RIGHTS

Apparently, patterned principles allow people to choose to expend upon themselves, but not upon others, those resources they are entitled to (or rather, receive) under some favored distributional pattern D_1. For if each of several persons chooses to expend some of his D_1 resources upon one other person, then that other person will receive more than his D_1 share, disturbing the favored distributional pattern. Maintaining a distributional pattern is individualism with a vengeance! Patterned distributional principles do not give people what entitlement principles do, only better distributed. For they do not give the right to choose what to do with what one has; they do not give the right to choose to pursue an end involving (intrinsically, or as a means) the enhancement of another's position. To such views, families are disturbing; for within a family occur transfers that upset the favored distributional pattern. Either families themselves become units to which distribution takes place, the column occupiers (on what rationale?), or loving behavior is forbidden. We should note in passing the ambivalent position of radicals toward the family. Its loving relationships are seen as a model to be emulated and extended across the whole society, at the same time that it is denounced as a suffocating institution to be broken and condemned as a focus of parochial concerns that interfere with achieving radical goals. Need we say that it is not appropriate to enforce across the wider society the relationships of love and care appropriate within a family, relationships which are voluntarily undertaken? Incidentally, love is an interesting instance of another relationship that is historical, in that (like justice) it depends upon what actually occurred. An adult may come to love another because of the other's characteristics; but it is the other person, and not the characteristics, that is loved. The love is not transferrable to someone else with the same characteristics, even to one who "scores" higher for these characteristics. And the love endures through changes of the characteristics that gave rise to it. One loves the particular person one actually encountered. Why love is historical, attaching to persons in this way and not to characteristics, is an interesting and puzzling question.

Proponents of patterned principles of distributive justice focus upon criteria for determining who is to receive holdings; they consider the reasons for which someone should have something, and also the total picture of holdings. Whether or not it is better to give than to receive, proponents of patterned principles ignore giving altogether. In considering the distribution of goods, income, and so forth, their theories are theories of recipient justice; they completely ignore any right a person might have to give something to someone. Even in exchanges where each party is simultaneously giver and recipient, patterned principles of justice focus only upon the recipient role and its supposed rights. Thus discussions tend to focus on whether people (should) have a right to inherit, rather than on whether people (should) have a right to bequeath or on whether persons who have a right to hold also have a right to choose that others hold in their place. I lack a good explanation of why the usual theories of distributive justice are so recipient oriented; ignoring givers and transferrers and their rights is of a piece with ignoring producers and their entitlements. But why is it *all* ignored?

Patterned principles of distributive justice necessitate *re*distributive activities. The likelihood is small that any actual freely-arrived-at set of holdings fits a given pattern; and the likelihood is nil that it will continue to fit the pattern as people exchange and give. From the point of view of an entitlement theory, redistribution is a serious matter indeed, involving, as it does, the violation of people's rights. (An exception is those takings that fall under the principle of the rectification of injustices.) From other points of view, also, it is serious.

Taxation of earnings from labor is on a par with forced labor.

Some persons find this claim obviously true: taking the earnings of *n* hours labor is like taking *n* hours from the person; it is like forcing the person to work *n* hours for another's purpose. Others find the claim absurd. But even these, *if* they object to forced labor, would oppose forcing unemployed hippies to work for the benefit of the needy. And they would also object to forcing each person to work five extra hours each week for the benefit of the needy. But a system that takes five hours' wages in taxes does not seem to them like one that forces someone to work five hours, since it offers the person forced a wider range of choice in activities than does taxation in kind with the particular labor specified. (But we can imagine a gradation of systems of forced labor, from one that specifies a particular activity, to one that gives a choice among two activities, to . . . ; and so on up.) Furthermore, people envisage a system with something like a proportional tax on everything above the amount necessary for basic needs. Some think this does not force someone to work extra hours, since there is no fixed number of extra hours he is forced to work, and since he can avoid the tax entirely by earning only enough to cover his basic needs. This is a very uncharacteristic view of forcing for those who *also* think people are forced to do something *whenever* the alternatives they face are considerably worse. However, *neither* view is correct. The fact that others intentionally intervene, in viola-tion of a side constraint against aggression, to threaten force to limit the alternatives, in this case to paying taxes or (presumably the worse alternative) bare subsistence, makes the taxation system one of forced labor and distinguishes it from other cases of limited choices which are not forcings.

The man who chooses to work longer to gain an income more than sufficient for his basic needs prefers some extra goods or services to the leisure and activities he could perform during the possible nonworking hours; whereas the man who chooses not to work the extra time prefers the leisure activities to the extra goods or services he could acquire by working more. Given this, if it would be illegitimate for a tax system to seize some of a man's leisure (forced labor) for the purpose of serving the needy, how can it be legitimate for a tax system to seize some of a man's goods for that purpose? Why should we treat the man whose happiness requires certain material goods or services differently from the man whose preferences and desires make such goods unnecessary for his happiness? Why should the man who prefers seeing a movie (and who has to earn money for a ticket) be open to the required call to aid the needy, while the person who prefers looking at a sunset (and hence need earn no extra money) is not? Indeed, isn't it surprising that redistributionists choose to ignore the man whose pleasures are so easily attainable without extra labor, while adding yet another burden to the poor unfortunate who must work for his pleasures? If anything, one would have expected the reverse. Why is the person with the nonmaterial or nonconsumption desire allowed to proceed unimpeded to his most favored feasible alternative, whereas the man whose pleasures or desires involve material things and who must work for extra money (thereby serving whomever considers his activities valuable enough to pay him) is constrained in what he can realize? Perhaps there is no difference in principle. And perhaps some think the answer concerns merely administrative convenience. (These questions and issues will not disturb those who think that forced labor to serve the needy or to realize some favored end-state pattern is acceptable.) In a fuller discussion we would have (and want) to extend our argument to include interest, entrepreneurial profits, and so on. Those who doubt that this extension can be carried through, and who draw the line here at taxation of income from labor, will have to state rather complicated patterned *historical* principles of distributive justice, since end-state principles would not distinguish *sources* of income in any way. It is enough for now to get away from end-state principles and to make clear how various patterned principles are dependent upon particular views about the sources or the illegitimacy or the lesser legitimacy of profits, interest, and so on; which particular views may well be mistaken.

What sort of right over others does a legally institutionalized end-state pattern give one? The central core of the notion of a property right in X, relative to which other parts of the notion are to be explained, is the right to determine what shall be done with X; the right to choose which of the constrained set of options concerning X shall be realized or attempted. The constraints are set by other principles or laws operating in the society; in our theory, by the Lockean rights people possess (under the minimal state). My property rights in my knife allow me to leave it where I will, but not in your chest. I may choose which of the acceptable options involving the knife is to be realized. This notion of property helps us to understand why earlier theorists spoke of people as having property in themselves and their labor. They viewed each person as having a right to decide what would become of himself and what he would do, and as having a right to reap the benefits of what he did.

This right of selecting the alternative to be realized from the constrained set of alternatives may be held by an *individual* or by a *group* with some procedure for reaching a joint decision; or the right may be passed back and forth, so that one year I decide what's to become of *X*, and the next year you do (with the alternative of destruction, perhaps, being excluded). Or, during the same time period, some types of decisions about *X* may be made by me, and others by you. And so on. We lack an adequate, fruitful, analytical apparatus for classifying the *types* of constraints on the set of options among which choices are to be made, and the *types* of ways decision powers can be held, divided, and amalgamated. A *theory* of property would, among other things, contain such a classification of constraints and decision modes, and from a small number of principles would follow a host of interesting statements about the *consequences* and effects of certain combinations of constraints and modes of decision.

When end-result principles of distributive justice are built into the legal structure of a society, they (as do most patterned principles) give each citizen an enforceable claim to some portion of the total social product; that is, to some portion of the sum total of the individually and jointly made products. This total product is produced by individuals laboring, using means of production others have saved to bring into existence, by people organizing production or creating means to produce new things or things in a new way. It is on this batch of individual activities that patterned distributional principles give each individual an enforceable claim. Each person has a claim to the activities and the products of other persons, independently of whether the other persons enter into particular relationships that give rise to these claims, and independently of whether they voluntarily take these claims upon themselves, in charity or in exchange for something.

Whether it is done through taxation on wages or on wages over a certain amount, or through seizure of profits, or through there being a big *social pot* so that it's not clear what's coming from where and what's going where, patterned principles of distributive justice involve appropriating the actions of other persons. Seizing the results of someone's labor is equivalent to seizing hours from him and directing him to carry on various activities. If people force you to do certain work, or unrewarded work, for a certain period of time, they decide what you are to do and what purposes your work is to serve apart from your decisions. This process whereby they take this decision from you makes them a *part-owner* of you; it gives them a property right in you. Just as having such partial control and power of decision, by right, over an animal or inanimate object would be to have a property right in it.

End-state and most patterned principles of distributive justice institute (partial) ownership by others of people and their actions and labor. These principles involve a shift from the classical liberals' notion of self-ownership to a notion of (partial) property rights in *other* people.

Considerations such as these confront end-state and other patterned conceptions of justice with the question of whether the actions necessary to achieve the selected pattern don't themselves violate moral side constraints. Any view holding that there are moral side constraints on actions, that not all moral considerations can be built into end-states that are to be achieved, must face the possibility that some of its goals are not achievable by any morally permissible available means. An entitlement theorist will face such conflicts in a society that deviates from the principles of justice for the generation of holdings, if and only if the only actions available to realize the principles themselves violate some moral constraints. Since deviation from the first two principles of justice (in acquisition and transfer) will involve other persons' direct and aggressive intervention to violate rights, and since moral constraints will not exclude defensive or retributive action in such cases, the entitlement theorist's problem rarely will be pressing. And whatever difficulties he has in applying the principle of rectification to persons who did not themselves violate the first two principles are difficulties in balancing the conflicting considerations so as correctly to formulate the complex principle of rectification itself; he will not violate moral side constraints by applying the principle. Proponents of patterned conceptions of justice, however, often will face head-on clashes (and poignant ones if they cherish each party to the clash) between moral side constraints on how individuals may be treated and their patterned conception of justice that presents an end-state or other pattern that *must* be realized.

May a person emigrate from a nation that has institutionalized some end-state or patterned distributional principle? For some principles (for example, Hayek's) emigration presents no theoretical problem. But for others it is a tricky matter. Consider a nation having a compulsory scheme of minimal social provision to aid the neediest (or one organized so as to maximize the position of the worst-off group); no one may opt out of participating in it. (None may say, "Don't compel me to contribute to others and don't provide for me via this compulsory mechanism if I am in need.") Everyone above a certain level is forced to contribute to aid the needy. But if emigration from the country were allowed, anyone could choose to move to another country that did not have compulsory social provision but otherwise was (as much as possible) identical. In such a case, the person's *only* motive for leaving would be to avoid participating in the compulsory scheme of social provision. And if he does leave, the needy in his initial country will receive no (compelled) help from him. What rationale yields the result that the person be permitted to emigrate, yet forbidden to stay and opt out of the compulsory scheme of social provision? If providing for the needy is of overriding importance, this does militate against allowing internal opting out; but it also speaks against allowing external emigration. (Would it also support, to some extent, the kidnapping of persons living in a place without compulsory social provision, who could be forced to make a contribution to the needy in your community?) Perhaps the crucial component of the position that allows emigration solely to avoid certain arrangements, while not allowing anyone internally to opt out of them, is a concern for fraternal feelings within the country. "We don't want anyone here who doesn't contribute, who doesn't care enough about the others to contribute." That concern, in this case, would have to be tied to the view that forced aiding tends to produce fraternal feelings between the aided and the aider (or perhaps merely to the view that the knowledge that someone or other voluntarily is not aiding produces unfraternal feelings).

THE RIGHT TO DO WRONG

Roger Pilon

Defenders of individual rights often appear to be defending speech or behavior that many people regard as highly offensive or even immoral. The point, of course, is to defend not the behavior itself but rather the right of adults to make their own decisions. Libertarians themselves may regard such actions as immoral while insisting that adults must be free to choose. Indeed, a concern for virtue should lead one to support individual freedom, because an action can hardly reflect individual virtue if it is coerced; it is the free choice of virtuous actions that deserves the label virtue. In this essay Roger Pilon, senior fellow at the Cato Institute, defends "the right to do wrong"—though not the actual *choice* to do wrong—by examining two controversial actions, flag-burning and racial discrimination.

Two questions that captured the attention of the American public in the spring of 1990 were whether we should ban the burning of the American flag and whether we should enact a new civil rights statute to broaden the rights of minorities, women, and others in the workplace. Those are distinct questions, to be sure, and have been seen as distinct by most of the public. Nevertheless, underlying them are certain common themes that go to the core of the American vision. . . .

When the Supreme Court [in 1990] found for the second time in as many years that a statute aimed at prohibiting the desecration of the American flag as a form of political protest was itself prohibited by the First Amendment to the Constitution, the Court did so by drawing upon the classic distinction between speech and its content. The statute's "restriction on expression cannot be justified without reference to the content of the regulated speech," the Court said. And "if there is a bedrock principle underlying the First Amendment, it is that the Government may not prohibit the expression of an idea simply because society finds the idea itself offensive or disagreeable."

This distinction between speech and its content is ancient, of course, finding its roots in antiquity, its modern expressions in the *philosophes* of the Enlightenment and the Founders of the American Republic. When Sir Winston Churchill observed in 1945 that "the United States is a land of free speech. Nowhere is speech freer—not even [in England] where we sedulously cultivate it even in its most repulsive forms," he was merely echoing thoughts attributed to Voltaire, that he may disapprove of what you say but would defend to the death your right to say it, and the ironic question of Benjamin Franklin: "Abuses of the freedom of speech ought to be repressed; but to whom are we to commit the power of doing it?" There is all the difference in the world between defending the right to speak and defending the speech that flows from the exercise of that right. Indeed, with perfect consistency one can condemn the burning of the flag, as most Americans do, while defending the right to burn it.

Yet for many—Americans and non-Americans alike—the distinction between speech and its content is difficult to grasp, and certainly difficult to endure. Some see the relatively explicit protections of the First Amendment as an impediment to some "right of the majority" to express its values through the democratic process. Others draw a distinction between speech and action, then claim that the First Amendment protects only the former—apparently unaware not only that speech takes many forms, many quite "active," but that all speech is action and, arguably, all action is, if not speech, at least expression. Still others point to such restrictions on speech as are found in the areas of endangerment (shouting "Fire!" in a crowded theater), defamation, and obscenity, assume those to reflect mere value or policy decisions, then ask why restrictions on flag desecration should be treated any differently.

Setting aside restrictions on obscenity as they pertain to adults, which are inexplicable anomalies in the jurisprudence of the First Amendment, the rationale for restricting speech that endangers or defames others is both persuasive and instructive. Indeed, when properly explicated, that rationale goes to the core of the American vision, as captured most generally in the Ninth Amendment, of which the First Amendment, among others, is simply a more specific manifestation. Stating that "the enumeration in the Constitution of certain rights shall not be construed to deny or disparage others retained by the people," the Ninth Amendment is fairly read as recognizing and establishing in law a general presumption in favor of liberty. Whether we call that presumption a "right to be let alone—the most comprehensive of rights and the right most valued by civilized men," as Justice Brandeis put it when exploring the idea of privacy, or a right to be free, a right to come and go as we please, to plan and live our own lives, that basic right is limited only by the equal right of others and by the express powers of government that are enumerated in the Constitution and in the constitutions of the various states. It is precisely because they implicate the rights of others, therefore, that acts that endanger or defame are not protected by the First Amendment, even when they are deemed to be "speech," whereas acts that do not implicate the rights of others are protected.

It is this fundamental principle, then, the principle of equal freedom, defined classically by our rights to life, liberty, and property, that constitutes the core of the American vision and serves as well to order systematically the countless examples of those rights—from speech to religion, contract, due process, and on and on. Far from being mere value or policy choices, when rationally related, those rights reflect a moral order that transcends our contingent values and preferences. That transcendent order—the higher or natural law, if you will—was captured most forcefully in our Declaration of Independence, of course, which states plainly that we are born free and equal, with equal moral rights to plan and live our own lives—even, by implication, when doing so offends others. Call it tolerance, call it respect: it is the mark of a free society that individuals are left free to pursue their own values, however wise or foolish, however enlightened or benighted, however pleasing or offensive to others.

But if that fundamental principle applies not simply to flag-

burning, nor even simply to speech, religion, and other First Amendment issues generally, but across the board—to all questions about
the relationship between the individual and his government—then
we cannot shirk from that application, however unpleasant or unpopular the results may be. We turn, then, to the second of our
debates and to the question whether the Civil Rights Act of 1990 is
a threat to our civil rights. Plainly, underlying that question is the
more basic question about just what our civil rights are. It is that
more basic question to which Professor [Richard] Epstein points
when he challenges not simply the proposed Civil Rights Act of 1990
but the assumptions underlying the Civil Rights Act of 1964 as well.
In the Washington of 1990, neither of those challenges, but especially
the latter, will earn one popular acclaim. If we are serious about getting to the heart of the matter, however, and about understanding
the core of the American vision, the fundamental questions must be
examined.

Now it would be one thing to respond to the basic question about
what our civil rights are by answering that those rights are what the
legislature says they are. That tack is all too familiar. In so responding, however, not only would we place our rights at the mercy of
majorities—or, if the public choice school of thought is correct, at the
mercy of special interests—but by doing so we would expose those
rights to the vagaries of popular opinion, which is precisely what we
have rights to protect us from. If our rights come and go according to
the winds of political fashion, then we live not under the rule of law
but under the rule of men. Indeed, it was precisely to secure the former that our Founders wrote a constitution in the first place, a constitution, as noted above, that was founded on the principle of equal
freedom, as defined by our rights to life, liberty, and property. Subject
those rights to the vagaries of public opinion and you undermine the
very foundations of that moral and legal order.

Yet that is precisely what has happened over a wide area of life,
including the especially wide area that is defined by our rights, or
freedom, of association. As Professor Epstein observes, the civil
rights acts that were enacted after the Civil War were intended simply
to ensure that freed slaves would have the same civil capacities, or
rights, as other free persons—rights to purchase and hold property,

to make and enforce contracts, to sue and be sued, and so on. That those newly recognized rights came to be frustrated, especially in the South, by Jim Crow is appalling, of course, for the Jim Crow restraints were in direct violation of the American vision that the civil rights acts were intended to secure. And insofar as the Civil Rights Act of 1964 eliminated Jim Crow, it is to be commended. But the idea behind the early civil rights acts was to give force at last to the principle of equal freedom upon which this nation was founded, however imperfect that founding. The idea was not, most decidedly, to recognize "rights" that were inconsistent with that principle.

With the Civil Rights Act of 1964, however, that precisely is what took place. Driven by the very real problem of discrimination, but failing utterly to distinguish between the appalling institution of public discrimination, in the form of Jim Crow, and its private counterpart, the authors of the 1964 act created a "right" against private discrimination on certain grounds and in certain contexts, which has been expanded over the years. That "right," of course, is nowhere to be found in the Constitution or in its underlying principles. Indeed, its enforcement is inconsistent with that document and with those principles. For if we do have a right to be free, to plan and live our own lives as we choose, limited only by the equal right of others, then we have a right to associate, or to refuse to associate, for whatever reasons we choose, or for no reason at all. That is what freedom is all about. Others may condemn our reasons—that too is a right. But if freedom and personal sovereignty mean anything, they mean the right to make those kinds of decisions for ourselves, even when they offend others.

None of this is to defend private discrimination, of course. Rather, as in the case of flag-burning, it is to defend the *right* to discriminate. For discrimination, like flag-burning, violates no rights of others, however offensive it may otherwise be. We have no more right to associate with those who do not want to associate with us, for whatever reason, than we have to be free from the offense that flag-burning gives. Fortunately, most Americans condemn both flag-burning and discrimination. But in doing so they make value judgments, which are very different from rational judgments about the rights we have. Indeed, the whole point of rights is to enable us to pursue our ends, especially our unpopular ends. We hardly need to invoke rights to pursue popular ends.

Enter, however, this "right against discrimination" and the issues are turned on their heads. Now we may no longer choose not to associate with someone for the proscribed reasons; indeed, we have an obligation not to discriminate on those grounds. But how do we enforce such a right? After all, those who are otherwise inclined to discriminate on one or more of the proscribed grounds are not likely to announce their reasons, thereby subjecting themselves to the sanctions of the act. The answer is that, save for those rare cases in which someone openly defies the act, we have to abandon an intent test, for all practical purposes, and look instead at the effects of an individual's actions. If an employer has a workforce in which blacks or women, say, are "underrepresented" with respect to the "relevant population," we presume, prima facie, that he has discriminated on those proscribed grounds (race and sex) and then ask him to prove that he has not. Thus does the burden shift—from the state to prove guilt to the defendant to prove his *innocence*—*not* because the statute explicitly requires it—far from it—but because practically that is the only way such a "right" can be enforced. For given such a statute, and the sanctions it imposes, people simply do not go around saying they discriminated for one of the wrong reasons. By the same token, however, people who discriminate for *other* reasons, and get their numbers wrong, will be swept into the maw of this statute, from which they will extricate themselves only if they are able to convince the court that those reasons are compelling.

Quotas, then, are no explicit part of the 1964 act, nor are they of the proposed 1990 act. But they are there all the same, every bit as real as if they were written in stone. For if an employer does not get his numbers right, the burden of proving his innocence is so onerous, and the penalties for failing to do so, especially under the 1990 act, so draconian, that for all practical purposes he will operate as if quotas were explicitly in the statute. Thus those who oppose quotas, but believe in this "right against discrimination," need to rethink their position. If they are serious about enforcing such a "right," then de facto quotas are inescapable.

We return, then, to the underlying issues that join these two debates. For at a deeper level, the approach we have taken to the problem of private discrimination—admittedly, a very real problem that cries out for condemnation—is itself an affront to our founding principles. We speak, after all, of the indivisibility of freedom. And we understand that idea and its applications, for the most part, in such areas of the Constitution as the First Amendment, where our rights are relatively clear. But the principle of those First Amendment rights—that individuals are and ought to be free to express their own values and live their own lives, however much they may offend others in the process—is perfectly general. Again, most Americans find flag-burning abhorrent, just as they find discrimination abhorrent. As long, however, as those who burn flags or those who discriminate do not violate the rights of others, their right to so behave should be protected.

Indeed, we have other, more peaceful and, ultimately, more effective means of dealing with such people. In the age of communication—local, national, and global—the force of moral suasion and public obloquy in areas such as these is far more effective and far less costly than any heavy-handed resort to law, with all its unintended consequences. We need to unleash this force, not disparage it by a too hasty, and ultimately misguided, resort to legal force. And we need in particular to be careful about compromising our fundamental, founding principles, not only when our ends are noble, but especially when they are noble.

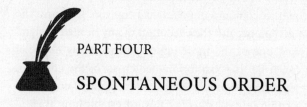

PART FOUR

SPONTANEOUS ORDER

The key insight of libertarian social analysis is the concept of spontaneous order. The historian Ralph Raico suggests that true liberalism is defined by the belief "that civil society—that is, the whole of the social order based on private property—by and large runs itself."

Such a belief is somewhat counterintuitive. As F. A. Hayek and Michael Polanyi discuss in the selections below, when we see an orderly process we naturally assume that someone has designed or planned it. Hayek says that we fail to distinguish between two kinds of order: the "made" or planned order, such as a business firm or other limited organization, and the "grown" or spontaneous order, such as the whole society or the market process. It is crucial to make this distinction, however, because the two kinds of order are very different. Notably, the made order is designed for a specific purpose, while the grown order reflects the different and often competing purposes of many individuals and enterprises.

Many great philosophers have failed to comprehend the existence of spontaneous order. Kant, for instance, despite his defense of individual rights, believed that peace and order could not exist without coercion. Karl Marx could see only "the anarchy of capitalist production," not the tremendous prosperity produced by the unplanned order that Adam Smith seventy-five years earlier had called "the simple system of natural liberty." Echoing and refuting Marx a century later, Ludwig von Mises wrote, "Production is anarchistic"—and it is precisely that unplanned, competitive process that generates economic growth.

Spontaneous order is not just the market. Libertarian scholars point to law, language, customs, and money as other important institutions that evolved without any central direction—in the words of Adam Smith's Scottish contemporary Adam Ferguson, they are "the result of human action, but not the execution of any human design." Carl Menger asked one of the most important questions in social science: "How can it be that institutions which serve the common welfare and are extremely significant for its development come into being without a common will directed toward establishing them?" That is the question that interested Adam Smith, Thomas Paine, Herbert Spencer, and F. A. Hayek.

The French Physiocrats of the eighteenth century expressed the concept of spontaneous order in their famous slogan, "*Laissez-faire, laissez-passer, le monde va de lui-même*" ("Let us do, leave us alone: The world runs by itself"). Adam Smith argued that:

> Little else is requisite to carry a State to the highest degree of opulence from the lowest barbarism, but peace, easy taxes, and a tolerable administration of justice, all the rest being brought about by the natural course of things. All governments which thwart this natural course, which force things into another channel, or which endeavor to arrest the progress of society at a particular point, are unnatural, and to support themselves are obliged to be oppressive and tyrannical.

The concept of a natural harmony in the world can be found in Eastern philosophy as well. Perhaps the classic statement is the *Tao Te Ching* of Lao-tzu, briefly excerpted here. The idea is found throughout the work of Adam Smith. Here we include his famous description of "the man of system," who treats individuals as chess pieces to be moved at will, from *The Theory of Moral Sentiments*. One of Thomas Paine's important theoretical contributions to libertarianism was to fuse a theory of justice—natural rights—with the social theory of spontaneous order.

The great twentieth-century theorist of spontaneous order was F. A. Hayek, who explored the topic in many books, including *The Constitution of Liberty, The Sensory Order, The Counter-Revolution of Science, The Fatal Conceit, Law, Legislation, and Liberty,* and essays in many collections. We include here his discussion of how a society can best coordinate all the decentralized knowledge that people possess to produce the highest level of economic output. In a later essay, he rescues the concept of order from authoritarians who have insisted that order rests on "command and obedience" and notes that we frequently err by trying to apply the rules appropriate to a small group, such as a family or village, to a large society: "If we were to apply the unmodified, uncurbed rules of the micro-cosmos (i.e., of the small band or troop, or of, say, our families) to the macro-cosmos (our wider civilization), as our instincts and sentimental yearnings often make us wish to do, *we would destroy it*. Yet if we were always to apply the rules of the extended order to our more intimate group-ings, *we would crush them*." That is, for instance, we would not want to operate within our families on the basis of the general rules of property rights and free exchange. Yet if we seek to extend the rules of the family—mutual love and moral desert—to the whole of society, we would be enmeshed in constant social conflict and would destroy the system that produces goods and services. Hayek's contemporary and friend, Michael Polanyi, also discusses planned and spontaneous orders, from the perspective of a scientist.

Our final selection in this section is from *Bionomics: The Inevita-bility of Capitalism* by Michael Rothschild, who explores the fascinat-ing parallels between evolution, ecosystems, and economic processes. The connection is an old one, of course: In fact, writes Stephen Jay Gould, the paleontologist and historian of science, "The theory of natural selection is a creative transfer to biology of Adam Smith's basic argument for a rational economy: the balance and order of na-ture does not arise from a higher, external (divine) control, or from the existence of laws operating directly upon the whole, but from struggle among individuals for their own benefits."

The theme running through these essays is twofold: that un-planned, competitive processes can produce order without central direction, and that a state's attempt to impose order or alter the re-sults of spontaneous processes is likely to produce discoordination, poverty, and social conflict.

HARMONY

Lao-tzu

Libertarian ideas of individualism, natural rights, and constitutional government arose in the West, though liberals and libertarians believe that they are applicable to all human societies. But elements of libertarian ideas in society can certainly be found in Eastern philosophy as well. One of the classic sources is the *Tao Te Ching,* thought to have been written in the sixth century B.C. by a scribe named Lao-tzu (or Laozi). *Tao* is sometimes translated "the Way," though another possible translation is "natural law." As used in Taoism, the Tao refers to the way of ways, the law of laws, the ultimate reality and its structure, expressed in *I Ching* as "The Tao consists of yin and yang [i.e., the Tao is the unity of two opposites]." Taoism is a political philosophy underlain by Taoist cosmology, the philosophy of paradoxes and of nonaction. Lao-tzu urges the ruler ("the sage") to refrain from acting, to accept the good with the bad, to let the people pursue their own actions. In the Taoist view, harmony can be achieved only through strife or competition. Taoism reflects an ancient Chinese attitude, also seen in the Soil-Breaking Song of the Farmers from one of the Chinese classics:

I work when the sun rises; I retreat when the sun sets.
I dig the well for water; I plow the field for food:
What use do I have for the emperor's power!

Such a conception is very similar to that of Adam Ferguson, Adam Smith, F. A. Hayek, and the other theorists of spontaneous order. Some libertarians consider the legendary Lao-tzu the first libertarian. These excerpts are from *The Way and Its Power: A Study of the Tao Te Ching and Its Place in Chinese Thought* by Arthur Waley (New York: Grove, 1958), with some revisions and additional translations by Kate Xiao Zhou, a professor of Chinese politics at the University of Hawaii.

———————

19

Exterminate the sage [the ruler] and discard the wisdom [of rule],
And the people will benefit a hundredfold.

32

Without law or compulsion, men would dwell in harmony.

42

All things carry the yin and embrace the yang.
They achieve harmony through their interaction.

57

The more prohibitions there are,
The poorer the people will be.

The more laws are promulgated,
The more thieves and bandits there will be.

Therefore a sage has said:
So long as I "do nothing" the people will of themselves be
    transformed.
So long as I love quietude, the people will of themselves go
    straight.
So long as I act only by inactivity the people will of themselves
    become prosperous.

75

The people starve because those above them eat too much tax-grain. That is the only reason why they starve. The people are difficult to keep in order because those above them interfere. That is the only reason why they are so difficult to keep in order.

THE MAN OF SYSTEM

Adam Smith

In this brief excerpt from *The Theory of Moral Sentiments,* Adam Smith illuminates two different visions of the world: the understanding of natural harmony and spontaneous order versus the conceit of "the man of system," who imagines that he can move people around like chess pieces to fulfill some plan. Modern governments are full of "men of system," who believe that the world would work much better if only individuals would cooperate with the man of system's plan.

———————

The man whose public spirit is prompted altogether by humanity and benevolence, will respect the established powers and privileges even of individuals, and still more those of the great orders and societies into which the state is divided. Though he should consider some of them as in some measure abusive, he will content himself with moderating what he often cannot annihilate without great violence. When he cannot conquer the rooted prejudices of the people by reason and persuasion, he will not attempt to subdue them by force, but will religiously observe what by Cicero is justly called the divine maxim of Plato, never to use violence to his country, no more than to his parents. He will accommodate, as well as he can, his public arrangements to the confirmed habits and prejudices of the people, and will remedy, as well as he can, the inconveniences which may flow from the want of those regulations which the people are averse to submit to. When he cannot establish the right, he will not disdain to ameliorate the wrong; but, like Solon, when he cannot establish the best system of laws, he will endeavour to establish the best that the people can bear.

The man of system, on the contrary, is apt to be very wise in his own conceit, and is often so enamoured with the supposed beauty of his own ideal plan of government, that he cannot suffer the smallest deviation from any part of it. He goes on to establish it completely and in all its parts, without any regard either to the great interests or to the strong prejudices which may oppose it: he seems to imagine that he can arrange the different members of a great society with as much ease as the hand arranges the different pieces upon a chess-board; he does not consider that the pieces upon the chess-board have no other principle of motion besides that which the hand impresses upon them; but that, in the great chess-board of human society, every single piece has a principle of motion of its own, altogether different from that which the legislature might choose to impress upon it. If those two principles coincide and act in the same direction, the game of human society will go on easily and harmoniously, and is very likely to be happy and successful. If they are opposite or different, the game will go on miserably, and the society must be at all times in the highest degree of disorder.

OF SOCIETY AND CIVILIZATION

Thomas Paine

In this selection from the second part of *The Rights of Man* (1791–92), Paine returns to a theme from *Common Sense:* the distinction between society and the state. Here he argues that the order naturally observed in human society is not the result of government. "It existed prior to government, and would exist if the formality of government was abolished." The need for co-operation in a market economy impels people to develop rules for living together. Paine points to the "order and harmony" that continued to exist in the American colonies when their British-run governments were abolished. Unlike the social philosophers of the Scottish Enlightenment, Paine ties this theory of natural harmony to a theory of justice: He argues that not only do all existing governments violate individual rights, they are unnecessary for creating social order.

Great part of that order which reigns among mankind is not the effect of government. It has its origin in the principles of society and the natural constitution of man. It existed prior to government, and would exist if the formality of government was abolished. The mutual dependence and reciprocal interest which man has upon man, and all the parts of a civilized community upon each other, create that great chain of connection which holds it together. The landholder, the farmer, the manufacturer, the merchant, the tradesman, and every occupation, prospers by the aid which each receives from the other, and from the whole. Common interest regulates their concerns, and forms their law; and the laws which common usage ordains, have a greater influence than the laws of government. In fine, society performs for itself almost everything which is ascribed to government.

To understand the nature and quantity of government proper for man, it is necessary to attend to his character. As Nature created him for social life, she fitted him for the station she intended. In all cases she made his natural wants greater than his individual powers. No one man is capable, without the aid of society, of supplying his own wants; and those wants, acting upon every individual, impel the whole of them into society, as naturally as gravitation acts to a centre.

But she has gone further. She has not only forced man into society, by a diversity of wants, which the reciprocal aid of each other can supply, but she has implanted in him a system of social affections, which, though not necessary to his existence, are essential to his happiness. There is no period in life when this love for society ceases to act. It begins and ends with our being.

If we examine, with attention, into the composition and constitution of man, the diversity of his wants, and the diversity of talents in different men for reciprocally accommodating the wants of each other, his propensity to society, and consequently to preserve the advantages resulting from it, we shall easily discover, that a great deal of what is called government is mere imposition.

Government is no farther necessary than to supply the few cases to which society and civilization are not conveniently competent; and instances are not wanting to show, that everything which government can usefully add thereto, has been performed by the common consent of society, without government.

For upwards of two years from the commencement of the American war, and to a longer period in several of the American States, there were no established forms of government. The old governments had been abolished, and the country was too much occupied in defence, to employ its attention in establishing new governments; yet during this interval, order and harmony were preserved as inviolate as in any country in Europe. There is a natural aptness in man, and more so in society, because it embraces a greater variety of abilities and resources, to accommodate itself to whatever situation it is in.

The instant formal government is abolished, society begins to act. A general association takes place, and common interest produces common security.

So far is it from being true, as has been pretended, that the abolition of any formal government is the dissolution of society, that it acts by a contrary impulse, and brings the latter the closer together. All that part of its organization which it had committed to its government, devolves again upon itself, and acts through its medium. When men, as well from natural instinct, as from reciprocal benefits, have habituated themselves to social and civilized life, there is always enough of its principles in practice to carry them through any changes they may find necessary or convenient to make in their government. In short, man is so naturally a creature of society, that it is almost impossible to put him out of it.

Formal government makes but a small part of civilized life; and when even the best that human wisdom can devise is established, it is a thing more in name and idea, than in fact. It is to the great and fundamental principles of society and civilization—to the common usage universally consented to, and mutually and reciprocally maintained—to the unceasing circulation of interest, which, passing through its million channels, invigorates the whole mass of civilized man—it is to these things, infinitely more than to anything else which even the best instituted government can perform, that the safety and prosperity of the individual and of the whole depends.

The more perfect civilization is, the less occasion has it for government, because the more does it regulate its own affairs, and govern itself; but so contrary is the practice of old governments to the reason of the case, that the expenses of them increase in the proportion they ought to diminish. It is but few general laws that civilized life requires, and those of such common usefulness, that whether they are enforced by the forms of government or not, the effect will be nearly the same. If we consider what the principles are that first condense men into society, and what the motives that regulate their mutual intercourse afterwards, we shall find, by the time we arrive at what is called government, that nearly the whole of the business is performed by the natural operation of the parts upon each other.

Man, with respect to all those matters, is more a creature of consistency than he is aware, or than governments would wish him to believe. All the great laws of society are laws of nature. Those of trade and commerce, whether with respect to the intercourse of individuals, or of nations, are laws of mutual and reciprocal interest. They are followed and obeyed, because it is the interest of the parties so to do, and not on account of any formal laws their governments may impose or interpose.

But how often is the natural propensity to society disturbed or destroyed by the operations of government! When the latter, instead of being ingrafted on the principles of the former, assumes to exist for itself, and acts by partialities of favour and oppression, it becomes the cause of the mischiefs it ought to prevent.

If we look back to the riots and tumults, which at various times have happened in England, we shall find, that they did not proceed from the want of a government, but that government was itself the generating cause; instead of consolidating society it divided it; it deprived it of its natural cohesion, and engendered discontents and disorders, which otherwise would not have existed. In those associations which men promiscuously form for the purpose of trade, or of any concern, in which government is totally out of the question, and in which they act merely on the principles of society, we see how naturally the various parties unite; and this shows, by comparison, that governments, so far from being always the cause or means of order, are often the destruction of it. The riots of 1780 had no other source than the remains of those prejudices, which the government itself had encouraged. But with respect to England there are also other causes.

Excess and inequality of taxation, however disguised in the means, never fail to appear in their effects. As a great mass of the community are thrown thereby into poverty and discontent, they are constantly on the brink of commotion; and deprived, as they unfortunately are, of the means of information, are easily heated to outrage. Whatever the apparent cause of any riots may be, the real one is always want of happiness. It shows that something is wrong in the system of government, that injures the felicity by which society is to be preserved.

But as fact is superior to reasoning, the instance of America presents itself to confirm these observations.—If there is a country in the world, where concord, according to common calculation, would be least expected, it is America. Made up, as it is, of people from different nations, accustomed to different forms and habits of government, speaking different languages, and more different in their modes of worship, it would appear that the union of such a people was impracticable; but by the simple operation of constructing government on the principles of society and the rights of man, every difficulty retires, and all the parts are brought into cordial unison. There, the poor are not oppressed, the rich are not privileged. Industry is not mortified by the splendid extravagance of a court rioting at its expense. Their taxes are few, because their government is just; and as there is nothing to render them wretched, there is nothing to engender riots and tumults.

A metaphysical man, like Mr Burke, would have tortured his invention to discover how such a people could be governed. He would have supposed that some must be managed by fraud, others by force, and all by some contrivance; that genius must be hired to impose upon ignorance, and show and parade to fascinate the vulgar. Lost in the abundance of his researches, he would have resolved and re-resolved, and finally overlooked the plain and easy road that lay directly before him.

One of the great advantages of the American Revolution has been, that it led to a discovery of the principles, and laid open the imposition, of governments. All the revolutions till then had been worked within the atmosphere of a court, and never on the great floor of a nation. The parties were always of the class of courtiers; and whatever was their rage for reformation, they carefully preserved the fraud of the profession.

In all cases they took care to represent government as a thing made up of mysteries, which only themselves understood; and they hid from the understanding of the nation, the only thing that was beneficial to know, namely, *That government is nothing more than a national association acting on the principles of society.*

Having thus endeavoured to show, that the social and civilized state of man is capable of performing within itself, almost everything necessary to its protection and government, it will be proper, on the other hand, to take a review of the present old governments, and examine whether their principles and practice are correspondent thereto.

THE USE OF KNOWLEDGE IN SOCIETY

F. A. Hayek

Friedrich A. Hayek (1899–1992) was the great twentieth-century scholar of spontaneous order. In a series of books he explored not only the principles of economics but the limits of rationalism and the spontaneous emergence of rules and order. He argued that the "rules of just conduct" in a complex society are the product of a long evolutionary process, not of rational design, and that we should thus be very cautious about seeking to alter the results of the spontaneous order. There is a tension in libertarian thought between respect for spontaneously emerged institutions and the use of reason to develop theories of individual rights and limited government. Some libertarian critics, especially those influenced by Rand and Rothbard, argue that Hayek's approach virtually renounces the idea that we can critically analyze society and government and recommend changes. In this 1945 essay, Hayek sets forth one of the important themes of his work: how society can best make use of "the dispersed bits of incomplete and frequently contradictory knowledge which all the separate individuals possess." He shows that full-blown socialism cannot work because only freely chosen prices in a system of private property can encapsulate all the information that is scattered throughout society and communicate it to economic actors. This essay helped to demonstrate *how* markets work in a more fully developed way than economists had previously achieved. One of the most influential articles in modern economics, it inspired, among many other things, an entire book: *Knowledge and Decisions* by Thomas Sowell (1980).

————————

1

What is the problem we wish to solve when we try to construct a rational economic order? On certain familiar assumptions the answer is simple enough. *If* we possess all the relevant information, *if* we can start out from a given system of preferences, and *if* we command complete knowledge of available means, the problem which remains is purely one of logic. That is, the answer to the question of what is the best use of the available means is implicit in our assumptions. The conditions which the solution of this optimum problem must satisfy have been fully worked out and can be stated best in mathematical form: put at their briefest, they are that the marginal rates of substitution between any two commodities or factors must be the same in all their different uses.

This, however, is emphatically *not* the economic problem which society faces. And the economic calculus which we have developed to solve this logical problem, though an important step toward the solution of the economic problem of society, does not yet provide an answer to it. The reason for this is that the "data" from which the economic calculus starts are never for the whole society "given" to a single mind which could work out the implications and can never be so given.

The peculiar character of the problem of a rational economic order is determined precisely by the fact that the knowledge of the circumstances of which we must make use never exists in concentrated or integrated form but solely as the dispersed bits of incomplete and frequently contradictory knowledge which all the separate individuals possess. The economic problem of society is thus not merely a problem of how to allocate "given" resources—if "given" is taken to mean given to a single mind which deliberately solves the problem set by these "data." It is rather a problem of how to secure the best use of resources known to any of the members of society, for ends whose relative importance only these individuals know. Or, to put it briefly, it is a problem of the utilization of knowledge which is not given to anyone in its totality.

This character of the fundamental problem has, I am afraid, been obscured rather than illuminated by many of the recent refinements of economic theory, particularly by many of the uses made of mathematics. Though the problem with which I want primarily to deal in this paper is the problem of a rational economic organization, I shall in its course be led again and again to point to its close connections with certain methodological questions. Many of the points I wish to make are indeed conclusions toward which diverse paths of reasoning have unexpectedly converged. But, as I now see these problems, this is no accident. It seems to me that many of the current disputes with regard to both economic theory and economic policy have their common origin in a misconception about the nature of the economic problem of society. This misconception in turn is due to an erroneous transfer to social phenomena of the habits of thought we have developed in dealing with the phenomena of nature.

2

In ordinary language we describe by the word "planning" the complex of interrelated decisions about the allocation of our available resources. All economic activity is in this sense planning; and in any society in which many people collaborate, this planning, whoever does it, will in some measure have to be based on knowledge which, in the first instance, is not given to the planner but to somebody else, which somehow will have to be conveyed to the planner. The various ways in which the knowledge on which people base their plans is communicated to them is the crucial problem for any theory explaining the economic process, and the problem of what is the best way of utilizing knowledge initially dispersed among all the people is at least one of the main problems of economic policy—or of designing an efficient economic system.

The answer to this question is closely connected with that other question which arises here, that of *who* is to do the planning. It is about this question that all the dispute about "economic planning" centers. This is not a dispute about whether planning is to be done or not. It is a dispute as to whether planning is to be done centrally, by one authority for the whole economic system, or is to be divided among many individuals. Planning in the specific sense in which the term is used in contemporary controversy necessarily means central planning—direction of the whole economic system according to one unified plan. Competition, on the other hand, means decentralized planning by many separate persons. The halfway house between the two, about which many people talk but which few like when they see it, is the delegation of planning to organized industries, or, in other words, monopolies.

Which of these systems is likely to be more efficient depends mainly on the question under which of them we can expect that fuller use will be made of the existing knowledge. This, in turn, depends on whether we are more likely to succeed in putting at the disposal of a single central authority all the knowledge which ought to be used but which is initially dispersed among many different individuals, or in conveying to the individuals such additional knowledge as they need in order to enable them to dovetail their plans with those of others.

3

It will at once be evident that on this point the position will be different with respect to different kinds of knowledge. The answer to our question will therefore largely turn on the relative importance of the different kinds of knowledge: those more likely to be at the disposal of particular individuals and those which we should with greater confidence expect to find in the possession of an authority made up of suitably chosen experts. If it is today so widely assumed that the latter will be in a better position, this is because one kind of knowledge, namely, scientific knowledge, occupies now so prominent a place in public imagination that we tend to forget that it is not the only kind that is relevant. It may be admitted that, as far as scientific knowledge is concerned, a body of suitably chosen experts may be in the best position to command all the best knowledge available—

though this is of course merely shifting the difficulty to the problem of selecting the experts. What I wish to point out is that, even assuming that this problem can be readily solved, it is only a small part of the wider problem.

Today it is almost heresy to suggest that scientific knowledge is not the sum of all knowledge. But a little reflection will show that there is beyond question a body of very important but unorganized knowledge which cannot possibly be called scientific in the sense of knowledge of general rules: the knowledge of the particular circumstances of time and place. It is with respect to this that practically every individual has some advantage over all others because he possesses unique information of which beneficial use might be made, but of which use can be made only if the decisions depending on it are left to him or are made with his active co-operation. We need to remember only how much we have to learn in any occupation after we have completed our theoretical training, how big a part of our working life we spend learning particular jobs, and how valuable an asset in all walks of life is knowledge of people, of local conditions, and of special circumstances. To know of and put to use a machine not fully employed, or somebody's skill which could be better utilized, or to be aware of a surplus stock which can be drawn upon during an interruption of supplies, is socially quite as useful as the knowledge of better alternative techniques. The shipper who earns his living from using otherwise empty or half-filled journeys of tramp-steamers, or the estate agent whose whole knowledge is almost exclusively one of temporary opportunities, or the *arbitrageur* who gains from local differences of commodity prices—are all performing eminently useful functions based on special knowledge of circumstances of the fleeting moment not known to others.

It is a curious fact that this sort of knowledge should today be generally regarded with a kind of contempt and that anyone who by such knowledge gains an advantage over somebody better equipped with theoretical or technical knowledge is thought to have acted almost disreputably. To gain an advantage from better knowledge of facilities of communication or transport is sometimes regarded as almost dishonest, although it is quite as important that society make use of the best opportunities in this respect as in using the latest scientific discoveries. This prejudice has in a considerable measure affected the attitude toward commerce in general compared with that toward production. Even economists who regard themselves as definitely immune to the crude materialist fallacies of the past constantly commit the same mistake where activities directed toward the acquisition of such practical knowledge are concerned—apparently because in their scheme of things all such knowledge is supposed to be "given." The common idea now seems to be that all such knowledge should as a matter of course be readily at the command of everybody, and the reproach of irrationality leveled against the existing economic order is frequently based on the fact that it is not so available. This view disregards the fact that the method by which such knowledge can be made as widely available as possible is precisely the problem to which we have to find an answer.

4

If it is fashionable today to minimize the importance of the knowledge of the particular circumstances of time and place, this is closely connected with the smaller importance which is now attached to change as such. Indeed, there are few points on which the assumptions made (usually only implicitly) by the "planners" differ from those of their opponents as much as with regard to the significance and frequency of changes which will make substantial alterations of production plans necessary. Of course, if detailed economic plans could be laid down for fairly long periods in advance and then closely adhered to, so that no further economic decisions of importance would be required, the task of drawing up a comprehensive plan governing all economic activity would be much less formidable.

It is, perhaps, worth stressing that economic problems arise always and only in consequence of change. As long as things continue as before, or at least as they were expected to, there arise no new problems requiring a decision, no need to form a new plan. The belief that changes, or at least day-to-day adjustments, have become less important in modern times implies the contention that economic problems also have become less important. This belief in the decreasing importance of change is, for that reason, usually held by the same people who argue that the importance of economic considerations has been driven into the background by the growing importance of technological knowledge.

Is it true that, with the elaborate apparatus of modern production, economic decisions are required only at long intervals, as when a new factory is to be erected or a new process to be introduced? Is it true that, once a plant has been built, the rest is all more or less mechanical, determined by the character of the plant, and leaving little to be changed in adapting to the ever changing circumstances of the moment?

The fairly widespread belief in the affirmative is not, as far as I can ascertain, borne out by the practical experience of the businessman. In a competitive industry at any rate—and such an industry alone can serve as a test—the task of keeping cost from rising requires constant struggle, absorbing a great part of the energy of the manager. How easy it is for an inefficient manager to dissipate the differentials on which profitability rests and that it is possible, with the same technical facilities, to produce with a great variety of costs are among the commonplaces of business experience which do not seem to be equally familiar in the study of the economist. The very strength of the desire, constantly voiced by producers and engineers, to be allowed to proceed untrammeled by considerations of money costs, is eloquent testimony to the extent to which these factors enter into their daily work.

One reason why economists are increasingly apt to forget about the constant small changes which make up the whole economic picture is probably their growing preoccupation with statistical aggregates, which show a very much greater stability than the movements of the detail. The comparative stability of the aggregates cannot, however, be accounted for—as the statisticians occasionally seem to be inclined to do—by the "law of large numbers" or the mutual compensation of random changes. The number of elements with which we have to deal is not large enough for such accidental forces to produce stability. The continuous flow of goods and services is maintained by constant deliberate adjustments, by new dispositions made every day in the light of circumstances not known the day before, by B stepping

in at once when A fails to deliver. Even the large and highly mech-
anized plant keeps going largely because of an environment upon
which it can draw for all sorts of unexpected needs: tiles for its roof,
stationery for its forms, and all the thousand and one kinds of equipment in which it cannot be self-contained and which the plans for the
operation of the plant require to be readily available in the market.

This is, perhaps, also the point where I should briefly mention the
fact that the sort of knowledge with which I have been concerned is
knowledge of the kind which by its nature cannot enter into statistics
and therefore cannot be conveyed to any central authority in statistical form. The statistics which such a central authority would have to
use would have to be arrived at precisely by abstracting from minor
differences between the things, by lumping together, as resources of
one kind, items which differ as regards location, quality, and other
particulars, in a way which may be very significant for the specific
decision. It follows from this that central planning based on statistical
information by its nature cannot take direct account of these circumstances of time and place and that the central planner will have to
find some way or other in which the decisions depending on them
can be left to the "man on the spot."

5

If we can agree that the economic problem of society is mainly one of
rapid adaptation to changes in the particular circumstances of time
and place, it would seem to follow that the ultimate decisions must
be left to the people who are familiar with these circumstances, who
know directly of the relevant changes and of the resources immediately available to meet them. We cannot expect that this problem
will be solved by first communicating all this knowledge to a central
board which, after integrating all knowledge, issues its orders. We
must solve it by some form of decentralization. But this answers only
part of our problem. We need decentralization because only thus can
we insure that the knowledge of the particular circumstances of time
and place will be promptly used. But the "man on the spot" cannot
decide solely on the basis of his limited but intimate knowledge of the

facts of his immediate surroundings. There still remains the problem of communicating to him such further information as he needs to fit his decisions into the whole pattern of changes of the larger economic system.

How much knowledge does he need to do so successfully? Which of the events which happen beyond the horizon of his immediate knowledge are of relevance to his immediate decision, and how much of them need he know?

There is hardly anything that happens anywhere in the world that *might* not have an effect on the decision he ought to make. But he need not know of these events as such, nor of *all* their effects. It does not matter for him *why* at the particular moment more screws of one size than of another are wanted, *why* paper bags are more readily available than canvas bags, or *why* skilled labor, or particular machine tools, have for the moment become more difficult to obtain. All that is significant for him is *how much more or less* difficult to procure they have become compared with other things with which he is also concerned, or how much more or less urgently wanted are the alternative things he produces or uses. It is always a question of the relative importance of the particular things with which he is concerned, and the causes which alter their relative importance are of no interest to him beyond the effect on those concrete things of his own environment.

It is in this connection that what I have called the "economic calculus" (or the Pure Logic of Choice) helps us, at least by analogy, to see how this problem can be solved, and in fact is being solved, by the price system. Even the single controlling mind, in possession of all the data for some small, self-contained economic system, would not—every time some small adjustment in the allocation of resources had to be made—go explicitly through all the relations between ends and means which might possibly be affected. It is indeed the great contribution of the Pure Logic of Choice that it has demonstrated conclusively that even such a single mind could solve this kind of problem only by constructing and constantly using rates of equivalence (or "values," or "marginal rates of substitution"), that is, by attaching to each kind of scarce resource a numerical index which cannot be derived from any property possessed by that particular thing, but which reflects, or in which is condensed, its significance in view of the whole means-end structure. In any small change he will have to consider only these quantitative indices (or "values") in which all the relevant information is concentrated; and, by adjusting the quantities one by one, he can appropriately rearrange his dispositions without having to solve the whole puzzle *ab initio* or without needing at any stage to survey it at once in all its ramifications.

Fundamentally, in a system in which the knowledge of the relevant facts is dispersed among many people, prices can act to co-ordinate the separate actions of different people in the same way as subjective values help the individual to co-ordinate the parts of his plan. It is worth contemplating for a moment a very simple and commonplace instance of the action of the price system to see what precisely it accomplishes. Assume that somewhere in the world a new opportunity for the use of some raw material, say, tin, has arisen, or that one of the sources of supply of tin has been eliminated. It does not matter for our purpose—and it is significant that it does not matter—which of these two causes has made tin more scarce. All that the users of tin need to know is that some of the tin they used to consume is now more profitably employed elsewhere and that, in consequence, they must economize tin. There is no need for the great majority of them even to know where the more urgent need has arisen, or in favor of what other needs they ought to husband the supply. If only some of them know directly of the new demand, and switch resources over to it, and if the people who are aware of the new gap thus created in turn fill it from still other sources, the effect will rapidly spread throughout the whole economic system and influence not only all the uses of tin but also those of its substitutes and the substitutes of these substitutes, the supply of all the things made of tin, and their substitutes, and so on; and all this without the great majority of those instrumental in bringing about these substitutions knowing anything at all about the original cause of these changes. The whole acts as one market, not because any of its members survey the whole field, but because their limited individual fields of vision sufficiently overlap so that through many intermediaries the relevant information is communicated to all. The mere fact that there is one price for any commodity—or rather that local prices are connected in a manner determined by the cost of transport, etc.—brings about the solution which (it is just conceptually possible) might have been arrived at by one single mind possessing all the information which is in fact dispersed among all the people involved in the process.

6

We must look at the price system as such a mechanism for communicating information if we want to understand its real function—a function which, of course, it fulfils less perfectly as prices grow more rigid. (Even when quoted prices have become quite rigid, however, the forces which would operate through changes in price still operate to a considerable extent through changes in the other terms of the contract.) The most significant fact about this system is the economy of knowledge with which it operates, or how little the individual participants need to know in order to be able to take the right action. In abbreviated form, by a kind of symbol, only the most essential information is passed on and passed on only to those concerned. It is more than a metaphor to describe the price system as a kind of machinery for registering change, or a system of telecommunications which enables individual producers to watch merely the movement of a few pointers, as an engineer might watch the hands of a few dials, in order to adjust their activities to changes of which they may never know more than is reflected in the price movement.

Of course, these adjustments are probably never "perfect" in the sense in which the economist conceives of them in his equilibrium analysis. But I fear that our theoretical habit of approaching the problem with the assumption of more or less perfect knowledge on the part of almost everyone has made us somewhat blind to the true function of the price mechanism and led us to apply rather misleading standards in judging its efficiency. The marvel is that in a case like that of a scarcity of one raw material, without an order being issued, without more than perhaps a handful of people knowing the cause, tens of thousands of people whose identity could not be ascertained by months of investigation, are made to use the material or its products more sparingly; that is, they move in the right direction. This is enough of a marvel even if, in a constantly changing world, not all will hit it off so perfectly that their profit rates will always be maintained at the same even or "normal" level.

I have deliberately used the word "marvel" to shock the reader out of the complacency with which we often take the working of this mechanism for granted. I am convinced that if it were the result of deliberate human design, and if the people guided by the price changes understood that their decisions have significance far beyond their immediate aim, this mechanism would have been acclaimed as one of the greatest triumphs of the human mind. Its misfortune is the double one that it is not the product of human design and that the people guided by it usually do not know why they are made to do what they do. But those who clamor for "conscious direction"—and who cannot believe that anything which has evolved without design (and even without our understanding it) should solve problems which we should not be able to solve consciously—should remember this: The problem is precisely how to extend the span of our utilization of resources beyond the span of the control of any one mind; and, therefore, how to dispense with the need of conscious control and how to provide inducements which will make the individuals do the desirable things without anyone having to tell them what to do.

The problem which we meet here is by no means peculiar to economics but arises in connection with nearly all truly social phenomena, with language and with most of our cultural inheritance, and constitutes really the central theoretical problem of all social science. As Alfred Whitehead has said in another connection, "It is a profoundly erroneous truism, repeated by all copy-books and by eminent people when they are making speeches, that we should cultivate the habit of thinking what we are doing. The precise opposite is the case. Civilization advances by extending the number of important operations which we can perform without thinking about them." This is of profound significance in the social field. We make constant use of formulas, symbols, and rules whose meaning we do not understand and through the use of which we avail ourselves of the assistance of knowledge which individually we do not possess. We have developed these practices and institutions by building upon habits and institutions which have proved successful in their own sphere and which have in turn become the foundation of the civilization we have built up.

The price system is just one of those formations which man has learned to use (though he is still very far from having learned to make the best use of it) after he had stumbled upon it without understanding it. Through it not only a division of labor but also a co-ordinated utilization of resources based on an equally divided knowledge has become possible. The people who like to deride any suggestion that this may be so usually distort the argument by insinuating that it asserts that by some miracle just that sort of system has spontaneously grown up which is best suited to modern civilization. It is the other way round: man has been able to develop that division of labor on which our civilization is based because he happened to stumble upon a method which made it possible. Had he not done so, he might still have developed some other, altogether different, type of civilization, something like the "state" of the termite ants, or some other altogether unimaginable type. All that we can say is that nobody has yet succeeded in designing an alternative system in which certain features of the existing one can be preserved which are dear even to those who most violently assail it—such as particularly the extent to which the individual can choose his pursuits and consequently freely use his own knowledge and skill.

7

It is in many ways fortunate that the dispute about the indispensability of the price system for any rational calculation in a complex society is now no longer conducted entirely between camps holding different political views. The thesis that without the price system we could not preserve a society based on such extensive division of labor as ours was greeted with a howl of derision when it was first advanced by Von Mises [in 1920]. Today the difficulties which some still find in accepting it are no longer mainly political, and this makes for an atmosphere much more conducive to reasonable discussion. When we find Leon Trotsky arguing that "economic accounting is unthinkable without market relations"; when Professor Oscar Lange promises Professor von Mises a statue in the marble halls of the future Central Planning Board; and when Professor Abba P. Lerner rediscovers Adam Smith and emphasizes that the essential utility of the price system consists in inducing the individual, while seeking his own interest, to do what is in the general interest, the differences can indeed no longer be ascribed to political prejudice. The remaining dissent seems clearly to be due to purely intellectual, and more particularly methodological, differences.

TWO KINDS OF ORDER

Michael Polanyi

Michael Polanyi (1891–1976) was a Hungarian-born chemist and philosopher of science. He wrote a great deal on academic freedom and on science as a competitive process, in such books as *Personal Knowledge, The Study of Man,* and *Science, Faith, and Society.* In *The Logic of Liberty* (1951), from which this selection is drawn, he examined science as a spontaneous order and then broadened his analysis to include other forms of spontaneous order, including the market process.

My argument for freedom in science bears a close resemblance to the classical doctrine of economic individualism. The scientists of the world are viewed as a team setting out to explore the existing openings for discovery and it is claimed that their efforts will be efficiently co-ordinated if—and only if—each is left to follow his own inclinations. This statement is very similar to Adam Smith's claim with regard to a team of business men, drawing on the same market of productive resources for the purpose of satisfying different parts of the same system of demand. Their efforts—he said—would be co-ordinated, as by an invisible hand, to the most economical utilization of the available resources.

These two systems of maximized utility are indeed based on similar principles; and more than that: they are only two examples of a whole set of parallel cases. There is a wide range of such systems in nature exhibiting similar types of order. They have been called systems of "dynamic order" by Köhler, whose designation I followed in an earlier writing; but I think it will be simpler to refer to them as systems of *spontaneous order.*

TWO KINDS OF ORDER

Wherever we see a well-ordered arrangement of things or men, we instinctively assume that someone has intentionally placed them in that way. A well-kept garden must have been laid out; a machine working properly must have been constructed and a company on parade must have been drilled and placed under command: that is the obvious way for order to emerge. Such a method of establishing order consists in limiting the freedom of things and men to stay or move about at their pleasure, by assigning to each a specific position in a pre-arranged plan.

But there exists another, less obviously determined type of order which is based on the opposite principle. The water in a jug settles down, filling the hollow of the vessel perfectly and in even density, up to the level of a horizontal plane which forms its free surface: a perfect arrangement such as no human artifice could reproduce, should the process of gravitation and cohesion, to which it is due, refuse to function for a moment. Yet any number of such containers of varied and complex shapes, joined to a system of communicating vessels, could be filled in the same perfect and uniform way up to a common horizontal plane—merely by letting a liquid come to rest in them.

In this second type of order no constraint is applied specifically to the individual particles; the forces from outside, like the resistance of the vessels and the forces of gravitation, take effect in an entirely indiscriminate fashion. The particles are thus free to obey the internal forces acting between them, and the resultant order represents the equilibrium between all the internal and external forces. . . .

This suggests that, while it may be possible to achieve certain socially desirable forms of co-ordination in society by allowing each individual to adjust his action to that of all the others (or to some state of affairs resulting from the action of all the others) there is no warrant to assume either (1) that any particular conceivable task of co-ordination can be attained by such a technique or (2) that any particular instance of free mutual adjustment between individuals will produce a desirable result. It warns us that even the most wonderful successes achieved by such adjustment will not be free of manifest shortcomings nor represent more than a relative optimum. But it suggests, nevertheless, that such tasks as a system of free adjustment may achieve, cannot be effectively performed by any other technique of co-ordination. . . .

SYSTEMS OF SPONTANEOUS ORDER IN SOCIETY

When order is achieved among human beings by allowing them to interact with each other on their own initiative—subject only to laws which uniformly apply to all of them—we have a system of spontaneous order in society. We may then say that the efforts of these individuals are co-ordinated by exercising their individual initiative and that this self-co-ordination justifies their liberty on public grounds.

The actions of such individuals are said to be free, for they are not determined by any *specific* command, whether of a superior or of a public authority; the compulsion to which they are subject is impersonal and general. There are dozens of aspects in which these individuals are not free. They are under compulsion to earn their living, they may be exploited by their employers, bullied by their families, deluded by their own vanity, and must all die; it is not claimed that they are free in any other sense than such as is expressly stated. How far such liberty is of intrinsic value and deserves protection, even apart from its social usefulness, is a question which I leave open at this stage and shall try to clarify later.

An aggregate of individual initiatives can lead to the establishment of spontaneous order only if each takes into account in its action what the others have done in the same context before. Where large numbers are involved, such mutual adjustment must be indirect; each individual adjusts himself to a state of affairs resulting from the foregoing actions of the rest. This requires that information about the state of affairs in question should be available to each member of the aggregate; as in the case of such communal states of affairs as the condition of various markets, the current achievements of scientific progress, or the position of the law up to date. We may add that for "individuals" we may read "corporations acting as individuals". . . .

SYSTEMS OF INTELLECTUAL ORDER

Of the systems of spontaneous order which form part of the intellectual life of society I shall take first the example of Law, and in particular Common Law.

Consider a judge sitting in court and deciding a difficult case. While pondering his decision, he refers consciously to dozens of precedents and unconsciously to many more. Before him numberless other judges have sat and decided according to statute, precedent, equity and convenience, as he himself will have to decide now; his mind, while he analyses the various aspects of the case, is in constant contact with theirs. And beyond the purely legal references, he senses the entire contemporary trend of opinions, the social medium as a whole. Not until he has established all these bearings of his case and responded to them in the light of his own professional conscience, will his decision acquire force of conviction and will he be ready to declare it.

The moment this point is reached and the judgment announced, the tide starts running backwards. The addition made to the Law by the decision just taken may be massive or slight; in either case it represents an interpretation of the hitherto existing Law, reinforcing or modifying its system in some respect. It makes it appear henceforth in a somewhat new light. Public opinion too has received a new response and a new stimulus. Every new decision in court gives guidance to all future judges for their decisions of cases yet unthought of.

The operation of Common Law thus constitutes a sequence of adjustments between succeeding judges, guided by a parallel interaction between the judges and the general public. The result is the ordered growth of the Common Law, steadily re-applying and re-interpreting the same fundamental rules and expanding them thus to a system of increasing scope and consistency. Such coherence and fitness as this system possesses at any time is the direct embodiment of the wisdom with which each consecutive judicial decision is adjusted to all those made before and to any justified changes in public opinion.

Accordingly, the operations of a judicial system of case law is an instance of spontaneous order in society. But we see that it differs profoundly from the systems of production or consumption by the fact that it achieves more than temporal advantages. While an economic system of spontaneous order co-ordinates individual actions merely to serve the momentary material interest of its participants, an orderly process of judicature deposits a valid and lasting system of legal thought.

The next example of spontaneous order brings us back to the opening theme of this book, which is Science. Every scientist in search of discovery is faced with the scientific results and opinions of all other scientists up to that time, which are summed up in textbooks or—for more recent works—in current publications and public discussions. In the setting of his problem, in the way in which he pursues it and reaches his conclusions, he follows the recognized methods of science with such personal variations as he thinks fit to apply.

The scientist differs from the judge in that he is not given a case to decide, but has to select his own problem for investigation. Early in life he specializes on certain branches of science which seem to fit his inclinations, and then through the years of his apprenticeship in research he keeps looking out for some problem specially suited to his gifts, by the pursuit of which he may hope to achieve important results. Since the credit for a new discovery goes to the scientist who first publishes it, each will be eager to publish his results as soon as he feels sure of them. This induces scientists to inform their colleagues without delay of their current progress. On the other hand, sharp sanctions are in operation against premature publication, and scientists whose conclusions have proved hasty suffer a serious loss in reputation; this guards scientific opinion from being confused by a flood of erroneous claims put in circulation by too ambitious investigators. Every new claim put forward by a scientist is received with a measure of scepticism by the scientific public, and the author may find it necessary to defend his claim against possible objections. Thus every proposed addition to the body of science is subjected to a regular process of scrutiny, the arguments on both sides being given public hearing before scientific opinion decides to accept or reject the new ideas in question.

In the way a scientist, wrestling with a problem, accepts as his premise a great mass of previously established knowledge and submits to the guidance of scientific standards, while taking also into account the whole trend of current scientific opinion, he resembles a judge referring to precedent and statute and interpreting them in the light of contemporary thought. But in the way the scientist selects a new problem to which he might apply his gifts to the best advantage, and, when discovery is achieved, puts forward his claims as soon as he is certain of their validity, pressing for their acceptance by the scientific public—the scientist acts more like a business man, who first searches for a new profitable application of the resources at his disposal and then hastens to advertise and commend his products to the consumers before anyone can forestall him.

The first method of adjustment is common to judges and scientists and is a process of *consultation*. The consistent growth of law and science derives from the consultative acts by which the dynamic systems of law and science are maintained. Turning on the other hand to business men, we find few consultative contacts between them. Though commercial ideas also keep growing continuously, their cultivation is not the main function of a commercial system. Mutual adjustment between business men is primarily guided by a striving for individual advantage, and we have seen that the same applies in a modified form to some important aspects of scientific work. In both these cases we have a *competitive* adjustment which, wherever it operates, tends to maximize total production and minimize cost. While "consultation" assures the systematic growth of science, the competitive forces at work in scientific life tend to bring about the most economic use both of the intellectual power and the material resources applied to the pursuit of discovery.

But something is yet missing in this analysis. The public discussion by which scientific claims are sifted before they can be accepted as established by science, is a process of mutual adjustment which is neither consultative nor competitive. This type of adjustment is exemplified by two opposing counsel trying to win over the jury to their own side. When such a discussion goes on in wider circles, each participant adjusts his arguments to what has been said before and thus all divergent and mutually exclusive aspects of a case are in turn revealed, the public being eventually persuaded to accept one (or some) and to reject the others. The persons participating in the controversy by which this result is achieved, may be said to co-operate in a system of spontaneous order. This type of coordination resembles a competitive order in view of the part played in it by the struggle of different individuals trying to achieve mutually exclusive advantages. But in a controversy that is both sincere and fair, the participants will primarily aim at presenting the truth, relying on it to prevail over error. Therefore, I suggest that co-ordination involved in a sincere and fair controversy should be classed separately as a system of *spontaneous order based on persuasion*. The mutual co-ordination of scientific activities is thus seen to include modes of interaction of all three kinds: consultation in the first place, competition as second in importance, and persuasion as third.

Law and science are only two among the many intellectual fields in society. Though no other activities of the mind form such precise systems as those of legal and scientific thought, they all prosper similarly by the mutually adjusted efforts of individual contributors. Thus language and writing are developed by individuals communicating through them with each other. Literature and the various arts, pictorial as well as musical; the crafts, including medicine, agriculture, manufacture and the various technical services; the whole body of religious, social and political thought—all these, and many other branches of human culture, are fostered by methods of spontaneous order similar to those described for science and law. Each of these fields represents a common heritage accessible to all, to which creative individuals in each successive generation respond in the form of proposed innovations, which, if accepted, are assimilated to the common heritage and passed on for the guidance of generations yet to come. . . .

POLYCENTRICITY

In the present essay I have hitherto been concerned with extending the concept of self-co-ordination—known since Adam Smith to operate within a market—to various other activities in the intellectual field and with clarifying the relationship between the economic and intellectual systems thus brought into analogy to each other. I have shown before that a task which is achieved spontaneously by mutual adjustment cannot be performed deliberately through a corporate body. Now I want to define certain social tasks which may or may not be manageable; but which, if manageable, can only be performed by spontaneous mutual adjustment. I shall pursue this aim by enlarging upon the concept of *polycentricity*. . . .

Hitherto I have talked only of polycentric problems that can be mathematically formulated, such as are commonly presented to the engineer and also occur all over the field of science, for example as the many-body problems of astronomy and atomic physics. In a wider sense, however, we may consider every problem of balancing a large number of elements as a polycentric task. The system of postural reflexes which keep us in equilibrium while sitting, standing or walking, performs a very complex polycentric task. And from this purely animal level we may ascend continuously to the highest intellectual, moral and artistic achievements. Wisdom is defined by Kant as a man's capacity to harmonize all his purposes in life; thus wisdom aims at a polycentric task. In a painting each patch of colour should bear a significant relation to every other patch. Mozart is quoted as saying that he could simultaneously hear all the notes of an opera which he had just finished composing. All art aims at polycentric harmonies. Between the reflex reactions and the supremely creative levels there are many intermediate levels of practical intelligence, which raise similar many-sided problems. A well-assorted menu will combine dishes and wines harmoniously and a wise gastronomer will adjust his helpings of each so as to make the most of all. A doctor will prescribe a cure for a trouble of the lungs, while considering also the heart, the kidneys and the digestion as well as the income and the family conditions of the patient. All these are polycentric tasks which cannot be mathematically formulated.

The solving of polycentric tasks of this kind is a characteristic ability of living beings and of animals in particular. On the lowest levels it may be identified with the capacity for homeostasis or purposive action, while its higher forms manifest man's power of intelligent judgment. In either case the balance is achieved by an organism re-acting to the whole range of impulses that reach it from all the "cen-tres" which it jointly takes into account. The organism evaluates their joint significance, whether reflexly or consciously, and, thus guided, produces a solution of the polycentric task, or achieves, at any rate, a measure of success in this direction.

Between such polycentric tasks which are *completely unformalized* and those of the engineer which are *completely formalized,* there is an intermediate range of tasks which I shall describe as *"theoretically formalized."*

Economic tasks fall into this class. In a wider sense all polycen-tric tasks are economic, for it is of the essence of all problems to be set within certain limiting conditions and a polycentric task always aims at making the best within these limits of a number of elements available for a joint purpose. But a problem becomes more narrowly economic if the numerous "elements" are different kinds of consum-able goods or different forms of resources applied to the production of these goods, and the limitation consists in the scarcity of these re-sources and of the goods produced from them. The particular kind of wisdom, or prudence, required to deal with such situations is called "economy" in the technical sense.

First among its oft-described exemplars is the prudent housewife, spreading her expenditure over all possible purchases so as to max-imize their total utility. Each item she spends should be balanced against every other item, this in turn being balanced against every other, and so on indefinitely. This is the polycentric task of the con-sumer's choice. Robinson Crusoe has an even more complex poly-centric task to solve if he wishes to balance every item of the simple needs and pleasures which he satisfies, both against each other and against every item of effort expended on gaining these satisfactions—while each effort in its turn would have to be balanced against every other effort and against each form of satisfaction to which it contrib-utes. This defines the polycentric task of self-subsistent production.

The judgment exercised by the shopping housewife or the self-subsistent farmer in carrying out their tasks has certain features which make it suitable for mathematical formulation, which it would be useless to attempt for other fields of prudence or to artistic decisions. The goods which are consumed and the labour expended can be specified quantitatively, or may at any rate be supposed to be so specifiable, without serious distortion of the facts. This has stimulated the setting up of mathematical equations illustrating the problems facing the housewife and the self-subsistent producer. The significance of these equations is, however, quite different from that of the mathematically expressed problems of engineering or astronomy, which I have described as fully formalized. For, firstly—and obviously—housewives and farmers know nothing about the equations which are supposed to set out their problems, nor would they understand them if they knew about them. And secondly, these equations cannot be evaluated, for the substitution-coefficients which enter into them cannot be measured and the symbols referring to these are therefore without numerical significance. These equations are valuable in exhibiting certain logical features of the problem to which they refer, but cannot be used for solving these problems. They offer a mathematical model of economic decisions. If the consumer could be represented by a robot, the function of the robot could be fully specified in mathematical terms and these would satisfy equations of the kind by which economic theory describes the consumer's problem. Similarly, a mechanical Robinson Crusoe would have to satisfy the mathematical theory of the self-subsistent producer. It is in this sense that I said that the economic problems to which I have referred are *theoretically formalizable*. Their mathematical formulation is significant only in theory, not in practice.

I should mention here that the economic problem facing industrial managers can also be theoretically formalized. It consists in the maximization of profits by transforming productive resources into articles that can be sold, particularly to consumers, both the resources and the products being valued at given current prices. The mathematical formulation of managerial functions is, once more, merely a mathematical model. A modern industrial manager will use more computations (directly or indirectly) than Robinson Crusoe, but most of the "data" on which he relies can obviously not be given numerical values, or brought into mathematically specifiable relations to each other.

The major result of economic theory is to show that an aggregate of individuals, solving as Producers and Consumers the problems theoretically assigned to them, would achieve self-co-ordination as if directed by an "invisible hand." The resulting system of spontaneous order is defined as a minimum of production costs, combined with a maximum utility of distribution.

MADE ORDERS AND SPONTANEOUS ORDERS

F. A. Hayek

In this selection from his 1973 book *Law, Legislation, and Liberty,* Hayek elaborates on the two kinds of order, "made" and "grown." He suggests that the made order may be referred to as an organization, the grown order as a spontaneous order. Classical Greek had two distinct words for the two kinds of order: *taxis* and *cosmos.* The British philosopher Michael Oakeshott made a related distinction between an "enterprise association," intentionally organized to achieve some purpose, and a "civil association," which comprised all the individuals and enterprises in the society. Organizations—which may be businesses, churches, clubs, cooperatives, or something else— usually have a specific purpose and are organized to achieve it. But the whole society, the *cosmos,* has no purpose of its own. It is formed by the actions of purposive individuals and organizations. The "fatal conceit," as Hayek put it in his last book, of the "man of system" is to think that society should be organized like a single enterprise to achieve a single purpose.

The central concept around which the discussion of this book will turn is that of order, and particularly the distinction between two kinds of order which we will provisionally call "made" and "grown" orders. Order is an indispensable concept for the discussion of all complex phenomena, in which it must largely play the role the concept of law plays in the analysis of simpler phenomena. There is no adequate term other than "order" by which we can describe it, although "system," "structure" or "pattern" may occasionally serve instead. The term "order" has, of course, a long history in the social sciences, but in recent times it has generally been avoided, largely because of the ambiguity of its meaning and its frequent association with authoritarian views. We cannot do without it, however, and shall have to guard against misinterpretation by sharply defining the general sense in which we shall employ it and then clearly distinguishing between the two different ways in which such order can originate.

By "order" we shall throughout describe *a state of affairs in which a multiplicity of elements of various kinds are so related to each other that we may learn from our acquaintance with some spatial or temporal part of the whole to form correct expectations concerning the rest, or at least expectations which have a good chance of proving correct.* It is clear that every society must in this sense possess an order and that such an order will often exist without having been deliberately created. As has been said by a distinguished social anthropologist, "that there is some order, consistency and constancy in social life, is obvious. If there were not, none of us would be able to go about our affairs or satisfy our most elementary needs."

Living as members of society and dependent for the satisfaction of most of our needs on various forms of co-operation with others, we depend for the effective pursuit of our aims clearly on the correspondence of the expectations concerning the actions of others on which our plans are based with what they will really do. This matching of the intentions and expectations that determine the actions of different individuals is the form in which order manifests itself in social life; and it will be the question of how such an order does come about that will be our immediate concern. The first answer to which our anthropomorphic habits of thought almost inevitably lead us is that it must be due to the design of some thinking mind. And because order has been generally interpreted as such a deliberate *arrangement* by somebody, the concept has become unpopular among most friends of liberty and has been favoured mainly by authoritarians. According to this interpretation order in society must rest on a relation of command and obedience, or a hierarchical structure of the whole of society in which the will of superiors, and ultimately of some single supreme authority, determines what each individual must do.

This authoritarian connotation of the concept of order derives, however, entirely from the belief that order can be created only by forces outside the system (or "exogenously"). It does not apply to an equilibrium set up from within (or "endogenously") such as that which the general theory of the market endeavours to explain. A spontaneous order of this kind has in many respects properties different from those of a made order.

THE TWO SOURCES OF ORDER

The study of spontaneous orders has long been the peculiar task of economic theory, although, of course, biology has from its beginning been concerned with that special kind of spontaneous order which we call an organism. Only recently has there arisen within the physical sciences under the name of cybernetics a special discipline which is also concerned with what are called self-organizing or self-generating systems.

The distinction of this kind of order from one which has been made by somebody putting the elements of a set in their places or directing their movements is indispensable for any understanding of the processes of society as well as for all social policy. There are several terms available for describing each kind of order. The made order which we have already referred to as an exogenous order or an arrangement may again be described as a construction, an artificial order or, especially where we have to deal with a directed social order, as an *organization*. The grown order, on the other hand, which we have referred to as a self-generating or endogenous order, is in English most conveniently described as a *spontaneous order*. Classical Greek was more fortunate in possessing distinct single words for the two kinds of order, namely *taxis* for a made order, such as, for example, an order of battle, and *kosmos* for a grown order, meaning originally "a right order in a state or a community." We shall occasionally avail ourselves of these Greek words as technical terms to describe the two kinds of order.

It would be no exaggeration to say that social theory begins with—

and has an object only because of—the discovery that there exist orderly structures which are the product of the action of many men but are not the result of human design. In some fields this is now universally accepted. Although there was a time when men believed that even language and morals had been "invented" by some genius of the past, everybody recognizes now that they are the outcome of a process of evolution whose results nobody foresaw or designed. But in other fields many people still treat with suspicion the claim that the patterns of interaction of many men can show an order that is of nobody's deliberate making; in the economic sphere, in particular, critics still pour uncomprehending ridicule on Adam Smith's expression of the "invisible hand" by which, in the language of his time, he described how man is led "to promote an end which was no part of his intentions." If indignant reformers still complain of the chaos of economic affairs, insinuating a complete absence of order, this is partly because they cannot conceive of an order which is not deliberately made, and partly because to them an order means something aiming at concrete purposes which is, as we shall see, what a spontaneous order cannot do.

We shall examine later (see below, in this volume) how that coincidence of expectations and plans is produced which characterizes the market order and the nature of the benefits we derive from it. For the moment we are concerned only with the fact that an order not made by man does exist and with the reasons why this is not more readily recognized. The main reason is that such orders as that of the market do not obtrude themselves on our senses but have to be traced by our intellect. We cannot see, or otherwise intuitively perceive, this order of meaningful actions, but are only able mentally to reconstruct it by tracing the relations that exist between the elements. We shall describe this feature by saying that it is an abstract and not a concrete order.

THE DISTINGUISHING PROPERTIES OF SPONTANEOUS ORDERS

One effect of our habitually identifying order with a made order or *taxis* is indeed that we tend to ascribe to all order certain properties which deliberate arrangements regularly, and with respect to some of these properties necessarily, possess. Such orders are relatively *simple* or at least necessarily confined to such moderate degrees of complexity as the maker can still survey; they are usually *concrete* in the sense just mentioned that their existence can be intuitively perceived by inspection; and, finally, having been made deliberately, they invariably do (or at one time did) *serve a purpose* of the maker. None of these characteristics necessarily belong to a spontaneous order or *kosmos*. Its degree of complexity is not limited to what a human mind can master. Its existence need not manifest itself to our senses but may be based on purely *abstract* relations which we can only mentally reconstruct. And not having been made it cannot legitimately be said to *have a particular purpose*, although our awareness of its existence may be extremely important for our successful pursuit of a great variety of different purposes.

Spontaneous orders are not necessarily complex, but unlike deliberate human arrangements, they may achieve any degree of complexity. One of our main contentions will be that very complex orders, comprising more particular facts than any brain could ascertain or manipulate, can be brought about only through forces inducing the formation of spontaneous orders.

Spontaneous orders need not be what we have called abstract, but they will often consist of a system of abstract relations between elements which are also defined only by abstract properties, and for this reason will not be intuitively perceivable and not recognizable except on the basis of a theory accounting for their character. The significance of the abstract character of such orders rests on the fact that they may persist while all the particular elements they comprise, and even the number of such elements, change. All that is necessary to preserve such an abstract order is that a certain structure of relationships be maintained, or that elements of a certain kind (but variable in number) continue to be related in a certain manner.

Most important, however, is the relation of a spontaneous order to the conception of purpose. Since such an order has not been created by an outside agency, the order as such also can have no purpose, although its existence may be very serviceable to the individuals which move within such order. But in a different sense it may well be said that the order rests on purposive action of its elements, when "purpose" would, of course, mean nothing more than that their actions tend to secure the preservation or restoration of that order. The use of "purposive" in this sense as a sort of "teleological shorthand," as it has been called by biologists, is unobjectionable so long as we do not imply an awareness of purpose of the part of the elements, but mean merely that the elements have acquired regularities of conduct conducive to the maintenance of the order—presumably because those who did act in certain ways had within the resulting order a better chance of survival than those who did not. In general, however, it is preferable to avoid in this connection the term "purpose" and to speak instead of "function." . . .

IN SOCIETY, RELIANCE ON SPONTANEOUS ORDER
BOTH EXTENDS AND LIMITS OUR POWERS OF CONTROL

Since a spontaneous order results from the individual elements adapting themselves to circumstances which directly affect only some of them, and which in their totality need not be known to anyone, it may extend to circumstances so complex that no mind can comprehend them all. Consequently, the concept becomes particularly important when we turn from mechanical to such "more highly organized" or essentially complex phenomena as we encounter in the realms of life, mind and society. Here we have to deal with "grown" structures with a degree of complexity which they have assumed and could assume only because they were produced by spontaneous ordering forces. They in consequence present us with peculiar difficulties in our effort to explain them as well as in any attempt to influence their character. Since we can know at most the rules observed by the elements of various kinds of which the structures are made up, but not all the individual elements and never all the particular circumstances in which each of them is placed, our knowledge will be restricted to the general character of the order which will form itself. And even where, as is true of a society of human beings, we may be in a position to alter at least some of the rules of conduct which the elements obey, we shall thereby be able to influence only the general character and not the detail of the resulting order.

This means that, though the use of spontaneous ordering forces enables us to induce the formation of an order of such a degree of complexity (namely comprising elements of such numbers, diversity and variety of conditions) as we could never master intellectually, or deliberately arrange, we will have less power over the details of such an order than we would of one which we produce by arrangement. In the case of spontaneous orders we may, by determining some of the factors which shape them, determine their abstract features, but we will have to leave the particulars to circumstances which we do not know. Thus, by relying on the spontaneously ordering forces, we can extend the scope or range of the order which we may induce to form, precisely because its particular manifestation will depend on many more circumstances than can be known to us—and in the case of a social order, because such an order will utilize the separate knowledge of all its several members, without this knowledge ever being concentrated in a single mind, or being subject to those processes of deliberate coordination and adaptation which a mind performs.

In consequence, the degree of power of control over the extended and more complex order will be much smaller than that which we could exercise over a made order or *taxis*. There will be many aspects of it over which we will possess no control at all, or which at least we shall not be able to alter without interfering with—and to that extent impeding—the forces producing the spontaneous order. Any desire we may have concerning the particular position of individual elements, or the relation between particular individuals or groups, could not be satisfied without upsetting the overall order. The kind of power which in this respect we would possess over a concrete arrangement or *taxis* we would not have over a spontaneous order where we would know, and be able to influence, only the abstract aspects. . . .

THE SPONTANEOUS ORDER OF SOCIETY IS MADE UP OF INDIVIDUALS AND ORGANIZATIONS

In any group of men of more than the smallest size, collaboration will always rest both on spontaneous order as well as on deliberate organization. There is no doubt that for many limited tasks organization is the most powerful method of effective co-ordination because it enables us to adapt the resulting order much more fully to our wishes, while where, because of the complexity of the circumstances to be taken into account, we must rely on the forces making for a spontaneous order, our power over the particular contents of this order is necessarily restricted.

That the two kinds of order will regularly coexist in every society of any degree of complexity does not mean, however, that we can combine them in any manner we like. What in fact we find in all free societies is that, although groups of men will join in organizations for the achievement of some particular ends, the co-ordination of the activities of all these separate organizations, as well as of the separate individuals, is brought about by the forces making for a spontaneous order. The family, the farm, the plant, the firm, the corporation and the various associations, and all the public institutions including government, are organizations which in turn are integrated into a more comprehensive spontaneous order. It is advisable to reserve the term "society" for this spontaneous overall order so that we may distinguish it from all the organized smaller groups which will exist within it, as well as from such smaller and more or less isolated groups as the horde, the tribe, or the clan, whose members will at least in some respects act under a central direction for common purposes. In some instances it will be the same group which at times, as when engaged in most of its daily routine, will operate as a spontaneous order maintained by the observation of conventional rules without the necessity of commands, while at other times, as when hunting, migrating, or fighting, it will be acting as an organization under the directing will of a chief.

The spontaneous order which we call a society also need not have such sharp boundaries as an organization will usually possess. There will often be a nucleus, or several nuclei, of more closely related individuals occupying a central position in a more loosely connected but more extensive order. Such particular societies within the Great Society may arise as the result of spatial proximity, or of some other special circumstances which produce closer relations among their members. And different partial societies of this sort will often overlap and every individual may, in addition to being a member of the Great

Society, be a member of numerous other spontaneous sub-orders or partial societies of this sort as well as of various organizations existing within the comprehensive Great Society.

Of the organizations existing within the Great Society one which regularly occupies a very special position will be that which we call government. Although it is conceivable that the spontaneous order which we call society may exist without government, if the minimum of rules required for the formation of such an order is observed without an organized apparatus for their enforcement, in most circumstances the organization which we call government becomes indispensable in order to assure that those rules are obeyed.

This particular function of government is somewhat like that of a maintenance squad of a factory, its object being not to produce any particular services or products to be consumed by the citizens, but rather to see that the mechanism which regulates the production of those goods and services is kept in working order. The purposes for which this machinery is currently being used will be determined by those who operate its parts and in the last resort by those who buy its products.

The same organization that is charged with keeping in order an operating structure which the individuals will use for their own purposes, will, however, in addition to the task of enforcing the rules on which that order rests, usually be expected also to render other services which the spontaneous order cannot produce adequately. These two distinct functions of government are usually not clearly separated; yet, as we shall see, the distinction between the coercive functions in which government enforces rules of conduct, and its service functions in which it need merely administer resources placed at its disposal, is of fundamental importance. In the second it is one organization among many and like the others part of a spontaneous overall order, while in the first it provides an essential condition for the preservation of that overall order.

In English it is possible, and has long been usual, to discuss these two types of order in terms of the distinction between "society" and "government." There is no need in the discussion of these problems, so long as only one country is concerned, to bring in the metaphysically charged term "state." It is largely under the influence of continental and particularly Hegelian thought that in the course of the last hundred years the practice of speaking of the "state" (preferably with a capital "S"), where "government" is more appropriate and precise, has come to be widely adopted. That which acts, or pursues a policy, is however always the organization of government; and it does not make for clarity to drag in the term "state" where "government" is quite sufficient. It becomes particularly misleading when "the state" rather than "government" is contrasted with "society" to indicate that the first is an organization and the second a spontaneous order.

THE RULES OF SPONTANEOUS ORDERS
AND THE RULES OF ORGANIZATION

One of our chief contentions will be that, though spontaneous order and organization will always coexist, it is still not possible to mix these two principles of order in any manner we like. If this is not more generally understood it is due to the fact that for the determination of both kinds of order we have to rely on rules, and that the important differences between the kinds of rules which the two different kinds of order require are generally not recognized.

To some extent every organization must rely also on rules and not only on specific commands. The reason here is the same as that which makes it necessary for a spontaneous order to rely solely on rules: namely that by guiding the actions of individuals by rules rather than specific commands it is possible to make use of knowledge which nobody possesses as a whole. Every organization in which the members are not mere tools of the organizer will determine by commands only the function to be performed by each member, the purposes to be achieved, and certain general aspects of the methods to be employed, and will leave the detail to be decided by the individuals on the basis of their respective knowledge and skills.

Organization encounters here the problem which any attempt to bring order into complex human activities meets: the organizer must wish the individuals who are to co-operate to make use of knowledge that he himself does not possess. In none but the most simple kind of organization is it conceivable that all the details of all activities are governed by a single mind. Certainly nobody has yet succeeded in deliberately arranging all the activities that go on in a complex society. If anyone did ever succeed in fully organizing such a society, it would no longer make use of many minds but would be altogether dependent on one mind; it would certainly not be very complex but extremely primitive—and so would soon be the mind whose knowledge and will determined everything. The facts which could enter into the design of such an order could be only those which were known and digested by this mind; and as only he could decide on action and thus gain experience, there would be none of that interplay of many minds in which alone mind can grow.

What distinguishes the rules which will govern action within an organization is that they must be rules for the performance of assigned tasks. They presuppose that the place of each individual in a fixed structure is determined by command and that the rules each individual must obey depend on the place which he has been assigned and on the particular ends which have been indicated for him by the commanding authority. The rules will thus regulate merely the detail of the action of appointed functionaries or agencies of government.

Rules of organization are thus necessarily subsidiary to commands, filling in the gaps left by the commands. Such rules will be different for the different members of the organization according to the different roles which have been assigned to them, and they will have to be interpreted in the light of the purposes determined by the commands. Without the assignment of a function and the determination of the ends to be pursued by particular commands, the bare abstract rule would not be sufficient to tell each individual what he must do.

By contrast, the rules governing a spontaneous order must be independent of purpose and be the same, if not necessarily for all members, at least for whole classes of members not individually designated by name. They must, as we shall see, be rules applicable to an unknown and indeterminable number of persons and instances. They will have to be applied by the individuals in the light of their respective knowledge and purposes; and their application will be independent of any common purpose, which the individual need not even know.

In the terms we have adopted this means that the general rules of law that a spontaneous order rests on aim at an abstract order, the particular or concrete content of which is not known or foreseen by anyone; while the commands as well as the rules which govern an organization serve particular results aimed at by those who are in command of the organization. The more complex the order aimed at, the greater will be that part of the separate actions which will have to be determined by circumstances not known to those who direct the whole, and the more dependent control will be on rules rather than on specific commands. In the most complex types of organizations, indeed, little more than the assignment of particular functions and the general aim will be determined by command of the supreme authority, while the performance of these functions will be regulated only by rules—yet by rules which at least to some degree are specific to the functions assigned to particular persons. Only when we pass from the biggest kind of organization, government, which as organization must still be dedicated to a circumscribed and determined set of specific purposes, to the overall order of the whole of society, do we find an order which relies solely on rules and is entirely spontaneous in character.

It is because it was not dependent on organization but grew up as a spontaneous order that the structure of modern society has attained that degree of complexity which it possesses and which far exceeds any that could have been achieved by deliberate organization. In fact, of course, the rules which made the growth of this complex order possible were initially not designed in expectation of that result; but those people who happened to adopt suitable rules developed a complex civilization which then often spread to others. To maintain that we must deliberately plan modern society because it has become so complex is therefore paradoxical, and the result of a complete misunderstanding of these circumstances. The fact is, rather, that we can preserve an order of such complexity not by the method of directing the members, but only indirectly by enforcing and improving the rules conducive to the formation of a spontaneous order.

We shall see that it is impossible, not only to replace the spontaneous order by organization and at the same time to utilize as much of the dispersed knowledge of all its members as possible, but also to improve or correct this order by interfering in it by direct commands. Such a combination of spontaneous order and organization it can never be rational to adopt. While it is sensible to supplement the commands determining an organization by subsidiary rules, and to use organizations as elements of a spontaneous order, it can never be advantageous to supplement the rules governing a spontaneous order by isolated and subsidiary commands concerning those activities where the actions are guided by the general rules of conduct. This is the gist of the argument against "interference" or "intervention" in the market order. The reason why such isolated commands requiring specific actions by members of the spontaneous order can never improve but must disrupt that order is that they will refer to a part of a system of interdependent actions determined by information and guided by purposes known only to the several acting persons but not to the directing authority. The spontaneous order arises from each element balancing all the various factors operating on it and by adjusting all its various actions to each other, a balance which will be destroyed if some of the actions are determined by another agency on the basis of different knowledge and in the service of different ends.

What the general argument against "interference" thus amounts to is that, although we can endeavour to improve a spontaneous order by revising the general rules on which it rests, and can supplement its results by the efforts of various organizations, we cannot improve the results by specific commands that deprive its members of the possibility of using their knowledge for their purposes.

We will have to consider throughout this book how these two kinds of rules have provided the model for two altogether different conceptions of law and how this has brought it about that authors using the same word "law" have in fact been speaking about different things. This comes out most clearly in the contrast we find throughout history between those to whom law and liberty were inseparable and those to whom the two were irreconcilable. We find one great tradition extending from the ancient Greeks and Cicero through the Middle Ages to the classical liberals like John Locke, David Hume, Immanuel Kant and the Scottish moral philosophers, down to various American statesmen of the nineteenth and twentieth centuries, for whom law and liberty could not exist apart from each other; while to Thomas Hobbes, Jeremy Bentham and many French thinkers and the modern legal positivists law of necessity means an encroachment on freedom. This apparent conflict between long lines of great thinkers does not mean that they arrived at opposite conclusions, but merely that they were using the word "law" in different senses.

ECONOMY AS ECOSYSTEM

Michael Rothschild

The economist William A. Niskanen, former member of the President's Council of Economic Advisers and later chairman of the Cato Institute, had three portraits on his wall: of Isaac Newton, Adam Smith, and Charles Darwin. Under each portrait was the legend "Order without Direction." But Michael Rothschild argues that economists went wrong by borrowing mechanical concepts from Newtonian physics rather than evolutionary thought from Darwinian biology. Darwin's theories of evolution and natural selection were influenced by his reading of Adam Smith and other classical economists, but later economists didn't appreciate the connection. Rothschild, a business consultant who founded the Bionomics Institute, argues in *Bionomics: The Inevitability of Capitalism* that information—genetic or economic—is the basis of both the environment and the market. Although Rothschild was not familiar with the work of Hayek and other "Austrian School" economists, his analysis is quite complementary to theirs.

Every organism is defined by the information in its genes, but a living thing also is defined by its relationships to its prey, competitors, and predators. In the same way, an organization is defined by its technology and by its associations with its suppliers, competitors, and customers. From a bionomic perspective, organisms and organizations are nodes in networks of relationships. As time passes and evolution proceeds, some nodes are wiped out and new ones crop up, triggering adjustments that ripple across each network. Constrained by its key relationships, each organism and each organization is held in its niche, pursuing the same goal—the survival of the genetic or technological information it carries.

In the ecosystem, resources flow up the food chain. Sunlight powers the entire system. Energy flows from plants to herbivores to predators. Completing the materials cycle, bacteria break down dead tissues and excrete chemical wastes that become nutrients for plants.

In the economy, resources flow up the value-added chain from mines and farms to fabricators, assemblers, and service firms. Human work powers the system. The economy's end products are used up by individual consumers. And, now that our awareness of environmental destruction finally is maturing, consumer wastes are beginning to be recycled to the bottom of the value-added chain.

Although ecosystems and economies share a basic architecture, several subtle differences distinguish these living networks. To comprehend fully their profound similarity, it is necessary to understand their superficial differences. For instance, ecologists define an organism's "niche"—its profession in the economy of nature—by cataloging the resources it consumes from the level *below* it in the food web. By contrast, when businesspeople speak of a company's "niche," they refer to its market position, its links to customers *above* it in the value-added web.

The inverted usages of the term *niche* stem from the basic difference between an ecosystem and an economy. In nature, the population of a species is constrained primarily by the availability of resources. Without sunlight, there are no plankton. Without plankton, there are no fish. The abundance of life at each level in a food web depends upon the "carrying capacity" of the resources immediately below. Ecosystems are "resource-limited" networks. Defining a species' niche—how it copes with scarcity—is the key to understanding its role in the ecosystem.

By contrast, an industry's size is limited by customer demand, not the availability of resources. Under capitalism, firms die for lack of paying customers, not for lack of supplies. Without demand for air travel, airlines cannot survive. Without demand from airlines, aircraft assemblers shut down. Without aircraft makers, avionics makers and engine builders vanish. At each level in a value-added web, organizational survival depends upon the layer of customers just above.

Limited resource supply restrains the growth of a species' population just as limited consumer demand holds back an industry's expansion. In this sense, economies are "consumer-limited" networks. The ecologist's "carrying capacity" is the businessperson's "market size." Describing an industry's niche—how it taps into limited consumer demand—is the key to understanding its role in the economy. Even though their uses of *niche* seem inverted, both ecologists and businesspeople apply the term to the growth-limiting factor.

At a deeper level, the contrast between these "resource-limited" and "consumer-limited" networks stems from a very basic difference between organisms and organizations. Organisms cannot live forever. They must produce offspring that survive long enough to yield their own progeny. When a predator kills a prey organism, it diminishes the survival prospects of the prey species' DNA. A fox cannot eat a rabbit without destroying the rabbit's reproductive capacity. To preserve the genetic code residing in its cells, a rabbit must avoid foxes until it has reproduced. As far as any rabbit is concerned, the world has far too many foxes.

Organizations face exactly the reverse situation. Since firms do not have finite lifespans, they can maintain their technology in perpetuity. Firms need not produce offspring capable of reproducing. Instead of generating baby organizations, companies convert resources into products. A company's technology shapes its product's features just as parents' genes determine their child's characteristics. But unlike offspring, which contain the genes needed to make more organisms, products cannot make more products. Products reflect the technological "genes" that shaped them, but they do not hold the information needed to produce more copies. Products are like the shells abandoned by molting crabs—shaped by the genes, but not alive.

Technology stays within the organization. Aircraft makers sell jetliners, not blueprints, to their airline customers. By applying its special expertise to purchased components, the aircraft maker adds real value to its resources. Under normal conditions, the amount the aircraft maker receives for a jetliner exceeds the cost of the resources used in its production. By reinvesting its profits in more technology, the aircraft builder improves its chances of long-term survival. In short, where a rabbit's survival is threatened by too many potential consumers, an aircraft maker's survival is threatened by too few.

Since the "motivations" of the players in these "resource-limited" and "consumer-limited" networks are inverted, it makes sense for organisms and organizations to practice contrary survival techniques. For instance, many species use camouflage to hide from their consumers. Some butterfly pupae imitate inedible objects, such as leaves and bird droppings. The colorations of moths and lizards often match the bark of the trees they inhabit. First-time visitors to rain forests often complain about an apparent scarcity of animal and insect life. In reality, creatures are abundant, but, given the intensity of rain-forest competition, their camouflage has evolved to such perfection that many species are all but invisible.

Following the opposite strategy, companies devote enormous resources to attracting consumers. Advertising, packaging, public relations, and all other forms of marketing—so often criticized as evidence of capitalism's pointless excess—are natural consequences of a "consumer-limited" system. Just as camouflage is essential to survival in a fiercely competitive ecosystem, grabbing the customers' attention is crucial in a vigorously competitive economy. In major urban centers—the "rain forests" of the global economy—competition is so severe that advertising reaches levels of sophistication not required in less crowded areas. . . .

The cacophony of choice in America's supermarkets strikes many observers as proof that capitalism has run amok. But, as demonstrated by the Soviets, the result of the alternative approach—where central planning stamps out both competition and diversity—has proved to be far worse—namely, nothing at all on the shelves. Along with incessant and obnoxious advertising, mind-numbing product variety is an inevitable consequence of vigorous competition in an immense consumer market.

Most Americans could probably live just as happily with fewer brands of breakfast cereal. But, obviously, somebody out there is paying good money for the stuff. No one is forcing supermarkets to carry Fruity Yummy Mummy. The products in the nation's supermarkets are the current winners in a never-ending struggle for shelf-space and market share. More than 80 percent of all new supermarket products don't even last a year. As in nature, the overwhelming majority of mutants do not find a niche and die a quick death.

Despite the economic efficiency of spontaneous market action, if the prime benefit of a competitive economy comes down to the freedom to choose between waxed and unwaxed dental floss, reasonable people might well question whether it's all worth the effort. But the creation of diverse choices is not merely a matter of fashioning gimmicks to satisfy consumer tastes. The proliferation of options pervades every aspect of economic life, including those of great social significance.

Like an amoeba, the economy is bound on all sides by its cost frontiers. Along each frontier, the competitive frenzy never lets up. In information, transportation, food, clothing, housing, health, energy, finance, and all the other economic sectors, firms differentiate their products to avoid head-on confrontation. Competition and innovation keep poking holes in and pushing back the cost frontiers, allowing the economy to extend itself into previously uninhabited regions. This is the source of economic expansion.

The daily events of the struggle are chaotic, messy, and unpredictable. The people involved are haunted by the risks and the unknowns. But beneath the economy's turbulent surface, competition compels an inexorable trend toward higher output at lower cost. By specializing, by concentrating their experience on a narrow set of problems, firms keep learning to squeeze more value from less resource.

In both ecosystem and economy, survival rewards efficiency. Inefficiency is punished by extinction. Attempting to escape scarcity, species as well as industries fragment into ever more-specialized offshoots. By adapting to the peculiarities of their niches, ecologic and economic life forms become more efficient at making offspring and products. Lacking any grand design other than the urge to escape threats to their continued existence, genes and technology spontaneously weave living webs of ever more-intricate filigree. The future details of these stunningly complex systems are unknowable, but their basic architecture and historical direction are quite clear and similar.

Ever since Darwin, the similarity of natural selection and economic competition has been obvious. But, until quite recently, it was impossible to develop a meaningful comparison. After all, the great bulk of thorough ecological research is a product of the last thirty years. Since no one knew the facts of ecologic competition, any attempt to draw a compelling comparison to economic competition was futile.

Beyond this, even if the biological knowledge had existed long ago, the hidden patterns of business competition were not well understood until recently. Prior to the widespread use of computers, precise data on market shares, costs, prices, and other key variables simply was not available. Even in the largest corporations, critical decisions were based on "seat-of-the-pants" intuition rather than rigorous competitive analysis.

Computers not only made analysis possible, they also radically accelerated the pace of business evolution. Industry life cycles and competitive scenarios that once stretched over decades now unfold in months or years. Together, time compression and accessible data revealed the underlying patterns of economic competition. Today, the study of competitive dynamics is standard fare in business schools. But, ironically, the professors never mention that nature has been playing by the same rules for eons.

PART FIVE

FREE MARKETS AND VOLUNTARY ORDER

Libertarianism is often closely identified with advocacy of free markets. That perception is entirely valid, but it may be overemphasized. The point of libertarianism is not so much to defend market relations per se—and certainly not capitalist forms of organization—as to defend individual freedom, civil society, and spontaneous order. The free market is the economic system that exists when individuals are allowed to acquire property and exchange it, subject only to the requirement that they not violate the rights of others. Markets are also the necessary form of order if human beings are to be able to cooperate to achieve complex purposes.

People often divide American organizations into three sectors: public, private, and nonprofit (or "independent"). Another division may be more fundamental: forced or free. There are essentially only two kinds of organizations, those that involve coercion and those that are entirely voluntary. The voluntary sector includes for-profit firms, clubs, churches and synagogues, and charitable organizations. All of these differ from government in one crucial way: They may not acquire resources or implement plans through coercion.

Analysis of markets is thus just the study of one form of voluntary order, that part in which people seek to achieve their own ends by cooperating and exchanging with others. Economists have played an important role in the development of libertarian thought because they have studied the spontaneous order of the market based on voluntary cooperation more carefully than other social scientists.

The fundamental problem that economists seek to solve is coordination. At the simplest level they ask, How does a city get fed? If the people of Philadelphia produce neither food nor beer nor televisions, how is it all those things are readily available to them? The process works so smoothly that we assume someone with a very powerful computer must plan it. The reality, of course, is that no one plans it, and that when someone *tries* to plan economic coordination, the result is discoordination and disaster.

Each individual plans for himself, of course, and business firms certainly plan their production processes. Why, then, a *New York Times* editorial asked in 1975, "is planning considered a good thing for individuals and business but a bad thing for the national economy?" The answer lies in the distinction between two types of organizations outlined by Hayek and Polanyi. Enterprises or associations plan because they are organized to achieve a single purpose and want to use their resources more effectively to achieve that purpose. A society doesn't have a single purpose; it is composed of thousands or millions of individuals, each with his or her own purpose. The attempt to produce a single plan would necessarily mean elevating some people's purposes over others. It would also mean a much reduced level of overall output, since the competitive market makes the best use of all the dispersed bits of knowledge that people in society have—about their own plans and values and local circumstances.

Some governments have produced impressive documents labeled "national production plans" that are in fact just summaries of the plans of all the businesses in society. Polanyi compares such "plans" to a manager of a chess team saying, "The plan of my team is to advance 45 pawns by one place, move 20 bishops by an average of three places, 15 castles by an average of four places, etc." It may be called a plan, but it is really "a nonsensical summary of an aggregate of plans."

Although the Spanish Scholastics, the French Physiocrats, and others had earlier made important advances in economic theory, Adam Smith is usually regarded as the founder of modern economic science, with his 1776 book *The Wealth of Nations*. Smith started out by explaining the importance of the division of labor—not just the greater production that it makes possible but the fact that it is essential to the development of a complex society. He went on to demonstrate the benefits of free international trade, an analysis that protectionists have tried unsuccessfully to rebut for more than two centuries. Smith called the market order "the simple system of natural liberty." Modern libertarians have similarly said that "capitalism is what happens when you let people alone."

Frédéric Bastiat was a great popularizer of the ideas of Smith and the French economists. One of his important essays stressed a fundamental issue in economic analysis: the difference between "what is seen and what is not seen." What is seen, he said, is the immediate effect of any expenditure, especially a government expenditure; what is often not seen is the opportunity cost—the money the taxpayer could not spend on his own purposes, for instance, because it was taxed away for some other purpose.

In 1922 Ludwig von Mises published a massive critique of the impracticability of socialism—its inability to solve the problem of "economic calculation" in the absence of property rights and prices. Had this reader appeared before the demise of Soviet communism, it would have included excerpts from *Socialism*. Today, however, with full-fledged socialism largely a matter of purely historical interest, it is Mises's critique of interventionism that is more relevant. In many of his writings Mises examined how one intervention into the smooth functioning of the market process creates problems that seem to require more intervention, generating a process of more and more government domination of the economy.

Hayek made some important contributions to economic theory in such books as *The Pure Theory of Capital* and *Prices and Production*. In most of his work, however, he examined the market as one kind of spontaneous order. In the excerpt here from *Law, Legislation, and Liberty*, he argues that the word "economy" can confuse our understanding of the market process: It is derived from the Greek for "household management" and can be used to mean a single household or firm but has also come to mean a national economy. But since there is strictly speaking no national economy but only a network of enterprises, Hayek suggests that we call the market order a "catallaxy," from a Greek verb meaning not only "to exchange" but "to welcome into the community" and "to change from enemy into friend."

Milton Friedman examines a noneconomic benefit of the market process: protecting individual freedom and civil liberty by limiting the role of the state and providing alternative sources of wealth and influence in society. Although we sometimes see basically capitalist countries with little political freedom, we never see a socialist country that is politically free. Under socialism, every action requires the approval of government: What central planner would allocate newsprint or television time to critics of the government? A pluralist society with strict protections for private property means that many people have the ability to advance ideas.

The demise of communism has taken the luster off the idea of economic planning. Although social engineers still advance planning schemes, they never call them planning but come up with terms such as industrial policy, economic democracy, or competitiveness policy. These days the most important argument for interference with the free-market order is redistribution of income through the welfare state. Bertrand de Jouvenel offers a perspective on the problems with the welfare state. De Jouvenel warns that redistribution usually involves "a redistribution of power from the individual to the State."

Since the Industrial Revolution, the impressive economic growth produced in market economies has encouraged the spread of markets around the world. Today it seems that the entire world is finally being brought into the global marketplace. But some countries' rulers—and some intellectuals—still resist the requirements of economic growth. They seek growth without pluralism, competition, and freedom of enterprise. David Ramsay Steele, the author of *From Marx to Mises*, wrote in 1979 about the first stirrings of capitalism in China. He cited a writer in the official *Beijing Review* who argued that China need not adopt free-market institutions in order to achieve a modern economy. "We should do better than the Japanese," the Chinese analyst wrote. "They have learnt from the United States not only computer science but striptease. For us it is a matter of acquiring the best of the developed capitalist countries while rejecting their philosophy." Steele responded:

> Visitors from less-developed countries have the habit of making out a mental shopping list of social institutions. . . . However, social institutions are not toy balloons. There can be no advanced industry without a market for factors of production. . . . Scientific and technological innovation cannot long flourish without the

sardonic, rational-critical, what's-it-really-worth way of thinking spilling over into every department of life.... The unplanned catallactic process known as the market ... is inconsistent with political regimentation of society into one lifestyle or way of thinking....

You play the game of catallaxy, or you do not play it. If you do not play it, you remain wretched. But if you play it, *you must play it*. You want computer science? Then you have to put up with striptease.

Free markets are the economic system of free people. That can be a frightening prospect for ruling elites, but it should be an inspiring vision for those who have no vested interest in the status quo.

THE DIVISION OF LABOR

Adam Smith

Adam Smith's 1776 book, *An Inquiry into the Nature and Causes of the Wealth of Nations,* is generally regarded as the foundation of modern economics. In these opening pages of the book Smith began by exploring the significance of the division of labor, going immediately to his famous example of a pin factory in which specialization allows a group of people to produce far more pins cooperatively than they could as individuals.

The greatest improvement in the productive powers of labour, and the greater part of the skill, dexterity, and judgment with which it is any where directed, or applied, seem to have been the effects of the division of labour.

The effects of the division of labour, in the general business of society, will be more easily understood, by considering in what manner it operates in some particular manufactures. It is commonly supposed to be carried furthest in some very trifling ones; not perhaps that it really is carried further in them than in others of more importance: but in those trifling manufactures which are destined to supply the small wants of but a small number of people, the whole number of workmen must necessarily be small; and those employed in every different branch of the work can often be collected into the same workhouse, and placed at once under the view of the spectator. In those great manufactures, on the contrary, which are destined to supply the great wants of the great body of the people, every different branch of the work employs so great a number of workmen, that it is impossible to collect them all into the same workhouse. We can seldom see more, at one time, than those employed in one single branch. Though in such manufactures, therefore, the work may really be divided into a much greater number of parts, than in those of a more trifling nature, the division is not near so obvious, and has accordingly been much less observed.

To take an example, therefore, from a very trifling manufacture; but one in which the division of labour has been very often taken notice of, the trade of the pin-maker; a workman not educated to this business (which the division of labour has rendered a distinct trade), nor acquainted with the use of the machinery employed in it (to the invention of which the same division of labour has probably given occasion), could scarce, perhaps, with his utmost industry, make one pin in a day, and certainly could not make twenty. But in the way in which this business is now carried on, not only the whole work is a peculiar trade, but it is divided into a number of branches, of which the greater part are likewise peculiar trades. One man draws out the wire, another straights it, a third cuts it, a fourth points it, a fifth grinds it at the top for receiving the head; to make the head requires two or three distinct operations; to put it on, is a peculiar business, to whiten the pins is another; it is even a trade by itself to put them into the paper; and the important business of making a pin is, in this manner, divided into about eighteen distinct operations, which, in some manufactories, are all performed by distinct hands, though in others the same man will sometimes perform two or three of them. I have seen a small manufactory of this kind where ten men only were employed, and where some of them consequently performed two or three distinct operations. But though they were very poor, and therefore but indifferently accommodated with the necessary machinery, they could, when they exerted themselves, make among them about twelve pounds of pins in a day. There are in a pound upwards of four thousand pins of a middling size. Those ten persons, therefore, could make among them upwards of forty-eight thousand pins in a day. Each person, therefore, making a tenth part of forty-eight thousand pins, might be considered as making four thousand eight hundred pins in a day. But if they had all wrought separately and independently, and without any of them having been educated to this peculiar business, they certainly could not each of them have made twenty, perhaps not one pin in a day; that is, certainly, not the two hundred and fortieth, perhaps not the four thousand eight hundredth part of what they are at present capable of performing, in consequence of a proper division and combination of their different operations.

In every other art and manufacture, the effects of the division of labour are similar to what they are in this very trifling one; though, in many of them, the labour can neither be so much subdivided, nor reduced to so great a simplicity of operation. The division of labour, however, so far as it can be introduced, occasions, in every art, a proportionable increase of the productive powers of labour. The separation of different trades and employments from one another, seems to have taken place, in consequence of this advantage. This separation too is generally carried furthest in those countries which enjoy the highest degree of industry and improvement; what is the work of one man in a rude state of society, being generally that of several in an improved one. . . .

This great increase of the quantity of work, which, in consequence of the division of labour, the same number of people are capable of performing, is owing to three different circumstances; first, to the increase of dexterity in every particular workman; secondly, to the saving of the time which is commonly lost in passing from one species of work to another; and lastly, to the invention of a great number of machines which facilitate and abridge labour, and enable one man to do the work of many. . . .

It is the great multiplication of the productions of all the different arts, in consequence of the division of labour, which occasions, in a well-governed society, that universal opulence which extends itself to the lowest ranks of the people. Every workman has a great quantity of his own work to dispose of beyond what he himself has occasion for; and every other workman being exactly in the same situation, he is enabled to exchange a great quantity of his own goods for a great quantity, or, what comes to the same thing, for the price of a great quantity of theirs. He supplies them abundantly with what they have occasion for, and they accommodate him as amply with what he has occasion for, and a general plenty diffuses itself through all the different ranks of the society.

SOCIETY AND SELF-INTEREST

Adam Smith

This selection contains Smith's widely quoted statement that "it is not from the benevolence of the butcher, the brewer, or the baker, that we expect our dinner, but from their regard to their own interest." But note that only a few sentences above Smith points out that "man has almost constant occasion for the help of his brethren." Each person's regard for his own interest is what impels us to cooperate through the market with more people than we could ever befriend.

––––––––––

This division of labour, from which so many advantages are derived, is not originally the effect of any human wisdom, which foresees and intends that general opulence to which it gives occasion. It is the necessary, though very slow and gradual, consequence of a certain propensity in human nature which has in view no such extensive utility; the propensity to truck, barter, and exchange one thing for another. . . .

In civilized society [man] stands at all times in need of the co-operation and assistance of great multitudes, while his whole life is scarce sufficient to gain the friendship of a few persons. In almost every other race of animals each individual, when it is grown up to maturity, is entirely independent, and in its natural state has occasion for the assistance of no other living creature. But man has almost constant occasion for the help of his brethren, and it is in vain for him to expect it from their benevolence only. He will be more likely to prevail if he can interest their self-love in his favour, and shew them that it is for their own advantage to do for him what he requires of them. Whoever offers to another a bargain of any kind, proposes to do this. Give me that which I want, and you shall have this which you want, is the meaning of every such offer; and it is in this manner that we obtain from one another the far greater part of those good offices which we stand in need of. It is not from the benevolence of the butcher, the brewer, or the baker, that we expect our dinner, but from their regard to their own interest. We address ourselves, not to their humanity but to their self-love, and never talk to them of our own necessities but of their advantages. Nobody but a beggar chuses to depend chiefly upon the benevolence of his fellow-citizens. Even a beggar does not depend upon it entirely. The charity of well-disposed people, indeed, supplies him with the whole fund of his subsistence. But though this principle ultimately provides him with all the nec-essaries of life which he has occasion for, it neither does nor can provide him with them as he has occasion for them. The greater part of his occasional wants are supplied in the same manner as those of other people, by treaty, by barter, and by purchase.

LABOR AND COMMERCE

Adam Smith

In these paragraphs Smith advances his labor theory of value, which ultimately proved a dead end for economics and was replaced by the subjective theory of value. He offers a skeptical view of businessmen and their attempt to conspire to raise prices. Note that Smith does *not* suggest that such attempts are likely to be successful in the absence of government help.

———————

As it is the power of exchanging that gives occasion to the division of labour, so the extent of this division must always be limited by the extent of that power, or, in other words, by the extent of the market. When the market is very small, no person can have any encouragement to dedicate himself entirely to one employment, for want of the power to exchange all that surplus part of the produce of his own labour, which is over and above his own consumption, for such parts of the produce of other men's labour as he has occasion for. . . .

Every man is rich or poor according to the degree in which he can afford to enjoy the necessaries, conveniencies, and amusements of human life. But after the division of labour has once thoroughly taken place, it is but a very small part of these with which a man's own labour can supply him. The far greater part of them he must derive from the labour of other people, and he must be rich or poor according to the quantity of that labour which he can command, or which he can afford to purchase. The value of any commodity, therefore, to the person who possesses it, and who means not to use or consume it himself, but to exchange it for other commodities, is equal to the quantity of labour which it enables him to purchase or command. Labour, therefore, is the real measure of the exchangeable value of all commodities.

The real price of every thing, what every thing really costs to the man who wants to acquire it, is the toil and trouble of acquiring it. What every thing is really worth to the man who has acquired it, and who wants to dispose of it or exchange it for something else, is the toil and trouble which it can save to himself.

People of the same trade seldom meet together, even for merriment and diversion, but the conversation ends in a conspiracy against the public, or in some contrivance to raise prices. It is impossible indeed to prevent such meetings, by any law which either could be executed, or would be consistent with liberty and justice. But though the law cannot hinder people of the same trade from sometimes assembling together, it ought to do nothing to facilitate such assemblies; much less to render them necessary.

FREE TRADE

Adam Smith

Since the publication of *The Wealth of Nations,* there has been
no intellectually respectable defense of protectionist trade
policies, though special interests have kept protectionism alive
until the present day. In these excerpts, Smith makes several
key points: that people working for their own gain are led, as if
"by an invisible hand," to promote the public good; that "nothing can be more absurd than this whole notion of the balance
of trade," since voluntary trade is always advantageous to both
sides; and that nations prosper when their trading partners
prosper.

———————

Every individual who employs his capital in the support of domestic
industry, necessarily endeavours so to direct that industry, that its
produce may be of the greatest possible value.

The produce of industry is what it adds to the subject or materials
upon which it is employed. In proportion as the value of this produce
is great or small, so will likewise be the profits of the employer. But
it is only for the sake of profit that any man employs a capital in the
support of industry; and he will always, therefore, endeavour to employ it in the support of that industry of which the produce is likely
to be of the greatest value, or to exchange for the greatest quantity
either of money or of other goods.

But the annual revenue of every society is always precisely equal to
the exchangeable value of the whole annual produce of its industry,

or rather is precisely the same thing with that exchangeable value. As every individual, therefore, endeavours as much as he can both to employ his capital in the support of domestic industry, and so to direct that industry that its produce may be of the greatest value; every individual necessarily labours to render the annual revenue of the society as great as he can. He generally, indeed, neither intends to promote the public interest, nor knows how much he is promoting it. By preferring the support of domestic to that of foreign industry, he intends only his own security; and by directing that industry in such a manner as its produce may be of the greatest value, he intends only his own gain, and he is in this, as in many other cases, led by an invisible hand to promote an end which was no part of his intention. Nor is it always the worse for the society that it was no part of it. By pursuing his own interest he frequently promotes that of the society more effectually than when he really intends to promote it. I have never known much good done by those who affected to trade for the public good. It is an affectation, indeed, not very common among merchants, and very few words need be employed in dissuading them from it.

What is the species of domestic industry which his capital can employ, and of which the produce is likely to be of the greatest value, every individual, it is evident, can, in his local situation, judge much better than any statesman or lawgiver can do for him. The statesman, who should attempt to direct private people in what manner they ought to employ their capitals, would not only load himself with a most unnecessary attention, but assume an authority which could safely be trusted, not only to no single person, but to no council or senate whatever, and which would nowhere be so dangerous as in the hands of a man who had folly and presumption enough to fancy himself fit to exercise it. . . .

The interest of a nation in its commercial relations to foreign nations is, like that of a merchant with regard to the different people with whom he deals, to buy as cheap and to sell as dear as possible. But it will be most likely to buy cheap, when by the most perfect freedom of trade it encourages all nations to bring to it the goods which it has occasion to purchase; and, for the same reason, it will be most likely to sell dear, when its markets are thus filled with the greatest number of buyers.

In the foregoing Part of this Chapter I have endeavoured to shew, even upon the principles of the commercial system, how unnecessary it is to lay extraordinary restraints upon the importation of goods from those countries with which the balance of trade is supposed to be disadvantageous.

Nothing, however, can be more absurd than this whole doctrine of the balance of trade, upon which, not only these restraints, but almost all the other regulations of commerce are founded. When two places trade with one another, this doctrine supposes that, if the balance be even, neither of them either loses or gains; but if it leans in any degree to one side, that one of them loses, and the other gains in proportion to its declension from the exact equilibrium. Both suppositions are false. A trade which is forced by means of bounties and monopolies, may be, and commonly is disadvantageous to the country in whose favour it is meant to be established, as I shall endeavour to shew hereafter. But that trade which, without force or constraint, is naturally and regularly carried on between any two places, is always advantageous, though not always equally so, to both. . . .

By such maxims as these, however, nations have been taught that their interest consisted in beggaring all their neighbours. Each nation has been made to look with an invidious eye upon the prosperity of all the nations with which it trades, and to consider their gain as its own loss. Commerce, which ought naturally to be, among nations, as among individuals, a bond of union and friendship, has become the most fertile source of discord and animosity. The capricious ambition of kings and ministers has not, during the present and the preceding century, been more fatal to the repose of Europe, than the impertinent jealousy of merchants and manufacturers. The violence and injustice of the rulers of mankind is an ancient evil, for which, I am afraid, the nature of human affairs can scarce admit of a remedy. But the mean rapacity, the monopolizing spirit of merchants and manufacturers, who neither are, nor ought to be, the rulers of mankind, though it cannot perhaps be corrected, may very easily be prevented from disturbing the tranquility of any body but themselves.

That it was the spirit of monopoly which originally both invented and propagated this doctrine, cannot be doubted; and they who first taught it were by no means such fools as they who believed it. In every country it always is and must be the interest of the great body of the people to buy whatever they want of those who sell it cheapest. The proposition is so very manifest, that it seems ridiculous to take any pains to prove it; nor could it ever have been called in question, had not the interested sophistry of merchants and manufacturers confounded the common sense of mankind. Their interest is, in this respect, directly opposite to that of the great body of the people.

The wealth of a neighbouring nation, however, though dangerous in war and politics, is certainly advantageous in trade. In a state of hostility it may enable our enemies to maintain fleets and armies superior to our own; but in a state of peace and commerce it must likewise enable them to exchange with us to a greater value, and to afford a better market, either for the immediate produce of our own industry, or for whatever is purchased with that produce. As a rich man is likely to be a better customer to the industrious people in his neighbourhood, than a poor, so is likewise a rich nation.

THE SIMPLE SYSTEM OF NATURAL LIBERTY

Adam Smith

In this very brief selection we find Smith's famous description of the free-enterprise system as "the obvious and simple system of natural liberty." He also identifies three functions of government in a system of natural liberty: protecting the society from invasion, protecting each member of society from injustice by others, and undertaking public works that individuals could not profitably do. Many later libertarians would argue that Smith's third function for government reflected a failure to apply his own principles, that the market process can produce any "public" work that is actually worth its cost.

It is thus that every system which endeavours, either, by extraordinary encouragements, to draw towards a particular species of industry a greater share of the capital of the society than what would naturally go to it; or, by extraordinary restraints, to force from a particular species of industry some share of the capital which would otherwise be employed in it; is in reality subversive of the great purpose which it means to promote. It retards, instead of accelerating, the progress of the society towards real wealth and greatness; and diminishes, instead of increasing, the real value of the annual produce of its land and labour.

All systems either of preference or of restraint, therefore, being thus completely taken away, the obvious and simple system of natural liberty establishes itself of its own accord. Every man, as long as he does not violate the laws of justice, is left perfectly free to pursue his own interest his own way, and to bring both his industry and capital into competition with those of any other man, or order of men. The sovereign is completely discharged from a duty, in the attempting to perform which he must always be exposed to innumerable delusions, and for the proper performance of which no human wisdom or knowledge could ever be sufficient; the duty of superintending the industry of private people, and of directing it towards the employments most suitable to the interest of the society. According to the system of natural liberty, the sovereign has only three duties to attend to; three duties of great importance, indeed, but plain and intelligible to common understandings: first, the duty of protecting the society from the violence and invasion of other independent societies; secondly, the duty of protecting, as far as possible, every member of the society from the injustice of oppression of every other member of it, or the duty of establishing an exact administration of justice; and, thirdly, the duty of erecting and maintaining certain public works and certain public institutions, which it can never be for the interest of any individual, or small number of individuals, to erect and maintain; because the profit could never repay the expence to any individual or small number of individuals, though it may frequently do much more than repay it to a great society.

WHAT IS SEEN AND WHAT IS NOT SEEN

Frédéric Bastiat

Joseph Schumpeter called Frédéric Bastiat (1801–50) "the most brilliant economic journalist who ever lived." His essays sparkle with wit and a passion for liberty. In "The Law," he denounced the "legal plunder" of laws that take property from one person to give it to another. In "The State," he concluded that "the state is the great fictitious entity by which everyone seeks to live at the expense of everyone else." In essays on free trade, he pointed out that a country's balance of trade would be improved if ships containing exports sank rather than returning with imports, and produced a mock "Candlemakers' Petition" demanding protection from foreign competition: the sun. In the essay excerpted here, he presented a basic economic insight: the difference between what is seen and what is not seen. What is seen is the immediate result of an action, such as the jobs created by government spending. What is not seen is the forgone activity, such as the jobs that would have been created by private investment had money not been taxed away. This insight was expanded to book length by another great economic journalist, Henry Hazlitt, in his 1946 book *Economics in One Lesson*. Whenever a Chamber of Commerce official proclaims that, after all, the hurricane's damage will mean a construction boom for the local economy, or a journalist writes that building a whole new capital city would improve a nation's economy, they are falling for the "broken window fallacy" identified by Bastiat in this 1850 essay.

In the economic sphere an act, a habit, an institution, a law produces not only one effect, but a series of effects. Of these effects, the first alone is immediate; it appears simultaneously with its cause; *it is seen.* The other effects emerge only subsequently; *they are not seen;* we are fortunate if we *foresee* them.

There is only one difference between a bad economist and a good one: the bad economist confines himself to the *visible* effect; the good economist takes into account both the effect that can be seen and those effects that must be *foreseen.*

Yet this difference is tremendous; for it almost always happens that when the immediate consequence is favorable, the later consequences are disastrous, and vice versa. Whence it follows that the bad economist pursues a small present good that will be followed by a great evil to come, while the good economist pursues a great good to come, at the risk of a small present evil.

The same thing, of course, is true of health and morals. Often, the sweeter the first fruit of a habit, the more bitter are its later fruits: for example, debauchery, sloth, prodigality. When a man is impressed by the effect *that is seen* and has not yet learned to discern the effects *that are not seen,* he indulges in deplorable habits, not only through natural inclination, but deliberately.

This explains man's necessarily painful evolution. Ignorance surrounds him at his cradle; therefore, he regulates his acts according to their first consequences, the only ones that, in his infancy, he can see. It is only after a long time that he learns to take account of the others. Two very different masters teach him this lesson: experience and foresight. Experience teaches efficaciously but brutally. It instructs us in all the effects of an act by making us feel them, and we cannot fail to learn eventually, from having been burned ourselves, that fire burns. I should prefer, in so far as possible, to replace this rude teacher with one more gentle: foresight. For that reason I shall investigate the consequences of several economic phenomena, contrasting those *that are seen* with those *that are not seen.*

1. THE BROKEN WINDOW

Have you ever been witness to the fury of that solid citizen, James Goodfellow, when his incorrigible son has happened to break a pane of glass? If you have been present at this spectacle, certainly you must also have observed that the onlookers, even if there are as many as thirty of them, seem with one accord to offer the unfortunate owner the selfsame consolation: "It's an ill wind that blows nobody some good. Such accidents keep industry going. Everybody has to make a living. What would become of the glaziers if no one ever broke a window?"

Now, this formula of condolence contains a whole theory that it is a good idea for us to expose, *flagrante delicto,* in this very simple case, since it is exactly the same as that which, unfortunately, underlies most of our economic institutions.

Suppose that it will cost six francs to repair the damage. If you mean that the accident gives six francs' worth of encouragement to the aforesaid industry, I agree. I do not contest it in any way; your reasoning is correct. The glazier will come, do his job, receive six francs, congratulate himself, and bless in his heart the careless child. *That is what is seen.*

But if, by way of deduction, you conclude, as happens only too often, that it is good to break windows, that it helps to circulate money, that it results in encouraging industry in general, I am obliged to cry out: That will never do! Your theory stops at *what is seen.* It does not take account of *what is not seen.*

It is not seen that, since our citizen has spent six francs for one thing, he will not be able to spend them for another. *It is not seen* that if he had not had a windowpane to replace, he would have replaced, for example, his worn-out shoes or added another book to his library. In brief, he would have put his six francs to some use or other for which he will not now have them.

Let us next consider industry *in general.* The window having been broken, the glass industry gets six francs' worth of encouragement; *that is what is seen.*

If the window had not been broken, the shoe industry (or some other) would have received six francs' worth of encouragement; *that is what is not seen.*

And if we were to take into consideration *what is not seen,* because it is a negative factor, as well as *what is seen,* because it is a positive factor, we should understand that there is no benefit to industry *in general* or to *national employment* as a whole, whether windows are broken or not broken.

Now let us consider James Goodfellow.

On the first hypothesis, that of the broken window, he spends six francs and has, neither more nor less than before, the enjoyment of one window.

On the second, that in which the accident did not happen, he would have spent six francs for new shoes and would have had the enjoyment of a pair of shoes as well as of a window.

Now, if James Goodfellow is part of society, we must conclude that society, considering its labors and its enjoyments, has lost the value of the broken window.

From which, by generalizing, we arrive at this unexpected conclusion: "Society loses the value of objects unnecessarily destroyed," and at this aphorism, which will make the hair of the protectionists stand on end: "To break, to destroy, to dissipate is not to encourage national employment," or more briefly: "Destruction is not profitable." . . .

The reader must apply himself to observe that there are not only two people, but three, in the little drama that I have presented. The one, James Goodfellow, represents the consumer, reduced by destruction to one enjoyment instead of two. The other, under the figure of the glazier, shows us the producer whose industry the accident encourages. The third is the shoemaker (or any other manufacturer) whose industry is correspondingly discouraged by the same cause. It is this third person who is always in the shadow, and who, personifying *what is not seen,* is an essential element of the problem. It is he who makes us understand how absurd it is to see a profit in destruction. It is he who will soon teach us that it is equally absurd to see a profit in trade restriction, which is, after all, nothing more nor less than partial destruction. So, if you get to the bottom of all the arguments advanced in favor of restrictionist measures, you will find only a paraphrase of that common cliché: *"What would become of the glaziers if no one ever broke any windows?"* ...

3. TAXES

Have you ever heard anyone say: "Taxes are the best investment; they are a life-giving dew. See how many families they keep alive, and follow in imagination their indirect effects on industry; they are infinite, as extensive as life itself."

To combat this doctrine, I am obliged to repeat the preceding refutation. ...

The advantages that government officials enjoy in drawing their salaries are *what is seen.* The benefits that result for their suppliers are also *what is seen.* They are right under your nose.

But the disadvantage that the taxpayers try to free themselves from is *what is not seen,* and the distress that results from it for the merchants who supply them is *something further that is not seen,* although it should stand out plainly enough to be seen intellectually.

When a government official spends on his own behalf one hundred sous more, this implies that a taxpayer spends on his own behalf one hundred sous the less. But the spending of the government official *is seen,* because it is done; while that of the taxpayer *is not seen,* because—alas!—he is prevented from doing it.

You compare the nation to a parched piece of land and the tax to a life-giving rain. So be it. But you should also ask yourself where this rain comes from, and whether it is not precisely the tax that draws the moisture from the soil and dries it up.

You should ask yourself further whether the soil receives more of this precious water from the rain than it loses by the evaporation?

What is quite certain is that, when James Goodfellow counts out a hundred sous to the tax collector, he receives nothing in return. When, then, a government official, in spending these hundred sous, returns them to James Goodfellow, it is for an equivalent value in wheat or in labor. The final result is a loss of five francs for James Goodfellow.

It is quite true that often, nearly always if you will, the government official renders an equivalent service to James Goodfellow. In this case there is no loss on either side; there is only an exchange. Therefore, my argument is not in any way concerned with useful functions. I say this: If you wish to create a government office, prove its usefulness. Demonstrate that to James Goodfellow it is worth the equivalent of what it costs him by virtue of the services it renders him. But apart from this intrinsic utility, do not cite, as an argument in favor of opening the new bureau, the advantage that it constitutes for the bureaucrat, his family, and those who supply his needs; do not allege that it encourages employment.

When James Goodfellow gives a hundred sous to a government official for a really useful service, this is exactly the same as when he gives a hundred sous to a shoemaker for a pair of shoes. It's a case of give-and-take, and the score is even. But when James Goodfellow hands over a hundred sous to a government official to receive no service for it or even to be subjected to inconveniences, it is as if he were to give his money to a thief. It serves no purpose to say that the official will spend these hundred sous for the great profit of our *national industry;* the more the thief can do with them, the more James Goodfellow could have done with them if he had not met on his way either the extralegal or the legal parasite.

Let us accustom ourselves, then, not to judge things solely by *what is seen,* but rather by *what is not seen. . . .*

5. PUBLIC WORKS

Nothing is more natural than that a nation, after making sure that a great enterprise will profit the community, should have such an enterprise carried out with funds collected from the citizenry. But I lose patience completely, I confess, when I hear alleged in support of such a resolution this economic fallacy: "Besides, it is a way of creating jobs for the workers."

The state opens a road, builds a palace, repairs a street, digs a canal; with these projects it gives jobs to certain workers. *That is what is seen.* But it deprives certain other laborers of employment. *That is what is not seen.*

Suppose a road is under construction. A thousand laborers arrive every morning, go home every evening, and receive their wages; that is certain. If the road had not been authorized, if funds for it had not been voted, these good people would have neither found this work nor earned these wages; that again is certain.

But is this all? . . .

In noting what the state is going to do with the millions of francs voted, do not neglect to note also what the taxpayers would have done—and can no longer do—with these same millions. You see, then, that a public enterprise is a coin with two sides. On one, the figure of a busy worker, with this device: *What is seen;* on the other, an unemployed worker, with this device: *What is not seen.*

The sophism that I am attacking in this essay is all the more dangerous when applied to public works, since it serves to justify the most foolishly prodigal enterprises. When a railroad or a bridge has real utility, it suffices to rely on this fact in arguing in its favor. But if one cannot do this, what does one do? One has recourse to this mumbo jumbo: "We must create jobs for the workers."

This means that the terraces of the Champ-de-Mars are ordered first to be built up and then to be torn down. The great Napoleon, it is said, thought he was doing philanthropic work when he had ditches dug and then filled in. He also said: "What difference does the result make? All we need is to see wealth spread among the laboring classes."

Let us get to the bottom of things. Money creates an illusion for us. To ask for co-operation, in the form of money, from all the citizens in a common enterprise is, in reality, to ask of them actual physical co-operation, for each one of them procures for himself by his labor the amount he is taxed. Now, if we were to gather together all the citizens and exact their services from them in order to have a piece of work performed that is useful to all, this would be understandable; their recompense would consist in the results of the work itself. But if, after being brought together, they were forced to build roads on which no one would travel, or palaces that no one would live in, all under the pretext of providing work for them, it would seem absurd, and they would certainly be justified in objecting: We will have none of that kind of work. We would rather work for ourselves.

Having the citizens contribute money, and not labor, changes nothing in the general results. But if labor were contributed, the loss would be shared by everyone. Where money is contributed, those whom the state keeps busy escape their share of the loss, while adding much more to that which their compatriots already have to suffer. . . .

6. MIDDLEMEN

Society is the aggregate of all the services that men perform for one another by compulsion or voluntarily, that is to say, *public services* and *private services*.

The first, imposed and regulated by the law, which is not always easy to change when necessary, can long outlive their usefulness and still retain the name of *public services,* even when they are no longer anything but public nuisances. The second are in the domain of the voluntary, i.e., of individual responsibility. Each gives and receives what he wishes, or what he can, after bargaining. These services are always presumed to have a real utility, exactly measured by their comparative value.

That is why the former are so often static, while the latter obey the law of progress.

While the exaggerated development of public services, with the waste of energies that it entails, tends to create a disastrous parasitism in society, it is rather strange that many modern schools of economic thought, attributing this characteristic to voluntary, private services, seek to transform the functions performed by the various occupations.

These schools of thought are vehement in their attack on those they call middlemen. They would willingly eliminate the capitalist, the banker, the speculator, the entrepreneur, the businessman, and the merchant, accusing them of interposing themselves between producer and consumer in order to fleece them both, without giving them anything of value. Or rather, the reformers would like to transfer to the state the work of the middlemen, for this work cannot be eliminated.

The sophism of the socialists on this point consists in showing the public what it pays to the *middlemen* for their services and in concealing what would have to be paid to the state. Once again we have the conflict between what strikes the eye and what is evidenced only to the mind, between *what is seen and what is not seen.*

It was especially in 1847 and on the occasion of the [European] famine that the socialist schools succeeded in popularizing their disastrous theory. They knew well that the most absurd propaganda always has some chance with men who are suffering; *malesuada fames.*

Then, with the aid of those high-sounding words: *Exploitation of man by man, speculation in hunger, monopoly,* they set themselves to blackening the name of business and throwing a veil over its benefits.

"Why," they said, "leave to merchants the task of getting foodstuffs from the United States and the Crimea? Why cannot the state, the departments, and the municipalities organize a provisioning service and set up warehouses for stockpiling? They would sell at *net cost,* and the people, the poor people, would be relieved of the tribute that they pay to free, i.e., selfish, individualistic, anarchical trade."

The tribute that the people pay to business, *is what is seen.* The tribute that the people would have to pay to the state or to its agents in the socialist system, *is what is not seen.*

What is this so-called tribute that people pay to business? It is this: that two men render each other a service in full freedom under the pressure of competition and at a price agreed on after bargaining.

When the stomach that is hungry is in Paris and the wheat that can satisfy it is in Odessa, the suffering will not cease until the wheat reaches the stomach. There are three ways to accomplish this: the hungry men can go themselves to find the wheat; they can put their trust in those who engage in this kind of business; or they can levy an assessment on themselves and charge public officials with the task.

Of these three methods, which is the most advantageous?

In all times, in all countries, the freer, the more enlightened, the more experienced men have been, the oftener have they *voluntarily* chosen the second. I confess that this is enough in my eyes to give the advantage to it. My mind refuses to admit that mankind at large deceives itself on a point that touches it so closely.

However, let us examine the question.

For thirty-six million citizens to depart for Odessa to get the wheat that they need is obviously impracticable. The first means is of no avail. The consumers cannot act by themselves; they are compelled to turn to middlemen, whether public officials or merchants.

However, let us observe that the first means would be the most natural. Fundamentally, it is the responsibility of whoever is hungry to get his own wheat. It is a *task* that concerns him; it is a *service* that he owes to himself. If someone else, whoever he may be, performs this *service* for him and takes the task on himself, this other person has a right to compensation. What I am saying here is that the services of *middlemen* involve a right to remuneration.

However that may be, since we must turn to what the socialists call a parasite, which of the two—the merchant or the public official—is the less demanding parasite?

Business (I assume it to be free, or else what point would there be in my argument?) is forced, by its own self-interest, to study the reasons, to ascertain day by day the condition of the crops, to receive reports from all parts of the world, to foresee needs, to take precautions. It has ships all ready, associates everywhere, and its immediate self-interest is to buy at the lowest possible price, to economize on all details of operation, and to attain the greatest results with the least effort. Not only French merchants, but merchants the whole world over are busy with provisioning France for the day of need; and if self-interest compels them to fulfill their task at the least expense, competition among them no less compels them to let the consumers profit from all the economies realized. Once the wheat has arrived, the businessman has an interest in selling it as soon as possible to cover his risks, realize his profits, and begin all over again, if there is an opportunity. Guided by the comparison of prices, private enterprise distributes food all over the world, always beginning at the point of greatest scarcity, that is, where the need is felt the most. It is thus impossible to imagine an *organization* better calculated to serve the interests of the hungry, and the beauty of this organization, not perceived by the socialists, comes precisely from the fact that it is free, i.e., voluntary. True, the consumer must pay the businessman for his expenses of cartage, of trans-shipment, of storage, of commissions, etc.; but under what system does the one who consumes the wheat avoid paying the expenses of shipping it to him? There is, besides, the necessity of paying also for *service rendered;* but, so far as the share of the middleman is concerned, it is reduced to a *minimum* by competition; and as to its justice, it would be strange for the artisans of Paris not to work for the merchants of Marseilles, when the merchants of Marseilles work for the artisans of Paris.

If, according to the socialist plan, the state takes the place of private businessmen in these transactions, what will happen? Pray, show me where there will be any economy for the public. Will it be in the retail price? But imagine the representatives of forty thousand municipalities arriving at Odessa on a given day, the day when the wheat is needed; imagine the effect on the price. Will the economy be effected in the shipping expenses? But will fewer ships, fewer sailors, fewer trans-shipments, fewer warehouses be needed, or are we to be relieved of the necessity for paying for all these things? Will the saving be effected in the profits of the businessmen? But did your representatives and public officials go to Odessa for nothing? Are they going to make the journey out of brotherly love? Will they not have to live? Will not their time have to be paid for? And do you think that this will not exceed a thousand times the two or three per cent that the merchant earns, a rate that he is prepared to guarantee?

And then, think of the difficulty of levying so many taxes to distribute so much food. Think of the injustices and abuses inseparable from such an enterprise. Think of the burden of responsibility that the government would have to bear.

The socialists who have invented these follies, and who in days of distress plant them in the minds of the masses, generously confer on themselves the title of "forward-looking" men, and there is a real danger that usage, that tyrant of language, will ratify both the word and the judgment it implies. "Forward-looking" assumes that these gentlemen can see ahead much further than ordinary people; that their only fault is to be too much in advance of their century; and that, if the time has not yet arrived when certain private services, allegedly parasitical, can be eliminated, the fault is with the public, which is far behind socialism. To *my* mind and knowledge, it is the contrary that is true, and I do not know to what barbaric century we should have to return to find on this point a level of understanding comparable to that of the socialists.

The modern socialist factions ceaselessly oppose free association in present-day society. They do not realize that a free society is a true association much superior to any of those that they concoct out of their fertile imaginations.

Let us elucidate this point with an example:

For a man, when he gets up in the morning, to be able to put on a suit of clothes, a piece of land has had to be enclosed, fertilized, drained, cultivated, planted with a certain kind of vegetation; flocks of sheep have had to feed on it; they have had to give their wool; this wool has had to be spun, woven, dyed, and converted into cloth; this cloth has had to be cut, sewn, and fashioned into a garment. And this series of operations implies a host of others; for it presupposes the use of farming implements, of sheep-folds, of factories, of coal, of machines, of carriages, etc.

If society were not a very real association, anyone who wanted a suit of clothes would be reduced to working in isolation, that is, to performing himself the innumerable operations in this series, from the first blow of the pickaxe that initiates it right down to the last thrust of the needle that terminates it.

But thanks to that readiness to associate which is the distinctive characteristic of our species, these operations have been distributed among a multitude of workers, and they keep subdividing themselves more and more for the common good to the point where, as consumption increases, a single specialized operation can support a new industry. Then comes the distribution of the proceeds, according to the portion of value each one has contributed to the total work. If this is not association, I should like to know what is.

Note that, since not one of the workers has produced the smallest particle of raw material from nothing, they are confined to rendering each other mutual services, to aiding each other for a common end; and that all can be considered, each group in relation to the others, as *middlemen.* If, for example, in the course of the operation, transportation becomes important enough to employ one person; spinning, a second; weaving, a third; why should the first one be considered more of a *parasite* than the others? Is there no need for transportation? Does not someone devote time and trouble to the task? Does he not spare his associates this time and trouble? Are they doing more than he, or just something different? Are they not all equally subject, in regard to their pay, that is, their share of the proceeds, to the law that restricts it to the *price agreed upon after bargaining*? Do not this division of labor and these arrangements, decided upon in full liberty, serve the common good? Do we, then, need a socialist, under the pretext of planning, to come and despotically destroy our voluntary arrangements, put an end to the division of labor, substitute isolated efforts for co-operative efforts, and reverse the progress of civilization?

SOCIALISM AND INTERVENTION

Ludwig von Mises

Mises may be best known for his devastating demonstration of the impracticability of true socialism, under which money, prices, and markets would be abolished. His student, F. A. Hayek, described the effect his book *Socialism* had:

> When *Socialism* first appeared in 1922, its impact was profound. It gradually but fundamentally altered the outlook of many of the young idealists returning to their university studies after World War I. I know, for I was one of them. . . . Socialism promised to fulfill our hopes for a more rational, more just world. And then came this book. Our hopes were dashed.

Despite Mises's critique, Western intellectuals and Eastern-bloc rulers continued to try to make socialism work for another seventy years. If this reader had been published before the fall of the Berlin Wall, it would have contained an excerpt from *Socialism*. But with socialism discredited everywhere outside the cloistered halls of academe, it seems more relevant to emphasize another of Mises's arguments: his analysis of intervention in the market. In a series of books and articles, ranging from his 1912 book *Theory of Money and Credit* to the posthumously published *Critique of Interventionism* (1977), Mises demonstrated that government attempts to intervene in the market process to bring about desired results always create distortions that lead to demands for further intervention. He focused especially on price controls, but we can see the same process at work in such areas as rent control, acreage allotments, and health insurance. This selection is from his 1927 book *Liberalism,* a brief introduction to liberal political and economic theory. Note that his argument that "state enterprises ... in Germany and Russia" do not constitute actual socialism reflects the fact that he was writing during Lenin's New Economic Policy, just before the sweeping nationalization that began in 1928.

THE IMPRACTICABILITY OF SOCIALISM

People are wont to consider socialism impracticable because they think that men lack the moral qualities demanded by a socialist society. It is feared that under socialism most men will not exhibit the same zeal in the performance of the duties and tasks assigned to them that they bring to their daily work in a social order based on private ownership of the means of production. In a capitalist society, every individual knows that the fruit of his labor is his own to enjoy, that his income increases or decreases according as the output of his labor is greater or smaller. In a socialist society, every individual will think that less depends on the efficiency of his own labor, since a fixed portion of the total output is due him in any case and the amount of the latter cannot be appreciably diminished by the loss resulting from the laziness of any one man. If, as is to be feared, such a conviction should become general, the productivity of labor in a socialist community would drop considerably.

The objection thus raised against socialism is completely sound, but it does not get to the heart of the matter. Were it possible in a socialist community to ascertain the output of the labor of every individual comrade with the same precision with which this is accomplished for each worker by means of economic calculation in the capitalist system, the practicability of socialism would not be dependent on the good will of every individual. Society would be in a position, at least within certain limits, to determine the share of the total output to be allotted to each worker on the basis of the extent of his contribution to production. What renders socialism impracticable is precisely the fact that calculation of this kind is impossible in a socialist society.

In the capitalist system, the calculation of profitability constitutes a guide that indicates to the individual whether the enterprise he is operating ought, under the given circumstances, to be in operation at all and whether it is being run in the most efficient possible way, i.e., at the least cost in factors of production. If an undertaking proves unprofitable, this means that the raw materials, half-finished goods, and labor that are needed in it are employed by other enterprises for an end that, from the standpoint of the consumers, is more urgent and more important, or for the same end, but in a more economical manner (i.e., with a smaller expenditure of capital and labor). When, for instance, hand weaving came to be unprofitable, this signified that the capital and labor employed in weaving by machine yield a greater output and that it is consequently uneconomical to adhere to a method of production in which the same input of capital and labor yields a smaller output.

If a new enterprise is being planned, one can calculate in advance whether it can be made profitable at all and in what way. If, for example, one has the intention of constructing a railroad line, one can, by estimating the traffic to be expected and its ability to pay the freight rates, calculate whether it pays to invest capital and labor in such an undertaking. If the result of this calculation shows that the projected railroad promises no profit, this is tantamount to saying that there is other, more urgent employment for the capital and the labor that the construction of the railroad would require; the world is not yet rich enough to be able to afford such an expenditure. But it is not only when the question arises whether or not a given undertaking is to be begun at all that the calculation of value and profitability is decisive; it controls every single step that the entrepreneur takes in the conduct of his business.

Capitalist economic calculation, which alone makes rational production possible, is based on monetary calculation. Only because the prices of all goods and services in the market can be expressed in terms of money is it possible for them, in spite of their heterogeneity, to enter into a calculation involving homogeneous units of measurement. In a socialist society, where all the means of production are owned by the community, and where, consequently, there is no market and no exchange of productive goods and services, there can also be no money prices for goods and services of higher order. Such a social system would thus, of necessity, be lacking in the means for the rational management of business enterprises, viz., economic calculation. For economic calculation cannot take place in the absence of a common denominator to which all the heterogeneous goods and services can be reduced.

Let us consider a quite simple case. For the construction of a railroad from A to B several routes are conceivable. Let us suppose that a mountain stands between A and B. The railroad can be made to run over the mountain, around the mountain, or, by way of a tunnel, through the mountain. In a capitalist society, it is a very easy matter to compute which line will prove the most profitable. One ascertains the cost involved in constructing each of the three lines and the differences in operating costs necessarily incurred by the anticipated traffic on each. From these quantities it is not difficult to determine which stretch of road will be the most profitable. A socialist society could not make such calculations. For it would have no possible way of reducing to a uniform standard of measurement all the heterogeneous quantities and qualities of goods and services that here come into consideration. In the face of the ordinary, everyday problems which the management of an economy presents, a socialist society would stand helpless, for it would have no possible way of keeping its accounts.

The prosperity that has made it possible for many more people to inhabit the earth today than in the precapitalist era is due solely to the capitalist method of lengthy chains of production, which necessarily requires monetary calculation. This is impossible under socialism. In vain have socialist writers labored to demonstrate how one could still manage even without monetary and price calculation. All their efforts in this respect have met with failure.

The leadership of a socialist society would thus be confronted by a problem that it could not possibly solve. It would not be able to decide which of the innumerable possible modes of procedure is the most rational. The resulting chaos in the economy would culminate quickly and irresistibly in universal impoverishment and a retrogression to the primitive conditions under which our ancestors once lived.

The socialist ideal, carried to its logical conclusion, would eventuate in a social order in which all the means of production were owned by the people as a whole. Production would be completely in the hands of the government, the center of power in society. It alone would determine what was to be produced and how, and in what way goods ready for consumption were to be distributed. It makes little difference whether we imagine this socialist state of the future as democratically constituted or otherwise. Even a democratic socialist state would necessarily constitute a tightly organized bureaucracy in which everyone, apart from the highest officials, though he might very well, in his capacity as a voter, have participated in some fashion in framing the directives issued by the central authority, would be in the subservient position of an administrator bound to carry them out obediently.

A socialist state of this kind is not comparable to the state enterprises, no matter how vast their scale, that we have seen developing in the last decades in Europe, especially in Germany and Russia. The latter all flourish *side by side with* private ownership of the means of production. They engage in commercial transactions with enterprises that capitalists own and manage, and they receive various stimuli from these enterprises that invigorate their own operation. State railroads, for instance, are provided by their suppliers, the manufacturers of locomotives, coaches, signal installations, and other equipment, with apparatus that has proved successful elsewhere in the operation of privately owned railroads. Thence they receive the incentive to institute innovations in order to keep up with the progress in technology and in methods of business management that is taking place all around them.

It is a matter of common knowledge that national and municipal enterprises have, on the whole, failed, that they are expensive and inefficient, and that they have to be subsidized out of tax funds just to maintain themselves in operation. Of course, where a public enterprise occupies a monopolistic position—as is, for instance, generally the case with municipal transportation facilities and electric light and power plants—the bad consequences of inefficiency need not always express themselves in visible financial failure. Under certain circumstances it may be possible to conceal it by making use of the opportunity open to the monopolist of raising the price of his products and services high enough to render these enterprises, in spite of their uneconomic management, still profitable. The lower productivity of the socialist method of production merely manifests itself differently here and is not so easily recognized as otherwise; essentially, however, the case remains the same.

But none of these experiments in the socialist management of enterprises can afford us any basis for judging what it would mean if the socialist ideal of the communal ownership of *all* means of production were to be realized. In the socialist society of the future, which will leave no room whatsoever for the free activity of private enterprises operating side by side with those owned and controlled by the state, the central planning board will lack entirely the gauge provided for the whole economy by the market and market prices. In the market, where all goods and services come to be traded, exchange ratios, expressed in money prices, may be determined for everything bought and sold. In a social order based on private property, it thus becomes possible to resort to monetary calculation in checking on the results of all economic activities. The social productivity of every economic transaction may be tested by the methods of bookkeeping and cost accounting. It yet remains to be shown that public enterprises are unable to make use of cost accounting in the same way as private enterprises do. Nevertheless, monetary calculation does give even governmental and communal enterprises some basis for judging the success or failure of their management. In a completely socialist economic system, this would be quite impossible, for in the absence of private ownership of the means of production, there could be no exchange of capital goods in the market and consequently neither money prices nor monetary calculation. The general management of a purely socialist society will therefore have no means of reducing to a common denominator the costs of production of all the heterogeneous commodities that it plans to produce.

Nor can this be achieved by setting expenditures in kind against savings in kind. One cannot calculate if it is not possible to reduce to a common medium of expression hours of labor of various grades, iron, coal, building materials of every kind, machines, and all the other things needed in the operation and management of different enterprises. Calculation is possible only when one is able to reduce to monetary terms all the goods under consideration. Of course, monetary calculation has its imperfections and deficiencies, but we have nothing better to put in its place. It suffices for the practical purposes of life as long as the monetary system is sound. If we were to renounce monetary calculation, every economic computation would become absolutely impossible.

This is the decisive objection that economics raises against the possibility of a socialist society. It must forgo the intellectual division of labor that consists in the cooperation of all entrepreneurs, landowners, and workers as producers and consumers in the formation of market prices. But without it, rationality, i.e., the possibility of economic calculation, is unthinkable.

INTERVENTIONISM

The socialist ideal is now beginning to lose more and more of its adherents. The penetrating economic and sociological investigations of the problems of socialism that have shown it to be impracticable have not remained without effect, and the failures in which socialist experiments everywhere have ended have disconcerted even its most enthusiastic supporters. Gradually people are once more beginning to realize that society cannot do without private property. Yet the hostile criticism to which the system of private ownership of the means of production has been subjected for decades has left behind such a strong prejudice against the capitalist system that, in spite of their knowledge of the inadequacy and impracticability of socialism, people cannot make up their minds to admit openly that they must return to liberal views on the question of property. To be sure, it is conceded that socialism, the communal ownership of the means of production, is altogether, or at least for the present, impracticable. But, on the other hand, it is asserted that unhampered private ownership of the means of production is also an evil. Thus people want to create a third way, a form of society standing midway between private ownership of the means of production, on the one hand, and communal ownership of the means of production, on the other. Private property will be permitted to exist, but the ways in which the means of production are employed by the entrepreneurs, capitalists, and landowners will be regulated, guided, and controlled by authoritarian decrees and prohibitions. In this way, one forms the conceptual image of a regulated market, of a capitalism circumscribed by authoritarian rules, of private property shorn of its allegedly harmful concomitant features by the intervention of the authorities.

One can best acquire an insight into the meaning and nature of this system by considering a few examples of the consequences of government interference. The crucial acts of intervention with which we have to deal aim at fixing the prices of goods and services at a height different from what the unhampered market would have determined.

In the case of prices formed on the unhampered market, or which would have been formed in the absence of interference on the part of the authorities, the costs of production are covered by the proceeds. If a lower price is decreed by the government, the proceeds will fall short of the costs. Merchants and manufacturers will, therefore, unless the storage of the goods involved would cause them to deteriorate rapidly in value, withhold their merchandise from the market in the hope of more favorable times, perhaps in the expectation that the government order will soon be rescinded. If the authorities do not want the goods concerned to disappear altogether from the market as a result of their interference, they cannot limit themselves to fixing the price; they must at the same time also decree that all stocks on hand be sold at the prescribed price.

But even this does not suffice. At the price determined on the unhampered market, supply and demand would have coincided. Now, because the price was fixed lower by government decree, the demand has increased while the supply has remained unchanged. The stocks on hand are not sufficient to satisfy fully all who are prepared to pay the prescribed price. A part of the demand will remain unsatisfied. The mechanism of the market, which otherwise tends to equalize supply and demand by means of price fluctuations, no longer operates. Now people who would have been prepared to pay the price prescribed by the authorities must leave the market with empty hands. Those who were on line earlier or who were in a position to exploit some personal connection with the sellers have already acquired the whole stock; the others have to go unprovided. If the government wishes to avoid this consequence of its intervention, which runs counter to its intentions, it must add rationing to price control and compulsory sale: a governmental regulation must determine how much of a commodity may be supplied to each individual applicant at the prescribed price.

But once the supplies already on hand at the moment of the government's intervention are exhausted, an incomparably more difficult problem arises. Since production is no longer profitable if the goods are to be sold at the price fixed by the government, it will be reduced or entirely suspended. If the government wishes to have production continue, it must compel the manufacturers to produce, and, to this end, it must also fix the prices of raw materials and half-finished goods and the wages of labor. Its decrees to this effect, however, cannot be limited to only the one or the few branches of production that the authorities wish to regulate because they deem their products especially important. They must encompass all branches of production. They must regulate the price of all commodities and all wages. In short, they must extend their control over the conduct of all entrepreneurs, capitalists, landowners, and workers. If some branches of production are left free, capital and labor will flow into these, and the government will fail to attain the goal that it wished to achieve by its first act of intervention. But the object of the authorities is that there should be an abundance of production in precisely that branch of industry which, because of the importance they attach to its products, they have especially singled out for regulation. It runs altogether counter to their design that precisely in consequence of their intervention this branch of production should be neglected.

It is therefore clearly evident that an attempt on the part of the government to interfere with the operation of the economic system based on private ownership of the means of production fails of the goal that its authors wished to achieve by means of it. It is, from the point of view of its authors, not only futile, but downright contrary to purpose, because it enormously augments the very "evil" that it was supposed to combat. Before the price controls were decreed, the commodity was, in the opinion of the government, too expensive; now it disappears from the market altogether. This, however, is not the result aimed at by the government, which wanted to make the commodity accessible to the consumer at a cheaper price. On the contrary: from its viewpoint, the absence of the commodity, the impossibility of securing it, must appear as by far the greater evil. In this sense one can say of the intervention of the authorities that it is futile and contrary to the purpose that it was intended to serve, and of the system of economic policy that attempts to operate by means of such acts of intervention that it is impracticable and unthinkable, that it contradicts economic logic.

If the government will not set things right again by desisting from its interference, i.e., by rescinding the price controls, then it must follow up the first step with others. To the prohibition against asking any price higher than the prescribed one it must add not only measures to compel the sale of all stocks on hand under a system of enforced rationing, but price ceilings on goods of higher order, wage controls, and, ultimately, compulsory labor for entrepreneurs and workers. And these regulations cannot be limited to one or a few branches of production, but must encompass them all. There is simply no other choice than this: either to abstain from interference in the free play of the market, or to delegate the entire management of production and distribution to the government. Either capitalism or socialism: there exists no middle way.

The mechanism of the series of events just described is well known to all who have witnessed the attempts of governments in time of war and during periods of inflation to fix prices by fiat. Everyone knows nowadays that government price controls had no other result than the disappearance from the market of the goods concerned. Wherever the government resorts to the fixing of prices, the result is always the same. When, for instance, the government fixes a ceiling on residential rents, a housing shortage immediately ensues. In Austria, the Social Democratic Party has virtually abolished residential rent. The consequence is that in the city of Vienna, for example, in spite of the fact that the population has declined considerably since the beginning of the World War and that several thousand new houses have been constructed by the municipality in the meantime, many thousands of persons are unable to find accommodations.

Let us take still another example: the fixing of minimum wage rates.

When the relationship between employer and employee is left undisturbed by legislative enactments or by violent measures on the part of trade unions, the wages paid by the employer for every type of labor are exactly as high as the increment of value that it adds to the materials in production. Wages cannot rise any higher than this because, if they did, the employer could no longer make a profit and hence would be compelled to discontinue a line of production that did not pay. But neither can wages fall any lower, because then the workers would turn to other branches of industry where they would be better rewarded, so that the employer would be forced to discontinue production because of a labor shortage.

There is, therefore, in the economy always a wage rate at which all workers find employment and every entrepreneur who wishes to undertake some enterprise still profitable at that wage finds workers. This wage rate is customarily called by economists the "static" or "natural" wage. It increases if, other things being equal, the number of workers diminishes; it decreases if, other things being equal, the available quantity of capital for which employment in production is sought suffers any diminution. However, one must, at the same time, observe that it is not quite precise to speak simply of "wages" and "labor." Labor services vary greatly in quality and quantity (calculated per unit of time), and so too do the wages of labor.

If the economy never varied from the stationary state, then in a labor market unhampered by interference on the part of the government or by coercion on the part of the labor unions there would be no unemployed. But the stationary state of society is merely an imaginary construction of economic theory, an intellectual expedient indispensable for our thinking, that enables us, by contrast, to form a clear conception of the processes actually taking place in the economy which surrounds us and in which we live. Life—fortunately, we hasten to add—is never at rest. There is never a standstill in the economy, but perpetual changes, movement, innovation, the continual emergence of the unprecedented. There are, accordingly, always branches of production that are being shut down or curtailed because the demand for their products has fallen off, and other branches of production that are being expanded or even embarked upon for the first time. If we think only of the last few decades, we can at once enumerate a great number of new industries that have sprung up: e.g., the automobile industry, the airplane industry, the motion picture industry, the rayon industry, the canned goods industry, and the radio broadcasting industry. These branches of industry today employ millions of workers, only some of whom have been drawn from the increase in population. Some came from branches of production that were shut down, and even more from those that, as a result of technological improvements, are now able to manage with fewer workers.

Occasionally the changes that occur in the relations among individual branches of production take place so slowly that no worker is obliged to shift to a new type of job; only young people, just beginning to earn their livelihood, will enter, in greater proportion, the new or expanding industries. Generally, however, in the capitalist system, with its rapid strides in improving human welfare, progress takes place too swiftly to spare individuals the necessity of adapting themselves to it. When, two hundred years or more ago, a young lad learned a craft, he could count on practicing it his whole life long in the way he had learned it, without any fear of being injured by his conservatism. Things are different today. The worker too must adjust himself to changing conditions, must add to what he has learned, or begin learning anew. He must leave occupations which no longer require the same number of workers as previously and enter one which has just come into being or which now needs more workers than before. But even if he remains in his old job, he must learn new techniques when circumstances demand it.

All this affects the worker in the form of changes in wage rates. If a particular branch of business employs relatively too many workers, it discharges some, and those discharged will not easily find new work in the same branch of business. The pressure on the labor market exercised by the discharged workers depresses wages in this branch of production. This, in turn, induces the worker to look for employment in those branches of production that wish to attract new workers and are therefore prepared to pay higher wages.

From this it becomes quite clear what must be done in order to satisfy the workers' desire for employment and for high wages. Wages in general cannot be pushed above the height that they would normally occupy in a market unhampered either by government interference or other institutional pressures without creating certain side effects that cannot be desirable for the worker. Wages can be driven up in an individual industry or an individual country if the transfer of workers from other industries or their immigration from other countries is prohibited. Such wage increases are effected at the expense of the workers whose entrance is barred. Their wages are now lower than they would have been if their freedom of movement had not been hindered. The rise in wages of one group is thus achieved at the expense of the others. This policy of obstructing the free movement of labor can benefit only the workers in countries and industries suffering from a relative labor shortage. In an industry or a country where this is not the case, there is only *one* thing that can raise wages: a rise in the general productivity of labor, whether by virtue of an increase in the capital available or through an improvement in the technological processes of production.

If, however, the government fixes minimum wages by law above the height of the static or natural wage, then the employers will find that they are no longer in a position to carry on successfully a number of enterprises that were still profitable when wages stood at the lower point. They will consequently curtail production and discharge workers. The effect of an artificial rise in wages, i.e., one imposed upon the market from the outside, is, therefore, the spread of unemployment.

Now, of course, no attempt is being made today to fix minimum wage rates by law on a large scale. But the position of power that the trade unions occupy has enabled them to do so even in the absence of any positive legislation to that effect. The fact that workers form unions for the purpose of bargaining with the employers does not, in and of itself, necessarily provoke disturbances in the operation of the market. Even the fact that they successfully arrogate to themselves the right to break, without notice, contracts duly entered into by them and to lay down their tools would not itself result in any further disturbance in the labor market. What does create a new situation in the labor market is the element of coercion involved in strikes and compulsory union membership that prevails today in most of the industrial countries of Europe. Since the unionized workers deny access to employment to those who are not members of their union, and resort to open violence during strikes to prevent other workers from taking the place of those on strike, the wage demands that the unions present to the employers have precisely the same force as government decrees fixing minimum wage rates. For the employer must, if he does not wish to shut down his whole enterprise, yield to the demands of the union. He must pay wages such that the volume of production has to be restricted, because what costs more to produce cannot find as large a market as what costs less. Thus, the higher wages exacted by the trade unions become a cause of unemployment.

The unemployment originating from this source differs entirely in extent and duration from that which arises from the changes constantly taking place in the kind and quality of the labor demanded in the market. If unemployment had its cause only in the fact that there is constant progress in industrial development, it could neither assume great proportions nor take on the character of a lasting institution. The workers who can no longer be employed in one branch of production soon find accommodation in others which are expanding or just coming into being. When workers enjoy freedom of movement and the shift from one industry to another is not impeded by legal and other obstacles of a similar kind, adjustment to new conditions takes place without too much difficulty and rather quickly. For the rest, the setting up of labor exchanges would contribute much toward reducing still further the extent of this type of unemployment.

But the unemployment produced by the interference of coercive agencies in the operation of the labor market is no transitory phenomenon continually appearing and disappearing. It is incurable as long as the cause that called it into existence continues to operate, i.e., as long as the law or the violence of the trade unions prevents wages from being reduced, by the pressure of the jobless seeking employment, to the level that they would have reached in the absence of interference on the part of the government or the unions, namely, the rate at which all those eager for work ultimately find it.

For the unemployed to be granted support by the government or by the unions only serves to enlarge the evil. If what is involved is a case of unemployment springing from dynamic changes in the economy, then the unemployment benefits only result in postponing the adjustment of the workers to the new conditions. The jobless worker who is on relief does not consider it necessary to look about for a new occupation if he no longer finds a position in his old one; at least, he allows more time to elapse before he decides to shift to a new occupation or to a new locality or before he reduces the wage rate he demands to that at which he could find work. If unemployment benefits are not set too low, one can say that as long as they are offered, unemployment cannot disappear.

If, however, the unemployment is produced by the artificial raising of the height of wage rates in consequence of the direct intervention of the government or of its toleration of coercive practices on the part of the trade unions, then the only question is who is to bear the costs involved, the employers or the workers. The state, the government, the community never do so; they load them either onto the employer or onto the worker or partially onto each. If the burden falls on the workers, then they are deprived entirely or partially of the fruits of the artificial wage increase they have received; they may even be made to bear more of these costs than the artificial wage increase yielded them. The employer can be saddled with the burden of unemployment benefits to some extent by having to pay a tax proportionate to the total amount of wages paid out by him. In this case, unemployment insurance, by raising the costs of labor, has the same effect as a further increase in wages above the static level: the profitability of the employment of labor is reduced, and the number of workers who still can be profitably engaged is concomitantly decreased. Thus, unemployment spreads even further, in an ever widening spiral. The employers can also be drawn on to pay the costs of the unemployment benefits by means of a tax on their profits or capital, without regard for the number of workers employed. But this too only tends to spread unemployment even further. For when capital is consumed or when the formation of new capital is at least slowed down, the conditions for the employment of labor become, *ceteris paribus,* less favorable.

It is obviously futile to attempt to eliminate unemployment by embarking upon a program of public works that would otherwise not have been undertaken. The necessary resources for such projects must be withdrawn by taxes or loans from the application they would otherwise have found. Unemployment in one industry can, in this way, be mitigated only to the extent that it is increased in another.

From whichever side we consider interventionism, it becomes evident that this system leads to a result that its originators and advocates did not intend and that, even from their standpoint, it must appear as a senseless, self-defeating, absurd policy.

REDISTRIBUTING POWER

Bertrand de Jouvenel

Libertarianism first arose in response to the old order of monarchy, state-enforced religion, and economic monopolies. No sooner had that enemy been largely vanquished in the West than a new adversary of liberty appeared: socialism. Now that full-blown socialism has also been decisively defeated in the West (along with fascism, which had a briefer life), the simple system of natural liberty is challenged primarily by social democracy and the welfare state. In this excerpt from *The Ethics of Redistribution,* the French scholar Bertrand de Jouvenel (1903–87) examines the morality of coercive redistribution of wealth and income. Unlike most critics of the welfare state, Jouvenel ignores economic or incentive problems to concentrate his analysis on redistribution's impact on freedom and culture. In particular, he suggests that high tax rates on the wealthy may reduce their ability to fund cultural activities, leading to demands that government support the arts and thus to increased state control over the culture.

THE EFFECT OF REDISTRIBUTION UPON SOCIETY

No one has attempted to draw the picture of the society which would result from radical redistribution, as called for by the logic of reasoning on the maximization of satisfactions. Even if one were to compromise on such a floor-and-ceiling society as we attempt to work out in the Appendix, it would still be one which would exclude the present modes of life of our leaders in every field, whether they are business-men, public servants, artists, intellectuals, or trade-unionists.

We have forbidden ourselves to contemplate any decrease in the activity of anyone, any lowering of production as a whole. But the reallocation of incomes would bring about a great shift in activities. The demand for some goods and services would be increased. The demand for others would drop or disappear. It is not beyond the skill of those economists who have specialized in consumer behavior to calculate roughly how far the demand of certain items would rise and how far the demand of certain others would drop.

A number of the present activities of our society would fade out for lack of a buyer. Thereby Wicksteed's "misdirection of productive activities" would be redressed. This great economist argued with feel-ing that inequality of income distorts the allocation of productive re-sources; efforts in a free market economy being directed to the point at which they will be best remunerated, the rich can draw such efforts away from the satisfaction of poor men's urgent wants to the satisfac-tion of rich men's whims. The big incomes are, so to speak, magnets attracting efforts away from their best application. In our reformed society, this evil would be done away with.

I for one would see without chagrin the disappearance of many ac-tivities which serve the richer, but no one surely would gladly accept the disappearance of all the activities which find their market in the classes enjoying more than £500 of net income. The production of all first-quality goods would cease. The skill they demand would be lost and the taste they shape would be coarsened. The production of artis-tic and intellectual goods would be affected first and foremost. Who could buy paintings? Who even could buy books other than pulp?

Can we reconcile ourselves to the loss suffered by civilization if creative intellectual and artistic activities fail to find a market? We must if we follow the logic of the felicific calculus. If the 2,000 guin-eas heretofore spent by 2,000 buyers of an original piece of historical or philosophical research are henceforth spent by 42,000 buyers of shilling books, aggregate satisfaction is very probably enhanced. There is therefore a gain to society, according to this mode of thought which represents society as a collection of independent consumers.

Felicific calculus, counting in units of satisfactions afforded to individuals, cannot enter into its accounts the loss involved in the suppression of the piece of research—a fact which, by the way, brings to light the radically individualistic assumptions of a viewpoint usually labeled socialistic.

In fact, and although this entails an intellectual inconsistency, the most eager champions of income redistribution are highly sensitive to the cultural losses involved. And they press upon us a strong restorative. It is true that individuals will not be able to build up private libraries; but there will be bigger and better and ever more numerous public libraries. It is true that the producer of the book will not be sustained by individual buyers; but the author will be given a public grant, and so forth. All advocates of extreme redistribution couple it with most generous measures of state support for the whole superstructure of cultural activities. This calls for two comments. We shall deal first with the measures of compensation and then with their significance.

THE MORE REDISTRIBUTION, THE MORE POWER TO THE STATE

Already, when stressing the loss of investment capital which would result from a redistribution of incomes, we found that the necessary counterpart of lopping off the tops of higher incomes was the diversion by the State from these incomes of as much, or almost as much, as they used to pour into investment; the assumption which followed logically was that the State would take care of investment: a great function, a great responsibility, and a great power.

Now we find that by making it impossible for individuals to support cultural activities out of their shrunken incomes, we have developed upon the State another great function, another great power.

It then follows that the State finances, and therefore chooses, investments; and that it finances cultural activities and must thenceforth choose which it supports. There being no private buyers left for books or paintings or other creative work, the State must support literature and the arts either as buyer or as provider of *beneficia* to the producers, or in both capacities.

This is a rather disquieting thought. How quickly this State mastery follows upon measures of redistribution we can judge by the enormous progress toward such mastery which has already followed from limited redistribution.

VALUES AND SATISFACTIONS

But the fact that redistributionists are eager to repair by State expenditure the degradation of higher activities which would result from redistribution left to itself is very significant. They want to prevent a loss of values. Does this make sense? In the whole process of reasoning which sought to justify redistribution rationally, it was assumed that the individual's satisfaction was to be maximized and that the maximization of the sum of individual satisfactions was to be sought. It was granted for argument's sake that the sum of individual satisfactions may be maximized when incomes are equalized. But in this condition of income equality, if it be the best, must not market values set by the buyers and the resulting allocation of resources be, *ex hypothesi,* the best and most desirable? Is it not in direct contradiction with this whole line of reasoning to resume production of items that are not now in demand?

By our redistribution process we have now, it is assumed, reached the condition of maximum welfare, where the sum of individual satisfactions is maximized. Is it not illogical immediately to move away from it?

Surely, when we achieve the distribution of incomes which, it is claimed, maximizes the sum of satisfactions, we must let this distribution of incomes exert its influence upon the allocation of resources and productive activities, for it is only through this adjustment that the distribution of incomes is made meaningful. And when resources are so allocated, we must not interfere with their disposition, since by doing so we shall, as a matter of course, decrease the sum of satisfactions. It is then an inconsistency, and a very blatant one, to intervene with state support for such cultural activities as do not find a market. Those who spontaneously correct their schemes of redistribution by schemes for such support are in fact denying that the ideal allocation of resources and activities is that which maximizes the sum of satisfactions.

But it is clear that by this denial the whole process of reasoning by which redistribution is justified falls to the ground. If we say that, although people would be better satisfied to spend a certain sum on needs they are more conscious of, we deprive them of this satisfaction in order to support a painter, we obviously lose the right to argue that James's income must go to the mass of the people because satisfaction will thereby be increased. For all we know, James may be supporting the painter. We cannot accept the criterion of maximizing satisfactions when we are destroying private incomes and then reject it when we are planning state expenditure.

The recognition that maximizing satisfactions may destroy values which we are all willing to restore at the cost of moving away from the position of maximal satisfaction destroys the criterion of maximizing satisfactions.

COMMERCIALIZATION OF VALUES

An important component of socialism was the ethical revolt against the sordid motivations of a commercial society, where everything, so the saying went, was done for money. It is, then, a paradoxical outcome of socialist policies that the services which were rendered without thought of reward should be on their way to disappearance, a number of these activities being turned into professions and therefore performed for a monetary reward. Only very careless thinking can represent modern society as one in which more and more things are freely given. Services which are paid for in bulk by taxation are not freely given. And how could they be, when the producers of these free services claim salaries equal or superior to those which reward services that the individual buys in the market? The only services which are truly free are those which are rendered by individuals exacting no payment for them; and these are most manifestly on the decline.

An unnoticed consequence of this development is that demand rules far more imperiously in our society of today than it did heretofore. Where there is no margin of leisure and income to enable individuals to offer free services, where all services can be offered only insofar as their performance is paid for, either by individual buyers or by the community, there is no opportunity of proffering services the want of which is not felt by a sufficient number of consumers or by the leaders of the community.

Let us take as an illustration the various investigations into working-class conditions made in the nineteenth century. Such work was at the time susceptible of being rewarded neither by the commercial market nor by the government. It was done at the cost of individuals such as Villermé or Charles Booth, who thought it necessary to focus public attention upon the sorry state of things. Their initiative has altered the course of history. But the very people whose politics have been shaped by the outcome of these investigations tend to make such individual moves impossible in the future. And had the institutions toward which we tend been active at the time, the lack of private and of public demand for such investigations, the lack of prospective gains on the market and of state credits earmarked for the purpose would have defeated the venture.

There is generally no market for new ideas. These have to be elaborated and set forth at the cost of the innovator or a few adepts. It is an arresting thought that the writing of Marx's *Das Kapital* was made possible only by Engels' benefactions out of untaxed profits. Marx did not have to sell his wares on the market, nor did he have to get his project accepted by a public foundation of learning. His career testifies to the social utility of surplus incomes. It is, of course, assumed by *Etatistes* of today that Marx under the new dispensation would benefit from ample and honorable public support. But it seems so to them because his idea is now an old one and is accepted as the prevailing prejudice of our time. An innovator as bold today as he was in his day would not get by the boards of control which administer public funds. Nor is this scandalous: It is not the business of those who administer the common chest to subsidize bold ideas. These have to be offered on the market for ideas by convinced venturers.

A REDISTRIBUTION OF POWER FROM
INDIVIDUALS TO THE STATE

Our examination of the redistributionist ideal in theory and practice has led us gradually away from our initial contrast between rich and poor toward quite another contrast—that between individuals on the one hand, and the State and minor corporate bodies on the other.

Pure redistribution would merely transfer income from the richer to the poorer. This could conceivably be achieved by a simple reverse-tax or subsidy handed to the recipients of lower incomes from the proceeds of a special tax on higher incomes. But this is not the procedure which has prevailed. The State sets up as trustee for the lower-income group and doles out services and benefits. In order to avoid the creation of a "protected class," a discrimination fatal to political equality, the tendency has been to extend the benefits and services upward to all members of society, to cheapen food and rents for the rich as well as the poor, to assist the well-to-do in illness equally with the needy. The cost of such services has soared . . . and is quite incapable of being met by taxation of the well-to-do. . . . In fact, the public authorities, so that they may give to all, must take from all. And from the study made by the E.C.A. mission to the United Kingdom, it appears that lower-income families taken as a whole pay more into the exchequer than they draw from it.

The more one considers the matter, the clearer it becomes that redistribution is in effect far less a redistribution of free income from the richer to the poorer, as we imagined, than a redistribution of power from the individual to the State.

REDISTRIBUTION INCIDENTAL TO CENTRALIZATION?

In our exploration, we have found ourselves repeatedly coming across centralization as the major implication of redistributionist policies. Insofar as the State amputates higher incomes, it must assume their saving and investment functions, and we come to the centralization of investment. Insofar as the amputated higher incomes fail to sustain certain social activities, the State must step in, subsidize these activities, and preside over them. Insofar as income becomes inadequate for the formation and expenses of those people who fulfill the more intricate or specialized social functions, the State must see to the formation and upkeep of this personnel. Thus, the consequence of redistribution is to expand the State's role. And conversely, as we have just seen, the expansion of the State's takings is made acceptable only by measures of redistribution.

We then may well wonder which of these two closely linked phenomena is predominant: whether it is redistribution or centralization. We may ask ourselves whether what we are dealing with is not a political even more than a social phenomenon. This political phenomenon consists in the demolition of the class enjoying "independent means" and in the massing of means in the hands of managers. This results in a transfer of power from individuals to officials, who tend to constitute a new ruling class as against that which is being destroyed. And there is a faint but quite perceptible trend toward immunity for this new class from some part of the fiscal measures directed at the former.

This leads the observer to wonder how far the demand for equality is directed against inequality itself and is thus a fundamental demand, and how far it is directed against a certain set of "unequals" and is thus an unconscious move in a change of *élites*.

THE RELATION BETWEEN ECONOMIC
FREEDOM AND POLITICAL FREEDOM

Milton Friedman

From 1962, when he published *Capitalism and Freedom*, until his death in 2006, Milton Friedman was the most important advocate of libertarian ideas in the United States. Through his books, his long-running column in *Newsweek*, his public television series *Free to Choose*, and countless speeches and television appearances, he consistently and eloquently made the case for individual freedom. Although his professional specialty was economics, for which he won the Nobel Prize in 1976, he expounded a wide-ranging libertarian agenda, notably including school choice, abolition of the draft, and decriminalization of illegal drugs. For most of his professional life Friedman was the most prominent member of the economics faculty at the University of Chicago, where a large group of scholars produced a stream of solid policy research on the failure of government intervention into the market process. Important figures there included Frank H. Knight, Aaron Director, Yale Brozen, Sam Peltzman, and other Nobel laureates including F. A. Hayek, George Stigler, Ronald Coase, Merton Miller, and Gary Becker. In this excerpt from *Capitalism and Freedom*, Friedman discusses the necessity of economic freedom and widely dispersed property ownership for civil and political liberties.

It is widely believed that politics and economics are separate and largely unconnected; that individual freedom is a political problem and material welfare an economic problem; and that any kind of political arrangements can be combined with any kind of economic arrangements. The chief contemporary manifestation of this idea is the advocacy of "democratic socialism" by many who condemn out of hand the restrictions on individual freedom imposed by "totalitarian socialism" in Russia and who are persuaded that it is possible for a country to adopt the essential features of Russian economic arrangements and yet to ensure individual freedom through political arrangements. The thesis of this chapter is that such a view is a delusion, that there is an intimate connection between economics and politics, that only certain combinations of political and economic arrangements are possible, and that in particular, a society which is socialist cannot also be democratic, in the sense of guaranteeing individual freedom.

Economic arrangements play a dual role in the promotion of a free society. On the one hand, freedom in economic arrangements is itself a component of freedom broadly understood, so economic freedom is an end in itself. In the second place, economic freedom is also an indispensable means toward the achievement of political freedom.

The first of these roles of economic freedom needs special emphasis because intellectuals in particular have a strong bias against regarding this aspect of freedom as important. They tend to express contempt for what they regard as material aspects of life, and to regard their own pursuit of allegedly higher values as on a different plane of significance and as deserving of special attention. For most citizens of the country, however, if not for the intellectual, the direct importance of economic freedom is at least comparable in significance to the indirect importance of economic freedom as a means to political freedom.

The citizen of Great Britain, who after World War II was not permitted to spend his vacation in the United States because of exchange control, was being deprived of an essential freedom no less than the citizen of the United States, who was denied the opportunity to spend his vacation in Russia because of his political views. The one was ostensibly an economic limitation on freedom and the other a political limitation, yet there is no essential difference between the two.

The citizen of the United States who is compelled by law to devote

something like 10 per cent of his income to the purchase of a particular kind of retirement contract, administered by the government,
is being deprived of a corresponding part of his personal freedom.
How strongly this deprivation may be felt and its closeness to the
deprivation of religious freedom, which all would regard as "civil"
or "political" rather than "economic," were dramatized by an episode
involving a group of farmers of the Amish sect. On grounds of principle, this group regarded compulsory federal old age programs as an
infringement of their personal individual freedom and refused to pay
taxes or accept benefits. As a result, some of their livestock were sold
by auction in order to satisfy claims for social security levies. True,
the number of citizens who regard compulsory old age insurance as
a deprivation of freedom may be few, but the believer in freedom has
never counted noses.

A citizen of the United States who under the laws of various states
is not free to follow the occupation of his own choosing unless he can
get a license for it, is likewise being deprived of an essential part of
his freedom. So is the man who would like to exchange some of his
goods with, say, a Swiss for a watch but is prevented from doing so by
a quota. So also is the Californian who was thrown into jail for selling Alka-Seltzer at a price below that set by the manufacturer under
so-called "fair trade" laws. So also is the farmer who cannot grow the
amount of wheat he wants. And so on. Clearly, economic freedom, in
and of itself, is an extremely important part of total freedom.

Viewed as a means to the end of political freedom, economic
arrangements are important because of their effect on the concentration or dispersion of power. The kind of economic organization that
provides economic freedom directly, namely, competitive capitalism,
also promotes political freedom because it separates economic power
from political power and in this way enables the one to offset the
other.

Historical evidence speaks with a single voice on the relation between political freedom and a free market. I know of no example in
time or place of a society that has been marked by a large measure of
political freedom, and that has not also used something comparable
to a free market to organize the bulk of economic activity.

Because we live in a largely free society, we tend to forget how limited is the span of time and the part of the globe for which there has ever been anything like political freedom: the typical state of mankind is tyranny, servitude, and misery. The nineteenth century and early twentieth century in the Western world stand out as striking exceptions to the general trend of historical development. Political freedom in this instance clearly came along with the free market and the development of capitalist institutions. So also did political freedom in the golden age of Greece and in the early days of the Roman era.

History suggests only that capitalism is a necessary condition for political freedom. Clearly it is not a sufficient condition. Fascist Italy and Fascist Spain, Germany at various times in the last seventy years, Japan before World Wars I and II, tzarist Russia in the decades before World War I—are all societies that cannot conceivably be described as politically free. Yet, in each, private enterprise was the dominant form of economic organization. It is therefore clearly possible to have economic arrangements that are fundamentally capitalist and political arrangements that are not free.

Even in those societies, the citizenry had a good deal more freedom than citizens of a modern totalitarian state like Russia or Nazi Germany, in which economic totalitarianism is combined with political totalitarianism. Even in Russia under the Tzars, it was possible for some citizens, under some circumstances, to change their jobs without getting permission from political authority because capitalism and the existence of private property provided some check to the centralized power of the state.

The relation between political and economic freedom is complex and by no means unilateral. In the early nineteenth century, Bentham and the Philosophical Radicals were inclined to regard political freedom as a means to economic freedom. They believed that the masses were being hampered by the restrictions that were being imposed upon them, and that if political reform gave the bulk of the people the vote, they would do what was good for them, which was to vote for laissez faire. In retrospect, one cannot say that they were wrong. There was a large measure of political reform that was accompanied by economic reform in the direction of a great deal of laissez faire.

An enormous increase in the well-being of the masses followed this change in economic arrangements.

The triumph of Benthamite liberalism in nineteenth-century England was followed by a reaction toward increasing intervention by government in economic affairs. This tendency to collectivism was greatly accelerated, both in England and elsewhere, by the two World Wars. Welfare rather than freedom became the dominant note in democratic countries. Recognizing the implicit threat to individualism, the intellectual descendants of the Philosophical Radicals—Dicey, Mises, Hayek, and Simons, to mention only a few—feared that a continued movement toward centralized control of economic activity would prove *The Road to Serfdom,* as Hayek entitled his penetrating analysis of the process. Their emphasis was on economic freedom as a means toward political freedom.

Events since the end of World War II display still a different relation between economic and political freedom. Collectivist economic planning has indeed interfered with individual freedom. At least in some countries, however, the result has not been the suppression of freedom, but the reversal of economic policy. England again provides the most striking example. The turning point was perhaps the "control of engagements" order which, despite great misgivings, the Labour party found it necessary to impose in order to carry out its economic policy. Fully enforced and carried through, the law would have involved centralized allocation of individuals to occupations. This conflicted so sharply with personal liberty that it was enforced in a negligible number of cases, and then repealed after the law had been in effect for only a short period. Its repeal ushered in a decided shift in economic policy, marked by reduced reliance on centralized "plans" and "programs," by the dismantling of many controls, and by increased emphasis on the private market. A similar shift in policy occurred in most other democratic countries.

The proximate explanation of these shifts in policy is the limited success of central planning or its outright failure to achieve stated objectives. However, this failure is itself to be attributed, at least in some measure, to the political implications of central planning and to an unwillingness to follow out its logic when doing so requires trampling rough-shod on treasured private rights. It may well be that the shift is only a temporary interruption in the collectivist trend of this century. Even so, it illustrates the close relation between political freedom and economic arrangements.

Historical evidence by itself can never be convincing. Perhaps it was sheer coincidence that the expansion of freedom occurred at the same time as the development of capitalist and market institutions. Why should there be a connection? What are the logical links between economic and political freedom? In discussing these questions we shall consider first the market as a direct component of freedom, and then the indirect relation between market arrangements and political freedom. A by-product will be an outline of the ideal economic arrangements for a free society.

As liberals, we take freedom of the individual, or perhaps the family, as our ultimate goal in judging social arrangements. Freedom as a value in this sense has to do with the interrelations among people; it has no meaning whatsoever to a Robinson Crusoe on an isolated island (without his Man Friday). Robinson Crusoe on his island is subject to "constraint," he has limited "power," and he has only a limited number of alternatives, but there is no problem of freedom in the sense that is relevant to our discussion. Similarly, in a society freedom has nothing to say about what an individual does with his freedom; it is not an all-embracing ethic. Indeed, a major aim of the liberal is to leave the ethical problem for the individual to wrestle with. The "really" important ethical problems are those that face an individual in a free society—what he should do with his freedom. There are thus two sets of values that a liberal will emphasize—the values that are relevant to relations among people, which is the context in which he assigns first priority to freedom; and the values that are relevant to the individual in the exercise of his freedom, which is the realm of individual ethics and philosophy.

The liberal conceives of men as imperfect beings. He regards the problem of social organization to be as much a negative problem of preventing "bad" people from doing harm as of enabling "good" people to do good; and, of course, "bad" and "good" people may be the same people, depending on who is judging them.

The basic problem of social organization is how to co-ordinate the economic activities of large numbers of people. Even in relatively backward societies, extensive division of labor and specialization of function is required to make effective use of available resources. In advanced societies, the scale on which co-ordination is needed, to take full advantage of the opportunities offered by modern science and technology, is enormously greater. Literally millions of people are involved in providing one another with their daily bread, let alone with their yearly automobiles. The challenge to the believer in liberty is to reconcile this widespread interdependence with individual freedom.

Fundamentally, there are only two ways of co-ordinating the economic activities of millions. One is central direction involving the use of coercion—the technique of the army and of the modern totalitarian state. The other is voluntary co-operation of individuals—the technique of the market place.

The possibility of co-ordination through voluntary co-operation rests on the elementary—yet frequently denied—proposition that both parties to an economic transaction benefit from it, *provided the transaction is bi-laterally voluntary and informed.*

Exchange can therefore bring about co-ordination without coercion. A working model of a society organized through voluntary exchange is a *free private enterprise exchange economy*—what we have been calling competitive capitalism.

In its simplest form, such a society consists of a number of independent households—a collection of Robinson Crusoes, as it were. Each household uses the resources it controls to produce goods and services that it exchanges for goods and services produced by other households, on terms mutually acceptable to the two parties to the bargain. It is thereby enabled to satisfy its wants indirectly by producing goods and services for others, rather than directly by producing goods for its own immediate use. The incentive for adopting this indirect route is, of course, the increased product made possible by division of labor and specialization of function. Since the household always has the alternative of producing directly for itself, it need not enter into any exchange unless it benefits from it. Hence, no exchange will take place unless both parties do benefit from it. Cooperation is thereby achieved without coercion.

Specialization of function and division of labor would not go far if the ultimate productive unit were the household. In a modern society, we have gone much farther. We have introduced enterprises which are intermediaries between individuals in their capacities as suppliers of service and as purchasers of goods. And similarly, specialization of function and division of labor could not go very far if we had to continue to rely on the barter of product for product. In consequence, money has been introduced as a means of facilitating exchange, and of enabling the acts of purchase and of sale to be separated into two parts.

Despite the important role of enterprises and of money in our actual economy, and despite the numerous and complex problems they raise, the central characteristic of the market technique of achieving co-ordination is fully displayed in the simple exchange economy that contains neither enterprises nor money. As in that simple model, so in the complex enterprise and money-exchange economy, co-operation is strictly individual and voluntary *provided*: (a) that enterprises are private, so that the ultimate contracting parties are individuals and (b) that individuals are effectively free to enter or not to enter into any particular exchange, so that every transaction is strictly voluntary.

It is far easier to state these provisos in general terms than to spell them out in detail, or to specify precisely the institutional arrangements most conducive to their maintenance. Indeed, much of technical economic literature is concerned with precisely these questions. The basic requisite is the maintenance of law and order to prevent physical coercion of one individual by another and to enforce contracts voluntarily entered into, thus giving substance to "private." Aside from this, perhaps the most difficult problems arise from monopoly—which inhibits effective freedom by denying individuals alternatives to the particular exchange—and from "neighborhood effects"—effects on third parties for which it is not feasible to charge or recompense them. These problems will be discussed in more detail in the following chapter.

So long as effective freedom of exchange is maintained, the central feature of the market organization of economic activity is that it prevents one person from interfering with another in respect of most of his activities. The consumer is protected from coercion by the seller because of the presence of other sellers with whom he can deal. The seller is protected from coercion by the consumer because of other consumers to whom he can sell. The employee is protected from coercion by the employer because of other employers for whom he can work, and so on. And the market does this impersonally and without centralized authority.

Indeed, a major source of objection to a free economy is precisely that it does this task so well. It gives people what they want instead of what a particular group thinks they ought to want. Underlying most arguments against the free market is a lack of belief in freedom itself.

The existence of a free market does not of course eliminate the need for government. On the contrary, government is essential both as a forum for determining the "rules of the game" and as an umpire to interpret and enforce the rules decided on. What the market does is to reduce greatly the range of issues that must be decided through political means, and thereby to minimize the extent to which government need participate directly in the game. The characteristic feature of action through political channels is that it tends to require or enforce substantial conformity. The great advantage of the market, on the other hand, is that it permits wide diversity. It is, in political terms, a system of proportional representation. Each man can vote, as it were, for the color of tie he wants and get it; he does not have to see what color the majority wants and then, if he is in the minority, submit.

It is this feature of the market that we refer to when we say that the market provides economic freedom. But this characteristic also has implications that go far beyond the narrowly economic. Political freedom means the absence of coercion of a man by his fellow men. The fundamental threat to freedom is power to coerce, be it in the hands of a monarch, a dictator, an oligarchy, or a momentary majority. The preservation of freedom requires the elimination of such concentration of power to the fullest possible extent and the dispersal and distribution of whatever power cannot be eliminated—a system of checks and balances. By removing the organization of economic activity from the control of political authority, the market eliminates this source of coercive power. It enables economic strength to be a check to political power rather than a reinforcement.

Economic power can be widely dispersed. There is no law of conservation which forces the growth of new centers of economic strength to be at the expense of existing centers. Political power, on the other hand, is more difficult to decentralize. There can be numerous small independent governments. But it is far more difficult to maintain numerous equipotent small centers of political power in a single large government than it is to have numerous centers of economic strength in a single large economy. There can be many millionaires in one large economy. But can there be more than one really outstanding leader, one person on whom the energies and enthusiasms of his countrymen are centered? If the central government gains power, it is likely to be at the expense of local governments. There seems to be something like a fixed total of political power to be distributed. Consequently, if economic power is joined to political power, concentration seems almost inevitable. On the other hand, if economic power is kept in separate hands from political power, it can serve as a check and a counter to political power.

The force of this abstract argument can perhaps best be demonstrated by example. Let us consider first, a hypothetical example that may help to bring out the principles involved, and then some actual examples from recent experience that illustrate the way in which the market works to preserve political freedom.

One feature of a free society is surely the freedom of individuals to advocate and propagandize openly for a radical change in the structure of the society—so long as the advocacy is restricted to persuasion and does not include force or other forms of coercion. It is a mark of the political freedom of a capitalist society that men can openly advocate and work for socialism. Equally, political freedom in a socialist society would require that men be free to advocate the introduction of capitalism. How could the freedom to advocate capitalism be preserved and protected in a socialist society?

In order for men to advocate anything, they must in the first place be able to earn a living. This already raises a problem in a socialist society, since all jobs are under the direct control of political authorities. It would take an act of self-denial whose difficulty is underlined by experience in the United States after World War II with the problem of "security" among Federal employees, for a socialist government to permit its employees to advocate policies directly contrary to official doctrine.

But let us suppose this act of self-denial to be achieved. For advocacy of capitalism to mean anything, the proponents must be able to finance their cause—to hold public meetings, publish pamphlets, buy radio time, issue newspapers and magazines, and so on. How could they raise the funds? There might and probably would be men in the socialist society with large incomes, perhaps even large capital sums in the form of government bonds and the like, but these would of necessity be high public officials. It is possible to conceive of a minor socialist official retaining his job although openly advocating capitalism. It strains credulity to imagine the socialist top brass financing such "subversive" activities.

The only recourse for funds would be to raise small amounts from a large number of minor officials. But this is no real answer. To tap these sources, many people would already have to be persuaded, and our whole problem is how to initiate and finance a campaign to do so. Radical movements in capitalist societies have never been financed this way. They have typically been supported by a few wealthy individuals who have become persuaded—by a Frederick Vanderbilt Field, or an Anita McCormick Blaine, or a Corliss Lamont, to mention a few names recently prominent, or by a Friedrich Engels, to go farther back. This is a role of inequality of wealth in preserving political freedom that is seldom noted—the role of the patron.

In a capitalist society, it is only necessary to convince a few wealthy people to get funds to launch any idea, however strange, and there are many such persons, many independent foci of support. And, indeed, it is not even necessary to persuade people or financial institutions with available funds of the soundness of the ideas to be propagated. It is only necessary to persuade them that the propagation can be financially successful; that the newspaper or magazine or book or other venture will be profitable. The competitive publisher, for example, cannot afford to publish only writing with which he personally agrees; his touchstone must be the likelihood that the market will be large enough to yield a satisfactory return on his investment.

In this way, the market breaks the vicious circle and makes it possible ultimately to finance such ventures by small amounts from many people without first persuading them. There are no such possibilities in the socialist society; there is only the all-powerful state.

Let us stretch our imagination and suppose that a socialist government is aware of this problem and is composed of people anxious to preserve freedom. Could it provide the funds? Perhaps, but it is difficult to see how. It could establish a bureau for subsidizing subversive propaganda. But how could it choose whom to support? If it gave to all who asked, it would shortly find itself out of funds, for socialism cannot repeal the elementary economic law that a sufficiently high price will call forth a large supply. Make the advocacy of radical causes sufficiently remunerative, and the supply of advocates will be unlimited.

Moreover, freedom to advocate unpopular causes does not require that such advocacy be without cost. On the contrary, no society could be stable if advocacy of radical change were costless, much less subsidized. It is entirely appropriate that men make sacrifices to advocate causes in which they deeply believe. Indeed, it is important to preserve freedom only for people who are willing to practice self-denial, for otherwise freedom degenerates into license and irresponsibility. What is essential is that the cost of advocating unpopular causes be tolerable and not prohibitive.

But we are not yet through. In a free market society, it is enough to have the funds. The suppliers of paper are as willing to sell it to the *Daily Worker* as to the *Wall Street Journal*. In a socialist society, it would not be enough to have the funds. The hypothetical supporter of capitalism would have to persuade a government factory making paper to sell to him, the government printing press to print his pamphlets, a government post office to distribute them among the people, a government agency to rent him a hall in which to talk, and so on.

Perhaps there is some way in which one could overcome these difficulties and preserve freedom in a socialist society. One cannot say it is utterly impossible. What is clear, however, is that there are very real difficulties in establishing institutions that will effectively preserve the possibility of dissent. So far as I know, none of the people who have been in favor of socialism and also in favor of freedom have really faced up to this issue, or made even a respectable start at developing the institutional arrangements that would permit freedom under socialism. By contrast, it is clear how a free market capitalist society fosters freedom.

A striking practical example of these abstract principles is the experience of Winston Churchill. From 1933 to the outbreak of World War II, Churchill was not permitted to talk over the British radio, which was, of course, a government monopoly administered by the British Broadcasting Corporation. Here was a leading citizen of his country, a Member of Parliament, a former cabinet minister, a man who was desperately trying by every device possible to persuade his countrymen to take steps to ward off the menace of Hitler's Germany. He was not permitted to talk over the radio to the British people because the BBC was a government monopoly and his position was too "controversial."

Another striking example, reported in the January 26, 1959 issue of *Time,* has to do with the "Blacklist Fadeout." Says the *Time* story,

> The Oscar-awarding ritual is Hollywood's biggest pitch for dignity, but two years ago dignity suffered. When one Robert Rich was announced as top writer for the *The Brave One,* he never stepped forward. Robert Rich was a pseudonym, masking one of about 150 writers . . . blacklisted by the industry since 1947 as suspected Communists or fellow travelers. The case was particularly embarrassing because the Motion Picture Academy had barred any Communist or Fifth Amendment pleader from Oscar competition. Last week both the Communist rule and the mystery of Rich's identity were suddenly rescripted.
>
> Rich turned out to be Dalton *(Johnny Got His Gun)* Trumbo, one of the original "Hollywood Ten" writers who refused to testify at the 1947 hearings on Communism in the movie industry. Said producer Frank King, who had stoutly insisted that Robert Rich was "a young guy in Spain with a beard": "We have an obligation to

our stockholders to buy the best script we can. Trumbo brought us *The Brave One* and we bought it." . . .

In effect it was the formal end of the Hollywood black list. For barred writers, the informal end came long ago. At least 15% of current Hollywood films are reportedly written by blacklist members. Said Producer King, "There are more ghosts in Hollywood than in Forest Lawn. Every company in town has used the work of blacklisted people. We're just the first to confirm what everybody knows."

One may believe, as I do, that communism would destroy all of our freedoms, one may be opposed to it as firmly and as strongly as possible, and yet, at the same time, also believe that in a free society it is intolerable for a man to be prevented from making voluntary arrangements with others that are mutually attractive because he believes in or is trying to promote communism. His freedom includes his freedom to promote communism. Freedom also, of course, includes the freedom of others not to deal with him under those circumstances. The Hollywood blacklist was an unfree act that destroys freedom because it was a collusive arrangement that used coercive means to prevent voluntary exchanges. It didn't work precisely because the market made it costly for people to preserve the blacklist. The commercial emphasis, the fact that people who are running enterprises have an incentive to make as much money as they can, protected the freedom of the individuals who were blacklisted by providing them with an alternative form of employment, and by giving people an incentive to employ them.

If Hollywood and the movie industry had been government enterprises or if in England it had been a question of employment by the British Broadcasting Corporation it is difficult to believe that the "Hollywood Ten" or their equivalent would have found employment. Equally, it is difficult to believe that under those circumstances, strong proponents of individualism and private enterprise—or indeed strong proponents of any view other than the status quo—would be able to get employment.

Another example of the role of the market in preserving political freedom, was revealed in our experience with McCarthyism. Entirely aside from the substantive issues involved, and the merits of the charges made, what protection did individuals, and in particular government employees, have against irresponsible accusations and probings into matters that it went against their conscience to reveal? Their appeal to the Fifth Amendment would have been a hollow mockery without an alternative to government employment.

Their fundamental protection was the existence of a private-market economy in which they could earn a living. Here again, the protection was not absolute. Many potential private employers were, rightly or wrongly, averse to hiring those pilloried. It may well be that there was far less justification for the costs imposed on many of the people involved than for the costs generally imposed on people who advocate unpopular causes. But the important point is that the costs were limited and not prohibitive, as they would have been if government employment had been the only possibility.

It is of interest to note that a disproportionately large fraction of the people involved apparently went into the most competitive sectors of the economy—small business, trade, farming—where the market approaches most closely the ideal free market. No one who buys bread knows whether the wheat from which it is made was grown by a Communist or a Republican, by a constitutionalist or a Fascist, or, for that matter, by a Negro or a white. This illustrates how an impersonal market separates economic activities from political views and protects men from being discriminated against in their economic activities for reasons that are irrelevant to their productivity—whether these reasons are associated with their views or their color.

As this example suggests, the groups in our society that have the most at stake in the preservation and strengthening of competitive capitalism are those minority groups which can most easily become the object of the distrust and enmity of the majority—the Negroes, the Jews, the foreign-born, to mention only the most obvious. Yet, paradoxically enough, the enemies of the free market—the Socialists and Communists—have been recruited in disproportionate measure from these groups. Instead of recognizing that the existence of the market has protected them from the attitudes of their fellow countrymen, they mistakenly attribute the residual discrimination to the market.

THE MARKET ORDER OR CATALLAXY

F. A. Hayek

In this essay from *Law, Legislation, and Liberty,* vol. 2, Hayek examines a particular kind of spontaneous order: the market process. Again he distinguishes between the "made" order—which in the market context he calls an "economy," such as a household, a firm, or some other organization—and the spontaneous order, which he prefers to call a "catallaxy" rather than an economy. He stresses that the Great Society is held together—that is, that people are enabled to cooperate across great distances—by economic relations, but that doesn't mean that "economic ends" predominate over others. "There are, in the last resort, no economic ends." Rather, people use economic *means* to achieve purposes that are ultimately noneconomic. Following the rules of just conduct allows more people to achieve more ends than any other system possibly could.

THE NATURE OF THE MARKET ORDER

In chapter 2 we have discussed the general character of all spontaneous orders. It is necessary now to examine more fully the special attributes possessed by the order of the market and the nature of the benefits we owe to it. This order serves our ends not merely, as all order does, by guiding us in our actions and by bringing about a certain correspondence between the expectations of the different persons, but also, in a sense which we must now make more precise, by increasing the prospects or chances of every one of a greater command over the various goods (i.e., commodities and services) than we are able to secure in any other way. We shall see, however, that this manner of co-ordinating individual actions will secure a high degree of coincidence of expectations and an effective utilization of the knowledge and skills of the several members only at the price of a constant disappointment of some expectations.

For a proper understanding of the character of this order it is essential that we free ourselves of the misleading associations suggested by its usual description as an "economy." An economy, in the strict sense of the word in which a household, a farm, or an enterprise can be called economies, consists of a complex of activities by which a given set of means is allocated in accordance with a unitary plan among the competing ends according to their relative importance. The market order serves no such single order of ends. What is commonly called a social or national economy is in this sense not a single economy but a network of many interlaced economies. Its order shares, as we shall see, with the order of an economy proper some formal characteristics but not the most important one: its activities are not governed by a single scale or hierarchy of ends. The belief that the economic activities of the individual members of society are or ought to be part of one economy in the strict sense of this term, and that what is commonly described as the economy of a country or a society ought to be ordered and judged by the same criteria as an economy proper, is a chief source of error in this field. But, whenever we speak of the economy of a country, or of the world, we are employing a term which suggests that these systems ought to be run on socialist lines and directed according to a single plan so as to serve a unitary system of ends.

While an economy proper is an organization in the technical sense in which we have defined that term, that is, a deliberate arrangement of the use of the means which are known to some single agency, the cosmos of the market neither is nor could be governed by such a single scale of ends; it serves the multiplicity of separate and incommensurable ends of all its separate members.

The confusion which has been created by the ambiguity of the word economy is so serious that for our present purposes it seems necessary to confine its use strictly to the original meaning in which it describes a complex of deliberately co-ordinated actions serving a single scale of ends, and to adopt another term to describe the system of numerous interrelated economies which constitute the market-order. Since the name "catallactics" has long ago been suggested for the science which deals with the market order and has more recently been revived, it would seem appropriate to adopt a corresponding term for the market order itself. The term "catallactics" was derived from the Greek verb *katallattein* (or *katallassein*) which meant, significantly, not only "to exchange" but also "to admit into the community" and "to change from enemy into friend." From it the adjective "catallactic" has been derived to serve in the place of "economic" to describe the kind of phenomena with which the science of catallactics deals. The ancient Greeks knew neither this term nor had a corresponding noun; if they had formed one it would probably have been *katallaxia*. From this we can form an English term *catallaxy* which we shall use to describe the order brought about by the mutual adjustment of many individual economies in a market. A catallaxy is thus the special kind of spontaneous order produced by the market through people acting within the rules of the law of property, tort and contract.

A FREE SOCIETY IS A PLURALISTIC SOCIETY
WITHOUT A COMMON HIERARCHY OF PARTICULAR ENDS

It is often made a reproach to the Great Society and its market order that it lacks an agreed ranking of ends. This, however, is in fact its great merit which makes individual freedom and all it values possible. The Great Society arose through the discovery that men can live together in peace and mutually benefiting each other without agreeing on the particular aims which they severally pursue. The discovery that by substituting abstract rules of conduct for obligatory concrete ends made it possible to extend the order of peace beyond the small groups pursuing the same ends, because it enabled each individual to gain from the skill and knowledge of others whom he need not even know and whose aims could be wholly different from his own.

The decisive step which made such peaceful collaboration possible in the absence of concrete common purposes was the adoption of barter or exchange. It was the simple recognition that different persons had different uses for the same things, and that often each of two individuals would benefit if he obtained something the other had, in return for his giving the other what he needed. All that was required to bring this about was that rules be recognized which determined what belonged to each, and how such property could be transferred by consent. There was no need for the parties to agree on the purposes which this transaction served. It is indeed characteristic of such acts of exchange that they serve different and independent purposes of each partner in the transaction, and that they thus assist the parties as means for different ends. The parties are in fact the more likely to benefit from exchange the more their needs differ. While within an organization the several members will assist each other to the extent that they are made to aim at the same purposes, in a catallaxy they are induced to contribute to the needs of others without caring or even knowing about them.

In the Great Society we all in fact contribute not only to the satisfaction of needs of which we do not know, but sometimes even to the achievement of ends of which we would disapprove if we knew about them. We cannot help this because we do not know for what purposes the goods or services which we supply to others will be used by them. That we assist in the realization of other people's aims without sharing them or even knowing them, and solely in order to achieve our own aims, is the source of strength of the Great Society. So long as collaboration presupposes common purposes, people with different aims are necessarily enemies who may fight each other for the same means; only the introduction of barter made it possible for the different individuals to be of use to each other without agreeing on the ultimate ends.

When this effect of exchange of making people mutually benefit each other without intending to do so was first clearly recognized, too much stress was laid on the resulting division of labour and on the fact that it was their "selfish" aims which led the different persons to render services to each other. This is much too narrow a view of the matter. Division of labour is extensively practised also within organizations; and the advantages of the spontaneous order do not depend on people being selfish in the ordinary sense of this word. The important point about the catallaxy is that it reconciles different knowledge and different purposes which, whether the individuals be selfish or not, will greatly differ from one person to another. It is because in the catallaxy men, while following their own interests, whether wholly egotistical or highly altruistic, will further the aims of many others, most of whom they will never know, that it is as an overall order so superior to any deliberate organization: in the Great Society the different members benefit from each other's efforts not only in spite of but often even because of their several aims being different.

Many people regard it as revolting that the Great Society has no common concrete purposes or, as we may say, that it is merely means-connected and not ends-connected. It is indeed true that the chief common purpose of all its members is the purely instrumental one of securing the formation of an abstract order which has no specific purposes but will enhance for all the prospects of achieving their respective purposes. The prevailing moral tradition, much of which still derives from the end-connected tribal society, makes people often regard this circumstance as a moral defect of the Great Society which ought to be remedied. Yet it was the very restriction of coercion to the observance of the negative rules of just conduct that made possible the integration into a peaceful order of individuals and groups which pursued different ends; and it is the absence of prescribed common ends which makes a society of free men all that it has come to mean to us.

Though the conception that a common scale of particular values is a good thing which ought, if necessary, to be enforced, is deeply founded in the history of the human race, its intellectual defence today is based mainly on the erroneous belief that such a common scale of ends is necessary for the integration of the individual activities into an order, and a necessary condition of peace. This error is, however, the greatest obstacle to the achievement of those very ends. A Great Society has nothing to do with, and is in fact irreconcilable with "solidarity" in the true sense of unitedness in the pursuit of known common goals. If we all occasionally feel that it is a good thing to have a common purpose with our fellows, and enjoy a sense of elation when we can act as members of a group aiming at common ends, this is an instinct which we have inherited from tribal society and which no doubt often still stands us in good stead whenever it is important that in a small group we should act in concert to meet a sudden emergency. It shows itself conspicuously when sometimes even the outbreak of war is felt as satisfying a craving for such a common purpose; and it manifests itself most clearly in modern times in the two greatest threats to a free civilization: nationalism and socialism.

Most of the knowledge on which we rely in the pursuit of our ends is the unintended by-product of others exploring the world in different directions from those we pursue ourselves because they are impelled by different aims; it would never have become available to us if only those ends were pursued which we regarded as desirable. To make it a condition for the membership of a society that one approved of, and deliberately supported, the concrete ends which one's fellow members serve, would eliminate the chief factor which makes for the advancement of such a society. Where agreement on concrete objects is a necessary condition of order and peace, and dissent a danger to the order of the society, where approval and censure depend on the concrete ends which particular actions serve, the forces for intellectual progress would be much confined. However much the existence of agreement on ends may in many respects smooth the course of life, the possibility of disagreement, or at least the lack of compulsion to agree on particular ends, is the basis of the kind of civilization which has grown up since the Greeks developed independent thought of the individual as the most effective method of advancement of the human mind.

THOUGH NOT A SINGLE ECONOMY, THE GREAT SOCIETY IS STILL HELD TOGETHER MAINLY BY WHAT VULGARLY ARE CALLED ECONOMIC RELATIONS

The misconception that the market order is an economy in the strict sense of the term is usually found combined with the denial that the

Great Society is held together by what are loosely called economic relations. These two views are frequently held by the same persons because it is certainly true that those deliberate organizations which are properly called economies are based on an agreement on common ends which in turn mostly are non-economic; while it is the great advantage of the spontaneous order of the market that it is merely means-connected and that, therefore, it makes agreement on ends unnecessary and a reconciliation of divergent purposes possible. What are commonly called economic relations are indeed relations determined by the fact that the use of all means is affected by the striving for those many different purposes. It is in this wide sense of the term "economic" that the interdependence or coherence of the parts of the Great Society is purely economic.

The suggestion that in this wide sense the only ties which hold the whole of a Great Society together are purely "economic" (more precisely "catallactic") arouses great emotional resistance. Yet the fact can hardly be denied; nor the fact that, in a society of the dimensions and complexity of a modern country or of the world, it can hardly be otherwise. Most people are still reluctant to accept the fact that it should be the disdained "cash-nexus" which holds the Great Society together, that the great ideal of the unity of mankind should in the last resort depend on the relations between the parts being governed by the striving for the better satisfaction of their material needs.

It is of course true that within the overall framework of the Great Society there exist numerous networks of other relations that are in no sense economic. But this does not alter the fact that it is the market order which makes peaceful reconciliation of the divergent purposes possible—and possible by a process which redounds to the benefit of all. That interdependence of all men, which is now in everybody's mouth and which tends to make all mankind One World, not only is the effect of the market order but could not have been brought about by any other means. What today connects the life of any European or American with what happens in Australia, Japan or Zaire are repercussions transmitted by the network of market relations. This is clearly seen when we reflect how little, for instance, all the technological possibilities of transportation and communication would matter if the conditions of production were the same in all the different parts of the world.

The benefits from the knowledge which others possess, including all the advances of science, reach us through channels provided and directed by the market mechanism. Even the degree to which we can participate in the aesthetic or moral strivings of men in other parts of the world we owe to the economic nexus. It is true that on the whole this dependence of every man on the actions of so many others is not a physical but what we call an economic fact. It is therefore a misunderstanding, caused by the misleading terms used, if the economists are sometimes accused of "pan-economism," a tendency to see everything from the economic angle, or, worse, wanting to make "economic purposes" prevail over all others. The truth is that catallactics is the science which describes the only overall order that comprehends nearly all mankind, and that the economist is therefore entitled to insist that conduciveness to that order be accepted as a standard by which all particular institutions are judged.

It is, however, a misunderstanding to represent this as an effort to make "economic ends" prevail over others. There are, in the last resort, no economic ends. The economic efforts of the individuals as well as the services which the market order renders to them, consist in an allocation of means for the competing ultimate purposes which are always non-economic. The task of all economic activity is to reconcile the competing ends by deciding for which of them the limited means are to be used. The market order reconciles the claims of the different non-economic ends by the only known process that benefits all—without, however, assuring that the more important comes before the less important, for the simple reason that there can exist in such a system no single ordering of needs. What it tends to bring about is merely a state of affairs in which no need is served at the cost of withdrawing a greater amount of means from the use for other needs than is necessary to satisfy it. The market is the only known method by which this can be achieved without an agreement on the relative importance of the different ultimate ends, and solely on the basis of a principle of reciprocity through which the opportunities of any person are likely to be greater than they would otherwise be.

THE AIM OF POLICY IN A SOCIETY OF FREE
MEN CANNOT BE A MAXIMUM OF FOREKNOWN
RESULTS BUT ONLY AN ABSTRACT ORDER

The erroneous interpretation of the catallaxy as an economy in the strict sense of this word frequently leads to attempts to evaluate the benefits which we derive from it in terms of the degree of satisfaction of a given order of ends. But, if the importance of the various demands is judged by the price offered, this approach, as has been pointed out innumerable times, by the critics of the market order even more frequently than by its defenders, involves us in a vicious circle: because the relative strength of the demand for the different goods and services to which the market will adjust their production is itself determined by the distribution of incomes which in turn is determined by the market mechanism. Many writers have concluded from this that if this scale of relative demands cannot without circular reasoning be accepted as the common scale of values, another scale of ends must be postulated if we are to judge the effectiveness of this market order.

The belief that there can be no rational policy without a common scale of concrete ends implies, however, an interpretation of the catallaxy as an economy proper and for this reason is misleading. Policy need not be guided by the striving for the achievement of particular results, but may be directed towards securing an abstract overall order of such character that it will secure for the members the best chance of achieving their different and largely unknown particular ends. The aim of policy in such a society would have to be to increase equally the chances for any unknown member of society of pursuing with success his equally unknown purposes, and to restrict the use of coercion (apart from the raising of taxes) to the enforcement of such rules as will, if universally applied, tend in this sense to improve everyone's opportunities.

A policy making use of the spontaneously ordering forces therefore cannot aim at a known maximum of particular results, but must aim at increasing, for any person picked out at random, the prospects that the overall effect of all changes required by that order will be to increase his chances of attaining his ends. We have seen that the common good in this sense is not a particular state of things but consists in an abstract order which in a free society must leave undetermined the degree to which the several particular needs will be met. The aim will have to be an order which will increase everybody's chances as much as possible—not at every moment, but only "on the whole" and in the long run.

Because the results of any economic policy must depend on the use made of the operation of the market by unknown persons guided by their own knowledge and their own aims, the goal of such a policy must be to provide a multi-purpose instrument which at no particular moment may be the one best adapted to the particular circumstances, but which will be the best for the great variety of circumstances likely to occur. If we had known those particular circumstances in advance, we could probably have better equipped ourselves to deal with them; but since we do not know them beforehand, we must be content with a less specialized instrument which will allow us to cope even with very unlikely events. . . .

SPECIFIC COMMANDS ("INTERFERENCE") IN A CATALLAXY CREATE DISORDER AND CAN NEVER BE JUST

A rule of just conduct serves the reconciliation of the different purposes of many individuals. A command serves the achievement of particular results. Unlike a rule of just conduct, it does not merely limit the range of choice of the individuals (or require them to satisfy expectations they have deliberately created) but commands them to act in a particular manner not required of other persons.

The term "interference" (or "intervention") is properly applied only to such specific orders which, unlike the rules of just conduct, do not serve merely the formation of a spontaneous order but aim at particular results. It was in this sense only that the classical economists used the term. They would not have applied it to the establishment or improvement of those generic rules which are required for the functioning of the market order and which they explicitly presupposed in their analysis.

Even in ordinary language "interference" implies the operation of a process that proceeds by itself on certain principles because its parts obey certain rules. We would not call it interference if we oiled a clockwork, or in any other way secured the conditions that a going mechanism required for its proper functioning. Only if we changed the position of any particular part in a manner which is not in accord with the general principle of its operation, such as shifting the hands of a clock, can it properly be said that we have interfered. The aim of interference thus is always to bring about a particular result which is different from that which would have been produced if the mechanism had been allowed unaided to follow its inherent principles. If the rules on which such a process proceeds are determined beforehand, the particular results it will produce at any one time will be independent of the momentary wishes of men.

The particular results that will be determined by altering a particular action of the system will always be inconsistent with its overall order: if they were not, they could have been achieved by changing the rules on which the system was henceforth to operate. Interference, if the term is properly used, is therefore by definition an isolated act of coercion, undertaken for the purpose of achieving a particular result, and without committing oneself to do the same in all instances where some circumstances defined by a rule are the same. It is, therefore, always an unjust act in which somebody is coerced (usually in the interest of a third) in circumstances where another would not be coerced, and for purposes which are not his own.

It is, moreover, an act which will always disrupt the overall order and will prevent that mutual adjustment of all its parts on which the spontaneous order rests. It will do this by preventing the persons to whom the specific commands are directed from adapting their actions to circumstances known to them, and by making them serve some particular ends which others are not required to serve, and which will be satisfied at the expense of some other unpredictable effects. Every act of interference thus creates a privilege in the sense that it will secure benefits to some at the expense of others, in a manner which cannot be justified by principles capable of general application. What in this respect the formation of a spontaneous order requires is what is also required by the confinement of all coercion to the enforcement of rules of just conduct: that coercion be used only where it is required by uniform rules equally applicable to all. . . .

THE GOOD SOCIETY IS ONE IN WHICH THE CHANCES OF ANYONE SELECTED AT RANDOM ARE LIKELY TO BE AS GREAT AS POSSIBLE

The conclusion to which our considerations lead is thus that we should regard as the most desirable order of society one which we would choose if we knew that our initial position in it would be decided purely by chance (such as the fact of our being born into a particular family). Since the attraction such chance would possess for any particular adult individual would probably be dependent on the particular skills, capacities and tastes he has already acquired, a better way of putting this would be to say that the best society would be that in which we would prefer to place our children if we knew that their position in it would be determined by lot. Very few people would probably in this case prefer a strictly egalitarian order. Yet, while one might, for instance, regard the kind of life lived in the past by the landed aristocracy as the most attractive kind of life, and would choose a society in which such a class existed if he were assured that he or his children would be a member of that class, he would probably decide differently if he knew that that position would be determined by drawing lots and that in consequence it would be much more probable that he would become an agricultural labourer. He would then very likely choose that very type of industrial society which did not offer such delectable plums to a few but offered better prospects to the great majority.

IF YOU'RE PAYING, I'LL HAVE TOP SIRLOIN

Russell Roberts

For centuries liberals worked to bring about governments based on the consent of the governed, though they disagreed a great deal on how democratic or republican forms of government could avoid the problems of both an unconstrained ruler and an unconstrained majoritarianism. Two centuries of experience with democratic decision making have persuaded many libertarians that democracies have a natural tendency to produce government bigger and more expensive than is either proper by libertarian standards or desirable to most citizens. This problem was explored beginning more than a century ago by the Italian public finance theorists such as Vilfredo Pareto, Giovanni Montemartini, Amilcare Puviani, and Luigi Einaudi, first president of the Italian Republic after World War II. In our own time it has been the central focus of the Public Choice school, in such books as *The Calculus of Consent* by James M. Buchanan and Gordon Tullock, *Theory of Public Choice* edited by Buchanan and Robert D. Tollison, *Bureaucracy and Representative Government* by William A. Niskanen, and *The Vote Motive* by Tullock. In this short essay from *The Wall Street Journal*, Russell Roberts, a research fellow at Stanford University's Hoover Institution, explains the process by which individuals as voters demand more government services than any of them would be willing to pay for directly as consumers.

As Congress tries to cut spending, I am reminded of an evening last fall at the St. Louis Repertory Theater, our local company. Before the curtain rose, the company's director appeared and encouraged us to vote against a ballot proposition to limit state taxes. He feared it would lead to reduced funding for the company.

I turned to the woman sitting next to me and asked her if she felt guilty knowing that her ticket was subsidized by some farmer in the "boot heel" of Missouri. No, she answered, he's probably getting something, too. She seemed to be implying that somehow it all evened out.

I left her alone. But I wanted to say: No, it doesn't even out. That's the whole idea behind much of what the government does. The subsidized theatergoer thinks she's getting a good deal, and so does the farmer. If it "evened out" for everybody, then matters would really be depressing: all that money shuffled around, all those people working for the IRS, all those marginal tax rates discouraging work effort just to get everybody to get the same deal.

Here in St. Louis we recently completed the Metrolink, a light rail system. It cost $380 million to build. We locals contributed zero out of pocket, except for the usual federal taxes. Shouldn't we feel guilty making people in California pay for our trips to the hockey arena downtown? No, say the beneficiaries. After all, we paid for BART in San Francisco, MARTA in Atlanta and all the other extraordinarily expensive, underutilized public transportation systems whose benefits fall far short of their costs. It's only fair that we get our turn at the trough.

This destructive justification reminds me of a very strange restaurant.

When you eat there, you usually spend about $6. You have a sandwich, fries and a drink. Of course you'd also enjoy dessert and a second drink, but they would cost an additional $4. The extra food isn't worth $4 to you, so you stick with the $6 meal.

Sometimes, you go to the restaurant with three friends. The four of you split the check evenly. You realize after a while that the $4 drink and dessert will end up costing you only $1 because the total tab is split four ways. Should you order the drink and dessert? If you're a nice person, you might want to spare your friends from having to subsidize your extravagance. Then it dawns on you that they may be ordering extras financed out of your pocket. But they're your friends. You wouldn't do that to each other.

But now suppose the tab is split not at each table but across the 100 diners at all the tables. Now adding the $4 drink and dessert costs only four cents. Splurging is easy to justify now. In fact, you won't just add a drink and dessert, you'll upgrade to the steak and add a bottle of wine.

Suppose you and everybody else orders $40 worth of food. The tab for the entire restaurant will be $4,000. Divided by the 100 diners, your bill comes to $40. Like my neighbor at the theater, you'll get your "fair share." But this outcome is a disaster. When you dined alone, you spent $6. The extra $34 of steak and other treats was not worth it. But in competition with the others, you chose a meal far out of your price range whose enjoyment fell far short of its cost.

Self-restraint goes unrewarded. If you go back to ordering your $6 meal in hopes of saving money, your tab will be close to $40 anyway, unless the other 99 diners cut back also. The good citizen starts to feel like a chump.

And so we read of the freshmen congressman eager to cut pork out of the budget but in trouble back home because local projects will also come under the knife. Instead of being proud to lead the way, he is forced to fight for the projects, to make sure his district gets its "fair share."

Matters get much worse when there are gluttons and drunkards at the restaurant mixing with dieters and teetotalers. The average tab might be $40, but some are eating $80 worth of food while others are stuck with salad and an iced tea. Those with modest appetites would like to flee the premises, but suppose it's the only restaurant in town and you're forced to eat there every night. Resentment and anger come naturally. And since it's the only restaurant in town, you can imagine the quality of the service.

Such a restaurant can be a happy place if the light eaters enjoy watching the gluttony of those who eat and drink with gusto. Many government programs generate a comparable range of support. But many do not.

How many Americans other than farmers benefit from agriculture subsidies? How many Americans other than train riders benefit from the Amtrak subsidy? How many Americans outside of the theater and its patrons benefit from the subsidy to the arts?

People who are overeating at the expense of others should be ashamed. The only way to avoid national indigestion is to close the government restaurant where few benefit at the expense of many.

PART SIX

PEACE AND INTERNATIONAL HARMONY

The classical liberals regarded war as the greatest scourge that state power could visit upon society. Like Christians, humanists, and many other people, they abhorred the mass murder that war entailed. But liberals added something else to the argument against war, as Ludwig von Mises points out in this section. Liberals recognized that war disrupts peaceful forms of cooperation: families, businesses, and civil society. It wreaks havoc on the whole process of social cooperation and long-range planning. Thus, preventing kings from putting their subjects at risk in unnecessary wars was one of liberalism's major goals. Adam Smith argued that little else was needed to create a happy and prosperous society but "peace, easy taxes, and a tolerable administration of justice."

Liberals also understood that war creates big government. Throughout history it has provided an excuse for governments to arrogate money and power to themselves and regiment society. Thomas Paine wrote that an observer of the British government would conclude "that taxes were not raised to carry on wars, but that wars were raised to carry on taxes." That is, it seemed that the English and other European governments engaged in quarreling *in order* "to fleece their countries by taxes." The early twentieth-century liberal Randolph Bourne wrote simply, "War is the health of the State"; it is the only way to create a herd instinct in a free people and the best way to extend the powers of government.

The American Founders, happy to be free of endless European wars, made peace and neutrality cardinal principles of their new government. Americans regarded the wide Atlantic Ocean as their great protection from European intrigues. "The true interest of the States," the Continental Congress resolved in 1783, "requires that they should be as little as possible engaged in the politics and controversies of European nations." George Washington wrote to a French friend in 1788, "Separated as we are by a world of water from other Nations, if we are wise we shall surely avoid being drawn into the labyrinth of their politics, and involved in their destructive wars." In his Farewell Address, Washington told the nation, "The great rule in conduct for us, in regard to foreign nations, is in extending our commercial relations to have with them as little political connection as possible." And Thomas Jefferson described American foreign policy in his First Inaugural Address this way: "Peace, commerce, and honest friendship with all nations—entangling alliances with none."

John Quincy Adams, son of a prominent Founder and himself a future president of the United States, enunciated the American view of foreign policy in a Fourth of July address in 1821, when he was President James Monroe's secretary of state:

> Wherever the standard of freedom and independence has been or shall be unfurled, there will [America's] heart, her benedictions and her prayers be. But she goes not abroad, in search of monsters to destroy. She is the well-wisher to the freedom and independence of all. She is the champion and vindicator only of her own. . . . She well knows that by once enlisting under other banners than her own, were they even the banners of foreign independence, she would involve herself beyond the power of extrication, in all the wars of interest and intrigue, of individual avarice, envy, and ambition, which assume the colors and usurp the standard of freedom. The fundamental maxims of her policy would insensibly change from *liberty* to *force*. . . . She might become the dictatress of the world. She would no longer be the ruler of her own spirit!

European liberals envied the peaceful American republic and made peace and free trade their cardinal principles. Building on the analysis of David Hume and Adam Smith, nineteenth-century English and French liberals pointed out that countries benefit from the prosperity of their neighbors, who have more to offer in trade. They insisted, "If goods don't cross borders, armies will." Richard Cobden, John Bright, and other English free-traders—often known as the Manchester School liberals—worked first to repeal the Corn Laws that kept the price of bread high in England and then to keep England out of unnecessary wars. Their counterparts on the Continent undertook similar efforts.

Before the liberal revolutions in Europe, kings and princes saw no need to justify their wars. It was taken for granted that kings would lead their subjects into war for personal glory or national aggrandizement. After the rapid triumph of liberalism, wars did not cease, but rulers at least had to offer a justification for going to war. After the end of the Napoleonic wars in 1815, liberal Europe enjoyed a century without a general Continental war, though the peace was broken by such outbreaks as wars of national unification and the Crimean War.

By the end of the nineteenth century, however, liberalism began to recede in the face of nationalism and socialism. Liberals such as E. L. Godkin, the founding editor of *The Nation,* mourned that there would be "international struggles on a terrific scale" before liberalism was again in the ascendancy. He was more horribly right than he could have imagined.

Not only did the wars of the twentieth century result in death and destruction on an unprecedented scale, they led to tremendous increases in statism of all sorts. The destruction of civil society in Russia, Central Europe, and China helped open the way for communist victories; and the harsh terms imposed on the defeated Germany in 1918, combined with a burdensome welfare state, created the conditions for the rise of National Socialism under Adolf Hitler. Even in the democratic countries war brought about a change in the relationship between the individual and the state. During World Wars I and II the United States government (like European governments) assumed powers it could have never have acquired in peacetime, powers such as wage and price controls, rationing, press restrictions, close control of labor and production, and astronomical tax rates. Constitutional restrictions on federal power were swiftly eroded. The lesson libertarians drew from the experience was that war was at best a terrible price that had to be paid for freedom and should be avoided whenever possible.

As the latter essays in this section point out, in the nuclear age it is especially important to avoid war. American libertarians argue that a policy of strategic independence would keep American citizens safe from foreign threats and avoid involving the United States in the futile task of policing the world.

COMMERCE IS THE GRAND PANACEA

Richard Cobden

Richard Cobden (1804–65) was born poor and became a successful manufacturer in Manchester, England. He was enormously influential in British politics as a writer, organizer, and member of Parliament. Along with the great orator John Bright, he led the Anti-Corn Law League, which agitated successfully for repeal of the tariff on grain. Cobden twice turned down positions in the British cabinet, preferring to retain his independence and the freedom to speak out on issues. After the repeal of the Corn Laws in 1846, he and Bright worked for reductions in government spending, for repeal of a tax on newspapers, and for peace and nonintervention. Naomi Churgin Miller summed up his views on foreign affairs in a 1973 edition of Cobden's *Political Writings:* "Against the doctrine of balance of power, Cobden urged the advantages of a policy of non-intervention; against recourse to armies and navies, he emphasized the greater power that derived from wealth, trade, and internal improvement; in place of war as a means of resolving international disputes, he argued for the wiser, pacific method of arbitration." This selection is from his 1835 pamphlet *England, Ireland, and America,* written just before the start of his long public career.

———

The middle and industrious classes of England can have no interest apart from the preservation of peace. The honours, the fame, the emoluments of war belong not to them; the battle-plain is the harvest-field of the aristocracy, watered with the blood of the people.

We know of no means by which a body of members in the re-formed House of Commons could so fairly achieve for itself the patriotic title of a national party, as by associating for the common object of deprecating all intervention on our part in continental pol-itics. Such a party might well comprise every representative of our manufacturing and commercial districts, and would, we doubt not, very soon embrace the majority of a powerful House of Commons. At some future election, we may probably see the test of *"no foreign politics"* applied to those who offer to become the representatives of free constituencies. Happy would it have been for us, and well for our posterity, had such a feeling predominated in this country fifty years ago! But although, since the peace, we have profited so little by the experience of the revolutionary wars as to seek a participation in all the subsequent continental squabbles, and though we are bound by treaties, or involved in guarantees, with almost every state of Europe; still the coming moment is only the more proper for adopting the true path of national policy, which always lies open to us. . . .

Nor do we think it would tend less to promote the ulterior benefit of our continental neighbours than our own, were Great Britain to refrain from participating in the conflicts that may arise around her. An onward movement of constitutional liberty must continue to be made by the less advanced nations of Europe, so long as one of its greatest families holds out the example of liberal and enlightened freedom. England, by calmly directing her undivided energies to the purifying of her own internal institutions, to the emancipation of her commerce—above all, to the unfettering of her press from its excise bonds—would, by thus serving as it were for the beacon of other na-tions, aid more effectually the cause of political progression all over the continent than she could possibly do by plunging herself into the strife of European wars.

For, let it never be forgotten, that it is not by means of war that states are rendered fit for the enjoyment of constitutional freedom; on the contrary, whilst terror and bloodshed reign in the land, in-volving men's minds in the extremities of hopes and fears, there can be no process of thought, no education going on, by which alone can a people be prepared for the enjoyment of rational liberty. Hence, after a struggle of twenty years, *begun in behalf of freedom,* no sooner had the wars of the French revolution terminated, than all the nations of the continent fell back again into their previous state of political servitude, and from which they have, ever since the peace, been *qualifying* to rescue themselves, by the gradual process of intellectual advancement. Those who, from an eager desire to aid civilisation, wish that Great Britain should interpose in the dissensions of neighbouring states, would do wisely to study, in the history of their own country, how well a people can, by the force and virtue of native elements, and without external assistance of any kind, work out their own political regeneration: they might learn too, by their own annals, that it is only when at peace with other states that a nation finds the leisure for looking within itself, and discovering the means to accomplish great domestic ameliorations.

To those generous spirits we would urge, that, in the present day, commerce is the grand panacea, which, like a beneficent medical discovery, will serve to inoculate with the healthy and saving taste for civilisation all the nations of the world. Not a bale of merchandise leaves our shores, but it bears the seeds of intelligence and fruitful thought to the members of some less enlightened community; not a merchant visits our seats of manufacturing industry, but he returns to his own country the missionary of freedom, peace, and good government—whilst our steam boats, that now visit every port of Europe, and our miraculous railroads, that are the talk of all nations, are the advertisements and vouchers for the value of our enlightened institutions.

NONINTERVENTION

Richard Cobden

In this 1850 speech in Parliament criticizing the British government's dispatch of naval forces to Greece in response to alleged violations of British citizens' property by the Greek government (known as the Don Pacifico affair), Cobden laid out the policy of nonintervention as a principle of foreign affairs.

I say, if you want to benefit nations who are struggling for their freedom, establish as one of the maxims of international law the principle of non-intervention. If you want to give a guarantee for peace, and as I believe, the surest guarantee for progress and freedom, lay down this principle, and act on it, that no foreign State has a right by force to interfere with the domestic concerns of another State, even to confer a benefit on it, without its own consent.

Do you want to benefit the Hungarians and Italians? I think I know more of them than most people in this country. I sympathised with them during their manly struggle for freedom, and I have admired and respected them not less in their hour of adversity. I will tell you the sentiments of the leading men of the Hungarians. . . .

These men say,—"We don't ask you to help us, or to come to our assistance. Establish such a principle as shall provide we shall not be interfered with by others." And what do the Italians say? They don't want the English to interfere with them, or to help them. "Leave us to ourselves," they say. "Establish the principle that we shall not be interfered with by foreigners."

I will answer the hon. and learned Gentleman's cheer. He seems to ask, How will you keep out Austria from Italy, and Russia from Hungary? I will give him an illustration of what I mean. Does he remember when Kossuth took refuge in Turkey, and that Austria and the Emperor of Russia demanded him back? I beg him to understand that this illustrious refugee was not saved by any intervention of the Foreign Secretary. Has it not been admitted that the Emperor of Russia gave up his claim before the courier arrived from England? What was it, then, that liberated them? It was the universal outbreak of public opinion and public indignation in Western Europe. And why had public opinion this power? Because this demand for the extradition of political offenders was a violation of the law of nations, which declares that persons who have committed political offences on one state shall find a sanctuary in another, and ought not to be delivered up. If our Government were always to act upon this principle of non-intervention, we should see the law of nations declaring itself as clearly against the invasion of a foreign country as it has spoken out against the extradition of political refugees. Let us begin, and set the example to other nations of this non-intervention. . . .

I believe the progress of freedom depends more upon the maintenance of peace, the spread of commerce, and the diffusion of education, than upon the labours of Cabinets or Foreign-offices. And if you can prevent those perturbations which have recently taken place abroad in consequence of your foreign policy, and if you will leave other nations in greater tranquillity, those ideas of freedom will continue to progress, and you need not trouble yourselves about them.

THE ECLIPSE OF LIBERALISM

The Nation

From its founding in 1865 and into the early twentieth century, *The Nation* was a liberal magazine, committed to individual rights, free markets, and peace. Its founding editor was E. L. Godkin, an Anglo-Irish follower of John Stuart Mill, Richard Cobden, and John Bright. In this editorial, published on August 9, 1900, and thought to have been written by Godkin, *The Nation* looked back on the glorious accomplishments of liberalism in the nineteenth century but mourned that liberalism was by century's end being eclipsed by nationalism and socialism. The editorialist's dire prediction of "international struggles on a terrific scale" before statism was again repudiated proved all too accurate.

As the nineteenth century draws to its close it is impossible not to contrast the political ideals now dominant with those of the preceding era. It was the rights of man which engaged the attention of the political thinkers of the eighteenth century. The world had suffered so much misery from the results of dynastic ambitions and jealousies, the masses of mankind were everywhere so burdened by the exactions of the superior classes, as to bring about a universal revulsion against the principle of authority. Government, it was plainly seen, had become the vehicle of oppression; and the methods by which it could be subordinated to the needs of individual development, and could be made to foster liberty rather than to suppress it, were the favorite study of the most enlightened philosophers. In opposition to the theory of divine right, whether of kings or demagogues, the doctrine of natural rights was set up. Humanity was exalted above human institutions, man was held superior to the State, and universal brotherhood supplanted the ideals of national power and glory.

These eighteenth-century ideas were the soil in which modern Liberalism flourished. Under their influence the demand for Constitutional Government arose. Rulers were to be the servants of the people, and were to be restrained and held in check by bills of rights and fundamental laws which defined the liberties proved by experience to be most important and most vulnerable. Hence arose the movement for Parliamentary reform in England, with its great outcome, the establishment of what was called free trade, but which was really the overthrow of many privileges besides those of the landlords. Hence arose the demands for Constitutional reform in all the countries of Europe; abortive and unsuccessful in certain respects, but frightening despots into a semblance of regard for human liberty, and into practical concessions which at least curbed despotic authority. Republics were established and Constitutions were ordained. The revolutions of 1848 proved the power of the spirit of Liberalism, and where despotism reasserted itself, it did so with fear and trembling.

To the principles and precepts of Liberalism the prodigious material progress of the age was largely due. Freed from the vexatious meddling of governments, men devoted themselves to their natural task, the bettering of their condition, with the wonderful results which surround us. But it now seems that its material comfort has blinded the eyes of the present generation to the cause which made it possible. In the politics of the world, Liberalism is a declining, almost a defunct force. The condition of the Liberal party in England is indeed parlous. There is actually talk of organizing a Liberal-Imperialist party; a combination of repugnant tendencies and theories as impossible as that of fire and water. On the other hand, there is a faction of so-called Liberals who so little understand their traditions as to make common cause with the Socialists. Only a remnant, old men for the most part, still uphold the Liberal doctrine, and when they are gone, it will have no champions.

True Liberalism has never been understood by the masses of the

French people; and while it has no more consistent and enlightened defenders than the select group of orthodox economists that still reverence the principles of Turgot and Say, there is no longer even a Liberal faction in the Chamber. Much the same is true of Spain, of Italy, and of Austria, while the present condition of Liberalism in Germany is in painful contrast with what it was less than a generation ago. In our country recent events show how much ground has been lost. The Declaration of Independence no longer arouses enthusiasm; it is an embarrassing instrument which requires to be explained away. The Constitution is said to be "outgrown"; and at all events the rights which it guarantees must be carefully reserved to our own citizens, and not allowed to human beings over whom we have purchased sovereignty. The great party which boasted that it had secured for the negro the rights of humanity and of citizenship, now listens in silence to the proclamation of white supremacy and makes no protest against the nullification of the Fifteenth Amendment. Its mouth is closed, for it has become "patriot only in pernicious toils," and the present boasts of this "champion of human kind" are

> "To mix with Kings in the low lust of sway. Yell in the hunt, and share the murderous prey;
> To insult the shrine of Liberty with spoils From freemen torn, to tempt and to betray."

Nationalism in the sense of national greed has supplanted Liberalism. It is an old foe under a new name. By making the aggrandizement of a particular nation a higher end than the welfare of mankind, it has sophisticated the moral sense of Christendom. Aristotle justified slavery, because Barbarians were "naturally" inferior to Greeks, and we have gone back to his philosophy. We hear no more of natural rights, but of inferior races, whose part it is to submit to the government of those whom God has made their superiors. The old fallacy of divine right has once more asserted its ruinous power, and before it is again repudiated there must be international struggles on a terrific scale. At home all criticism of the foreign policy of our rulers is denounced as unpatriotic. They must not be changed, for the national policy must be continuous. Abroad, the rulers of every country must hasten to every scene of territorial plunder, that they may secure their share. To succeed in these predatory expeditions the restraints of parliamentary, even of party, government must be cast aside. The Czar of Russia and the Emperor of Germany have a free hand in China; they are not hampered by constitutions or by representatives of the common people. Lord Salisbury is more embarrassed, and the President of the United States is, according to our Constitution, helpless without the support of Congress. That is what our Imperialists mean by saying that we have outgrown the Constitution.

PEACE

Ludwig von Mises

In this excerpt from *Liberalism,* Mises lays out the liberal case against war. To the humanitarian argument, he adds the positive analysis that war disrupts cooperation and commerce; only peace makes possible the division of labor across long distances and national boundaries. In the nineteenth century, it seemed that liberalism had forever eliminated the possibility of war in Europe, but the twentieth-century ideologies of "socialism, nationalism, protectionism, imperialism, statism, and militarism" had caused it to return. Mises, writing in 1927, could not yet know just how true that lament was.

There are high-minded men who detest war because it brings death and suffering. However much one may admire their humanitarianism, their argument against war, in being based on philanthropic grounds, seems to lose much or all of its force when we consider the statements of the supporters and proponents of war. The latter by no means deny that war brings with it pain and sorrow. Nevertheless, they believe it is through war and war alone that mankind is able to make progress. War is the father of all things, said a Greek philosopher, and thousands have repeated it after him. Man degenerates in time of peace. Only war awakens in him slumbering talents and powers and imbues him with sublime ideals. If war were to be abolished, mankind would decay into indolence and stagnation.

It is difficult or even impossible to refute this line of reasoning on the part of the advocates of war if the only objection to war that one can think of is that it demands sacrifices. For the proponents of war are of the opinion that these sacrifices are not made in vain and that they are well worth making. If it were really true that war is the father of all things, then the human sacrifices it requires would be necessary to further the general welfare and the progress of humanity. One might lament the sacrifices, one might even strive to reduce their number, but one would not be warranted in wanting to abolish war and to bring about eternal peace.

The liberal critique of the argument in favor of war is fundamentally different from that of the humanitarians. It starts from the premise that not war, but peace, is the father of all things. What alone enables mankind to advance and distinguishes man from the animals is social cooperation. It is labor alone that is productive; it creates wealth and therewith lays the outward foundations for the inward flowering of man. War only destroys; it cannot create. War, carnage, destruction, and devastation we have in common with the predatory beasts of the jungle; constructive labor is our distinctively human characteristic. The liberal abhors war, not, like the humanitarian, in spite of the fact that it has beneficial consequences, but because it has only harmful ones.

The peace-loving humanitarian approaches the mighty potentate and addresses him thus: "Do not make war, even though you have the prospect of furthering your own welfare by a victory. Be noble and magnanimous and renounce the tempting victory even if it means a sacrifice for you and the loss of an advantage." The liberal thinks otherwise. He is convinced that victorious war is an evil even for the victor, that peace is always better than war. He demands no sacrifice from the stronger, but only that he should come to realize where his true interests lie and should learn to understand that peace is for him, the stronger, just as advantageous as it is for the weaker.

When a peace-loving nation is attacked by a bellicose enemy, it must offer resistance and do everything to ward off the onslaught. Heroic deeds performed in such a war by those fighting for their freedom and their lives are entirely praiseworthy, and one rightly extols the manliness and courage of such fighters. Here daring, intrepidity, and contempt for death are praiseworthy because they are in the service of a good end. But people have made the mistake of representing these soldierly virtues as absolute virtues, as qualities good in and for themselves, without consideration of the end they serve. Whoever holds this opinion must, to be consistent, likewise acknowledge as noble virtues the daring, intrepidity, and contempt for death of the robber. In fact, however, there is nothing good or bad in and of itself. Human actions become good or bad only through the end that they serve and the consequences they entail. Even Leonidas would not be worthy of the esteem in which we hold him if he had fallen, not as the defender of his homeland, but as the leader of an invading army intent on robbing a peaceful people of its freedom and possessions.

How harmful war is to the development of human civilization becomes clearly apparent once one understands the advantages derived from the division of labor. The division of labor turns the self-sufficient individual into the *Zoon politikon* dependent on his fellow men, the social animal of which Aristotle spoke. Hostilities between one animal and another, or between one savage and another, in no way alter the economic basis of their existence. The matter is quite different when a quarrel that has to be decided by an appeal to arms breaks out among the members of a community in which labor is divided. In such a society each individual has a specialized function; no one is any longer in a position to live independently, because all have need of one another's aid and support. Self-sufficient farmers, who produce on their own farms everything that they and their families need, can make war on one another. But when a village divides into factions, with the smith on one side and the shoemaker on the other, one faction will have to suffer from want of shoes, and the other from want of tools and weapons. Civil war destroys the division of labor inasmuch as it compels each group to content itself with the labor of its own adherents.

If the possibility of such hostilities had been considered likely in the first place, the division of labor would never have been allowed to develop to the point where, in case a fight really did break out, one would have to suffer privation. The progressive intensification of the division of labor is possible only in a society in which there is an assurance of lasting peace. Only under the shelter of such security can the division of labor develop. In the absence of this prerequisite, the division of labor does not extend beyond the limits of the village or even of the individual household. The division of labor between town and country—with the peasants of the surrounding villages furnishing grain, cattle, milk, and butter to the town in exchange for the manufactured products of the townsfolk—already presupposes that peace is assured at least within the region in question. If the division of labor is to embrace a whole nation, civil war must lie outside the realm of possibility; if it is to encompass the whole world, lasting peace among nations must be assured.

Everyone today would regard it as utterly senseless for a modern metropolis like London or Berlin to prepare to make war on the inhabitants of the adjacent countryside. Yet for many centuries the towns of Europe kept this possibility in mind and made economic provision for it. There were towns whose fortifications were, from the very beginning, so constructed that in case of need they could hold out for a while by keeping cattle and growing grain within the town walls.

At the beginning of the nineteenth century by far the greater part of the inhabited world was still divided into a number of economic regions that were, by and large, self-sufficient. Even in the more highly developed areas of Europe, the needs of a region were met, for the most part, by the production of the region itself. Trade that went beyond the narrow confines of the immediate vicinity was relatively insignificant and comprised, by and large, only such commodities as could not be produced in the area itself because of climatic conditions. In by far the greater part of the world, however, the production of the village itself supplied almost all the needs of its inhabitants. For these villagers, a disturbance in trade relations caused by war did not generally mean any impairment of their economic well-being. But even the inhabitants of the more advanced countries of Europe did not suffer very severely in time of war. If the Continental System, which Napoleon I imposed on Europe in order to exclude from the continent English goods and those coming from across the ocean only by way of England, had been enforced even more rigorously than it was, it would have still inflicted on the inhabitants of the continent hardly any appreciable privations. They would, of course, have had to do without coffee and sugar, cotton and cotton goods, spices, and many rare kinds of wood; but all these things then played only a subordinate role in the households of the great masses.

The development of a complex network of international economic relations is a product of nineteenth-century liberalism and capitalism. They alone made possible the extensive specialization of modern production with its concomitant improvement in technology. In order to provide the family of an English worker with all it consumes and desires, every nation of the five continents cooperates. Tea for the breakfast table is provided by Japan or Ceylon, coffee by Brazil or Java, sugar by the West Indies, meat by Australia or Argentina, cotton from America or Egypt, hides for leather from India or Russia, and so on. And in exchange for these things, English goods go to all parts of the world, to the most remote and out-of-the-way villages and farmsteads. This development was possible and conceivable only because, with the triumph of liberal principles, people no longer took seriously the idea that a great war could ever again break out. In the golden age of liberalism, war among members of the white race was generally considered a thing of the past.

But events have turned out quite differently. Liberal ideas and programs were supplanted by socialism, nationalism, protectionism, imperialism, statism, and militarism. Whereas Kant and Von Humboldt, Bentham and Cobden had sung the praises of eternal peace, the spokesmen of a later age never tired of extolling war, both civil and international. And their success came only all too soon. The result was the [First] World War, which has given our age a kind of object lesson on the incompatibility between war and the division of labor.

THE CASE FOR STRATEGIC DISENGAGEMENT

Earl C. Ravenal

Like Richard Cobden, Earl Ravenal was a businessman before he began writing about foreign policy. Ravenal, a former official in the Office of the Secretary of Defense, has been Professor of International Affairs at the Georgetown University School of Foreign Service, senior fellow at the Cato Institute, and author of several books, including *Never Again: Learning from America's Foreign Policy Failures* and *Designing Defense for a New World Order.* For more than twenty years he made the case for nonintervention as American foreign policy, pointing out the costs and risks of military alliances and intervention around the world. In this 1973 essay he makes a moral and pragmatic case for "strategic disengagement" by the United States.

Characteristic of American foreign policy since World War II has been the quest for a certain minimum of world order and a practical maximum of American control. Successive schemes for the regulation of power—collective security, bipolar confrontation, and now perhaps the balance of power—have differed in their objects and style. But interventionism—structuring the external political-military environment and determining the behavior of other nations, whether in collaboration, conflict, or contention with them—has been the main underlying dimension of our policy. There has been no serious substantive challenge to this premise since the eve of our entry into World War II. The last "great debate," in 1951, over the dispatch of American troops to Europe, was about implementation and constitutional procedure.

How the world might look now had the United States not exercised itself for these thirty years, and how it might look thirty years from now if we were to cease exercising ourselves, are open to conjecture. More certain are the failures of deterrence and the costs of war and readiness. These speculations and reflections are materials for a larger debate about the critical objects and operational style of our foreign policy.

It is time for such a debate. We are at a turning point in our conception of the shape of the international system and our perception of the necessities and responsibilities it imposes on our foreign policy. This is more than the feeling that any year of crisis is a turning point, and more than the hope that after the tunnel of a long and obscure war we must be emerging into a new valley. Rather, longer historical perspective and larger categories of analysis indicate that the second of the major structural systems that followed World War II—bipolar confrontation—has been played out, and a new, but severely limited, set of alternative international systems is pending as both object and determinant of American foreign policy.

These are the alternatives: (1) A limited constellation of powerful nations or blocs, all fully engaged and all with a stake in preserving the system, even at the cost of occasional forcible exercises; differing politically and contending economically, but observing certain "mutual restraints" or rules of engagement—in short, a balance of power. And (2) a more extensive and less-ordered dispersion of nation-states, great, large, and medium in size and "weight," with relative power a less critical factor in assessing and constructing relationships; agnostic about maintaining the shape and tone of the system as a whole, and not bound to restrain other—especially distant—nations for the sake of their own security or the integrity of the system. The latter system has no conventional verbal handle. We might call it "general unalignment," or "a pluralism of unaligned states." It is the baseline condition, the limiting case, of the international system—actually a quasi-anarchy, the situation that is reached if the major nations stop striving to impose external order. This system—or perhaps nonsystem—is the only present alternative to the balance of power (objective conditions not favoring the imposition of universal domination, the achievement of collective security, or the restoration of alliance leadership and bipolar confrontation); and it may well be its historical successor.

This analysis might seem abstract and impractical, were it not for the fact that several successive Administrations have been sensitive to these large-scale alternatives and convinced of the importance of establishing a version of the balance of power. In particular, the Nixon-Kissinger Administration seemed to be aware of the restricted palette of foreign-policy choice, which it characterized prejudicially as "engagement" (the rhetorical concomitant of the balance of power) or "isolationism" (the presumed counterpart of international anarchy). But to describe the choice in such flat terms is to efface the moral dimension of a foreign policy. For example, the balance of power—seen as a policy rather than a system—should be defined not simply by its main dimension of interventionism (or its euphemism, "engagement"), but also by another dimension: that of amoralism.

Similarly, the alternative policy orientation of nonintervention should be defined two-dimensionally: It can be either amoral or moral. Amoral noninterventionism *is* "isolationism." It connotes Fortress America, narrow prejudice, and active xenophobia. It is hard to subscribe to this isolationism; but it may be fair to abstain from its further condemnation, if only because this condemnation has become a mindless litany, and because the diametrically opposite course of national action—moralistic interventionism—has often led beyond the point of general damage to the brink of universal disaster.

The other, moral, style of noninterventionism is not isolationism at all. Rather, it reflects (a) a strict and consistent principle of non-intervention in the political-military order, and (b) a concern for constructive contact with the world. Such a foreign policy orientation might be called "strategic disengagement."

Thus, the balance of power, as system or policy, is neither an inevitable development nor a unique response. The "other" major international system, general unalignment, is a possible world—even a probable world, in time. And the "other" major foreign policy orientation, strategic disengagement, is a viable mode of behavior for the United States, indeed an appropriate mode if the international system continues to evolve toward a more diffused condition.

Unfortunately, the rhetoric of disengagement, unless it is presented meretriciously as a "new internationalism," is not appealing. Particularly in seasons of peace and reconciliation, it may seem ungenerous to project skepticism about the future of world order, and to prescribe the curtailment of international ambition and the pursuit of national immunity. And it is bound to be diminishing for Americans—who are used to hearing that their identity depends on a special responsibility for world order—to be told that they ought to give up their honorable pretensions and to live modestly, like other nations.

But international politics is full of ironies, and not the least of them is that the desire to do good often leads to objective harm. Private virtues are often public vices; national virtues are often international vices. Even the most attractive motives, caring and helping, can be a source of danger and destruction. Conversely, even the private vice of indifference to disorder might, in this imperfect world of fragmented sovereignties, translate into the public virtues of preserving internal integrity and respecting external reality. If we can recognize these ironies of international politics, why should we resist their codification in a coherent scheme of national conduct?

Strategic disengagement is both a policy and the end-state of a policy. It can be defined, first, by exclusion—by differentiating it from other positions that are critical or limitationist. It is not the "old isolationism"; it has no xenophobic animus and does not entail autarky. . . .

And finally, strategic disengagement is not to be equated with "appeasement." The salient aspect of Munich—apart from the fact that the United States did not even participate—is that the powers that did conceive that short-lived solution *imposed* it on Czechoslovakia in an extension of *active* diplomatic meddling—the very opposite of disengagement. Similarly, the proposal of unilateral withdrawal from Indochina—which was buried by the actual Vietnam settlement—was falsely characterized by its opponents: They likened it to "conniving at the overthrow of our South Vietnamese ally" in order to negotiate our exit from the war. Such a duplicitous course was a highly *conditional* alternative and *would* have constituted appeasement. In absolute contrast, unilateral withdrawal was a completely *unconditional* position—though it would have had extensive implications.

A second way to define strategic disengagement is by its connotations. Its keynote is large-scale adjustment to the international system, rather than detailed control of it. It is a prescription for an orderly withdrawal from our political-military commitments to other nations and from our military positions overseas, in a deliberate and measured fashion, with the timetable determined by our unilateral judgment but responsive to opportune circumstances and to the sensibilities of our allies and the conduct of our adversaries. Above all, it would be paced, not precipitate. To reach the end-state of the disengaged posture might take one or even two decades of initiatives and diplomacy.

Strategic disengagement comprises two syndromes: The first centers on the dissolution of alliances and includes rehabilitation of the civilized concept of neutrality, respect for international law (even if often its observance is asymmetrical and its sanctions only symbolic), and relations with any effective government regardless of its complexion. The second centers on a strict but limited definition of national security and includes acceptance of revolutionary change in the world, acquiescence even in the forcible rearrangement of other countries, and adoption of second-chance military strategies. . . .

Why do it? Why adopt a policy of strategic disengagement? In doing anything, one either initiates, hoping to achieve some gain or improvement, or responds, adjusting to a situation. Strategic disengagement has elements of both, but more of the latter. It is an anticipatory adjustment—a long, major adaptation to an evolutionary process in the international system and a basic social situation in the United States.

Nevertheless, there are some benefits, though these are not so much reasons for doing it as reasons for being glad to have done it. First, this posture does have tangible consequences for defense preparations—force structures, weapons systems, and budgets. Though cost saving might not be the main determinant of this policy, it is not a contemptible byproduct. In fact, the only way honestly to achieve meaningful defense budget cuts ... is to execute a far-reaching program of strategic disengagement.

Another positive reason for strategic disengagement is to avoid the possible moral "costs" of conflict. These costs are not negligible and impose their own constraints in the form of international diplomatic reactions and domestic social pressures, which might limit our ability to persevere in a conflict. Moral costs can attach either to indecisive conflicts protracted by self-limitation or, conversely, to decisive measures to end conflict.

But the principal reason for strategic disengagement is to make an adjustment that will have sufficient coherence to weather a future of perplexing variations in the pressure of circumstances and the incidence of accidental events. . . .

Strategic disengagement depends on the ability, in logic and in fact, to maintain two distinctions. The first is the separation of strategic interests from other concerns, and the sympathetic pursuit of those other nonstrategic concerns in collaborative international bodies and in our own unilateral acts; disengagement should not affect commercial relations, humanitarian expressions, or cultural contacts.

The second is the distinction of objective from nonobjective factors. The key to this is the concept of equanimity (or "indifference"). This is *not* an attitude of negligence or unconcern or rejection; it is an acceptance of situations and consequences.

This equanimity is "objective" in several senses of the word: (1) It refers to an *objective* policy orientation, not a subjective psychological state; (2) It is directed to the *objects* of our policy—whether they be the international system as a whole, or particular allied nations, threatened resources, or strategic situations—not the style of our policy-making or its specific values. And in the last resort, it is not even our sympathy for these objects of our policy, or our formal "commitments" to them, but what we consider their strategic *necessity* that implicates us in foreign conflict and virtually dictates our intervention.

Thus, if we are to achieve disengagement, we must make our policy deliberately neutral toward a wide range of differential strategic conditions and outcomes in the world. We will be able to afford this orientation only if we hedge and insulate. But even these are not enough. To sustain a strict and consistent disengagement, our decision-making system must adjust its most fundamental presumptions—about the relevance of threats, the calculus of risks, and the nature of the national interest. These are the primal categories that mold our response to strategic challenge, despite apparent shifts in surface values.

Nevertheless, in final ethical terms, we are left with an unsatisfactory choice: whether to choose the sins of commission and intervention, or the sins of omission and disengagement. We may have to resolve this dilemma on the basis of the Kantian categorical imperative: We cannot control the behavior of others; we can only behave as we will others to behave—though we expect little reciprocity or symmetry. Admittedly, this is not a self-executing policy. But, at least in moral theory, it could be a self-fulfilling prophecy.

TOWARD STRATEGIC INDEPENDENCE

Ted Galen Carpenter

Ted Galen Carpenter is senior fellow for defense and foreign policy studies at the Cato Institute and the author of several books, including *A Search for Enemies: America's Alliances after the Cold War* and *The Captive Press: Foreign Policy Crises and the First Amendment*. He argues that a policy of strategic independence would best protect American liberty and encourage world peace. Like other libertarian noninterventionists, Carpenter makes clear that noninterventionism is not isolationism. Rather, it is a policy of military and political nonintervention combined with substantial economic and cultural contact across national borders.

America's security policy is adrift without a compass in a turbulent post–Cold War world. The Clinton administration has shown little understanding of the necessary balance between military capabilities and military commitments. Even worse, the administration has failed to understand that even the United States—an economic and military superpower—cannot police the world. The Prussian leader Frederick the Great once warned that he who attempts to defend everything defends nothing. US security policy exhibits precisely that defect.

Instead of continuing to pursue an expensive and dangerous policy of global interventionism, the United States has the opportunity to adopt a new approach: strategic independence. This new policy would mean that the US would use military forces solely for defending America's vital security interests. Implementing strategic independence would entail several dramatic changes in Washington's foreign policy: 1) the United States would decline to participate militarily in UN peacekeeping operations—indeed, America's political and financial commitment to the United Nations would be greatly circumscribed; 2) US Cold War alliances would be phased out before the end of the decade, in most cases; 3) the United States would explicitly reject a global policing role, whether acting unilaterally, in combination with regional allies, or through the United Nations; and 4) perhaps most important, the United States would adopt the role of the balancer of last resort in the international system, rather than the intervenor of first resort.

AMERICA'S STRATEGIC OVEREXTENSION

The Clinton administration shows a disturbing inability to discriminate between those developments in the international system that are essential to America's security, and those that are peripheral or irrelevant. US policymakers frequently act as though everything, everywhere is important to US interests. Thus, the administration has preserved all of Washington's Cold War security obligations, and has even sought to upgrade some of them, such as the mission of policing the Persian Gulf region. The administration has also sought to add new security commitments, proposing to enlarge NATO to include the nations of Central and Eastern Europe. Additionally, the administration has involved the United States in multilateral peacekeeping and nation-building missions in places such as Somalia and Haiti. The inevitable result is strategic overextension.

Such an approach is unnecessary, as well as undesirable. Given the absence of a superpower adversary, the United States has no need to continue subsidizing the defense of allies in Western Europe and East Asia. Although these allies prefer to rely on the United States, they have the population and economic resources to build whatever military forces they need to protect themselves from lesser threats. Just as domestic welfare expenditures foster an unhealthy mentality of dependence on the part of recipients, so too do international military welfare subsidies foster unhealthy mentalities of dependence.

The financial benefits that Washington's security dependents receive are considerable—and it is understandable that they wish to continue the arrangement—but the benefits to the United States are less apparent. The principal justification offered by US policymakers is that a dominant US role around the world helps preserve "stability," and prevents the reemergence of the great destructive power rivalries that led to previous wars. Accordingly, the United States does not want Japan or the major powers of Western Europe to even aspire to play more active military roles, because such assertiveness might prove disruptive.

Although there is some validity to that argument, the costs and risks entailed in preserving US dominance are extremely high. Not only does a "smothering" strategy require US forces to risk involvement in actual or potential conflicts which have little direct relevance to America's security, but such a strategy requires that the United States maintains a much larger—and more costly—military than would otherwise be necessary. It is Washington's global-policing role that accounts for the huge disparity between US military spending and the spending levels of other industrial countries.

If, instead of encouraging the prosperous West European and East Asian nations to remain forever dependent on the United States for their security, Washington would encourage them to take responsibility for their own defense, the United States could then grasp the opportunity to take advantage of a post–Cold War world in which there are new, multiple centers of power. America can receive indirect benefits from more vigorous defense efforts by other major democratic nations which, to protect their own vital interests, will be compelled to contain threats and promote stability in their respective regions.

Preserving Washington's Cold War alliances is a dubious decision from the standpoint of American interests; expanding those commitments is even more ill-advised. Proposals to enlarge NATO, for example, would entangle the United States in the myriad disputes of Central and Eastern Europe. Enlarging NATO would fatally undercut the position of Russia's democratic faction and give the ultranationalists an ideal issue to exploit; it would risk a confrontation with Moscow over a region in which Russia has political, economic, and security interests going back generations; and, it would involve the United States in quarrels and conflicts among the Central and East European nations themselves.

America's legitimate European interests do not warrant taking such risks. The primary interest of the United States is preventing a hostile power from dominating the Continent and thereby posing a serious threat to America's own security. Such a danger is utterly improbable in the foreseeable future. In any case, it is imperative to distinguish between a conflict which threatens to undermine the European balance of power, and the assortment of petty conflicts now taking place in portions of Eastern Europe that have little relevance outside the immediate region. For the United States to become entangled in such wars would be a misguided attempt to micromanage the Continent's security.

DEFINING VITAL INTERESTS

The European example illustrates a larger point. US policymakers must be more cautious and discriminating about the concept of vital interests. When President Clinton contended that the United States had vital interest at stake in Haiti—citing the desire to promote democracy in the Western Hemisphere as an example—he demonstrated a failure to grasp the concept.

To constitute a vital US interest, a development must have a direct, immediate, and substantial connection to America's physical survival, political independence, or domestic liberty. Anything that does not reach that threshold is a secondary interest, a peripheral interest, or, in many cases, not a valid security interest at all. It is also important to stress that "vital" means essential or indispensable, not merely relevant or desirable. Democracy in Haiti and elsewhere in the hemisphere is indeed desirable, but it is hardly indispensable to America's well-being. There have been dictatorships in Haiti—as well as in Caribbean and Latin American countries—without any discernibly adverse impact on the security of the United States.

The concept of a vital interest also has an operational definition. A vital interest is something for which the United States must be prepared to wage a major war, if necessary. That sobering factor alone should be enough to discourage US policymakers from using the term in a casual fashion, or in making security commitments that the United States would be unwise to fulfill.

THE SIGNIFICANCE OF THE DEMISE OF THE SOVIET THREAT

Although the collapse of the Soviet Union did not change the nature of America's vital interests, it did radically alter the global-threat environment. During the Cold War, it was possible to argue that conflicts which appeared to have only local or regional importance were, in fact, much more significant because they frequently involved Soviet surrogates. Whatever validity that argument may have had, it is no longer relevant. Without the Soviet factor, most conflicts that are taking place in various regions are parochial. They may be of importance to the parties involved—and perhaps to neighboring states—but they have no serious potential to menace the United States.

The demise of the Soviet threat altered the global-threat environment in another important way. Throughout the Cold War, conventional wisdom held that only the United States could neutralize the military threat posed by another superpower. That argument was probably overdone, even during the Cold War. Although no single nation other than the United States had the wherewithal to counter the power of the USSR, an alliance of several medium-size nations might well have been able to do so. In particular, the major countries of Western Europe, once they had recovered from the devastation of World War II, should have been capable of containing Soviet expansionism—at least in Europe.

In any case, the argument has no relevance today. There is no superpower threat, and regional powers are capable of neutralizing lesser threats without the aid of the United States. The notion that the European Union—with a collective population of more than 370 million, a gross domestic product of $7.5 trillion a year, and more than

2 million troops—cannot contain Serb expansionism strains credulity. Similarly, the argument that Japan, South Korea, Russia, China,
and the other powers of East Asia cannot address the threat posed
by North Korea's nuclear program is unfounded. Americans who
contend that only the United States can solve such problems exhibit a
disturbing national hubris. The leaders of other countries who make
the same contention have the ulterior motive of wanting the United
States to continue assuming an unwarranted portion of the costs and
risks of international security.

America should position itself as the balancer of last resort in the
international system. In other words, the United States should maintain sufficient forces to backstop the efforts of other powers were an
unusually potent expansionist threat to emerge, and were those powers unable to contain it with their own resources. Such a breakdown
of regional containment efforts is rare, and, given the absence of any
credible candidate to become a global hegemonic threat comparable
to Nazi Germany or the Soviet Union, the need is remote for the
United States to use military force to implement the balancer role in
the foreseeable future.

AVOIDING UNNECESSARY UN ENTANGLEMENTS

A security strategy based on the defense of vital American interests
would leave no room for signing on to peacekeeping or nation-
building enterprises directed by the United Nations. The Clinton
administration has retreated somewhat from its initial enthusiasm
for UN military missions. At one time, the administration considered contributing US troops to a permanent UN peacekeeping
force, and seemed willing to subordinate US military personnel to
UN command. The ineptitude that the United Nations displayed in
conducting its missions in Somalia and Bosnia has apparently caused
administration officials to advocate a more cautious policy.

Nevertheless, the administration remains too willing to commit
US troops to dubious UN missions that have little relevance to the
security of the United States. The debacle in Somalia was a warning
of the dangers entailed by involvement in such operations. Yet the

administration indicates that the United States is willing to provide forces—perhaps including ground troops—to extricate UN peace-keepers from Bosnia if that mission is terminated.

In addition to problems of excessive costs and risks, the United States would be wise to avoid involvement in UN peacekeeping operations for another reason: it is important to maximize America's decision-making autonomy and preserve the widest array of policy alternatives whenever possible. An interventionist policy within a global collective security arrangement may be the worst of all possible options. Unilateral interventionism, at least, leaves US officials complete latitude to determine when, where, and under what conditions to use the nation's armed forces. Working through the UN Security Council to reach such decisions reduces that flexibility and creates another layer of risk. That hindrance is especially troublesome if Washington is serious about collaborating in collective security operations, and is not merely seeking to use the United Nations as a multilateral facade for US objectives. Other powers are going to insist on *quid pro quos* for supporting measures desired by Washington. The calls by Britain and France—Western Europe's two permanent members on the Security Council—for the United States to assume its "fair share" of the risks in the UN's Bosnia peacekeeping mission are omens of such pressures.

REJECTING THE "LIGHT-SWITCH" MODEL OF US ENGAGEMENT

Whenever dissident policy experts suggest pruning Washington's overgrown global security commitments, defenders of the *status quo* invariably cry "isolationism." That view is essentially the light-switch theory of America's engagement in the world—that there can be only two possible positions: on or off. According to this theory, either the United States continues to pursue an indiscriminate global interventionist policy, which requires putting American military personnel at risk in such places as Somalia, Haiti, and Bosnia, or it adopts a "Fortress America" strategy and "cuts itself off from the world."

Such a contention is a red herring. No serious analyst advocates creating a hermit republic. It is entirely possible to adopt a security policy between the extremes of global interventionism—which is essentially the current US policy—and Fortress America. Moreover, there are different forms of engagement in world affairs, of which the political-military version is merely one form. Economic connections and influence are crucial, and seem to be growing in importance. Diplomatic and cultural engagement is also significant, especially in the age of the information revolution.

There is no reason why the United States must have identical positions along each axis of engagement. It is entirely feasible to have extensive economic and cultural relations with the rest of the world— and have an active and creative diplomacy—without playing the role of world policeman. It is only in the area of military engagement that the United States needs to retrench.

A policy of strategic independence is based on a more modest and sustainable world-role for the United States. It takes into account the fundamental changes that have occurred in the world in recent years, and seeks to position the United States to benefit from an emerging multi-polar political, economic, and military environment. It would end the promiscuously interventionist policy that requires a military budget larger than those of all other industrial powers combined, and that has placed American military personnel at risk in such strategically irrelevant places as Somalia and Haiti. A new security strategy would enable the United States to substantially reduce its military budget and force structure while more-than-adequately protecting national security.

Strategic independence also would be a policy consistent with the values of a constitutional republic based on the principle of limited government. The lives, freedoms, and financial resources of the American people are not rightfully available for whatever missions suit the whims of political leaders. The US government has constitutional and moral responsibilities to protect the security and liberty of the American republic. It has neither constitutional nor moral writs to risk lives and resources to police the planet, promote democracy, or advance other aims on the bureaucracy's foreign policy agenda.

PART SEVEN

THE LIBERTARIAN FUTURE

The basic insights of libertarianism—decentralization of power, individualism, imprescriptible rights, spontaneous order, voluntary exchange, and peace—provide a framework both for understanding the world and for constructing a social order in which people can use their knowledge to pursue happiness. A social and political order largely based on those insights, characterized by the rule of law, freedom of religion and expression, secure property rights, and relatively free markets, has spread throughout the West and beyond, freeing individuals to improve their own lives and in the process to transform the world. Karl Marx, misconstruing liberalism as the "rule" of the bourgeoisie, described the results of liberal society more than a century ago:

> The bourgeoisie, during its rule of scarce one hundred years, has created more massive and more colossal productive forces than have all preceding generations together. Subjection of nature's forces to man, machinery, application of chemistry to industry and agriculture, steam navigation, railways, electric telegraphs, clearing of whole continents for cultivation, canalization of rivers, whole populations conjured out of the ground—what earlier century had even a presentiment that such productive forces slumbered in the lap of social labor?

Now that liberalism has shown the world that progress is possible, present generations can have at least a presentiment of the kinds of changes that the world may yet witness. For a century now, from Edward Bellamy to Isaac Asimov to many of the celebrated futurists of our own time, intellectuals have had the odd idea that an increasingly complex world would require bigger and more comprehensive government. Planning to cope with change has been the watchword. Every day one can read in the world's great newspapers that a new study or presidential commission finds a new policy needed to deal with mass transit, or education, or technological change, or bioethics, or inequality, or the environment, or whatever. Each new policy, it turns out, requires the transfer of more authority from civil society to political society, from the process of voluntary association and exchange to the regime of command and control.

But is it really plausible that coercive planning will lead us forward, to a world of technology and material prosperity and social arrangements that we cannot even imagine? Had we entrusted the planning of the twentieth century to government, our society today would look like the Soviet Union—except that if the entire capitalist world had been brought under the thumb of coercive planners, there would have been no country to produce the technological advances that the Soviet Union was able to borrow. If we want to see technological progress and a higher standard of living in the future—with the gradual reduction of disease, poverty, and ignorance—we really have no choice but freedom.

The libertarian attitude toward change may seem contradictory to some readers. Libertarians embrace the prospect of economic, technological, and cultural change, yet they insist on a firm adherence to longstanding and stable principles of government. There is no contradiction. As all the authors in this section explicitly or implicitly acknowledge, the libertarian principles of John Locke and Adam Smith, of the American Revolution and the Constitution, create a *framework for progress*. When we protect the individual's right to think, to communicate, to create, to exchange—when we hold strictly to the rules of private property, free exchange, and consent—we create a society in which change can occur. Every deviation from those rules—every use of government to bring about some particular person's idea of better results—serves to inhibit progress.

In this section, Samuel Brittan points to the similarities between competitive capitalism and the "counterculture" values of the 1960s, a point that would have seemed obvious to earlier generations of liber-

als but has been lost in the odd late-twentieth-century separation be-
tween the advocates of free enterprise and the advocates of personal
freedom. Antonio Martino, Richard Cornuelle, and Mario Vargas
Llosa point to some political and intellectual challenges confronting
libertarians in the postcommunist era. Norman Macrae and Michael
Prowse contend that coercive government is a relic of the Industrial
Age that will soon pass from the scene. Peter Pitsch and John Perry
Barlow discuss the implications of the Information Age.

Lynn Scarlett looks at a particularly important issue of the coming
era—environmental protection—in the light of the libertarian principles found throughout this book. She concludes, "Centralized, top-
down rule making is ill-suited to addressing environmental problems
in a complex, dynamic world in which most relevant information is
location-specific and different people have very different priorities." It
is a central message of libertarianism that one could substitute almost
any topic for the words "environmental problems" in that sentence,
and it would still be true.

CAPITALISM AND THE PERMISSIVE SOCIETY

Samuel Brittan

In the latter half of the twentieth century the advocates of personal freedom and of economic freedom often found themselves on opposite ends of the political spectrum, with supporters of economic liberty lining up with Republicans or the British Conservative party and those who defend civil liberties and personal freedom becoming Democrats or Labour party supporters. In the eighteenth and nineteenth centuries no such distinction was made, and those who favored freedom—both personal and economic—were found in the liberal movement. The logical connection among various liberties remains, however, and in this essay Samuel Brittan argues that "competitive capitalism is the biggest single force acting on the side of what it is fashionable to call 'permissiveness,' but what was once known as personal liberty." Writing in 1973, Brittan pointed out that although capitalists and the young people of the sixties regarded each other as the enemy, both the market economy and the "counterculture" were based on the idea of "doing your own thing." Brittan was a longtime columnist for the *Financial Times* and Honorary Professor of Politics at the University of Warwick. He is the author of many books, including *Left or Right: The Bogus Dilemma* and *A Restatement of Economic Liberalism,* in which this essay appeared. He was knighted in 1993.

The values of competitive capitalism have a great deal in common with contemporary attitudes, and in particular with contemporary radical attitudes. Above all they share a similar stress on allowing people to do, to the maximum feasible extent, what they feel inclined to do rather than conform to the wishes of authority, custom or convention. Under a competitive system, the businessman will make money by catering for whatever it is that people wish to do—by providing pop records, or nude shows, or candyfloss. He will not make anything by providing what the establishment thinks is good for them. An individual citizen is free to maximise his income by using his abilities (and his capital if he has any) to cater for public tastes. But he does not have to. He can go for the easiest or most congenial job, or the one with the most leisure; or, like most of us he can find some compromise between these alternatives. In any case his life-style is his own. He can concentrate on personal pleasure, social service at home, the relief of poverty abroad, or any combination of these and numerous other activities.

Competitive capitalism is far from being the sole or dominating force of our society and Galbraith is right to force this on our attention. But to the extent that it prevails, competitive capitalism is the biggest single force acting on the side of what it is fashionable to call "permissiveness," but what was once known as personal liberty. Business enterprise can, of course, thrive and prosper alongside a great deal of "moral" prohibitions and prescriptions, whether enforced by law or public opinion. But the profit motive will always be kicking against such restraints and seeking to widen the range of what is permissible—whether it is a nineteenth-century publisher launching an attack on orthodox religion or a twentieth-century theatrical or film producer challenging conventional concepts of decency and decorum. The profit motive will act both to stretch the existing law and as a force for its liberalisation.

As against these advantages it is often alleged that competitive capitalism is based on the false values of the "consumer society." Critics of this sort often forget that the great virtue of the consumer society is that no one is forced to consume. There may be middle class, or middle age pressures in that direction (and plenty of "trendy" pressures of other sorts among the young); but social pressures are not the same as edicts enforced by the police, and the rise of the "counter-culture" has itself set up pressures of an opposite kind, and the range of effective choice has been extended. To the extent that the competitive element prevails, a citizen can be equally indifferent to right-wing attacks on the self-indulgence of modern youth and to the traditional left-wing demand that all economic activity be channelled into some higher national purpose. The ethos of the market economy can be summed up in the vernacular as "doing your own thing." A capitalist market economy is not, of course, an equal society. But it is a powerful agent for disrupting existing class barriers and official hierarchies. Indeed, commercial societies are notorious, among those who dislike this aspect, for bringing new people and families to the fore and undermining traditional status barriers.

The expression "competitive capitalism" is used here in its broadest possible meaning. It does not exclude the existence of a substantial public sector; nor does it prevent the state from carrying out a great many functions which are required if the market is to transmit people's preferences effectively—and this includes a great many measures in the anti-pollution field. But the emphasis is on the profit motive, consumer choice and competition. The conditions required for these activities to lead to tolerable results will be discussed in greater detail in later essays. The aim of this introductory chapter is to state the issue in its simplest terms; and rather than take refuge in terms such as "mixed economy" or "social market economy," I shall stick to the more provocative term "competitive capitalism." I would add, however, that "competitive capitalism" is not a partisan slogan. When it comes to the test of practical application, it has at least as many opponents among Conservatives as among Labour supporters, and among businessmen as among trade unionists.

THE HISTORICAL CONTEXT

The reasons why people hold certain beliefs have no bearing on their validity; to suppose otherwise would be to fall into the same intellectual trap as the worst Marxist or Freudian camp followers (it is not a trap that Marx, and above all Freud would have been guilty of themselves). Examination of the roots of widely held views can, all the same, be useful in explaining why people persist in holding them, despite rational arguments to the contrary, and why the latter fail to make a sufficient impression.

In the discussion that follows I shall begin with a reference to the historical background, go on to the features of the contemporary behaviour of businessmen and others in authority, which seem to confirm the worst suspicions of their critics, and then describe some of the other causes of the rise of anti-capitalist sentiment. With these matters out of the way, the path will be clear for a discussion of the New Left critique of capitalism and of the prospects of dealing with evils such as poverty and "alienation" under alternative systems. This may seem a reversal of the logical order; but the treatment adopted may be more illuminating for the non-specialist reader who wants to put the economic arguments into a broader context.

Modern ideals of personal freedom, and the accompanying political, economic and legal beliefs, emerged from the religious writers of the seventeenth century and the political and economic philosophers of the eighteenth and nineteenth centuries. Yet, during the period when these ideals formed part of the public philosophy of the country, they were both less important to human welfare and more hedged around with stultifying qualifications than they are today when their credentials are so widely challenged. The period of English history when the capitalist ideal of freedom was most widely acknowledged was the mid-nineteenth century—the age of Peel and Gladstone. Yet, in many ways and for many people, it must have been a very unattractive time in which to live; and economic liberals would do well to acknowledge this fact.

The point most frequently made is, of course, that although living standards were rapidly improving, the mass of people were too poor to enjoy their freedom. This stricture needs to be more carefully stated than it often is. Freedom is not the same as absence of poverty; and to say that a labourer in the 1870s, or an Egyptian peasant today is "not really free" is a confusion of thought. If freedom is defined so that the absence of poverty is a necessary condition of its existence, two different values become confused, distinctions which exist in real life are obliterated, and language is impoverished. It is better to stick to the negative concept of freedom, but say that where the majority of the people hardly earn enough to cover their bare physical requirements, freedom may be less important as a goal than an increase of wealth.

The above, however, is well-trodden ground. What is less often pointed out is the limited number of people to whom even the legal freedoms of the nineteenth century applied. Personal liberty was effectively limited to male heads of households over 21. Women and children had as few rights as the subjects of the Eastern despots so much condemned in the Liberal literature of the period; and the same applied to anyone who had once volunteered for the Army or Navy. If freedom is defined as the absence of coercion, there was precious little for a schoolboy or soldier of the period, both of whom were also victims of the passion for flagellation which was (and to some extent still is) the real English sickness. Even for adult heads of households, freedom was carefully circumscribed. There was freedom to start up a business enterprise, freedom to emigrate and freedom to move money over frontiers (all freedoms which we despise at our peril). But in view of the very great powers still in the hands of local JPs, and the ferocious maximum penalties on the statute book, there was far more discretionary power of one individual over another than nostalgic admirers of the Victorian era would admit.

Apart from this, the prohibitions in the law and custom of the land were numerous and oppressive. Whether E. M. Forster's novel *Maurice* is good or bad as a work of literature, one can only recoil with horror at the revelations of the weight of the legal and the social penalties—and above all the burden of guilt—imposed on those whose impulses were not in keeping with the official sexual mores. Among those with "normal" tastes promiscuity abounded, and was tolerated provided that it was not publicly admitted and the pretences were maintained.

The important point, however, is that both the political and economic philosophy and the capitalist practices of a century ago set in motion a train of events and ideas which eventually undermined the status-ridden conventional society of the time and brought into being the more tolerant England of today. Indeed, the basic arguments for the so-called "permissive" morality were developed by thinkers in the nineteenth-century liberal tradition from John Stuart Mill onwards (one has only to think of his lifelong campaign against the subjection of women—the genuine article before which "Women's Lib" groups pall). Many of the classical ideas of nineteenth-century liberalism did not come on the statute book until the 1960s. The battle is still far from won, as can be seen from the sentences still passed on "obscene publications" or the hysterical and vindictive attitude adopted by so many authority figures towards the problem of drugs.

Growing prosperity and leisure have meanwhile increased the importance and desirability of individual freedom for the mass of the population. The paradox is that just when personal liberty is beginning to govern the life-style of a generation, the economic system which makes it possible has become intensely antipathetic to a great many of that generation's most articulate members. The old opposition to competitive capitalism from the puritan Left that instinctively felt (even when it denied this) that the Fabian state *did* know better, has been succeeded—just when it seemed about to fade away—by fresh opposition from the "New Left," which is rightly suspicious of all authority, has no lingering affection for Joseph Stalin (and is Marxist only because that seems a far-out thing to be), but which identifies "capitalism" with "the system" and, in its headier movements, has brought back semi-serious talks of "the revolution." (To take "the revolution" seriously is acceptable at many expense account lunches. It is equally "trendy" to discuss it semi-facetiously; the one thing that is out-and-out "square" is to be seriously opposed to it.)

THE RISE OF THE WORD MAN

Another characteristic of capitalism is that it tends to nourish in its own midst an anti-capitalistic culture. This was explained many years ago by Joseph Schumpeter in *Capitalism, Socialism and Democracy*, a work largely written before and at the beginning of the Second World War, and which is more up-to-date than most works currently off the press. His basic thesis was that capitalism was killing itself by its own achievements.

Capitalist civilisation is above all rationalist. It is anti-heroic and anti-mystical. The spirit that animates it is the very opposite of "Theirs not to reason why, theirs but to do or die." The successful capitalist is forced by circumstances to query the way everything is done and endeavour to try and find a better way. If he relies on a traditional, mystical or ceremonial justification of existing practices, he will be overtaken by someone else and may well sink into oblivion. The breakdown of theological authority, the rise of the scientific spirit and the growth of capitalism were interrelated phenomena. A new ethic arose in the seventeenth century and had grown to fruition by the nineteenth, which blessed empirical and logical enquiry, denigrated the claims of authority and legitimised the profit motive (*inter alia* by removing the mediaeval restraints on usury and the notion of "just price").

THE NEW LEFT ATTACK

So much for the climate of opinion in which capitalism now operates. What, however, are the main objections to competition and the profit motive actually put forward by the new generation of radicals? The New Left critics differ from both their Marxist and their Fabian forerunners in being equally distrustful of market forces and of central planning or bureaucracy in any form. This revival of the more utopian and anarchic strain is a welcome change from the paternalism and emphasis on state power which have for so long characterised socialist movements. Indeed, it ought to make a dialogue between the New Left and the market economists possible in a way it was not possible with either the Webbs or the Stalinist Communists. (Professor Lindbeck cites the case of a pseudonymous writer of the Chicago free market school who, by using a flamboyant style sprinkled with four letter words, at first reading gives the impression of being somewhere on the anarchist wing of the New Left.)

Unfortunately, the fatal flaw in the economic outlook of the New Left is the belief that one does not have to choose between a market and a command economy or between varying mixtures of the two; and that there is a third ethically preferable system which would rely on more spontaneous and less selfish motives. A large part of Assar Lindbeck's *The Political Economy of the New Left* is taken up with a sympathetic but relentless analysis of this fallacy; and I find it strange that Paul Samuelson should give the impression in his polemical foreword that the book will make an impartial or hostile observer take New Left economics more seriously. The opposite effect seems to me far more likely.

Lindbeck conveniently summarises the standard problems of any society which have caused generations of economists to doubt that one can have an economy dispensing with both markets and bureaucratic commands. These are the needs:

1. to obtain information about people's preferences;
2. to allocate men, machines, land, building and other resources in accordance with these preferences;
3. to decide which production techniques to use;
4. to create incentives to avoid unnecessarily costly methods, to invest, to develop new technologies and products; and
5. (and perhaps most important) to co-ordinate the desires of millions of individuals, firms and households.

This list is provided not by Friedman or Hayek, but by a Swedish Social Democrat whose book is offered to us by Samuelson as an antidote to the former writers. I would only add that four at least of these requirements do not depend on selfishness but on the need for co-ordinating and signalling devices which would still exist even if we could rely more on people's goodwill. Remarks such as Adam Smith's about addressing ourselves not to the "humanity" but to the "self-love" of others and Alfred Marshall's about men's motives "in the ordinary business of life" give a misleading impression. Even if people were actuated by benevolence, they would still need to know what jobs to do and what methods to use to satisfy other people's desires most efficiently, and a coordinating mechanism would be required. At most we could dispense with the fourth item on the list—incentives. Even then the profits or opportunities for high earnings would still be indispensable as *signals,* although any excess wealth gained by following them might eventually be given away to charitable organisations.

Galbraith's influence on the New Left has, as Lindbeck has pointed out, strengthened its temptation to ignore the inconvenient problem of co-ordination. Galbraith fails to explain how the few large firms on which he concentrates—let alone millions of householders and individuals—co-ordinate their activities. He concentrates on planning within firms, and many readers overlook the fact that he has said nothing about relations between firms, except by quasi-mystical references to the "technostructure."

Lindbeck also lays to rest the illusion that computers could take over from markets the functions just listed. This belief is more characteristic of the old technocratic Left than of the New Left; but the latter might be inclined to clutch at it as a straw. Complicated messages about preferences, product qualities and information on production processes cannot be coded onto a computer. This is more than a practical impossibility. Even if consumers could immediately translate into computer language their preferences between an indefinitely large set of alternatives made possible by technology, they do not themselves know how they would react to new kinds of goods or changes in quality or innovation in general, for the simple reason that people do not always know how they themselves will react in hypothetical circumstances. Even when it comes to communicating details of production processes it is difficult to envisage how the specifics of "knowing how" could be put into a computer. Moreover, all this effort, even if successful, would simply reproduce the data already presented by prices, profits and sales figures.

A dominant feature of New Left thinking, again powerfully stimulated by Galbraith, is a denial that the market does allow people to "do their own thing." Consumer wants, it is alleged, are artificially fabricated by advertising and other sales techniques. . . .

Such writers do not, however, go to the lengths of the New Left and some of its prophets in asserting that firms can create a demand for whatever goods they choose to produce. As Lindbeck has pointed out, the latter is a new form of "Say's Law"—so much attacked by Keynes for giving too *favourable* an impression of the capitalist system—which asserted that supply created its own demand and which thereby denied the possibility of a depression. The new form of the law seems to assert that this is true, not merely for the economy as a whole, but for each individual firm or product.

The belief is quite false. Simply because firms do not limit themselves to supplying demands felt by the human race when it left the Garden of Eden, but actively build up a market for their products, this does not mean that they can impose whatever they like on a defenceless public. The British motor industry has not been able to prevent consumers from buying more imported cars; Cunard has been unable to prevent a fall in demand for passenger shipping lines; the Coal Board has been unable to prevent a switch to other fuels; and there are countless other examples. Marketing studies suggest that among products regarded as "technical successes" only perhaps 10–20 per cent survive market and prelaunching studies, while of those that are launched one-third to one-half are withdrawn as failures within one year.

There are two extreme and equally absurd prevalent models of the role of the consumer. There is, on the one hand, the view that people have innate tastes which firms exist to satisfy. Hardly any reputable economist, however orthodox, has ever explicitly held this view; but there are incautious statements, particularly in American textbooks, which give credence to this allegation of Galbraith's. At the other extreme is the view to which Galbraith himself comes perilously close, that sees consumers as plastic clay on which the advertisers can impose any shape they like. In fact, salesmanship is part of the process of increasing the range of alternatives of which people are aware. Like many other technological and cultural techniques, it develops desires of which people were not aware before and—the point must be conceded—causes some people to be more dissatisfied with their lot than they otherwise would be. This is part of the price of freedom of communication. Nearly all the products of civilisation—arts, sports and recreations, just as much as running water, telephones or labour-saving gadgets—have been invented and sold to people who were not spontaneously asking for any of them, but were glad to have them when they arrived. It is part of the function of a market economy to suggest new possibilities to people which they are then free to accept or reject. It may be that commercial advertising increases demand for consumer goods relative to "public goods," leisure or a pleasant environment. But politicians, writers and journalists can and do propagandise in the opposite direction; the activities of the New Left are themselves part of the free market in ideas, and by no means the least successful part of it.

None of this means that the situation in regard to advertising or consumer information is incapable of reform. If advertisers really discovered and used forms of subliminal advertising, which exercised a literally hypnotic effect which people were powerless to resist, the case for legal prohibition of these forms would be strong. On the positive side, much more could be done to encourage the provision of information and views on products from points of view other than the producer's. There is a case for state encouragement and financial support of consumer bodies. It is still too difficult to organise or finance anything analogous to the political "Opposition" in the commercial sphere.

Another objection to markets, which does not fit very easily with a belief in a "permissive" morality, but which is sometimes heard from the same camp, is that the exercise of choice itself involves costs and inconvenience which some people do not wish to bear. In many aspects of life an attempt to survey the total range of options would be impractical, because the consumer lacks the knowledge to make it, or irrational, because the benefits are too trivial in relation to the time and effort expended; and there may be advantages in voluntarily delegating the choice to others. Investment and unit trusts spare the investor the bother of selecting his own securities; organisations such as the AAA and *The Good Food Guide* select hotels and restaurants and group them into convenient grades. Travel agents offer both package and individual tours for people who cannot be bothered to make their own arrangements. There are excellent "flower clubs" which, for a fixed annual subscription, arrange a weekly delivery of the flowers that happen to give the best value for money at the time of year. This gives access to both expertise and to economies of bulk purchasing which most individuals could not hope to have acting on their own. Every encouragement should be given to such methods of delegating choice; and we can all exercise our own preferences about which purchases to delegate, and to whom. . . .

By all means let us experiment with every sort of choice for giving people more say in the organisations in which they work—although my own feeling is that what people most want is, in the first place, to be informed in advance so that decisions are not sprung upon them and secondly, to be consulted so that they can express their views before it is too late, rather than to attempt themselves the tasks of management.

Another point, not generally realised, is that to the extent that workers really want to have a say in management, those firms who are responsive will find it easier to attract workers. Thus, if there is a real demand for greater workers' participation (although not for expropriating the owners), this too can be brought about by the market.

If the above remarks seem a little removed from reality, the main reason lies in the part played by the restrictionist activities of the trade unions themselves. Catering for minority tastes in, say, hours of work, or in preference for a more relaxed tempo of work, is a costly business. It can be costly because of the kind of preferences involved, or simply because they are minority tastes and an employer who caters for them will have to do more searching around for staff. These are real costs, which would exist in a non-capitalist society; and an employee who wishes to be treated in this way must expect smaller take-home pay. Unfortunately the insistence of union activists on levelling up all wage differentials between workers of comparable skills would soon discourage any employer who tried to cater for such minority tastes or attitudes. . . .

A TURN OF THE TIDE?

Yet, although these parallels are ominous, the comparison with the late Roman Empire shows only one of several roads along which we might travel. There are also more hopeful possibilities. The great advance of technology brings with it an immense range of options which were quite unknown to most societies before the twentieth century. For all the excesses cited on previous pages, the spirit of most of those who "opt out" is more critical, less submissive to some mystical fate than that of the Manichaeans, neoplatonists or early Christian monks.

The instinctive revolt against a life grimly devoted to work and promotion is soundly based. There is a healthy mean between the superstitious worship of the Gross National Product and a belief in the sanctity of poverty. Behind the clichés about the "quality of life" and "the environment" is a well-founded suspicion of false goals which we are free not to follow.

The mistake of too many radicals is (a) to underestimate the forces working against the cosy "New Industrial State" that many business leaders would admittedly love to establish and (b) to overrate the potentialities and gravely underestimate the risk of political accountability as a check on economic power. But their rejection of all the many arrangements and institutions which are neither responsible to the consumer through the market, nor politically accountable, nor subject to known laws, is sound and admirable.

In time they may come to see that the remedy is neither to indulge in nostalgia for a pre-industrial age, nor to talk about "the revolution," but to promote an effective market in which all costs and benefits are properly priced and which are regulated by deliberately impersonal processes. More simply and crudely, there is a need to restore the entrepreneurial and even buccaneering element in capitalism at the expense of the managerial one. Then, given a proper framework of law, taxes and subsidies, we shall have no more Concordes or other loss-making home-based technological industries and produce more of the things that people actually want, whether these be leisure, peace and quiet, or a less hectic pattern of living, more consumer goods, or some combination of all of these.

The "guerrilla capitalist" battling against the monopoly of the Post Office or broadcasting authorities is a small sign of a change in the direction of youthful energy and dissent. There are signs that some of those who "opt out" are trying their luck at small scale entrepreneurial activities of their own, supplying many services on a personal, flexible basis impossible to the large public and private bureaucracies. Certainly the time is ripe for a realignment in which the more thoughtful members of the New Left and the more radical advocates of competitive free enterprise realise that they have a common interest in opposing the corporate industrial state.

There are built-in forces in modern society providing a ready audience for specious anti-capitalist propaganda which I have repeatedly emphasised in this prologue. But in optimistic moods I am impressed by the limits to human gullibility. There is a chance—how large I cannot predict—that the modern mixed economy will develop in a less materialist direction through the development of the attitudes and of institutions of a free society rather than through coercion from above or below. The revolt of young people against the pattern of their lives being decided by others or by impersonal forces they cannot influence is fundamentally justified. Precisely the same arguments are to be found in the classical defences of free markets, private property and limited government. Until recently technological limitations were such that freedom could be important only in the lives of a fortunate minority. It is now possible for all who are not afraid of it.

LIBERALISM IN THE COMING DECADE

Antonio Martino

Antonio Martino is professor of economics at the University of Rome. He has served as foreign minister and defense minister of Italy. This article is based on his presidential address to the Mont Pelerin Society, the international society of classical liberal scholars, in 1990. Martino argues that despite the collapse of state socialism, liberalism still faces many challenges: from coercive environmentalism, petty regulation of our personal lives, and the continuing growth of government spending, taxation, and borrowing.

In the midst of great historical changes, some reflections on the role of liberal thinkers in today's world seem appropriate. According to historian Max Hartwell, "The common objective of those who met in Mont Pèlerin in 1947 was undoubtedly to halt and reverse current political, social, economic and intellectual trends towards socialism, and to ensure the revival of liberalism."

In the light of recent history, it would be tempting to conclude that those trends have in fact been reversed, liberalism has been revived, and the society has achieved its purpose. While the differences between the world of 1947 and that of today are undeniable, it is far from clear that our mission has been completed. It seems to me that liberty is still facing gigantic obstacles on both sides of the collapsed iron curtain and in the rest of the world. Let me mention just a few of the obstacles that may confront us in the next 10 years.

THE COLLAPSE OF COMMUNISM

The memorable events of the past several months in what are now called the ECCs (ex-communist countries) have stimulated the hopes of freedom fighters all over the world. There is no doubt that the events of 1989 provide conclusive evidence of the collapse of communism both as a viable form of economic organization and as a political system, because it has been proven beyond any doubt that communism was inefficient and not based on the consent of the governed. Although those realizations are hardly new for liberals, it is certainly pleasant to see one's political views so clearly confirmed.

The pace of change in the past months has been so rapid that even our wildest hopes have not been able to keep up with it. Yet a word of caution is probably needed. In many ECCs the demand for political freedom has translated itself into free (or quasi-free) elections resulting in the defeat of the formerly ruling Communist party. That is undoubtedly a desirable change per se, but to those of us who believe in freedom, the real question is whether the introduction of elements of political democracy in some East European countries will start a process that leads to the liberalization of those societies. In other words, will the change from totalitarian rule to electoral democracy widen the range of free choices open to individuals in their everyday lives, or will it be just a cosmetic change that will leave nearly everything else unchanged?

There is no doubt that, as a political decisionmaking mechanism, democracy is superior to its alternatives. But, for a liberal, electoral democracy is not the only issue. A liberal agrees with Herbert Spencer that "the real issue is whether the lives of citizens are more interfered with than they were; not the nature of the agency which interferes with them."

Or, as Milton Friedman has recently remarked:

The unprecedented political upheavals that believers in human freedom have welcomed with so much joy can be the prelude to comparable economic miracles, but that is far from inevitable. They can equally be the prelude to a continuation of collectivism under a different set of rules. Everything depends on the political will of the people, the economic understanding of their leaders, and the ability of those leaders to persuade the public to support the radical measures that are necessary.

The first signs are not necessarily encouraging. In many cases, the paralysis of action has prompted extravagance of language but no appreciable change. East European countries do not seem to have yet embarked on radical reforms that promise to transform them into workable free-market economies. In many cases, that has been due to the fact, pointed out by James M. Buchanan, that both in the East and in the West, "the loss of faith in politics, in socialism broadly defined, has not . . . been accompanied by any demonstrable renewal or reconversion to a faith in markets."

As for the economic understanding of communist leaders, in an article entitled "Pricing in USSR between Supply and Demand," Anatolij Derjabin recommended a radical reform of retail prices, lamenting, for example, that the price of milk was proportional to its fat content rather than its protein content, "as in most other countries"!

After so many decades of planning mythology, misunderstanding of the market is hardly surprising. But what I fear is that the superior prosperity of market economies has generated the delusion that all that is needed to promote economic growth is to imitate some of the *external* features of our economies, while leaving everything else unchanged. A good example is the notion that the dismal performance of communist economies is due to bad management. That is wrong. Management is not the problem. Market economies are not efficient because by chance they have been endowed with superior managers. They have better managers *because* they are efficient. It is the market that provides the filter mechanism required to make sure that only managers who make the correct decisions survive and prosper. *Superior management is the consequence of market efficiency, not its cause.*

I often compare the apparent beliefs of some East European reformers with those of the "cargo cult"—Pacific islanders who, after World War II, watched Western soldiers clear an expanse of land and build a tower. When the islanders saw that the clearing and tower attracted huge metallic birds laden with precious commodities, they built fake landing strips and control towers in the hope that a cornucopia of goods would fall from the sky. The same kind of wishful thinking is reflected in the idea, heard frequently in Eastern Europe these days, that prosperity can be achieved by simply extolling the virtues of "market socialism" and "structural transformation" (whatever those words mean) in the absence of private property rights, freedom of contract, free trade, and a functioning price system.

It would be grossly unfair, however, to generalize the imperfect understanding of the free-market system shown by some leaders in Eastern Europe and ignore the existence of a surprisingly large number of dedicated freedom fighters who have cultivated liberal ideas, often at substantial personal costs. They remind us of a new and important task for Western liberals—debating the innumerable problems posed by the transition from socialism to capitalism. That is a very difficult assignment; there is no magic formula, no "model," for the transformation of a planned economy into a competitive one.

We have nothing to teach the ECCs. Our record in dismantling the innumerable bits of socialism that have proliferated in our own countries over the decades is not sensational. Rather, we have a lot to learn from the ECCs. We could sharpen our understanding of the nature of the problem by discussing the difficulties encountered by our friends in Eastern Europe. In return, we could provide them with the kind of invaluable encouragement that associating with other liberals has given many of us.

The debate on liberal ideas in an international forum is more necessary to our friends from the East than it is to us. That task alone would be sufficient to fill the liberal agenda for the next decade.

IS FREEDOM WINNING?

While the problems faced by East European countries are numerous, serious, and unprecedented, liberty in our "free" countries is not immune to new and formidable predicaments. The reason is simple and very well known: *while socialism is dead, statism is not.* We have, for the moment at least, freed ourselves from the danger of wholesale socialism, but we are still facing the gradual but continuous erosion of our liberties. And, since a free country is one in which there is no particular individual to blame for the existing tyranny, we can only reproach ourselves for what is happening.

Capitalism's current problems, according to the *Economist,* are three: the environment; the increase in government spending, taxing, and borrowing that results from the interplay of pressure groups; and the growth of an "underclass" due mostly to the failure of public schools.

Environmentalism is one of the main causes of the new wave of statism. The threat of environmentalism is subtle and deadly. Its plausibility makes it acceptable even to reasonable believers in freedom; its appeal to the uninformed is enormous; the half-baked scientific assertions used to justify all kinds of government intervention for the sake of the environment require extensive information on the part of those who wish to criticize them. And the problem is made worse by the many environmentalists who deliberately suppress any evidence that the bases of their proposals are questionable. Environmentalism poses a future risk to liberty that is as serious as that posed by wholesale socialism in the past.

Believers in freedom have already done extensive work on alternative, free-market solutions to environmental problems. What is needed now is more interdisciplinary research by collaborating scientists and economists. Such research should be a high priority for liberal scholars in the near future.

Another threat comes from the enormous variety of "small" restrictions on our personal freedoms that are continuously being introduced in the name of safety, health, and other lofty ideals. Each of them, taken by itself, seems trivial. Taken together, they amount to a wholesale attack on our independence.

The purpose of the law has been distorted, so that now the state, instead "of protecting, as far as possible, every member of the society from the injustice or oppression of every other member of it," as Adam Smith put it, tries to protect individuals *from themselves,* destroying the very concept of personal responsibility in the process.

The welfare state, "public" health care in particular, has gradually instilled the notion that we do not own our health. The results of that view are schizophrenic. On the one hand, the increase in life expectancy becomes the cause of national anxiety, since an aging population imposes costs "on society." A good example was given by a recent *Washington Post* article that explained that "smokers 'save' the Social Security system hundreds of billions of dollars. Certainly this does not mean that decreased smoking would not be socially beneficial. In fact, it is probably one of the most cost-effective ways of increasing average longevity. It does indicate, however, that if people alter their behavior in a manner which extends life expectancy, then this must be recognized by our national retirement program." At this point, the patriotic citizen does not know what to do. If he lives dangerously, he imperils the financial future of the public health system. If he decides to live a long, healthy life, Social Security is in trouble.

On the other hand, since "the government" pays for our medical care, we are not free to live our lives in a manner that is deemed unhealthy by the authorities. The standard argument for the panoply of restrictions on activities considered unhealthy is that people who engage in them are more likely to get sick and "impose a cost on society." As a result, what is deemed dangerous or unhealthy is banned, and what is considered healthy or otherwise beneficial is made compulsory: speed limits; helmets for motorcyclists; seat belts; restrictions on the sale of pornographic material and the consumption of drugs, alcohol, and tobacco; and so on. We are heading toward a society in which dangerous sports will not be permitted, pedestrians will be required to have licenses, obesity will be illegal, and what we are allowed to eat will be determined by the National Dieting Board!

If you think that is ridiculous, exaggerated, or paradoxical, think of the European Economic Community's toy regulations. As pointed out by Digby Anderson:

> The contemporary obsession with safety, especially safety for children, has found its true bureaucratic home in the EEC.... Committees have now recommended the statutory minimum dimensions of marbles based on the average width of toddlers' throats so that the Community shall protect its young from swallowing them. Or perhaps it is so that they *will* be able to swallow them rather than get them stuck: it's not clear.... The pea in a whistle may be governed by regulation as to its toxicity lest someone tread on a whistle, the pea escape, be picked up and chewed

by a child desperately looking for a pre-EEC-ban-style marble. I'm unsure about whether such peas will have to be the size of tennis balls (for marbleish reasons) and how huge post-1990 whistles will have to be to incorporate them.

Examples of absurd pretenses for intruding into our privacy and regulating our lives could fill several volumes. Their absurdity should not make us forget the danger they pose to our liberty. Think of the bill signed by representatives of all political parties in Italy that, if approved, would have forbidden television on Saturday for the lofty purpose of forcing people to spend more time talking to their families. And what should we make of a society in which a citizen who is considered old and mature enough to pay taxes, enter into a labor contract, get married, drive a car, participate in determining the political future of his country by voting, or risk his life in its defense is not considered old or responsible enough to go into a bar and drink a beer? Yet that is what is happening in the "land of the free and the home of the brave."

Whatever we intend to do, we would be well advised to follow Laurence Peter's advice. "Do it now! There may be a law against it tomorrow."

I believe it is more important today to ask the question that Spencer asked more than a century ago. "In past times Liberalism habitually stood for individual freedom *versus* State-coercion. . . . How is it that . . . Liberalism has to an increasing extent adopted the policy of dictating the actions of citizens, and, by consequence, diminishing the range throughout which their actions remain free?"

The last set of problems involves both new and old challenges to a liberal order. Liberals have for years advocated the introduction of choice in education as a way to impose the discipline of competition on inefficient public school systems. We have not made much progress in that area, despite the production of a substantial body of theoretical work, so it seems appropriate to analyze the reasons for our failure and look for a way to overcome the political and bureaucratic obstructions that so far have prevented experimentation. However, the growth of an underclass is not the result of the failure of public schools alone; it is the most visible symptom of the failure of the entire welfare state. While freedom fighters have consistently criticized welfare statism, we are still divided on the alternatives that have so far been proposed—the negative income tax, for example. Finally, we cannot hope to dismantle the existing welfare state unless we can suggest a plausible alternative. Liberal alternatives to welfare should be a high priority for our scholars.

GROWTH OF GOVERNMENT AND THE FUTURE OF LIBERTY

By far the most pressing problem plaguing contemporary capitalism is our old nemesis, the growth of government spending, taxation, and borrowing. In most countries, the tendencies of the past have continued undisturbed, despite the dramatic change in political rhetoric. In my own country, the 1980s witnessed repeated pronouncements on the part of all governments about the need to contain spending, taxation, and borrowing. The results have been disappointing, to say the least. From 1980 to 1989 public-sector spending increased from 43.5 to 54 percent of GDP, public-sector revenue went from 35 to 43.3 percent, and net borrowing from 8.5 to 10.7 percent. Public debt more than doubled in real terms, reaching the astronomical figure of roughly $900 billion. If the trends that prevailed in the 1980s are allowed to continue through the 1990s, in the year 2000 public spending in Italy could absorb 75 percent of gross domestic product, while explicit taxation could amount to 60 percent. That would spell the end of our freedom and prosperity.

The explanation of the contrast between good intentions and appalling results is simple: the growth of government is not a managerial problem that can be solved by changing managers. It is a problem of rules: without an effective set of constitutional constraints, political incentives will always and everywhere result in the uninterrupted growth of spending and taxation. In the words of James Buchanan, "There will be no escape from the protectionist-mercantilist regime that now threatens to be characteristic of the post-socialist politics in both Western and Eastern countries so long as we allow the ordinary or natural outcomes of majoritarian democratic processes to operate without adequate constitutional constraints." That is why I believe that discussion of a fiscal and monetary constitution should continue to be a high priority on the liberal agenda—all the more so because there still is no consensus among liberals on the most effective way to constrain government.

Any constitutional solution must address the problem of the relationship among the various levels of government. Federalism is today advocated as the appropriate framework for the peaceful coexistence of different geographic, ethnic, or linguistic groups within the same country. Whether in South Africa or Canada, the USSR or China, the EEC or nation-states like Italy, Spain, or even the United Kingdom, the decentralization of government seems to offer the kind of flexible structure needed to accommodate regional differences within a country. Federalism also allows experimentation with the competition among policies. The debate on public policy problems can then leave the abstract and dogmatic domain of ideological confrontation for the more pragmatic and potentially fruitful approach of comparing the concrete results of various policy solutions.

But federalism could also offer a healthy check on total government power and on its tendency to grow over time. It is no accident that federal structures, such as those of Switzerland or the United States, have often been more successful in containing the growth of government than have nonfederal ones.

Unfortunately, the ideals of federalism can be betrayed and corrupted. Witness the EEC's experience and the growth of *eurodirigisme*. We clearly face the additional task of devising constitutional constraints on the central power in federal structures to prevent them from evolving into the kind of centralized leviathan they were supposed to replace.

On the economic front, an important potential problem seems to be a shortage of savings. Keynes's prediction that "as a rule . . . a greater *proportion* of income [is] saved as real income increases" has been belied by the evidence. In many countries, including my own, the savings ratio has steadily declined as real income has increased. Such a tendency is obviously reinforced by demographic trends. Should it continue, it would constrain our growth potential. Demography and related issues, such as immigration, which have not always been prominent on the liberal research agenda, deserve more careful scrutiny.

THE DURABILITY OF IDEAS

Whether ideas make a difference is an important question for us. It seems to me that liberal ideas may not prevail in practice at the time of their conception but that they are more durable than their socialist counterparts.

Keynes's notorious view that in the long run we are all dead was wrong. We always *live* in the long run. Today is the last day of a long run that started sometime in the distant past. Yet, in a sense, Keynes was right: he *is* dead. Forty-four years after his demise, Keynes is dead both physically and intellectually; very little is left of his intellectual legacy. That is so because "the ideas of economists and political philosophers . . . are more powerful than is commonly understood" *only when they are right,* when they are in accordance with logic and evidence.

The ideas of great liberal thinkers have lasted much longer. It is because of the durability of the liberal tradition, which has survived the dark years of the socialist consensus, that we can enjoy the excitement of our times. The events of 1989 confirm beyond any doubt the view of Milton and Rose Friedman that "the force of ideas, propelled by the pressure of events, is clearly no respecter of geography or ideology or party label." The consequences, however, of the intellectual legacy of socialism will continue to exist long after their intellectual roots have fallen into disrepute. We therefore face the urgent task of showing how intellectual change can be translated into changes in public policy.

CONCLUSION

We live in an exciting but complex world. Few of us would disagree with the comment of Alphonso X, "the learned" King of Castile (1252–84), a medieval patron of astronomy, who is quoted as saying, "if the Lord Almighty had consulted me before embarking on the Creation, I would have recommended something simpler."

The problems confronting us are numerous and intricate. Those that I have mentioned are only a few of the many difficulties that confront the future of liberty in today's world. By themselves, they could fill the liberal research agenda for the next decade. But that agenda will *always* be full, for the obvious reason that we shall never win. We cannot win, not because of any intrinsic weakness in our philosophy but because individual liberty is destined to be continuously challenged. Furthermore, our duty is to be ahead of our times, to offer a perspective on desirable future developments. We are doomed to be constantly ahead of politics.

THE POWER AND POVERTY
OF LIBERTARIAN THOUGHT

Richard Cornuelle

Richard Cornuelle (1927–2011) was a businessman and the author of *Reclaiming the American Dream,* which explored the ways that the nonprofit sector of civil society can solve social problems. In this article he urges that libertarians turn their attention from socialism—which finally proved as unworkable as Mises had predicted—to two new challenges: understanding civil society and voluntary social action as well as they understand markets, and bringing the principles of individualism and enterprise into the workplace.

If the collapse of communism caught the CIA and others unawares, it was certainly no surprise to the students of Ludwig von Mises. We had been expecting it for 40 years. With a confidence no less certain because we had acquired it fortuitously, we knew socialism was doomed and we knew why.

Now everyone knows what we knew; the one big thing the libertarians knew and could explain better than anyone else—that the invisible hand of the market is a more reliable organizer of the economic life of nations than the visible hand of the state—is suddenly the newest universal. The collapse of the communist economies has at last put to rest one of the great unsettled questions of modern times, which absorbed an unreasonable share of the world's intellectual energy for nearly a century. Libertarians had it right from the very beginning.

The assimilation of this enlightenment into everyday affairs will be a long and uncertain process. It may take years, for example, for the people of the Russian republics to accept the idea that the acquisitive private vices they have been conditioned for three generations to repress must now be indulged in the public interest. But socialism is dead, its ponderous "how to" literature has become waste paper, and history has exonerated libertarian scholarship.

NEW CHALLENGES FOR LIBERTARIANS

The irony is that while the libertarians waited for nearly a century for acceptance, the sun shone on them for only a moment. Their central proposition was promptly absorbed into the conventional wisdom and is no longer interesting. Now the unsettled questions are in new and less familiar territory. The dialogue is shifting to ground for which, regrettably, the libertarians are no better prepared than anyone else.

Libertarian thought is wonderfully sound as far as it goes, but there are two gaping holes in it that are now taking on a decisive importance. For one thing, there is no very distinct libertarian vision of community—of social as distinct from economic process—outside the state; the alluring libertarian contention that society would work better if the state could somehow be limited to keeping the peace and enforcing contracts has to be taken largely on faith. Nor have libertarians confronted the disabling hypocrisy of the capitalist rationale, which insists that while capitalists must have extensive freedom of action, their employees may have much less. Their analysis of how an invisible hand arranges economic resources rationally without authoritarian direction stopped abruptly at the factory gate. Inside factories and offices, the heavy, visible hand of management continues to rule with only token opposition.

The repudiation of communist economics is shifting the intellectual action from a battle in which the libertarians held the high ground to one where they hold no ground at all. From the beginning and almost to the end, communism drew its legitimacy from its ends rather than its means, from the powerful echo of its original promises to protect ordinary people from the hazards of life in a capitalist society. Large numbers of working people and their intellectual surrogates still feel in their bones that an unfettered free market is a jungle, that workers do not get their fair share of what they produce, that capitalism so degrades and disorients working people that they cannot make mature decisions about their own welfare, that it pollutes the streams and waters the whiskey, that it creates an acrid social atmosphere in which the smell of money works its way indelibly into the fabric of everything, that it leaves undone or poorly done all the things a good society needs most, and finally that capitalism is given by its nature to large arrhythmic spasms, and the burden of this abiding economic insecurity falls primarily on working people.

In fact, the essentials of this nightmare were most brutally realized in the Soviet Union where the members of a new ruling class lived like Western rock stars on unearned income and the simplest human and material requirements of ordinary people were ignored entirely. Economic insecurity, far from being eliminated, was collectivized. And after a while the theory of worker control was small comfort to workers in rigidly regimented and politicized workplaces. But in spite of those disappointments, the belief in the propriety of the Marxian indictment of capitalism persists with a remarkable intensity, certainly in the East and to a considerable extent everywhere. The Marxian prescription, or at least its economic ingredient, may be in disrepute, but Marx continues to control the social agenda from his grave in Highgate.

In this context, the Soviet debacle is simply the victory of the reformers of the left over the revolutionaries of the left, settling once for all the historic tactical debate whether to tame capitalism or replace it. The supporting premise of the reformist view is that Marx's analysis of the perils of capitalism is more or less correct, but that the way to right the alleged wrongs is not to overthrow capitalism but to domesticate it—treating it like one of those factory-produced chickens, giving it just enough freedom of movement to stay a little healthy and just enough nourishment to get a little fat—and then use the wealth it produces to provide whatever working people need and are too poor or improvident to provide for themselves. This is the new consensus: democratic political institutions, a closely watched and guided market economy, and a welfare or service state with a broad charter to keep the society fair and fit for human habitation. This now-fashionable arrangement is to be found with only superficial variations throughout the industrialized world, in countries as culturally diverse as Japan, Sweden, England, and the United States.

This "system," to which the newly non-Communist nations are thoughtlessly gravitating—variously called social democracy, democratic socialism, or market socialism—is the only game in town, but it is everywhere, and particularly in the United States, showing signs of strain. Eastern European countries may only have jumped out of the fire and into the frying pan. They, along with the rest of the developed world's democracies, are staring down the barrel of the same non sequitur: if it is true that the state is bound by its nature to bungle the business of making steel or shoes, what makes us think it is any better at the vastly more complex responsibilities of the modern full-service state: educating the children, providing pensions and health care, eliminating unemployment, protecting depositors from the imprudence of their bankers, and providing hundreds of other services, presumably necessary but beyond the reach of the market, not just for the few who have been left behind, but for practically everyone?

In fact, the incompetence of the state as social engineer is by now almost as well documented as its incompetence as economic manager. The 1930s and 40s produced a large, ardent literature that imagined the boundless possibilities of activist government. The 1960s, 70s, and 80s produced a literature of an entirely different sort—sadder, saner, sometimes hair-raising chronicles of the failures of the state's efforts to improve society. In the United States, the early work in this genre was done by a handful of libertarian and conservative scholars. In time, they were joined by many of their former "liberal" adversaries—those Irving Kristol said had been mugged by reality. They became the born-again conservatives, the "neo-conservatives." One by one, disillusioned liberals defected, wrote a penitential monograph about how this or that promising government program had failed in practice, until their ranks were so nearly emptied of objectivity and common sense that one of their number called for a new, "rational" liberalism and thus gave birth to "neo-liberalism," which joined in the fun. Now the literature documenting the failure of state action has become almost as immense, impenetrable, and depressing as government itself.

Thus, the American service state, our not very original version of social democracy, an undertaking now at least three times as large as the whole Soviet economy, is no longer sustained either by logic or by any record of practical success. It is becoming clear that we have confused the state's blustering eagerness to take responsibility with an innate capacity to exercise it. The American service state survives and flourishes only because an invincible political majority is convinced that its failing programs must be continued because they are essential and because there are, or seem to be, no alternatives. The so-called Reagan revolution was bogus—a disguised tax revolt. It was not an effort to repeal the service state but to preserve it—and to substitute debt or inflation for taxation as a way of paying its politically irreducible costs. But the illusion that gave the Reagan program its ephemeral plausibility has already faded, and America's social democracy is in a bind from which there is no apparent escape. The status quo is impossible to defend and impossible to change. The American polity has reached a kind of dead end, and libertarian thought, in its present state of development, doesn't help.

Thanks in large part to libertarian scholarship, there is a well-understood alternative to the strictly economic half of the traditional socialist program—state operation of the nation's economic institutions—its farms, factories, banks, and power plants. In this sector, libertarians know what they are for. A highly developed literature explains precisely why a centrally planned economy can't work, but it also explains with a practiced clarity how free markets do work and why. There is a well-traveled pathway to change. If a nation decides to desocialize its mail service or its rum distilleries, it can issue shares and sell them outright to the public, or it can decriminalize competition and stop subsidizing the state operation. Libertarians can demonstrate how competitive services would come into being overnight and why, in time, they would work better and cost less than the state system they had replaced. Given the political will, privatizing partial socialism in countries where free capital markets exist, as Mrs. Thatcher and others have demonstrated, is a comparatively straightforward business.

PRIVATIZING SOCIAL SERVICES

Privatizing the other half of a socialist program, the social services
that remain when the last state enterprise has been privatized—the
part that is practically indistinguishable from the democratic West's
social service states—is a task of an altogether different order. If there
are alternatives to the state's failing efforts to get rid of Skid Row,
eliminate involuntary unemployment, eradicate illiteracy, provide
reasonable pensions, treat the indigent sick, detoxify the environment, among a thousand other problems that beset and perplex an
industrial society, there is only the dimmest awareness of them, and
certainly no confidence that they would work. (That is one of the reasons Americans sound so confused when they talk to opinion poll-
sters, saying usually that government programs are failing miserably
and ought to be expanded.)

Here, libertarians can respond only by stretching market theory
beyond its natural limits. They understand economic process; increasingly they understand political process (libertarian James Buchanan won a Nobel prize in economics for his work in public choice
theory); but their understanding of *social* process is scarcely developed at all. Thus, the service state is immune to libertarian thought
in its present, unfinished condition. However, there is gathering
evidence that there are half-forgotten, potentially powerful, largely
dormant social forces in the society that might, in time, become a
serious alternative to state social action. This dimension of society is
practically begging to be rediscovered, explored, and understood. It
has a glorious past, an ambiguous present, and possibly a considerable future.

Before America's Great Depression, after a century and a half of
remarkable growth, there was a formidable alternative to government
action for almost every aspect of the public business from disease
control to economic stabilization. Tocqueville had considered the
habit of aggressive and imaginative voluntary action in the public
interest—neither commercial on the one hand nor governmental
on the other—the most distinctive and promising aspect of the developing American polity. When the crash came in 1929, this third
dimension or "sector" of society (now increasingly called the "inde-

pendent" sector) had become so large and complex as to be literally indescribable in any reasonable space. Nor had anyone catalogued its elements or assessed its total contribution to the general welfare. Even now, the organizations of the independent sector are waiting to be counted and classified.

America's overall institutional landscape consists of one federal government, 50 state governments, and, at last count, about 80,000 local governments of various shapes and sizes. There are more than 10 million commercial entities, ranging from bootblacks and push-cart peddlers to giant conglomerate corporations. And running through and among and around all those like glue are the institutions of the third, independent sector, several million of them altogether. The variety of their purposes is staggering. There are hundreds of universities, elementary and secondary schools, thousands of hospitals, museums, symphony orchestras, and libraries, hundreds of thousands of mutual aid groups like Alcoholics Anonymous, to mention only a few of its more visible entities. Its institutions range from the giant Teachers' Insurance and Annuity Association, now the world's largest nongovernmental pension provider with assets of more than $80 billion, to a clearinghouse through which amputees can trade their useless left or right shoes or gloves. Any list of its activities of reasonable length is bound to be a distortion.

How we could mislay a sector of society of this size and scope is something of a mystery. Perhaps the decline of this dimension of American pluralism began when Woodrow Wilson, the schoolmaster president, set out to use his extraordinary wartime powers to jail all our most gallant, original, and entertaining misfits and "rationalize" American society. In any case, by 1946 the American tradition of independent action on the public business had been buried alive— an accidental casualty of Wilson, two wars that greatly improved the health of the state, a thoroughly demoralizing depression, and, finally, the politically captivating Keynesian contention that, in a presumably mature economy, government spending was often its own justification. This gave government a decisive advantage in the continuing contention for social responsibility, and the independent sector stopped growing. Many of its forms have survived and since the 1960s a tentative renaissance has begun, but for half a century the third sector was in limbo, the victim of an unexamined supposition that in an industrial society, independent social action was technologically obsolete.

So while there can be no doubt about the existence of a third sector, there are everywhere understandable doubts about its fitness as a competitor for the vast responsibilities of the welfare state. Given the present state of social thought, it is as hard to believe in the utility and virility of independent social action as it was to believe in the rationality and moral legitimacy of free markets before *The Fable of the Bees* and *The Wealth of Nations*. We need now to understand voluntary social process as completely as we understand market process, and libertarians could again show the way.

CENTRAL PLANNING IN ONE FIRM?

As the dust settles on the ruins of the socialist epoch, a second crippling deficiency of libertarian thought is becoming more visible and embarrassing. The economic methodology that the Russians have lately found unworkable still governs the internal affairs of firms in capitalist and socialist countries alike. An economy presumably works best if it is not administered from the top; a factory presumably works best if it is.

In Adam Smith's hypothetical pin factory, the work was divided and specialized—and hence much more productive. That perception (and a dozen other converging circumstances) became the basis for the industrial era. Another element drew less attention: the method used to coordinate the efforts of these specialized workers was borrowed from the army, the principal previous undertaking that had involved substantial numbers of specialized participants. The necessary coordination was accomplished by regimentation, some people giving orders and others taking them. This primitive method survives in the modern corporation along with its military vocabulary: officers, rank and file, line, staff, chain of command, and the like.

When freemen went to work in factories, their status was not unlike that of the iron-collared serfs who had preceded them. Their employment was a kind of voluntary indenture, tacitly renewed each day, in which the worker agreed to submit to supervision for a certain number of hours for an agreed-upon amount of pay. Workers were free in one sense but painfully unfree in another. Feudalism had only moved indoors. The movement to civilize this relationship began immediately and has been more or less continuous. Workplaces have been made safer, lighter, warmer, and more agreeable. Wages are higher, hours shorter, and an accumulation of law and custom has elaborated the rights of employees and put limits on the prerogatives of employers. But the system has never been altered elementally. Working people are far, far freer than slaves or indentured servants, but they are not as free as their bosses and not nearly as free as they might be.

The economic consequences of regimentation are enormous: productivity is undoubtedly much lower than it could be, and the need to translate work, which is boundless, into jobs, which are finite, is a primal cause of unemployment. But the most serious consequences are more urgently human ones. A nation of employees, subordinated to a hierarchy, however restrained and benign, is politicized in the sense that much of employees' effort must be spent pleasing the powers that be in ways that are entirely unrelated to the work itself. In a society that is forever boasting of its dedication to democratic ideals, employees are, however affluent they may have become, members of a subordinate, unmistakably lower, class.

The regimentation of work has created a political majority whose attitudes about themselves and their world are heavily conditioned by a lifelong habit of subordination—what Hayek has called an "employee mentality." How can people see the value of independence and self-propulsion when they work in a system in which they are dependent and subordinate? There is little in their daily experience that would cause them to conclude that a society is kept alive by a continuous process of adaptation, led by independent, enterprising people. They see society as something static—something to be administered. Employed people can scarcely be expected to revere qualities they have been carefully instructed to repress. Instead, they tend to become what the way they work requires: politicized, unimaginative, unenterprising, petty, security-obsessed, and passive. Thomas Jefferson, enchanted as he was by labor-saving machinery, still feared that industrialization would produce a breed of working people so altered by daily subordination that they would be unfit for self-government.

Here, the problem of the unworkable, unaffordable, and un-touchable welfare state and the problem of workplace regimentation converge. In America's long march to its distinctive brand of social democracy, there came into being something Marx could not have anticipated: a working class with proletarian status but middle-class means. Now, the overwhelming majority of Americans, in their working-class capacity, consider themselves entitled to an ever-expanding range of social services, which in their middle-class capacity they pay for in taxes they find increasingly unreasonable.

The search for ways to liberate working people from their pro-letarian status has a long history. Most of the many experiments in workplace reform, accepting the apparent necessity for politicized workplaces, have sought to give workers more political power, and the flaw in this approach sometimes reveals itself palpably when workers in worker-managed plants strike against themselves. But now there is movement toward more elemental reform that would depoliticize workplaces entirely, make each worker self-supervising, and base compensation on some credible estimate of the value each person adds to whatever product or service the firm produces, in effect bringing the principles of the free market into the plant. But without a legitimatizing rationale, something the libertarians are best equipped to provide, this is bound to be a confused and halting process.

A THEORY OF COMMUNITY

Libertarians, to their enduring credit, believe passionately in the power of ideas. They learned from Hayek that socialism was always and everywhere an intellectual movement before it could become a mass movement—and that any successful anti-socialist effort would have to be built on an unshakable intellectual foundation. That has been the central article of faith that has sustained the movement since it began to rebuild itself in the 1940s and 50s. Libertarians are, perhaps inevitably, something of a joke as political activists, but the communist collapse is evidence of the immense power of an intellectual movement which, just 40 years ago, would have fitted into a phone booth. Now history is beckoning from a somewhat different direction, one that many libertarians will find forbidding. The lack of a coherent, comprehensive vision of voluntary community has forced libertarians, unnecessarily, I think, into an individualist emphasis, a suspicious aversion to any kind of collective activity beyond the commercial, in spite of the fact that the libertarian movement is, itself, a voluntary collective with a strong sense of solidarity and remarkable power.

The chronic crisis of the world's social democracies is putting democratic political institutions under increasing stress. We may be in process of fulfilling the familiar prophecy, often made by some of political democracy's most passionate enthusiasts, that democratic societies are inherently unstable and self-destructive. It seems more than ever clear that the several forms of pluralism are interdependent—that the lack of economic pluralism imperils political pluralism and vice versa—and now our two-dimensional societies are showing unnerving signs of instability. It may be that a renaissance of the third, less familiar pluralism—the social pluralism manifested in the institutions of the independent sector—is essential to the survival of the other two; moreover, it may be that regimented working people will have great difficulty building and maintaining free societies and that history has suddenly redefined the task of libertarian scholarship.

I believe Mises himself would have welcomed enthusiastically the continuing enlargement of libertarian thought. Unique among economists, his knowledge of economics was so complete that he understood its limitations. In *Human Action* he said, with his customary clarity, that in the vast spectrum of human activities, economics treated only a slice, those which result in an exchange. Mises knew that economics is the beginning of the inquiry into the nature and metabolism of human action and certainly not the end of it.

THE CULTURE OF LIBERTY

Mario Vargas Llosa

Mario Vargas Llosa is a Peruvian novelist and essayist. His works include *Conversation in the Cathedral* and *The War of the End of the World*. Once a socialist like so many Latin American intellectuals, in 1990 he ran for the presidency of Peru on a free-market liberal platform. In this essay, delivered at a 1991 Democracy Commission conference in Managua, Nicaragua, he urges Latin Americans to create a culture of liberty and individual responsibility, rejecting the mercantilism, economic nationalism, and statism that have long created poverty and social division across the region. He allows a larger role for the state than most libertarians would, but in the Latin American context his essay is radically liberal.

───────

It is said that the fashionable curse during the Chinese Cultural Revolution was, "May you live in interesting times." Our times would doubtless qualify—we cannot complain on that score. Over the last few years almost every day has brought fresh surprises, leaving us to gape at each new breakthrough for freedom: the fall of the Berlin Wall and the subsequent reunification of Germany; the overthrow of Nicolae Ceauşescu in Romania; Václav Havel's stunning rise from the depths of prison to the presidency of Czechoslovakia; Violeta Chamorro's upset victory in the Nicaraguan elections; and the democratization of Haiti.

We are still rubbing our eyes at some of the things we see on our television screens. There is, for example, the sight of Red Square teeming with demonstrators calling for an end to Soviet repression in the Baltics and demanding free elections throughout the USSR. Everywhere, it seems, communist parties are expiring or seeking to survive (as in Italy) by changing their names and disowning such essential features of Marxism-Leninism as class struggle, centralized planning, and social ownership of the means of production. We are witnessing the abandonment of all the myths, stereotypes, arguments, and methods that gave birth to communism, made it grow, put a third of the human race under its yoke of servitude and terror, and finally led to its self-destruction.

Under the circumstances, great pronouncements are difficult to avoid. Are we not launching a new era in human history? The term "history" is one of many concepts that has been prostituted by ideology. Appeals to history have served as alibis for the grand intellectual deceptions of our times; history has been invoked in our century to justify genocide and the basest political crimes ever recorded.

Should we, then, join Francis Fukuyama in claiming that communism's last gasp marks the true "end of history" in the Hegelian sense? I think we should not. On the contrary, events in the Soviet Union and Eastern Europe have unexpectedly revitalized the very notion of "history." Humanity is now free of the blinders and fictions that Marxism—orthodox or heterodox—imposed upon it for so long. Humankind's taste for healthy risk-taking has been restored, as has its instinct for free improvisation undertaken in defiance of all reductionist conceptual schemes.

Today, we can confirm the position that Karl Popper, Friedrich Hayek, and Raymond Aron always held in opposition to thinkers like Machiavelli, Vico, Marx, Spengler, and Toynbee. The former insisted, rightly, that history is never "written" before it happens; it does not proceed according to some script determined by God, nature, reason, or the class struggle and the means of production. History is rather a continuous and variable creation that can move through the most unexpected turns, evolutions, involutions, and contradictions. Its complexity always threatens to sweep away those who attempt to predict and explain it.

We are right to be thrilled by current trends such as the resurgence of the individual vis-à-vis the state; of economic freedom versus central planning; of private property and enterprise versus collectivism and statism; of liberal democracy versus dictatorship and mercantilism. But let us not fool ourselves. None of this was "written." No hidden force, waiting in the catacombs of obscurantism and terror that impoverished and humiliated entire peoples, led to the fall of Ceaușescu, the triumph of Solidarity, or the demolition of the wall that divided Berlin. These victories—and all the others like them that have recently inspired totalitarianism's foes—were hard-won by the stubborn resistance of victims, sometimes aided by the desperation of communist oligarchs. These latter, brought face-to-face with the need for drastic change by communism's inability to solve pressing economic and social problems, found themselves haunted by the unmitigated national catastrophes that failure to reform would surely bring about.

The victory of freedom over totalitarianism has been overwhelming, but it is far from fully secured. Indeed, the toughest part of the struggle lies ahead. The dismantling of statism and the dispersal of the economic and political power expropriated by a despotic bureaucracy are exceedingly complex tasks. They are demanding enormous sacrifices from those peoples who still labor under the illusion that political democracy and economic liberty provide instant solutions to all problems. These peoples need to overcome the legacy of stupefaction and rigidity that collectivism has left behind. They must restore their sense of individual responsibility. They must put to rest the alienating assumption, fostered by communism, that all problems must be referred first to the state for solution, and only as a last resort to themselves. Bringing about such a profound and widespread change of ingrained attitudes is a far more daunting challenge than ousting petty tyrants ever was.

For countries like Poland, Hungary, Romania, Bulgaria, Czechoslovakia, and the Soviet Union, then, the true revolutionary task has barely begun. The job is nothing short of staggering: to build the foundations of a free society on the ruins of socialism. This will require citizens who know that without economic freedom there can be no political liberty, much less any progress. They must also learn that a market economy needs discipline, firm rules, risk-taking, initiative, and above all, plenty of hard work and sacrifice. The culture of success—that extraordinary wellspring of prosperity that sustains all advanced democratic societies—also demands that entrepreneurs and companies accept the risk of failure without expecting the state to cushion all their falls.

Accepting this new-found liberty, then, means standing ready to pay the piper for inefficiency or miscalculation. The competitive market generates the most efficiency and creates the most wealth of any economic system, but it is also cold and merciless toward inefficiency. It is best, I think, to take this sobering truth into account right now, at the threshold of the new era. Freedom, which is always necessary for progress and justice, exacts a price that people must pay daily if they wish to remain free. No country, neither the most prosperous nor the one with the longest democratic tradition, is exempt from this danger.

What is happening in Eastern Europe is also happening, though in a less obvious and much less spectacular way, in Latin America. Here it is a slow, indirect process, not always conscious, but still visible to the dispassionate observer. Except for Cuba, all our dictatorships have given way to civilian governments. Democratic regimes— although admittedly with varying degrees of legitimacy—govern our countries from the Rio Grande to the Straits of Magellan. The case of Nicaragua, our host country, is especially significant. No more so, however, than Paraguay, Chile, or Haiti. Violent revolutionary myths have also lost their power to sway more than a few young people, peasants, and workers. Some radical academics and intellectuals (along with other unassimilated and marginal sectors), while still capable of causing considerable harm, are day by day coming to be regarded as eccentrics with no real popular support.

The real change, however, is that welcome signs of pragmatism and modernization are starting to spring up all over Latin America in spite of (or perhaps because of) the great economic crisis we confront. With rare exceptions, few governments still dare to follow the Keynesian model that has wreaked so much havoc and continues to do so. A renewed liberalism—in the classical sense—is making headway in the region as a healthy alternative to the worn-out notions of "internal development" and "import substitution."

Some approach the task with enthusiasm, some with reluctance, while others do not know exactly why they are doing it, yet almost all the new governments are starting to take necessary, if sometimes small, steps to attack the root causes of poverty. It is a great achievement of our own era in comparison to previous ones that the evil of poverty has become curable, as long as the ailing country has the will to get better.

This means, in social and economic terms, the will to modernize, to clean up, and to cut the state down to the proper size for ensuring order, justice, and liberty. It means fostering the right to create wealth in an open system, based on merit, without bureaucratic privileges and interference. It also means that the state must assume responsibility for ensuring that each generation will enjoy that which, together with liberty, is the basis of all democratic societies—namely, equality of opportunity.

Little by little, Latin America is learning that a government "redistributes" more intelligently by offering outstanding public education than by smothering private enterprise with oppressive taxes, and by making sure that private property is accessible to the largest number rather than by harassing those who have property already.

Economic nationalism—which along with cultural nationalism is one of the most tenacious aberrations in our history—is beginning to show signs of receding at last. Nationalism has contributed substantially to the underdevelopment of Latin America. Yet slowly we are learning that health does not derive from fortifying our borders, but from opening them up wide and going out into the world to capture markets for our products, along with the technology and capital and ideas that the world can offer us to develop our resources and create the jobs that we so urgently need.

Given this new cultural climate, many would now admit that the much-touted regional integration of Latin America never worked because it was always hampered by the "nationalist spirit." It was promoted as a defense against the rest of the world and its notorious "imperialism," but came a cropper because each Latin American country tried to use regional unity for its own benefit, not for that of others.

Now that growing numbers of Latin Americans finally seem

to be learning that highest of political virtues—common sense—integration is starting to be understood in its modern sense: as a joining together to speed Latin America's integration with the rest of humanity. Entering into today's world with an awareness of possibilities, of risks, and of markets is the best way for poor and backward countries like our own to start being modern—that is, prosperous. Without prosperity, there is little true freedom, for freedom in poverty is at best a precarious and limited sort of freedom.

Let us be rid of nationalism, which has bloodied and divided us, and in whose name we have wasted enormous resources in order to arm ourselves against one another. These resources would have been much better spent fighting the real enemies of any nation, which are not its neighbors but rather hunger, ignorance, and backwardness. It is essential that we not backslide into the sorts of methods that bad governments use to muzzle their critics. Let there be no more intimidating talk about alleged "threats from foreign enemies" or the supposed need for absolute "national unity." We need to work diligently to overcome reciprocal mistrust, solving problems peacefully as they arise. We must also keep struggling to ensure that barriers between our nations are lowered by the beneficent power of friendship, common interests, and the shared consciousness that only by working together can we exorcise those persistent demons that have kept us so far behind other, more prosperous regions of the world.

Fortunately, the number of Latin Americans who can distinguish clearly between nationalism and patriotism is growing all the time. While patriotism, as Dr. Johnson observed, may sometimes serve as the last refuge of scoundrels, it is more often a generous, unselfish sentiment of love for the land where one was born and one's ancestors died. It represents a moral and emotional commitment to the web of historical, geographical, and cultural references that frame the destiny of every individual. But even patriotism, with all its beautiful and noble qualities, cannot be made obligatory without degrading it, any more than would be the case for such private experiences as sex, friendship, faith, and love.

In these times of upheaval and wonder, even capitalism—that most odious of words, so greatly feared by Latin American politicians—is starting to wend its way ever so subtly and delicately into our public vocabulary. Shorn of frightening old connotations, it comes down objectively to this: it is the system that, despite its limitations and flaws, has made possible the greatest progress in collective welfare, social security, human rights, and individual liberty that history has ever seen.

Let me hasten to add that this does not necessarily mean that because of capitalism, human happiness has been measurably increased. Happiness is not something to be measured according to social coordinates, only individual ones. That is why, as Karl Popper says, happiness is not the duty of governments. Those who try to achieve it for everyone—"holistic" governments like those of Fidel Castro, the Shiite ayatollahs of Iran, or the superstitious antediluvians of the People's Republic of China—tend to turn their societies into a hell. Happiness, which is mysterious and variable, like poetry, concerns only oneself and one's intimates; there are no formulas to produce it and no explanations to decipher it.

It needs to be recognized that the quickest way out of poverty is a clear and resolute decision for the market, private enterprise, and individual initiative. As a necessary first step, we must reject statism, collectivism, and populist demagogy. To avoid serious confusion we must insist upon the sharp distinction that separates genuine capitalism—which, for clarity, we might call liberal and which we have never actually had—from those adulterated forms of rentier or mercantile capitalism that have always been present until now in Latin America.

Cozy agreements between political authorities and influential business groups aimed at giving the latter monopoly privileges and exemptions from competition—that is, from having to exert themselves to satisfy the demands of the consumer—have been inexhaustible sources of inefficiency and corruption in our economies. Corruption is inevitable when the success of an enterprise depends not on the market but on some bureaucrat signing a decree. Such a system warps both business and the businessman, who must focus his ingenuity and efforts not on serving the consumer, but on obtaining state privileges. Mercantilism has been one of the principal causes of our underdevelopment, and of the discrimination and injustices that our societies visit upon the poor. Mercantilism has made

THE CULTURE OF LIBERTY   [491]

legality a privilege accessible only to those with "pull," and thus has condemned the poor to seeking opportunities for work and profit at the margins, in the so-called informal economy. Such an existence is admittedly precarious, but free. In some ways, the informals are the harbingers of an authentic popular capitalism for Latin America.

Ending mercantilism is a moral and political imperative fully as urgent as eradicating the social and economic "reforms" that in our societies have led to the nationalization of businesses, the collectivization of land, and the entrenchment of statism. Mercantilism, collectivism, and statism are all different expressions of the same phenomenon that strangles individual initiative, makes the bureaucrat instead of the businessman or the worker the protagonist of productive life, stimulates inefficiency and corruption, legitimates discrimination and privilege, and, sooner or later, brings about the erosion and disappearance of liberty.

Establishing a free economy that banishes monopolies and guarantees everyone access to markets governed by simple, clear, and equitable rules will not weaken Latin America's nation-states. On the contrary, it will strengthen them by giving them the authority and credibility they now lack. Despite their size, they are too weak and impotent to provide the basic services expected of them: health, security, justice, education, and a minimal infrastructure.

But denying the state the right to intervene as producer in order to allow it more efficiently to fulfill its role as arbitrator and promoter of economic life does not mean exempting it from its essential responsibilities. Among these, for example, is keeping the market free of interference and distortions that sap its efficiency and promote abuses. Another is continual improvement of the system of justice, since without a fair, strong, and universal judicial system that all citizens, especially the poor, can rely on to defend their rights, there can be no functioning market economy. Finally and most especially, there must be efforts to promote the ownership of property among those who still have none. Private property is not theft, as Proudhon held, but rather the sign and sustenance of liberty.

A liberal state is inconceivable without a policy of support for the disabled and the infirm, for the person who because of age, nature, or fate is not able to provide for himself and would be crushed if subjected to the strict laws of the market. Critics of the liberal state often charge that it is systematically inhumane. But when and where did Adam Smith or the other great classical liberal thinkers propose that the state be indifferent toward the weak? The truth is that liberal democracies have the best record in the world when it comes to protecting the aged and children, as well as insuring against unemployment, industrial accidents, and illness.

Above all, there is an order, the cultural order, in which the liberal state has the obligation to take initiatives, to invest resources, and to promote action and participation by everyone. Making cultural benefits accessible to all and stimulating curiosity, interest, and pleasure in what the human imagination and artistic spirit are capable of inventing to counteract life's shortcomings—these are the ways to ensure that people's sensibilities and critical faculties remain sharp, promoting that permanent dissatisfaction without which there can be no social renewal. Nothing keeps this kind of healthy discontent awake and stimulated like a rich cultural life.

It goes without saying that the state should not "direct," or even nudge, cultural activity one inch beyond what it needs to be free and autonomous. The state's function is to guarantee that culture is diverse, abundant, and open to every current and influence, because only thus exposed to challenges and competition can it remain close to experience and help people live, believe, and hope.

Culture has no need for protection, since when it exists in an authentic sense, it protects itself much better than any government could. But states certainly have a duty to give everyone the means of acquiring and producing culture; that is, to provide the education and minimally adequate life circumstances that allow people to enjoy it.

An intense cultural activity, furthermore, is one of the ways in which the liberal state can exorcise a danger that seems to be a congenital affliction of capitalist society: a certain dehumanization of life, a materialism that isolates the individual, destroys the family, and fosters selfishness, loneliness, skepticism, snobbishness, cynicism, and other forms of spiritual emptiness. No modern industrial society has been capable of meeting this challenge effectively; in all of them, high standards of living and large-scale material progress have weakened the sense of social solidarity that, paradoxically, tends to be very strong in primitive communities. This weakening has in turn generated a proliferation of wildly irrational cults and rites that seem to derive their appeal from an unconscious need for a sense of the sacred that we have somehow lost but apparently cannot live without.

The drug subculture that has become perhaps the most formidable present-day backlash against reason amounts to a rejection of that quality of enlightenment which forms the very backbone of the culture of liberty. Drugs seem to provide one of the most extreme ways of expressing—particularly in highly advanced countries—that perennial hunger for transcendence and the absolute that previously was satisfied by magic, myth, and religion.

Those of us who are struggling to modernize our countries by means of the only system that brings prosperity without diminishing freedom should learn a lesson from all this. We must formulate a speedy and imaginative response to these dangers, by establishing a system of patronage for culture, for human creativity in all its myriad forms and bold expressions, for the artistic enterprise, critical thought, research, experimentation, and intellectual exercise. Also, whatever may be our personal religious convictions, we must inspire the development of a deeply spiritual life, since, for the great majority, religion seems to be the most effective vehicle in our tradition for curbing the death wish, expressing solidarity, advancing respect for ethical codes, promoting coexistence and order, and generally maintaining peace and taming the savage desires that all humans, even those seemingly most civilized, harbor within ourselves.

In my youth, as an avid reader of the French existentialists, I came to believe that man determines his own destiny by constantly choosing from among the various possibilities that his changing circumstances present to him. This belief helped me, I think, to become the writer that ever since childhood I had always dreamed of being. But today, after having passed through many perils, I tell myself somewhat sadly that individual destinies are perhaps influenced as much by circumstances and luck as by the freely choosing will.

Yet the "history" of an individual is not "written" in advance any more than is the "history" of a whole society. We must "write" our lines, day by day, without abdicating our right to choose, but knowing that our choices may occasionally do nothing more than confirm—openly and ethically, we hope—that which has already been chosen for us by circumstances and by others. This is cause neither for mourning nor celebration; this is life as we must live it, cherishing the whole experience of this terrible and inspiring adventure.

For Latin Americans today, the challenge could not be clearer, or more urgent. We must transform our countries into nations that are in step with their times, with no more hunger or violence, with freedom and with work, so that all may achieve a decent existence through their own efforts. It will be difficult, though assuredly not impossible, to realize the promises held by the culture of liberty that now seems to be radiating out in all directions around the globe. The expansive and lively ideas of this culture have been found workable elsewhere, and they remain capable of overcoming the barbarity of underdevelopment everywhere in the world.

GOVERNMENTS IN DECLINE

Norman Macrae

Norman Macrae (1923–2010) was a longtime editor of *The Economist* and author of *The 2025 Report: A Concise History of the Future 1975–2025*. In this essay, based on his remarks at a 1992 Mexico City conference sponsored by the Cato Institute and the Centro de Investigaciones Sobre la Libre Empresa, he offers an optimistic vision of the free and prosperous future that markets and technology will make possible in the twenty-first century.

My favorite anti-every-forecaster story, especially at an inter-American conference, concerns the Canadian politician who once said that his Canada faced a limitless future because it was going to combine American efficiency with the British system of government and French culture.

And then, under his premiership, the poor devils temporarily got British efficiency. And the French system of government. And American culture. The specific forecasts I now offer may in some respects be subject to the same Pickwickian margin of error.

In 1981 I was writing a book (published in 1984) that was called in Britain *The 2024 Report: A Concise History of the Future 1974–2024*. And the next year the American version was *The 2025 Report: A Concise History of the Future 1975–2025*. And the French version was *Le Rapport deux mille vingt-six*. In this age of the word processor it is convenient marginally to amend future history as it goes along.

In all versions of the book, fortunately, the main thesis for the first decade proved right. The book recorded in 1981 that communism did not survive the 1980s. In all editions, the old Soviet Disunion had by 1992 broken up into a confederation of 17 successor republics, which were all trying to follow sensible Thatcherite or Reaganite economic policies, although they did not initially work. The name "confederation" and the number 17 have proved wrong, but you can't win them all. In one edition of the book, the Berlin Wall came down on Heilige Nacht, Christmas Eve, 1989. Since in real history it came down in November 1989, the optimistic forecasts that I now offer on other matters—including the coming end of politicians—may prove, by that analogy, about six weeks too pessimistic.

In the decade of the 1980s, it was clear that the thing due to disappear, now that the Soviet Union had become a genuinely educated country, was the illogical monster called communism. In the three or so decades from these 1990s, the thing that will disappear, in educated societies, is the illogical monster called government. In the 1870s Gladstone's supposedly very left-wing Liberal government absorbed 6 percent of Britain's gross national product in government expenditure, at a time when it held one-fifth of the world in fee as the British Empire. By the late 1980s Thatcher's supposedly right-wing Conservative government absorbed 44 percent of GNP in government expenditure. All of you could cite similar absurdities in your own countries, which really can't survive now that we've seen what government expenditure does to steelworks in Omsk. Once we are educated—which may mean once we have moved education from the system that provided state steelworks in Omsk to a market or voucher system—we the people won't allow politicians to spend so much of our money for us any more. That change was already certain before its prospects were speeded by the third and greatest transport revolution.

The first transport revolution dated from Watt's invention of the steam engine in the 1780s. As the consequent railways exploded across Britain, the first Duke of Wellington, he of Waterloo, warned, "My lords, these iron horses will enable the working classes to move about." Which was very shrewd of the old boy. Before then the average Englishman never moved more than six miles from his birthplace, so he pulled his forelock to the local squire or duke. The railways created the Americas, and did all sorts of other disturbing things, but I am glad they did. The second transport revolution started by coincidence in the 1880s when two Germans, Daimler and Benz, who I think never met, invented the internal combustion engine, and then Henry Ford put civilization on wheels. That changed all our lives until this third and greatest transport revolution, which started by coincidence in the 1980s.

The third transport revolution is telecommunications allied with the computer. The crucial change that revolution brings is that the majority of brainworkers are not going to have to live near their workplaces. They are going to be able to stare into computer screens and communicate through them, from their own homes in pleasant parts of the world, with the cost of communication not depending on distance. "Brainworkers" will at first mean the majority of decision-making workers—zapping at a keystroke across the world, not merely instructions and market orders, but capital, knowledge, patents, accounts, analysis, knowhow. Some time in the next century "brainworkers" will plausibly mean the majority of all workers in rich areas. If politicians try to boss us or charge too high taxes, brainworkers will go away and telecommute from Tahiti. Countries that choose to have too high taxes or too fussy regulations will be residually inhabited mainly by dummies.

LIFE IN THE 2020S

I have been playing in my mind with likely social patterns of the 2020s for quite a while now, and I have altered my original concepts sufficiently little to have more or less come to believe in them. So here goes. I will start in the 2020s with a family called McGonagle. That is a Scottish name, and I place the family initially in Scotland, although they could well be the Gomez family of California or Acapulco. But you will be better able than I to ponder what will by then be the rather small differences between such mobile brainworkers as the Gomezes and the McGonagles, and I hope you realize that the worst forecasts at the start of a transport revolution are from those who get into intellectual bed with the cautious. In 1903 the Mercedes company said, amid many "hear, hears," that it realized there would never be as many as 1 million automobiles worldwide. The reason was that it was implausible that as many as 1 million artisans world-wide would be trainable as chauffeurs.

Anyway, my McGonagles of 2020 are a typical nuclear family of father and mother plus two early-teenage children. Left-wing sociologists say the nuclear family is due to disappear. That is not the only reason for supposing the nuclear family will make a dramatic come-back right across the world. Another reason is that father and mother will more often be working from home in the telecommuting age, just as they did at the beginning of the twentieth century when more than 70 percent of North American families were being brought up on farms, and children had chores to do. That is a recipe for closer knit nuclear families. So is fear of awful sexual diseases, the Hegelian cycle between puritanism and prurience, and much else.

In 2020 Mrs. McGonagle has a rather well paid market research job. She sits at her computer in her village in Scotland analyzing figures from computerized check-out points all over the world and advises small, and some large, businesses what and where the market opportunities are for just-in-time inventory rebuilding. To Father McGonagle in 2020 I'll give the lower powered because less do-it-this-instant job of helping to fill one of umpteen competitive international databases. Mr. McGonagle thus has more time to be housefather to the young teenagers. I'm putting the McGonagle family in 2020 in a community in Scotland that centers particularly on a golf course and a renownedly good village school, because I know such a community. The village school does not yet telecommute into the learning-system database most suitable for each individual child, but by 2020 it will.

By 2020 my guess is that this sort of Scottish or California or Mexican community will quite usually have chosen as its local government rule by an insurance company, perhaps Dutch founded but turned fully international. Lots of insurance companies will be offering contracts on roughly the following lines: we will take from you such and such a level of property tax or poll tax and make a profit from that while offering you (a) environmental services that receive at least an AB rating from your and our choice of environmental audit agency, plus (b) a crime rate that will not exceed such and such, plus (c) various other measured services. If performance falls below targets, the insurance company will have to pay back some of the property tax already levied. If the Bush administration fails to cut drug-related crime, it does not—watch its lips—have to pay back some of your wasted taxes.

The McGonagle family in 2021 has a problem because the elder teenage boy has committed some hooligan or vandal offense. The Dutch insurance company therefore wants to impose a special surcharge on the McGonagles' property tax, and this Dutch company does not keep such offenses secret as some other insurance companies do. The McGonagles therefore feel they want to move out. They call up one of the databases that put several thousand lifestyles all over the world on offer.

Those range from rather authoritarian, expensive lifestyles to rather hippie communes. The authoritarian lifestyle might be in an expensive hotel. If a reader celebrated my glad tidings about 2020 by rising delightedly in a hotel dining room and streaking naked round the tables, I suspect that the hotel management would suggest diplomatically that he leave tomorrow, even if the request was undemocratic because a majority of the diners liked the sight. At the other extreme there might be some communes of bearded vegetarian pacifists who bicycled around forbidding automobiles and allowing free marijuana and enforcing free love. If people wanted such lifestyles well away from me, it would not be for me to forbid them, although I would personally prefer that entry to such communes be permitted only after a certain age. Perhaps after people had made the metamorphosis from teenagers to human beings.

Between those extremes there will be lots of alternative versions of the insurance company-ruled communities and even weirdo communities that prefer to elect local politicians. The McGonagles could take their choice, and they might perhaps move to New Zealand or Rio de Janeiro or one of what will by then be the 13,000 lovely tropical islands of Indonesia. Mother and father could continue their present employment from there, and there would not even be interruption of schooling, because it will be possible to telecommute into learning systems. One snag is obviously that the very popular communities will not want many more people streaming in. There will therefore be some version of a transfer fee, with the Dutch insurance company saying delightedly, "Three more families want to join our community and are offering to pay an entrance fee of such and such, which will cut your property tax and aid our profit." Other communities will be positively wanting new entrants because they will not be viable at their present size.

FREE TRADE AND FUTURE PROSPERITY

You will ask whether, above local rule by insurance companies or whatever, there will not have to be some more central government for some purposes, especially redistribution of income from the rich to some of the poor. Yes indeed, and I am fearful of appearing to repeat the famous sermon by a Scots divine. "Fifteenthly, ma friends, we come here to a verra great deeficultee. Let us look it firmly in the face, and pass on." At present I feel that I have a duty to talk more directly of a free-trade area for the Americas, and how you can best fit it in with the marvelous choice of lifestyle to come.

I am an ardent supporter of a free-trade area for the Americas—a big one from Hudson Bay to the Horn, not just the piddly one from Yukon to Yucatan. You have some lessons to learn from our European Community, mostly negative ones. The first lesson is "For God's sake don't have a coordinating body of bureaucrats like the Brussels Commission, or a Parliament of the Americas, or nonsense organizations like that." We set up a free-trade area in Western Europe and then created a Brussels Commission to turn it back into corrupt protectionism. Brussels's Common Agricultural Policy consists of paying five times the world price to farmers in rich countries and blocking cheaper food imports from more efficient poor countries. We thereby impede the development of farming in poor areas where the main threat to health is undernourishment, while piling up huge food mountains in areas where the main threat to health is obesity.

Within the Americas you should go for full free trade in everything. You should try to abolish nontariff barriers, even if at first the abolition cannot be very well policed. Contrary to the EC model,

I do not think you should have a common external tariff against the outside world (e.g., I do not think Mexico's tariff or other barriers against Japanese or Taiwanese goods need be the same as U.S. barriers). Our experience in the EC is that a common external tariff brings the worst protectionist pressures against American and other goods, pressures that are usually muttered to Brussels in French. Indeed, I think it could be sensible for some countries to be in the free-trade area of the Americas, while also individually having free trade with all the world, including sensible "encouragement of dumping" legislation. If some fool of a country is subsidizing its exports of particular things, they will almost always be things going into glut, so developing countries should avoid those industries and might as well get for their own people the nice cheap goods that foreign fools of taxpayers help provide.

I know that some old-fashioned people will ask, "What is the point of a free-trade area of the Americas, if other countries are to have free-trading access to parts of the bloc?" I believe such people totally misunderstand the future of successful business corporations. There are not going to be nationally based corporations anymore, and they aren't going to have long-lasting lines of production in settled places. To me the business of the future is in some way exemplified by the American garment seller called The Limited, although I am sure its model can be improved. Each evening The Limited gathers from its stores across the United States the computer check of the clothes sold that day. That computer printout becomes the cutting order for workshops in Asia the next day. Four days later, a Boeing leaves Hong Kong carrying the replenishment for The Limited's inventories just in time. That will be the pattern of tomorrow's manufacturing, and several huge factors are about to accelerate it.

TWO, THREE, MANY HONG KONGS

One is that vast India and China are about to enter that sort of subcontracting world. With Hong Kong and Taiwan you ain't seen nothing yet. In Western Europe we can see the educated ex-communist world to our east. A highly skilled worker in Czechoslovakia today has one-fifteenth of the average wage of a German worker, who is often a guest worker less educated than the Czechoslovak. Of course, the whole German automobile industry is going to move east. With a free-trade area of the Americas, I am sure that some Mexicans hope that Detroit will move to Mexico. God help you; have you seen Detroit recently? The automobile industry of tomorrow will make components in many different places. In the General Motors building in Detroit, executives sit above the assembly line and pass labored analyses to each other by hand. Their equivalents in Toyota in Japan give their production orders to any point on the globe with a few strokes on their computers.

You in Latin America may say some of this is bad news. You will not be intending to drop to a Chinese or even ex-communist standard of life. But I think you underestimate the extent to which you will have advantages, provided a free-trade area of the Americas helps establish English and Spanish as the world's two main business languages. You may also underestimate the speed of change. One Japanese machine toolmaker says that, compared with the early 1980s, a component factory in a developing country already needs only about one-fifth as much space and about one-sixth as many workers, but tighter tying in to the schedules and much greater flexibility of manufacturing because established lines of production are not going to last as long. Compared with distant China or Prague, Latin America will have advantages for U.S. corporations.

I agree that American business habits bring one disadvantage, together with many advantages. The more successful experience of Japan suggests that there is one profession in which America has 20 times more incumbents than a civilized country should. "The first thing we do," recommends the admirable leader of the peasants' revolt in Shakespeare's *Henry VI,* "we kill all the lawyers." That sensible social reform does not need to be carried to extremes, but the United States is overrun with lawyers, like Australia used to be with rabbits. You should not allow your free-trade area of the Americas to fall prey to that affliction.

You will note that I have assumed a free-trade area will have free movement of goods, capital, and knowledge, but not I fear of people. I think inflow of people will be controlled by very local governments, who, unfortunately, will do it more efficiently than national governments whose border guards happily can't succeed. There is also the problem that lines of products will be shorter lasting, here today and in India tomorrow, so people doing manual jobs will be out of work more frequently. But there will be mitigations; Latin American businesses will be well placed to profit from the work of market researchers such as Mrs. McGonagle, who determines what American inventories suddenly need to be filled where. I think the new plants and other workplaces will be able to switch products more quickly. As a last resort, I also think people will be more mobile. If underemployment hits some areas, the people will be studying databases to find out where jobs are; and retraining through computer-based learning will be quicker.

FINDING TASKS FOR CENTRAL GOVERNMENT

The final question is what jobs central government—or regional or international government—will still do. I think there are two: (a) defense and (b) what we call redistribution in English, but you in America call welfare, with a snarl.

As regards defense. In my *2024 Report* the 1990s are called the decade of the gunboats, with the sole superpower the United States (supported by the ex-Soviet Disunion) firing conventional missiles, down individual windows from 500 miles away, to kill Third World dictators or the terrorists they support, especially when they are about to develop nuclear arms. Something like that is liable to be needed with Saddam, maybe soon with North Korea, and maybe together with peacekeeping forces in parts of the Soviet Disunion if its breakup goes awkward with all those nuclear warheads lying around and unemployed nuclear scientists hirable cheap. In the book there is an outcry during the next decade that too much of the world policeman's role is being undertaken by the United States and ex-Soviet Union, so (and I quote) "a demand goes up that the gunboat role be internationalized without anybody at first being clear what that could conceivably mean." I envisage that by 2024 the nearest thing left to an army or navy or air force anywhere is an anti-emergency force paid on performance contract by some very much reformed United Nations.

I made some other naughty forecasts about defense, and (very broadly) still stand by them. Whereas in 1984 military expenditure took around 5 percent of gross world product, I think by 2024 it takes only about 0.01 percent. We should henceforth get weapons in the cheapest market. Because Japan has been active in consumer electronics but not in defense electronics, consumer electronics have got cheaper and cheaper and defense electronics more and more expensive, often without working. The soldiers of the anti-emergency force will come from people who like to be soldiers, Gurkhas and various warlike tribes in India. The demise of national armies, to quote again, "does not take place because of any great international conference. It comes because owning national armies is absurdly uneconomic." I'm afraid I particularly criticize some Latin American governments who seem to me to have kept large conscript armies mainly to fight their own people.

We turn to redistribution. I think the world will need some sort of numéraire for international transactions—maybe the dollar or some replacement for the dollar in a free-trade area of the Americas, an ecu in a widening European Community, perhaps special drawing rights on the International Monetary Fund if we happily go very international. I am not saying local currencies should have a fixed exchange rate against those numéraires; I hope and believe they will float. But I do think we will have to end aid from the governments of rich countries to the governments of poor countries; one reason for the poverty of the latter is that government spends too much of national income already.

I would hope for IMF help along the following lines. First, if poor countries are adopting policies that would genuinely bring non-inflationary growth, and if they are held up only by the fact that those policies would initially turn them into external deficit, then I could see special drawing rights being created for them. Some say that such deliberate creation of credit would be very inflationary. In the *2024 Report* I say optimistically that in only one year between 2000 and 2024 has the creation of new IMF credit increased world money supply by more than 0.2 percent, and I admit I would accept that level of inflation.

Second, and more important, I envisage performance contracts round the world. At present, if a medical team keeps an 87-year-old millionaire in Texas alive in great pain for an extra three weeks, it is liable to draw $50,000 from his catastrophe insurance. If a team sharply cuts death rates in poor areas of Africa by introducing cheap and probably computerized medical facilities, by changing diets and fresh water systems, there is no market mechanism whereby it can earn a penny. I think we will move to performance contracts, which will have the great advantage of keeping politicians in the poor countries further out of the way. I don't think those contracts can be offered by institutions based on one man, one vote. They will more likely be based on systems of one dollar, one vote, which to some extent the IMF already is. I could see the system moving toward contracts for raising earning power in the poorest parts of the world above minimum human needs. But if we are going into such international welfare systems, it will be important to remember the new research on poverty. Although 14 percent of the people in the United States are said to be below the poverty line, an American runs less than a 1 percent risk of staying long in poverty, provided she or he does three things: completes high school, gets and stays married, and sticks for a year in a first job even if it pays only minimum wage. In spreading assaults on poverty round the world, I think we will have to introduce performance contracts geared to those criteria.

I always like to end my pontificating with an anti-pontificatory story. When President de Gaulle carried out his state visits to Latin America in the 1960s in a French battle cruiser, it is said that he stood beside his admiral as the cruiser came into the main port of Ecuador and asked, "Do you know the name of the president of this little country?" The admiral replied that he didn't, but they had a chap back at Admiralty who knew that sort of thing. So the message went out. "Make from the president of the French Republic to Captain Henri Dubois, Quai d'Orsay, top presidential priority. Message: 'Do you know the name of the president of Ecuador?'—signed de Gaulle." Well, the captain was thoroughly intimidated so he spluttered out a terse one-word reply, "Oui." The next message was more in the style of the de Gaulle we newspapermen knew. "Oui, quoi? Imbécile." As they approached the saluting base on shore, the terrified bureaucrat's second replay came. "Oui, mon général." I think we will have to stop saying, "Oui, mon général," and I rejoice that [we] are blazing the way like a meteor toward just that.

PATERNALIST GOVERNMENT IS OUT OF DATE

Michael Prowse

Michael Prowse has been a correspondent and editor for leading British newspapers. In this 1995 essay, based on remarks
delivered at the Institute of Economic Affairs and published
in *The Independent,* he describes his own intellectual odyssey
from state paternalism to libertarianism. He argues that the
issue separating the libertarian from the paternalist is not virtue, compassion, or community, all of which are valued by both
philosophies, but rather the question of coercion versus voluntary cooperation.

A decade ago I believed you could not be a compassionate, caring
person unless you believed in big government. For me, as for many
others, government and compassion were synonymous. I accepted
that market forces had some uses in promoting economic efficiency.
But I thought the government had to intervene in countless ways to
prevent "market failure." And I believed it had a duty to redistribute
resources on a massive scale to ensure social justice. I subscribed, in
short, to policies now known as "new Labour."

Such views now strike me as entirely natural for somebody
brought up in a welfare state. Like many in my generation I enjoyed
free education (at university as well as at school) and free health
care. I expected state support should I become unemployed or
should I simply lose the taste for work. And I looked forward to an
income-linked state pension.

I began to question this kind of state paternalism for two reasons: because the world began to change in the late Eighties and because I fell under new intellectual influences. To a British audience it may seem puzzling to argue that changes in the political climate encouraged a move away from paternalism. After all, the free-market movement reached its apogee of influence in about 1987. Today the conventional wisdom is that Thatcherism put too much emphasis on individualism and not enough on community.

Yet, taking a wider view, the free-market case has been greatly strengthened since the late Eighties. The demise of Communism in eastern Europe and the former Soviet Union, and the burgeoning of the capitalist spirit in China and much of the Third World, are among the most significant political events of the century. This change, which I did not expect, profoundly influenced my thinking.

Equally important, a move from London to Washington in 1990 gave me a strikingly different perspective on events. Bill Clinton won the 1992 election only by packaging himself as a quasi-conservative committed to "ending welfare as we know it." He then shifted sharply to the left. But the reaction in last November's congressional elections was remarkable. The Republican vote in the House of Representatives rose by about a third compared with the last mid-term election in 1990—the biggest swing since the late Twenties, when the Democrats enjoyed a comparable surge in support.

I see this as evidence that the conservative revolution that began with Ronald Reagan is gaining, not losing, momentum. Newt Gingrich has sparked a more profound debate about the role of government than anything seen in the Eighties.

It is certainly more profound than the limited debate in Europe about the future of the welfare state which is driven, it seems, purely by financial considerations. And there seems no doubt that the US is now moving in a conservative/libertarian direction. The question is not whether there will be less government and a devolution of powers from Washington to the states and localities, but how quickly this will occur.

Yet in an important sense the US is merely returning to its pre–Great Depression traditions. The revolution that created America was an impassioned and principled rejection of government—British government. For 200 years, ordinary Americans have had a much greater distrust of government—any government—than Britons. Seeing this at first hand, I have felt my own convictions about the role of the state begin to shift.

Intellectually, I have been influenced by the "classical liberal" writers of the seventeenth and eighteenth centuries and by two modern schools of thought: "Austrian" economics, which has increased my confidence in markets; and US "public choice" theory, which diminished my faith in government.

Austrian theory starts from far more plausible assumptions than traditional neoclassical theory. Markets are not assumed to "fail" merely because they do not meet the efficiency conditions dreamt up by mathematical economists. They are seen rather as a discovery process—a way of utilising knowledge that is distributed among millions of individual participants and that is not, even in principle, available to any central department.

Markets are superior to governments for at least three fundamental reasons: they disseminate and process information more rapidly; they rely on more decision takers; and they provide, through the profit motive, an in-built incentive for agents to use this knowledge efficiently to promote ends valued by fellow citizens.

Public choice theory, for its part, explains precisely why government failure is more likely than market failure. It reminds us that individuals do not cease to be self-interested when they enter public service. I do not deny that bureaucrats (like private business people) can sometimes be altruistic. But they have a powerful, countervailing incentive to do whatever will further their careers; their actions will often be determined by factors internal to their organisations.

Usually they will have an incentive to increase the power and prestige of their arm of government, which is one reason why the public sector has a natural tendency to expand. In any case, the self-interest of public officials will be less effectively channelled into virtuous paths than will that of private agents subject to the discipline of market competition.

So what role do I now think government should play?

The first point I would emphasise is how far the world has strayed in this century from classical liberal principles. I was struck by a line in a review by Martin Taylor, of Barclays Bank, of *The State We're In* by Will Hutton. Mr Taylor was not impressed by Mr Hutton's general argument but he did concede that "too much individualism is bad for too many individuals," or words to that effect.

That somebody as sensible as Mr Taylor can believe that Britain suffers from an excess of individualism strikes me as profoundly alarming. In retrospect, the Thatcher years saw, at best, a tiny move in this direction: the growth of public spending was not checked; the state did not withdraw from any of its traditional functions. How can anyone talk seriously of an excess of individualism when government spending (including transfers) accounts for more than 43 per cent of GDP against less than 41 per cent in 1979, the last year of Labour government?

Do we really need a state this large? If we do, what does this tell us about the assumed capacity of individuals to look after themselves? A small proportion of individuals at the bottom of the ability/income spectrum perhaps need assistance. But it is surely ridiculous to assume, as we usually do, that most people cannot manage without the state as a crutch.

I am not saying that most people should assume greater responsibility primarily to save the state money. The cost is important: the tax burden imposed by the welfare state clearly undermines incentives and retards growth. But the real argument cuts deeper. Individuals should assume responsibility for these basic duties because doing so will make them stronger, better and, in the long run, happier human beings. The strongest argument against dependency on government is that it cripples individuals' capacity for self-development.

This raises what is perhaps the fundamental question: how large a state should classical liberals support? I will assume, for the sake of argument, that there is a case for a minimal state that protects individuals against internal and external threats to person and property and upholds rights of contract. The question then is how to justify a larger than minimal state. The traditional answer is in two ways: the state is necessary to provide certain "public goods" and in order to redistribute resources from rich to poor.

The public goods defence of government is much weaker than is usually assumed. The classic definition of a public good is that it is non-excludable and jointly supplied. Non-excludable means that those who do not pay cannot be prevented from enjoying the good. Jointly supplied means that my consumption of the good does not limit what is available for you. An example of a true public good is the deterrence effect of national defence.

Most so-called public spending is not on services meeting this technical definition of a public good: education does not meet the criteria, nor do pensions or health care. I believe we greatly underestimate the ability of individuals to provide collective goods through voluntary co-operation: lack of faith in voluntary action is one of the bitter legacies of big government.

That leaves redistribution as the real justification for today's outsized states. Why is this argument so potent? One reason, sadly, is that many people are motivated by envy. If you doubt this, just consider the furore over executive pay in the UK. In the US there is no such fuss because there is less of a tradition of resentment at the good fortune of others, even though pay and wealth inequalities are larger than in Britain.

Envy is fuelled by the popularity of the distributive or "cake" theory of justice. According to this, income or wealth is supposed to be just there, to be magically generated out of nothing. But a dynamic "entitlement" theory of justice is surely far more realistic. As Robert Nozick pointed out, goods and entitlements-to-goods are created simultaneously; without the entitlements there would be no goods. The size of the cake is not predetermined. No one plans the distribution effected by market forces. There is no guiding intelligence. So, as Friedrich von Hayek argued, it is strictly meaningless to think of a distribution as fair or unfair. It just is.

So how would I sum up the libertarian or individualistic credo to which I now subscribe?

The fundamental belief is that we as individuals, in almost all circumstances, are the best judges of what makes us happy. We should thus be as free as possible to make choices for ourselves. Restraints are necessary, as John Stuart Mill argued, only to prevent us harming or violating the rights of others.

Allowing individuals to make as many choices as possible for themselves is not an argument for greed or materialism. For all I care, everyone can spend their days meditating or tending their gardens. I do not care if the GDP shrinks. What matters is that the pattern of activity reflects people's free choices.

To be a libertarian is not to lack virtue or compassion. It is to recognise that benevolence is a quality of individuals, not of governments. The loudness with which people demand higher taxes on others is not a measure of their benevolence. The only plausible gauge of personal benevolence is our willingness voluntarily to give money to others. I believe a libertarian society would stimulate individual moral growth and, with it, true compassion for the less fortunate.

Individualism, as I understand it, is not opposed to community. I am in favour of clubs, associations and co-operative ventures of every conceivable kind. There should be as many and as varied a set of associations as people want. The one essential condition is that they should be voluntary.

Here we encounter what is perhaps the fundamental difference between the libertarian and the paternalist. The libertarian believes passionately in voluntary co-operation (and especially that brought about by market transactions). The paternalist believes in coercion, in the forcible raising of taxes and the collective management of resources by a supposedly enlightened elite. The libertarian wants the many to take decisions for themselves; the paternalist wants the few to take decisions for the many.

There is no longer any question in my mind that the former philosophy is superior: voluntary action is preferable to coercion. Libertarianism would bolster the economy, strengthen personal morality and create more individual freedom. I thus find it hard to understand why anybody wishes to defend the paternalist status quo.

"CREATIVE DESTRUCTION"
AND THE INNOVATION AGE

Peter K. Pitsch

Peter Pitsch is a lawyer and economist with thirty years' experience in telecommunications policy. In this selection based on his 1996 book *The Innovation Age* he argues that Hayek's concept of spontaneous order and Schumpeter's emphasis on the "creative destruction" of the market process are even more relevant to the Innovation Age than they were to the industrial era.

Revolutionary developments in computer and fiber optic technologies have radically altered the way we process and communicate information today. This has led to a new awareness of information as central to economic activity, and has produced a widespread belief that the world is entering a new "Information Age." As consumers and businesses adjust to the opportunities created by these new digital technologies, they are transforming the economy. Alvin and Heidi Toffler characterize these developments as "the third wave" of change, comparable in importance to man's adoption of agriculture 8,000 years ago ("the first wave") and the industrial revolution in Europe and the U.S. in the nineteenth century ("the second wave"). The Tofflers predict that the means of production, distribution, marketing, entertainment, and communication will become "deconcentrated," as the digital revolution reduces the importance of economies of scale and lowers the cost of decentralized and diversified approaches.

Although the societal transformations that are occurring are profound and knowledge-driven, it would be a mistake to view them as discrete, predictable, or a onetime phenomenon. Rather, the defining feature of this new era will be continuing and accelerating change. Thus, the Information Age could be more appropriately termed the "Innovation Age." The new era of change will be increasingly complex and uncertain, dynamic and unpredictable. Standard "static" economic analysis will become less useful. Understanding and living with this era of change will require us to come to terms with the resulting complexity and dynamism.

In the first half of this century, two Austrian-born economists, Friedrich Hayek and Joseph Schumpeter, provided such a framework for analysis. Long recognized for their insights on the workings of the market and its comparative advantages over socialism and central planning, Hayek's and Schumpeter's analyses are even more relevant to today's increasingly complex, fast-changing global economy. Hayek and Schumpeter are economic prophets for the Innovation Age. Their insights provide a basis for understanding our future economy and the government's role in it. A new, market-based approach to regulation is called for. This is especially true for telecommunications—the regulated half of the digital revolution.

HAYEK'S SPONTANEOUS ORDER

Hayek is best known for his 1944 classic, *The Road to Serfdom,* in which he warned that the loss of economic freedom eventually leads to the loss of civil liberty as well. Perhaps his most important work, however, was on the nature and operation of markets found in *The Constitution of Liberty* and related philosophical essays. There he expounds on how effective human institutions such as markets develop spontaneously without the benefit of any overt planning. Indeed, Hayek contends that markets work far better than "planned economies," because they "utilize the knowledge and skill of all members of society to a much greater extent than would be possible in any order created by central direction."

One of the best illustrations of this phenomenon, according to

Hayek, is the price mechanism. Economic theory has developed an impressive system of equations showing how prices are determined by the desires, the resources, and the knowledge of all market participants. But Hayek contends that it would be absurd to think that anyone could ever ascertain all the particular data needed to use those mathematical equations to arrive at the numerical determination of prices. He warns:

> Their purpose is exclusively to describe the general character of the order that will form itself. Since this order implies the existence of certain relations between the elements, and the actual presence or absence of such relations can be ascertained, the prediction of such an order can be shown to be false, and the theory will thus be empirically testable. But we shall always be able to predict only the general character of the order and not its detail.

In emphasizing the enormous complexity that lies beneath the market system, Hayek is advising government policymakers to be cautious in attempting to redesign it. He says, "It is high time . . . that we take our ignorance more seriously."

SCHUMPETER'S CREATIVE DESTRUCTION

Joseph Schumpeter, like Hayek, recognized the complexity of the economic process, believed capitalism was superior to socialism, and was leery of regulatory tinkering. In 1942, as an economics professor at Harvard University, he published *Capitalism, Socialism, and Democracy*, the culmination of four decades of thought. In that book, he characterizes the market process as an organic one in which considerable time is required for the separate elements to reveal their true features and ultimate effects. For Schumpeter, however, the defining feature and the key to understanding the fundamental workings and benefits of capitalism is its dynamism:

> The fundamental impulse that sets and keeps the capitalist engine in motion comes from the new consumers' goods, the new

methods of production or transportation, the new markets, the
new forms of industrial organization that capitalist enterprise
creates . . . the same process of industrial mutation—if I may use
that biological term—that incessantly revolutionizes the economic
structure from within, incessantly destroying the old one, incessantly creating a new one. This process of Creative Destruction is
the essential fact about capitalism.

Schumpeter's creative destruction hardly makes for a complacent
existence for the participants. Businesses will be enticed to compete
vigorously for "spectacular prizes," even though in the end most
will receive only modest compensation. It is the resulting creative
destruction that "in the long run expands output and brings down
prices," but it is a "competition which commands a decisive cost or
quality advantage and which strikes not at the margins of the profits
and outputs of the existing firms but at their foundations and their
very lives."

Schumpeter believed that the benefits of these successive innovations are so great that they outweigh even the economic drag created
by monopoly. The cost reductions from farm machinery, steel mills,
and airplanes dwarf the static losses that might arise because the
industries that produce these modern wonders do not meet the conditions of perfect competition. Morever, the nature of most monopolies operates to reduce the losses predicted by the static monopoly
model:

It is hardly necessary to point out that competition of the kind we
now have in mind acts not only when in being but also when it is
merely an ever-present threat. It disciplines before it attacks.

Indeed, Schumpeter believed that departures from the conditions
of perfect competition may in many instances benefit consumers and
that regulators must therefore exercise great care in attempting to
remedy them.

COMPELLING NEW CIRCUMSTANCES

Although Hayek and Schumpeter are familiar names in the pantheon of economists, their insights have all too seldom been given the weight they deserve. Perhaps this is understandable because their views bring into question the usefulness of much of the static efficiency analysis that is the main subject of economic textbooks. Nonetheless, both men recognized long ago the importance of knowledge to the workings of an economic system. Modern economic developments are now making their insights more compelling with the passing of every day.

The globalization of markets has added a new dimension to an already complex business environment. The collapse of communism in the Soviet bloc countries and the reduction of tax, tariff, and other barriers to foreign investment in many of the so-called developing countries promise to effect dramatic increases in economic growth rates in these areas. The reduction of trade barriers has expanded markets and increased the scope of specialization and the intensity of competition. To name two frequently cited examples, financial markets are becoming borderless and the work force global.

Likewise, uncertainty has increased as the pace of innovation has accelerated across a broad range of technical fronts. Economics tells us that accelerating change will increase uncertainty, because bigger changes require more time for users to recognize fully all the opportunities they create. The dramatic price and quality changes that innovation causes will produce unanticipated and delayed reactions as businesses and consumers learn how to exploit and adapt to these changes. For example, personal computers were initially used as a better way to type letters; only later did they facilitate the flattening of corporate hierarchies as the "networked workplace" eliminated the need for intermediaries.

In the digital information processing field alone, for example, we can expect continuing major advances in semiconductors, optoelectronics, parallel processing, storage, object programming, computer "agents," speech recognition, wireless technologies, switches, and compression techniques. Such a broad range of change among competing and complementary technologies can be expected to create numerous unanticipated interactions. Furthermore, the retarding effect that a dominant firm's embedded base might have on its incentive to innovate will become less important as the pace of technical change quickens.

Also, technical change has elevated the importance of Schumpeter's notion of creative destruction. The overthrow of IBM's "big iron" mainframe computers by the personal computer is a spectacular example of creative destruction. In the five years after 1987, IBM lost two-thirds of its market value—more than $70 billion. Microsoft, Lotus, Novell, Apple, Compaq, Dell, and Intel collectively now have market capitalization totaling more than $80 billion, and the benefits to consumers and business users from the personal computer have been incalculable. Moreover, the environment of creative destruction persists. Andrew Groves, the CEO of market leader Intel, has explained his competitive strategy with a quip: "Only the paranoid survive."

LAMARCKIAN INNOVATION

The compelling nature of the Hayekian and Schumpeterian perspectives in the Innovation Age is well illustrated by Michael Rothschild's comparison of the modern economy to an ecosystem. In *Bionomics,* Rothschild develops detailed analogies between biological systems and economic activity. Although he does not explicitly refer to Hayek, Rothschild sees economies and ecosystems as complex, spontaneous orders that no one designed. Rothschild criticizes traditional economic modes of analysis for virtually ignoring the role of growth and change in economies. In his view, modern economics sees the economy as a machine that can be explained by Isaac Newton's mechanics, when in reality economies are much more like ecosystems and better explained by Charles Darwin's concepts of evolution and natural selection. Machines do not change on their own or grow. Economies are in a constant state of change and are continually adapting to internal and external factors.

As Rothschild recognizes, however, the ecosystem analogy does not capture one important feature of economic change: whereas organisms in an ecosystem change through relatively rare gene mutation, economic participants can change through their own efforts. In this regard, economies better fit Jean-Baptiste Lamarck's (mistaken) view of biological evolution. Lamarck theorized that animals passed on acquired traits to their offspring. For example, he argued that the giraffe developed a long neck because giraffes who "stretched" their necks to reach ever-higher leaves passed on this trait to their offspring.

This mode of change speeds up the rate of economic advance for two important reasons. First, Lamarckian change does not have to wait for beneficial genetic mutations to occur. As Hayek and Schumpeter recognized, the market fosters such beneficial change and quickly spreads its effects throughout the economy through voluntary, for-profit transactions. Often such a change will simply be an idea and have the attributes of what economists call a "public" good. That is, once an idea is learned, it costs little to pass on and will be virtually free to others. Many innovations—such as the supermarket, minivan, facsimile machine, and cordless phone—have been copied quickly at little or no cost using existing technologies. Second, as Rothschild observes, economic change stems largely from recorded information that now exists outside human DNA. Unlike an ecosystem, the growth of this "corpus" of information is not inherently limited to a set number of chromosomes. Rather, it can actually grow geometrically as a result of the increasing specialization and beneficial interactions between subsets of knowledge that are likely to occur more frequently as the volume of knowledge expands.

THE CASE FOR HUMILITY

This analysis compels us to recognize that predicting what will happen in the Innovation Age, not to mention regulating it, must be undertaken with humility. The increasing complexity and uncertainty in the economy are making an already tough job increasingly difficult. The difficulty of the job facing today's futurist can be illustrated by picturing a simple (straight line) graph depicting the progress of technical capability from today into the future. The two dimensions are time (x) and technical capability (y). On the one hand, increasing complexity makes it increasingly difficult to predict the slope of this line, because we do not know which particular technical modalities will become state-of-the-art or what real improvements they will generate. On the other hand, it has become more likely that the technical status quo (the y-intercept) will change radically.

Schumpeter would warn us that explosive change in some shape or form is more likely than ever. Predicting that the status quo will continue is therefore not a wise course. This is borne out by the rapid increase in economic growth rates. At the turn of the century, a country growing at 4 percent per year would have been considered to have a high growth rate. Now something closer to 10 percent would be in order. Starting in 1780, it took Britain 60 years to double its output per person. Beginning in 1880, Japan achieved this feat in 34 years. Starting in 1966, South Korea did it in 11 years.

Hayek, in turn, would warn us against the conceit of "knowing" more than we can know. Simplified or "hero-based" analyses almost certainly will be too simplistic. Often, market processes mask the fact that a wealth of possibilities and trade-offs exist. Robert Fogel's analysis of the overall impact of American railroads illustrates this point. Fogel found that even the railroad had not been vital to the economic growth that occurred during the nineteenth century. Despite the railroad's rapid growth, eventual dominance of inland transportation, and enormous use of capital, it did not make an overwhelming contribution to the productive potential of the economy. (Canals and other forms of water transportation often provided an effective alternative means of shipping during this period.) Economic growth was a consequence of numerous innovations developed over the course of several centuries that were applied to a broad spectrum of economic processes.

REGULATING IN THE INNOVATION AGE

Increasing complexity and accelerating technical advances should change how we approach regulation. First, the daunting web of interconnections that now underlies the "spontaneous order" should give policymakers pause as they seek to "improve" on the marketplace. That is especially true in the many instances where such regulation is intended to protect the status quo from technical change. The substantial efficiency gains from innovation will likely be more diffuse and even harder to trace than they were in the past, although the loss from job displacement will be concrete and immediate. The short-term political appeal of giving in to this temptation will increase, but we must recognize that the costs of protecting the status quo from technical change will increase even more dramatically.

Second, the faster the potential rate of innovation, the more important dynamic considerations become and the greater the care that must be taken to assure that regulations designed to address efficiency concerns do not have the unintended effect of retarding innovation. In Schumpeter's words,

> A system—any system, economic or other—that at every given point of time fully utilizes its possibilities to the best advantage may yet in the long run be inferior to a system that does so at no given point of time, because the latter's failure to do so may be a condition for the level or speed of long-run performance. . . .

CONCLUSION

The choice of a regulatory framework that recognizes the complex and dynamic nature of our economy, as opposed to one that is based on "static," intrusive regulatory policy, is crucial to the future. This choice is especially important in telecommunications. As Hayek and Schumpeter would have known, the wealth of our nation—and its citizens—hangs in the balance.

EVOLUTIONARY ECOLOGY

Lynn Scarlett

Lynn Scarlett has studied environmental issues at the Department of the Interior and the Nature Conservancy. In this article from *Reason* magazine, she offers a libertarian perspective on an issue that is crucially important for the future: protecting the environment. Drawing on all the ideas developed in this book, she points to the importance of property rights, common law, decentralized knowledge, competition, and market process in environmental protection.

———

The 25th anniversary of Earth Day came and went last year, with little fanfare and no public demand for more environmental laws. The new Republican Congress tried, and mostly failed, to enact reforms designed to lessen the burden of environmental regulation. Behind the scenes and in public forums, various schools of environmental reform debated and discussed. They talked cost-benefit analysis and "takings" compensation, emissions trading and "win-win" environmentalism. They disagreed about many things, including basic principles. But there was general consensus about two ideas: that environmental goals are important, and that the current structure of regulation isn't that great.

Environmental policy is finally growing up. But to make genuine improvements, rather than merely tinker around the edges, we first need to understand where the demand for environmental regulation comes from, and where it went wrong. And we need a vision of how environmental policy might be set right—of the general principles and concepts that might guide a new environmentalism.

Environmentalism is not, as its critics sometimes portray it, simply a New Age ideology foisted upon an unwilling public. The environmental *movement* has important ideological components, but the demand for cleaner air and water or for wilderness and species preservation is not that different from the demand for any other good. As living standards rise, people want to buy more environmental "goods." Pollution is as old as human activity, but only recently have we been rich enough to worry about it.

Looking across countries, University of Chicago economist Don Coursey finds a clear correlation between increased wealth, measured by per capita GDP, and increased allegiance to environmental protection. As incomes rise, per capita expenditures on pollution control increase—a phenomenon Coursey observes in most advanced industrialized nations. The amount of land set aside for protection also rises with GDP. Green groups may decry economic growth, but it is growth itself that makes environmental protection possible and popular.

Coursey's work also points up a fact often forgotten in public discussions: "The environment" is not an all-or-nothing good, but a bundle of different goods. In surveys, he asks people to indicate how much they'd be willing to spend to preserve different species. The results are wildly varied. Animals like the bald eagle and grizzly bear consistently rank high, while spiders, beetles, snakes, and snails are barely valued. The varied costs of real-world regulations reflect this distinction: Coursey calculates the amount spent to preserve a single Florida panther at $4.8 million, compared to a mere $1.17 to preserve a single Painted Snake Coil Forest Snail.

Political maneuvering may produce such disparate results, but the law does not actually recognize such distinctions, or the implicit tradeoffs they express. It declares species protection, like many other environmental goods, an absolute. Early environmentalist thinking—influential to this day—did not recognize environmental values as some goods among many but rather proclaimed them preminent: Earth First! A California regulator describes his state's water policy this way: "If Mother Nature didn't put it in, you had to take it out—

everything—that was the goal. This drove us to rigid, grossly exuberant attempts at clean up."

This absolutism suggests one way that environmental policy went wrong. It did not recognize that quality of life resides in pursuit of multiple values. People seek shelter, nourishment, health, security, learning, fairness, companionship, freedom, and personal comfort together with environmental protection. They even seek many, sometimes competing, environmental goals. They don't agree on how to marshal their resources (and time) in pursuit of these many goals. And it is often difficult for outsiders—or even individuals themselves—to know in advance how they would prefer to trade off among different values.

Competing values are not unique to the environmental arena. In fact, people make such tradeoffs every day. They also deal with another conundrum of environmental policy: the "knowledge problem."

On the one hand, environmental problems involve matters of "general" knowledge, scientific knowledge of facts that are constant across time and space. In some cases, the general knowledge is a matter of settled understanding: the boiling point of water, for instance, or the bonding patterns of chemicals. In others, it is a matter of ongoing research and scientific contention. General knowledge includes such still-controversial issues as the health hazards of various substances or the effects of CFCs on the ozone layer. Much environmental debate takes place over issues of general knowledge, and these questions are important. But they aren't the whole story.

Environmental problems and problem solving also often involve "specific" knowledge—the knowledge of time, place, and experience described by Nobel laureate F. A. Hayek in "The Use of Knowledge in Society." This information varies by circumstance and location and may change over time. Specific knowledge is decentralized—it resides on the factory floor, at a particular Superfund site, or on a specific farm.

The impacts of a landfill in a desert will differ from those near the Florida Everglades. Emitting effluent into a fast-moving stream is different from emitting waste into a pond. Using two coats of paint will have different effects than using just one coat. Resource use and emissions associated with cloth and disposable diapers will depend on how many are used each day, what kinds of disposal systems are available, and where those systems are located. Nor are environmental effects the only important specific knowledge relevant to environmental issues—tradeoffs between environmental goods and other goods may vary from situation to situation. These kinds of details do not reside in the minds of bureaucrats in Washington. Yet it is this kind of knowledge that is often most relevant to understanding environmental problems and possible remedies.

Again, there is nothing unique to environmental issues about the knowledge problem. It is a fundamental aspect of human life, something people cope with all the time.

If, for instance, an environment-loving outdoorsman wishes to equip himself for mountain climbing, he may need to buy a special jacket (among much other gear). Deciding what to buy requires tradeoffs: First, he's devoting his financial resources to a jacket, rather than to something else, and his free time to mountain climbing. Then he must decide what characteristics he wants: how much insulation, how much durability, what sort of pockets or hood, and so on—all keeping in mind the continuing tradeoff between money he spends on the jacket and money he could spend on something else. He looks at brand names and reputations. He finds out what sort of return policies and customer service the jacket maker has.

The outdoorsman has specific knowledge. He knows what mountains he wishes to climb, and at what time of year. He knows whether he's an occasional climber, or a devotee. He knows whether he wants a lot of help from a sales clerk, or simply the best price. He knows his size and his favorite color. The jacket maker, too, has specific knowledge: of supplies, of tradeoffs between design features and costs, of distribution channels, of changing patterns of demand. No one centrally decides a single jacket policy for all U.S. mountain climbers.

But behind all these considerations lie a host of social and business institutions, from the Uniform Commercial Code and product liability law to standard sizes, specialty magazines, and outdoor-equipment shops. Overcoming the knowledge and values problems is not easy or cost-free, even in well-developed markets. Companies spend millions of dollars on marketing in an attempt to better understand and address consumer values. They draw on general knowledge—on, for instance, scientific research on physiology or the properties of jacket materials. They wear-test products and adjust to ever-changing information about suppliers. They respond to the unexpected: a cold snap that sends jacket demand up, a supplier's zipper redesign, a sudden change of fashion. Throughout all these processes, they receive constant feedback, direct and indirect, from customers and suppliers.

For "ordinary" goods like jackets, we have hundreds of years of institutional evolution to make markets work, to address the problems of values and knowledge. Some of those institutions involve government policy. Many do not.

Environmental goods present special challenges because of the characteristics of these goods. But meeting those challenges has been unnecessarily difficult. For too long environmental policy has been shaped by people who demanded that environmental values trump all other considerations and who assumed that a regulatory elite possessed all necessary knowledge. Rather than figuring out how to perfect or create institutions that would allow a market for environmental goods to develop and flourish, they have been bent on opposing and destroying markets. They have seen markets not as processes for addressing values and conveying knowledge but as symbols of base commercialism and greed. This moralistic approach is finally fading. We can now begin to examine what sorts of institutions different environmental goods require—to explore a new environmental vision.

For 20 years, some of the most effective proponents of "free market environmentalism" have come out of the New Resource Economics school of thought. These economists, mostly based in the Western United States, focus on the environmental goods most easily incorporated into traditional institutions of property rights—and, perhaps not coincidentally, the oldest areas of U.S. environmental policy, dating back to the Progressive Era. Their starting premise is that individuals are predominantly self-interested. New Resource Economics then explores how different ownership settings and decision-making institutions shape incentives for stewardship.

"Actual or potential owners have incentives to use their resources efficiently," write economists Richard Stroup and John Baden, neatly summing up their thesis. Owners enjoy the fruits of efficient resource use and land stewardship through enhanced returns on their investment and maintenance of their property's value over time.

Environmental problems arise, in this model, when resources are unowned. This is the famous "tragedy of the commons," in which resources are "owned" by everyone and thus effectively by no one, because they can be used indiscriminately by everyone. Each person has an incentive to consume as much as possible, as fast as possible, rather than to preserve and protect resources for future use. According to this view, institutions, not perverse people, are the genesis of environmental problems.

"The same people who nearly destroyed the buffalo population," write Stroup and Baden, "posed no threat to the more valuable beef cattle raised on the western range. In that instance more clearly defined property rights resulted in the proliferation of beef cattle while the imperfect, if not altogether absent, property rights to the buffalo led to its near elimination."

Translated into policy, the insights of these economists encourage experiments in market creation. Environmental writer Tom Wolf describes a "Ranching for Wildlife" program in Colorado that borrows from the ideas of New Resource Economists. In the Sangre de Cristo Mountains, elk on public and private lands compete with cattle for forage. The challenge, suggests Wolf, is "to figure out how ranchers can capture value from the elk."

Hunters will pay as much as $8,000 for a license to hunt a trophy elk. But until Colorado passed its Ranching for Wildlife program, landowners were unable to take part in potential revenue from sale of hunting licenses. To cattle ranchers, then, elk were merely pests. Under Ranching for Wildlife, the state still "owns" the wildlife, but owners of large ranches can auction off, at whatever price the market will bear, a designated number of hunting licenses that guarantee trophy elk. The program, in effect, has partially privatized elk-hunting rights. Participating ranch owners now manage their lands to provide suitable habitat for elk. They also guard vigilantly against poaching of young bull elk.

One of the advantages of "privatizing" resource and land-use decisions through various property rights arrangements is that these arrangements reduce the need for consensus. Goals, such as wilderness preservation, can be pursued through private land purchases that, unlike public preservation activities, do not require majority voter approval.

Wedding their work to the pioneering work of Nobel laureate economist James Buchanan and Gordon Tullock on "public choice theory," the New Resource Economists are also able to explain some of the perversities that keep surfacing in public lands management. The U.S. Forest Service, for instance, has incentives enshrined in law that encourage it to allow large-scale timber cutting even when the logging costs more than the Forest Service takes in. Because bureaucrats have no rights to the resources they manage, Stroup and Baden argue, "Even when [they] are highly trained, competent, and well intended, the information and incentives they face do not encourage either sensitive or efficient resource management."

Most environmental issues are not, however, quite that simple. Incentives and self-interest are always present, but they are not the whole story.

Markets work for jackets and, with a little work, for elk because these goods have certain characteristics that make transactions relatively simple. It's possible to clearly specify who owns what, to identify buyers and sellers, and to convey all the necessary information for trades to take place. As a result, the market operates as a discovery process to address the knowledge and value problems—and to encourage improvements over time, such as better jacket brands or improved elk forage.

In other cases, however, things aren't so clearly defined. There are frictions: hard-to-divide goods, parties too numerous or scattered to be identified, vital information that isn't easily shared or easily known, blurry property lines. Institutions must evolve to deal with these hard cases.

One such institution is the common law. The common-law approach asks, "What happens when one person's sphere of activity conflicts with another person's?" The result is a focus on the concepts of liability, nuisance, and trespass; the role of courts in evaluating harms and benefits; and their role in resolving conflicts by clarifying the scope of different intersecting rights.

This blurry realm is not confined to a few difficult air pollution problems (and, in fact, common law may not work well for air pollution). Anywhere people congregate, conflicts emerge over sights, smells, and physical invasions that include everything from factory smoke to ugly houses to one neighbor's leaves falling on another's yard. They also include potentially big nuisances such as toxic air emissions or discharges of waste into water bodies.

The common-law framework offers a means of further clarifying rights and refining just what "enjoyment and use" of one's property means. It is thus both a mechanism for conflict resolution and a means of discovering the scope and limit of rights.

Consider an apartment building with a noisy air-conditioning unit that disturbs a neighbor. Asked for injunctive relief, one tool of common law, the court may emphasize the neighbor's rights, requiring the apartment owner to eliminate the air conditioner noise—unless the neighbor agrees to some other arrangement. Or it may assign the owner the rights, declaring that the neighbor must put up with the noise unless he can make a deal with the owner. In actual conflicts, injunctive relief usually balances the two interests. "The law of nuisance," says Chicago economist Coursey, "actually would tend to use a rule that looked like a combination . . . : the apartment owner may make noise with impunity up to some critical level, and, if the apartment owner makes more than the critical level of noise, the single family may obtain an order of the court directing the apartment owner to reduce the noise down to the critical level."

In his famous "Coase theorem," Nobel laureate Ronald Coase developed the theoretical underpinnings of this sort of institution. In a friction-free world, where there are no "transaction costs," he argued, it doesn't matter which side is given the rights, because the two parties can always make a deal. (This calculation covers only the question of whether activities will occur, not issues of fairness, where distribution of rights does matter.) If your air conditioner is making noise you have every right to make, I can pay you to stop; if, on the other hand, you have no right to a noisy air conditioner without my permission, you can pay me to grant that permission. Problems arise in the real world, however, because transactions aren't free and the way rights are defined affects the cost of reaching agreement. So social institutions, such as courts, step in and assign rights to minimize conflict and maximize wealth, at least in theory.

Common-law tradition embodies a discovery process that clarifies and refines rights boundaries and obligations in those blurry realms where different sets of rights intersect. Common law tends to follow precedent, and precedent can only be disturbed by private parties bringing new cases with slightly different circumstances or new arguments. As the law gets better and better at maximizing the welfare of the parties in a particular kind of case, fewer and fewer such cases will be brought. As a result, the common law tends to settle on fairly efficient rules—those that make the value pie larger. Private parties then bargain "in the shadow" of settled law, dividing a larger pie than they would under rules not tested over time.

Common law, write economists Bruce Yandle and Roger Meiners, "continues to evolve. Changing preferences and improved understanding of pollution problems continuously enter the arena of law." And, unlike statutes, common law takes into account the particular circumstances of specific situations.

The common law can work to mediate disputes between discrete, identifiable parties. But, concede Yandle and Meiners, "It is hard to imagine how common law could address urban auto emission control, ozone layer problems, and global warming, to the extent that the science of those problems becomes more settled." In such cases, it is much too difficult to identify a clear-cut "polluter" and a clear-cut "plaintiff." Either most people fall simultaneously into both categories or the cost of dividing the environmental good—clean air, an undisturbed ozone layer, etc.—is much too high (sometimes approaching infinity).

Yet the problems of knowledge and values remain, and so does the demand for environmental goods. The trick for environmental reformers is to develop a vision of evolving institutions that permits different sorts of institutions to address different kinds of issues, and to do so at the appropriate decision-making level. It helps to think of this challenge as a sequence of interrelated questions, a decision tree based on the characteristics of the particular environmental goods involved.

In some cases, what is needed is not political rule making but business institutions, analogous to standard sizes and outdoor-equipment trade shows. In these cases, environmental goods are divisible, rights are assignable, and we are in the ordinary realm of markets, where entrepreneurs are rewarded for finding ways to address the knowledge and value problems effectively. Here the only issue is allowing time for institutions to evolve on their own.

Markets for some recyclables, for instance, are hampered because buyers and sellers sometimes lack information about available supplies and demand, and uniform quality is not guaranteed. These problems resemble those of many farm commodities in the 1800s. One remedy is to mimic the experience of corn farmers a century ago: Establish a coordinated process for trading in recyclables. The recent creation of electronic listing of some recyclables with the Chicago Board of Trade is a first step in this direction.

This approach differs markedly from political activists' calls to mandate recycled content in products. Those proposed mandates simply override the specific knowledge of circumstances so critical to efficient resource use. For example, mandating high levels of recycled content in certain paperboard products can require adding extra virgin (nonwaste) fiber to maintain adequate strength of the paperboard. The result is a heavier product that uses more total fiber.

Often, however, environmental goods are indivisible and present challenges to ordinary markets. Faced with these "market failures," the traditional response from the green movement has been to substitute government coercion for individual choice. Yet absolutist regulation that suppresses knowledge and imposes a single value hierarchy is not the only way to achieve such goals as clean air. It is possible to create evolvable institutions that, while they are not as simple or politically neutral as traditional markets, capture much relevant information about knowledge and values.

Traditional regulations, such as technology prescriptions and resource-use mandates, ignore the location-specific and ever-changing information critical to all production and consumption decisions. Performance standards, by contrast, allow individuals and firms to figure out how best to achieve the stated standards: to lower overall air pollution to a certain level, for instance. This is the central insight of economists who have articulated the case for market-oriented regulations like the tradeable permits scheme set forth in the 1990 Clean Air Act Amendments.

Tradeable permit schemes and pollution charges provide flexibility to producers (and consumers, in the case of vehicle emission charges) that should, in the long run, result in more efficient responses to air pollution problems. These approaches still require top-down goal-setting, and they are still therefore subject to political pressures that don't affect the market for jackets. In setting such standards, general scientific knowledge is critical, and often a matter of dispute.

But the problem of indivisibility—especially in the case of air pollution—makes some sort of collective goal-setting inevitable. The number of affected parties makes common-law approaches or voluntary bargaining cumbersome, given today's technologies. What is attractive about tradeable permit schemes is their potential to prepare the groundwork for creating enforceable "clean air rights" over time. For this to happen, however, legislators need to eliminate all the current language that insists these pollution credits are not rights—language that renders investment in such credits uncertain.

Tradeable permits and pollution charges are promising mechanisms. But even if we decide they are the right mechanisms to address a certain environmental problem, we still must ask who the affected parties are—who is breathing the air in question—and where, then, the goal-setting ought to be done. For three decades, we've taken for granted the idea that there should be one single environmental standard for the whole nation. But understanding the roles of knowledge and values in defining and pricing environmental goods suggests that that may not be the case. For some problems, impacts are strictly local and narrowly circumscribed. Other environmental problems may impose regional, or even global, impacts. The locus of impact should help determine where decision-making authority resides.

If most relevant knowledge is location-specific and dynamic, decisions about "how clean is clean" and what remedies to use should take place closest to where the problem occurs. For air-emission problems, that might mean a local air basin. For decisions about siting a hazardous waste facility, that might mean bargaining between landowners adjacent to the site and the site owner.

The rationale for using decentralized bargaining approaches to address environmental problems lies not with any mystical faith that small is always beautiful, nor with the now-faddish notion that all that is good must come from communities. The rationale for these approaches builds, instead, on two premises. One is the importance of decentralized information in understanding and remedying environmental problems. The other is the importance of finding ways for real people affected by real conflicts of social space to undertake their own balancing act among competing values.

Several years ago, when the Mobro garbage barge out of Islip, New York, roamed the high seas in search of a place to unload its unappetizing cargo, nightly newscasters regaled viewers with tales of the NIMBY (not-in-my-backyard) problem. People increasingly don't want landfills—or any other "nuisance" facility—sited in their communities. But people do want to be able to throw out their waste, and the trash must go somewhere.

Political edicts directing communities to site landfills are one possible remedy. But such edicts simply override the concerns and preferences of affected individuals. Bargaining between would-be landfill operators and local communities offers another option—one already used by waste management companies. Sometimes called YIMBY-FAP (yes, in my backyard, for a price), these arrangements involve negotiations in which landfill operators offer a package of protections and benefits, including compensation, to affected landowners—or sometimes entire communities—in exchange for permission to site a landfill. The costs of the landfill are thus borne by all its customers, rather than only the property owners in the surrounding area. (The same principle applies in legal reforms aimed at requiring government "takings" compensation to landowners who bear the cost of such policies as wetlands protection. Society as a whole is buying an environmental good, and all the "purchasers" should bear the cost.)

These bargaining processes have shed light on several important decision-making conundrums.

First, surveys of New York citizens showed that acceptance of benefit packages depends on how the package is offered. Early direct involvement in the bargaining process is important to participants.

Second, perceptions matter. Just as people may "irrationally" want to buy cars with tail fins, so too they may "irrationally" dislike living next to a landfill, even if it poses no health hazards. In our study, "Too Little, Too Late? Host-Community Benefits and Siting Solid Waste Facilities," economist Rodney Fort and I note that "perception costs might be portrayed as distortions of reality, or as the inability of lay people correctly to assess the problem, but individuals will react according to their perceptions. . . . The [perception] costs are real regardless of whether public perception is viewed as correct or rational by policy makers, scientists, and technical experts."

Technocratically minded environmental reformers fear that public perceptions will yield irrational demands, driving up costs to solve environmental problems—whether those problems involve building landfills or cleaning up Superfund sites. Those fears do not appear to be justified in circumstances where citizens face *both* the risks associated with a facility and enjoy directly the benefits—in the form of lower costs or higher compensation—associated with a particular remedy. Bargaining itself may serve as a discovery process, revealing more accurate information about both risks and benefits.

Unbounded fears may, in fact, be more likely to drive decisions toward "zero risk" in centralized decision processes. There, the costs of decisions are spread over an entire population, while the benefits from pursuing pristine clean-ups are enjoyed by those few near a particular site. The few then have an incentive to invest heavily in lobbying, while the many do not—with obvious results. Experience with many EPA regulations, and the very high cost per year of life saved associated with those regulations, confirms this observation.

The contrast between costly Superfund site clean-ups, which have occurred in a top-down, regulatory framework directed by the EPA, and more recent local remediation of abandoned industrial sites through negotiated settlements offers further testament to this point. Processes that create closer links between those who pay for clean-up costs and those who enjoy the benefits of clean-up offer a discipline missing from traditional top-down approaches. The locally negotiated clean-ups have, in general, been achieved at a fraction of the cost for Superfund sites.

Not all indivisible environmental problems will be well-suited to collective-negotiation processes, however. In a very imperfect world, sometimes national, state, or local restrictions may be the best we can do.

What distinguishes these circumstances? They involve a high degree of public consensus—even among the regulated parties—that limits or "injunctions" against the activity are appropriate. These are those very rare cases in which everyone would be better off if an environmentally damaging practice were ended, but where there will always be incentives to "cheat" unless a restriction can be enforced by law.

Most environmental problems do not share these characteristics, but some problems may come close—as in the use and discharge of acute, well-understood toxins into the air or water. Consider two examples: the case of the "mad hatter" and the problem of cadmium discharges into water in Japan. The term "mad hatter" came from the severe effects of using mercury in the hatter's trade to make felt hats. And in 1950s Japan, mining operations discharged cadmium into water that eventually found its way into the food supply, causing Itai-Itai ("ouch-ouch") disease that results in demineralization of bones. When the source of the disease was pinpointed in 1968, the Japanese government set strict effluent standards for cadmium and prohibited consumption of rice with cadmium concentrations above a specific standard.

In each of these cases, uniform standards on the handling, use, or disposal of these materials might reduce harm, coincide with broad-based public values, and lessen transaction costs associated with case-by-case bargaining or court remedies. In effect, a legal ban enforces a cartel, in which everyone in the industry is able to stop using the dangerous chemicals because they know their competitors will have to stop, too.

Such standards need not always emerge through government actions. When acute problems of this kind become known, the marketplace itself sometimes moves to eliminate use of the offending toxins. For example, after it became clear that vapors from chromium-plating processes resulted in serious health problems for workers, the costs from worker compensation claims drove industries to find ways of safely containing the vapors.

The same kind of evolution occurred among dentists in their use of mercury amalgams. The government did not ban the use of such amalgams. However, dentists found ways of minimizing exposures to the mercury vapors created during the preparation of amalgams, and some dentists turned to substitutes. Trade associations, trade unions, professional organizations, and consumer groups often promote these kinds of changes by monitoring safety issues relevant to their members.

Whether uniform standards ought to be considered will be a function of the level of consensus regarding whether some action should be taken; the clarity of knowledge about the causation of a problem and the level of risk associated with the problem. Where problems are indivisible, risks posed by the problem are extremely high, and causes of those risks are well-understood, public rules offer a plausible solution.

Clearly, an environmental vision based on evolving institutions will not please everyone. It acknowledges tradeoffs among values, and it admits both the necessity and the limits of political decision making—positions guaranteed to upset both traditional environmentalists and free market absolutists. It does not promise a perfect world, merely a slowly improving one. And it faces squarely the underlying problem with current environmental regulations: Centralized, top-down rule making is ill-suited to addressing environmental problems in a complex, dynamic world in which most relevant information is location-specific and different people have very different priorities.

Applying such a vision cannot be a matter of waving a single legislative wand. Three decades of statutes have created layer upon layer of regulations. But Congress could start with a few basic reforms. The National Environmental Policy Institute is exploring ways to craft a single statute that would phase in devolution of most environmental decisions to states. The concept is worth pursuing. Devolution to states does not really go far enough, since, ultimately, what is needed is further decentralization to local communities and, where feasible, privatization of environmental decisions. But devolution to the states is a good place to start in any reform agenda.

Similarly, Congress needs to get the EPA out of the business of prospectively approving state and local environmental protection programs. Under the Clean Air Act, for example, Congress sets air-emission standards and states are delegated responsibility for developing State Implementation Plans. Using computer models and other criteria, the EPA assesses those plans to determine whether they comply with federal law. States get full emission-reduction "credits" when the EPA's computer models show a state program achieving over time some estimated pollution reduction. But this means the EPA's assumptions about everything from population growth to commuting patterns, not actual pollution levels, determine the outcome. The process prevents experimentation. It locks states into using technologies or programs that the EPA thinks—but has not necessarily demonstrated—will work. Eliminating the prospective approval process would give states the latitude to design programs they believe will achieve emission reductions, and to evaluate and adjust those programs based on real-world data.

Above all, what is needed is a fundamental shift away from an approach that is primarily regulatory and punitive to one that emphasizes bargaining, improvement in information flows, and incentives for stewardship. The 1995 House proposals regarding takings compensation are essential to realigning the incentive equation.

Turning environmental policy in the direction of more bargaining is likely to require experimentation and many varied measures. But a place to start is in revising approaches to environmental enforcement. Current approaches have blurred any distinctions between intent and accident; the line between civil and criminal cases is not always clear; sentencing guidelines bear little logical relationship to the scope of alleged crimes.

In recent soul-searching, business leaders and legislators who led the 1995 regulatory reform effort of the 104th Congress opined that their reform vision was the right one. It was, they concluded, only their message that was inadequate. This self-appraisal is too generous.

Their message was inadequate *because* their vision was not well thought out. Pieces of that vision—such as the need to realign private incentives through takings compensation—were on target. But bills to require cost-benefit analysis and risk assessment really targeted only a symptom—high costs and skewed goals—without looking at the more fundamental problem. Would-be reformers adopted a mirror image of their opponents' technocratic, top-down approach without thinking seriously about how to ensure environmental protection in a world in which environmental goods are widely valued.

The movement toward environmental reform will not, however, disappear. And, in the long run, the past year's setbacks may provide an important opportunity: an occasion to reflect seriously not only on the politics of environmental regulation but on the alternatives to traditional methods. We have a chance to get it right this time, but only if we are willing to invest in developing a dynamic vision.

THE FUTURE OF GOVERNMENT

John Perry Barlow

John Perry Barlow is a rancher, a former lyricist for the Grateful Dead, and a cofounder of the Electronic Frontier Foundation. In this essay he addresses one of the key questions for politics in the next few years: How will the Information Age affect politics and government? Like many libertarians, he argues that as information empowers individuals, fewer people will be willing to put up with coercive government.

There are still factories on this planet, but the industrial era is over. There is still admiration for the fruits of reason, but the age of reason is over. We are no longer modern. We are no longer even postmodern. We are now pre-something else.

Most of our speculation about the history of the future will look ridiculous to our descendants. The more alert of us know one thing with certainty: Massive, accelerating change is taking place. While most of it is driven by digital technology, it will affect far more than the way we communicate at a distance. It will attack our identities, it will amputate our very bodies, and it will rip at every stable power relationship in which we have sought refuge for the last 200 years.

Nearly all of the large institutions in this world—whether corporations, nation-states, political parties, or trade unions—evolved in a mutually augmenting spiral with the rise of industry. Just as they arose to serve the Industrial Revolution, so they will fall as it departs, and the coup de grâce will be delivered by huge webs of rapidly moving information that will render them irrelevant. Many federal governments are already both fibrillating with data-shock and increasingly incapable of convincing the taxpayers who support them that they are getting anything like their money's worth. I think it is unlikely that there will be a federal government left on the planet in 50 years.

And what will come in the wake? Howling anarchy? Crushing totalitarianism? Neither? Both? We don't know. But just as, at the dawn of the industrial age, Thomas Jefferson, James Madison, Thomas Paine, Jean-Jacques Rousseau, and company were able to contemplate the future of government without knowing what would ultimately be governed, we have, as they did, a blank canvas upon which to sketch in outline the *novus ordo saeculorum,* the new cycle of the ages. Like them, we have entered a new social context in which the old and tangled growths of power haven't taken root and so have no moral or practical claim to sovereignty. Back then, that context was the New World. For us, it's the new frontier of cyberspace, even more limitless in its perils and opportunities than the unexplored North American continent.

The electronic environment hardly lends itself to the purposes or methods of imposed government. It is difficult to enforce a credible order upon people whose activities can take place in any terrestrial jurisdiction on the planet, and whose actions can easily be made invisible. It is difficult to imagine a democracy in which the self has no clear definition. It is difficult to silence people who have at their disposal a medium that can carry one's ideas to the rest of humanity without revealing the location of one's body.

We're looking at a dream of liberty that would have both exhilarated and terrified Jefferson. It's time to ask the question he would have asked: If the old methods of government won't work in the virtual dimension, how are the inhabitants of cyberspace to, as Jefferson wrote in the Declaration of Independence, "institute new Government, laying its Foundation on such Principles and organizing its Powers in such Form, as to them shall seem most likely to effect their Safety and Happiness"?

We can be reasonably sure that it will not be easy to impose order on anything as slippery as a virtual body politic. It will be possible for a government to crack down on Internet sites full of sex and sedition, but those forms of expression can as easily bloom in any place on the earth where the love of freedom is greater than the fear of the unknown. Even though that is no longer the case in America, I am confident there will always be havens in the Net for free, radical bits.

I look to see the biggest renaissance of the city-state since, well, the Renaissance. Those open nerve centers of information and culture that are already forming in the Net—New York, Hong Kong, Berlin, Amsterdam, Los Angeles, Silicon Valley—are starting to exhibit autonomy from the terrestrial powers into whose jurisdiction they purportedly fall. But what about the Net itself? I think public life will always be a little wild in there. People will be able to erect walls of cryptography behind which they can create an infinity of social experiments, but cyberspace as a whole will be ungovernable by the old model of imposed will.

Instead, it will have governance—culture, ethical codes, an understanding of mutual self-interest. In an environment that literally wires perceptions into one another, it's likely that shared experiences will be common. At least, that's what I'm hoping for.

Because one thing is clear to me. We are at the end of the world as we know it. Our grandchildren will obtain their order by methods we cannot imagine; our legacy to them should be a virtual landscape open to all the possibilities they might try. Let's be ancestors for them as great as Jefferson and Madison were to us. Let's leave them freedom. They can decide how much of it they're brave enough to keep.

The Literature of Liberty

Tom G. Palmer

No one collection can do justice to the richness of libertarianism or to the range of problems to which one can apply libertarian insights in illuminating or practical ways, but the reader you hold in your hands provides a good overview of libertarian thought. The reader includes a number of the canonical works of the libertarian traditions, either excerpted or in their entirety. This short guide is a supplement to those texts, intended for those who wish to explore further the foundations, implications, and promise of libertarianism. (I have not generally listed works already represented in this reader, although those that are merely excerpted often merit reading in full.) In addition to works written from a libertarian perspective, or which have contributed to the development of libertarianism, I have included some contemporary and classic works that are critical of the libertarian approach, ranging from Plato's criticism of voluntary social organization to contemporary conservative, socialist, and social democratic criticisms. Libertarianism is central to virtually all of the currently exciting debates in ethical theory, political science, economics, history, and the other humane sciences, as well as to actual political struggles across the globe, and it is important to see libertarianism, not only as its proponents see it, but from the perspective of its critics as well.

Such a bibliographical guide could be organized in any number of ways (chronological/historical, thematic, by schools or countries), and each has its advantages. I have organized this guide so that the reader can first review broad introductions to the subject and then delve into more specific issues. Accordingly, I have organized the material into eight categories: (I) contemporary or relatively recent general works on libertarianism; (II) the history of civilization from a libertarian perspective; (III) imprescriptible individual rights; (IV) spontaneous order; (V) free markets and voluntary organization; (VI) justice and political organization; (VII) violence and the state; and (VIII) classical and contemporary works that are directly critical of libertarianism. The topic divisions are somewhat arbitrary, precisely because so many of the ideas are mutually reinforcing and therefore likely to be found treated in the same book or essay. I conclude with the critics of libertarianism in order to allow the reader the opportunity to see the issues from at least two perspectives, to think through some difficult problems, and to decide for herself which arguments she finds most convincing. No one perspective is likely to have all the answers, or even to ask all of the interesting and important questions, and it is only through dialogue with other views—through criticism and hard thinking—that libertarianism is likely to grow and flourish, and to make possible a better, freer, more peaceful, prosperous, and just world.

Readers trying to find an authoritative once-and-for-all answer to every question are likely to be disappointed, for not all the writers here discussed agree on all questions, and many of the most interesting works were written as criticisms of other libertarian or classical liberal writers. Broad agreement on the value and importance of imprescriptible rights to life, liberty, and property is the hallmark of the libertarian approach, but libertarianism remains a lively and exciting field for the thoughtful and creative, rather than merely a set of canonical answers. What is perhaps most remarkable about modern libertarianism is the way it illuminates the world, both morally and scientifically. Libertarianism offers both moral imperatives for peace and voluntary cooperation and a rich understanding of the spontaneous order made possible by such voluntary cooperation. The complement to the latter is the explication of the ways in which coercive intervention can disorder the world and set in motion complex trains of unintended consequences, often with catastrophically negative consequences.

The guide is, by necessity, somewhat eccentric—reflecting my own reading and the interests that have guided me over the years—and most definitely incomplete. I certainly anticipate objections from readers who will complain that works were excluded that were better, or more important, or "more libertarian" than works that were included. As excuse for the absence of important works, I can only plead the limitations of space. To the objection that works are included to which some may object, on the grounds that the are not "plumb line" libertarian texts, I respond with the words of the late Henry Hazlitt, formerly economics editor at the *New York Times* and columnist for *Newsweek*, and the author of the extraordinarily influential book *Economics in One Lesson*, in his own bibliography of libertarianism, *The Free Man's Library* (Princeton: Van Nostrand, 1956):

> In an effort to answer as many as possible of such objections in advance, I should like to say here that the inclusion of a book in this bibliography certainly does not imply that I myself subscribe to every doctrine or sentence in that book or that I think that every opinion it

enunciates is an essential part of the libertarian or individualist tradition. What inclusion does imply is that in my judgment the book . . . makes on net balance a factual or theoretical contribution to the philosophy of individualism, and that at least some readers may derive from it a fuller understanding of that philosophy (pp. 7–8).

Partly because this bibliography is so much smaller than Hazlitt's, which listed 550 books, I have employed more fine-grained selection criteria and have not included the many criticisms of totalitarianism that appeared in his 1956 listing, when the totalitarian state was a very present threat to liberty. The selection I have made, which is drawn entirely from material available in English, is far from comprehensive, but those who wish to read and study further will find that each book or essay invariably leads to others.

I. GENERAL WORKS ON LIBERTARIANISM

In my opinion, the finest short introduction to libertarianism is David Boaz's book *Libertarianism: A Primer* (New York: Free Press, 1997), which was revised and retitled *The Libertarian Mind: A Manifesto for Freedom* in 2015. It's clear, nonjargonistic, and very substantive. Boaz, the editor of *The Libertarian Reader*, in which this bibliographical essay is published, has been for years the executive vice president of the Cato Institute, the world's premier libertarian think tank, and has written on public policy, political science, economics, and moral philosophy. I know of no finer general book on libertarian thought.

At the risk of tooting my own horn, I recommend as a helpful introduction an edited collection of short essays (including some I wrote), *Why Liberty: Your Life, Your Choices, Your Future* (Ottawa, Ill.: Jameson, 2013). I had the honor of editing the essays, most of which were written by members of the youth group Students for Liberty.

Those seeking a more detailed intellectual/historical exposition of libertarian thought would benefit from George H. Smith's masterful book *The System of Liberty: Themes in the History of Classical Liberalism* (New York: Cambridge University Press, 2013). Smith is not only learned and erudite, but also a fine teacher with a talent for explaining complex matters in simple language. A useful collection of classical liberal texts from the eighteenth and nineteenth centuries can be found in E. K. Bramsted and K. J. Melhuish, eds., *Western Liberalism: A History in Documents from Locke to Croce* (New York: Longman, 1978); the collection also includes nonlibertarian "social liberals" of the late nineteenth and twentieth centuries.

Among the more prolific libertarian writers of the last century was undoubtedly Murray N. Rothbard, whose writings ranged from his own area of academic training—economics—to political science, ethics, history, international affairs, and much more. In the 1970s he turned his attention to writing a "manifesto" of libertarianism, which appeared in two editions under the name *For a New Liberty: The Libertarian Manifesto* (2nd ed.; New York: Macmillan, 1978). That book provides a good overview of the libertarian worldview, although the chapters on public policy issues and on the organized libertarian movement are by now quite dated.

Rothbard had published many articles and books in the 1950s and 1960s arguing against the legitimacy of the state (in American English, usually referred to as "government," although that term implies the impossibility of "voluntary government," which Rothbard favored). The distinguished philosopher Robert Nozick found Rothbard's arguments a powerful case against the legitimacy of the state, and he was moved by Rothbard's challenge to write his own tremendously successful and brilliant book defending the strictly limited state, *Anarchy, State, and Utopia* (New York: Basic Books, 1974). Nozick's book has come to enjoy a canonical status among academics, who typically assign a chapter or two to students as "the" libertarian case, with little appreciation of the broader tradition of libertarian thinking and scholarship within which Nozick's work took shape. The issue of whether the state can be justified has been taken up by many other libertarian philosophers; a notably stimulating work is Michael Huemer's *The Problem of Political Authority: An Examination of the Right to Coerce and the Duty to Obey* (New York: Palgrave Macmillan, 2013).

Nozick started his enterprise with the explicit assumption, stated in the first sentence of *Anarchy, State, and Utopia*, that "individuals have rights, and there are things no person or group may do to them (without violating those rights)," an assumption shared with other libertarians, and then attempted to answer the question "How much room do individual rights leave for the state?" His response was that a very limited state, dedicated to protecting individual rights, is legitimate and consistent with individual rights. In the process of defending the (strictly) limited state, Nozick articulated many provocative ideas in his witty and dazzling book, and offered a direct and strong criticism of John Rawls's then recently published and widely acclaimed defense of the redistributive welfare state, *A Theory of Justice* (Cambridge: Harvard University Press, 1971). Largely because of his remarks on Rawls and the extraordinary power of his intellect, Nozick's book was taken quite seriously by academic philosophers and political theorists, many of whom had not before read any contemporary libertarian (or classical liberal) material and thus considered Nozick's work to be the only articulation and defense of libertarianism available. Since Nozick was writing to defend the limited state and did not justify his starting assumption that individuals have rights, that led some academics to dismiss libertarianism as "without foundations," in the words of the philosopher Thomas Nagel. When read in light of the explicit statement of the book's purpose, however, that criticism is misdirected, or should have been directed at some other book attempting to make another argument. (Other contemporary philosophers have taken up the task of justifying the strong claim that individuals have rights, and I will introduce a few of them shortly.)

A list of "general" works on libertarianism certainly must include the enormously popular essays of the best-selling novelist-philosopher Ayn Rand. Some of her better works, along with essays by three collaborators (psychologist Nathaniel Branden, historian Robert Hessen, and Alan Greenspan, who later became Federal Reserve chairman), can be found in the collection *Capitalism: The Unknown Ideal* (New York: New American Library, 1966). Presented in vivid and dramatic language, the essays represent an attempted synthesis of Rand's political philosophy. Unlike most of her other books, which deal with her theories of popular culture, art, personal morality, metaphysical truths, epistemology, and the many other issues to which Rand turned her formidable intellect, the essays in this volume are more narrowly political and libertarian. Rand, who escaped the Soviet Union, was strongly influenced in developing her political philosophy by the libertarian writers Isabel Paterson (originally from Canada) and Rose Wilder Lane, as well as the Austrian economist Ludwig von Mises, who had fled the Nazi advance in Europe. (It should be noted that Rand's dramatic style—so important to an artist—sometimes led to oversimplification, as in her characterization of "big business" as "America's persecuted minority"; her efforts to defend businesspeople from the kind of scapegoating directed at Jews in National Socialist Germany or at the "bourgeoisie" in her native Russia led her to downplay the efforts of many involved in "business" to get special favors from the state and to restrain the activities of their competitors. For such favor-seeking businesspeople, those who dealt in what she called "the aristocracy of pull," she had only contempt.) One remarkable thing about Rand's approach that distinguished it from so much previous thinking—and that is certainly a prominent feature of the essays in this collection—is that she offered a distinctively *moral* defense of an economic system based on voluntary cooperation and exchange; it was not that people were not "good enough" for socialism, but that socialism was not good enough for people.

Two significant contributors to modern libertarian thought from Austria were Ludwig von Mises and F. A. Hayek, both articulate defenders of the older tradition of liberalism against the new threat of totalitarianism in the twentieth century. Mises published his positive political philosophy in his book *Liberalism* in German in 1927 (Indianapolis: Liberty Fund, 2005). Hayek, who went on to win the Nobel Prize in economics in 1974, set forth his views on political matters in a number of books. Taken together, those books reveal a gradual evolution in Hayek's political thought. They include his extraordinarily influential book *The Road to Serfdom* (Chicago: University of Chicago Press, 1944), which undoubtedly represents one of the intellectual and political turning points of the century; *The Constitution of*

Liberty (Chicago: University of Chicago Press, 1960); and his three-volume *Law, Legislation, and Liberty* (Chicago: University of Chicago Press, 1973, 1976, 1979). Another Nobel Prize–winning economist whose works have been enormously influential in the post–World War II libertarian movement is Milton Friedman, who, with his wife, Rose Friedman, wrote eloquently about the loss of freedom due to growing state power. Milton Friedman's *Capitalism and Freedom* (Chicago: University of Chicago Press, 1962) was groundbreaking, and Milton and Rose Friedman's *Free to Choose* (New York: Harcourt Brace Jovanovich, 1980) introduced millions to libertarian ideas, especially through the television series associated with the book.

Political scientist Norman P. Barry's *On Classical Liberalism and Libertarianism* (New York: St. Martin's, 1987) presents a useful overview of libertarian thought, focusing mainly on twentieth-century writers. An attempt to place libertarianism on a "contractarian" foundation and to defend it from various criticisms can be found in philosopher Jan Narveson's *The Libertarian Idea* (Philadelphia: Temple University Press, 1988). A rigorous attempt to place libertarianism (or thoroughgoing classical liberalism) on a foundation of well-formulated axioms is available in economist Anthony de Jasay's *Choice, Contract, Consent: A Restatement of Liberalism* (London: Institute of Economic Affairs, 1991), and in other books by that prolific social scientist and commentator. Law professor Richard A. Epstein has produced powerful defenses of a broadly libertarian approach, including what he considers to be defensible but tightly delimited deviations from strict libertarianism, in his *Simple Rules for a Complex World* (Cambridge: Harvard University Press, 1995), *Skepticism and Freedom* (Chicago: University of Chicago Press, 2003), and other books, including his most recent major work, *The Classical Liberal Constitution: The Uncertain Quest for Limited Government* (Cambridge: Harvard University Press, 2014).

I must mention a little favorite of mine, *Liberty Against Power: Essays by Roy A. Childs, Jr.*, Joan Kennedy Taylor, ed. (San Francisco: Fox & Wilkes, 1994), a collection of essays by the late libertarian scholar Roy A. Childs, Jr., which includes a selection of his scholarly articles, popular essays, journalistic pieces, speeches, and reviews. Childs, an autodidact and independent scholar who did not go to college, exercised an enormous influence on a generation of libertarian scholars, many of whom are now well-known professors, and kept up a vast and learned correspondence with distinguished academics, artists, musicians, businesspeople, journalists, and politicians. (He was one of the brightest and most dazzling personalities I have ever known and remains an inspiration to me and to many other libertarians.) The volume has a foreword by the famous libertarian psychiatrist Thomas Szasz.

A few other short and rather personal introductions to libertarian thought are worth mentioning. The social scientist Charles Murray in his book *What It Means to Be a Libertarian: A Personal Interpretation* (New York: Broadway, 1997) proposes some basic tests and a general framework for evaluating public policies against a background of libertarian principles. Harvard economics professor Jeffrey Miron's *Libertarianism, from A to Z* (New York: Basic Books, 2010) offers short essays (many of which originated as blog posts) on topics arranged in alphabetical order. (It's an admirable short work, but suffers from a lack of documentation of the evidence to justify some of the claims.) Georgetown University philosopher Jason Brennan's *Libertarianism: What Everyone Needs to Know* (Oxford: Oxford University Press, 2012) offers an introduction to the libertarian movement that is informed by his own "social justice" perspective on libertarianism. Brian Doherty's *Radicals for Capitalism: A Freewheeling History of the Modern American Libertarian Movement* (New York: PublicAffairs, 2007) delivers on the book's subtitle. It's focused on the United States, detailed and often entertaining, but may sometimes dwell a bit too much on colorful, but deservedly obscure, figures.

My own book *Realizing Freedom: Libertarian Theory, History, and Practice* (2nd rev. ed.; Washington, D.C.: Cato Institute, 2014) offers introductory essays on libertarian thought (the first is "Why Be Libertarian?") and a mix of historical, economic, ethical, and practical applications of libertarian thought to particular issues.

Finally, *The Encyclopedia of Libertarianism* (Thousand Oaks, Calif.: Sage, 2008), edited by Ronald Hamowy, brings together hundreds of entries on topics from Abolitionism to Mary Wollstonecraft.

II. THE HISTORY OF CIVILIZATION FROM A LIBERTARIAN PERSPECTIVE

One way of understanding the history of modern civilization is as a constant struggle between liberty and power. That was how it was understood by the historian John Emerich Edward Dalberg Acton, known as Lord Acton. There are many available editions of his writings, as well as a number of fine biographies. Paradoxically, precisely because of his vast and unequaled learning (he read and annotated tens of thousands of books in his lifetime and was fluent in a mind-boggling number of languages), Acton never wrote a complete book. He fell prey to the mistake of allowing the best to be the enemy of good, as he always knew that there was more that could be learned before committing his views to print. Thus, his planned great history of liberty has been referred to as "the greatest book never written," but his collected essays and reviews run to many volumes. Especially noteworthy are his essays "Nationality," "The History of Freedom in Antiquity," "The History of Freedom in Christianity," and "Inaugural Lecture on the Study of History," all of which are available in a volume edited by J. Rufus Fears, *Selected Writings of Lord Acton, Vol. I: Essays in the History of Liberty* (Indianapolis: Liberty Classics,

1985). It was Acton who summed up his study of thousands of years of history in the now famous phrase: "Power tends to corrupt and absolute power corrupts absolutely."

A sweeping treatment of history as a struggle between liberty and power can be found in the work of the sociologist Alexander Rüstow, who opposed the National Socialists in Germany and then went into exile as Hitler destroyed the last remnants of continental European libertarianism. During his exile Rüstow strove to understand how the monstrosity of collectivism could emerge in a civilized country such as Germany, and the result was a massive work in social theory, which was abridged and edited by his son Dankwart Rüstow and published in English as *Freedom and Domination: A Historical Critique of Civilization* (Princeton: Princeton University Press, 1980).

Another approach, resting on philosophical underpinnings quite different from those of either Acton or Rüstow (although he influenced both), can be found in the work of the nineteenth-century German legal historian Otto von Gierke, who distinguished between the principles of association (*Genossenschaft*) and domination or lordship (*Herrschaft*) and who saw both as operative in shaping modern social relations. A good selection from his work is available in *Community in Historical Perspective*, Antony Black, ed. (Cambridge: Cambridge University Press, 1990).

Generally, libertarians distinguish society from the state, Thomas Paine famously argued in 1776 in his pamphlet *Common Sense* that

> SOME writers have so confounded society with government, as to leave little or no distinction between them; whereas they are not only different, but have different origins. Society is produced by our wants, and government by our wickedness; the former promotes our happiness POSITIVELY by uniting our affections, the latter NEGATIVELY by restraining our vices. The one encourages intercourse, the other creates distinctions. The first is a patron, the last a punisher.
>
> Society in every state is a blessing, but Government, even in its best state, is but a necessary evil; in its worst state an intolerable one.

Libertarians see such accomplishments as the rule of law, individual rights, toleration, and peace as victories won in a long struggle against power, and institutions such as representative government, the separation of powers, equality before the law, juries, and independent courts as devices to bring the state itself—the organized system of plunder and domination—under law.

Just as there are histories of states (indeed so much of what most people think of as "history" is merely the chronicling of power, of kings and queens, courts and coups, wars and conquests), there are also histories of civil society, of the market, of property and law, of productive work and exchange, of voluntary cooperation. A good place to start is with the history of the revival of commercial civilization in Europe after the barbarian conquests, found in the work of Henri Pirenne, notably his very readable and popular *Medieval Cities: Their Origins and the Revival of Trade* (1925; Princeton: Princeton University Press, 1974). The birth and growth of commercial society are examined in many works. Two of the more outstanding are Robert S. Lopez, *The Commercial Revolution of the Middle Ages, 950–1350* (Cambridge: Cambridge University Press, 1976), and John Brewer and Roy Porter, eds., *Consumption and the World of Goods* (London: Routledge, 1996). A sophisticated and accessible treatment of the rise of "capitalism" can be found in Nathan Rosenberg and L. E. Birdzell, Jr., *How the West Grew Rich* (New York: Basic Books, 1986). An exceptionally fine and very readable work on the topic is the economic historian Deirdre N. McCloskey's *Bourgeois Dignity* (Chicago: University of Chicago Press, 2010), which seeks to explain "the great fact," namely, the staggering, almost incomprehensible rise in living standards for average people in the last two centuries. McCloskey tests every theory of economic growth I had ever heard of (and some I had not) against the evidence and concludes that what best accounts for modern widespread (and ever spreading) prosperity is "the Bourgeois Deal": "Let me get very rich by buying innovations low and selling them high (and do please refrain from stealing from me, or interfering), and I'll make *you* pretty rich, too" (p. 70).

Similar accounts of the emergence of civil society, or the extended order of modern "capitalism," can be found in E. L. Jones, *The European Miracle* (Cambridge: Cambridge University Press, 1981), which locates the source of European economic and legal progress in the radical fragmentation of power on that continent, and Hayek's last book, *The Fatal Conceit: The Errors of Socialism* (Chicago: University of Chicago Press, 1988), which offers a sweeping account of the rise of liberal civilization. A primary feature of these accounts is the role played in the development of modern liberty by the fragmentation of power. Political fragmentation and commercial civilization (with movable forms of wealth, as Benjamin Constant emphasizes in his essay in this reader) lower the individual's cost of exit from an oppressive political situation. Because people could escape from one political system to another, rulers and potential rulers had to compete among themselves to attract or maintain their base of taxpayers. Furthermore, in Europe political power was rarely unitary in any one territory, but was usually at least shared (and disputed!) by the church and the secular authorities, unlike the situation in other areas of the world, where the king claimed either the title of head priest or of God it/him/herself, something unthinkable in the Judeo-Christian worldview. In Europe, because of the competition between church and state and among different kinds of secular authorities, liberty was able to grow up in the "jurisdictional cracks" between the different powers; individuals and groups were able to play powers off against one another, generally resulting in greater security of rights for the individual. A brilliant account of that history of "legal pluralism" and "jurisdictional cracks" is found in the legal historian Harold J. Berman's *Law and Revolution: The Formation of the Western Legal Tradition* (Cambridge: Harvard University Press, 1983).

III. IMPRESCRIPTIBLE INDIVIDUAL RIGHTS

The source or justification of rights has always been a contentious issue among libertarian thinkers. Whether individuals have rights in virtue of their utility, their correspondence to the demands of pure reason, divine revelation, or for some other reason may be a matter of great concern. For myself, rather than seeing different kinds of justifications arriving at the same general conclusion as a problem, I prefer to see such convergence of arguments as a kind of "fail-safe" mechanism: If many different nonexclusive arguments all converge on the same conclusion, we can be more sure of its truth than if only one of those arguments led us there, and the others led to other conclusions.

In any case, in the history of political thought "natural law" arguments and arguments from "utility," for example, were not generally seen as in opposition, for one comes to understand nature only indirectly, through experience, whether in the physical sciences or in the moral sciences, and the sign of a good institution is its good consequences, or utility. What is characteristic of the libertarian approach to rights and distinguishes it from others is that basic rights are held to be "imprescriptible," meaning that fundamental rights are not gifts or mere dispensations from power—whether king or parliament, commissar or congressman—but have moral force before and independently of particular political arrangements. Rights are what individuals bring to politics, not what they take out. When political society works properly, what individuals derive from government is security for rights; their previously justified rights are what they enter into political arrangements to secure. Imprescriptible rights are thus not subject to "prescription"; they are neither handed out by authoritative figures, as doctors hand out prescriptions for drugs, nor subject to being arbitrarily taken away without injustice.

One of the finest histories of the idea of natural rights is Brian Tierney, *The Idea of Natural Rights* (Grand Rapids, Mich.: Wm. B. Eerdmans, 2001). Another useful historical account of the origins of natural rights theories is Richard Tuck's *Natural Rights Theories: Their Origin and Development* (Cambridge: Cambridge University Press, 1979). (While Tuck's knowledge and scholarship are truly impressive, a useful supplement to his book can be found in an article by Tierney, "Tuck on Rights: Some Medieval Problems," *History of Political Thought* 4, no. 3 [Winter 1983]. Tuck himself extended his account in his essay "The 'Modern' Theory of Natural Law," in

The Languages of Political Theory in Early-Modern Europe, Anthony Pagden, ed. (Cambridge: Cambridge University Press, 1987). Another account by a distinguished philosopher, Fred D. Miller, Jr.'s, *Nature, Justice, and Rights in Aristotle's Politics* (Oxford: Oxford University Press, 1995), argues that the roots of modern rights theory can be found in Aristotle, that "Locke's theory of 'the Law of Nature' is a direct descendant of Aristotle's theory of natural justice," and that in Aristotle's writings can be found a theory of "rights based on nature."

Especially important in the history of libertarianism are the contributions of the Spanish School of Salamanca, whose members articulated so much of the foundation of the modern libertarian synthesis of spontaneous order and individual rights. An early work that outlined the contributions to the understanding of self-regulating free societies was Marjorie Grice-Hutchinson, *The School of Salamanca: Readings in Spanish Monetary Theory, 1544–1605* (Oxford: Clarendon Press, 1952). The members of the School of Salamanca were concerned with much more than monetary theory, however, and laid out much of the general framework of what was to emerge as classical liberalism. One writer whose defense of the rights of the Indians contributed greatly to the modern libertarian idea of imprescriptible individual rights is Francisco de Vitoria, whose "On the American Indians" (in Francisco de Vitoria, *Political Writings*, Anthony Pagden and Jeremy Lawrance, eds. [Cambridge: Cambridge University Press 1991]) exercised a great influence on later rights theorists. Vitoria concluded that the Indians were not the "natural slaves" of which Aristotle had written, and that "the barbarians undoubtedly possessed as true dominion, both public and private, as any Christians. That is to say, they could not be robbed of their property . . . on the grounds that they were not true masters (*ueri domini*)."

Vitoria drew on the writings of one of the great lawyer-popes of the thirteenth century, Innocent IV, who had insisted that to deprive unbelievers ("infidels," including Jews and Muslims) of life, liberty, property was unjust: "Lordship, possession, and jurisdiction can belong to infidels licitly and without sin, for these things are made not only for the faithful but for every rational creature as has been said." (Innocent's arguments can be found in the outstanding collection edited by Brian Tierney, *The Crisis of Church and State, 1050–1300* [Toronto: University of Toronto Press, 1988], along with many other documents important to the development of libertarianism.)

Particularly active in the struggle to protect the rights of the Indians was Bartolomé de Las Casas, who defended their rights in a famous debate with Juan Ginés de Sepúlveda in Valladolid in 1550 (Las Casas's arguments were later published as a book; see his *In Defense of the Indians* [c. 1552 ; DeKalb: Northern Illinois University Press, 1992]), and who wrote eloquently to alert European readers to the horrors visited on the native peoples by their conquerors (see his *The Devastation of the Indies: A Brief Account* [1552; Baltimore: Johns Hopkins University Press, 1992]).

The proto-libertarians of the School of Salamanca succeeded in establishing a vigorous defense of the rights of every human being to life, liberty, and property, which is truly one of the great accomplishments of our civilization. Even if honored more in the breach than in practice for many years, the principle of imprescriptible individual rights was established as a moral norm, and that principle spurred the later emancipation of slaves, the equalization of rights between men and women, and at least some degree of restraint in the treatment of the helpless, whose lot in earlier years was to be destroyed if they could not be enslaved.

What emerged from that tradition and from those debates was the idea that to be a moral agent was to be able to take responsibility for one's actions, referred to as "dominium," or self-mastery, which entailed that one had the *right* to fulfill one's responsibilities, essentially on the grounds that "ought implies can." That idea was expressed in English by the phrase "a property in one's person," an idea advanced by such figures as the English Leveller Richard Overton (see the selection in this reader) and the more widely known English physician, philosopher, and activist for liberty, John Locke (see the selections in this reader). Locke brought together into an appealing synthesis ideas about property, consent, contract, and the origins and limits of legitimate government. Locke's influence on the modern world, as on modern libertarianism, is inestimable. It is, of course, especially obvious in the American Declaration of Independence, which articulated libertarian ideals for a worldwide audience. Locke brought together those important ideals in his *Two Treatises of Government*, the first of which is mainly a refutation of the arguments for absolutism of Sir Robert Filmer, while the second contains more of Locke's own arguments on behalf of individual liberty and limited government. The language remains remarkably readable, but it is advisable to obtain one of the annotated editions for footnotes explaining references that may be obscure to contemporary readers. (Locke's arguments are clearly restated, defended from criticism, and applied to new problems and issues—not always in ways entirely consistent with libertarian approaches— by A. John Simmons in *The Lockean Theory of Rights* [Princeton: Princeton University Press, 1992].)

Contrary to the interpretation given to these developments by socialist historians (such as C. B. Macpherson, whose *The Political Theory of Possessive Individualism* [Oxford: Oxford University Press, 1962] has misled thousands upon thousands of university students), the idea of property was not a sneaky trick to justify the wealth of a nascent bourgeoisie, but was articulated first and foremost in defense of such groups as the defeated American Indians and persecuted religious dissenters. (The absurd interpretation of the idea of property in one's person as a kind of trick to justify "capitalist inequality" has been restated, on the basis of a mass of historical errors, by Attracta Ingram in her sustained screed against libertarianism, *A Political Theory of Rights* [Oxford: Clarendon Press, 1994]. Being uninformed about the historical record, Ingram ultimately has to rely on what she refers to as the "intuitive plausibility" [p. 75] of her misrepresentation of history as an argument against property in one's person.) The connection between the idea of property in one's person (sometimes referred to as "self-ownership") and freedom of conscience is nicely laid out by the philosopher/historian George H. Smith in his historical survey "Philosophies of Toleration" (in George H. Smith, *Atheism, Ayn Rand, and Other Heresies* [Buffalo, N.Y.: Prometheus, 1991]).

The history of the application of the idea of property to *alienable* objects (the more common use of the term "property" by contemporary writers) is traced and explained in the philosopher Stephen Buckle's very readable *Natural Law and the Theory of Property: Grotius to Hume* (Oxford: Oxford University Press, 1991).

The classical accounts of individual rights canvassed in the literature above tended to focus on the issue of responsibility for one's actions, or "dominium" (an issue to which F. A. Hayek returned in the chapter "Responsibility and Freedom" in *The Constitution of Liberty* [Chicago: University of Chicago Press, 1960]). The idea has been restated in contemporary times in a somewhat more analytical way (focusing on the analysis of concepts or essences) by Ayn Rand and the philosophers she has inspired. Rand's own arguments, which are somewhat fragmentary (being found scattered over a variety of her essays), have been reconstructed by the philosopher Eric Mack in his essay "The Fundamental Moral Elements on Rand's Theory of Rights," in *The Philosophic Thought of Ayn Rand*, Douglas J. Den Uyl and Douglas B. Rasmussen, eds. (Chicago: University of Illinois Press, 1986). The idea that rights are a requirement of the life of a living reasoning entity, which is central to Rand's philosophy, is explored further in Tibor R. Machan's *Individuals and Their Rights* (La Salle, Ill.: Open Court, 1989) and in Douglas Rasmussen and Douglas J. Den Uyl's *Liberty and Nature: An Aristotelian Defense of Liberal Order* (LaSalle, Ill.: Open Court, 1991), both of which defend versions of "moral realism." Taking their cue from Aristotle's *Nicomachean Ethics*, Rasmussen and Den Uyl stress the importance of "self-direction" to human flourishing, a theme that also plays a role in the philosophically rather different account offered by the libertarian philosopher Loren E. Lomasky. In *Persons, Rights, and the Moral Community* (Oxford: Oxford University Press, 1987), Lomasky argues that human beings are "project pursuers," with the right to choose and pursue their own life projects.

Another illuminating approach to rights draws on the "transcendental" form of argument pioneered by Immanuel Kant, who (to simplify matters a bit) started with the accepted truths of arithmetic, Euclidean geometry, and Newtonian physics and then asked what would have to be true for these sciences to generate knowledge. Analogously, the libertarian bioethicist H. Tristram Engelhardt, Jr., has asked what would have to be true for the pluralistic extended order, or civil society, to exist; he presented a theory of two "tiers" of morality, the abstract rules of the free society, which provide a mere framework for social coexistence and cooperation; and the concrete customs, injunctions, and requirements of particular religious or philosophical or communal moralities, which provide the content of moral lives. This theory is set out in its general form and then applied to concrete problems and issues in biomedical ethics by Engelhardt in his book *The Foundations of Bioethics* (Oxford: Oxford University Press, 1986). (Interestingly, that transcendental argument has some affinity with the "hypothetical imperative" argument advanced by such thinkers as Samuel Pufendorf, who stressed "sociality" as the foundation of the rules of justice: If you wish to live with other humans in peace and harmony, *then* certain things are necessary, such as rights, rules of just conduct, and property. See Pufendorf's *On the Duty of Man and Citizen* [1673; Cambridge: Cambridge University Press, 1991] and Craig L. Carr, ed., *The Political Writings of Samuel Pufendorf* [Oxford: Oxford University Press, 1994].)

The best recent work in the tradition of "hypothetical imperatives," which also draws heavily on the insights of F. A. Hayek on knowledge and a deep understanding of legal processes, is Randy E. Barnett's *The Structure of Liberty: Justice and the Rule of Law* (Oxford: Oxford University Press, 2014).

An account that begins with the nature of rights as such and derives consistent systems of justice is offered by the University of Manchester philosopher Hillel Steiner, who has emphasized the issue of "compossibility" as a necessary characteristic of genuine rights. A set of compossible rights includes only rights that can be exercised at the same time without entailing conflicts. The rights entailed by property in one's person fulfill that requirement, whereas various alleged "welfare rights," "national rights," and so forth do not. Steiner's principal work is *An Essay on Rights* (Oxford: Blackwell, 1994), which is a dazzling display of analytical rigor, leading to sometimes unexpected results, including a number from which libertarians would typically dissent. (Notably, Steiner endorses what has come to be known as a "Georgist" position on land and natural resources, after the nineteenth-century economist Henry George, according to which all have a right to an equal share of naturally occurring resources, rather than the Lockean position that all have an equal right to appropriate. As the reader can easily imagine, such a seemingly slight difference in terms yields extraordinarily different conclusions.)

Another contemporary philosopher who has presented a strong defense of property in one's person (or "self-ownership") is Eric Mack, whose essays defending this approach include "Agent-Relativity of Value, Deontic Restraints, and Self-Ownership," in R. G. Frey and Christopher W. Morris, eds., *Value, Welfare, and Morality* (Cambridge: Cambridge University Press, 1993) and "Personal Integrity, Practical Recognition, and Rights," *The Monist* 76, no. 1 (January 1993). Mack applies the principle of property in one's person to the particular issue of whether profits from voluntary exchange are justified (in a somewhat technical discussion of the work of philosopher David Gauthier) in his essay "Rights to Natural Talents and Pure Profits: A Critique of Gauthier on Rights and Economic Rent," in Robin Cowan and Mario J. Rizzo, eds., *Profits and Morality* (Chicago: University of Chicago Press, 1995). (The volume edited by Cowan and Rizzo also contains interesting discussions of the right to earn profits by the economist Israel Kirzner, who delineates the economic concept of profit and defends a "finders-keepers" rule of appropriation, and Jan Narveson, who defends market exchange and justly earned profits from a number of criticisms.)

Other accounts have stressed the general utility of rights. Notable in such accounts are those emphasizing the central role of rights in generating beneficial social cooperation. An interesting example of this kind of argument is found in the British economist Robert Sugden's essay "Labour, Property, and the Morality of Markets," in *The Market in History*, B. L. Anderson and A. J. H. Latham, eds. (London: Croom Helm, 1986). A similar approach is taken by the economist and law professor David Friedman in his essay "A Positive Account of Property Rights," in Ellen Frankel Paul, Fred D. Miller, Jr., and Jeffrey Paul, eds., *Property Rights* (Cambridge: Cambridge University Press, 1994). Both Sugden and Friedman advance "self-ownership" as a salient, or prominent, solution to the problem of who gets to control the "most scarce" of all resources: you and your body.

It is sometimes objected that groups can have rights, too (or perhaps even that groups *are* the basic rights holders, and that individuals are the ones who *may* have rights, too, when the group decides to bestow them, meaning, of course, that they can be taken away again). This issue has again taken center stage in current discussions of such issues as "affirmative action," the rights of aboriginal tribes, and other concrete issues. A well-thought-out and nuanced treatment of the issue is offered by the political scientist Chandran Kukathas in his essay "Are There Any Cultural Rights?," *Political Theory* 20, no. 1 (February 1992). (The social democratic philosopher Will Kymlicka criticizes Kukathas in the same issue of *Political Theory*, and Kukathas responds in vol. 20, no. 4 [November 1992].)

The extension of recognized imprescriptible rights is to a large extent the measure of civilization. One way of viewing the history of liberty is as the history of the recognition of rights among ever wider groups. The struggle for the rights of women is represented in this reader, notably by Mary Wollstonecraft and the Grimké sisters, but additional treatments of this important subject can be found in Wendy McElroy, ed., *Freedom, Feminism, and the State* (New York: Holmes & Meier, 1991). A defense of modern liberal society, focusing on the possibility of "role complexity" and emphasizing the liberation of women from imposed roles, is offered by Rose Laub Coser, *In Defense of Modernity: Role Complexity and Individual Autonomy* (Stanford: Stanford University Press, 1991). A modern restatement of individualist feminism is Joan Kennedy Taylor, *Reclaiming the Mainstream: Individualist Feminism Rediscovered* (Buffalo, N.Y.: Prometheus, 1992). An inspiring account of women who struggled for their own rights and the rights of others can be found in John Blundell's *Ladies for Liberty: Women Who Made a Difference in American History* (New York: Algora, 2011).

It would not be appropriate to conclude a discussion of the literature of rights without pointing again to the important work by Robert Nozick that was mentioned in the first section of this essay, *Anarchy, State, and Utopia* (New York: Basic Books, 1974). Many things could be said about this interesting and challenging book, but in this context Nozick's construal of individual rights as "side constraints" on acceptable behavior is especially noteworthy. Nozick argued against what he called a "utilitarianism of rights," that is, the view that what we are all called morally to do is to minimize the amount of rights violation, even if we have to violate rights in the process. In response to such views, Nozick argued that the rights of others serve as constraints on our behavior, and not as a quantity to be maximized. Rights are important moral signposts, for they guide us in what we ought to do or refrain from doing. Rights are action-guiding, and systems that require a God's-eye view (as so many of the "positive" welfare rights views do, with various conflicting rights being balanced against each other—and against other interests—by some all-powerful agency) hardly qualify as systems of rights at all.

IV. SPONTANEOUS ORDER

Libertarianism as a *political* theory can perhaps best be understood as the integration of two mutually reinforcing theories, one "normative" (containing "ought" statements) and the other "positive" (containing "is" statements). The normative theory is a theory of individual rights; the positive theory is a theory of how order comes about. To understand how those two themes are related, consider the following: If respect for individual rights were to be shown to lead, not to order and prosperity, but to chaos, the destruction of civilization, and famine, few would uphold such alleged rights, and those who did would certainly be held the enemies of mankind. Those who can see order only when there is a conscious ordering mind—socialists, totalitarians, monarchical absolutists, and the like—fear just such consequences from individual rights. But if it can be shown that a multitude of individuals exercising a set of "compossible" rights (as described above, in the section on imprescriptible rights) generates, not chaos, but order, cooperation, and the progressive advance of human well-being, then respect for the dignity and autonomy of the individual would be seen to be not only compatible with, but even a necessary precondition for, the achievement of social coordination, prosperity, and high civilization. Individual rights and spontaneous order are complementary elements of libertarianism.

The study of how order can emerge as an unintended consequence of the actions of many individuals is usually referred to as the study of "spontaneous order," and that field of study is a central element of libertarian political economy.

Thomas Paine recognized the immense attractiveness of that integration of order and rights. He defended natural and imprescriptible rights in *The Rights of Man, Part I* (1791): "Natural rights are those which always appertain to man in the right of his existence." That was reinforced in *The Rights of Man, Part II* (1792) with a most remarkable observation: "For upwards of two years from the commencement of the American war, and a longer period in several of the American states, there were no established forms of government. The old governments had been abolished, and the country was too much occupied in defense to employ its attention in establishing new governments; yet during this interval order and harmony were preserved as inviolate as in any country in Europe." (That section is excerpted in this reader.) The advocates of royal power predicted chaos, disorder, disruption, and mass mayhem if one iota of the royal power were to be challenged, yet Paine observed that the power of the state was not merely attenuated, but was *completely* absent, and still people continued to farm, to engage in manufacturing, to trade, to respect one another, and to live in "order and harmony." The question of how that could be—and the conditions propitious for such spontaneous order—has been a major topic of research for libertarian scholars and social scientists.

Paine was not, of course, the first to make the connection between social order and individual rights (the School of Salamanca had explored that territory long before), but as a forceful writer and popularizer he understood the attractiveness of a political theory that integrated a theory of justice (imprescriptible rights) and a theory of society (spontaneous order). The intellectual history of the theory of spontaneous order is mapped out by the polymath economist F. A. Hayek in his essay "The Results of Human Action but Not of Human Design" in *Studies in Philosophy, Politics, and Economics* (Chicago: University of Chicago Press, 1967), which traces the theme from ancient to modern times.

The observation of the self-regulating order of the free market was a most important impetus to the development of classical liberal (or libertarian) systems of political economy. As the English writer Charles Davenant noted in his 1695 pamphlet, *A Memorial Concerning the Coyn of England*, price controls were ineffective, because "Nor can any law hinder B, C, & D from supplying their Wants [for in the] Naturall Course of Trade, Each Commodity will find its Price. . . . The supream power can do many things, but it cannot alter the Laws of Nature, of which the most originall is, That every man should preserve himself." Joyce Appleby comments on this passage, noting:

> Economic writers had discovered the underlying regularity in free market activity. Where moralists had long urged that necessity knows no law, the economic analysts who pursued price back to demand had discovered a lawfulness in necessity, and in doing so they had come upon a possibility and a reality. The reality was that individuals making decisions about their own persons and property were the determiners of price in the market. The possibility was that the economic rationalism of market participants could supply the order to the economy formerly secured through authority (Joyce Appleby, *Economic Thought and Ideology in Seventeenth-Century England* [Princeton: Princeton University Press, 1978], pp. 187–88).

A seminal figure in the development of the idea of spontaneous order, often quoted and cited by Hayek, was the Scottish thinker Adam Ferguson. In his famous book of 1767, Ferguson pointed out that "nations stumble upon establishments, which are indeed the result of human action, but not the execution of any human design" (see Adam Ferguson, *An Essay on the History of Civil Society* [1767; Cambridge: Cambridge University Press, 1995]). A good overview of the contributions of the thinkers of the Scottish Enlightenment is found in Ronald Hamowy's brief work *The Scottish Enlightenment and the Theory of Spontaneous Order* (Carbondale: Southern Illinois University Press, 1987).

The study of spontaneous order has hardly been limited to economic phenomena. Michael Polanyi, a Hungarian chemist, economist, and philosopher, was moved to reject socialism and embrace free market liberalism by his realization that the order of science was not, and could not be, "planned." When socialist intellectuals announced—as they were wont to do before the collapse of the socialist paradigm—that under "planned science" such-and-such would be discovered in year x, and another fact or theory or principle would be discovered in the next year, all in accordance with a rational plan for society, Polanyi realized that this sort of planning or social engineering was absurd, that one could not "plan" scientific progress. Scientific progress simply did not work that way, as Polanyi knew from personal experience. Polanyi applied his considerable intellect to understanding how order could emerge as an unintended consequence of human action, with special—but not exclusive—reference to the natural sciences, in the essays collected as *The Logic of Liberty* (Chicago: University of Chicago Press, 1951). Another classical liberal thinker and philosopher of science, Sir Karl

Popper, has pointed out that the idea that one could predict one's future knowledge in the way the socialists insisted was philosophically incoherent: If one could predict one's future knowledge, then one would already know it, and the problem of discovery would simply be assumed away. (Popper criticized the idea of historical prediction in his brilliant book *The Poverty of Historicism* [Boston: Beacon, 1957]; his critique of collectivist philosophy appeared in *The Open Society and Its Enemies* [Princeton: Princeton University Press, 1950], largely a criticism of Plato, Hegel, and Marx. Other essays on liberty and the open society appeared in *Conjectures and Refutations: The Growth of Scientific Knowledge* [New York: Harper & Row, 1968]; especially noteworthy are the essays "Public Opinion and Liberal Principles" and "Utopia and Violence.") Arguments informed by an examination of the history of science have been employed against both "fundamentalist" and "politically correct" attempts to restrict freedom of expression by the journalist Jonathan Rauch in *Kindly Inquisitors: The New Attacks on Free Thought* (2nd ed.; Chicago: University of Chicago Press, 2013).

The noted Italian jurist Bruno Leoni turned his attention to the subject of law itself—the very paradigm of order based on command, in the worldview of anti-libertarians—and showed how law is also a system of spontaneous order. Some of his more important English-language lectures and essays are collected together as *Freedom and the Law* (3rd ed.; Indianapolis: Liberty Press, 1991) (especially noteworthy is his essay "The Law as Individual Claim") and as *Law, Liberty, and the Competitive Market*, Carlo Lottieri, ed. (New Brunswick, N.J.: Transaction, 2008). Much of the discipline that has come to be known as "law and economics" can be traced to the work of Leoni and other libertarian scholars (for example, the Nobel laureate Ronald Coase, whose work will be discussed later), and has focused attention on understanding how the legal institutions that shape the market, such as property and contract, have emerged over time without themselves being "planned" by anyone. The scientific literature that has appeared in recent decades is enormous, but a good basic overview is provided by the Icelandic economist Thráinn Eggertsson in *Economic Behavior and Institutions* (Cambridge: Cambridge University Press, 1990) and by Oliver E. Williamson in *The Economic Institutions of Capitalism* (New York: Free Press, 1985).

There is also a vast literature that uses the mathematical and conceptual apparatus of game theory, or the formal study of strategic interaction, to study the emergence of spontaneous order and cooperation. A particularly good introduction to those themes is found in the English economist Robert Sugden's *The Economics of Rights, Co-operation, and Welfare* (Oxford: Basil Blackwell, 1986), which also provides a helpful introduction for the nonspecialist to the techniques and theorems of game theory. (Sugden provides in a way a masterful updating of the work of David Hume on the emergence of spontaneous order.) A more mathematically challenging and technical approach is found in Michael Taylor's *The Possibility of Cooperation* (Cambridge: Cambridge University Press, 1987). A pathbreaking use of the theory of games, using computerized tournaments between programmed strategies to study how cooperation can emerge even under specified adverse conditions (known as the "prisoner's dilemma"), is found in the political scientist Robert Axelrod's *The Evolution of Cooperation* (New York: Basic Books, 1984).

The study of spontaneous order has been most systematically undertaken by economists, whose enterprise was placed on that track by Adam Smith, who used the metaphor of the "invisible hand" (already prominent in discussions of the subject) in his work *An Inquiry into the Nature and Causes of the Wealth of Nations* (1776) to describe how man "is led to promote an end which is no part of his intentions." Smith thereby set much of the scientific research agenda of economics for the next two centuries. (An even more radical perspective was offered by the Nobel laureate James Buchanan in a comment, "Order Defined in the Process of Its Emergence," in which he argued "that the 'order' of the market emerges *only* from the *process* of voluntary exchange among the participating individuals. The 'order' is, itself, defined as the outcome of the *process* that generates it. The 'it,' the allocation-distribution result, does not, and cannot, exist independently of the trading process. Absent this process, there is and can be no 'order.'" ("Comments on 'The Tradition of Spontaneous Order' by Norman Barry," *Literature of Liberty* [1982; Library of Economics and Liberty, April 29, 2014], http://www.econlib.org/library/Essays/LtrLbrty/bryRF1.html.)

A particularly noteworthy work that helped to place modern social sciences on a secure foundation and that emphasized the tracing of complex systems of order to the actions of individuals is the Austrian economist Carl Menger's *Problems of Economics and Sociology* (1883; Urbana: University of Illinois Press, 1963).

This idea of spontaneous order, even within the study of economic phenomena, is not limited to the study of the price system of the market economy but has been extended to the institution of money itself, the means through which price ratios are expressed. Carl Menger, in *Principles of Economics* (1871; New York: New York University Press, 1981), showed how money emerges as an unintended by-product of barter and thereby makes possible ever more complex forms of exchange. Institutions that provide complex monetary instruments, such as banknotes, also emerged as the unintended by-products of acts of saving and lending. The history of "free banking," in which spontaneous monetary orders and complex systems of economic coordination are the results of voluntary interactions, is examined by economist Lawrence H. White in *Free Banking in Britain: Theory, Experience, and Debate, 1800–1845* (Cambridge: Cambridge University Press, 1984), and the economic analysis of free banking is undertaken by economist George A. Selgin in *The Theory of Free Banking: Money Supply Under Competitive Note Issue* (Totowa, N.J.: Rowman & Littlefield, 1988). (Both White and Selgin present evidence that free banking systems offer greater stability, without economic cycles, than do systems of centralized state-controlled banking.) Those studies of free banking are important not only because they offer the possibility of a society in which it is not necessary for the state to control the "commanding heights" of the economy, with all of the potential for abuse and malfeasance that the power represents, but also because they show that order can and does emerge precisely where it is so often assumed to be impossible.

The omnipresence and manifest importance of the price system of the market economy has offered a fertile field to economists interested in the study of spontaneous order (see Hayek's seminal essay "The Use of Knowledge in Society" in this reader), and it is understandable therefore that the systematic study of spontaneous order should have reached a higher state of development in its field, but that should not blind us to the importance of spontaneous order in law, morality, and many other kinds of human interactions.

V. FREE MARKETS AND VOLUNTARY ORGANIZATION

It may help to examine the market system and its importance in libertarian thought by seeing it in light of the problem of spontaneous order discussed in the previous section. Socialists see markets and see disorder, chaos, and irrationality, and insist that rationality simply demands that order be imposed on this anarchistic system by the state. Karl Marx himself complained of the "anarchy" of "capitalist production," a complaint that would come to be characteristic of almost all criticisms of free market economies. The remedy such critics offered was to replace markets with one form or another of conscious direction by state authorities.

The issue of whether socialism could in fact create order, rather than chaos, was raised by Ludwig von Mises in his 1920 essay "Economic Calculation in the Socialist Commonwealth." That and other essays are available in F. A. Hayek, ed., *Collectivist Economic Planning: Critical Studies on the Possibilities of Socialism* (1935; Clifton, N.J.: Augustus M. Kelley, 1975). Mises argued in that essay and in his later work *Socialism: An Economic and Sociological Analysis* (1922; Indianapolis: Liberty Fund, 1981) that socialist planners would not be able to determine how to achieve the ends they set forth, for they would not know what was the least costly method of production in the absence of the prices (or exchange ratios) that are generated through exchanges of property rights in a market. "Socialism," he concluded, "is the abolition of rational economy." That challenge to socialism led naturally to greater interest in how markets solve the problems of economic calculation, an issue addressed by F. A. Hayek in "The Use of Knowledge in

Society," presented in this reader, and the integration of the understanding of the market economy into the general theme of spontaneous order that I have argued above is central to modern libertarianism. (Other good treatments of the socialist calculation problem include Don Lavoie's *Rivalry and Central Planning: The Socialist Calculation Debate Reconsidered* [Cambridge: Cambridge University Press, 1985] and his more popular and accessible *National Economic Planning: What Is Left?* [Cambridge, Mass.: Ballinger, 1985], as well as David Ramsay Steele's *From Marx to Mises: Post-Capitalist Society and the Challenge of Economic Calculation* [La Salle, Ill.: Open Court, 1992], while the problem of how dispersed knowledge is made useful in complex social orders is examined in some detail by Thomas Sowell in *Knowledge and Decisions* [New York: Basic Books, 1980].)

A number of economics treatises have been written that offer the reader a thorough introduction to understanding the market economy; numerous economics textbooks also serve that function. It would be impossible to do justice to them, or even barely to scratch the surface of the extant economics literature, but one work is especially noteworthy for those interested in exploring libertarian political economy: Ludwig von Mises, *Human Action: A Treatise on Economics* (New Haven: Yale University Press, 1949, and many subsequent editions), which is far more than merely a treatise on economics. Mises offers a systematic view of the problems of social organization, from psychology to capital theory. Some people treat that book almost as a sacred text, which is a shame, as it is full of insights and ideas that deserve careful consideration.

A useful, but somewhat old-fashioned (in language), work for someone entering into the study of economics for the very first time is Henry Hazlitt's short book, published in 1946, *Economics in One Lesson* (2nd ed.; New Rochelle, N.Y.: Arlington House, 1985), which updates and applies the insights of the great classical economists to issues of contemporary policy. The insights are important, but are only a beginning in the study of economics.

Markets are significant for the way in which they can overcome racism, tribalism, and irrational prejudice and can replace enmity and war with friendship and peace. As F. A. Hayek was fond of pointing out, the ancient Greek verb *katallásso* means to welcome into one's village, to reconcile, to change an enemy into a friend, or to exchange. Historian Geoffrey Parker noted in his study of the Dutch rebellion against the taxing and religious policies of the Spanish king that there was "violent opposition" to his policies because "so many heretics came to Antwerp to trade that its prosperity would be ruined if a resident inquisition were introduced" (*The Dutch Revolt* [New York: Viking Penguin, 1988], p. 47).

Despite all of the language of "market takeovers" and "price wars," the market is a forum for voluntary persuasion, as Adam Smith emphasized in his *Lectures on Jurisprudence* when discussing the price system: "If we should enquire into the principle in the human mind on which this disposition of trucking [i.e., of trading] is founded, it is clearly on the natural inclination every one has to persuade. The offering of a shilling, which to us appears to have so plain and simple a meaning, is in reality offering an argument to persuade one to do so and so as it is for his interest" (Adam Smith, *Lectures on Jurisprudence* [Indianapolis: Liberty Classics, 1982], p. 352).

It is often argued that markets are fine for many or even most purposes, but that they systematically fail and must be supplemented or overridden by coercive state power. This "market failure" approach argues that the state must either intervene to change the conditions of trade for the production and exchange of certain goods and services (usually referred to, somewhat misleadingly, as "regulation"; on the changing meaning of "regulate," see Randy E. Barnett, "The Original Meaning of the Commerce Clause," *University of Chicago Law Review* 68 [2001]) or produce the goods and services itself (usually referred to as the production of "public goods").

A useful application of the insights gained from the socialist calculation debate to government's regulatory interventions into a fundamentally market economy is found in Israel M. Kirzner's essay "The Perils of Regulation," in his book *Discovery and the Capitalist Process* (Chicago: University of Chicago Press, 1985), which argues that coercive regulation by the state short-circuits the market's discovery processes. There is, in addition, an enormous volume of published empirical research on the issue of "government failure" and the harmful consequences for consumers of the edicts of governmental regulatory agencies. (A visit to the library to inspect such journals as the *Journal of Political Economy, The Journal of Law & Economics, The American Economic Review, The Cato Journal, Public Choice, Regulation,* or any number of others would give the reader a taste of the literature available.) Some of the main themes derived from that vast array of studies of government failure and the free market alternative are presented in a popular style in *Free to Choose* (New York: Harcourt Brace Jovanovich, 1980) by Milton and Rose Friedman, especially the chapters "Who Protects the Consumer?" and "Who Protects the Worker?," and in *Government Failure: A Primer in Public Choice* (Washington, D.C.: Cato Institute, 2002) by Gordon Tullock, Arthur Seldon, and Gordon L. Brady.

The issue of public goods, which plays so large a role in the justification of governmental coercion, has also generated a substantial literature, both critical of the state's ability to produce authentically "public" goods and revealing of how voluntary organization succeeds in producing public goods. In general, public goods are defined by references to two characteristics: Once a public good is produced, it may be costly to exclude noncontributors from its enjoyment (exclusion costs); and the consumption of the good by one person does not diminish the consumption of the good by another (nonrivalrous consumption). The standard example of a public good that could not be produced on the market was for many years the lighthouse, which throws out its light beam to be seen by all, whether they have paid or not (one cannot exclude the nonpayers from seeing it), and sighting the beam does not necessarily mean that there is "less" of a beam for another to see (nonrivalrous consumption). This paradigm case was examined by Nobel laureate in economics Ronald Coase in a classic essay, "The Lighthouse in Economics" (*The Journal of Law & Economics* 17, no. 2 [October 1974]; reprinted in R. H. Coase, *The Firm, the Market, and the Law* [Chicago: University of Chicago Press, 1988]), which examined the actual history of how lighthouses were produced in England and concluded that "economists should not use the lighthouse as an example of a service which could only be provided by the government." (The issue has generated some controversy, since British lighthouse owners were granted the right to collect fees from ships docking in ports for having benefited from the lighthouse service.) Many similar examples, along with classic essays on the topic (including Paul Samuelson's seminal case for state provisions of public goods), are collected by Tyler Cowen in *Public Goods and Market Failures: A Critical Examination* (New Brunswick, N.J.: Transaction, 1992).

Two other especially good treatments of the issue of public goods, tying in the economic aspects with ethical questions about fairness and justice, are Anthony de Jasay, *Social Contract, Free Ride: A Study of the Public Goods Problem* (Oxford: Oxford University Press, 1989), and David Schmidtz, *The Limits of Government: An Essay on the Public Goods Argument* (Boulder, Colo.: Westview, 1991).

One subclass of the public goods argument concerns the environment. "Environmental economics" has become especially relevant in recent years, as many policy debates have emerged regarding the proper role of government in this area. Ronald Coase, again, set much of the research agenda in this area with his essay "The Problem of Social Cost" (*The Journal of Law & Economics* 3 [October 1960]; reprinted in *The Firm, the Market, and the Law*), in which he showed that the problem of "externalities" (smoke is normally considered a "negative externality," because it harms people who were not part of the decision to produce the smoke) could be understood in terms of a lack of property rights; most externality problems arise from government's failure to define clearly or to protect property rights. A very readable primer on the economics of the environment, using a property rights approach, is *Free Market Environmentalism* (New York: Palgrave Macmillan, 2001) by Terry L. Anderson and Donald R. Leal. Many economic and ethical perspectives on environmental issues, including libertarian approaches, are gathered in David Schmidtz and Elizabeth Willott, eds., *Environmental Ethics: What Really Matters, What Really Works* (2nd ed.; Oxford: Oxford University Press, 2011). A helpful application of free market environmental approaches to a particular issue is Terry L. Anderson, Brandon Scarborough, and Lawrence R. Watson, *Tapping Water Markets* (New York: Routledge & Resources for the Future, 2012).

An important objection that has been raised against markets is that they fail to generate a proper "distribution" of income: Markets are unfair, or generate politically unstable distributions of wealth, or are responsible for "the rich getting richer, and the poor getting poorer." There are many issues tied up in those claims, but two good libertarian analyses of the ethics of redistributionism, employing economic reasoning but abstracting from the practical issues of incentives to produce when the fruits of one's labor are taken away, are the French political scientist Bertrand de Jouvenel's brilliant essay *The Ethics of Redistribution* (1951; Indianapolis: Liberty Press, 1990) (excerpted in this reader) and the German economist Ludwig Lachmann's essay "The Market Economy and the Distribution of Wealth" (in Ludwig Lachmann, *Capital, Expectations, and the Market Process*, Walter E. Grinder, ed. [Kansas City: Sheed Andrews and McMeel, 1977]) in which Lachmann distinguishes between "ownership" (or property), which is a legal concept, and "wealth," which is an economic concept. Wealth can change dramatically without any changes in ownership, as the value of one's property goes up and down due to the valuation of it by others and their estimation of how it will fit into their production plans. Thus, as Lachmann shows, "The market process is . . . a leveling process. In a market economy a process of redistribution of wealth is taking place all the time before which those outwardly similar processes which modern politicians are in the habit of instituting, pale into comparative insignificance." (Lachmann's essay is also reprinted in Tom G. Palmer, ed., *The Morality of Capitalism* [Ottawa, Ill.: Jameson, 2011].)

Of course, attempts to alter the ever-changing pattern of wealth holdings by force, through taxation and other forms of coercive redistribution of property, can generate most unwelcome consequences, as the contemporary experience with the welfare state shows. A careful empirical study of the effects of redistribution on the poor in America was undertaken by the social scientist Charles Murray and published as his pathbreaking *Losing Ground: American Social Policy, 1950–1980* (New York: Basic Books, 1984), which pointed out the growth of dependency and the breakdown of family life and civil society brought about by the welfare state. Not only does the welfare state undercut institutions such as the family, but it also systematically displaces the many other institutions of civil society by which the poor are assisted and solidarity is fostered. The long-neglected history of "mutual aid" has recently received renewed attention, thanks partly to the careful historical research of the British historian and political scientist David Green, especially in his study of the voluntary provision of medical care in Britain, *Working Class Patients and the Medical Establishment: Self-Help in Britain from the Mid-Nineteenth Century to 1948* (New York: St. Martin's 1985), which shows how the libertarian working people's organizations of earlier years fought against socialized medicine; and in his more recent study *Reinventing Civil Society: The Rediscovery of Welfare Without Politics* (London: Institute of Economic Affairs, 1993). The American scene has been studied by the historian David T. Beito, notably in *From Mutual Aid to the Welfare State: Fraternal Societies and Social Services, 1890–1967* (Chapel Hill: University of North Carolina Press, 2000), and by Richard C. Cornuelle, in *Reclaiming the American Dream: The Role of Private Individuals and Voluntary Associations* (New Brunswick, N.J.: Transaction, 1993). As Cornuelle and others have pointed out, the free society is a society characterized by voluntary relations, of which market exchanges are only one category. A wide range of organizations are possible, and common under freedom, including charities, self-help associations (such as Alcoholics Anonymous, an organization of recovering alcoholics who help each other to overcome their weaknesses), religious institutions, and much more. Just as socialism displaces profit-making firms from producing goods, so welfare statism displaces mutual aid organizations, families, and religious and fraternal organizations from producing solidarity, upward social mobility, and care for the least fortunate. A number of essays on this topic, including two by Beito and Green, are reprinted in *After the Welfare State* (Ottawa, Ill.: Jameson, 2012); in addition to editing the book, I contributed several essays on the political economy and history of the welfare state and an extended treatment of classical liberal approaches to poverty, the latter of which originally appeared in *Poverty and Morality* (Cambridge: Cambridge University Press, 2010), edited by William A. Galston and Peter H. Hoffenberg.

An especially important application of the understanding of markets is the maintenance of harmony and concord among people of different races, religious creeds, and nations. As markets are forums for persuasion, so they are opportunities for peaceful cooperation. A good introduction to the economic analysis of racial relations is the work of the economist and historian Thomas Sowell, *Markets and Minorities* (New York: Basic Books, 1982). The deleterious effects on minorities of state intervention in the market are examined in Walter Williams, *Race and Economics: How Much Can Be Blamed on Discrimination?* (Stanford: Hoover Institution Press, 2011). The history of "Jim Crow" laws, which forcibly separated African Americans and whites and relegated African Americans to "the back of the bus," is set forth by economic historian Jennifer Roback in a number of studies, including "Southern Labor Law in the Jim Crow Era: Exploitative or Competitive?," *University of Chicago Law Review* 51 (Fall 1984), and "The Political Economy of Segregation: The Case of Segregated Streetcars," *The Journal of Economic History* 46 (December 1986). Law professor David Bernstein, in "Roots of the 'Underclass': The Decline of Laissez Faire Jurisprudence and the Rise of Racist Labor Legislation," *American University Law Review* 43 (Fall 1993), and "Licensing Laws: A Historical Example of the Use of Government

Regulatory Power Against African-Americans," *San Diego Law Review* 31 (Winter 1994), has examined racially neutral regulations that had the effect and generally the purpose of restricting economic opportunity for African Americans.

Finally, it should be noted that although markets are not "perfect," neither is any other form of human interaction. Those who identify "market failure" by comparing the outcome of market interactions with some ideal outcome should do the same with government. Rather than simply comparing imperfect markets with perfect government, which is the typical approach of critics of the market, one should compare imperfect markets with imperfect government. In his witty book *Capitalism* (Oxford: Basil Blackwell, 1990), Arthur Seldon turns the tables on anti-libertarians and compares imperfect governments with perfect markets, a clever move to show how unreasonable many proposals for substituting government coercion for market persuasion really are.

VI. JUSTICE AND POLITICAL ORGANIZATION

It was claimed above that a belief in imprescriptible individual rights is a hallmark of libertarianism. Rights necessarily entail obligations on others. It is therefore a hallmark of libertarianism to maintain that all humans are under certain obligations. But what are those obligations? In general, we can say that the obligations are of a "negative" kind, that is, that one abstain from action harmful to the rights of others. Such obligations are universal, in the sense that they are binding on all moral agents, and "compossible," in the sense that they are all simultaneously possible of realization.

Of course, there are "positive" obligations, as well, such as the obligation to pay a dollar for the cup of coffee I drank this morning. That obligation is a particular one: I (and no one else) must pay the owner of the café (and no one else) an agreed-upon amount for the cup of coffee. John Locke and others in the libertarian tradition have insisted that all such particular obligations have to be based on consent. In contrast, nationalists, socialists, racists, and other sorts of collectivists typically insist that one has a multitude of particular obligations to which one did *not* consent, but to which one was born, as a member of a particular nation, class, or race. (Some of the better articulated of these ideas are discussed in the last section, under the rubric of "communitarian" critics of libertarianism.)

Contract was a central element of Roman law, as the great Roman jurist Gaius noted in his famous *Institutes*: "We turn now to obligations. They divide first into two: all obligations arise from a contract or from a delict" (a delict is a violation of law or offense to another). The argument that government should be based on the principles of contract, which played so important a role in the American founding (see the Declaration of Independence, reprinted in this reader), has a long history. The noted historian

Quentin Skinner has stated, in his *Foundations of Modern Political Thought: Volume 2, The Age of Reformation* (Cambridge: Cambridge University Press, 1978), "The idea that any legitimate polity must originate in an act of consent was of course a scholastic commonplace, one which the followers of Ockham no less than Aquinas had always emphasized" (p. 163). A typical example of the importance of consent, and of the retained right of the people to "alter or abolish" (in Thomas Jefferson's phrase) government when it overstepped its legitimate bounds, was found in the ancient coronation ceremony of the kings of Aragón, in which the peers declared: "We who are as good as you, make you our king, on condition that you keep and observe our privileges and liberties; and if not, not."

That principle was carefully enunciated by the brilliant Whig writer Algernon Sidney, who was executed by the English king's forces (and was therefore referred to by Jefferson as "the Martyr Sidney"), when he identified himself in his *Discourses Concerning Government* (1698; Thomas G. West, ed., Indianapolis: Liberty Classics, 1990) as, "I, who deny any power to be just that is not founded upon consent." John Locke insisted in his *Second Treatise of Government* that "no Government can have a right to obedience from a people who have not freely consented to it."

Rights play an important role in arguments about the legitimacy of government, for, as Thomas Jefferson insisted in the Declaration of Independence, some of our rights are *inalienable*. Even if we were to want to give those rights away to another person, we could not do so; it would be a violation of our very nature. "Voluntary slavery" is impossible, much as a spherical cube or a living corpse is impossible. Thus, a tyrannical government that attempted to destroy us or to take away all of our liberties would be ipso facto illegitimate; there are limits to the legitimate power of government, even when it has been constituted through initial acts of consent. The standard or canonical libertarian account of the origins and limitations of legitimate government remains John Locke's *Second Treatise of Government*, especially the chapters "Of the Beginning of Political Societies" and "Of the Dissolution of Government." The argument that one has nonconsensual particular obligations to particular political organizations is subjected to withering criticisms by A. John Simmons in *Moral Principles and Political Obligations* (Princeton: Princeton University Press, 1979) and in his later updating of Locke's philosophy of government, *On the Edge of Anarchy: Locke, Consent, and the Limits of Society* (Princeton: Princeton University Press, 1993).

Various attempts have been made to reconcile government—or institutions to protect individual rights—with consent, that is, to establish the legitimacy of government. It is certainly clear that most governments (or states, to use the more precise term) around the world did not originate in acts of consent on the part of the populations over which they rule. (Dictatorships, absolute monarchies, and the like are obvious examples.) To that extent, libertarians would certainly reject these governments' claims to exercise legitimate authority. Indeed, Lysander Spooner (in his essay in this reader) and other radical libertarians argued that all existing states were illegitimate, and that no one is bound to obey them, except in so far as their command coincides with one's natural and universally valid obligations to respect the rights of others.

Some libertarians have argued that business firms competing in free markets can provide defense from aggression more efficiently than monopoly states, and without violating fundamental rights in the process. There is evidence to support the claim, as there are far more private law enforcement agents (security guards, bail bondsmen, bounty hunters, and so on) in America than there are governmentally employed police; and rights violations by private security guards, while greater than zero, are a tiny fraction of rights violations by members of the police and other state enforcement agencies. For how nonstate actors enforce law, see John A. Chamberlin, "Bounty Hunters: Can the Criminal Justice System Live Without Them?," *University of Illinois Law Review* 1998, no. 4, pp. 1175–1205; as Chamberlin points out, "Approximately 35,000 defendants jump bail annually, and an astonishing 87% are brought back to justice by bounty hunters." The only study I have found of killings by police in the United States stated, "Police justifiably kill on average nearly 400 felons each year." The definitions underlying the study's methods were noteworthy: "In this report, killings by police are referred to as 'justifiable homicides' and the persons that police kill are referred to as 'felons.' These terms reflect the view of the police agencies that provide the data used in this report." Report of the Bureau of Justice Statistics of the Office of Justice Programs of the U.S. Department of Justice, "Policing and Homicide, 1976–98: Justifiable Homicide by Police, Police Officers Murdered by Felons" (Jodi M. Brown and Patrick A. Langan, March 2001, NCJ 180987). Libertarian journalist Radley Balko has argued that out-of-control police present an ever greater threat to life and liberty in America in *Rise of the Warrior Cop: The Militarization of America's Police Forces* (New York: PublicAffairs, 2013).

Murray N. Rothbard argued in *For a New Liberty: The Libertarian Manifesto* (2nd ed.; New York: Macmillan, 1978) that the state was not needed to provide law and order. (The claim that the state is incompatible with rights inspired Robert Nozick to defend strictly limited monopoly government in his *Anarchy, State, and Utopia* [New York: Basic Books, 1974], in which Nozick offered an ingenious argument for limited government that would not violate rights.) Rothbard's argument, that protection from aggression can be considered a service to be provided on the market, has also been defended by law professor (and former prosecutor) Randy E. Barnett in a two-part essay, "Pursuing Justice in a Free Society: Part One—Power vs.

Liberty; Part Two—Crime Prevention and the Legal Order" (*Criminal Justice Ethics*, Summer/Fall 1985, Winter/Spring 1986). The economist Bruce Benson presents a useful history and economic analysis of voluntary provision of law in *The Enterprise of Law: Justice Without the State* (Oakland, Calif.: Independent Institute, 2011). (Such approaches typically rest on the claim that restitution, or making the victim whole again, is preferable to punishment or harming the perpetrator without making the victim whole again, and that the incentive to obtain restitution can drive a more efficient and humane legal system. Two scholarly and fascinating studies of how a stateless society with a restitution-based legal system functioned are found in William Ian Miller's *Bloodtaking and Peacemaking: Feud, Law, and Society in Saga Iceland* [Chicago: University of Chicago Press, 1990] and Jesse Byock's *Viking Age Iceland* [New York: Penguin, 2001]. The conditions of medieval Iceland were rather different than today, but the stateless social order they created was more peaceful and orderly than those of comparable state-governed societies.)

Harvard psychologist Steven Pinker has argued in *The Better Angels of Our Nature: Why Violence Has Declined* (New York: Viking, 2011) that the rise of the state and its monopolization (or attempted monopolization) of the legitimate use of force was a major factor in the decline of the human experience of violence. (Pinker also argues that property rights, freedom of trade, and other institutions contributed to the further decline of violence. The book is a very rich and stimulating source of insight about violence—what causes it and what reduces it.)

The model that Rothbard advocated is easily misunderstood, as it sometimes seems from his writings that law and justice are merely commodities to be purchased like hamburgers or lawn fertilizer on a free market. But since law and justice are what define markets, it seems rather odd, if not contradictory, to see them as goods to be sold on markets. That misunderstanding can be corrected by examining contractual models of government, in which one does not "buy" particular commodities, but agrees to sets of rules that are subsequently binding on one. Especially illuminating are those accounts that take as their starting point actually existing contractual governments, such as neighborhood associations, condominium associations, and "proprietary communities." Economists Donald J. Boudreaux and Randall G. Holcombe provide a model of the contractual provision of public goods, including arbitration and security, in their essay "Government by Contract" (*Public Finance Quarterly* 17, no. 3 [July 1989]); and Fred Foldvary expands greatly on this approach in his outstanding work *Public Goods and Private Communities: The Market Provision of Social Services* (Aldershot, U.K.: Edward Elgar, 1994).

Other libertarians, citing the difficulties of obtaining the unanimity of consent that would be necessary to generate such legitimacy, have established unanimity as an ideal toward which one might aspire, even if it is never to be realized. Especially influential examples of this approach from the field of "public choice" or "constitutional economics" can be found in the work of James Buchanan and Gordon Tullock, notably *The Calculus of Consent* (Ann Arbor: University of Michigan, 1962), and in Buchanan's *The Limits of Liberty: Between Anarchy and Leviathan* (Chicago: University of Chicago Press, 1975). (A similar "second-best" approach to the legitimacy of government is found in Richard A. Epstein's *Simple Rules for a Complex World* [Cambridge: Harvard University Press, 1995].) A more recent libertarian work that brings careful examination of incentives and consequences to public policy is Mark Pennington's *Robust Political Economy: Classical Liberalism and the Future of Public Policy* (Northampton, Mass.: Edward Elgar, 2011). Pennington, a professor of public policy and political economy at King's College, University of London, defines "a robust set of institutions" as "one that generates beneficial results even under the least favourable conditions." It is a modern updating of the insight of James Madison, primary author of the United States Constitution, who argued in Federalist No. 10 that "It is in vain to say that enlightened statesmen will be able to adjust these clashing interests, and render them all subservient to the public good. Enlightened statesmen will not always be at the helm."

VII. VIOLENCE AND THE STATE

If it is the case that most states around the world are illegitimate, how did they come to have the unjust powers that they effectively claim? The historical answer is fairly clear, as Thomas Paine noted in *Common Sense* in dismissing the claims to legitimacy of the English monarchy: "No man in his senses can say that their claim under William the Conqueror is a very honourable one. A French bastard landing with an armed banditti, and establishing himself king of England against the consent of the natives, is in plain terms a very paltry rascally original.—It certainly hath no divinity in it." States originate in conquest and flourish through war.

If we consider the issue of the origins of states from the perspective of the different means to the accumulation of wealth (by no means the only way to consider the issue, but certainly a fruitful one), we may turn to a useful treatise by the German sociologist Franz Oppenheimer, *The State* (1914; New York: Free Life Editions, 1975). Oppenheimer noted that "there are two fundamentally opposed means whereby man, requiring sustenance, is impelled to obtain the necessary means for satisfying his desires. These are work and robbery, one's own labor and the forcible appropriation of the labor of others." The former he termed "the economic means" and the latter "the political means." "The state," he wrote, "is an organization of the political means." (The thesis that states originated in acts of conquest was woven through the history of civilization by Alexander Rüstow in his *Freedom and Domination:*

A Historical Critique of Civilization [Princeton: Princeton University Press, 1980], discussed earlier.)

The thesis that "war makes the state, and states make war" has been advanced by Charles Tilly (notably in his essay "War Making and State Making as Organized Crime," in Peter B. Evans, Dietrich Rueschemeyer, and Theda Skocpol, eds., *Bringing the State Back In* [Cambridge: Cambridge University Press, 1985], and in his book *Coercion, Capital, and European States, AD 990–1992* [Oxford: Blackwell, 1992]) and presented in a more accessible form by political scientist Bruce D. Porter in his *War and the Rise of the State: The Military Foundations of Modern Politics* (New York: Free Press, 1994). (Another careful study of this theme by a distinguished historian is Otto Hintze, "Military Organization and the Organization of the State," in Felix Gilbert, ed., *The Historical Essays of Otto Hintze* [Oxford: Oxford University Press, 1975].) A horrifying tabulation of how many people have been killed by states in this century is presented by political scientist R. J. Rummel in *Death by Government* (New Brunswick, N.J.: Transaction, 1994). He tabulates 169,202,000 human beings systematically killed by governments, between 1900 and 1987, "including genocide, politicide, and mass murder," but excluding "war dead." (p. 4) Libertarians typically ask how one can expect an institution with such a bloody and savage record to accomplish all the wondrous and humanitarian ends assigned to it by collectivists. That is no refutation of the collectivist arguments, of course, but it should at least raise questions about the appropriateness of the means chosen to the attainment of the ends. That the association of the state with war is not limited to the distant historical past is made evident by the experience of the twentieth century, when state power has grown by leaps and bounds through war. A good historical study of the growth of the American state and its association with war is found in the economic historian Robert Higgs's *Crisis and Leviathan: Critical Episodes in the Growth of American Government* (Oxford: Oxford University Press, 1987) and his *Depression, War, and Cold War: Challenging the Myths of Conflict and Prosperity* (Oakland, Calif.: Independent Institute, 2009).

It is frequently assumed that the emergence of militarily organized territorial monopolies over violence (that is, states), extending their powers through conquest, is the only conceivable or even normal form of political organization. Counterexamples are presented by Hendrik Spruyt in *The Sovereign State and Its Competitors* (Princeton: Princeton University Press, 1994), which examines other forms of political organization, often of a far more voluntary nature, such as the Hanseatic League of German merchants, and forms of nonterritorial organizations, such as the Roman Church and the Holy Roman Empire. (An eye-opening comparison of state-governed and stateless peoples is found in James C. Scott, *The Art of Not Being Governed* [New Haven: Yale University Press, 2010]; mountain people, who are often studied as examples of "prehistoric man," are in fact not prehistoric, but are refugees from the taxes, genocide, slave raids, conscription, religious repression, and social controls imposed by predatory states. Scott's work helps us to understand state formation and its impact on societies.)

Institutions that have seized and legitimized territorial monopolies have an advantage in their ability to "socialize" costs, that is, to spread costs over a "captive" population. By imposing relatively small costs on large numbers of people, wealth can be accumulated and delivered to relatively small numbers of people. That process is sometimes referred to in the technical economics literature as "rent-seeking," and it is made possible by the different "transaction costs" faced by large and small groups. As Milton Friedman has observed, in every country where farmers form a large majority of the population, they are brutally oppressed and squeezed for the benefit of the much smaller urban population. But wherever farmers are in the minority, they manage to squeeze enormous sums of money from the much larger urban population, through governmentally guaranteed high prices, government purchase of surpluses at above-market rates, acreage allotments, payments not to farm, and on and on. That seems a paradox, at least in democracies. But it is easily understood when we realize that the costs of becoming informed and of organizing (identifying one another as having common interests, coming together, agreeing on ends, and so forth) can be very high for large groups, but disproportionately smaller for smaller groups. As the sociologist Gaetano Mosca noted in his classic study of group conflict:

> The dominion of an organized minority, obeying a single impulse, over the unorganized majority, is inevitable. The power of any minority is irresistible as against each single individual in the majority, who stands alone before the totality of the organized minority. At the same time, the minority is organized for the very reason that it is a minority. A hundred men acting in concert, with a common understanding, will triumph over a thousand men who are not in accord and can therefore be dealt with one by one. Meanwhile it will be easier for the former to act in concert and have a mutual understanding simply because they are a hundred and not a thousand. It follows that the larger the political community, the smaller will the proportion of the governing minority to the governed majority be, and the more difficult it will be for the majority to organize for reaction against the minority (Gaetano Mosca, *The Ruling Class* [1896; New York: McGraw-Hill, 1939], p. 53).

The study of wealth transfers of that kind was of great interest to the members of the Italian school in fiscal theory, who raised the topic to the status of a science. Noteworthy among them were the social scientist

Vilfredo Pareto (see Vilfredo Pareto, *Sociological Writings*, S. E. Finer, ed. [Totowa, N.J.: Rowman & Littlefield, 1976], especially pp. 114–20, 137–42, 162–64, 270, 276–78, 315, and 317–18 on what he termed "spoliation"). Pareto and his colleagues revealed the phenomenon of "rational ignorance" and its role in perpetuating the tyranny of special interests. As Pareto noted, "Very many economic matters are so complicated that few people have even a superficial understanding of them. Amongst the people who use sugar there is not one in a thousand who is aware of the appropriation of wealth that goes on under the system of production-subsidies." Pareto explained how the state can disperse costs over large groups and concentrate benefits among small groups through a simple story:

> Let us suppose that in a country of thirty million inhabitants it is proposed, under some pretext or other, to get each citizen to pay out one franc, and to distribute the total amount amongst thirty persons. Every one of the donors will give up one franc a year; every one of the beneficiaries will receive one million francs a year. The two groups will differ very greatly in their response to the situation. Those who hope to gain a million a year will know no rest by day or night. They will win newspapers over to their interest by financial inducements and drum up support from all quarters. A discreet hand will warm the palm of needy legislators, even of ministers [of government]. . . . In contrast, the individual who is threatened with losing one franc a year—even if he is fully aware of what is afoot—will not for so small a thing forgo a picnic in the country, or fall out with useful or congenial friends, or get on the wrong side of the mayor or the *prefet*! In these circumstances the outcome is not in doubt: the spoliators will win hands down.

Other pioneers of the scientific study of government policy include Giovanni Montemartini (see "The Fundamental Principles of a Pure Theory of Public Finance," in *Classics in the Theory of Public Finance*, Richard A. Musgrave and Alan T. Peacock, eds. [3rd ed.; New York: St. Martin's, 1994]), Amilcare Puviani, Maffeo Pantaleoni, and the first president of the postwar Italian Republic, Luigi Einaudi. Nobel laureate in economics James Buchanan offers a study of the roots of public choice economics in the Italian school in his essay "'La Scienze delle Finanze': The Italian Tradition in Fiscal Theory," in James Buchanan, *Fiscal Theory and Political Economy* (Chapel Hill: University of North Carolina Press, 1960).

Since in complex societies that have progressed beyond simple lord/peasant arrangements of social differentiation virtually every person is a member of some economic or social minority, each person faces a similar incentive to try to extract wealth from the many through special favors and subsidies. Thus, as Frédéric Bastiat observed, in modern times, "The state is the great fictitious entity by which everyone seeks to live at the expense of everyone else" ("The State," in Frédéric Bastiat, *Selected Essays on Political Economy* [Irvington-on-Hudson, N.Y.: Foundation for Economic Education, 1968]). The coercive extraction of wealth is often referred to (rather unfortunately) in the economics literature as "rent-seeking," a term, according to James Buchanan, "designed to describe behavior in institutional settings where individual efforts to maximize value generate social waste rather than social surplus." The study of the system of what Bastiat called "reciprocal plunder" and technical economists refer to as the "rent-seeking society" has generated a massive literature, which would be impossible to survey here. A good place to start, however, would be James M. Buchanan, Robert D. Tollison, and Gordon Tullock, eds., *Toward a Theory of the Rent-Seeking Society* (College Station: Texas A&M University Press, 1980).

What libertarians conclude from historical study and from economic and sociological analysis of the activity of the state is that, if the state cannot be replaced by other—voluntary—forms of organization, it must certainly be carefully limited. Even if necessary, the state remains what Thomas Paine termed in *Common Sense* "a necessary evil," one that must always be watched over and guarded against. In the 1798 Kentucky Resolutions protesting the Alien and Sedition Acts, Thomas Jefferson maintained that "free government is founded in jealousy, not in confidence; it is jealousy and not confidence which prescribes limited constitutions, to bind down those whom we are obliged to trust with power." Domestically, the state must be restrained by the constitution and a vigilant population, and in foreign relations it must be held back from opportunities for conflict with foreign states. In his Farewell Address, George Washington counseled, "the great rule of conduct for us, in regard to foreign Nations is in extending our commercial relations to have with them as little *political* connection as possible." It is principally for that reason—the maintenance of peace and international harmony—that libertarians have favored freedom of trade, for in engaging in trade, ties of amity and interest are established, and occasions for war avoided. (That theme is explored extensively in *Peace, Love, and Liberty* [Ottawa, Ill.: Jameson, 2014], which I have edited and to which I contributed several chapters.) As Washington maintained in the Farewell Address, "Harmony, liberal intercourse with all nations, are recommended by policy, humanity and interest." (A good collection of Washington's writings is W. B. Allen, ed., *George Washington: A Collection* [Indianapolis: Liberty Classics, 1988]. Most of Jefferson's essential writings can be found in Merrill D. Peterson, ed., *The Portable Jefferson* [New York: Viking, 1975].)

A modern restatement of a libertarian case for limiting government through the Constitution is provided by Randy E. Barnett in his original and stimulating work *Restoring the Lost Constitution: The Presumption of Liberty* (Princeton: Princeton University Press, 2004).

VIII. CRITICS OF LIBERTARIANISM

As long as people have yearned for a society of free and equal individuals, in which relations between people are determined by consent, rather than by coercion, there have been critics who have argued that such a system would be unworkable, chaotic, or immoral, that individuals would be alienated and deracinated, or that voluntary cooperation on a large scale is impossible because the interests of individuals are inherently conflicting and can only result in violence.

Perhaps the earliest, and probably the most influential and brilliantly presented, of such criticism is to be found in *The Republic*, the dialogue written by the Greek philosopher Plato. Many of the ideas of the so-called Sophists (now largely a term of abuse, thanks to the brilliant polemics of Plato, their relentless critic) can be identified as proto-libertarian, and as defenses of the emerging liberty, commerce, and toleration (relative to its predecessors and neighbors) of the Greek world. In Book II of *The Republic*, Adeimantus and Socrates discuss the emergence of markets, voluntary coordination, and what we would call civil society, and Adeimantus concludes that justice lies in "some need . . . men have of one another" (372a), a view that foreshadows David Hume and the thinkers of the Scottish Enlightenment. That line of thought is interrupted by Glaucon, who describes such a city as "a city of sows" (372d). Plato then has Socrates assert that the desire for luxury among such men will lead to conflict with their neighbors, for "the land, of course, which was sufficient for feeding the men who were then, will now be small although it was sufficient. . . . Then we must cut off a piece of our neighbors' land, if we are going to have sufficient for pasture and tillage, and they in turn from ours, if they let themselves go to the unlimited acquisition of money overstepping the boundaries of the necessary . . . [and] after that won't we go to war as a consequence, Glaucon?" (372d–e). And with war will come the state, and the end of the voluntary society.

That argument alleging an ultimate irreconcilability of human ends and aspirations also plays a role in the thinking of many critics of libertarianism—notably among collectivist racial and national ideologies, according to which the interests of different races or nations are in irreconcilable conflict—and has proven a formidable opponent to libertarian views. One of the most brilliant critics of libertarianism was the German legal theorist Carl Schmitt, who in *The Concept of the Political* (1932; Chicago: University of Chicago Press, 2007), posited that "the specific political distinction . . . can be reduced to that between friend and enemy." Schmitt's influence has grown on both the anti-libertarian "right" and the anti-libertarian "left." Libertarians have argued against the thesis that conflict is definitive of human society for centuries. The economist Jean-Baptiste Say argued in 1803 in his *Treatise on Political Economy* that "Nations will be taught to know that they have really no interest in fighting one another; that they are sure to suffer all the calamities incident to defeat, while the advantages of success are altogether illusory." (Say's economic case for peace is examined and carefully explained by Emmanuel Martin, "The Economics of Peace," in Tom G. Palmer, ed., *Peace, Love, and Liberty* [Ottawa, Ill.: Jameson, 2014].)

Ludwig von Mises, drawing on David Ricardo's theory of "comparative advantage," showed the possibility of human cooperation when rules of just conduct are in place in *Human Action: A Treatise on Economics* (New Haven: Yale University Press, 1949, and many subsequent editions). As Mises noted:

> The fundamental facts that brought about cooperation, society, and civilization and transformed the animal man into a human being are the facts that work performed under the division of labor is more productive than isolated work and that man's reason is capable of recognizing this truth. But for these facts men would have forever remained deadly foes of one another, irreconcilable rivals in their endeavors to secure a portion of the scarce supply of means of sustenance provided by nature. Each would have been forced to view all other men as his enemies; his craving for the satisfaction of his own appetites would have brought him into an implacable conflict with all his neighbors. No sympathy could possibly develop under such a state of affairs.

The locus classicus of the claim that libertarianism leads to alienation and atomism is found in the writings of Karl Marx, another enormously influential critic of libertarianism, who argued in his essay "On the Jewish Question" that civil society, as libertarians understand it, is based on a "decomposition of man" such that man's "essence is no longer in community but in difference." Thus, to achieve man's true essence, we must insist not on individual rights, which merely separate one person from another, but instead on the primacy of the political community. (As the anthropologist Ernest Gellner pointed out in his *Conditions of Liberty: Civil Society and Its Rivals* [New York: Viking Penguin, 1994]), the experience of "real socialism" was that it led "not to a newly restored social man, but to something closer to total atomization than perhaps any previous society had known.") There is a great deal of literature that is critical of Marxism, but especially useful for its critique of the philosophy behind it (and not merely of the politics of Marxist states or of the impossibility of economic calculation without money prices) is the British philosopher H. B. Acton's work *The Illusion of the Epoch: Marxism-Leninism as a Philosophical Creed* (1955; London: Routledge & Kegan Paul, 1972). (See also Acton's defense of the morality of market exchanges in *The Morals of Markets and Related Essays*, David Gordon and Jeremy Shearmur, eds. [Indianapolis: Liberty Press, 1993].)

An especially prominent line of criticism of libertarianism—related to that offered by Marx—is that libertarians have fundamentally misunderstood the nature of freedom. This issue was already canvassed by Benjamin Constant in the essay included in this book, but it has been revived by Charles Taylor (whose work is discussed below) and by others who have argued that "real freedom" is a matter of how much "self-control" (over one's passions, for example) one has, or how much one is able to participate in collective decisions, or how much power (or wealth) one has to attain one's ends, or some complex combination of these factors.

A recent defense—offered on the basis of a new stipulation of the meaning of freedom—of redistributive socialism, and of a "right" to be supported through the coerced taxation of others, even if one refuses to work, has been advanced by Philippe Van Parijs in his book *Real Freedom for All: What (If Anything) Can Justify Capitalism?* (Oxford: Oxford University Press, 1995), which argues for the right—as a requirement of "real freedom"—of the deliberately indolent to be supported by money coercively taken from others. Merely "formal freedom" (of the sort defended by libertarians) allegedly consists of "security" and "self-ownership," but "real" freedom adds to the list "opportunity." Thus, two persons may be formally free to swim across a lake, but only the good swimmer is "really" free to do so, and it is this "real" freedom that really matters. A similar line of argument is found in Alan Haworth's *Anti-libertarianism: Markets, Philosophy, and Myth* (London: Routledge, 1994), in which the author claims that what has come to be known as libertarianism is in fact "anti-libertarian," because it does not guarantee the enjoyment of "real" freedom, which evidently requires extensive coercion for its realization.

We can, of course, stipulate that we will use freedom to mean one thing, and not another, or that we will use freedom to mean power, or wealth, or good character, or whatever, but we already have perfectly good words for those things (power, wealth, and good character), and saying that "freedom" will be used to refer to one of those things offers us little help in examining difficult problems of justice. (A useful collection of essays on the nature of freedom, including a variety of views, is found in a volume edited by David Miller, *Liberty* [Oxford: Oxford University Press, 1991]; in the selection from F. A. Hayek's book *The Constitution of Liberty* [Chicago: University of Chicago Press, 1960], Hayek defends the traditional view that liberty refers to freedom from dependence on the arbitrary will of another human.)

A collection of essays critical of libertarianism on the grounds that both freedom *and* equality have been misunderstood by libertarians is Stephen Darwall, ed., *Equal Freedom* (Ann Arbor: University of Michigan Press, 1995). Darwall points out that liberty and equality are sometimes seen as conflicting ideals, but that

> there are senses in which, on anyone's view, liberty and equality are not conflicting but interdependent and mutually reinforcing ideals.

Central to libertarianism, for instance, is the doctrine that all persons have equal moral standing by virtue of holding identical natural rights not to be harmed in their "life, health, liberty, or possessions" (in Locke's phrase). Liberty, in the broad sense of freedom from these harms, is a value *among equals*; it is realized when everyone's rights are respected equally. In advancing an ideal of liberty, therefore, the libertarian simultaneously puts forward an ideal of equality. He interprets both as complementary aspects of a comprehensive conception of justice.

The essays in the book, by distinguished socialist and social democratic philosophers, "can all be read as critiques of libertarianism," that is, as showing that some alternative notion of freedom or equality is superior to the libertarian "complementary" conception. The arguments are varied and ingenious and each deserves its own response, but one general response offered by libertarians is unaddressed: When some have the power to "equalize" the possessions or conditions of all others, those with the power to do so will be elevated in power above the rest, who will no longer be equal to them. Experience shows that those with greater political power typically use their greater political power to extract and secure greater wealth, as well. Equality of freedom, or equality before the law, but also equality of economic condition may be incompatible with the existence of the power to impose equality of condition. That problem was eloquently stated by F. A. Hayek in *The Road to Serfdom* (Chicago: University of Chicago Press, 1944), especially in the chapters "Who, Whom?" and "Why the Worst Get on Top," as well as by George Orwell, in whose 1945 novel *Animal Farm* the principle that "All animals are equal" is transmuted into "All animals are equal, but some animals are more equal than others."

Another particularly ingenious line of criticism of libertarianism has been developed by the Oxford philosopher and Marxist theorist G. A. Cohen and presented in his book *Self-Ownership, Freedom, and Equality* (Cambridge: Cambridge University Press, 1995), which is largely a sustained critique of Robert Nozick. (Much of Cohen's argument is fairly technical and rests on contestable claims about the nature of rationality, bargaining theory, and other matters, so it is really for advanced readers who have already read Nozick.) Cohen's arguments against libertarianism, along with many others, figure prominently in the treatments of libertarianism presented by the political theorist Will Kymlicka in his book *Contemporary Political Philosophy: An Introduction* (Oxford: Oxford University Press, 1990), Chapter 4, and by the socialist political scientist Attracta Ingram, in her book *A Political Theory of Rights* (Oxford: Oxford University Press, 1994).

Cohen seeks to undercut libertarianism by denying that property in one's person ("self-ownership") leads to a system of private property in alienable objects ("world ownership"). (Cohen rejects the idea of property in one's person, as well, but he is willing to assume it for the sake of argument.) In *Self-Ownership, Freedom, and Equality*, Cohen "entertained an alternative to Nozick's 'up for grabs' hypothesis about the external world, to wit, that it is jointly owned by everyone, with each having a veto over its prospective use. And I showed that final equality of condition is assured when the egalitarian hypothesis about ownership of external resources is conjoined with the thesis of self-ownership." In the process, however, Cohen made several errors in bargaining theory (he assumed that there is a uniquely rational bargaining strategy with determinate results) and he confused the various scenarios he describes. Of equal significance, however, is that a situation in which every resource in the world is "jointly owned by everyone, with each having a veto over its prospective use" is not justified by Cohen; it was considered and rejected as implausible several hundred years ago by John Locke, who noted in section 28 of his *Second Treatise of Government*, "If such a consent as that was necessary, Mankind had starved, notwithstanding the Plenty God had given him." The philosopher Jan Narveson responds to some of Cohen's arguments in *The Libertarian Idea* (Philadelphia: Temple University Press, 1988), and I pointed out the failures of his argument in "G. A. Cohen on Self-Ownership, Property, and Equality" (*Critical Review* 12, no. 3 [Summer 1998]; reprinted in my own *Realizing Freedom: Libertarian Theory, History, and Practice* [2nd rev. ed.; Washington, D.C.: Cato Institute, 2014].)

Another set of arguments rejecting the claim that each person has a property in his person can be found in philosopher Richard Arneson's essays "Lockean Self-Ownership: Towards a Demolition" (*Political Studies* 39, no. 1 [1991]), which manages to assert both that "self-ownership is not nearly so determinate as competing conceptions" (a remarkably dubious and unsupported claim) and that "it is obvious that self-ownership conflicts with even the most minimal requirements of humanity" (also unsupported, but evidence that Arneson does not share a libertarian view of the possibility of spontaneous order); and "Property Rights in Persons" (*Social Philosophy and Policy* 9, no. 1 [1992]), in which he "bites the bullet" and argues that "the egalitarian should agree with Nozick that horizontal equity may require forced labor if there is to be redistribution to aid the needy" and that "forced labor can be a morally acceptable state policy." As Arneson notes,

Judged by the criteria of enforcement of self-ownership, welfare-state liberalism and socialism appear to involve the moral equivalent of lord and serf relations. The response of the egalitarian welfarist is that elimination of feudalism is morally progressive, because feudalism's characteristic personal property relations dictate resource transfers from disadvantaged persons to already advantaged persons. The property rights in persons instituted by welfare-state liberalism and socialism, though superficially similar, are different in the morally crucial respect that (when rationally organized) they dictate resource transfers from better-off persons to worse-off persons.

Arneson's honesty is commendable, though he does not indicate what happens when "the property rights in persons instituted by welfare-state liberalism and socialism" are not "rationally organized," nor why we would ever expect such systems of power and violence to be systematically organized in the way he might prefer. (That reflects the regular failure of anti-libertarian thinkers to distinguish between intentions and consequences. That simple distinction is a hallmark of libertarian political economy.)

The distinguished British academic Raymond Plant integrates libertarian thinkers into his treatment of current issues in political philosophy in his *Modern Political Thought* (Oxford: Blackwell, 1991), contrasting libertarian views with conservative and socialist ideologies in an interesting way. Norman P. Barry's *An Introduction to Modern Political Theory* (3rd ed.; London: Macmillan, 1995) also places libertarian views in the context of modern political theory. (Both are more fair in their presentation of libertarian views, as well as of other views with which they may personally disagree, than most other introductory works in political theory.)

A work that is highly polemical in tone and intent, and which challenges the classical libertarian distinction between intentions and consequences, is Albert O. Hirschman's small tome *The Rhetoric of Reaction: Perversity, Futility, Jeopardy* (Cambridge: Harvard University Press, 1991). (Hirschman's work is highly rhetorical itself, and conflates a variety of views—tarring them all with the same brush, so the work is not principally about libertarianism, but about the form of the argument that "good consequences" do not always flow from "good intentions.") Perhaps the best "refutation" of this view is simply to point to the many insights that are gained by considering the unintended consequences of actions. The essay "What Is Seen and What Is Not Seen" by Frédéric Bastiat in this reader is a good response to those who fail to distinguish between intentions and consequences.

The general theme of an alleged conflict between the community and individual liberty has been articulated by the modern "communitarian" critics of liberalism. "Communitarianism" is a term not always embraced by those to whom it is applied, but it is a useful way of grouping together a number of thinkers who, while they may in other respects be considered "leftist" or "rightist," generally reject moral individualism and insist on the primacy of community, which is almost always assumed without further argument to mean the state.

Charles Taylor, a prominent communitarian, has offered especially direct criticisms of libertarianism in his essays "Atomism" and "What's Wrong with Negative Liberty" (both available in his *Philosophy and the Human Sci-*

ences: Philosophical Papers [Cambridge: Cambridge University Press, 1985], pp. 187–210 and 211–29). Among a number of criticisms, Taylor argues that freedom should be understood as a capacity, rather than as a relation to other people, and that a precondition of such a capacity is belonging to a certain kind of society that can foster that capacity, which claim he calls the "social thesis." Thus, "an assertion of the primacy of rights is impossible; for to assert the rights in question is to affirm the capacities, and granted the social thesis is true concerning these capacities, this commits us to an obligation to belong." And the obligation to belong entails the obligation to submit to the taxes, controls, victimless crime laws, prohibitions, and other edicts of the state. The non sequiturs that essay contains are numerous, but perhaps the most notable among them is the claim that submission to political society is necessary for the development of the capacity for choice. He does, however, leave a hole for the informed historical critique of the communitarian enterprise. (History is rarely a strong suit among communitarian critics of libertarianism, who usually substitute a priori musings for actual knowledge of historical events.) As Taylor admits, "Now it is possible that a society and culture propitious for freedom might arise from the spontaneous association of anarchist communes. But it seems much more likely from the historical record that we need rather some species of political society." As medieval historians have pointed out many a time, it was *precisely* among the revolutionary ("anarchist" if you will) communes of Europe (more commonly known today as cities) that liberty and individualism flourished. (The work of Henri Pirenne, *Medieval Cities: Their Origins and the Revival of Trade* [1925; Princeton: Princeton University Press, 1974], cited in Section II above, is a good place to start, but many other works in European history tell the same story.) As the historian Antony Black noted in his *Guilds and Civil Society in European Political Thought from the Twelfth Century to the Present* (Ithaca, N.Y.: Cornell University Press, 1984), "*Commune* was used as a rallying cry by early towns in defense of their liberties" (p. 49), and, "The crucial point about both guilds and communes was that here *individuation and association went hand in hand. One achieved liberty by *belonging* to this kind of group" (p. 65). Liberty did not emerge in the great states and empires founded on conquest, but in the guilds, communes, and other associations founded on freely given consent.

One general theme in the communitarian criticism has been that individuals are "constituted" by their communities, rather than the other way around, and that among the factors that constitute a person are his or her obligations. Thus, rather than particular obligations being a matter of choice, we have—and are constituted as moral agents by—given obligations: obligations to a caste, clan, nation, or state. That view was set forth by the Harvard philosopher Michael Sandel in his *Liberalism and the Limits of Justice* (Cambridge: Cambridge University Press, 1982), which is largely a critique

of two social democratic "liberals," John Rawls and Ronald Dworkin, showing the anti-liberal collectivist foundations of their views and how they are
incompatible with the elements of liberal individualism they espouse. Sandel
also argues that because "shared understandings" are constitutive of what
we are, and because those "comprehend a wider subject than the individual
alone, whether a family or tribe or city or class or nation or people, to this
extent they define a community in a constitutive sense." It is a short jump
to the conclusion that individualism is fundamentally mistaken, and that
"the bounds of the self are no longer fixed, individuated in advance and
given prior to experience." That means that the "self" in question is not a
numerically individuated biological person (Bill, or Mary, or Kareem, or
Gabriela), but the "self" made up of all of them. That argument, which is a
commonplace of collectivist metaphysics, is refuted by the philosopher John
J. Haldane ("Individuals and the Theory of Justice," *Ratio* 27, no. 2 [Decem-
ber 1985]), who argues straightforwardly that "features can only be shared
if they attach to bearers which are at base numerically diverse." The "epistemological" route to collectivism (or wholism) that Sandel takes was already
taken in the thirteenth century (by the Latin Averroists such as Siger of Bra-
bant) and rebutted by Thomas Aquinas, who articulated the case for moral
and metaphysical individualism in his great defense of individualism, *On the
Unity of the Intellect Against the Averroists* (Milwaukee: Marquette University
Press, 1968). Thomas refuted essentially the same argument on behalf of the
proposition that the human race had only one intellect, or one soul. Against
that, Thomas argued that understandings or ideas can be shared by many
people without our having to posit one intellect in which those ideas would
be located, that the notion "is absurd and contrary to human life (for it
would not be necessary to take counsel or make laws)," and therefore that "it
follows that the intellect is united to use in such a way that it and we constitute what is truly one being." (Sandel addressed libertarian ideas directly in
his book *Justice* [New York: Farrar, Straus & Giroux, 2009] and offered one
reason for rejecting libertarianism: that libertarianism could not immediately offer a decisive and definitive answer to a particularly bizarre, revolting,
and singular case that happened to have stumped the entire German legal
system. In another book, *What Money Can't Buy: The Moral Limits of Markets* [New York: Farrar, Straus & Giroux, 2012], Sandel criticizes voluntary
market exchanges as "corrosive" and "degrading" and for "displacing" other
norms, without ever considering whether nonmarket norms—such as racial,
ethnic, religious, or caste discrimination—that are displaced by markets
might be inferior.)

Another communitarian argument has been advanced by the socialist
and nationalist Oxford philosopher David Miller, who has effectively en-
dorsed Hayek's contention that socialism and robust welfare states rest on
a foundation of tribalism and anti-cosmopolitanism. Miller defends the

propagation of national "myths" (akin to Plato's "noble lies") as the grounds for obligations to the socialist or redistributive state, notably in his book *On Nationality* (Oxford: Oxford University Press, 1995). As Miller notes, "The redistributive policies of the kind favoured by socialists are likely to demand a considerable degree of social solidarity if they are to win popular consent, and for that reason socialists should be more strongly committed than classical liberals to the nation-state as an institution that can make such solidarity politically effective." One fairly obvious libertarian response to the nationalist approach is simply to point to the horrors of twentieth-century nationalism and collectivism, but deeper philosophical responses are available, as well, which can offer an account for the bad consequences of nationalism. Notable among them is the book *Nationalism* (4th ed.; Oxford: Blackwell, 1993), by Elie Kedourie, which subjects the philosophy of nationalism to withering criticism. Another critic of nationalistic and socialist thinking was the Austrian economist Ludwig von Mises, who argued in his *Nation, State, and Economy* (1919; New York: New York University Press, 1983) that the existence of different nations and cultures provides an argument for *limiting* the state, rather than imposing nationalist uniformity to achieve socialist or welfare-statist goals: "Whoever wants peace among nations must seek to limit the state and its influence most strictly."

The general "communitarian" theme has been favored by "right-wing" critics of libertarianism, even if they rarely explicate their metaphysical wholism to the degree that "left-wing" communitarian critics often do. (Notably, libertarians typically reject the "left-right" dichotomy as offering, at the least, a nonexhaustive choice, and that is reflected in the criticisms of libertarianism by both self-identified "left" and "right.") The metaphysical foundations of classical liberalism were systematically attacked by the German philosopher Martin Heidegger, whose dense prose has challenged generations of scholars and inspired generations of students to think that they were reading something profound. His entire worldview was collectivist and anti-libertarian, as has been made clear by the publication of his work from the period of the National Socialist dictatorship; for Heidegger *Dasein* did not refer to the existence of any individual being, as some had supposed, but rather to the existence of the German Volk, and *Sein*, or being, referred to the State, which Heidegger considered the being of the German people. (Heidegger's hatred of individualism and classical liberalism is revealed at length in Emmanuel Faye, *Heidegger: The Introduction of Nazism into Philosophy in Light of the Unpublished Seminars of 1933–1935* [New Haven: Yale University Press, 2009].) The anti-libertarian ideas of Martin Heidegger, Carl Schmitt, and others of that era have been resurrected recently in the writings of European "New Right" thinkers, such as the "National Bolshevik" and "Eurasianist" thinker Alexander Dugin of Moscow State University; his book *The Fourth Political Theory* (London: Arktos, 2012) is a thinly disguised restatement of National Socialist doctrines, with the focus on Russia, rather than Germany.

A particularly biting, polemical, and even personal attack on libertarianism was offered by a venerable figure of post–World War II American conservatism, Russell Kirk, in his essay "Libertarians: The Chirping Sectaries," in George W. Carey, ed., *Freedom and Virtue: The Conservative/Libertarian Debate* (Lanham, Md.: University Press of America, 1984), which contains a number of essays on the issues dividing libertarians and conservatives. It has never been entirely clear just what the term "conservatism" means in American politics, so it should be noted that Kirk's essay represents at least one conservative viewpoint that differs from the libertarian viewpoint in virtually every respect, from the significance of the individual to the roots of order to the nature of the state.

Kirk and other conservatives often quote Edmund Burke as an opponent of libertarian ideals, but Burke was in fact more complex, and a less forced reading would see him as advancing a particular version of the classical liberal or libertarian understanding of civil society and individual liberty. That deserves some explanation, for Burke has come to be associated in the public mind almost exclusively with one book, his *Reflections on the Revolution in France*, a book in which can be found many wise libertarian insights, as well as a very few truly absurd statements, the latter of which have come to color the appreciation of the book by later audiences. Among the absurd and even embarrassing statements is his description of the queen of France:

> Surely never lighted on this orb, which she hardly seemed to touch, a more delightful vision. . . . Little did I dream that I should live to see such disasters fallen upon her in a nation of gallant men, in a nation of men of honour and of cavaliers. I thought ten thousand swords must have leaped from their scabbards to avenge even a look that threatened her with insult.—But the age of chivalry is gone.—That of sophisters, oeconomists, and calculators, has succeeded; and the glory of Europe is extinguished for ever.

That rhetorical excess is an embarrassment to Burke's memory. But a few silly passages should not blind us to the brilliance of his critique of the events in France, from the confiscation of the church's property to finance the inherited debts of the state to the replacement of gold and silver by paper money.

Burke had defended the American Revolution, which he distinguished from the French Revolution by the Americans' defense of historically situated rights. The heart of Burke's criticism of the revolution in France is his objection to abstract rights, or rights justified in purely abstract terms, rather than to historically situated rights. In his defense of the Glorious Revolution of 1688 in the *Reflections* Burke wrote that "the Revolution was made to preserve our *antient* indisputable laws and liberties, and that *antient* constitution of government which is our only security for law and liberty." As he pointed out, the greatest English legal scholars "are industrious to prove the pedigree of our liberties." Rights that are merely abstractly formulated (such as the "rights of man") are, in this view, less likely to be stable and to secure liberty than are rights that have a "pedigree," that have emerged over time, enjoy the legitimacy of a tradition, and are understood to be the inheritance of a free people. One may certainly contest that claim, but it is consistent with, and has even proven a great contributor to, the growth of modern libertarianism. (A recent biography that shows Burke as a liberal is Conor Cruise O'Brien's *The Great Melody: A Thematic Biography of Edmund Burke* [Chicago: University of Chicago Press, 1992].)

An influential conservative criticism of the libertarian idea that the state should limit itself to prohibiting well-defined harms to others and should not "legislate morality" is found in James Fitzjames Stephen's *Liberty, Equality, Fraternity* (1873; Indianapolis: Liberty Classics, 1993), which offered a defense of coercion as the foundation of religion and morality. The belief that, absent a coercive power to maintain morality, humans would simply run riot, and that the purpose of state power is to "make men moral," has also been defended by the British jurist Patrick Devlin in *The Enforcement of Morals* (1965; Oxford: Oxford University Press, 1996), although Devlin later retracted his defense of sodomy laws; and by the conservative Princeton philosopher Robert P. George in *Making Men Moral: Civil Liberties and Public Morality* (Oxford: Oxford University Press, 1993). (George has been a very active campaigner against rights for gay people.) Libertarians have called for eliminating "crimes without victims." They have responded to those who wish to use coercion to "make men moral" with a variety of arguments, including arguments based on autonomy (offered by John Stuart Mill; see the selections in this reader), and on the distinction between vices and crimes (see the abolitionist and temperance advocate Lysander Spooner's 1875 essay "Vices Are Not Crimes," in George H. Smith, ed., *The Lysander Spooner Reader* [San Francisco: Fox & Wilkes, 1992]). Further, the many empirical studies of the terrible consequences of attempts to impose morality on society (increases in violent crime due to the perverse incentives of black markets, diversion of scarce police resources from apprehending violent criminals, corruption of the police, and much more) offer strong reasons to oppose imposition of moral norms through force and coercion, rather than cultivating morality through the use of persuasion and example. (Good examples of such studies are Jeffrey A. Miron's *Drug War Crimes: The Consequences of Prohibition* [Oakland, Calif.: Independent Institute, 2004); David W. Rasmussen and Bruce L. Benson's *The Economic Anatomy of a Drug War* [Lanham, Md.: Rowman & Littlefield, 1994]; Ronald Hamowy, ed., *Dealing with Drugs: Consequences of Government Control* [Cambridge, Mass.: Ballinger, 1987]; Richard A. Posner's *Sex and Reason* [Cambridge: Harvard University Press, 1992], in which a distinguished judge and law professor argues, largely on utilitarian grounds, that individual rights and self-ownership should be the rule; and Richard A. Epstein's *Bargaining with the State* [Princeton: Princeton University Press, 1993], which examines the problems that arise from the power of the state selectively to distribute benefits and burdens, mandates and prohibitions.)

CONCLUSION

No short listing or essay can really do justice to the wealth of insights offered by libertarian thinkers. The test is not, however, how much they have written, but how much their ideas help us to understand the world and to guide us as we try to live lives of decency, justice, compassion, and humanity. Judged against that standard, I believe that libertarianism is superior to other theories or organized belief systems. But whether you agree with me is for you to decide.

Tom G. Palmer is the executive vice president for international programs at the Atlas Network and a senior fellow at the Cato Institute, where he directs Cato University.

Sources

In many instances, footnotes have been removed from the readings for reasons of space.

Thomas Paine, "Of the Origin and Design of Government," from *Common Sense,* included in *The Thomas Paine Reader,* Michael Foot and Isaac Kramnick, eds. (1776; Harmondsworth, England: Penguin, 1987), pp. 67–79.

James Madison, "The Federalist No. 10," from *The Federalist* (New York: Random House, Modern Library, 1937), pp. 53–62.

Alexis de Tocqueville, "What Sort of Despotism Democratic Nations Have to Fear," from *Democracy in America,* Volume Two, Henry Reeve, trans. (New Rochelle, N.Y.: Arlington House), pp. 335–40.

John Stuart Mill, "Objections to Government Interference," from *On Liberty and Other Essays* (Oxford: Oxford University Press, 1991), pp. 13–14, 121–23.

H. L. Mencken, "More of the Same," *American Mercury,* February 1925, included in *A Mencken Chrestomathy,* H. L. Mencken, ed. (New York: Vintage Books, 1982), pp. 146–48. Reprinted by permission of Alfred A. Knopf, Inc.

Isabel Paterson, "The Humanitarian with the Guillotine," from *The God of the Machine* (Caldwell, Idaho: Caxton, 1968), pp. 247–63.

Murray N. Rothbard, "The State," from *For a New Liberty* (New York: Collier, 1978), pp. 45–69. Reprinted by permission of the Center for Independent Thought.

Richard A. Epstein, "Self-Interest and the Constitution," reprinted with permission from the *Journal of Legal Education,* Vol. 37, No. 2 (June 1987).

John Locke, "Understanding Can Not Be Compelled," from *A Letter Concerning Toleration* (Buffalo, N.Y.: Prometheus, 1990), pp. 18–65.

Adam Smith, "Justice and Beneficence," from *The Theory of Moral Sentiments* (Indianapolis: Liberty Classics, 1976), pp. 166–67, 203–07, 254–55.

Mary Wollstonecraft, "The Subjugation of Women," from *A Vindication of the Rights of Woman,* Sylvana Tomaselli, ed. (Cambridge: Cambridge University Press, 1995), pp. 69–70, 107–08, 235–41.

Benjamin Constant, "The Liberty of the Ancients Compared With That of the Moderns," from *Benjamin Constant: Political Writings,* Biancamaria Fontana, ed. and trans. (Cambridge: Cambridge University Press, 1988), pp. 309–28. Reprinted with the permission of Cambridge University Press.

Alexis de Tocqueville, "Associations in Civil Life," from *Democracy in America,* Volume Two, Henry Reeve, trans. (New Rochelle, N.Y.: Arlington House), pp. 114–18.

Alexis de Tocqueville, "Interest Rightly Understood," from *Democracy in America,* Volume Two, Henry Reeve, trans. (New Rochelle, N.Y.: Arlington House), pp. 129–32.

William Lloyd Garrison, "Man Cannot Hold Property in Man," from Declaration of Sentiments of the American Anti-Slavery Convention, *Selections from the Writings and Speeches of William Lloyd Garrison* (Boston: Wallcut, 1852), pp. 66–70, excerpted in *Free Government in the Making,* Alpheus Thomas Mason, ed. (New York: Oxford University Press, 1965), pp. 508–10.

Frederick Douglass, "Letter to His Old Master" and "The Nature of Slavery," from *My Bondage and My Freedom* (New York: Arno, 1969), pp. 421–40.

Frederick Douglass, Fourth of July Oration, from *The Frederick Douglass Papers,* Series One, Volume 2 (New Haven: Yale University Press, 1979), pp. 360–86.

William Ellery Channing, "A Human Being Cannot Be Justly Owned," from *Slavery,* included in *Free Government in the Making,* Alpheus

Thomas Mason, ed. (New York: Oxford University Press, 1965), pp. 510–14.

Angelika Grimké, "Rights and Responsibilities of Women," from *Letters to Catherine E. Beecher,* excerpted in *Freedom, Feminism and the State,* Wendy McElroy, ed. (Washington: Cato Institute, 1982), pp. 29–31.

Sarah Grimké, "Woman as a Moral Being," from *Letters on the Equality of the Sexes and the Condition of Women,* excerpted in *Freedom, Feminism, and the State,* Wendy McElroy, ed. (Washington: Cato Institute, 1982), pp. 122–27.

John Stuart Mill, "Of Individuality," from *On Liberty and Other Essays,* John Gray, ed. (Oxford: Oxford University Press, 1991), pp. 21, 63–83, 116–18.

Ludwig von Mises, "On Equality and Inequality," *Modern Age* (Spring 1961). Reprinted by permission of Intercollegiate Studies Institute.

Charles Murray, "The Tendrils of Community," from *In Pursuit: Of Happiness and Good Government* (New York: Simon & Schuster, 1988), pp. 273–78. Reprinted by permission of Charles Murray.

Doug Bandow, "Private Prejudice, Private Remedy," *The Freeman* (July 1996). Reprinted by permission of Foundation for Economic Education.

Richard Overton, "An Arrow Against All Tyrants," from *The Levellers in the English Revolution,* G. E. Aylmer, ed. (Ithaca, N.Y.: Cornell University Press, 1975).

John Locke, "Of Property and Government," from *Second Treatise of Government,* included in *Two Treatises of Government,* Mark Goldie, ed. (London: Everyman, 1995), pp. 128–30, 163–65, 178–89, 216, 222–33, 238–40.

David Hume, "Justice and Property," from *A Treatise of Human Nature,* 2d ed., L. A. Selby-Bigge, ed. (Oxford: Clarendon, 1978), pp. 484–88, 494–98, 514, 526.

Immanuel Kant, "Equality of Rights," from *Kant: Political Writings,* Hans Reiss, ed., H. B. Nisbet, trans. (Cambridge: Cambridge University Press, 1991), pp. 73–85, 137.

Herbert Spencer, "The Right to Ignore the State," from *Social Statics* (New York: Robert Schalkenbach Foundation, 1970), pp. 185–90.

Lysander Spooner, "The Constitution of No Authority," from *No Treason,* Number VI (Colorado Springs: Ralph Myles, 1973), pp. 11–24, 57.

Ayn Rand, interviewed by Alvin Toffler, *Playboy* (March 1964). Reprinted by permission of *Playboy* and Alvin Toffler.

Douglas J. Den Uyl and Douglas B. Rasmussen, "Ayn Rand on Rights and Capitalism," from *The Philosophic Thought of Ayn Rand,* Douglas J. Den Uyl and Douglas B. Rasmussen, eds. (Urbana and Chicago: University of Illinois, 1984), pp. 165–80. Reprinted by permission of University of Illinois Press.

Robert Nozick, "The Entitlement Theory of Justice," from *Anarchy, State, and Utopia* (New York: Basic Books, 1974), pp. 149–74. Copyright © 1974 by Basic Books. Reprinted by permission of Basic Books, a division of HarperCollins Publishers, Inc.

Roger Pilon, "The Right to Do Wrong," from *Flag-Burning, Discrimination, and the Right to Do Wrong,* Roger Pilon, ed. (Washington, D.C.: Cato Institute, Center for Constitutional Studies, 1990).

Lao-tzu, "Harmony," from *The Way and Its Power: A Study of the Tao Te Ching and Its Place in Chinese Thought* by Arthur Waley (New York: Grove Press, 1958), with additional translations by Kate Xiao Zhou.

Adam Smith, "The Man of System," from *The Theory of Moral Sentiments* (Indianapolis: Liberty Classics, 1976), pp. 380–81.

Thomas Paine, "Of Society and Civilization," from *The Rights of Man,* included in *The Thomas Paine Reader,* Michael Foot and Isaac Kramnick, eds. (Harmondsworth, England: Penguin, 1987), pp. 266–70.

F. A. Hayek, "The Use of Knowledge in Society," from *Individualism and Economic Order* (Chicago: University of Chicago Press, 1948), pp. 77–89. Copyright © 1948 University of Chicago.

Michael Polanyi, "Two Kinds of Order," from *The Logic of Liberty* (Chicago: University of Chicago Press, 1951), pp. 154–65, 170, 176–78.

F. A. Hayek, "Made Orders and Spontaneous Orders," from *Law, Legislation, and Liberty*, Volume 1 (Chicago: University of Chicago Press, 1973), pp. 35–52. Copyright © 1973 by F. A. Hayek.

Michael Rothschild, "Economy as Ecosystem," from *Bionomics: The Inevitability of Capitalism* (New York: Henry Holt, 1990), pp. 213–25. Copyright © 1990 by Michael Rothschild. Reprinted by permission of Henry Holt and Company, Inc.

Adam Smith, "The Division of Labor," from *An Inquiry into the Nature and Causes of the Wealth of Nations*, Edwin Cannan, ed. (New York: Random House, Modern Library, 1937), pp. 3–11.

Adam Smith, "Society and Self-Interest," from *The Wealth of Nations*, pp. 13–15.

Adam Smith, "Labor and Commerce," from *The Wealth of Nations*, pp. 17, 30, 128.

Adam Smith, "Free Trade," from *The Wealth of Nations*, pp. 422–23, 431, 455–61.

Adam Smith, "The Simple System of Natural Liberty," from *The Wealth of Nations*, pp. 650–51.

Frédéric Bastiat, "What Is Seen and What Is Not Seen," from *Selected Essays on Political Economy*, George B. de Huszar, ed., Seymour Cain, trans. (Irvington-on-Hudson, N.Y.: Foundation for Economic Education, 1964), pp. 1–24. Reprinted by permission of Foundation for Economic Education.

Ludwig von Mises, "Socialism and Intervention," from *Liberalism*, Ralph Raico, trans. (Irvington-on-Hudson, N.Y.: Foundation for Economic Education, 1985), pp. 70–85. Reprinted by permission of Bettina Bien Greaves.

Bertrand de Jouvenel, "Redistributing Power," from *The Ethics of Redistribution* (Indianapolis: Liberty Press, 1990), pp. 40–48, 70–80.

Milton Friedman, "The Relation Between Economic Freedom and Political Freedom," from *Capitalism and Freedom* (Chicago: University of Chicago Press, 1962), pp. 7–21. Copyright © 1962 by University of Chicago Press.

F. A. Hayek, "The Market Order or Catallaxy," from *Law, Legislation, and Liberty,* Volume Two (Chicago: University of Chicago Press, 1976), pp. 107–32. Copyright © 1976 by F. A. Hayek.

Russell Roberts, "If You're Paying, I'll Have Top Sirloin," reprinted with permission from *Wall Street Journal,* May 18, 1995.

Richard Cobden, "Commerce Is the Grand Panacea," from *England, Ireland, and America,* in *The Political Writings of Richard Cobden* (1903: New York: Garland, 1973), pp. 31–36.

Richard Cobden, "Nonintervention," from *Speeches by Richard Cobden, M. P.* (1870), Volume Two, pp. 225–27.

"The Eclipse of Liberalism," *The Nation* (August 9, 1900).

Ludwig von Mises, "Peace," from *Liberalism,* Ralph Raico, trans. (Irvington-on-Hudson, N.Y.: Foundation for Economic Education, 1985), pp. 23–27. Reprinted by permission of Bettina Bien Greaves.

Earl C. Ravenal, "The Case for Strategic Disengagement," *Foreign Affairs* (April 1973). Copyright © 1973 by Council on Foreign Relations, Inc.

Ted Galen Carpenter, "Toward Strategic Independence," *Brown Journal of World Affairs* (Summer 1995).

Samuel Brittan, "Capitalism and the Permissive Society," from *A Restatement of Economic Liberalism* (London: Macmillan, 1989), pp. 1–34. Reprinted by permission of Samuel Brittan.

Antonio Martino, "Liberalism in the Coming Decade," from *Cato Policy Report* (November/December 1990). Reprinted by permission of Antonio Martino.

Richard Cornuelle, "The Power and Poverty of Libertarian Thought," *Times Literary Supplement* (April 5, 1991). Reprinted by permission of Richard Cornuelle.

Mario Vargas Llosa, "The Culture of Liberty," from *Journal of Democracy* (Fall 1991), pp. 25–33. Reprinted by permission of The Johns Hopkins University Press.

About the Editor

David Boaz is the executive vice president of the Cato Institute, which the *Economist* calls "America's leading libertarian think-tank," and the author of *Libertarianism: A Primer* (revised, updated, and retitled as *The Libertarian Mind: A Manifesto for Freedom*). He is the former editor of *New Guard* magazine and was executive director of the Council for a Competitive Economy prior to joining Cato. He is a frequent guest on national television and radio shows, and his articles have been published in the *Wall Street Journal,* the *New York Times,* the *Washington Post,* the *Los Angeles Times,* and the *Encyclopedia Britannica.* He is the author of *The Politics of Freedom* and the coauthor of *The Libertarian Vote: Swing Voters, Tea Parties, and the Fiscally Conservative, Socially Liberal Center.* He is also the editor of *Toward Liberty: The Idea That Is Changing the World; Left, Right & Babyboom; Liberating Schools: Education in the Inner City; The Crisis in Drug Prohibition;* and *The Cato Handbook for Policymakers.*

Don't miss the revised, updated, and retitled edition of David Boaz's classic book *Libertarianism: A Primer*, which was praised as uniting **"history, philosophy, economics, and law—spiced with just the right anecdotes—to bring alive a vital tradition of American political thought that deserves to be honored today"** (Richard A. Epstein, New York Unversity School of Law).

The

Libertarian

Mind

Revised and updated edition of *Libertarianism: A Primer*

A MANIFESTO FOR FREEDOM

David Boaz

Executive Vice President, Cato Institute